Nicaragua

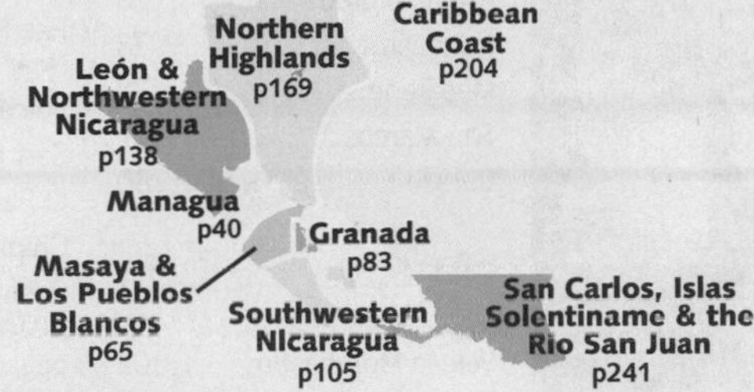

THIS EDITION WRITTEN AND RESEARCHED BY

Alex Egerton

Greg Benchwick

PLAN YOUR TRIP

STUDIO ONE-ONE / GETTY IMAGES ©

WILDLIFE P282

SEAN MURPHY / GETTY IMAGES ©

SURFING P33

ON THE ROAD

Contents

UNDERSTAND

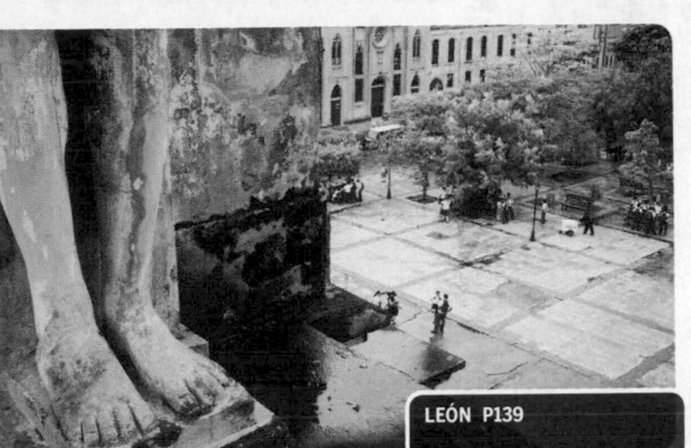

LEÓN P139

SURVIVAL GUIDE

SPECIAL FEATURES

Welcome to Nicaragua

Affable Nicaragua embraces travelers with offerings of volcanic landscapes, colonial architecture, sensational beaches and pristine forests that range from breathtaking to downright incredible.

Beaches

Whether it's dipping your toes into the crystalline Caribbean or paddling out to the crashing waves of the pounding Pacific, Nicaragua's beaches always deliver the goods. The big barrels of Rivas are revered in surfing circles while the clear waters of the Corn Islands are superb for snorkeling. More sedentary beach bums can choose between accessible slices of sand lined with fine restaurants and happening bars or natural affairs backed by a wall of rainforest. Even the best beaches in the country are refreshingly free of development, so you can experience them just as nature intended.

Outdoor Adventures

Looking for the ultimate rush? Nicaragua's diverse geography, intense energy and anything-goes attitude is perfect for exhilarating outdoor adventures. Get ready to check a whole gamut of new experiences off your list including: surfing down an active volcano, diving through underwater caves, canoeing through alligator-infested wetlands, swimming across sea channels between tiny white-sand islands and landing a 90-plus-kg tarpon beneath a Spanish fortress in the middle of the jungle. There's no signs, no crowds and no holding back.

Colonial Splendor

Nicaragua's colonial splendor comes in two distinct, but equally appealing, flavors. The elegant streetscapes of Granada have been entrancing travelers for centuries with their architectural grace. It's Nicaragua's best-preserved colonial town and boasts a meticulously restored cathedral, well-groomed plaza and perfectly maintained mansions that shelter lush internal courtyards. Far less polished, working-class León offers a different colonial experience where your crumbling 300-year-old houses come interspersed with revolutionary murals and architectural masterpieces housing corner stores. It's a vibrant city that, while proud of its heritage, is too busy to feel like a museum.

Getting off the Beaten Track

There are few destinations with such beauty that are as undeveloped as Nicaragua. Before you know it, you've dropped off the tourist trail and into a world of majestic mountains, cooperative farms, wetlands thronged with wildlife and empty jungle-clad beaches. Forge on and discover remote indigenous communities, overgrown pre-Columbian ruins and untouched rainforests. No matter how far you go, you'll always find friendly locals who are more than willing to share their culture with strangers.

Why I Love Nicaragua

By Alex Egerton, Author

Upon arriving in Nicaragua, like so many others I was captivated by the youthful energy and crumbling colonial charm of León, a city quite unlike others I had known. But after settling down there I soon identified the unparalleled adventure opportunities that were waiting on my doorstep and up and left to the wild Caribbean Coast. Now I live on the placid shores of Pearl Lagoon where I spend most of my spare time paddling my sea kayaks around the bays, up the jungle creeks and around the stunning Pearl Keys. Every trip's a new experience.

For more about our authors, see page 320

Above: A bungalow on Little Corn Island

Nicaragua

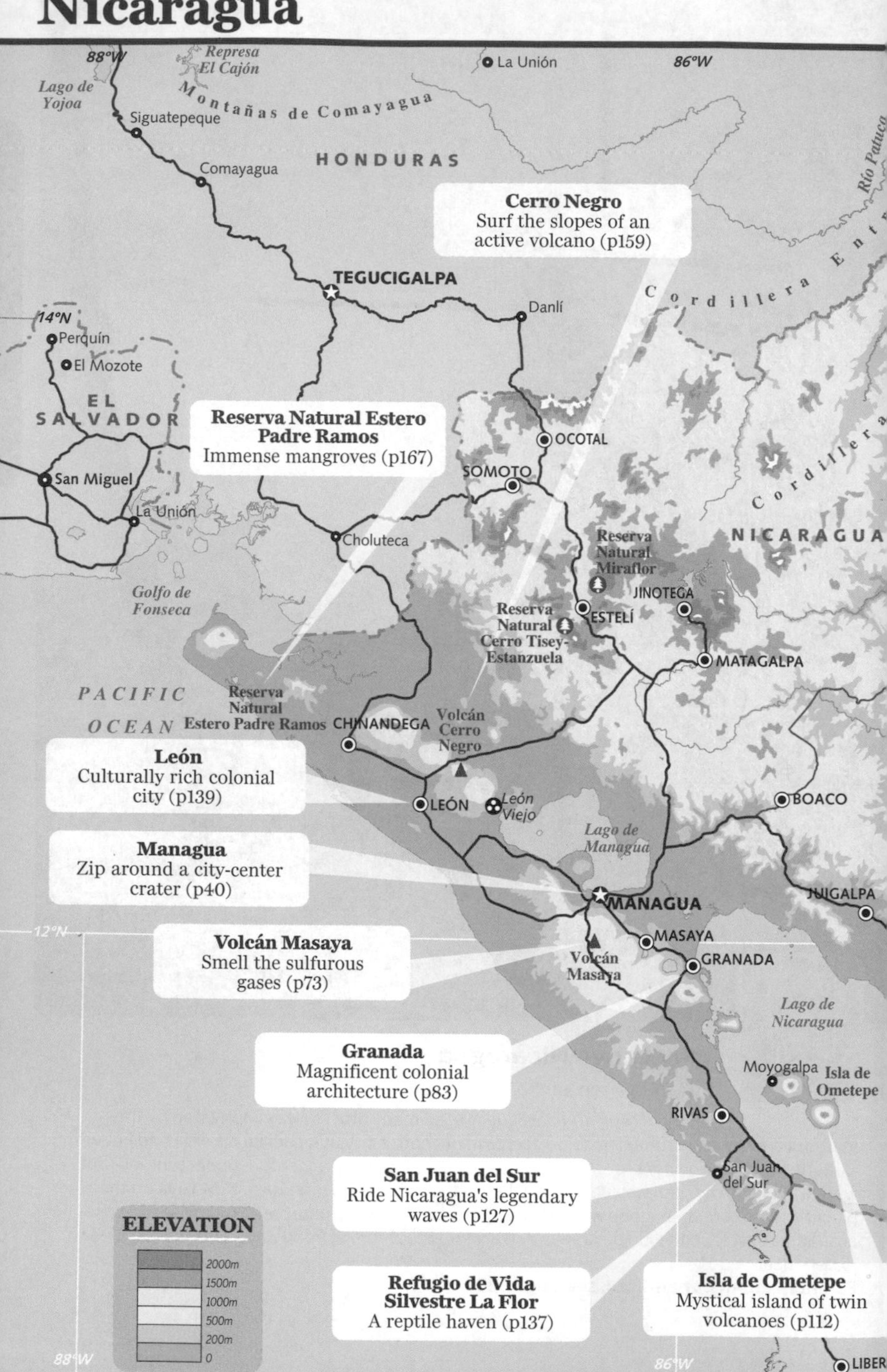

Cerro Negro
Surf the slopes of an active volcano (p159)
Reserva Natural Estero Padre Ramos
Immense mangroves (p167)
León
Culturally rich colonial city (p139)
Managua
Zip around a city-center crater (p40)
Volcán Masaya
Smell the sulfurous gases (p73)
Granada
Magnificent colonial architecture (p83)
San Juan del Sur
Ride Nicaragua's legendary waves (p127)
Refugio de Vida Silvestre La Flor
A reptile haven (p137)
Isla de Ometepe
Mystical island of twin volcanoes (p112)
ELEVATION
2000m
1500m
1000m
500m
200m
0
88°W
86°W
14°N
12°N
HONDURAS
EL SALVADOR
NICARAGUA
PACIFIC OCEAN
Represa El Cajón
Lago de Yojoa
Montañas de Comayagua
La Unión
Siguatepeque
Comayagua
TEGUCIGALPA
Danlí
Río Patuca
Cordillera Entr
Perquín
El Mozote
San Miguel
La Unión
Golfo de Fonseca
Choluteca
OCOTAL
SOMOTO
Cordillera
Reserva Natural Miraflor
JINOTEGA
ESTELÍ
Reserva Natural Cerro Tisey-Estanzuela
MATAGALPA
Reserva Natural Estero Padre Ramos
CHINANDEGA
Volcán Cerro Negro
LEÓN
León Viejo
Lago de Managua
BOACO
MANAGUA
JUIGALPA
MASAYA
GRANADA
Volcán Masaya
Lago de Nicaragua
Moyogalpa
Isla de Ometepe
RIVAS
San Juan del Sur
LIBER
El Coco

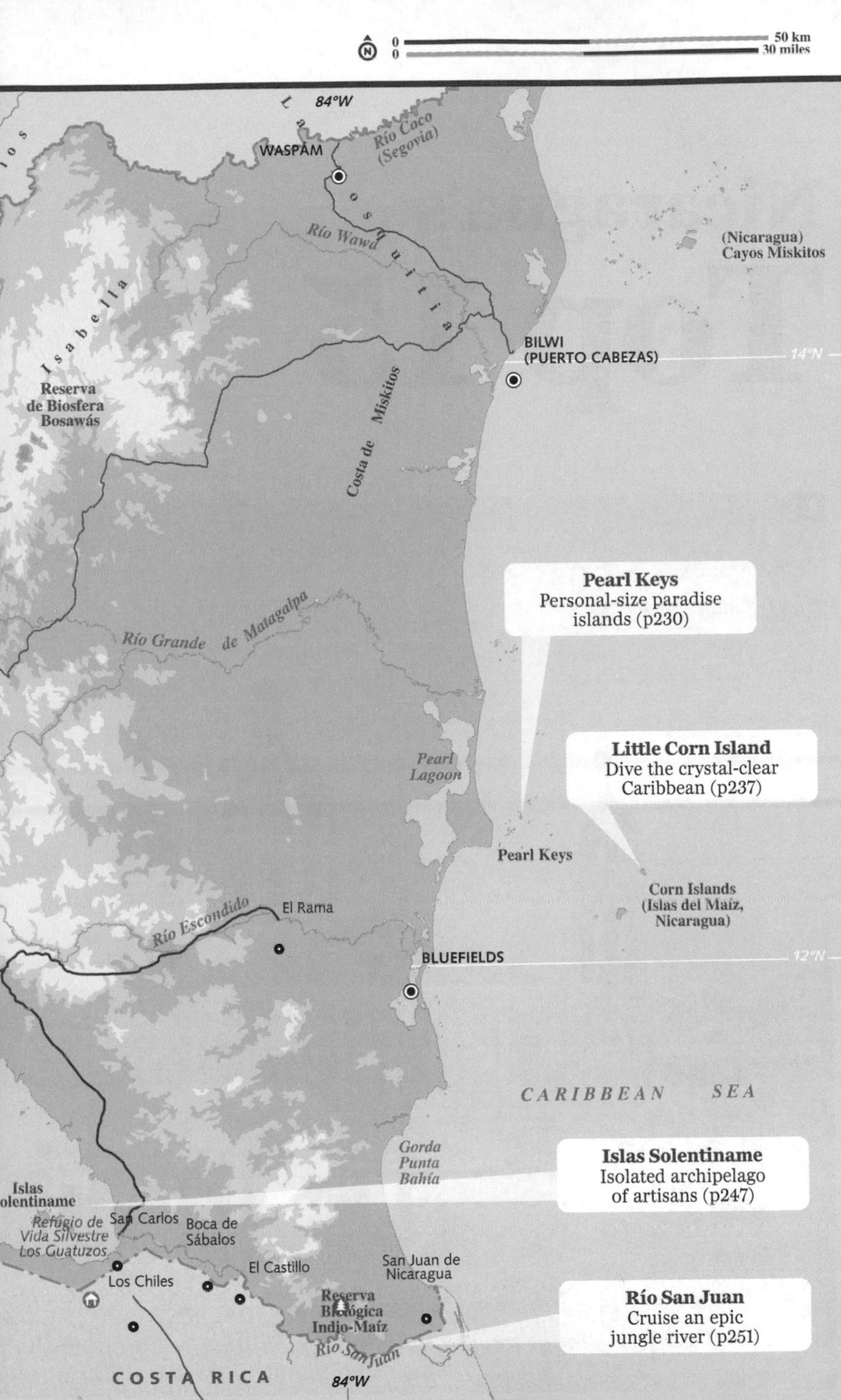

0
50 km
0
30 miles
84°W
WASPAM
Río Coco (Segovia)
La Mosquitia
Río Wawa
(Nicaragua) Cayos Miskitos
Isabella
BILWI (PUERTO CABEZAS)
14°N
Reserva de Biosfera Bosawás
Costa de Miskitos
Pearl Keys
Personal-size paradise islands (p230)
Río Grande de Matagalpa
Little Corn Island
Dive the crystal-clear Caribbean (p237)
Pearl Lagoon
Pearl Keys
Corn Islands (Islas del Maíz, Nicaragua)
El Rama
Río Escondido
BLUEFIELDS
12°N
CARIBBEAN SEA
Gorda Punta Bahía
Islas Solentiname
Isolated archipelago of artisans (p247)
Islas Solentiname
Refugio de Vida Silvestre Los Guatuzos
San Carlos
Boca de Sábalos
El Castillo
San Juan de Nicaragua
Los Chiles
Reserva Biológica Indio-Maíz
Río San Juan
Cruise an epic jungle river (p251)
Río San Juan
COSTA RICA
84°W
Tortuguero

Nicaragua's Top 15

1

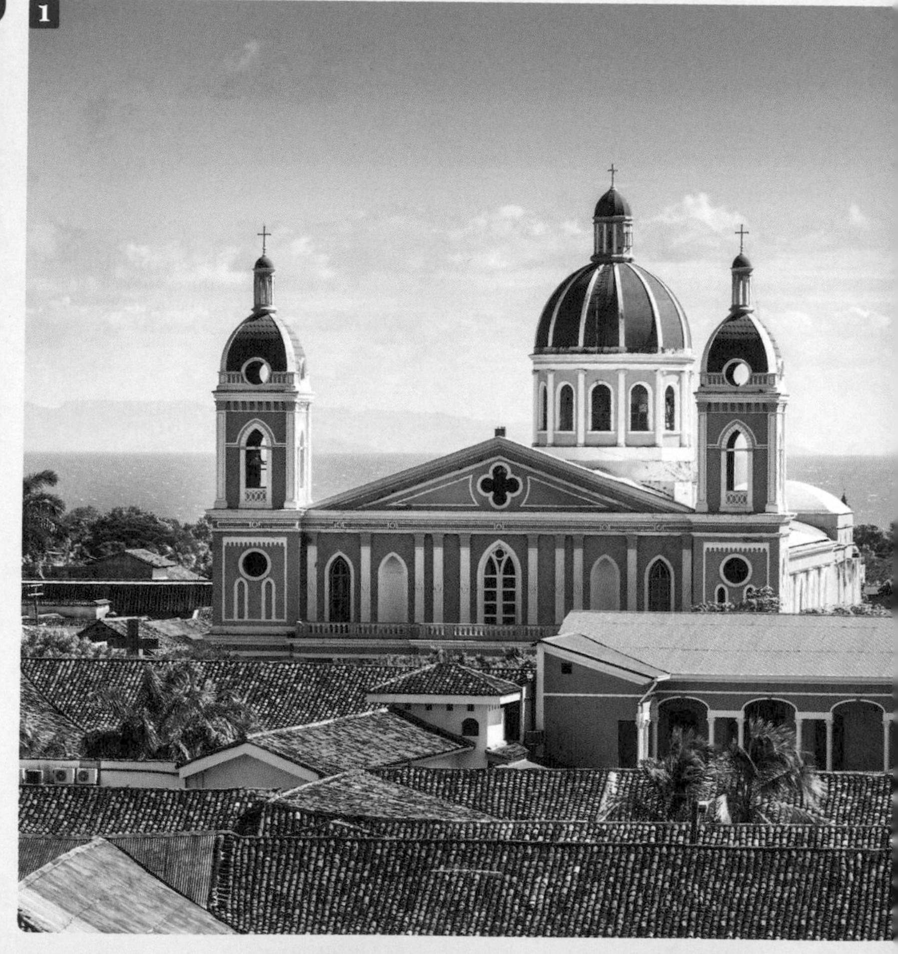

Granada

1 Granada (p83) is a town of immense and palpable magnetism. At the heart of the city's charms are the picture-perfect cobblestone streets, polychromatic colonial homes and churches, and a lilting air that brings the city's spirited past into present-day tight focus. Most trips here begin and end on foot, and simply dawdling from gallery to restaurant to colonial church can take up the better part of a day. From there, it's off to explore the myriad wild areas, islands, volcanoes and artisan villages nearby. Catedral de Granada

Little Corn Island

2 With no cars and no noise, just white-sand beaches and secluded coves mixing it with the crystal-clear Caribbean, Little Corn Island (p237) is the paramount place to take a break from the big city. There is plenty to keep you occupied during the day, including diving with hammerhead sharks and through underground caves, kitesurfing the stiff breeze and scrambling over jungle-covered headlands. And there's just enough to do at night, too. Add some great food to the mix and it's no surprise that many find it so hard to leave.

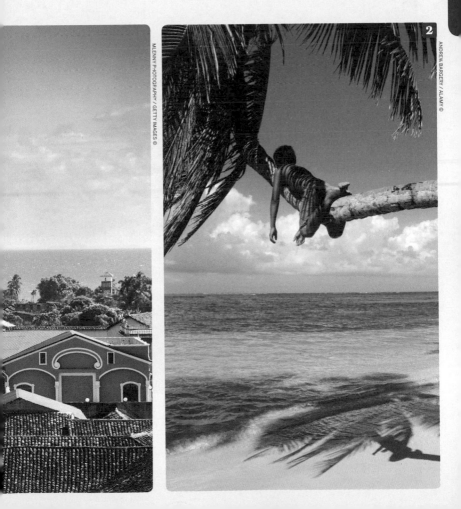

2

León

3 A royal city with revolutionary undercurrents, León both enchants and baffles. Within the city, you'll find an artsy, slightly edgy vibe originally fueled by the Sandinista revolution and now by the university (p148) and a 120-horsepower party scene. Come sunrise, you can spend a good day exploring the Catedral (p143), museums and downtown area, before heading out to honey-blonde beaches, volcanoes and Old West cowboy towns. View from León Catedral

Isla de Ometepe

4 Lago de Nicaragua's beloved centerpiece, Isla de Ometepe (p112) has it all: twin volcanoes, lush hillsides cut by walking tracks, archaeological remains, ziplines, monkeys and birdlife, waterfalls, lapping waves at your doorstep, and a laid-back island air that keeps travelers in the now as they make their way through this lost paradise found again. At the heart of the island's charms are the cool hostels, camping areas and peaced-out traveler scenes. Custom-fit your experience from high-end luxury lodges to groovy-groupie hippie huts.

3

4

PETE NIESEN / ALAMY ©

MARVIN DEL CID / GETTY IMAGES ©

Río San Juan

5 Once favored by pirates and prospectors as a path to riches, today the Río San Juan is exalted by nature lovers. All along the river, scores of birds nest on branches overhanging its slow surging waters while its lower reaches are dominated by the Reserva Biológica Indio-Maíz (p256), an impenetrable jungle that shelters jaguars and troupes of noisy monkeys. The only artificial attraction along the river's entire length is the grand Spanish fort (p254) over the rapids at El Castillo.

Pearl Keys

6 As you approach the dozen tiny islands ringed by snow-white sand and brilliant Caribbean waters that make up the Pearl Keys (p230), you will enter the realms of the ultimate shipwreck fantasy. Fortunately, you'll be marooned with a capable Creole guide that will cook up a spectacular seafood meal and source ice-cold beers from a mysterious supply, leaving you more time to swim, snorkel, spot sea turtles, or just lie back in your hammock and take in the idyllic panoramic views.

Coffee Country

7 A visit to Nicaragua's coffee zone is about more than just sipping plenty of joe, it's about getting out and seeing where it all comes from. Hike among the bushes shaded by ethereal cloud forest around Jinotega (p189) and pick ripe cherries alongside your hosts in a community farming cooperative near Matagalpa (p194). And why stop there when you can follow the beans to the roasting plant and then learn to identify flavors in a cupping session. After this, you'll savor your morning cup in a whole new way.

Coffee beans from the mountains of Matagalpa

CHRISTIAN HEEB / GETTY IMAGES ©

Surfing near San Juan del Sur

8 Nicaragua sparked into international stardom on the wake of tanned-and-toned surfer dudes and dudettes. And the surfing scene north and south of regional hub San Juan del Sur (p127) remains cooled-back, reefed-out, soulful and downright brilliant. The stars of the scene are the long rideable waves that fit the bill for surfers of all abilities, but the chillaxed surf camps, beach parties and cool breezes add to the vibe, making a beach vacation here work for everybody in your crew (even the boogie boarders).

Turtles at La Flor

9 Head to Nicaragua's southern Pacific coast between July and January to witness sea turtles by the thousands come to shore to lay their eggs at Refugio de Vida Silvestre La Flor (p137). There's a decent beach here, as well, but the highlight is a night tour (generally from nearby San Juan del Sur), where, if you're lucky, you'll see a leatherback or olive ridley mama come to shore to lay her eggs at the end of one of nature's most inspiring and remarkable journeys.

Islas Solentiname

10 The Islas Solentiname (p247) are straight out of a fairy tale. You simply must visit in order to experience the magic of this remote jungle-covered archipelago where a community of exceptionally talented artists live and work among the wild animals that are their inspiration. It's a place where an enlightened priest inspired a village to construct a handsome church alive with the sounds of nature and shooting stars illuminate the speckled night sky. Even having been there, you still find it hard to believe it's real. Woman painting a balsa-wood carved chicken

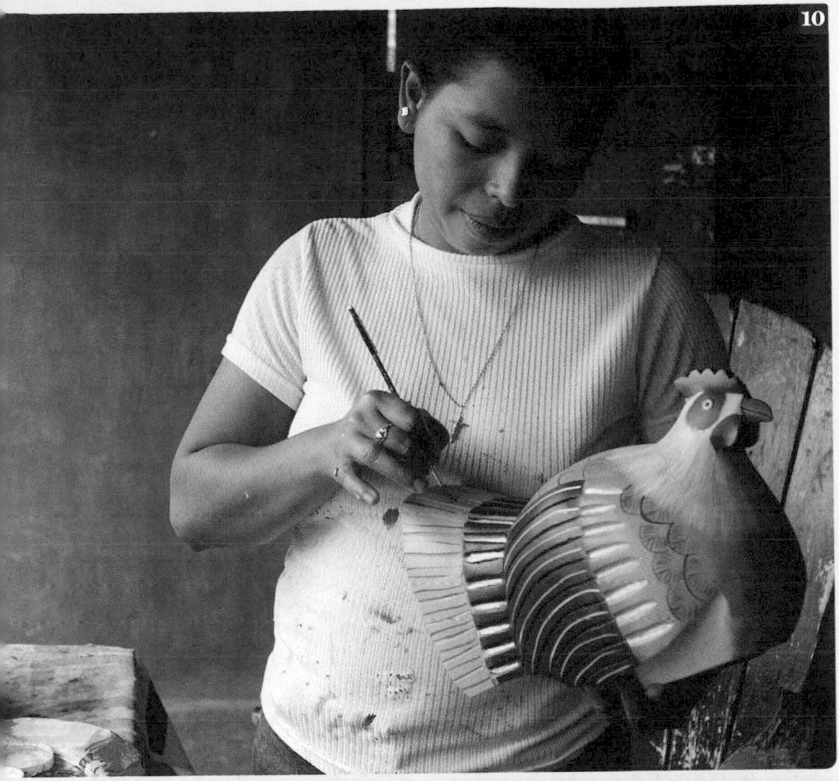

Volcán Masaya

11 Hovering above the artisan villages of Nicaragua's Central Plateau, the smoldering Volcán Masaya and its surrounding national park (p73) are a singular highlight not to be missed by volcanophiles, nature lovers and adventure seekers alike. This is one of the region's most active volcanoes, and it's pretty exciting to see the sulfurous columns of gas billow toward the sky as you relish the million-dollar views. Super-fun short treks take you to lava caves and butterfly gardens. Come sunset, an eerie bat tour tops off your adventure.

JANE SWEENEY / GETTY IMAGES ©

Wildlife-Watching

12 From the colorful parakeets flying over busy Managua to ubiquitous iguanas scratching across your hotel roof, exotic wildlife is everywhere in Nicaragua. Dedicate some energy to the pursuit and you'll discover some truly phenomenal natural spectacles. Head into the rugged rainforest-covered mountains of the Bosawás (p214) to spot three types of monkeys, toucans and tapirs, while reptile fans will not want to miss getting close to the alligators of Los Guatuzos (p251). Wherever you go, keep your binoculars handy. Baby green iguana

Canopy Tour in Managua

13 Big-brawling Managua doesn't make it onto many traveler top 10 lists, and one of the best parts of visiting this city is getting away. But you won't have to go far. Within the city's confines, the Parque Historico Nacional Loma de Tiscapa (p43) is home to the silhouetted statue of Augusto Sandino and was once the site of the presidential palace. Today the highlight of the park is a homegrown canopy-tour operation that swings you through the lush foliage. Zipline canopy tour, Parque Historico Nacional Loma de Tiscapa

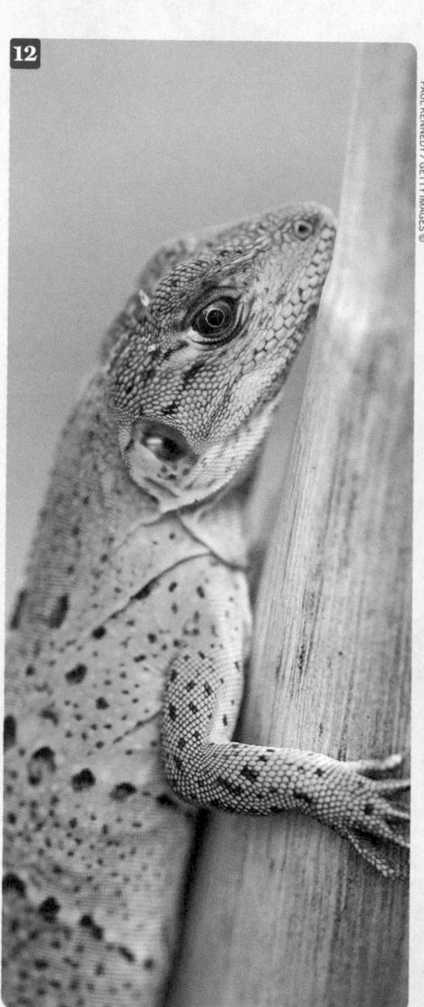
12

13

Volcano Boarding on Cerro Negro

14 What goes up must come down. But why walk, when you can strap on a custom-built volcano board and rip-roar your way down a slope of fine volcanic ash? That's the genesis of volcano surfing. And one of the best spots on the planet to dig this new adrenaline sport is atop 700-plus-meter Volcán Cerro Negro in northwestern Nicaragua's Reserva Natural Pilas–El Hoyo (p159). Tour operators in León will even provide you with cool jumpsuits for your dusty-bottomed descent.

Reserva Natural Estero Padre Ramos

15 The Reserva Natural Estero Padre Ramos (p167) is a vast nature reserve located in the far northwestern corner of Nicaragua. The largest remaining mangrove forest in Central America, the reserve is home to ocelots, alligators and a universe's worth of birds. While this is a wild corner of Nicaragua, basic tourist services will get you into the spider-webbing mangrove forest, to the beaches where sea turtles lay their eggs and good surf dominates, and into local communities.

Need to Know

For more information, see Survival Guide p290

Currency
Córdoba (C$)

Language
Spanish

Visas
Generally not required for stays up to three months.

Money
ATMs in most large towns. Credit cards accepted in larger hotels and restaurants.

Cell Phones
Local SIM cards work in any unblocked North American or Latin American phone. Other phones may need to be set to roaming.

Time
Central Standard Time (GMT/UTC minus six hours)

When to Go

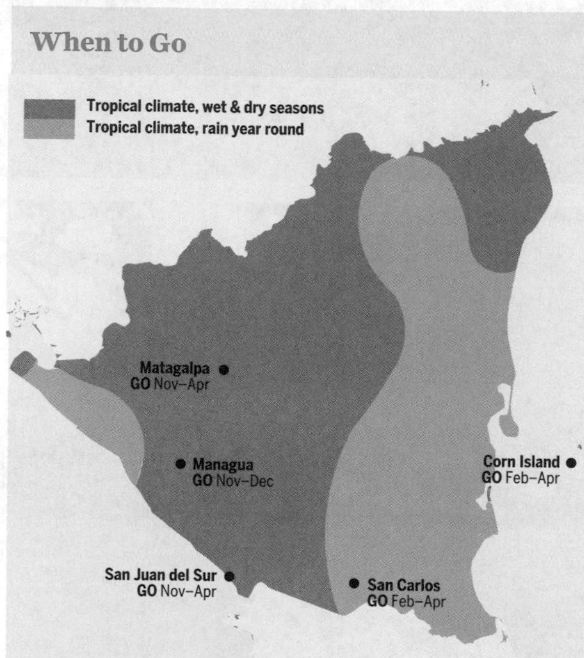

High Season
(Dec–Apr)

- Prices increase by up to 25% in popular tourist spots.
- Make reservations in advance for beach-side accommodations.
- Hot, sunny and dry conditions throughout the country.

Shoulder
(Nov)

- Rains ease throughout the Pacific but Caribbean still wet.
- Cool weather and green countryside make for best trekking.
- Coffee harvest energizes northern region.

Low Season
(May–Oct)

- Heavy rains make some roads in rural areas difficult to pass and mountain hiking trails slippery.
- Biggest swell on Pacific side pulls a crowd to the best breaks.
- Advanced reservations generally not necessary.

Websites

Lonely Planet (www.lonelyplanet.com) A comprehensive online overview of the country for travelers.

Vianica.com (www.vianica.com/traveling) Log on to this interactive map and click on your route to find Nicaraguan road conditions, travel-time estimates and more.

Intur (www.visitanicaragua.com/ingles) The official government website is in English and Spanish, with lots of cheerful, vague information and an awesome photo gallery.

Latin American Network Information Center (www.lanic.utexas.edu/la/ca/nicaragua) An excellent portal with academic and tourism-oriented offerings.

Important Numbers

Nicaragua country code	☎ 505
International access code	☎ 00
Fire (from cell phones)	☎ 115 ☎ 911
Police	☎ 118
Ambulance	☎ 128

Exchange Rates

Australia	A$1	24.95
Canada	C$1	24.21
Euro zone	€1	32.44
Japan	¥100	25.89
New Zealand	NZ$1	20.20
Serbia	100DIN	€0.88
UK	£1	38.19
US	US$1	24.30

For current exchange rates see www.xe.com

Daily Costs

Budget: Less than US$25

- Guesthouse: US$10-15
- Typical meal: US$4
- Museum admission: US$2
- Local bus: US$0.15

Midrange: US$25-75

- Midrange hotel: US$20-40
- Restaurant meal: US$10-12
- Adventure tour: US$25
- Short taxi ride: US$2

Top End: More than US$75

- Luxury hotel: US$80
- Gourmet meal: US$18
- Car hire: US$40
- Internal flight: US$100

Opening Hours

Opening hours vary wildly in Nicaragua as there are many informal and family-run establishments. General office hours are from 9am to 5pm. Some offices and shops, especially in rural areas, close for lunch from noon to 2pm. Government departments usually only attend the public in the mornings, but this varies between departments. Cheaper eateries usually open for breakfast and lunch while more formal restaurants serve lunch and dinner.

Banks 8:30am–4:30pm

Bars noon–midnight

Clubs 8pm–3am

Government Offices 8am–1pm

Museums 9am–noon & 2–5pm

Restaurants noon–10pm

Shops 9am–6pm

Arriving in Nicaragua

Managua International Airport (p60) Official taxis inside the airport meet all incoming flights and charge around US$20 to most local destinations. During the day, cheaper licensed collective taxis wait outside the domestic terminal. If you're heading out of Managua, it's possible to prearrange a pick-up with a private shuttle service.

Getting Around

Transport in Nicaragua is functional rather than comfortable and probably more chaotic than you are used to.

Flights Domestic flights are moderately priced and the fastest way to get you where you're going; however, they only serve more far-off destinations. They are often slightly delayed, but rarely canceled.

Car Renting a car enables travel at your own pace and access to off-the-beaten-track destinations. There is not much traffic on the roads and driving in Nicaragua is fairly stress-free (once you learn how to handle the traffic cops).

Buses Nicaragua's fleet of old-school buses are slow and uncomfortable but will get you anywhere you want to go for next to nothing. There are more comfortable, but far from luxurious, coach services to some long-distance destinations.

For much more on transport , see p298

First Time Nicaragua

For more information, see Survival Guide (p290)

Checklist

- Make sure your passport is valid for at least six months
- Check latest visa requirements online (see p296)
- Arrange travel insurance with medical evacuation cover (see p294)
- Inform your debit/credit card issuer that you are traveling to Central America
- Organize vaccinations against hepatitis A and typhoid and consult your doctor about malaria prophylactics

What to Pack

- Sturdy walking shoes
- Comfortable sports sandals
- Insect repellent containing DEET
- An emergency supply of US dollars in small bills
- A two-pronged electrical adapter
- A lightweight raincoat capable of resisting tropical downpours
- Contact lens solution and other personal toiletries

Top Tips for Your Trip

- Always go for a window seat in public transport, the landscapes are absolutely breathtaking.
- Take some Spanish classes at the beginning of your trip. Nicaraguans are outgoing and friendly but few have foreign-language skills.
- Hire local guides wherever possible, they're cheap and you'll learn not only about the attraction you're visiting but also about the culture.

What to Wear

The heat in Nicaragua can be oppressive, so you'll probably spend most of your time in lightweight t-shirts and shorts or cotton trousers. If you're heading to the northern highlands, you'll probably make use of a medium pullover for the cool evenings.

Note that in general, men in Nicaragua don't wear shorts unless practicing sports. Go for jeans and short-sleeved shirt or polo shirt if you are going out with locals.

On the beach women going topless is almost never acceptable and in rural areas bikinis may draw unwanted attention; consider swimming in shorts and a t-shirt like the locals.

Sleeping

Outside absolute peak periods in major tourist destinations, it's rarely necessary to reserve accommodations in advance in Nicaragua. See p290 for more accommodation information.

- **Hospedajes** These cheap guesthouses are often family run and are sometimes the only option in smaller towns.
- **Hotels** Larger, more polished and less personal; they offer more facilities including reception and often a restaurant.
- **Hostels** Traveler's hostels with dormitories and common areas are only found in the main tourist areas.
- **Ecolodges** Usually at the higher end of the market, these offer comfortable rooms surrounded by nature.

Money

ATMs are widespread in most midsized towns in Nicaragua, but you'll need to stock up on cash before heading to rural areas. Visa is the most widely accepted card followed by cards on the MasterCard network. Amex is not generally accepted. Most Nicaraguan ATMs charge a fee (around US$3) on top of what your bank charges.

Credit cards are widely accepted in larger towns but rarely in rural areas apart from in higher end hotels. US dollars are the alternative currency and are widely accepted, but for smaller items using Córdobas is cheaper and easier.

It's worth carrying an emergency supply of dollars in case you have problems with your card.

For more information, see p294.

Bargaining

All-out haggling is not really part of Nicaraguan culture; however, a few back-and-forths at an outdoor market or over a hotel room is considered acceptable.

Tipping

Tipping is not widespread in Nicaragua except in the following situations:

➡ **Guides** Tipping guides is recommended as this often makes up the lion's share of their salary.

➡ **Restaurants** A tip of around 10% is expected for table service. Some higher end restaurants automatically add this to the bill.

ERIC L. WHEATER / GETTY IMAGES ©

Girl in Nueva Segovia

Etiquette

➡ **Greetings** A firm handshake for men and a peck on the cheek for women.

➡ **Titles** When addressing Nicaraguans add Don (for men) or Doña (for women) before their given name.

➡ **Drinking** If you are sharing a bottle of rum, use the supplied shot glass to measure your drink; don't poor freely from the bottle.

Language

Even in major tourist destinations, very few Nicaraguans speak English. However, Nicaraguans are outgoing and friendly and will patiently listen if you make the effort to communicate. Learning a few basic phrases in Spanish will make traveling in Nicaragua a much more rewarding experience and is highly recommended if you plan on traveling to remote rural destinations. Hiring a translator to accompany you around town or on longer trips is affordable – ask at your hotel.

On the Caribbean coast English speakers will have no problem communicating with Creole residents, although it may take some getting use to the accent and grammar.

See Language (p303) for more information.

If You Like

Beaches

The Pacific has the waves, the Caribbean's got the reefs.

Little Corn Island Brilliant turquoise waters meet snow white sand in secluded coves on this enchanted isle. (p237)

Playa El Coco A spectacular stretch of sparkling sand framed by imposing forest-covered headlands. (p137)

Pearl Keys Live out your shipwreck fantasies beneath the coconut palms on this group of tiny, idyllic Caribbean islands. (p230)

El Ostional Charming fishing village with a sweeping brown-sand beach. (p137)

Playa Aserradores Long, smooth stretch of sand with a powerful, hollow beach break. (p166)

Volcanoes

Volcán Masaya Watch parakeets return to nest among clouds of sulfuric gases above visible pools of lava. (p73)

Volcán Maderas Hike up through cloud forest to reach a chilly jade green crater lake. (p123)

Volcán Momotombo Perched regally at the top of Lago de Managua, its perfect cone is a symbol of Nicaragua. (p158)

Volcán Cosigüina Climb the remnants of what was Central America's biggest volcano to look out over three countries. (p168)

Volcán Mombacho Accessible cloud forest with great hiking and even better bird-watching. (p102)

Colonial Towns

Granada Charge your batteries, Nicaragua's wonderfully preserved colonial showpiece lays on the charm from the moment you get off the bus. (p83)

León Energetic and unpretentious, this gregarious city has stunning colonial streetscapes, awe-inspiring churches and fine cosmopolitan eateries. (p139)

Ciudad Antigua Boasting a remarkable Moorish-influenced 17th-century church, this is one of Nicaragua's oldest towns. (p185)

San Rafael del Norte Surrounded by peaks, this charming small town is centered around the light-filled Templo Parroquial San Rafael Arcángel. (p187)

IF YOU LIKE... CIGARS

Make sure to join some factory tours in Estelí (p173) where you can watch classic stogies being hand rolled.

Coffee

Matagalpa and Jinotega departments have the pedigree but Estelí and little-visited Nueva Segovia also produce some outstanding beans.

La Bastilla Ecolodge Hike through immense shade-grown coffee plantations before improving your cupping skills at the laboratory. (p192)

San Ramón Try your hand picking coffee beans at local farms then visit a community roasting plant. (p200)

Selva Negra Follow the coffee from bush to cup or just sit by the mist-covered lake and enjoy a fresh brewed mug. (p201)

Área Protegida Miraflor Combine your coffee tour with a spot of bird-watching or a visit to waterfalls surrounded by cloud forest.(p177)

Wildlife

Refugio de Vida Silvestre La Flor Watching thousands of marine turtles arriving on this beach to lay their eggs is one

(Above) Coffee beans
(Below) Chestnut-mandibled toucan

of Latin America's superlative nature experiences. (p137)

Refugio Bartola Don rubber boots and head out into the jungle to spot three kinds of monkeys, fluorescent frogs and maybe even a tapir. (p256)

Volcán Mombacho Accessible cloud forest with great hiking and even better bird-watching. (p102)

Refugio de Vida Silvestre Los Guatuzos Perfectly preserved wetlands with fantastic bird-watching during the day and action-packed crocodile-spotting at night. (p251)

Islas Solentiname Bring binoculars to spot some of the thousands of migratory birds nesting in this remote archipelago. (p247)

Reserva Natural Macizos de Peñas Blancas Clinging to magnificent mountain peaks, this jungle is home to pumas, jaguars and ocelots. (p201)

Outdoor Adventure

Volcano boarding Volcán Cerro Negro is one of the few places on the planet to tick this deranged adventure sport off your list. (p148)

Kayaking and canoeing Paddle through the mangroves of Padre Ramos (p167), down the mighty Río San Juan (p254) or around majestic Isla de Ometepe. (p112)

Tubing Float with the current down the narrow **Cañon de Somoto**. (p182)

Diving Head to the Corn Islands for cave and reef dives in crystal-clear Caribbean waters. (p231)

Surfing Base yourself in San Juan del Sur, a vibrant beach town surrounded by top-class breaks. (p127)

Month by Month

TOP EVENTS

Noche de Agüizotes, October

Maypole, May

Turtle-Watching at La Flor, October

International Poetry Festival, February

Semana Santa in León, March/April

January

Perfect beach weather in the Pacific region with almost nonstop sunshine – expect bigger crowds and more expensive accommodations.

Baseball Finals

Stadiums get packed for the finals of the Liga Nacional de Beisbol Nicaraguense (Nicaraguan National Baseball League; www.lnbp.com.ni). Catch games at the Estadio Denis Martínez in Managua.

February

Crowds thin out but it's still all sunshine, making this one of the best times to plan a beach break. It can be uncomfortably hot in cities.

International Poetry Festival

Top Spanish-language wordsmiths from around the globe gather for this festival (www.festivalpoesianicaragua.com) in Granada with regular readings and more low-key fringe events.

March

The heat wave continues with soaring temperatures and dry conditions. Whether it falls in March or April, Easter is big business: prices spike, accommodations sell out and beaches get packed.

San Lazaro

Head to Masaya on the weekend before Palm Sunday for this religious festival that involves getting dressed up in bizarre costumes – even local dogs get in on the act.

Semana Santa in Léon

Easter is a major event all over the country but nowhere does it quite like León, where the traditional fireworks and parades are accompanied by sawdust mosaics and a sandcastle competition.

April

More sunshine, this time accompanied by big surf in the Pacific and calm seas throughout the Caribbean. After Easter crowds drop dramatically.

Surf's Up!

The combination of big swells along the Pacific and bright sunshine bring optimal conditions (and big crowds) to many of Nicaragua's best surf breaks, including the acclaimed Popoyo.

May

Low season gets underway with sunshine still sticking around but by the end of the month the skies open, marking the beginning of the wet season.

Maypole

Bluefields celebrates fertility with a series of neighborhood block parties culminating in the bright and boisterous carnival on the last Saturday of the month and the closing Tulululu when the entire town takes a midnight romp through the streets accompanied by a brass band.

June

Heavy rains drench the entire country, bringing significantly cooler temperatures but turning some rural roads into impassable pools of mud.

San Juan Bautista

The normally serene flower-growing town of Catarina is transformed by this wild festival in honor of San Juan Bautista, featuring dancing, ceremonial fights and music.

July

Rains continue unabated throughout the country. Most hiking trails are now muddy but many waterfalls are at their very best.

Aniversario de la Revolución

Dress in red and black and head to the plaza in Managua to celebrate the revolution alongside hard-drinking Sandinista supporters bussed in from all over the country. Or check out the bohemian fringe event in San Antonio.

August

Rains generally ease a little in the Pacific with most days enjoying stretches of sunshine. Meanwhile, the Caribbean experiences one of its wettest months.

Santo Domingo de Guzmán

Managua's biggest religious procession sees believers covering themselves in pitch-black used motor oil to accompany a tiny statue of the saint in his journey from the hills of Santo Domingo into the heart of the capital.

Crab Soup

Corn Island celebrates the end of slavery with a parade, concerts, plenty of beer and free ginger bread and bowls of crab soup for everyone.

September

The height of hurricane season in the Caribbean may disrupt travel plans, but when there are no storms the weather is generally bright and there are great deals on accommodations.

Feria del Maíz

The farmers of Nueva Segovia descend on the northern town of Jalapa for a celebration of everything corn. There's corn clothes, corn altars and corn dances, not to mention plenty of *chicha* (fermented corn drink).

October

Rains return with a vengeance throughout the Pacific with frequent heavy downpours in the afternoons. Traveler numbers are at their lowest.

Turtle-Watching at La Flor

Refugio de Vida Silvestre La Flor is the backdrop for one of nature's most amazing spectacles when olive ridley turtles arrive en mass (sometimes up to 3000 in one night) to lay their eggs on the sandy shores.

Noche de Agüizotes

This spooky festival in Masaya brings to life characters from horror stories of the colonial period with elaborate costumes. Keep an eye out for the headless priest.

November

Things get moving again following the easing of the rains. Travelers spread out throughout the country and the festival season warms up.

Garifuna Week

Nicaragua's Garifuna community celebrate their rich cultural heritage with drums, dancing and gastronomy in the remote community of Orinoco on the shores of Laguna de Perlas.

Carnival Acuático

Dancers from all over the country travel to San Carlos for this colorful parade of floats on the Río San Juan accompanied by concerts and a food fair on the waterfront.

December

The end of the rains in the Pacific region sees the high season begin in earnest.

La Griteria

Celebrated on the eve of the Immaculate Concepcíon, La Griteria sees hordes of children going from door to door singing songs to the Virgin Mary and receiving candies. It's celebrated throughout the country but León gets into it with unrivaled vigor.

ROLF RICHARDSON / ALAMY ©

Plan Your Trip

Itineraries

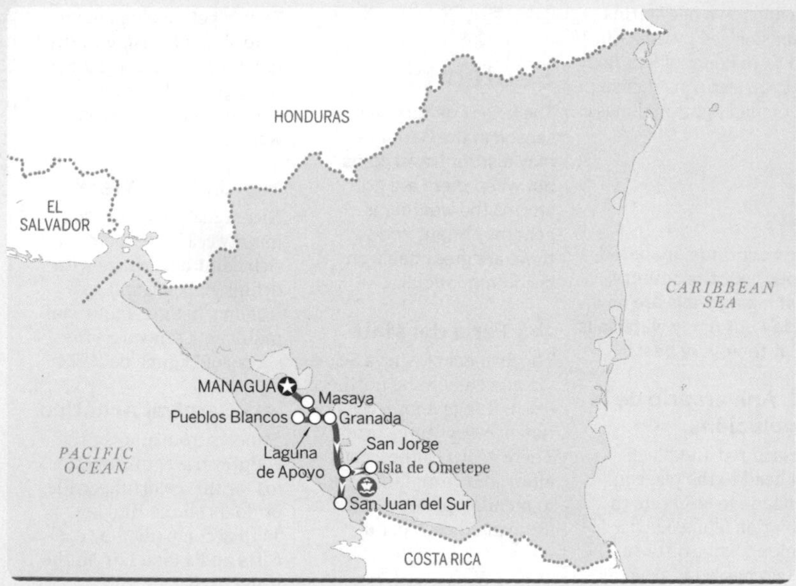

Stunning Southwest

If you've got limited time in Nicaragua, a trip through the southwest is big on awesome and small on hours in the bus. The region is a condensed wonderland of barreling surf, volcanoes, crater lakes, colonial towns and artisan villages that includes many of Nicaragua's must-see highlights.

Fly into **Managua** (p40) and take in the view across town from Sandino's silhouette on the Loma de Tiscapa before heading south and descending into the lush crater at **Laguna de Apoyo** (p75) for the night. Spend the next day swimming in the rich sulfuric waters or spotting birds and howler monkeys in the forest, before enjoying the spectacular night sky.

The following morning, visit the artisan workshops of the nearby **Pueblos Blancos** (p76), including the pottery cooperative at San Juan del Oriente.

Then head 30 minutes down the road for some colonial splendor in charismatic **Granada** (p83). Spend three nights taking in the wonderful streetscapes, visiting the museums and churches, and dining in the fine restaurants. While you're here make

Cascada San Ramón, Isla de Ometepe

day trips to kayak through the islets just offshore and hike among the cloud forest atop Volcán Mombacho.

Next head down the highway to San Jorge, from where you'll take the ferry across to the out-of-this world **Isla de Ometepe** (p112) with its twin volcanoes and endless outdoor activities. Spend one night among the howler monkeys at Reserva Charco Verde and another at the base of Volcán Maderas, from where you can hike to the crater lake surrounded by cloud forest.

Then head across the isthmus to the surfing capital of **San Juan de Sur** (p127), where you'll spend three days lazing on the splendid surrounding beaches or surfing some of the many excellent breaks in the area. Take a day trip to the charming fishing village of El Ostional or, if you're lucky, to watch sea turtles arrive en masse at Refugio de Vida Silvestre La Flor. In the evenings, work your way though the happening beachfront bars and restaurants.

On your way back to Managua, stop off at **Masaya** (p67) to shop for souvenirs and gifts in the excellent Mercado Artesanías (National Artisans Market) and visit the hammock workshops.

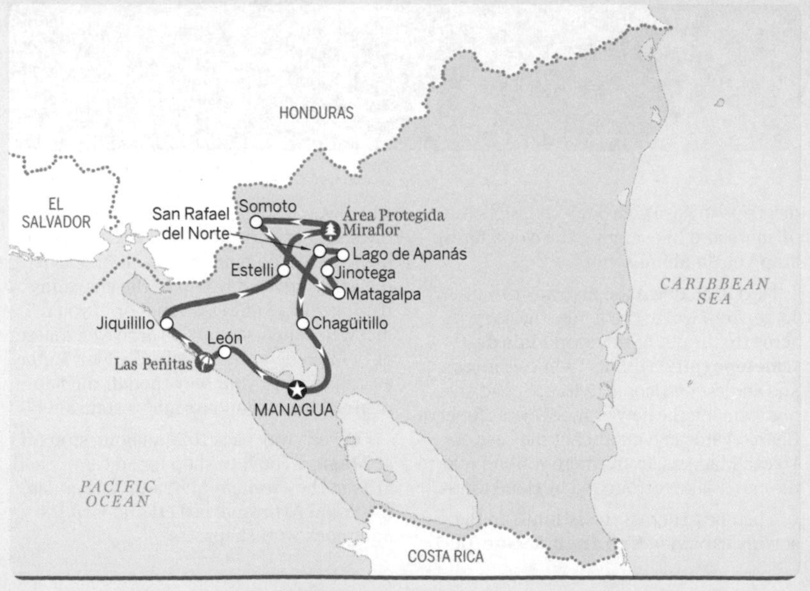
HONDURAS
EL SALVADOR
San Rafael del Norte
Somoto
Área Protegida Miraflor
Lago de Apanás
Estelli
Jinotega
Matagalpa
CARIBBEAN SEA
Jiquilillo
Chagüitillo
León
Las Peñitas
MANAGUA
PACIFIC OCEAN
COSTA RICA

MARIO LOPEZ/EPA/CORBIS ©

Northern Loop

Rich in nature and revolutionary culture, northern Nicaragua serves rugged and refined equally. In one trip you'll go from sipping organic coffee at the source to surfing an active volcano. Charge your batteries, you'll want to take plenty of pictures or no one will believe you when you get home.

Upon arrival skip through **Managua** (p40) and head for the crumbling colonial beauty of **León** (p139) to give Nicaragua the fantastic introduction it deserves. Spend three days exploring this endearing city on foot, visiting fascinating museums, spacious mansions and glorious churches. If you're feeling energetic, hike one of the nearby volcanoes or surf the slopes of Cerro Negro.

From León head out west to the beach at **Las Peñitas** (p156) and find a spot in a sand-floor beachside bar for the spectacular sunset. In the morning make an early start to travel north to **Jiquilillo** (p166) and spend a couple of days soaking up the ambience in this pretty fishing village and paddling through the mangroves of the nearby Reserva Natural Estero Padre Ramos.

Then travel across the Maribios Volcanic chain and into the mountains to **Estelí** (p172), where you can visit cigar factories and check out the revolutionary murals. After a couple of days head into mountains in the **Área Protegida Miraflor** (p177) for two days of horseback riding, wildlife-spotting and farm-culture immersion.

Move on to **Somoto** (p181) and to Monumento Nacional Cañon de Somoto to swim, jump and rappel your way through the canyon.

Next morning travel to **Matagalpa** (p194) for a few caffeine-fuelled days picking coffee beans and hiking on local plantations. Continue climbing higher into the mountains, stopping at the gorgeous Selva Negra coffee estate, before arriving in **Jinotega** (p188), gateway to the cloud forests of Reserva Natural Cerro Datanlí–El Diablo. Spend a day in town to climb Cerro la Cruz and then spend a couple of days hiking in the reserve.

Give your muscles a break with a boat cruise on **Lago de Apanás** (p193) before continuing on to **San Rafael del Norte** (p187) to visit one of Nicaragua's most magnificent churches or fly through the pine forest on a zipline. On your way back to Managua call in at **Chagüitillo** (p202) to view the pre-Columbian petroglyphs.

LATITUDESTOCK - TTL / GETTY IMAGES ©

Top: Monumento Nacional Cañon de Somoto
Bottom: Iglesia de La Recolección, León

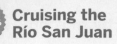

2 WEEKS Cruising the Río San Juan

The southeast corner of Nicaragua is an unparalleled playground for nature lovers of all dispositions, boasting both comfortable eco-retreats and more strenuous adventures among lush wetlands and towering rainforests that are filled with fascinating ruins, colorful reptiles and first-class birdlife.

From **Managua** (p40) fly or bus it to **San Carlos** (p244) or pick up the ferry in Granada or Ometepe. Dedicate a morning to checking out the old Spanish fort and waterfront before taking the afternoon boat over to the enchanted archipelago of the **Islas Solentiname** (p247). Spend a night on both Isla San Fernando and Isla Mancarrón, following jungle trails to in situ petroglyphs, swimming in the clear waters and visiting local artist workshops.

From Mancarrón, charter a boat to the **Río Papaturro** (p251) in the Refugio de Vida Silvestre Los Guatuzos, stopping to spot the amazing birdlife at some of the smaller islands on the way. Hike through the thick monkey-inhabited forest or kayak in the wetlands before heading out on an alligator safari in the evening.

Next take the public boat back to San Carlos to pick up a riverboat down the Río San Juan to **Boca de Sábalos** (p252), a small river town surrounded by steamy jungle. Take a tour to a local cacao plantation and chocolate factory or simply relax on your hotel balcony and spot aquatic birds on the banks of the majestic river.

After two nights in Sabalos, continue downstream to **El Castillo** (p254), where an imposing Spanish fort looms over the rapids. Spend two days here riding horses through the rolling green hills and feasting on giant river shrimp.

The following stop is the **Refugio Bartola** (p256) biological station, with a network of trails through towering old-growth forest and kayaks to paddle up the narrow jungle-clad Río Bartola to crystal-clear swimming holes.

Continue the journey by picking up a riverboat heading downriver to **San Juan de Nicaragua** (p257), where the Río San Juan pours into the Caribbean Sea. Give yourself three days to explore the ruins of Greytown, spot manatees in hidden lagoons and head up the Río Indio into the heart of the Reserva Biológica Indio-Maíz. From San Juan fly direct back to Managua.

Top: El Castillo fort overlooking the Río San Juan
Bottom: Capuchin monkeys

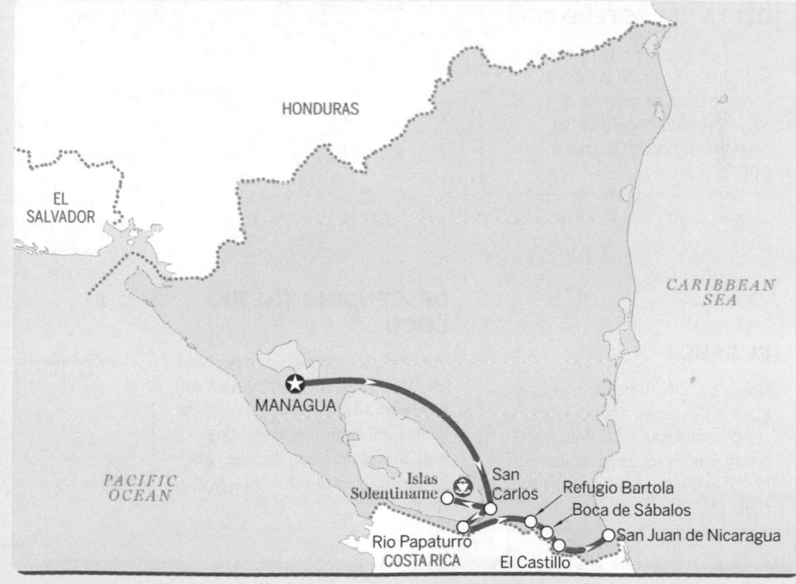
HONDURAS
EL SALVADOR
CARIBBEAN SEA
MANAGUA
PACIFIC OCEAN
Islas Solentiname
San Carlos
Refugio Bartola
Boca de Sábalos
San Juan de Nicaragua
Rio Papaturro
COSTA RICA
El Castillo

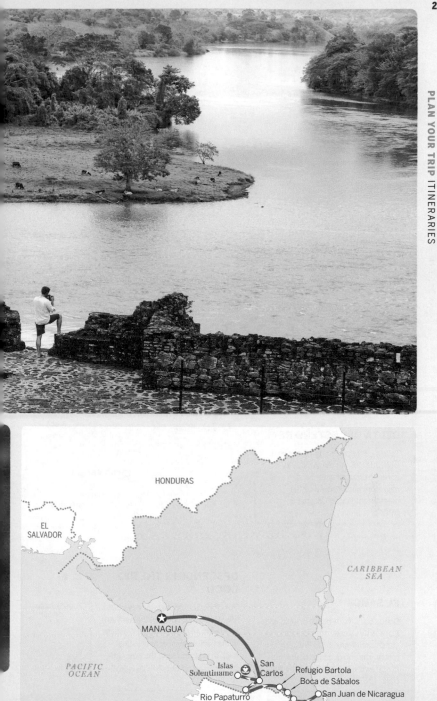

Off the Beaten Track: Nicaragua

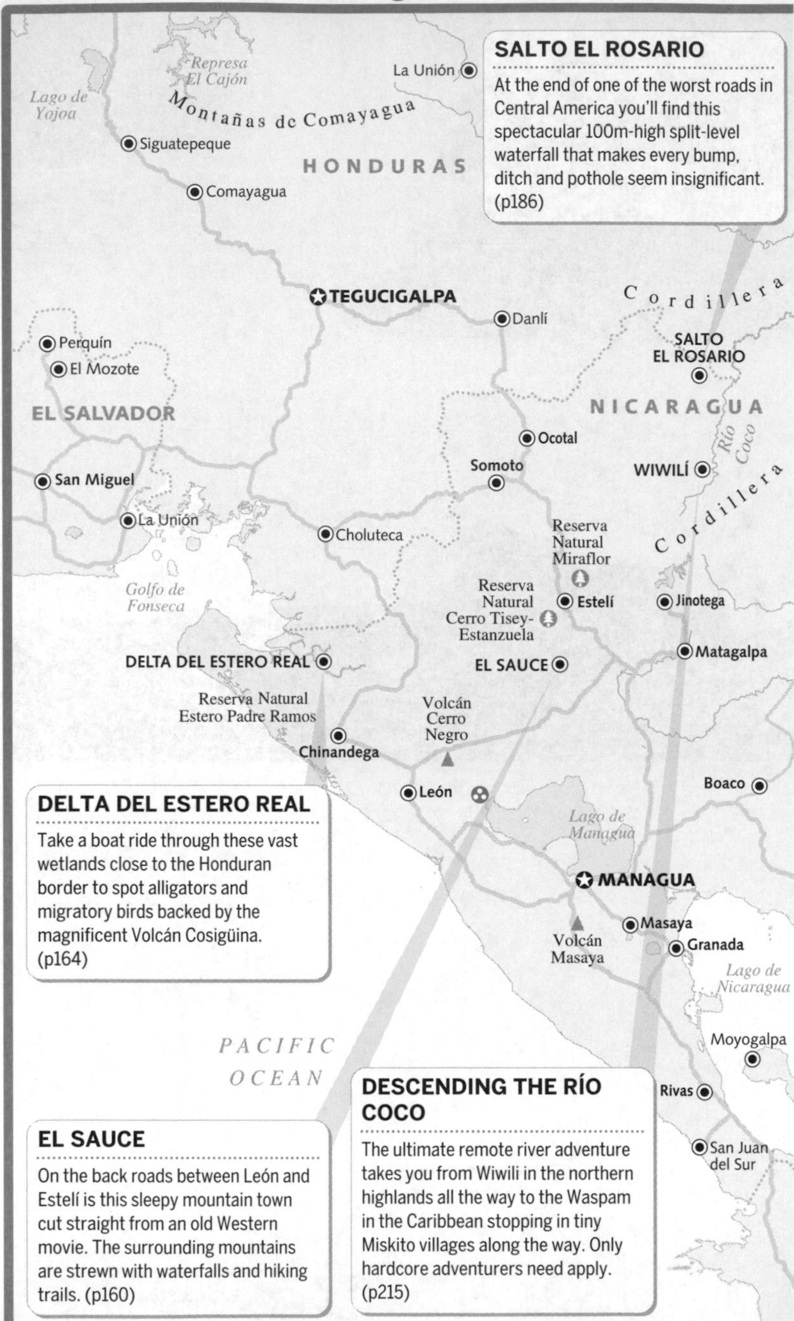
SALTO EL ROSARIO
At the end of one of the worst roads in Central America you'll find this spectacular 100m-high split-level waterfall that makes every bump, ditch and pothole seem insignificant. (p186)
DELTA DEL ESTERO REAL
Take a boat ride through these vast wetlands close to the Honduran border to spot alligators and migratory birds backed by the magnificent Volcán Cosigüina. (p164)
EL SAUCE
On the back roads between León and Estelí is this sleepy mountain town cut straight from an old Western movie. The surrounding mountains are strewn with waterfalls and hiking trails. (p160)
DESCENDING THE RÍO COCO
The ultimate remote river adventure takes you from Wiwili in the northern highlands all the way to the Waspam in the Caribbean stopping in tiny Miskito villages along the way. Only hardcore adventurers need apply. (p215)
Represa El Cajón
Lago de Yojoa
Montañas de Comayagua
La Unión
Siguatepeque
Comayagua
HONDURAS
TEGUCIGALPA
Danlí
Cordillera
Perquín
El Mozote
SALTO EL ROSARIO
EL SALVADOR
NICARAGUA
Ocotal
Río Coco
San Miguel
Somoto
WIWILÍ
Cordillera
La Unión
Choluteca
Reserva Natural Miraflor
Golfo de Fonseca
Reserva Natural Cerro Tisey-Estanzuela
Estelí
Jinotega
DELTA DEL ESTERO REAL
EL SAUCE
Matagalpa
Reserva Natural Estero Padre Ramos
Volcán Cerro Negro
Chinandega
León
Boaco
Lago de Managua
MANAGUA
Masaya
Volcán Masaya
Granada
Lago de Nicaragua
PACIFIC OCEAN
Moyogalpa
Rivas
San Juan del Sur

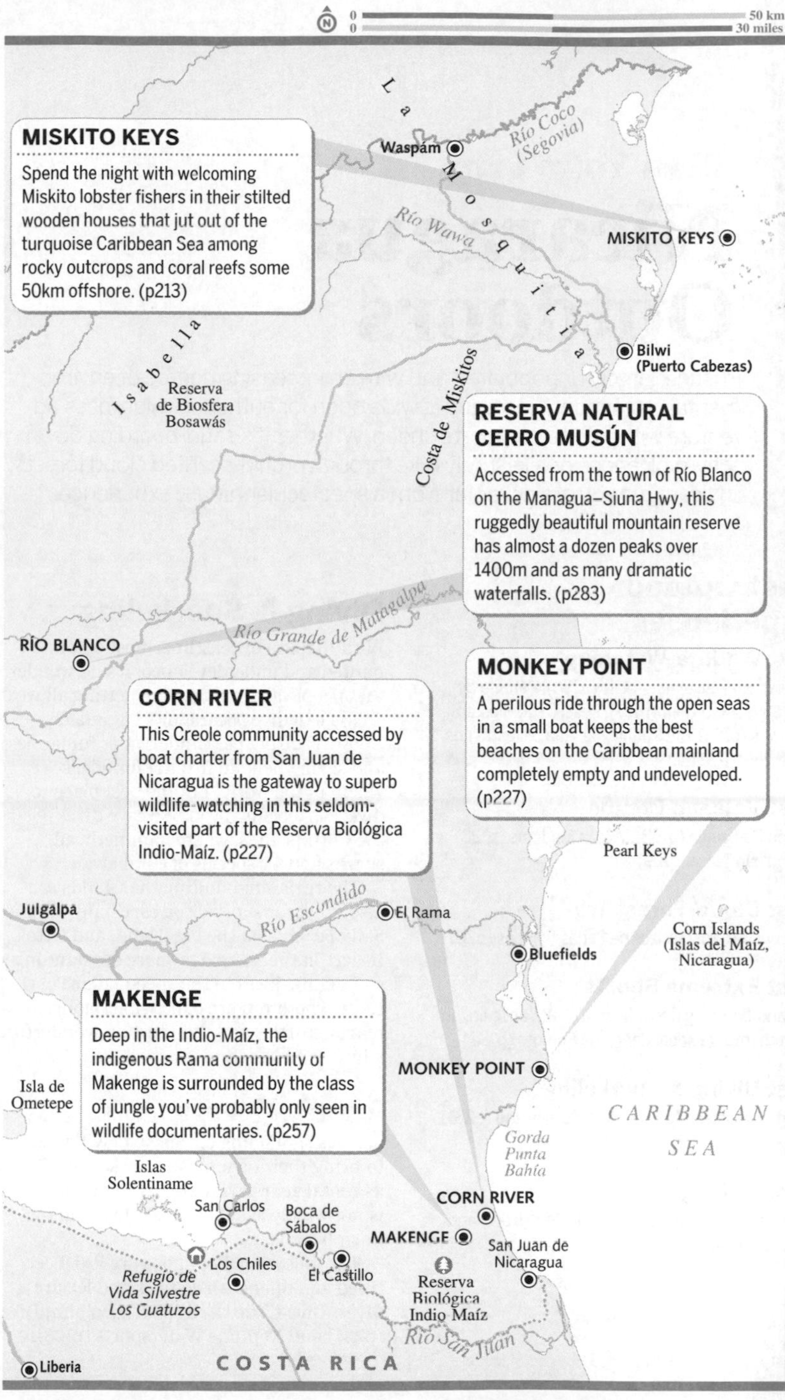

0 50 km
0 30 miles
MISKITO KEYS
Spend the night with welcoming Miskito lobster fishers in their stilted wooden houses that jut out of the turquoise Caribbean Sea among rocky outcrops and coral reefs some 50km offshore. (p213)
La Mosquitia
Waspám
Río Coco (Segovia)
Río Wawa
MISKITO KEYS
Bilwi (Puerto Cabezas)
Isabella
Reserva de Biosfera Bosawás
Costa de Miskitos
RESERVA NATURAL CERRO MUSÚN
Accessed from the town of Río Blanco on the Managua–Siuna Hwy, this ruggedly beautiful mountain reserve has almost a dozen peaks over 1400m and as many dramatic waterfalls. (p283)
Río Grande de Matagalpa
RÍO BLANCO
MONKEY POINT
A perilous ride through the open seas in a small boat keeps the best beaches on the Caribbean mainland completely empty and undeveloped. (p227)
CORN RIVER
This Creole community accessed by boat charter from San Juan de Nicaragua is the gateway to superb wildlife-watching in this seldom-visited part of the Reserva Biológica Indio-Maíz. (p227)
Pearl Keys
Julgalpa
Río Escondido
El Rama
Bluefields
Corn Islands (Islas del Maíz, Nicaragua)
MAKENGE
Deep in the Indio-Maíz, the indigenous Rama community of Makenge is surrounded by the class of jungle you've probably only seen in wildlife documentaries. (p257)
MONKEY POINT
Isla de Ometepe
CARIBBEAN SEA
Gorda Punta Bahía
Islas Solentiname
San Carlos
Boca de Sábalos
CORN RIVER
MAKENGE
San Juan de Nicaragua
Refugio de Vida Silvestre Los Guatuzos
Los Chiles
El Castillo
Reserva Biológica Indio Maíz
Río San Juan
Liberia
COSTA RICA

Plan Your Trip

Nicaragua Outdoors

Pristine, largely unpopulated and with an increasing degree of environmental protection, Nicaragua is wide open for authentic wilderness adventure without the corporate sheen. Whether it's sand-boarding down active volcanoes or a leisurely hike through orchid-scented cloud forests, in Nicaragua you are never far from a spectacular nature experience.

Best Outdoor Experiences

Best Wildlife-Watching

Reserva Biológica Indio-Maíz (p256), Refugio de Vida Silvestre La Flor (p137), Reserva de Biosfera Bosawás (p214) and Refugio de Vida Silvestre Los Guatuzos (p251)

Best Volcano Climbs

Volcán Cosigüina (p168), Volcán Maderas (p123) and Volcán Telica (p159)

Best Cloud-Forest Trek

Reserva Natural Macizos de Peñas Blancas (p201)

Best Extreme Sports

Volcano-boarding Cerro Negro (p148), abseiling in Monumento Nacional Cañon de Somoto (p182)

Best Diving & Snorkeling

Great Corn Island (p231), Little Corn Island (p231) and Pearl Keys (p230)

Best Fishing

Río San Juan (p251), San Juan del Sur (p127) and Río Escondido (p224)

Diving & Snorkeling

With 1040km of coastline, most of it untainted and underdeveloped, it's no wonder that people are interested in getting all wet.

You can dive Nicaragua's Laguna de Apoyo, cruising past underwater fumaroles and saying hello to fish not found elsewhere in the world. But the best place to dive – especially if you like cave dives – is the Corn Islands, where hammerhead sharks and 40 species of coral await.

The reefs surrounding the islands are also great for snorkeling, especially around Sally Peachie on the big island, and Otto Beach on the *islita*. For more outstanding snorkeling, head to the spectacular Pearl Keys, where you are can swim among marine turtles and then rest on wonderful white-sand beaches.

Make it Happen

Serious snorkeling enthusiasts will want to bring their own mask, snorkel and fins as rental gear varies greatly in quality and is not widely available apart from on the Corn Islands.

The following dive shops are PADI certified and offer both courses and leisure dives: Dive Little Corn (p237), Dolphin Dive (p237) and Neptune Watersports (p128).

Hiking

Thanks to an unlikely environmental consciousness (the Nicaraguan government found time to protect dozens of wilderness areas during the turbulent 1980s) and the war, which probably did more to save the rainforests than Unesco did in most countries, there's a lot of fairly pristine forest out there to see.

Some of the most interesting and easily accessible are at Área Protegida Miraflor, Reserva Natural Macizos de Peñas Blancas and Reserva Natural Cerro Datanlí–El Diablo.

The climbs with the real cachet, however, are any of the dozens of volcanoes, including the Maribios chain, Volcán Cosigüina and the volcanoes of Isla Ometepe. And if you're into dominating nature, consider the full-day climb to the peak of Cerro Mogotón (2106m), Nicaragua's highest mountain.

Make it Happen

Guides are usually recommended (and sometimes compulsory) for hikes in all but the best-developed natural parks and reserves, particularly for the volcanoes. Even on easy hikes, guides can almost always find things you never would. In smaller towns, ask about guides at the *alcaldía* (mayor's office), usually right on the Parque Central (central park).

Base yourself in the hiking havens of Estelí, Matagalpa or Jinotega to explore the mountains of the north. For volcanoes, the best access is from León.

There are a number of companies offering organized hikes. The following are recommended:

Quetzaltrekkers (p148) Nonprofit outift in León offering high-adventure volcano climbs.

Tree Huggers (p173) Based in Estelí, offers hikes around Estelí including to Área Protegida Miraflor and Cañon de Somoto.

Matagalpa Tours (p195) Matagalpa outfit, with treks to Reserva Naturals Cerro Apante, Datanlí, Peñas Blancas and other more off-the-beaten-track destinations.

Surfing

The center of Nicaraguan surfing remains San Juan del Sur, giving rise to a wave of surf camps and strongholds spreading northward to the holy grail of Nicaraguan wave-riding, Popoyo, past flawless beach breaks, scary-fun lava point breaks and lots of barrels, when conditions are right. Playa Gigante has the greatest concentration of surf camps, where all-inclusive means room, meals and boat rides out to the best waves in the area every day. North of Popoyo, despite some excellent surfing, services are thin; surfing on the Caribbean coast is possible, but there's no infrastructure and not much information available.

The best breaks often require boats to get to, not just because they're offshore, but because housing developments along the coast block land access. To make up for it, southern Nicaragua is caressed by an almost constant offshore wind, perhaps

HIKING GEAR CHECKLIST

Trekking for leisure is not particularly popular among Nicaraguans and quality gear is hard to find on the ground. If you plan on getting of the beaten track, make sure to bring the following:

- **Comfortable footwear** Consider both leather hiking boots for long days in the mountains and comfortable, sturdy sports sandals for treks involving river crossings.
- **Water purification tablets**
- **Lightweight sleeping bag** Believe it or not it does actually get cold in mountainous regions of Nicaragua.
- **Hammock** Indispensable for long boat rides or taking a break in the jungle high above the creepy crawlies of the forest floor.
- **Tent** If you find one in Nicaragua, it's likely to be bulky and barely waterproof. Bring a lightweight hiking model from home.

caused by the presence of Lago de Nicaragua and Lago de Managua.

Make it Happen

Nicaragua has great waves year-round. March to November is considered the best time to surf, with the biggest waves usually in March, April and October (consistently 1m to 2m, frequently 3m to 4m). November to March is the dry season, with smaller waves (averaging under 2m) but better weather – this is the best time for beginners.

Water temperatures average around mid-20°C (mid-70°F) year-round, but from December to April an upwelling offshore means that the water's temperature can drop; consider bringing a long-sleeve wetsuit top.

You can buy, sell and rent boards in San Juan del Sur and Popoyo, but it's generally better to bring your own board (consider selling it when you leave).

Numerous surfing outfits offer everything from one-on-one instruction to week-long all-inclusive surf packages. Listings are provided in the closest city to the waves.

Swimming

From sunny Pacific beaches to cool crater lakes, and lots of rivers and waterfalls, you'll always find places to put your bathing suit to work.

There are eight major crater lakes, with excellent swimming at Laguna de Apoyo, surrounded by lodging options, or undeveloped Laguna de Asososca, near León.

Isla de Ometepe has some excellent swimming opportunities, including the remarkable natural sand jetty at Punta Jesús María and the mineral-rich waters of La Presa Ojo de Agua.

The best beach swims are at some of the stunning coves around San Juan del

BEST BREAKS

Here are some favorite waves, which we've listed northeast to southwest. All of these beaches are on the Pacific coast. For a comprehensive list of the best breaks pick up a map (US$8) from **Surf Maps** (www.surfmaps.com).

- **Playa Aserradores** (p166) Just northeast of Chinandega, the beach is also called Boom-wavos for the powerful, hollow beach break making all that noise. There's another left five minutes offshore and plenty more waves around.
- **El Corinto** (p165) One of the best waves in the country goes almost unsurfed out there beyond Playa Paso Caballos, but it's boat access only; just north is a river-mouth break with left-breaking peaks.
- **Poneloya and Las Peñitas** (p155) Only decent surfing, but the easiest access on Nicaragua's north Pacific, just 20km from León.
- **Puerto Sandino** (p157) The stretch from Puerto Sandino to El Velero has half a dozen reef and rocky-bottomed beach breaks, including one spectacular left.
- **Playa Huehuete** (p82) Now is that golden time between when the road is paved and when the gated communities go up: check out the point, beach and river-mouth break now!
- **Playa Popoyo** (p126) This collection of sandy-floored surf lodges may be Nicaragua's next bona fide surf town, with at least four named waves: Popoyo, a right and left point break; aggressive Bus Stop; fast and rocky-floored Cobra; and the best wave in the region, Emergencias, with a left for the longboards and hollow right for short boards.
- **Playa Gigante** (p125) Accessing another handful of named waves, most of them a boat ride away, it's no wonder that surf lodges are springing up all over this beautiful beach.
- **Playa Maderas** (p135) Sometimes called Los Playones, this excellent surf spot with easy access from San Juan del Sur has a slow wave with two rights and two lefts that's perfect for beginners.

Sur and in the crystal-clear waters of the Caribbean around the Pearl Keys and the Corn Islands.

Wildlife

Nicaragua is home to an impressive array of tropical ecosystems, each offering their own outstanding wildlife-spotting opportunities.

The best spots to see big animals is in the tropical rainforests of the Reserva Bíologica Indio-Maíz and the Reserva de Biosfera Bosawás. One of the rarest ecosystems in the world is the cloud forest, a cool, misty tropical rainforest above 1200m, offering opportunities for seeing wildlife, most famously colorful quetzals and orchids. The easiest to see is at Volcán Mombacho, with easy access from Granada.

Nicaragua's Pacific coast is a haven for literally hundreds of thousands of nesting turtles each year, and some of their nesting sites are surprisingly accessible. In the San Juan del Sur area, you're within easy reach of Refugio de Vida Silvestre La Flor and Refugio de Vida Silvestre Río Escalante Chacocente. There's more turtle action further north at Reserva Natural Volcán Cosigüina.

Birders will also be drawn to Nicaragua's sweet-water wetlands and jungle-lined rivers, which offer outstanding birding opportunities.

BEST BIRDING SPOTS

➡ **Islas Solentiname** (p247) Tiny islands with Nicaragua's highest concentration of birdlife including tiger herons and flocks of roseate spoonbills.

➡ **Boca de Sábalos** (p252) Pick your spot along the river and observe a fantastic array of waterfowl and rainforest species without moving a muscle.

➡ **Área Protegida Miraflor** (p177) Accessible cloud forest boasting quetzals and toucans.

➡ **Refugio de Vida Silvestre Los Guatuzos** (p251) Immense wetlands home to around 400 bird species.

Regions at a Glance

Stretching from the sizzling Pacific with its colonial treasures, smoking volcanoes and superb surf beaches to the crystalline Caribbean with its indigenous communities and islands that groove to an altogether different tune, Nicaragua's geographical diversity is topped only by the range of cultures living within its boundaries.

The country is crowned in the north by spectacular mountain ranges covered in a patchwork of small farms, coffee plantations and cloud forest that offer great hiking and bird-watching opportunities. In the south you'll find the largest freshwater lake in Central America, with more outdoor activities than you could dream of cramming into your itinerary, wetlands brimming with birdlife and the virgin rainforests of the magnificent Río San Juan.

Managua

History
Nightlife
Culture

Walking the Town

Managua is a twisted, toiled, visceral hive of activity. Just bopping through town can be fun. Spin through the crumbling areas around the Plaza de la Revolución before walking up to the volcano's rim at Loma de Tiscapa.

Where Wild Grows

This town knows how to party. And while you'll definitely want to keep your senses about you, a diesel-charged night in the rock-roarious lounges and dancehalls along Carretera a Masaya is a rite of passage.

Dig Deep

This is the cultural fulcrum of a nation. The university offers great guerrilla learning opportunities, and there are museums and cultural houses, street artists and underground poets.

p40

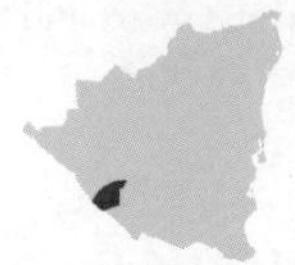

Masaya & Los Pueblos Blancos

Shopping
Culture
Outdoors

Crafts Central

Masaya has the best crafts market in all of Nicaragua. Beyond its Technicolor stalls, you'll find unique artisan workshops in the compact and neat little villages throughout this region.

Cultural Encounters

This region allows for broad-faced encounters with locals. Take the time to volunteer or learn Spanish and you'll experience the place on a whole new level.

From the Fire & the Deeps

Volcán Masaya offers great hiking trips, never-ending vistas and the all-too-real chance of being blown to smithereens in a pyroclastic burst of light. Southward, you'll come across the unrelenting beauty of Laguna de Apoyo.

p65

Granada

History
Eating
Walking

From the Pirate's Cup

Granada's history is as complex as it gets. This fleeting imprint is evidenced on nearly every corner. You'll see it in the city's architecture, its festivals, art and living culture.

A Gastronome's Delight

The city's vibrant restaurant scene will keep foodies busy for several hours each day. There's fusion, mind-blowing local steaks and experimental spots that cater to travelers of all palates.

Move

A city of movement, age-old grace and continued evolution, Granada is the place to walk till you drop. If that fails, head out by launch to explore a mythical island archipelago with monkey islands, fortresses and birds aplenty.

p83

Southwestern Nicaragua

Surf
Beauty
Wilderness

Charge It!

You don't get better surf at many other places in the world. After you hit dawn patrol at legendary spots like Playas Hermosa and Madera, you can chill out in your beachfront hammock paradise.

Islands in the Stream

Isla de Ometepe is a paradise lost. Get here now to discover petroglyphs, climb volcanoes, kayak to lost coves and chill out in cool travelers' enclaves on the edge of the wild.

Go Beyond

There are lost beaches, tough-and-ready inland towns, unique windows into rural Nicaraguan life, and wildlife preserves where turtles arrive by the thousands and birds of paradise caw madly from the forest canopy.

p105

León & Northwestern Nicaragua

History
Volcanoes
Outdoors

Revolutionary Roots

León is where the revolution was televised. And to this day, fiery rhetoric flows from this intellectual powerhouse. The partying here ain't bad either...

The Rim of Fire

The fire theme continues down below and up above in the large nature preserves that encircle massive volcanoes, forgotten islets and wide-open spaces of the interior. Come sunset, the sun lights up the Pacific night.

Explorers Club

Head north and you get further from the tourist track and closer to the wild. There are volcanoes that seldom see a climber and estuaries whose dreadlocked fingers only see a human wake once in a blue moon.

p138

Northern Highlands

Nature
Adventure
Coffee

Pristine Forests

Nature lovers will have no shortage of opportunities to spot nesting quetzals, toucans and boisterous howler monkeys among the region's swaths of precious cloud forest.

Authentic Adventure

Whether it's a mountainous trek to a hidden waterfall or tubing through an ancient canyon, the northern region offers unlimited opportunity for off-the-beaten path adventure.

Coffee Culture

The shade-grown plantations of northern Nicaragua produce classic gourmet coffees. Get into the fields and see where it comes from or go one step better and pick some beans yourself.

p169

Caribbean Coast

Beaches
Food
Culture

Pristine Shores

Romantic tropical islands with turquoise-fringed white-sand beaches shaded by coconut palms anyone? While you may find such idyllic beauty elsewhere, you won't find them as empty or undeveloped as these.

Home-Style Cooking

The coast has delicious seafood, most famously in its signature dish *'rundown'*. But *costeño* cooking goes way beyond fresh lobster, so grab a glass of seaweed punch and follow your nose to the wonderful unsigned bakeries.

Original Rhythms

Big on culture, the Caribbean coast's maypole rhythms and Miskito pop provide the soundtrack for performances by Nicaragua's best dancers.

p204

San Carlos, Islas Solentiname & the Río San Juan

Wildlife
Outdoors
Art

Bird-Watching

The remote Islas Solentiname is a haven for migratory waterbirds, and the Río San Juan is home to a grand variety of both aquatic and rainforest species.

Aquatic Adventures

The Río San Juan department is the ultimate boating playground, with kayak and canoe adventures, or alligator-spotting motorboat safaris.

A Community of Artists

A visit to the isolated island workshops and studios offers fascinating insights into the Primitivist paintings and bright balsa carvings from the Islas Solentiname.

p241

On the Road

Managua

POP 1,028,800 / ELEV 90M

Includes ➡

Best Places to Eat

- Doña Pilar (p52)
- Tercer Ojo (p52)
- La Casa de Los Nogueras (p53)

Best Places to Stay

- Managua Backpackers Inn (p51)
- Hotel Contempo (p51)
- Hotel Europeo (p50)

Why Go?

Managua is a shambles. It is chaotic and broken, poetic and mesmerizing, all at the same time.

And while most travelers are now skipping the city altogether – and arranging quick airport transfers from nearby Granada – stay a day or two and you will see that big, bad Managua ain't so bad after all, and that this truly is the heartstring that holds the nation's culture, commerce and conscious together.

Aside from diving into the whir of a magnificent beehive of honking horns, sprawling markets, garbage and rancor, this low-rise city with its improbable trees, remarkable street art and spirited monuments also gives you easy access to nearby lagoons, nature reserves at Montebelli and Chocoyero-El Brujo, a smattering of fun beaches like Pochomil, and the hot springs at El Trapiche.

When to Go

September through April is the best time of year for birdwatching. It is also good for turtle tours at nearby beaches and wild encounters in the lagoons and natural attractions just outside the city.

December through April are the dry months. Coming around now makes plying the city's streets easier, market days drier and chance encounters just a little more pleasant. Hotels can be a bit pricey during this time and during Semana Santa, so book ahead.

The best festival days are for the annual Taxi Grand Prix, the last week in March, the Day of the Revolution on July 19 or the Festival of Santo Domingo, the first 10 days in August.

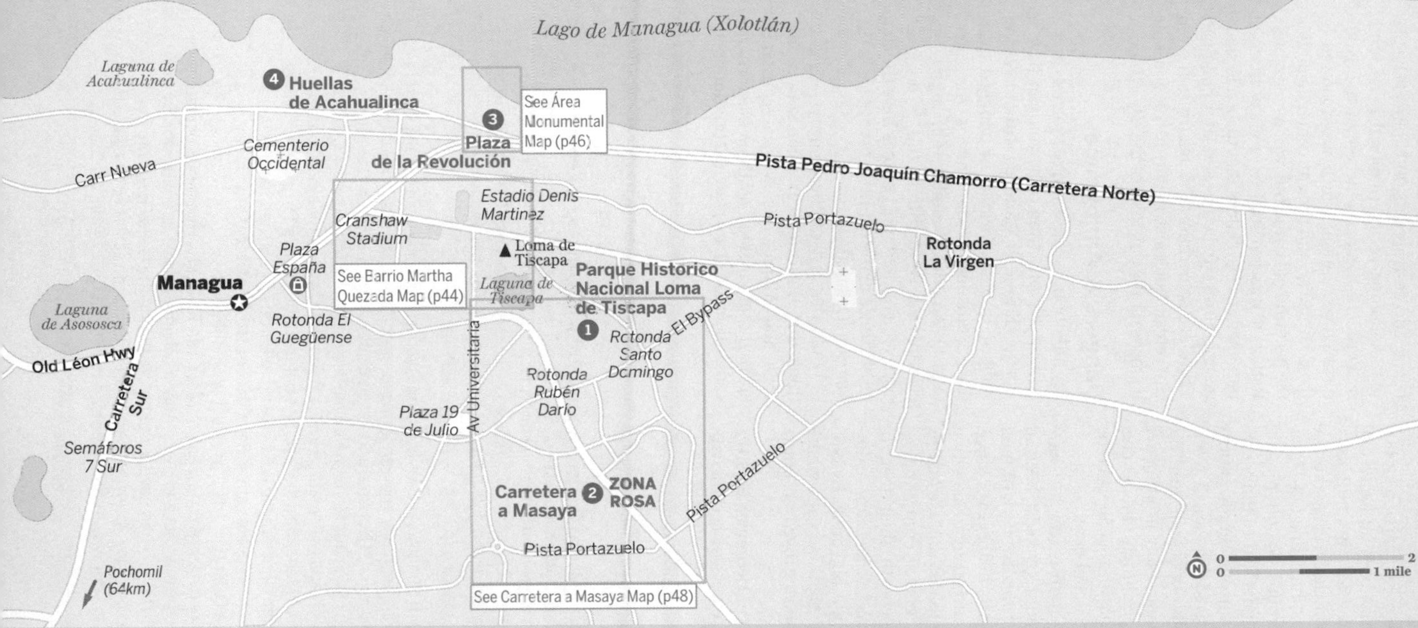

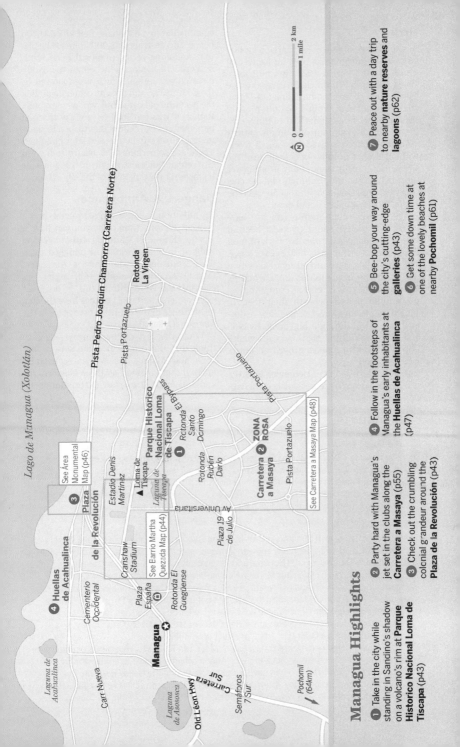

Managua Highlights

1 Take in the city while standing in Sandino's shadow on a volcano's rim at **Parque Historico Nacional Loma de Tiscapa** (p43)

2 Party hard with Managua's jet set in the clubs along the **Carretera a Masaya** (p55)

3 Check out the crumbling colonial grandeur around the **Plaza de la Revolución** (p43)

4 Follow in the footsteps of Managua's early inhabitants at the **Huellas de Acahualinca** (p47)

5 Bee-bop your way around the city's cutting-edge **galleries** (p43)

6 Get some down time at one of the lovely beaches at nearby **Pochomil** (p61)

7 Peace out with a day trip to nearby **nature reserves** and **lagoons** (p62)

History

A fishing encampment as early as 6000 years ago, Managua has been an important trading center for at least two millennia. When Spanish chronicler Fernández de Oviedo arrived in 1528, he estimated Managua's population at around 40,000; most of these original inhabitants fled to the Sierritas, the small mountains just south, shortly after the Spanish arrived. The small town, without even a hospital or school until the 1750s, didn't really achieve any prominence until 1852, when the seemingly endless civil war between Granada and León was resolved by placing the capital here.

The clever compromise might have worked out better had a geologist been at hand: Managua sits atop a network of fault lines that have shaped its history ever since. The late 1800s were rocked by quakes that destroyed the new capital's infrastructure, with churches and banks crumbling as the ground flowed beneath their feet. In 1931 the epicenter was the stadium – dozens were killed during a big game. In 1968 a single powerful jolt right beneath what's now Metrocentro mall destroyed an entire neighborhood.

And on the evening of December 23, 1972, a series of powerful tremors rocked the city, culminating in a 6.2 quake that killed 11,000 people and destroyed 53,000 homes. The blatant siphoning of international relief funds by President Somoza touched off the Sandinista-led revolution, which was followed by the Contra War, and the city center, including the beautiful old cathedral, was never rebuilt. Rather, it was replaced by a crazy maze of unnamed streets, shacks that turned to shanties that turned to homes and later buildings. There are some efforts to resurrect the old city center, but most new construction now happens on the outskirts of the city center.

Dangers & Annoyances

Pay attention, because you're probably going to hear this one time only: you can have a wonderful time in Managua without getting stabbed, robbed, beaten or mugged even once. Statistically, Managua is the safest Central American capital (although, considering the competition, this is no great achievement) and most crimes here (in fact, most crimes in the country) take place in the Mercado Oriental.

While the rest of the country seems to think that the capital is some sort of war zone and Managuans will be constantly amazed that you *walked* three blocks *alone* and still made it to your destination, stay-

MANAGUA IN...

One Day

If you wake up in Barrio Martha Quezada, you can just walk to the top of **Loma de Tiscapa** and the unmissable silhouette of **Sandino**. Then grab a cab (negotiating your fare beforehand!) to **Huellas de Acahualinca** for ancient history, then **Área Monumental** for the modern version. If nothing's on at **Teatro Nacional Rubén Darío** that night, enjoy a mellow evening of live music at **La Casa de los Mejía Godoy**.

Three Days

After communing with Sandino and Momotombo, you'll even have time to take the **Tiscapa Canopy Tour**, then really enjoy the museums and monuments, and grab tickets for a show at Teatro Nacional Rubén Darío; discuss afterward at **Bar La Cavanga**.

The next morning, check out Managua's lively art scene at **Epikentro** or **Códice**, followed by a sandwich and coffee at the lovely **Casa del Café**. After lunch, grab a little down time in one of Managua's leafy **parks** before hitting **Zona Hippo's** for some predinner drinks. After dinner, make your way up to Parque El Carmen where you can catch some experimental theater at **La Sala de Teatro Justo Rufino Garay**, or a poetry reading or live DJ at **Bar Art Café**, just down the road.

Day three is for shopping: grab souvenirs at **Mercado Roberto Huembes** or resupply for the hinterlands at the markets and malls. After lunch in exclusive Altamira, stop by the **Catedral Metropolitana**. Then have a nap before hitting the Bello Horizonte neighborhood, where you can enjoy your pizza to a mariachi soundtrack at **Pizzeria Los Idolos** before making your way to **Mrs Sponge** to get your groove on, Caribbean style, for your last night out.

ing safe here requires no greater amount of street smarts than you'd use in any major city from New York to New Delhi. Don't flash expensive items, look at the map *before* leaving your hotel/restaurant, carry only as much money as you're realistically going to need for the day, money belts go INSIDE your clothing, don't wander around drunk alone at night, and if you get lost, hail a cab.

It's fairly obvious which neighborhoods to avoid (and there's no real reason to go there, anyway), but if you do find yourself surrounded by abandoned houses and tattooed guys hanging out on street corners, turn around and go back the way you came.

The Barrio Martha Quezada has a particularly bad rep. It's fine in the daytime but gets sketchy at night, particularly on the unlit streets leading to the Plaza Inter mall. The neighborhood gets progressively worse the further north you go past Calle 27 de Mayo, and this area should be avoided day and night.

Sights & Activities

Managua's sights are few and, with the exception of the often deserted Área Monumental, far between. Taxis are a cheap and worthwhile investment in Managua's muggy climate.

Barrio Martha Quezada & Around

Since the days of the *internacionalistas* (idealistic visitors who came during the revolutionary years in the 1980s), Barrio Martha Quezada has been the city's budget-travel headquarters. It has easy access to Plaza Inter Mall and most international buses. Better to take a cab here at night.

Parque Histórico Nacional Loma de Tiscapa PARK
(8am-8pm Tue-Sun) Home to what's easily Managua's most recognizable landmark, Sandino's somber silhouette, this national historic park was once the site of the Casa Presidencial, where Sandino and his men were executed in 1934; what looks like a dilapidated parking structure was for decades one of Nicaragua's most notorious prisons.

You can see Sandino, hastily erected by the departing Frente Sandinista de Liberación Nacional (FSLN; Sandinista National Liberation Front) government after its electoral loss in 1990, from almost anywhere in town; begin your ascent at the Crowne Plaza. You'll pass **Monumento Roosevelt** (Map p44), constructed in 1939, with lovely lake views, which is today a memorial to those killed in the revolution.

The top of **Loma de Tiscapa** is actually the lip of Volcán Tiscapa's beautiful little crater lake, with incredible views of the city, both cathedrals and Volcán Momotombo, plus **Canopy Tiscapa** (Map p44; 8893 5017; canopytiscapa@yahoo.com; per person US$15), a small but fun 1.2km, three-platform, 25-minute tour. Keep in mind that, despite a vigorous clean-up campaign, the lake is polluted with untreated sewage.

Arboretum Nacional GARDENS
(National Arboretum; Map p44; admission US$0.30; 8am-5pm Mon-Fri) These modest gardens, inconveniently located halfway between Barrio Martha Quezada and the Plaza Monumental on Av Bolívar (well, it's convenient if you're making the hot 40-minute walk between them), features more than 200 species of plants divided into Nicaragua's five major life zones.

Of these only the dry tropical forest and central lowlands look happy. Your fee includes a guided tour, where you'll see a *madriño,* the national tree, and *sacuanjoche,* the national flower.

Epikentro Gallery ART GALLERY
(Map p44; www.epikentrogallery.com; Canal 2, 2c N, 2c O) Straddling the divide between fine and contemporary art.

Galeria Praxis ART GALLERY
(Map p44; 2266 3563; uniondeartesplasticos@yahoo.es; Embajada de Alemania, 1c O, 1c N; 10am-5:30pm Mon-Fri, to 2pm Sat) A fine collection of contemporary art at this artist-run collective.

Plaza de la Revolución & El Malecón

This quiet collection of pre-earthquake and post-revolutionary monuments, parks, museums and government offices was once the pulsing heart of Managua; the *malecón* (pier), a pleasant stroll from the Plaza de la Revolución, once overlooked a living lake lined with restaurants and festivities. Then came the 1972 earthquake, and two decades of war and privation, and the center was all but abandoned.

But slowly – little by little, as they say in Nicaragua – it is being resuscitated. Government buildings have been rebuilt and trees

Barrio Martha Quezada

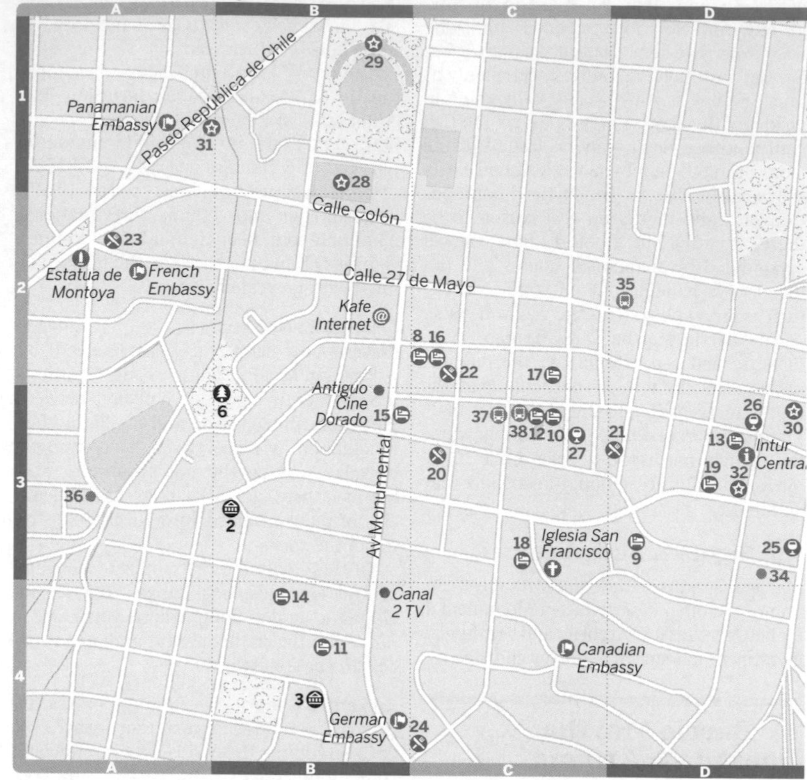

replanted, and ramshackle restaurants once again host cheerful after-church crowds on the lakefront.

Plaza de la Revolución PARK
(Map p46) Inaugurated in 1899 by national hero and original anti-American General José Santos Zelaya, this open plaza has been the scene of countless protests, parades, romances and more. On the northeast of the plaza rests the **tomb** of Sandinista commander Carlos Fonseca.

Antigua Catedral CATHEDRAL
(Map p46) The hollow shell of Managua's Old Cathedral remains Managua's most poignant metaphor, shattered by the 1972 earthquake and, despite promises, never restored. Though still beautiful and serene, attended by stone angels and dappled in golden light, it is empty and off-limits; the cathedral without a heart, in the city without a center.

Palacio de la Cultura y Biblioteca Nacional MUSEUM
(Map p46; admission US$2; ⏲8am-5pm Mon-Fri, 9am-4pm Sat & Sun) Adjacent to the cathedral, the 1935 palace houses the **Museo Nacional** (Map p46; admission US$2; ⏲8am-5pm). The timeline starts only 500 million years ago, as Nicaragua is one of the newest places on earth, and takes visitors through the formation of the lakes and volcanoes – not to mention gold mines – before getting to pre-Columbian statuary and one of the best pottery collections in the country, all well signed and explained.

Other exhibits whiz through the Spanish-colonial period before landing in the Sandino, then the Sandinista, eras. Above the main staircase is a mural of revolutionary movements in the Americas by Mexican artist Arnold Belkin, and there's also a room tracing 500 years of art (most from the 1970s).

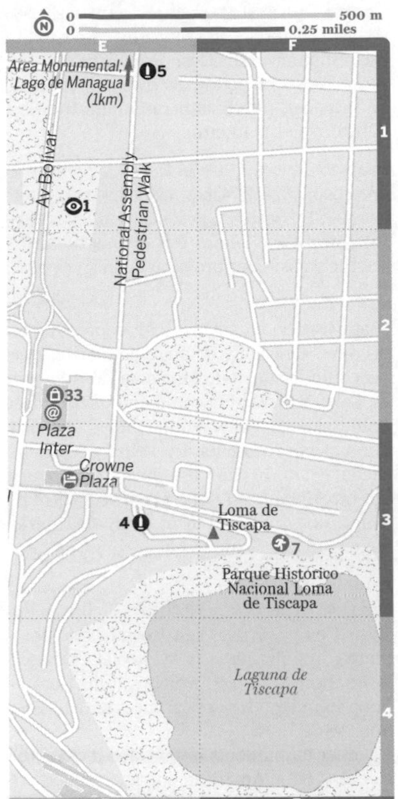

Barrio Martha Quezada

Sights
1 Arboretum Nacional E1
2 Epikentro Gallery B3
3 Galeria Praxis B4
4 Monumento Roosevelt E3
5 National Assembly Pedestrian Walk E1
6 Parque El Carmén B3

Activities, Courses & Tours
7 Canopy Tiscapa F3

Sleeping
8 Casa de Huéspedes Santos C2
9 Casa Linda B & B D3
10 Casa Vanegas C3
11 Hostal Casa El Madroño B4
12 Hostal Dulce Sueño C3
13 Hotel El Conquistador D3
14 Hotel Europeo B4
15 Hotel Los Felipe B3
16 Hotel y Apartamento Los Cisneros C2
17 Jardín de Italia C2
18 La Posada del Angel C3
19 Mansión Teodolinda D3

Eating
20 Cafetín Mirna C3
21 Cafetín Tonalli D3
22 Doña Pilar C2
23 Licuados Ananda A2
24 Restaurante Santa Fe C4

Drinking & Nightlife
25 Caramanchel D3
26 El Grillito D3
27 Shannon Bar C3

Entertainment
Cinema Plaza Inter .... (see 33)
28 Estadio Cranshaw B1
29 Estadio Denis Martínez B1
30 La Casa de los Mejía Godoy D3
31 Ruta Maya A1
32 Tabú D3

Shopping
33 Plaza Inter E2

Transport
34 Alamo D3
35 Central Line D2
King Quality .... (see 30)
36 Lugo A3
37 Tica Bus C3
38 Transporte del Sol C3

Admission includes a 30-minute guided tour in Spanish.

Casa del Pueblo BUILDING

(Map p46) This was rebuilt during the Alemán years with the help of the Taiwanese government as offices for the president, but is now home to the controversial Consejos de Poder CiudadanoCPCs (CPCs).

Monumento a Rubén Darío MONUMENT

(Map p46) On the lake side of Plaza de la Revolución, this monument was refurbished after the original 1933 statue fell into graffitied disrepair. A group of artists did a guerrilla installation, veiling the city's shame from public view and demanding poetic justice. In 1998 the cash-strapped government bowed to public opinion and, with Texaco Oil's help, restored the likeness of Nicaragua's favorite son.

Área Monumental

Top Sights

1 Plaza de la Revolución........................B2

Sights

2 Antigua Catedral................................B2
3 Casa del Pueblo................................B2
4 Centro Cultural Managua..................A3
5 Concha Acústica................................A1
6 Estatua al Soldado............................A3
7 Malecón..A1
8 Monumento a Rubén Darío................A2
9 Monumento al Trabajador Nicaragüense..................................B3
Museo Nacional..........................(see 10)
10 Palacio de la Cultura y Biblioteca Nacional..........................B3
11 Parque de la Paz...............................B3
Teatro Nacional Rubén Darío.....(see 15)
12 Tomb of Carlos Fonseca....................A2

Activities, Courses & Tours

13 Puerto Salvador Allende....................A1

Entertainment

14 Bar La Cavanga.................................B3
15 Teatro Nacional Rubén Darío............A2

Centro Cultural Managua CULTURAL BUILDING
(Map p46; Plaza de la Revolución, 1c S) Located in the remnants of the Gran Hotel, this cultural center hosts changing art exhibits, concerts and dances, plus handicrafts fairs the first Saturday of the month.

Teatro Nacional Rubén Darío BUILDING
(Map p46; ☎2222-7426; www.tnrubendario.gob.ni; tours US$1; ⏲guided tours 9am-noon & 1-4pm Mon-Fri) Toward the lake is this oblong theatre – see the website for program details.

Malecón WATERFRONT
(Map p46) The *malecón* is a bit depressing on off days, especially if you're pondering how we could let Lago de Managua (also known as Lake Xolotlán) become one of the most polluted bodies of water in Central America. Foreign governments are helping clean up the lake, and in the meantime families turn out on Sunday and partiers on weekend evenings, not to swim but to enjoy the quirky collection of seaside kiosks.

Concha Acústica MONUMENT
(Map p46) The trippy Acoustic Shell was designed by US artist Glen Howard and completed in July 2005. It overlooks **Plaza de la Fé Juan Pablo II**, which commemorates Pope John Paul II's appearances here in 1983 and 1996.

Other monuments in this area include the statue of Latin American liberation superhero **Simón Bolívar**, donated by the government of Venezuela in 1997; slightly overgrown **Plaza de la Cultura de Guatemala**; and the unabashedly political, disturbingly disproportionate **Estatua al Soldado** (Map p46) (Nameless Guerrilla Soldier) on the western side of Av Bolívar, catercorner to the Centro Cultural Managua. 'Workers and *campesinos* onward till the end,' reads the inscription, which explains the pickax, if not the assault rifle with a Sandinista flag sticking out of it. A block away, the **Monumento al Trabajador Nicaragüense** (Map p46) – another uncomfortably contorted sculpture, this one commissioned by the Liberals – celebrates the Nicaraguan worker with a bronzed, rather hunchbacked couple who look like they need a vacation and decent health care.

Parque de la Paz PARK
(Map p46) Managua's Peace Park, with its signature lighthouse, is a lasting symbol of the challenges and hopes facing a poor nation emerging from war. The park was in-

augurated in 1990 by then President Violeta Barrios de Chamorro. The concept in and of itself is quite beautiful. Within the park, they interred machines guns, pistols and even a tank in concrete – symbolically burying Nicaragua's bellicose past. Since then, the reflection pool has been drained, every brass plaque has been stolen, and even the generators and wiring for the lights have been pinched. This park is notorious for muggings – come in the middle of the day, without valuables and in a group. Try asking a guard to walk with you.

National Assembly Pedestrian Walk PUBLIC ART
(Map p44; Avenida Central) East of the National Assembly along Avenida Central is a pedestrian walk with open-air exhibits on Nicaragua's history, featuring everything from historic photos of Sandino to evocative pictures of pre-Earthquake Managua. It is sometimes closed to the public.

Puerto Salvador Allende BOAT TOUR
(Map p46; ☎2222-2745; www.epn.com.ni) This relatively modern port offers 45-minute boat tours Tuesday to Sunday to Isla del Amor at 11am, 1pm, 3pm and 5pm (US$3 to US$5). You can also head out Friday to Sunday at 10am and 1pm for a two-hour tour to the small village of San Francisco Libre (US$8).

Other Neighborhoods

Huellas de Acahualinca ARCHAEOLOGICAL SITE
(☎2266-5774; admission US$4, photography fee US$1; ⌚9am-4pm) Discovered by miners in 1874, these fossilized tracks record the passage of perhaps 10 people – men, women and children – as well as birds, raccoons and deer across the muddy shores of Lago de Managua some 6000 years ago. Despite early speculation that they were running from a volcanic eruption, forensics specialists have determined that these folks were in no hurry – and oddly enough, were fairly tall, between 145cm and 160cm.

The excavation was undertaken by the Carnegie Foundation in 1941 and 1942, and unearthed 14 layers, or 4m, of earth. They found some later Chorotega ceramics (about 2m down) and other intriguing artifacts, though there's no money to take it further. There is, however, a nifty on-site museum, with human skulls, a fossilized bison track and lots of ceramics, and your fee includes a Spanish-language tour of the whole shebang. Don't skip this one; it's an international treasure.

The best way here is by taxi (US$2 to US$4 per person).

Catedral Metropolitana CATHEDRAL
(Map p48; www.catedralmga.blogspot.com) Just north of the Metrocentro mall is an unforgettable Managua landmark and the

ESCAPE THE CHAOS IN MANAGUA'S GREEN SPACES

Tired of honking horns, screeching hawkers, pollution and litter? Take an afternoon breather in one of Managua's green areas. For your safety, only visit park areas during the day.

Parque Japonés (Map p48; Star City, 2c E) This not-particularly-Japanese park, nestled in the back blocks of the Metrocentro area, is a great place for a bit of time out – there are plenty of trees, some walking tracks and a couple of good playgrounds to keep the kids happy.

Parque El Carmén (Map p44; Antiguo Cine Dorado, 2c O) A couple of blocks from Martha Quezada's concrete jungle, this surprisingly pretty park is a little slice of suburbia, with kids riding bikes, a playground, and a kiosk selling snacks and cold drinks. The park is surrounded by some fairly opulent homes, including that of President Ortega – if your taxi driver doesn't know it, tell him '*donde vive Daniel*' (where Daniel lives).

Parque Las Palmas (Estatua de Montoya, 3c O, 50m N) A cute and shady little neighborhood park with the requisite benches, snack kiosks and even a laid-back bar in the middle.

Parque Las Piedrecitas (Carretera Sur, Km 6) Although it packs out on weekends with family groups, midweek this park on the western edge of the city is a slice of tranquility. There are great views of nearby Laguna Asososca, and very average food available at the kiosk – bring a picnic. Any bus heading along the Carr Sur toward Jinotepe can drop you at the entrance. Taxis charge about US$2.50 per person.

Carretera a Masaya

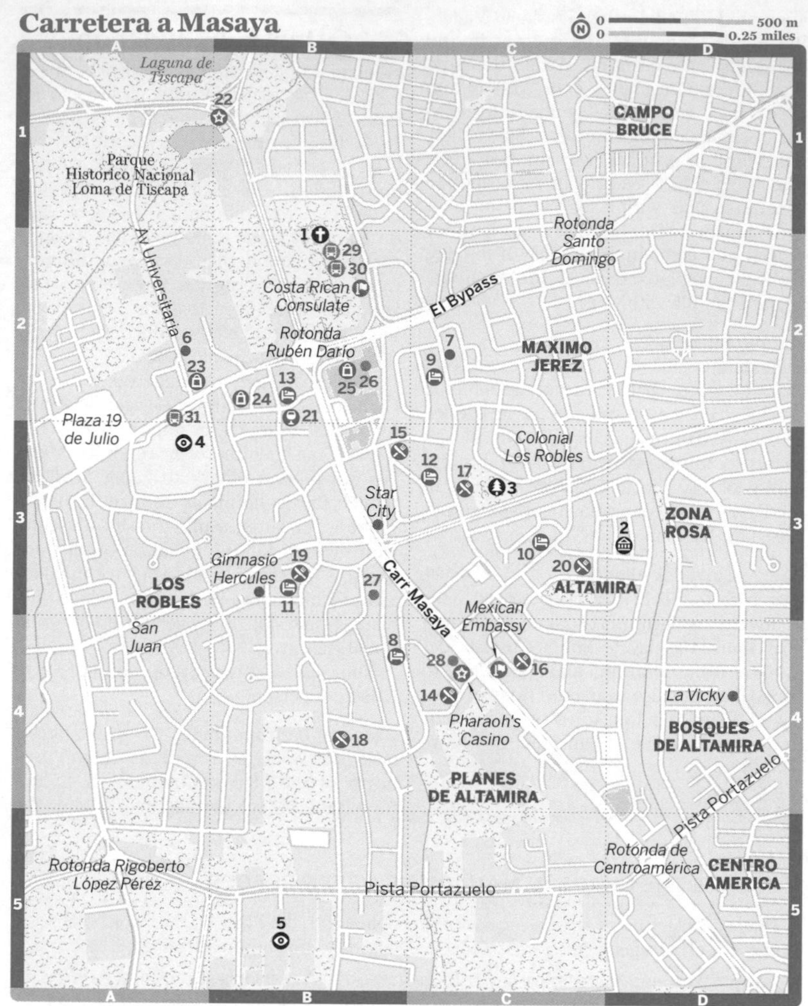

hemisphere's newest cathedral, an architectural marvel that leaves most visitors, well, scratching their heads. It's not a mosque, really: the 63 cupolas (or breasts, or eggs; speculation continues) symbolize Nicaragua's 63 Catholic churches, and also provide structural support during earthquakes – a good thing, since it sits astride a fault line.

Códice Espacio Cultural ART GALLERY

(Map p48; www.galeriacodice.com; Hotel Colón, 1c S, 2½c E) The best place to catch really cutting-edge contemporary art in Managua.

UCA UNIVERSITY

(Universidad Centro America; Map p48; www.uca.edu.ni; Rotonda Rubén Darío, 500m O) Founded in 1960 as a Jesuit school, this is one of Nicaragua's premier universities, with a science- and alternative-technology-heavy curriculum, Che Guevara sculptures, and vegetarian eateries out front. Worth a wander, in particular is the Centro Historia Militar, with relics from Sandino to the Sandinistas.

UNAN UNIVERSITY

(Universidad Nacional Autónoma de Nicaragua; Map p48; www.unan.edu.ni; Enitel Villa Fontana, 500m O) The Managua branch of Nicaragua's old-

Carretera a Masaya

Sights
1 Catedral Metropolitana B2
2 Códice Espacio Cultural D3
3 Parque Japonés C3
4 UCA A3
5 UNAN B5

Activities, Courses & Tours
6 La Academia Nicaragüense de la Danza A2
7 Viva Spanish School C2

Sleeping
8 Casa Naranja B4
9 Hotel Brandt's C2
10 Hotel Colón C3
Hotel Los Pinos .... (see 11)
11 Hotel Los Robles B3
12 Managua Backpackers Inn C3
13 Seminole Plaza Hotel B2

Eating
14 Cocina Doña Haydee C4
El Garabato .... (see 19)
15 El Muelle B3
La Casa de Los Nogueras .... (see 11)
16 La Casa del Café C4
17 La Hora del Taco C3
La Marseilles .... (see 11)
La Terraza Peruana .... (see 8)
Marea Alta .... (see 13)
18 Pan e Vino B4
19 Tercer Ojo B3
20 Yan Yan Siu C3

Drinking & Nightlife
21 Zona Hippo's B2

Entertainment
Metrocentro Cinemark .... (see 25)
22 Zona Latino B1

Shopping
23 El Parnaso A2
24 Librería Hispamer B2
Mama Delfina .... (see 18)
25 Metrocentro B2
Simplemente Madera .... (see 18)

Transport
26 Avis B2
27 Copa Airlines B3
Delta Airlines .... (see 19)
28 Easy Rent-a-car C4
29 Transnica B2
30 Transnica B2
31 UCA Minivans A2

est university (the original is in León, the former capital) was founded in 1958 and has more than 24,000 students.

Courses

Alianza Francesa COURSE
(☎2267-2811; www.alianzafrancesa.org.ni; Planes de Altamira, de la Embajada de México ½c N) Offers classes in painting, drawing, French, German and Portuguese, along with occasional art exhibits and poetry readings.

La Academia Nicaragüense de la Danza DANCE CLASS
(Map p48; ☎2277 5557; asociacionartistas@turbonett.com; UCA, 50m N, Av Universitaria) Offers a huge range of dance classes (salsa, merengue, reggaetón, folk, ballet, flamenco and belly, to name a few) for about US$25 per month.

Viva Spanish School LANGUAGE COURSE
(Map p48; ☎2270-2339; www.vivaspanishschool.com; Edificio FNI, 2c S) Highly recommended by long-term volunteers and NGO workers, classes here start at US$175 for a 20 hour week. Homestays can be arranged for an additional US$135 per week.

Festivals & Events

In addition to enthusiastic celebrations of national events, Managua has its own parties.

Annual Taxi Grand Prix EVENT
(Last week in March) Drivers modify a licensed taxi's exhaust system, then head to the pit at the Antigua Catedral. The roads of central Managua are closed off and dozens of five-car, five-lap races scream through the city, but only one will win a brand-new cab.

Day of the Revolution NATIONAL HOLIDAY
(July 19) You'll finally understand why people still love Daniel Ortega when you see the master work a crowd of 100,000 red-and-black-flag-waving faithful.

Festival of Santo Domingo de Guzmán RELIGIOUS
(August 1 to August 10) Managua's *fiestas patronales* (patron saint parties) feature a carnival, sporting events, *hípicos* (horse parades) and a procession of *diablitos,* which takes Santo Domingo to his country shrine at the Sierritas de Managua, followed by music and fireworks.

Sleeping

Most budget travelers stay in Barrio Martha Quezada, about 10 square blocks of fairly strollable streets, although crime is on the rise. But there are other options, from the posh boutique hotels of the Carretera a Masaya to more modest midrange options in Bolonia, convenient to Barrio Martha Quezada's collection of backpacker-oriented businesses.

Barrio Martha Quezada & Around

Better known to *taxistas* as 'Tica bus,' the international bus terminal upon which the barrio (district) is centered, Martha Quezada's been hosting shoestringers for a generation. Just to the south, the leafier, more upscale residential neighborhood of Bolonia has a handful of relaxed boutique hotels. Directions here are usually given from Canal Dos (Canal 2).

Hotel Los Felipe HOTEL **$**
(Map p44; 2222-6501; www.hotellosfelipe.net.ni; Tica Bus, 1½c O; s/d with fan US$15/20, with air-con US$25/30;) If you're planning on doing anything more than crashing the night and moving on, this is where you want to be. Rooms are a decent size, spotless and dotted around a lush garden with a (relatively) huge pool. Small discounts apply for more than three days, bigger ones for a month.

Casa Vanegas HOTEL **$**
(Map p44; 2222-4043; casavanegas1@hotmail.com; Tica Bus, 1c O; s/d US$12/20, s without bathroom $12;) Clean and secure, this friendly family-run spot offers decent-sized, unexciting rooms around a small patio. Hammocks, a spacious lounge area, cable TV and a shared kitchen make it a good option.

Hostal Dulce Sueño HOTEL **$**
(Map p44; 2228-4195; www.hostaldulcesueno.com; Tica Bus, 70m E; s/d US$10/16;) This simple guesthouse has spotless, no-frills rooms, and a central patio with a TV and a shared kitchen. It's a few steps from the Tica bus terminal, but this block is reputedly quite dangerous at night.

Jardín de Italia HOTEL **$**
(Map p44; 2222-7967; www.jardindeitalia.com; Tica Bus, 1c E, ½c N; r per person US$10;) Rooms, done out in cutesy, homey decorations, run alongside a pretty garden. The rooms are passable, but the service is just a bit odd.

Casa de Huéspedes Santos HOTEL **$**
(Map p44; 2222-3713; www.casadehuespedessantos.com.ni; Tica Bus, 1c N, 1½ O; r per person US$7;) This rambling classic has a variety of rooms arranged around a couple of covered courtyards. The murals, the layout and the vibe are either artsy, quirky or just plain grungy, depending on your point of view. For a few bucks more, you can do a whole lot better.

Hotel y Apartamento Los Cisneros HOTEL **$$**
(Map p44; 2222-3235; www.hotelloscisneros.com; Tica Bus, 1c N, 1½ O; s/d with fan US$30/40, with air-con US$46/56, apt from US$40;) A great deal with quirky, colorful, relative luxury, it's got hot water, phones, art and potted plants everywhere. The apartments are basically just big rooms with a kitchenette, but they're upstairs and you get your own balcony and hammock.

Casa Linda B&B B&B **$$**
(Map p44; 2266 8575; casalindamanagua@yahoo.com; 2c N, 170m O, Hospital Militar; s/d incl breakfast US$30/40;) This simple family home-turned-hotel has fairly large rooms that can be a bit musty at times. All in all, there's an overall feel of cheeriness here, making it a decent midrange bet in a central location.

★**Hotel Europeo** HOTEL **$$$**
(Map p44; 2268-2130; www.hoteleuropeo.com.ni; Canal 2, 75m O; s/d/tr incl breakfast US$67/80/94;) A favorite high-end pick in central Managua, the Europeo wins big points for its clean business-style rooms, thatched-roof restaurant out back, large gardens and fun pool. But the real kicker is that all profits from the hotel go to benefit the Dianova Nicaragua Foundation – nice!

La Posada del Angel BOUTIQUE HOTEL **$$$**
(Map p44; 2268-7228; www.hotelposadadelangel.com.ni; frente Iglesia San Francisco; s/d incl breakfast US$58/72;) The best valued top-end hotel in the downtown area, this large converted neo-Colonial-style house has huge rooms (get one upstairs) with plenty of antiques, Persian rugs and polished balustrades. Breakfast is served on the grassy lawn out back, where a good-sized pool awaits.

Hotel El Conquistador BUSINESS HOTEL **$$$**
(Map p44; ☎2222-4789; www.hotelelconquistador.info; Esso, 1c O, 1½c S; s/d incl breakfast US$47/58; P ❄ 📶) One of the few hotels with any real style in the area, the Conquistador masks itself as a business hotel, but the granny quilts and wrought-iron bedstands reveal a homespun bed and breakfast at heart. Rooms are big and comfortable – go for corner room number 5, with windows on two walls.

Mansión Teodolinda BUSINESS HOTEL **$$$**
(Map p44; ☎2228-1050; www.teodolinda.com.ni; Intur, 1c S, 1c O; s/d US$70/77; P ❄ @ 📶 🏊) The Teodolinda offers up some decent-sized rooms with all the business-class amenities. Good nightlife and restaurants are all within a block's walk, but for the price, many will opt for a place along the Carretera a Masaya.

Hostal Casa El Madroño HOTEL **$$$**
(Map p44; ☎2266-6657; www.hostalcasaelmadrono.com; Hospital Su Medico, ½c O; s/d incl breakfast US$50/60; ❄ @ 📶) The well-decked-out, carpeted rooms here are ridiculously big. Most have two king-sized beds, and there's still enough room to swing various cats – if that's what you're into. Go for room number 8 out the back – it's like a separate little house.

Centro Commercial & Carretera a Masaya

Although this cluster of upscale neighborhoods includes Metrocentro mall and Managua's busiest intersection, walking around these shady side streets is rather nice, plus it's convenient to the country's best hotels and discos. Of course, you'll pay for it.

Managua Backpackers Inn HOSTEL **$**
(Map p48; ☎2267-0006; www.managuahostel.com; El Muelle, 75m S; dm with fan/air-con US$10/14, s/d without bathroom $23/29, d with air-con $34; P ❄ @ 📶 🏊) In the quiet suburb of Los Robles, this is the best hostel in Managua. It is minutes away from the Metrocentro mall and endless nightlife and restaurant options. Rooms are basic but breezy, open and comfortable. And all the hostel amenities are here – DVD room, good-sized pool, well-stocked kitchen and heaps of tourist info.

Hotel Brandt's BOUTIQUE HOTEL **$$**
(Map p48; ☎2277-1884; www.brandtshotel.com.ni; Colonial Los Robles No 132, Bancentro Carretera a Masaya 2cE, 150m N; s/d incl breakfast US$64/70; ❄ 📶) This reasonably priced boutique in the tony Los Robles neighborhood has clean, modern, airy rooms with a contempo-casual feel. It only allows greys, browns, blacks and whites into the simple color scheme, and some may miss the vibrant colors of other colonial boutiques. But for moderno-philes, this is a great pick.

Hotel Contempo BOUTIQUE HOTEL **$$$**
(☎2264-9160; www.contempohb.com; Carretera a Masaya, Km 11, 400m O, Residencial las praderas; r US$100-200; P ❄ @ 📶 🏊) This modern boutique is one of the finest in all of Managua. We only wish it were a little more centrally located, but the large ultramodern rooms with flatscreens, MP3 docks, funked-out architecture and cool attention to detail are delightful. The gardens and pool area are equally impressive, as is the contemporary restaurant and top-notch service.

Casa Naranja BOUTIQUE HOTEL **$$$**
(Map p48; ☎2277 3403; www.hotelcasanaranja.com; Tip Top, 75m O; s/d/ste incl breakfast US$99/117/152; P ❄ @ 📶 🏊) This cozy boutique is one of your best bets for high-end accommodations. The rooms leave a little to be desired on the luxury-and-attention-to-detail scale, but are spacious and simply decorated with colonial-style furniture. The real draw is the house itself, a visual delight with cool, stylish interiors and a jungly backyard with its own dip pool.

Hotel Los Robles HOTEL **$$$**
(Map p48; ☎2267-3008; www.hotellosrobles.com; La Marseillaise, 30m S; s/d incl breakfast US$85/102; ❄ 📶 🏊) This Spanish-colonial-style hotel is absolutely flawless, from the attractively landscaped courtyard, centered on a burbling marble fountain, to the antique-style wooden furnishings and the modern amenities of the comfortable rooms. The airy neighborhood adds to the attraction, making this one of Managua's best top-end hotels.

Hotel Colón HOTEL **$$$**
(Map p48; ☎2278-2490; www.hcolon.net; Edificio BAC, 2c E; s/d incl breakfast US$60/70; P ❄ @ 📶) This neo-Colonial option offers easy access to nearby nightlife in the Zona Rosa. The pastel building and common areas are quite cheery. The rooms are modern and spacious, but are poorly lit and in sore need of renovation.

Hotel Los Pinos HOTEL **$$$**
(Map p48; ☎2270-0761; www.hotelospinos.info; Gimnasio Hercules, 1c S, ½c E; s/d incl breakfast US$64/75; P ❄ @ 📶 🏊) This private home

converted into a hotel is located in a great neighborhood, but lacks the charms of other higher-end options. The rooms are modern and spacious with minimalist decorations. They look into a neat garden and cheerful patio area dominated by a big swimming pool.

Seminole Plaza Hotel BUSINESS HOTEL **$$$**
(Map p48; 2270-0061; www.seminoleplaza.com; BanCentro Carretera a Masaya, 1c O, 1c S; s/d incl breakfast US$111/122;) Business class gone baroque crazy means gilt accents and art coupled with flawless concierge service, surprisingly modern rooms (though the bathrooms could use an update) and fun old-school touches like a shoeshine stand. There's a free airport shuttle service.

Other Neighborhoods

Nicaragua Guest House GUESTHOUSE **$**
(2249-8963; www.3dp.ch/nicaragua; Rotonda de La Virgen, 2c S, 2½c O; s/d with fan US$15/20, with air-con $28/35;) Basic but comfortable rooms a short ride from all the action in the Bello Horizonte neighborhood. The only catch? The 11pm curfew.

Camino Real BUSINESS HOTEL **$$$**
(2255-5888; http://www.caminoreal.com.ni; Carretera Norte, Km 9.5; r US$80-130;) Got an early flight? The Camino Real is just seconds from the airport.

Eating

Go budget in Barrio Martha Quezada or upscale on Carretera a Masaya.

Barrio Martha Quezada & Around

This area caters to businesspeople and backpackers, so prices are good. Want variety? Try Plaza Inter.

★ **Doña Pilar** NICARAGUAN **$**
(Map p44; Tica Bus, 1c O, ½c N; dishes US$2-4; 6-9pm Mon-Sat) Doña Pilar's been here for years, and this popular evening *fritanga* (sidewalk grill) is a neighborhood institution, both for her juicy, crispy barbecue chicken and the range of ever-so-slightly greasy tacos and enchiladas. A great introduction to typical Nicaraguan cuisine, with huge side servings of *gallo pinto* (rice and beans), chopped pickled cabbage and plantain chips.

Cafetín Tonalli NICARAGUAN **$**
(Map p44; Tica Bus, 2c E, ½c S; dishes US$2-6; breakfast & lunch Mon-Sat) If you're jonesing for some *pan integral* (wholewheat bread), this is the place to be. Breakfast can be on the disappointing side, but the homemade set lunches are delicious, served up in a leafy garden out back. Fresh-baked goodies are for sale in the bakery. The cafe is run by a women's co-op.

Licuados Ananda VEGETERIAN **$**
(Map p44; frente Estatua de Montoya; mains US$1-4, lunch buffet US$2.50;) Enjoy vegetarian goodies and 50 kinds of *licuados* (fruit and veggie juices; US$1) on this spacious patio overlooking lush gardens; the lunch buffet is from 11am to 3pm.

Cafetín Mirna NICARAGUAN **$**
(Map p44; Tica Bus, 1c O, 1c S; US$2-5) Everyone loves a big breakfast here, with fluffy pancakes, fabulous fresh juices and a good lunch buffet, too. It's a tradition.

Restaurante Santa Fe MEXICAN **$$**
(Map p44; Canal 2, 2c S; mains US$4-12) Despite the name, there's no green chili at this quality Tex-Mex spot, with a huge bar, good enchiladas and renowned steak.

Centro Commercial & Carretera a Masaya

Metrocentro and Galerias Santo Domingo malls both have large food courts, the latter is a bit more upscale.

Tercer Ojo FUSION **$$**
(Map p48; Seminole Plaza, 3½c S; mains US$5-14;) Managua's best fusion restaurant doesn't even really bother fusing – it just goes straight out for delicious Asian flavors that you can't get anywhere else in the country (apart from its sister restaurant in Granada). A wide balcony for street-side people-watching adds to the appeal.

Cocina Doña Haydee NICARAGUAN **$$**
(Map p48; lacocina.com.ni; Pharaoh's Casino, 1c O; mains US$3-8; breakfast, lunch & dinner) This spot does rustic right, all the way down to the traditional costumes and classic menu, from *gallo pinto* to *guiso de chilote* (cheese soup with baby corn) to steak with all the trimmings.

La Terraza Peruana PERUVIAN $$
(Map p48; www.laterrazaperuana.com; Tip Top, 100m O; mains US$5-12; ⏲ lunch & dinner Tue-Sun) A casual but refined Peruvian restaurant set on a cool front balcony overlooking a leafy side street, La Terraza has a huge menu that takes you from coastal to high Andean cuisine. With advance notice you can order such Peruvian classics as *cuy* (roasted guinea pig).

La Casa del Café CAFE $$
(Map p48; www.casadelcafe.com.ni; Lacmiel, 1c E, ½c S; sandwiches US$6; ⏲ 8am-7pm) Grab a table on the spacious and airy upstairs balcony and you'll find it hard to leave. All your regular and gourmet coffee options are available (including a very satisfying frozen mochaccino), plus a range of good-sized sandwiches and a couple of decent breakfast options.

La Hora del Taco MEXICAN $$
(Map p48; Monte de los Olivos 1c N; mains US$4.50-7.50; ⏲ lunch & dinner) This sprawling Mexican bar and restaurant has a well considered menu that includes standards like nachos and fajitas plus a few southern Mexican favorites like *cochinita pibil* (suckling pig).

El Garabato NICARAGUAN $$
(Map p48; Seminole Plaza, 3½c S; mains US$6-10) An artsy sort of place (for this side of town, anyway), serving up carefully prepared versions of traditional Nica dishes like *vigorón* (steamed yucca and pork rinds), *nacatamales* (banana-leaf wrapped bundles of cornmeal, meat, vegetables and herbs) and *repocheta* (cheese-stuffed tortillas).

Pan e Vino ITALIAN $$
(Map p48; Enitel Villa Fontana, 200m N; mains US$7-12) Getting the thumbs up from Italian expats, this stylish yet unpretentious place does good-sized pasta plates and crunchy-crusted pizzas. It has a small but decent selection of Italian, Spanish and Chilean wines (US$18 to US$25 per bottle).

El Muelle SEAFOOD $$
(Map p48; frente Chamán; mains US$6-12) Set behind a line of trees on a busy street, this surprisingly tranquil place serves up a range of seafood plates, including a tasty garlic shrimp (US$9) and fish done pretty much any way you want it.

La Casa de Los Nogueras EUROPEAN $$$
(Map p48; Avenida Principal Los Robles 17; mains US$14-25; ⏲ lunch & dinner Mon-Sat) One of the toniest restaurants in town, this cozy European bistro has delightful art, a wonderful garden out back for alfresco eating and top-notch but overly formal service. Note, no shorts allowed.

La Marseilles FRENCH $$$
(Map p48; ☎ 2277-0224; www.lamarseillaise-nicaragua.com; Seminole Plaza, 4c S; mains US$12-20; ⏲ Mon-Sat) The gold standard in Nicaraguan fine dining has tastefully art-bedecked walls, outstanding wine pairings and authentic French cuisine. Make reservations.

Marea Alta SEAFOOD $$$
(Map p48; ☎ 2278-2459; Seminole Plaza, 1c S; meals US$6-18) Managua gets a good supply of seafood, and this is one of the most highly respected fish restaurants in town. With an enviable corner location in the middle of the bar district, people-watching opportunities are endless. From the fish burger to the USDA imported beef, it's all good, but we recommend the lobster risotto.

Yan Yan Siu CHINESE $$$
(Map p48; Hotel Colón, 50m E, Los Robles; mains US$9-20; ❄) The best Chinese restaurant in town has friendly service, a rambling menu that takes you from seafood favorites to savory soups and old standards like Kung Pao chicken.

Bello Horizonte

Managua's *other* nightlife zone has a predictably good range of places to eat. Prices (and decor) are a lot more humble out here, and you're unlikely to see another tourist (or, refreshingly, a menu in dollars).

Pizzeria Los Idolos PIZZERIA $$
(frente Rotonda Bello Horizonte; pizzas US$4-8) Right at the center of this busy neighborhood, this legendary pizza joint serves up OK pies (beware the Hawaiian, though, with its glazed-pineapple topping). The real reason you're here, however, is for the atmosphere. Kick back, grab a beer and watch as the dueling mariachis battle it out.

Cocina de Doña Haydee NICARAGUAN $$
(Rotonda Bello Horizonte, 70m E; dishes US$4-8) Adding a bit of refinement to the area, this spin-off of the popular Los Robles restaurant offers the same range of well-presented, carefully prepared traditional Nica dishes.

Don Pez SEAFOOD $$
(Rotonda Bello Horizonte, 1c E; dishes US$6-11) The best seafood restaurant in the area, the

Don also grills a pretty mean steak. It's hard to pass up the surf-and-turf platter (fish, shrimp and beef).

Drinking & Nightlife

Bars & Pubs

There are bars all over town, but the best ones can be found in Barrio Martha Quezada, around the Metrocentro mall and at the Rotonda Bello Horizonte. Take a cab home!

Shannon Bar IRISH PUB
(Map p44; Tica Bus, 1c E, ½c S) The classic bar in this area, this Irish pub is an expat gathering spot and one of the only places in town where you can get a cold Guinness tallboy.

Caramanchel BAR
(Map p44; Crowne Plaza, 1c S, ½c E) For the extremely down-to-earth, bohemian side of Bolonia, hit the dance floor at this mostly outdoor neighborhood bar. Dress is extremely casual (jeans and flip-flops OK), and the DJ spins laidback dance tunes into the early morning.

El Grillito BAR
(Map p44; Intur, ½c N) There are a few little outdoor bars like this in the area, but this one consistently gets a good crowd. A range of snacks and more substantial meals are on the menu and the music volume is conversation-friendly.

Zona Hippo's BAR
(Map p48; Seminole Plaza, 1c S; ⊙noon-2am) Wanna go where everybody knows your name? Globalization has arrived and it's called Hippo's Grill & Tavern, with nine different burgers, next door to affiliated Woody's Sports Bar, with 15 types of hot wings. Both have Caesar salads, plenty of 'flair,' nonthreatening rock music and very full bars.

El Puerto BAR
(Rotonda Bello Horizonte, 80m E) Ignore the lame disco out back (there are much better ones in the area); this is the place to grab a beer on the front deck and do a bit of people-watching, before slipping inside for a couple of games of pool on surprisingly good tables.

Entertainment

Managua is far and away the country's boho-life capital. There are dozens of venues around town that occasionally have live music, folkloric dance, alternative theater, poetry readings and other cultural offerings. Thursday editions of *La Prensa* and *El Nuevo Diario* have good listings. **Nicaragua Bacanal** (www.bacanalnica.com) has lots of photos and some information.

Take a walk through the UCA (p48) to see what's on.

Performing Arts

INCH PERFORMING ARTS
(Instituto Nicaragüense de Cultura Hispanica; ☎2276-0733; nichispanica@gmail.com; Av del Campo 40-42, Las Colinas; ⊙9am-3pm Mon-Fri) In the very ritzy hill suburb of Las Colinas to the south of town, this center hosts some of the city's best cultural events, including cinema, theater, art and photography exhibitions, concerts and art-themed workshops.

Bar Art Café LIVE MUSIC
(Estatua de Montoya, 3c O, 50m N; ⊙Wed-Sat) Always worth a look, this bohemian little space in front of Parque Las Palmas hosts poetry and open-mic nights on Wednesday, electronica DJs on Thursday and other underground-type events the rest of the week.

Cinemas

Alhambra Cine VIP CINEMA
(tickets US$8) VIP service at the movies.

Cinema Plaza Inter CINEMA
(Map p44; tickets US$2) At Plaza Inter, close to Barrio Martha Quezada. Films are screened with subtitles.

La Sala de Teatro Justo Rufino Garay THEATER
(☎2266 3714; www.rufinos.org; Estatua de Montoya, 3c O, 20m N; tickets US$2) Artsy movies at 7pm Wednesday.

Metrocentro Cinemark CINEMA
(Map p48; tickets US$2.50) This bigger-is-better mall has six screens and shows blockbuster movies.

Gay & Lesbian Venues

Tabú GAY
(Map p44; Intur, 100m S) One of the few gay bars with any longevity in town. Tabu's dance floor gets going on weekends.

Lounge

Reef LOUNGE
(Galeria Santo Domingo) The most popular spot in the emerging *zona viva* (nightlife zone) out back of the Santo Domingo mall, this is a favorite pre-dance spot for scenesters.

Live Music

La Casa de los Mejía Godoy LIVE MUSIC

(Map p44; ☎2222-6110; www.losmejiagodoy.com; frente Crowne Plaza; cover US$8-15) Living legends Carlos and Luis Enrique Mejía Godoy, whose folk-music explorations into the heart of Nicaraguan culture have become church hymns and revolutionary standards since they first started laying down riffs in the 1960s, have moved from their original intimate venue to larger premises with a restaurant. Make reservations if you're planning on seeing the brothers play. Opening hours vary.

Bar La Cavanga LIVE MUSIC

(Map p46; Centro Cultural Managua; cover US$4; ⏲Thu-Sat) Take a taxi out to this 1950s-era gem, which stages live folk and jazz shows in the sketchy neighborhood near the Antigua Catedral.

Ruta Maya LIVE MUSIC

(Map p44; ☎2268-0698; www.rutamaya.com.ni; Estatua de Montoya, 150m E; cover US$1-5) Look around for flyers (or check the website) for happenings at this thatch-roofed venue. You get everything from Bee Gees cover bands to Caribbean *palo de mayo* to *son nicaragüense* (traditional Nicaraguan folk music). Barbecued meat is the specialty on the menu, and dinner shows are worth booking ahead for.

Carretera a Masaya Discos

Dress up to club it around here. Club owners seem particularly keen to have women in their establishments – many places charge US$2.50 admission for women and three times that much for men.

Moods DANCE

(www.moodsclubmanagua.com; Galeria Santo Domingo; cover US$3-10) Pretty much *the* club in town, with a dress code, Euro styling, imported DJs, dry ice, polished chrome, laser lighting…you get the picture. It's south of the city.

Zona Latino DANCE

(Map p48; Rotonda Rubén Darío, 600m N) This is the place to be for Latin grooves: salsa, merengue and *cumbia* (Colombian dance tunes) are in heavy rotation at this sprawling club in an oddly removed location.

Bello Horizonte Discos

Dubbed 'the heart of Nicaribeña,' Bello Horizonte is home to the largest concentration of Caribbean-descended Nicaraguans in Managua. Clubs out here have a predictably Atlantic coast flavor, with a heavier reggae, soca and *punta* (traditional Garifuna dance involving much hip movement) influence than their counterparts down south.

Charlie's Bar DANCE

(Rotonda Bello Horizonte, 60m E; cover US$1) The original and still one of the best, Charlie keeps the dance floor packed with a good selection of new hits and classics, all in the Caribbean vein.

Mrs Sponge DANCE

(Rotonda Bello Horizonte, 50m E; cover incl drink US$2) Who knows how they came up with the name. The small dance floor features a stripper pole. In case you were interested.

Luna de los Sueños DANCE

(Rotonda Bello Horizonte, 50m E; cover incl drink US$2) Sharing a parking lot with Mrs Sponge, this place is into Latin grooves like *cumbia* and *bacchata*.

Theater

Teatro Nacional Rubén Darío THEATER

(Map p46; ☎2266-3630; www.tnrubendario.gob.ni; Área Monumental) One of the few Managua buildings to survive the 1972 earthquake, this groovy theatre often has big-name international offerings on the main stage. It's worth trying to catch some experimental jazz or performance art in the smaller Sala Experimental Pilar Aguirre.

La Sala de Teatro Justo Rufino Garay THEATER

(☎2266 3714; www.rufinos.org; Estatua de Montoya, 3c O, 20m N; tickets US$5) Fans of alternative theater should check the program at this small, not-for-profit theater space, which specializes in experimental, contemporary works, often with a political bent. Plays are generally staged on Friday and Saturday nights.

Sports

Estadio Denis Martínez (Map p44) is the national baseball stadium, and is absolutely packed between mid-November and early April, when Nicaragua's four professional teams, including the Managua Bóers, compete in the national championships. Get stats, schedules and more at the **Liga de Beisbol Profesional** (www.lnbp.com.ni) website.

Reflecting football's secondary status in Nicaragua, **Estadio Cranshaw** (Map p44) is a more humble affair that squats in the shadows of its big brother, just to the south. There has long been talk of constructing a larger stadium, near UNAN; the **Nicaraguan Football Association** (www.fenifut.org.ni) will have the latest.

Shopping

Boutiques are clustered in Altamira, with standouts being **Mama Delfina** (Map p48; Enitel Villa Fontana, 200m N), with top-quality *artisanías* (handicrafts), and **Simplemente Madera** (Map p48; www.simplementamadera.com; Enitel Villa Fontana, 200m N), a fascinating place to browse even if you don't go home with the organically shaped wood furniture.

Markets and malls:

Galeria Santo Domingo MALL
(Carretera a Masaya, Km 8) See and be seen at the discos, eateries and shops of Managua's most upscale mall.

Mercado Oriental MARKET
Stash your cash in a couple of places (sock, bra) and try to find a local guide for Central America's largest market and scariest shopping experience.

Mercado Roberto Huembes HANDICRAFTS
This is more than just the southbound bus terminal; it has the best selection of souvenirs in Managua, from all over the country.

Metrocentro MALL
(Map p48) Upscale mall with restaurants, cinemas and more.

Plaza Inter MALL
(Map p44) Adjacent to Barrio Martha Quezada, it's convenient, with a cinema (with subtitled movies), lots of discount shops, a couple of department stores and a solid food court.

Bookstores

Managua has a great selection of bookstores – if you can read Spanish. There are better selections of English-language books in San Juan del Sur and Granada. UCA and UNAN both have excellent libraries.

El Parnaso BOOKS
(Map p48; Rotonda Rubén Darío, 300m O) Across from the UCA, this lefty bookstore also has a great selection of magazines.

Librería Hispamer BOOKS
(Map p48; www.hispamer.com.ni; UCA, 1c E, 1c N) This bookstore has the country's best selection of Nicaraguan and Latin American literature, history and poetry, plus local news and arts periodicals.

Orientation

The Interamericana (Pan-American Hwy) enters Managua from the southwest, via Jinotepe, as Carretera Sur, and exits to the northeast, past the airport toward Matagalpa and El Rama, as Carretera Norte. Running southeast from Metrocentro and Rotonda Rubén Darío is Carretera a Masaya, along which Managua's swankiest discos, restaurants and malls can be found. Heading west are Carretera Nueva and Carretera Vieja (New and Old Hwys) to León. Managua has hundreds of neighborhoods stretched between these highways, and not even the kamikaze *taxistas* (taxi drivers) know them all.

Área Monumental, on the lakefront site of Managua's pre-1972 downtown, is home to the Museo Nacional, Casa Presidencial (Presidential Palace) and Teatro Rubén Darío. It's connected by Av Bolívar, a major thoroughfare, to the Plaza Inter shopping mall, Loma de Tiscapa and Barrio Martha Quezada, with most services for budget travelers. To the southwest are Barrio Bolonia, with midrange accommodations, and Plaza España, next to Rotonda El Güegüense, with banks, travel agencies and airline offices.

To the southeast is Managua's modern commercial center, a 2km strip of Carretera a Masaya extending southeast from Metrocentro mall and Rotonda Rubén Darío through the cluster of glittering restaurants and bars known as Zona Rosa, as well as swanky Los Robles and Altamira, two of Managua's most exclusive neighborhoods. West of Rotonda Rubén Darío is Universidad Centro America (UCA), with left-wing bookstores and microbuses to most major regional cities, including Granada and Masaya.

Rotonda Bello Horizonte, located east of the Área Monumental, is a nightlife district with a few budget lodging options.

MAPS

Free maps of Managua are widely available at Intur and most hotels, but none of them are particularly detailed. If you're headed out into wilder Nicaragua, pick up topos and maps of Nicaragua's major protected areas at **Marena Central** (☎2263-2830; www.marena.gob.ni; Carretera Norte, Km 12.5), or check out Ineter (p294), which has excellent maps of the entire country.

Information

EMERGENCY

Ambulance (Cruz Roja; ☎128) Red Cross.

Fire (☎emergency 115, nonemergency 2222-6406)

Police (☎emergency 118, nonemergency 2249-5714)

IMMIGRATION OFFICES

Migración (Dirección de Migración y Extranjeria; ☎2244-3989; www.migob.gob.ni/dgme; semaf Tenderí, 200m N) The main office is located near the Ciudad Jardín area, but there's

NAVIGATING MANAGUA

As in other Nicaraguan cities and towns, only Managua's major roads are named. Large buildings, *rotondas* (traffic circles) and traffic lights serve as de facto points of reference, and locations are described in terms of their direction and distance, usually in *cuadras* (blocks) from these points. Many of these reference points no longer exist, and thus addresses may begin with something like '*de donde fue Sandy's*' (from where Sandy's used to be...).

In Managua, a special system is used for the cardinal points, whereby *al lago* (to the lake) means 'north' while *a la montaña* (to the mountains) means 'south.' *Arriba* (up) is 'east' toward the sunrise, while *abajo* (down) is 'west' and toward the sunset. Thus one might hear: '*del antiguo Cine Dorado, una cuadra al lago y dos cuadras arriba*' ('from the old Cine Dorado, one block toward the lake and two blocks up'), meaning one block north and two blocks east.

Confused? You get used to it (and you may be consoled to know that the rest of the country uses the same system, except with the cardinal points named). Listings in this section give the 'address' in Spanish – but we use the cardinal points, N *(norte)*, S *(sur)*, E *(este)* and O *(oeste)*, and C for *cuadra* – so you can ask locals for help or just let the cab driver figure it out.

a much more convenient branch office (no phone) in the Metrocentro shopping mall.

INTERNET ACCESS

Internet access is fast and plentiful, averaging US$0.70 per minute at cafes all over town. Wi-fi can be found in most hotels and even some restaurants. Internet cafes in Barrio Martha Quezada:

Kafe Internet (per hr US$0.70)

Plaza Inter (per hr US$2) Beside the food court, making sipping and surfing a breeze.

LAUNDRY

Laundry services are sadly lacking here, but most hotels offer laundry (in cheaper places, by hand, so allow time to dry). If your hotel doesn't do laundry, try the one next door.

MEDICAL SERVICES

There are scores of pharmacies, some open 24 hours (just knock), and the nation's best hospitals.

Hospital Alemán-Nicaragüense (☎2249-3368; Carretera Norte, Km 6) Has some German-speaking staff and modern equipment.

Hospital Bautista (☎2264-9020; www.hospitalbautistanicaragua.com; Casa Ricardo Morales Aviles, 2c S, 1½c E, Barrio Largaespada) Your best bet, with some English-speaking staff.

Hospital Metropolitano Vivian Pellas (☎2255-6900; www.metropolitano.com.ni; Carretera a Masaya, Km 9.75) State of the art facility.

MONEY

Managua has scores of banks and ATMs, most on the Visa/Plus system. BAC, with machines at Metrocentro mall, Managua International Airport and Plaza España, accepts MasterCard/Cirrus debit cards and gives US dollars and córdobas. Any bank can change US dollars.

POST & TELEPHONE

Most people are now calling using VOIP.

Palacio de Correos (Plaza de la Revolución, 2c O) The main post office (inside the former Enitel building) has poste restante services (mail is held for up to 45 days).

TOURIST INFORMATION

Ben Linder House (☎2266-4363; www.casabenlinder.org; de donde fue el Banco Popular, 2c N, 2c E, Monseñor Lezcano) This cultural center primarily serves the English-speaking volunteer community, with weekly presentations and discussion groups on Thursday at 8:30am, but stop by any time to see the amazing murals and chat.

Intur Central (Nicaraguan Institute of Tourism; ☎2254-5191; www.visitanicaragua.com/ingles; Crowne Plaza, 1c S, 1c O; ⏲8am-12:30pm & 1:30am-5pm Mon-Fri) The flagship office of Nicaragua's official tourist-info organization has heaps of flyers, but getting tips from the staff can be tough. There's another office in the international terminal at the airport.

Marena Central (Ministry of the Environment & Natural Resources; ☎2263-2830; www.marena.gob.ni; Carretera Norte, Km 12.5) Bring ID to the inconveniently located headquarters (out past the airport, a US$8 taxi ride) to access maps, flyers and management plans for most of Nicaragua's 82 protected areas.

Getting There & Away

AIR

Managua International Airport (MGA; www.eaai.com.ni; Carretera Norte, Km 13) is a small, manageable airport located about 30 to 45 minutes from most hotels. **Intur** (8am-10pm) has an office inside the international terminal, next to the luggage belt in the arrivals area, where English-speaking staff can recommend hotels, confirm flights and share flyers.

The smaller, more chaotic domestic terminal is adjacent to the main building. The following airlines fly from Managua:

Aerocaribbean (www.fly-aerocaribbean.com; Managua International Airport) Flies from Managua to Havana, Cuba.

American Airlines (2255-9095; www.aa.com; Plaza España, 3c S) Two flights daily to Miami.

Copa Airlines (Map p48; 2267-0045; www.copaair.com; Ofiplaza Bldg, 2nd level, Bldg 5) One daily flight to Houston via Star Alliance code share.

Delta Airlines (Map p48; 2254-8130; www.delta.com; Seminole Plaza, 31/2c S) Daily flights to Atlanta.

Grupo Taca (RUC; 2266-3136; www.taca.com; Plaza España) Daily flights to Miami, Los Angeles and several Latin American cities.

La Costeña (2263-2142; www.lacostena.com.ni; Managua International Airport) The domestic carrier has regular service to Bluefields, the Corn Islands, Las Minas, Puerto Cabezas and Waspán.

BUS

Managua is the main transportation hub for the country, with four major national bus and van terminals, plus a handful of international bus lines, most grouped in Barrio Martha Quezada.

International Buses

Tica Bus (p299) is in a newly remodeled terminal in the heart of Barrio Martha Quezada.

NATIONAL BUS SERVICES FROM MANAGUA

DESTINATION	COST (US$)	DURATION (hr)	DEPARTURES	FREQUENCY	LEAVES FROM
Boaco	$2	3	4am-6:30pm	every 15min	Mayoreo
Carazo (serving Diriamba & Jinotepe)	$1	1	4:30am-6:20pm	every 20min	Bóer
Chinandega/ El Viejo	$2.50	2½	5am-7pm	every 30min	Bóer
Chinandega minibus	$3	2	4am-6pm	when full	Bóer
El Rama *expreso*	$7.50	5	2pm, 6:10pm & 10pm	3 daily	Mayoreo
El Rama *ordinario*	$7.50	5	4:30am, 6am, 7am, 8:45am & 11:30am	5 daily	Mayoreo
El Sauce	$3	3	7:30am, 2:30 & 4pm	3 daily	Bóer
Esquipulas	$3	4	6:25am, 8:20am, 12:25pm, 1:25pm, 2:50pm & 3:50pm	6 daily	Mayoreo
Estelí	$3	2	5:45am-5:45pm	hourly	Mayoreo
Granada	$0.75	1	4am-6pm	every 15min	Huembes
Granada minibus	$1.25	1	6am-8pm	when full	UCA
Jinotega	$3.50	4	4am-5:30pm	hourly	Mayoreo
Jinotepe minibus	$1.15	1	5:20am-8:30pm	when full	UCA
Juigalpa	$2	4	3:15am-10pm	every 20min	Mayoreo
La Paz Centro	$0.90	1½	6:15am-8pm	every 30min	Bóer
León *expreso* (via New Hwy & La Paz Centro)	$1.85	1½	10am-6:30pm	every 2hr	Bóer
León *ordinario* (via Old Hwy)	$1.50	2	5am-7pm	every 20min	Bóer

Costa Rica (US$29 to US$40, 10 hours, 6am, 7am, 8am, 8:30am, 9am, 10am and noon) For Liberia and San José.

Guatemala (US$55, 30 hours, 5am and 11am) There is a continuing service to Tapachula, Mexico (US$69, 48 hours).

Honduras (US$23, seven hours, 5am) There is a continuing service from Tegucigalpa to San Pedro Sula (US$31, 11 hours).

Panama City (US$92, 34 hours) Via San José.

San Salvador (US$34 to US$49, 11 hours, 5am and 11am)

King Quality (Map p44; ☎2222-2075; www.king-qualityca.com; Calle 27 de Mayo, frente Plaza Inter) has in-flight...er, in-ride meal service, and less intense air-conditioning.

Costa Rica (US$44, eight hours, 1:30pm)

El Salvador (US$53, 10 hours, 3am) For San Salvador.

Guatemala (US$75, 32 hours, 3am) For Guatemala City.

Honduras (US$44, 10 hours, 3am) For Tegucigalpa.

Transnica (Map p4 transnica.com) is the over the other side of th

Costa Rica (US$23, nine h and 10am) There's a luxury bu noon; for San José.

Honduras (US$29, 10 hours, 5am) Fo Tegucigalpa.

Del Sol Bus (p299) has one bus leaving fo Salvador (US$45) and continuing to Guatem City (US$70) at 4am daily.

Central Line (Map p44; ☎2254-5431; www.transportescentralline.com; Calle 27 de Mayo, 4½c O, Esso) offers services to San José, Costa Rica (US$23, eight hours, 10am), with stops in Masaya and Liberia.

National Buses & Minivans

Buses leave from three main places: **Mercado Roberto Huembes** for Granada, Masaya and southwest Nicaragua; **Mercado Israel Lewites** (☎2265 2152; Bóer), commonly known as Bóer, for León and the northern Pacific; and

DESTINATION	COST (US$)	DURATION (hr)	DEPARTURES	FREQUENCY	LEAVES FROM
León minibus	$2.75	1½	4am-6pm	when full	Bóer
León minibus	$2.75	1½	5am-9:15pm	when full	UCA
Masatepe minibus	$1.10	1	6:30am-6:30pm	every 20min	Huembes
Masaya	$0.50	1	5:30am-9pm	every 30min	Huembes
Masaya minibus	$0.75	½	6am-9pm	when full	UCA
Matagalpa	$2.10	2¾	3am-6pm	hourly	Mayoreo
Mateare	$0.30	40min	5:50am-6:30pm	every 2hr	Bóer
Nagarote	$0.70	1	5am-8pm	every 30min	Bóer
Naindame	$1	1½	11am-3:30pm	every 20min	Huembes
Ocotal	$4.25	3½	5am-5pm	hourly	Mayoreo
Peñas Blancas	$3.50	3	10am & 4pm	2 daily	Huembes
Pochomil/ Masachapa	$1.10	2	6am-7pm	every 20min	Bóer
Río Blanco	$5	4	9:15am-12:15pm	hourly	Mayoreo
Rivas *expreso*	$3.25	1½	4am-6pm	every 30min	Huembes
Rivas *ordinario*	$2	2	4am-6pm	every 30min	Huembes
San Carlos	$7.50	9	5am, 6am, 7am, 1pm,	6 daily	Mayoreo
San Juan del Sur	$3.25	2½	10am & 4pm	2 daily	Huembes
San Marcos minibus	$1	1	4am-6pm	when full	Huembes
Siuna	$9	10-12	4:30am, 3pm & 5pm	3 daily	Mayoreo
Somoto	$4	4	7:15am, 9:45am, 11am, 12:45pm, 1:45pm, 2pm, 3:45pm & 4:45pm	8 daily	Mayoreo
Ticuantepe minibus	$0.35	40min	4am-6pm	when full	Huembes

729, Rama
ean coast
so leave
rural
ster, more
e to take
ounced
dinario

ouses
pular
cene is not
y and the direct airport departure, meaning you don't have to cab into town to catch an onward bus. Managua Backpackers offers shuttles to San Juan del Sur (US$70), León (US$50) and Granada (US$35) for one to four people. **Paxeos** (☎2552-8291; www.paxeos.com) serves Granada (US$40) and León ($70) for up to three people, and **Adelante Express** (☎8850-6070; www.adelanteexpress.com) serves San Juan del Sur (US$45 per person, three hours, leaving Managua's airport at 1pm daily).

CAR

Driving in Managua is a fool's errand – take a cab. Once you get out of the city, it's easy enough.

Alamo (Map p44; ☎2277-1117; www.alamonicaragua.com; Hospital Militar, 100m E)

Avis (Map p48; ☎Airport 2233-3011; www.avis.com) Has a desk at the Metrocentro Intercontinental.

Budget (☎2278-9504; www.budget.com.ni) Office is at Holiday Inn, Pista Juan Pablo II.

Easy Rent-a-car (Map p48; ☎2270-0654; www.easyrentacar.com.ni; Carretera a Masaya, Km 7.5)

Hertz (☎Airport 2233-1237; www.hertz.com.ni)

Lugo (Map p44; ☎2266-4477; www.lugorentacar.com.ni; Canal 2, 2c N, 3c O, Managua)

Getting Around

TO/FROM THE AIRPORT

The airport is 11km from town and has its special, more expensive taxis (US$15 to US$20 to most Managua destinations), which don't pick up passengers. At night this is worth it, but during the day you can just run across the very busy Carretera Norte to the bus stop, where *colectivo* taxis cost US$5 to go into town. Even cheaper (and only advisable during broad daylight) are regular buses, charging US$0.20 for the ride all the way to Mercado Roberto Huembes. Look for buses with 'Huembes' above the windshield.

BUS

Local buses are frequent and crowded. They're also known for their professional pickpockets, but stay alert and you'll be fine. Routes run every 10 minutes from 4:45am to 6pm, then every 15 minutes until 10pm. Buses do not generally stop en route – look for the nearest bus shelter. The fare is US$0.15. Useful routes:

No 101 Linda Vista to Mercado Mayoreo, via Rotonda Bello Horizonte.

No 109 Plaza de la República to Mercado Roberto Huembes, stopping en route at Plaza Inter.

No 110 Mercado Israel Lewites (Bóer) to Mercado Mayoreo, via UCA, Metrocentro, Rotonda de Centroamérica, Mercado Roberto Huembes and Mercado Iván Montenegro.

No 116 Estatua de Montoya, Plaza Inter, Mercado Oriental and Rotonda Bello Horizonte.

No 118 From Parque Las Piedrecitas, heads down Carretera Sur, then east, passing by Mercado Israel Lewites (Bóer), Rotonda El Güegüense (Plaza España), Plaza Inter and Mercado Oriental on its way to Mercado Mayoreo.

No 119 From Linda Vista to Mercado Roberto Huembes, with stops at Rotonda El Güegüense and UCA.

CAR & MOTORCYCLE

Driving in Managua is not recommended at night – even if you have a rental car, consider getting a taxi, and make sure your car is in a guarded lot. Night drivers should keep their windows rolled up and stay alert.

TAXI

Most taxis in Managua are *colectivos*, which pick up passengers as they go. There are also more expensive private taxis based at the airport, shopping malls, Mercado Roberto Huembes and other places. These are safer, but regular taxis also always congregate close by. Licensed taxis have red plates and the driver's ID above the dash; if yours doesn't, you're in a pirate taxi. This is probably OK, but don't go to the ATM, and beware of scams no matter what kind of taxi you're in. At night, take only licensed taxis – there has been an increase in reports of taxi drivers robbing passengers after dark.

Fares are US$1 to US$4 per person within the city. From Barrio Martha Quezada, taxis go to the airport (US$6/8/12 for one/two/three people), Mercado Roberto Huembes (US$2/3 for one/two people), Mercado Israel Lewites (US$1.50/2), Mayoreo (US$4/5), Zona Rosa (US$2/3) and Huellas de Acahualinca (US$2/3). Prices rise at night.

AROUND MANAGUA

Pacific Beaches

Not even 50km (but at least two hours by bus) from Managua are some surprisingly pretty beaches, that cater mostly to national tourists.

Masachapa & Pochomil

The twin towns of Masachapa and Pochomil are so close together that they might as well be one. You arrive in Masachapa, a small fishing village with a handful of bars, hotels and restaurants on the beach.

Buses and pedicabs ply the 2km between Masachapa and the government-operated **Centro Turistico Pochomil** (car/pedestrian US$1/free) tourist center. This run-down tourist ghetto has about 30 businesses, mostly waterfront restaurants and bars, almost all with *palapa* (thatched) roofs, fronting a truly spectacular beach.

There is no ATM in either town, so bring plenty of cash.

Activities

There's great surfing – a left point break just north of Montelimar, and a hollow right reef break to the south; Quizala, a beach break, is closer to Masachapa. South to Pochomil there are scores of smallish, predictable peaks that would be perfect to learn on.

There's a suprisingly clean river between Masachapa and Pochomil that makes for a fun dip.

Mesachapa Surf and Sportfishing SURFING
(☎8984-2464; www.sanjuandelsursurf.com; 200m E of beach on Main Rd, Mesachapa) This small operation rents surf boards (US$20 per day), takes you on sunset cruises (US$25 per person) or can charter surf/fish safaris (half-/full day US$285/420). Want to learn

Around Managua

WORTH A TRIP

EASY DAY TRIPS FROM MANAGUA

There are several worthwhile day trips just outside of Managua.

- **Lagunas De Xiloá & Apoyeque** Half a dozen crater lakes lie near Managua. The best for swimming is Laguna de Xiloá, on the Península de Chiltepe, about 20km northwest of Managua off the road to León. It's a steep 30 minute hike from Laguna de Xiloá to less accessible but more picturesque Laguna de Apoyeque, deep within a steep crater. Take bus 110 from UCA to Ciudad Sandino, where you can catch an onward bus to the lagoons.
- **Mateare** Back out on the main highway, take a right to get to this lazy little fishing village sloping down to the banks of Lago de Managua. From here, you can hire a boat for around US$80 (up to seven people), to take you to Isla Momotombo. Look out for snakes. Buses leave Mateare's parque central every two hours between 6am and 6pm for the 40-minute ride to Managua's Mercado Israel Lewites; the fare is US$0.35.
- **El Trapiche** Located 22km from Managua in the town of Tipitapa, the **Centro Turístico El Trapiche** (admission US$0.25; 7am-6pm) has therapeutic waters surrounded by gardens and restaurants. Buses to Tipitapa depart from Mercado Roberto Huembes.
- **Pacific Beaches** Just two hours away.
- **Nature Reserves** Try Montebelli or Volcán Masaya.
- **Villages** Masaya and it's surrounding villages are close by, as is the small town of Ticuantepe.

how to surf? Sign up for a US$40 day-long lesson, including board rental.

Sleeping

Most hotels are located along the road to Pochomil. To get there cross the river to the south of Mesachapa, heading east along a dirt road from the gas station.

Hospedaje Flipper HOTEL $
(2269-6509; Masachapa; r US$17) Right at the entrance to Mesachapa, this is the cheapest option in town, with OK cement rooms and cleanish private bathrooms; it caters to couples on a beach break.

Hotel Bahía HOTEL $$
(8396-6254; road to Pochomil; s/d US$30/40; P) Over the river, heading south, follow the signs to this cheerful place, a threadbare but woodsy lot with pretty cabins, plain-Jane rooms with itchy sheets, and a couple of swimming pools that may be clean. It's just across the road from the beach.

Hotel Vista HOTEL $$
(2269-0115; Masachapa; s/d US$35/40; P) New rooms were being built at press time, but all in all, there was a rather unkempt feel, though we love that you're right on the beach. Even if it's full, the restaurant has a great deck looking out to sea.

Hotel Vistamar RESORT $$$
(2265-8099; www.vistamarhotel.com; road to Pochomil; s/d incl all meals US$100/150; P) This is one of the prettiest hotels on this stretch of coast; accommodation is in two-story wooden bungalows – get an upstairs room for views and breezes. Three swimming pools, an on-site day spa and a gorgeous stretch of white-sand beach seal the deal. Check here for turtle tours or volunteer ops with its turtle release program.

Hotel Summer HOTEL $$$
(2269-7754; Masachapa; s/d US$58/70; P) Well overpriced, but right on the water, this has a big pool and smallish, pastel-hued rooms with cable TV. If you eat at the restaurant, you can use the pool here, too.

Getting There & Away

Buses arrive first at Masachapa – if you're planning on staying here, get off at the *empalme* (T junction). Buses run from Pochomil and Masachapa through to Managua's Mercado Israel Lewites (US$1.10, two hours) every 20 minutes from 8am to 6pm.

Montelimar

You'll be going the all-inclusive route if you stay around Montelimar. What's the draw? Amazing beaches, some decent surf breaks and a resort bigger than a city.

Sights

Montelimar Cave CAVE

This has several petroglyphs that show traces of red and blue pigment, suggesting that all these monochromatic carvings were once a bit showier.

Sleeping

Barceló Montelimar Beach Resort RESORT **$$$**

(☎1800-2200; www.barcelomontelimarbeach.com; Montelimar; r from US$200 all inclusive; P ⊖ ❄ @ ≋) Formerly the Somozas' summer home, this resort does it right: it's got well stocked rooms and bungalows, four huge pools, tennis courts, discos, restaurants, beauty parlors, and even miniature golf. Prices are all inclusive – food, beer, rum and most activities. Day-trippers can visit the casino for free, or pay US$50 per person for use of all facilities. If you just want to use the ATM, tell the gatekeeper 'casino.' Works like a charm.

Los Cardones Hotel Ecológico LODGE **$$$**

(☎8364-5925; www.loscardones.com; s/d from US$99/150 all inclusive) North of Montelimar, this rustic eco-lodge has great food and some of the best surfing in Nicaragua just steps away from your hammock. Owners also offer fishing, snorkeling and horseback riding, and sea turtles lay their eggs on the beach. The whole operation is not only low impact (solar energy, composting) but also family friendly, with breaks for kids under 12. They want you to stay at least three nights, and prices are very all-inclusive – check the website for details. An expert left point break, a right reef point, and beach breaks just offshore make this a surfing paradise. From Managua, head toward the beach until California, then follow the signs 15km to Los Cardones. Or, take the bus from Managua's Mercado Israel Lewites to San Cayetano (US$0.70, one hour, every 45 minutes, 4am to 9pm), get off in California and stick your thumb out.

Ticuantepe

POP 10,300 / ELEV 360M

Just 19km from Managua, Ticuantepe is a refreshing escape from the sweltering city, with temperatures ranging from 22°C to 28°C (71°F to 82°F). It's on the western rim of the Complejo Ventarrón Volcanic (Ventarrón Volcanic Complex), across from Nindirí and Masaya.

Occupied for at least 2500 years by the Matagalpa nation, Ticuantepe is today the

TAXI CAB CONFESSIONS: DANGERS, SCAMS & STAYING SAFE

- Express kidnappings – where a taxi driver holds the passenger hostage by knifepoint and then takes them to ATMs around town until their bank is depleted – are on the rise in Managua, and have also been reported in Granada, Masaya, San Juan del Sur and San Jorge. Here's a few top tips to stay safe.
- **Take radio taxis with a bubble on top** There are thousands of illegal cabs in Managua. The ones with the bubble on the roof and/or red plates are considered safer. There should be a nametag with the driver's information on the dashboard. These are registered with a company, and can be ordered by phone.
- **Ask your hotel to call you a cab** But don't trust just anybody. There are reports of people being kidnapped after a friendly stranger on the street helped them hail a cab.
- **Take cabs after dark** In the downtown area, you should take cabs after the sun sets. Around Carretera a Masaya, you should take them after 10pm. A general rule, if women and kids are walking around, you are probably safe to walk. Don't risk even a short two-block walk at night.
- **Know the price** While prices change, at the time of writing it was about US$1 to $1.50 for short trips less than 5km. For trips between the city center and Carretera a Masaya, you can expect to pay around US$2 to US$4 depending on the time of day and where you are going.
- **Agree to a price before getting in** And ask if you will be going as a *colectivo* (collective that stops to pick up other passengers) or *privado* (private).
- **Make sure the cab takes you where you want to go** Often cabbies will say a certain hotel is closed just to take you to a spot where they get a commission.

service center for an enormous and productive agricultural region, colloquially known as the Valle de las Piñas (Valley of Pineapples).

Sights & Activities

Museo Arqueológico Municipal Raúl Rojas MUSEUM
(⌚9am 4pm Mon-Sat) FREE The closest thing to a tourist attraction in town, with more than 50 stone and ceramic pieces dug up in the immediate era, plus an impressive mural of Ticuantepe c AD 1200. If it's closed, you may be able to gain entry by asking at the *alcaldía* (mayor's office) next door.

Pared de Serpientes ARCHAEOLOGICAL SITE
One of the most important petroglyphs in the region, the tantalizingly entitled Wall of Snakes has more than 25 beautifully preserved serpent-related drawings, and is evidently within easy walking distance of town. Unfortunately, it's on private property (ask Cantur, downtown, about guides).

Parque Zoológico Edgar Lang Sacasa ZOO
(adult/child US$0.70/0.30; ⌚8:30am-5pm Tue-Sun) At Km 16 on the Masaya Hwy, this has local wildlife and a few African species lounging listlessly in smallish enclosures; the nutria sure are cute, though. Bring insect repellent.

Cerro Ventarrón HIKING
There's a quiet trail climbing dormant Cerro Ventarrón: go southeast on the dirt road by Comedor Bianca for about an hour on foot, then enjoy the views of Masaya.

Sleeping & Eating

Hotel la Borgoña HOTEL **$$**
(☎2279-5552; r US$30; P ❄ ≋) There's no lodging in town, but a couple of kilometers down the road to San Marcos is this hotel with OK rooms, good beds, a great pool and a decent restaurant on-site.

Las Pithayas NICARAGUAN **$$**
(Carratera a Ticuantepe, Km 18; dishes US$3-8) On the road into town, serving good steaks and *típica* (regional specialties) under a huge thatched roof beside a fantastic swimming pool.

Mi Viejo NICARAGUAN **$$**
(Carretera a Masaya, Km 17.5; dishes US$3-6; ⌚7am-8:30pm; ❄) This place out on the main highway has an excellent selection of steaks served in a friendly thatched-roof setting.

Getting There & Away

Microbuses to Managua (Mercado Roberto Huembes; US$0.30, 40 minutes) and San Marcos (US$0.50, one hour) leave from the parque central when full (about every 20 minutes). You can catch a taxi or *moto* (motor cycle) to the area reserves.

Reserva Natural Chocoyero–El Brujo

This deep, Y-shaped valley 23km south of Managua has a small, 184-hectare **natural reserve** (☎8864-8652; admission US$4) that was originally created to safeguard almost one-third of Managua's water supply. **El Brujo** (The Wizard) is a waterfall that seems to disappear underground, separated by a 400m cliff from **El Chocoyero** (Place of Parakeets), the less immediately impressive cascade. Show up at around 3pm and you'll see bands of parakeets come screaming home for their evening gossip.

It may just have the most comfortable public campsites in Nicaragua (per person US$4), and you can rent a small tent for just US$10 more. Hiking guides or a nighttime bat tour cost US$5.

The reserve is 7km away from where the Managua–La Concepción bus drops you off, so it's much easier to get a cab in Ticuantepe (about US$10). If you're driving from Managua, after going 14km on the main road, turn west to Ticuantepe and La Concepción; at Km 21.5 a dirt road goes to the entrance.

Montibelli Reserva Privada

Make reservations in advance to visit one of Nicaragua's best **private reserves** (☎2270-4287; www.montibelli.com; camping/cabinas US$35/$40 ; ⌚Tue-Sun). It has excellent birding, almost 40 species of butterfly, great food and wonderful guided hikes. On the **Los Balcones trail**, you can see yellow and brown orependola birds, best known for their unique nests that swing like mossy pendulums from the trees. The **Mirador trail** offers spectacular views of Volcán Masaya, Cerro Ventarrón and Mombacho.

The reserve also organizes package deals geared toward students and scientists, including camping for groups of at least 10 people, including five meals, guided hikes and other activities. To get here, take a *moto* (US$2) from the Ticuantepe bus stop. The well-signed turnoff for the reserve is at Km 19 of Carretera Ticuantepe–La Concepción (or La Concha); it's another 2.5km to the reserve.

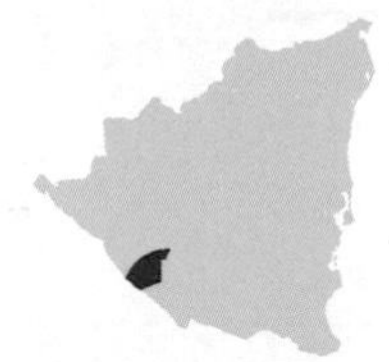

Masaya & Los Pueblos Blancos

Includes ➡

Best Places to Stay

- San Simian (p75)
- Centro Ecoturístico Flor de Pochote (p79)
- La Mariposa Spanish School & Eco Hotel (p79)

Best Festivals

- San Juan Bautista (p77)
- Santa Ana (p77)
- Virgen de la Candelaria (p77)

Why Go?

Nicaragua's *meseta central* (central plateau) offers a picturesque patchwork of lagoons, steamy volcanic peaks and sleepy colonial villages. Not many people stay here for more than a short day-trip from nearby Granada, leaving plenty of room for exploration and singular encounters with the region's remarkable natural, cultural and artistic imprint.

While trawling Masaya's well-stocked artisan market is obligatory, real fans of the craftsmanship on display should get out to the Pueblos Blancos. The Laguna de Apoyo is another must-see: its clear turquoise waters and laid-back waterfront lodges offer a splendid natural respite.

Towering over all of this is mighty Volcán Masaya, where hiking trails take you to lava-filled craters and bat-infested caves.

Sloping down from the *meseta* are the Carazo towns – pleasant stopovers on the way to a wild and remote stretch of coast.

When to Go

Thursday evenings rock in Masaya with the Jueves de Verbena. Stay the evening to sample local food, watch folkloric dances, and stroll through the large crafts market and museum.

December through August is the dry season. Coming around this time makes hiking around Volcán Masaya or skinny dipping in Laguna de Apoyo all the better. Come early in the season for green everywhere.

Sunday is the traditional market day throughout the region. It adds a brimming energy you won't feel other days of the week. There's also a good chance you'll find yourself smack dab in the middle of a religious or cultural festival.

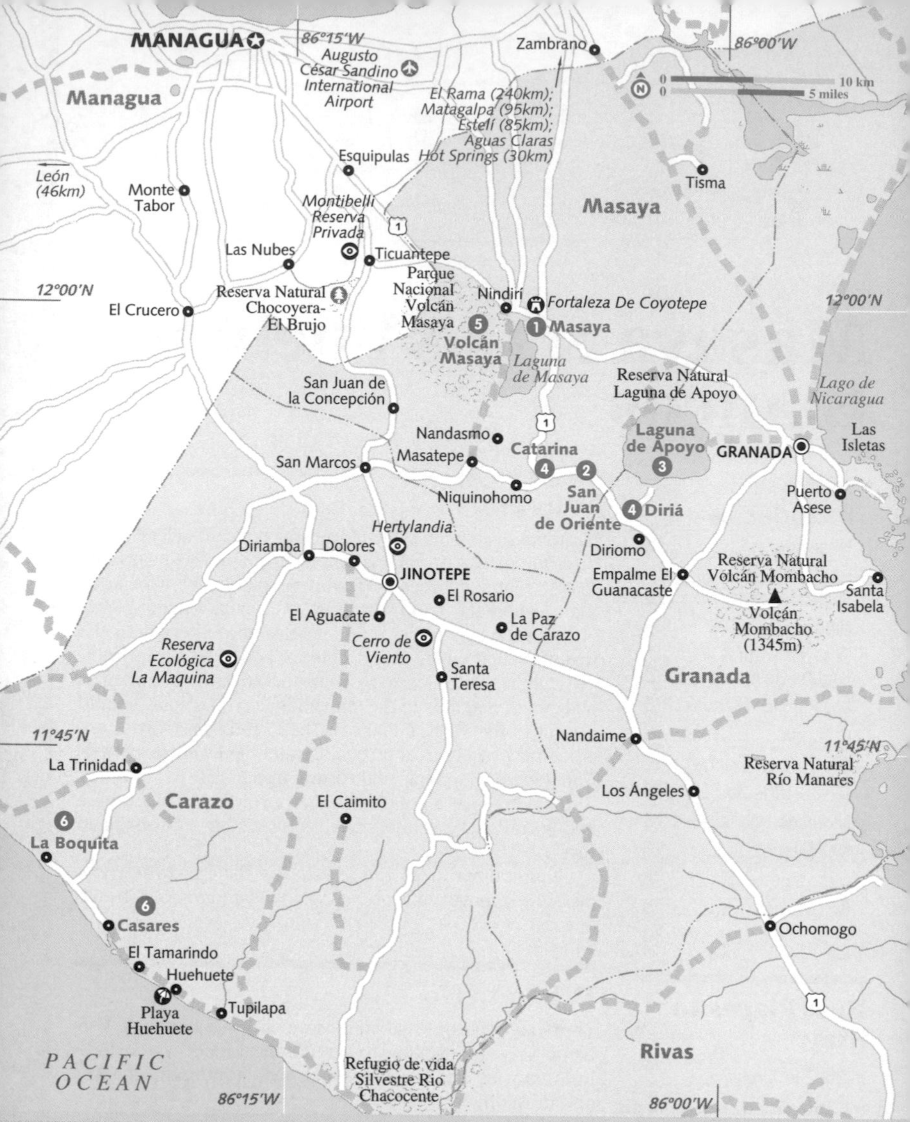

Masaya & Los Pueblos Blancos Highlights

1. Shop till you drop at the country's most famous handicraft market, the **Mercado Artesanías** (p67), in Masaya
2. Watch history repeat itself as potters in the workshops of **San Juan de Oriente** (p77) continue the centuries-old craft of ceramics production
3. Take a dip in the **Laguna de Apoyo** (p75), said to be the cleanest water in the whole country
4. Peer into that gorgeous lagoon from the spectacular lookouts at **Catarina** (p76) and **Diriá** (p78)
5. Drive to the 'gates of hell,' then take a full-moon hike up gassy, tempestuous **Volcán Masaya** (p73)
6. Pioneer virgin waves in lost beach towns like **La Boquita** (p82) and **Casares** (p82)

History

A thriving population center long before the arrival of the Spanish, Masaya and the network of small towns that surround it show signs of Chorotega inhabitation for at least the last 3000 years. While Masaya is without doubt the modern-day regional center, in pre-Colombian times the tiny town of Diriá was the Chorotega capital, a place where 28 chieftains would meet every seven years to elect a new leader.

The region's claim to fame, *artesanías* (handicrafts), has a long tradition, too – as far back as 1548 the Spanish required Masaya to provide hammocks and shoes for the colonizers as a tribute.

Masaya gained official status as a town in 1819, predating Nicaraguan independence by only two years. The delay was most likely due to the fierce fighting spirit of the locals – their opposition to the Spanish in 1529, William Walker in 1856, US Marines in 1912 and the Guardia Nacional throughout the revolution is legendary.

These last skirmishes took a particular toll on the region, none more so than when, in 1977, the Masaya suburb of Monimbó rose up against Somoza forces. During the struggle much of the town's colonial architecture was destroyed. As if that weren't enough, a massive earthquake in 2000 badly damaged the majority of the remaining historical buildings, many of which today await funding in order to be properly restored.

MASAYA

POP 166,500 / ELEV 240M

Coming from Granada, Masaya may seem a bit down at heel. This is a very workaday little town, unexceptional but for two things – a wonderful, crumbling *malecón* (waterfront walkway) and the famous artisan market, Mercado Artesanías, where you can stock up for every birthday, Christmas and anniversary for the rest of your life without buying two of the same thing. Nicaraguan tourists, by the way, always make sure their visit coincides with one of Masaya's many spectacular festivals, and there are cultural exhibitions and dances every Thursday evening.

Masaya is 29km southeast of Managua and 16km northwest of Granada. The city sits at the edge of Laguna de Masaya, beyond which rises Volcán Masaya, which can be visited on day trips from here or Granada.

Sights & Activities

One of the best ways to see the town is in a **horse-drawn carriage**, about US$2.50 per person for the grand tour. If you're here between Thursday and Sunday, consider taking the cute little **tourist train** (US$2) from Hotel Madera's Inn on a 40-minute guided tour of Masaya. Highlights include the *malecón*, Iglesia de San Jerónimo and the 1926 **old train station** (Av Zelaya), which unfortunately remains closed to the public.

★ Mercado Artesanías MARKET

(National Artisans Market, Mercado Viejo or Old Market) The 1888 Mercado Artesanías is a somewhat incongruous, black-basalt Gothic structure with a Spanish-fortress motif, including turrets, towers and oversized gates. Despite a major fire in 1966, it was used as a regular market until 1978, when Somoza's Guardia Nacional all but leveled it.

Today it's a wonderful place to stroll, with attractive booths separated by wide and breezy walkways, showcasing the highest-quality crafts in the country.

Museo del Folklore MUSEUM

(Mercado Artesanías; admission US$2; ⌚8am-5pm Fri-Wed, 8am-7pm Thu) This new museum inside the Mercado Artesanías walls focuses on dance, local myths and the cultural traditions of Masaya.

Malecón & Laguna de Masaya WATERFRONT

Seven blocks west of the parque central is one of the most inspiring views in a region famed for them: the view across Laguna de Masaya to the smoking Santiago crater. The attractive, if crumbling, *malecón* was constructed in 1944, when you could still swim, drink or fish in the impressive lagoon. Things have changed. Several trails carved into the volcanic crater millennia ago lead from a humble collection of restaurant-bars down to the water.

Museo y Galería de Héroes y Martires MUSEUM

(Av San Jerónimo, parque central 1½c N; ⌚8am-noon & 1-5pm Mon-Fri) FREE Inside the *alcaldía* (mayor's office), this museum honors Masayans who gave their lives during the revolution. There are walls of photos and interesting displays of bomb-building materials and weapons, as well as personal effects including musical instruments and a few Chorotegan funeral urns.

LOCAL KNOWLEDGE

'MONIMBÓ IS NICARAGUA!'

Masaya may have been declared the 'Cradle of National Folklore,' but the folklore of Masaya is the folklore of Monimbó. Once the region's most important indigenous city, this famous Masaya neighborhood, centered on Iglesia San Sebastián, is still populated mainly by people of Chorotegan descent.

In many ways Monimbó remains a world apart: indigenous government structures such as the Council of Elders are still in place, if largely relegated to ceremonial status.

One reason for Monimbó's cultural autonomy is its celebrated history of almost continuous rebellion against the Spaniards and other occupiers. Most recently, in 1977, the people of Monimbó famously attacked Somoza's feared Guardia Nacional, using homemade weapons – contact bombs, machetes and lances – produced by their own artisans and craftspeople. They held the barrio for a week.

After the battle, the Monimboseños donned traditional Spanish masks, borrowed from folkloric dances that ridiculed those occupiers, and denounced to the newspapers the abuses and atrocities of the Guardia Nacional. The country was inspired by the barrio's spectacular resistance, and streets across the nation echoed with the battle cry, 'Monimbó is Nicaragua!' Ernesto Cardenal wrote that the masked Monimboseños had declared their barrio 'Free Nicaragua.' And in the end, Masaya and Monimbó were among the first cities to see a complete withdrawal of Somoza's troops.

Festivals & Traditions

➜ **St Lazarus** The week before Easter, the Iglesia María Magdalena fills with devotees dressed up as children, witches, space aliens and more. A special Mass is followed by food and corn liquor for all.

➜ **Los Agüizotes** This celebration features spirits of the dead and characters from indigenous horror stories (many originating during the Spanish conquest). The Headless Priest and La Carreta Nagua (The Chariot of Death) are used throughout the year to scare children into better behavior, but on the last Friday in October they make their way through the streets of Monimbó and Masaya. Costumes are prepared the night before in a ceremony called **La Vela del Candil (Candle Vigil)**. The costumes are placed on a table with a large candle in the middle, and those watching over it throughout the night keep themselves awake with fireworks, live music, alcohol and dancing.

Fortaleza De Coyotepe FORT
(admission US$0.70; ⏲8am-6pm) Built in 1893 atop Cerro de los Coyotes, this eerie fortress witnessed the last stand of Benjamín Zeledón, the 1912 hero of resistance to US intervention. The marines managed to take the fortress, watched all the while by a young man named Sandino, who vowed his revenge. In the end it would also be the Guardia Nacional's last stronghold, overrun during the Sandinistas' final 1979 offensive.

It's worth the climb just for the view: Laguna de Masaya, Lago de Managua, Volcán Mombacho and, if it's clear, Volcán Momotombo, rising red and black above Managua. Your entrance fee includes a Spanish-language tour of the underground prison, detailing each atrocity.

You can walk 2km north on the Interamericana (Pan-American Hwy), but it's worth getting a Managua-bound bus (US$0.30) or taxi (US$1) to avoid the scary traffic. Taxis charge extra to take you up the steep hill. Otherwise it's a sweaty half-hour hike.

Churches & Plazas

There are 12 major barrios (neighborhoods) in Masaya, all of which were once separate communities with their own churches, plazas and identities: Monimbó, San Jerónimo, Santa Teresa, Villa Bosco Monge, Aserrio, Santa Susana, Las Malvinas, El Palomar, La Ceibita, Cerro Fortaleza de Coyotepe, Sylvio Renazco and Cerro la Barranca.

At the center of it all is the 1750 **Parroquia de la Asunción**, an attractive but scarred late-baroque beauty that the Spanish government has offered to help repair. It watches over the parque central, formally known as **Parque 17 de Octubre**, in honor of the 1977 fire fight that pitted local residents against Somoza's Guardia Nacional.

Monimbó is Masaya's most famous neighborhood, its ancient center now marked by the 1935 **Iglesia San Sebastián** (cnr Av Real de Monimbó & Calle Las Cuatro Esquinas). Perhaps more important, **Iglesia María Magdalena** (Av Magdalena), sort of the female counterpart to San Sebastián, is where many of Monimbó's most important festivals begin or end.

Although **Iglesia San Juan** (cnr Av El Tope & Calle Central) is usually closed to the public, check out the surrounding neighborhood strung between La Asunción and the lake, with more than a dozen hammock workshops and factories. Other churches worth seeing include the more modern **Iglesia de San Miguel** (Calle San Miguel, Mercado Nuevo, 1c E), whose resident San Miguel Arcángel makes the rounds during the procession of St Jerome, and 1848 **Iglesia San Juan**, small, simple and much nicer inside than out.

Parroquia El Calvario (Calle El Calvario, Parque Central, 7c E) is a squat colonial structure with no spire, most remarkable for the extra-gory statues of Jesus and the thieves being crucified, right at the entrance. Those are original – the rest had to be remodeled after the earthquake of 2000.

Among the major buildings worst hit by the earthquake, which also destroyed about 80 homes, was 1928 **Iglesia de San Jerónimo** (cnr Av San Jerónimo & Calle Palo Blanco), the spiritual heart of Masaya and one of the most recognizable silhouettes on the skyline.

Tours

Masaya Tours TOUR
(☎8666-7754; in front of Museo del Folklore) This home-grown operation offers trips to the nearby pueblos (US$25 per person), Volcán Masaya (US$35) and other tourist spots. The juices here are great, too!

Festivals & Events

Jueves de Verbena CULTURAL
(⊙5pm Thu) Once a week this has food, music and ballet *folklorico* at the Mercado Artesanías; most Granada tour outfits offer this as a weekly add-on to their regular Masaya trips.

La Virgen de la Asunción RELIGIOUS
(⊙March 16) Better known as the Virgin of the Burning Finger or the Festival of the Cross; the town's top Virgin is taken to the lake for a blessing of the waters and a good look at the slender protrusion of lava that threatened the town during the 1772 eruption, until she stopped it.

Jesús del Rescate RELIGIOUS
(⊙April 3) Scores of *carretas* (ox carts) begin their journey from Masaya to San Jorge.

San Lázaro RELIGIOUS
(⊙week before Palm Sunday) Includes a procession of costumed dogs.

Día de la Virgen de la Asunción RELIGIOUS
(⊙August 15) Everyone's favorite patron saint, María Magdelena, is hoisted atop the shoulders of revelers for her annual tour of Monimbó; fireworks are involved.

San Jerónimo RELIGIOUS
(⊙September 30) Officially it's eight days of festivities, but folks have stretched out Nicaragua's most famous festival to three months. The patron saint (in the guise of a bearded *campesino* named 'Tata Chombó,' or 'Doctor of the Poor') is taken from the Iglesia de San Jerónimo altar and borne around Masaya while traditional dances are performed, including Mozote y Verga, a mock battle that ends with peacemaking ceremonies to commemorate the September peace treaties of 1856, 1912 and 1979. Fireworks, marimbas, parades, drag queens and more make this a fiesta to remember.

Noche de Agüizotes CULTURAL
(last Friday in October) Not to be confused with Halloween or Day of the Dead, this spooky festival features legends come to life and ghosts of the dead, plus the costumed living parading through the streets.

El Toro Venado CULTURAL
(⊙last Sunday of October, third Sunday of November) This dance involves a mythical creature that is half bull, half deer (read: half Spanish, half indigenous), and whose mission is to make fun of the rest of the fair.

Baille de los Diablitos CULTURAL
(⊙last Sunday of November) Little devils dance in honor of Mephistopheles and San Jerónimo.

Sleeping

Most lodging is clustered about four blocks north of Parroquia de la Asunción, along Av Zelaya.

Masaya

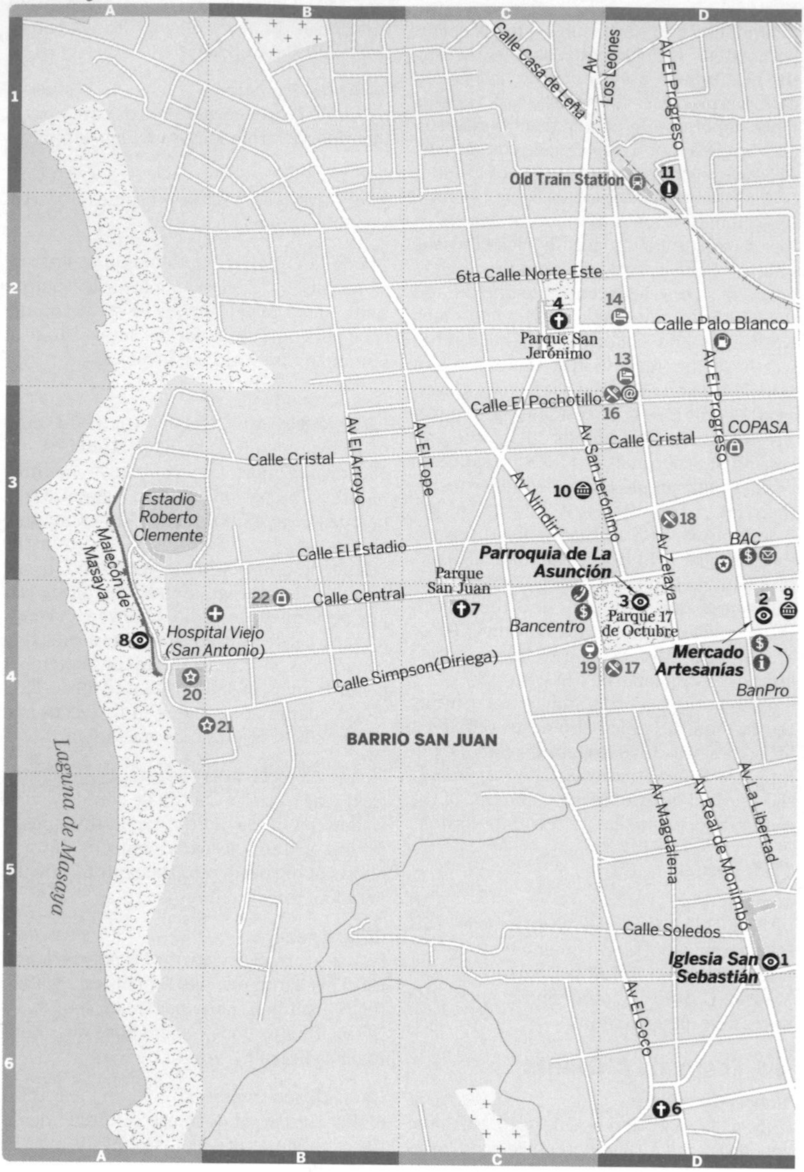

Hostal Mi Casa HOSTEL $
(☎2522-2500; mantonabermudez@hotmail.com; Av Zelaya; dm/r US$7/20, r with air-con $25; P ❄ 📶) Mi Casa has a nice garden area dominated by chattering birds. The three-bed dorm rooms have private bathrooms, making this a step up for the shared-room set.

Hotel Madera's Inn HOTEL $
(☎2522-5825; www.hotelmaderasinn.com; Av Zelaya, Iglesia San Jerónimo, 1c E, ½c N; dm/d US$5/15,

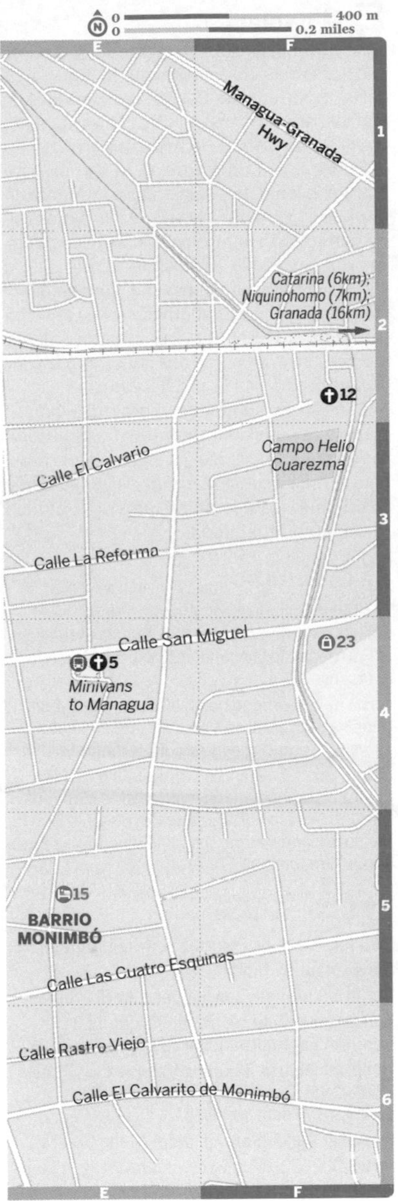

Masaya

Top Sights

1 Iglesia San Sebastián ... D5
2 Mercado Artesanías ... D4
3 Parroquia de La Asunción ... D4

Sights

4 Iglesia de San Jerónimo ... C2
5 Iglesia de San Miguel ... E4
6 Iglesia María Magdalena ... D6
7 Iglesia San Juan ... C4
8 Malecón & Laguna de Masaya ... A4
9 Museo del Folklore ... D4
10 Museo y Galería de Héroes y Martires ... C3
11 Old Train Station ... D1
12 Parroquia El Calvario ... F2

Activities, Courses & Tours

Masaya Tours ... (see 9)
Tourist Train ... (see 14)

Sleeping

13 Hostal Mi Casa ... D2
14 Hotel Madera's Inn ... D2
15 Hotel Monimbó ... E5

Eating

16 Fruti Fruti ... D3
17 La Ronda ... D4
18 Taquería La Jarochita ... D3

Drinking & Nightlife

19 Mezon La Terraza ... C4

Entertainment

20 Coco Jamboo ... A4
21 El Toro Loco ... B4

Shopping

22 Hammock Factories ... B4
23 Mercado Municipal Ernesto Fernández (Mercado Nuevo) ... F4

tr with air-con $45; ❄ 📶) One of your best bets in Masaya is simple and a bit smokey. But there are nice firm mattresses and friendly service – ask for a room upstairs. There's an annex across the street with dorm rooms sleeping four that can get a bit cramped with just a fan to keep you cool.

Hotel Monimbó HOTEL $$

(☎2522-6867; hotelmonimbo04@hotmail.com; Iglesia San Sebastián, 1c E, 1½c N; s/d US$25/30; P ❄ @) An odd location, stuck out in the mostly residential heart of Monimbó, south of town, but the rooms are surprisingly good: spacious and spotless, facing a trim little garden.

Eating

Inexpensive *comedores* (basic eateries) cling to the outside of the Mercado Municipal Ernesto Fernández, just outside the bus terminal. Plastic baggies of *vigorón* (mashed yucca topped with coleslaw and pork rinds), fruit salad and *gallo pinto* (blended rice and beans) can be had for less than US$1, a sit-down meal with a drink for around US$2. There's also snack stalls on the Parque 17 de Octubre and in the Mercado Artesanías.

Fruti Fruti SANDWICHES **$**
(Av Zelaya, parque central, 3c N; snacks US$2-6; ⏲7am-10pm) Fruit smoothies, cold sandwiches, salads and snacks served with a smile in spotless surrounds make this a fine stop.

Taquería La Jarochita MEXICAN **$$**
(Av Zelaya, parque central, 1c N; dishes US$7-12; ⏲11:30am-late) All your Tex-Mex faves are here, served up in a stately and elegant atmosphere. Get in early for a balcony seat out front and watch the world go by.

La Ronda NICARAGUAN **$$**
(Calle San Miguel, frente parque central; dishes US$4-6; ⏲lunch & dinner Tue-Sun) This bar-restaurant right on the main plaza has juicy steaks, cold beers and a friendly atmosphere.

Drinking

Mezon La Terraza BAR
(Av Nindirí, frente parque central; ⏲noon-late Tue-Sat) This small bar overlooking the park features loud music, a *very* young crowd and plenty of rum. Your call.

Entertainment

Discos are clustered around the entrance to the *malecón* – go for a walk and see which thumping beat suits you best.

Coco Jamboo DANCE
(⏲9pm-3am Fri-Sun) Danceheads opt for this big club at the southern end of the *malecón,* where a cheesy good time can usually be had.

El Toro Loco DANCE
(cover US$2.50; ⏲Thu-Sun) Gets packed on Thursday for reggae night, and pumps out the Latin pop, reggaeton and *bacchata* (romantic Dominican dance music) the rest of the week.

Shopping

Masaya's major claim to fame is shopping, and savvy buyers come here to find great deals on Nicaragua's finest handicrafts. Tours and taxi drivers drop you off at Masaya's main crafts market, Mercado Artesanías (p67).

Public buses drop you off in the massive bus lot behind the huge, chaotic **Mercado Municipal Ernesto Fernández**, a more typical market with unrefrigerated meat counters, colorful vegetable stands, toiletries and a wide selection of somewhat lower-quality handicrafts, cigars, handmade shoes and fun souvenirs at discount prices crammed under the hot, busy tents. Pay attention, watch your backpack and wallet, and have fun.

Can't stop shopping? There are handicrafts workshops all over town. **Hammock factories** congregate in Barrio San Juan, between La Asunción and the lagoon, while wood and leather workshops are hidden throughout Monimbó.

Orientation

The Mercado Municipal (Mercado Nuevo) and main bus station are about six blocks to the east of Parroquia de la Asunción, past the Mercado Artesanías.

The neighborhood north of La Asunción contains most of Masaya's restaurants and hotels, as well as famed Iglesia de San Jerónimo.

Continue for about 1km and you'll reach the old train station and the main road to Managua. The entrance to Fortaleza de Coyotepe is 2km to the north, and Parque Nacional Volcán Masaya is about 7km further.

Information

BAC (cnr Calle La Reforma & Av El Progreso)
Bancentro (Av Nindiri)
BanPro (cnr Calle San Miguel & Av El Progreso)
Enitel (Calle Central, frente Parque 17 de Octubre) For international calls.
Hospital Hilario Sanchez Vásquez (☎2522-2778; Calle San Miguel) This hospital has emergency-room services.
Hospital Viejo (San Antonio) (Calle Central)
Intur (☎2522-7615; www.visitanicaragua.com/ingles; Av El Progreso, Mercado Artesanías, ½c S) This well-funded office with English-speaking staff sells a fairly useful, if distorted, map (with lots of factoids in English) and has broad information about the region.
Kablenet Café (Av Zelaya, Iglesia San Jerónimo, 1c E, 1c S; per hr US$0.70)
Police Station (Calle La Reforma)
Post Office (Calle La Reforma)

Getting There & Around

Taxis and horse-drawn carriages both charge around US$0.75 for a ride across town.

Minivans to Managua's Universidad Centro America (US$0.80, 30 minutes) leave the park in front of Iglesia de San Miguel when full. Other buses and minivans arrive and depart from the **bus terminal** at the eastern side of the Mercado Municipal.

Parque Nacional Volcán Masaya

The Spaniards said this was the gate to hell, and put the Bobadilla cross (named for the priest who planted it) atop a now sadly inaccessible cliff. **Volcán Masaya** (☎2528-1444; admission US$4, 3hr guided tour) US$15; ⊙9am-4:45pm) is the most heavily venting volcano in Nicaragua, and in a more litigious nation there is no way you would ever be allowed to drive up to the lip of a volcanic cone as volatile as the Santiago crater.

There's always lava bubbling at the bottom (you probably won't see it, though), and a column of sulfurous gases rising above; in 2001 an eruption hurled heated rocks 500m into the air, damaging cars and narrowly missing people.

But you have to go. Masaya is already inside the volcano, an enormous and ancient crater called El Ventarrón, with a barely perceptible rim that runs from Ticuantepe to Masatepe, and around the Laguna de Masaya. Try to arrive in the afternoon, when the crater's thousands of *chocoyos* (parakeets) return to their nests in the crater walls, apparently unharmed by the billowing toxic gases.

There are more than 20km of hiking trails. Shorter, mostly accessible treks require **guides** (per group US$0.70 to US$2), which you pay for with your admission (tips are additional and you need at least five people to head out on the tour). **Sendero Los Coyotes** (1.5km) meanders through lava-strewn fields and dry tropical forest; **Sendero El Comalito** (2km) takes you to a smaller cone surrounded by fumaroles; and **Sendero Las Cuevas** (1½ hours) lets you explore the very cool lava tunnels of Tzinancanostoc, with bats.

There are also longer hikes (5km to 6km) to lookout points and large rocks that don't require guides (although you could certainly arrange them for around US$15 for three hours). If you speak Spanish, ask your guide to show you around the attractive **museum** (admission free) at the visitor center, with impressive natural-history displays and beautiful murals, and the **butterfly garden**.

MASAYA & MESETA ARTS & CRAFTS

Masaya itself has been famous since the days before the arrival of the Spanish for its excellent craftsmanship, including leather, woodcrafts and so much more. Intur (p72) has an excellent map of town showing where the various workshops are – you're welcome to drop in, have a look around and, of course, buy something.

Top Buys

- **Hammocks** (US$10 to US$20 for the simple ones, US$25 to US$50 for the nice ones) Bulky but beautiful, Nicaragua's signature craft is made right here in Masaya.
- **Naive paintings and balsawood carvings** (US$8 to US$200) Glowing colors and tropical subjects are a window on the exotic Islas Solentiname.
- **Black ceramics** (US$3 to US$20) Typical of Matagalpa and Jinotega; smooth, heavy ceramics are specially fired for a deep black sheen.
- **Natural fiber weavings** (US$3 to US$10) Whether it's the light, flexible *jipijapa* hats of Camoapa, the elaborately patterned reed mats from Masatepe, or even the woven palm-leaf crickets (US$0.25) that every enterprising eight year old in Nicaragua has on offer, you'll find it here.
- **Carved jícara shells** (US$1 to US$5) You've probably seen the shiny green seeds hanging from the rangy-looking trees, one of the first plants ever domesticated – not for food, but for the shell. Carvings on durable cups and bowls range from simple to stunning, and are priced accordingly.
- **Soapstone sculptures** (US$20 to US$50) They don't take up much space, but these sensually smooth marmolina sculptures from San Juan de Limay will weigh you down.

The park entrance is 7km north of Masaya. You pay for your entry and guided hikes at the entrance gate, and you'll receive a handy brochure with a map and useful information in Spanish and English. It's 5km of paved road to the crater and **Plaza de Oviedo**, which honors the intrepid priest who went down into the volcano with a sample dish, to find out whether or not the lava was (as he suspected) pure gold. It wasn't, but folks were still impressed enough with the feat to name the parking lot after him. Park officials limit your time here to just five minutes. From here, community-run **horseback-riding tours** (US$4) can take you toward the summit.

There's a night tour (US$10 per person, 5pm to 7pm) where you can witness millions of bats leaving a nearby cave... spooky.

Sleeping & Eating

Hotel Volcán Masaya HOTEL **$$**
(2522-7114; s/d US$27/37) There's no camping, but this place, right by the park entrance, has bare but comfortable rooms complete with screened-in porches. It only serves breakfast (US$2) and snacks, and restaurants are a long walk along the busy road; consider bringing food with you.

Getting There & Away

Any Managua-bound bus from Masaya or Granada can drop you at the entrance, but it's a steep, hot climb to the crater; hitching is definitely possible. Consider taking a round-trip taxi from Masaya (US$8) or Granada (US$15), including an hour's wait at the top. Most tour outfits in Granada come here as part of a Masaya day trip, including the markets and Catarina overlook, for around US$15 per person.

Nindirí

POP 17,300

Only 3km north of Masaya, the much more adorable town of Nindirí may have been even more important than Monimbó during the Chorotega era. Archaeological treasures abound, as you'll see at tiny **Museo Tendirí** (8954-0570; parque central, 1c N; donations accepted; 8am-noon & 2-5pm Mon-Fri). Vast quantities of priceless ceramics, ancient sculptures and colonial-era artifacts (3000 in all) have been crammed into this cheerfully dilapidated building.

If the lady who runs the museum is out, you could check out the 1529 Catholic **church**, which has been left in adobe simplicity by subsequent renovations. It's home to Cristo del Volcán, credited with stopping a lava flow from destroying the town during the 1772 eruption that opened the Santiago crater.

Adventurous souls could take the short hike to **Cascadas Cailagua** and **petroglyphs**. Start at the cemetery close to the Nindirí *empalme* (junction): take the road through the cemetery until you get to the three green crosses; make a right and follow the trail through the gap in the fence and across the field. The waterfall would be more attractive without the litter (and raw sewage), but check out the wall of petroglyphs nearby.

Unfortunately, there are no hotels in Nindirí, but tour operator **Harold Ramos** (8629-1983) can be found in the **Colegio Oreana Teresa** (parque central, 2½c O). He can arrange lodging in the city (per person US$6) or countryside (US$5). Meals cost US$3 extra.

BUS SERVICES FROM MASAYA

DESTINATION	COST (US$)	DURATION (hr)	DEPARTURES	FREQUENCY
Carazo (San Marcos, Diriamba and Jinotepe)	$0.30-0.50	1¼	5am-6pm	every 20min
Catarina, Diriomo & Diriá	$0.30-0.50	40min	6am-5pm	every 20min
Catarina, San Juan de Oriente, Niquinohomo, Masatepe & San Marcos	$0.50	1¼	5am-6pm	every 20min
Granada	$0.50	40min	5am-6pm	every 20min
Laguna de Apoyo entrance	$0.35	20min	5am-5pm	every 20min
Managua	$0.50	1	4:30am-5:10pm	every 20min
Matagalpa	$3	3	5:30am & 6am	-
Ticuantepe	$0.50	45min	6am-5pm	every 20min

In Nindirí, the best eats in town are at **La Llamarada** (parque central, 3c S; dishes US$4-7; ⊗closed Tue), where you can gorge yourself on huge set meals – the *bistec encebollado* (beef with fried onions) truly is worth writing home about.

Reserva Natural Laguna De Apoyo

A vision in sapphire set into a lush forest crater, this 200m-deep, 200-centuries-old crater lake is said to be the country's cleanest and deepest. The warm undersea fumaroles feed the healing and slightly salty waters, howler monkeys bark overhead every morning and there's a cooled-back air that make this a favorite respite for peace-seeking travelers.

While technically considered a natural reserve (free for foot traffic, US$1 entrance for cars), this wild area has plenty of hotels dotting the lake's shore and limited environmental protections from the various agencies that claim jurisdiction. Tread lightly.

Many visitors are content with just taking in the view from the crater's edge in Catarina or Diriá. But it's worth making your way to the bottom for one of the finest swims you'll ever enjoy. A tiny town lies at the bottom of the paved road into the crater, accessible via an often unsigned turnoff about 15km north of Granada along the Carretera a Masaya. All directions given here are from El Triangulo – the T intersection where the road splits once it hits the waterfront, either heading to the right (south) or left (north).

Activities

There's a free **beach** at the bottom of the road; look for the trail just to the right of the T intersection. Otherwise, pay a few dollars to any of the hotels for day-use privileges at their docks.

Apoyo Dive Center DIVING
(☎8631-1890; Triangulo, 500m N; one tank US$40) Located in the Hotel Selva Sur, this PADI operation also has certification courses.

Estación Biológica DIVING
(☎8882-3992; www.gaianicaragua.org; Triangulo 1km N; one tank US$60) This ecological research station hosts scientists studying the region's endemic fish population and offers dives for PADI-certified divers. Expect 30 feet of visibility, dives down to 30m and fleeting glimpses of guapote and mojada fish, along with the fumeroles.

Spanish School Laguna de Apoyo LANGUAGE COURSE
(☎8882-3992; www.gaianicaragua.org; Triangulo, 1km N) Located at the Estación Biológica, this school offers 20 hours of language instruction plus room and board for US$240.

Sleeping & Eating

There's a basic store 50m north of the T intersection. Otherwise, most hotels also have restaurants.

Monkey Hut HOSTEL $
(☎8887-3546; www.themonkeyhut.net; Triangulo, 450m N; dm/d/cabin US$14/34/56; P 📶) Operated by Granada's popular Bearded Monkey hostel, this waterfront property has a beautiful dock (US$6 day use for nonguests), lots of toys (including free kayaks), beer on the honor system, a shared kitchen, and a swimming hole the size of a volcanic crater. It sells snacks.

Paradiso Hotel HOSTEL $
(www.paradisolaguna.com; Triangulo, 550m N; dm US$10, r with/without bathroom US$40/25; P ❄ @ 📶) The large 12-bed dorm has lake views, making this a good bet for budgeteers. The private rooms and boring brick architecture leave a bit to be desired, as do the grounds. But you get a large terrace, private dock, kayaks, restaurant and shared kitchen.

Pucha's Inn INN $
(☎2522 5505; Triangulo, 1.5km N; r US$20) Simple budget rooms a bit up the hill from the water's edge. There's no restaurant here, but you can use the kitchen. If you're coming, call ahead as the place is often left unattended. The hotel is badly signposted – coming up the hill, look for a big pink house on your right, with a church in front; the side road to the hotel runs between them toward the lake.

★ **San Simian** BUNGALOW $$$
(☎8850-8101; www.sansimian.com; Triangulo, 3km S; cabins incl breakfast US$55; P 📶) These beautiful little cabins blend into the jungly hillside. Most have stone-walled, alfresco bathrooms, and all have big-screened windows, mosquito nets over the beds, and plenty of air and light. This place books up quick, so reserve at least a week in advance. You get free use of kayaks and innertubes from the hotel's dock.

La Orquidea GUESTHOUSE **$$$**
(☎8872-1866; www.laorquideanicaragua.com; Triangulo, 1.8km N; d/q incl breakfast US$60/140; P 📶) If you can rent the whole house for four people, this is the place to stay. You get your own living room, gorgeous, spacious rooms – there's just two bedrooms – with big windows leading out onto balconies with excellent lagoon views. The water's a short walk down the hill.

Posada la Abuela CABINS **$$$**
(☎8880-0368; www.posadaecologicalaabuela.com; Triangulo, 2.4km N; cabins incl breakfast US$70; P ❄) On a steep hillside leading down to the water, these cute little cabins are comfortable enough to make you feel at home (with coffeemaker and fridge) but still have a rustic touch, giving a sense of adventure. These are the nicest grounds along the lake, and the restaurant and dock offer spectacular lake views.

The Villas at Apoyo APARTMENT **$$$**
(☎2552-8200; www.thevillasatapoyo.com; Triangulo 1km S; apt US$75, cabin US$85-105, q US$125-180; P ❄ 📶 🏊) Running up the hill from the lakeside road, these luxury condos lack the great lake views that other spots have, and are missing direct beach access, but with kitchens, living rooms, a pool and plenty of room to spread out, they are a good option for families.

Pájaro Azul GUESTHOUSE **$$$**
(☎8539-0779; Triangulo, 1.5km S; campsite per person/s/apt US$16/50/100; ❄) Big groups need only apply for this lakefront guesthouse that sleeps up to seven. But if you all want to hang out, it has excellent grounds, a shared kitchen, and slightly cramped and dark rooms. Camping is in a nearby lot.

Norome NICARAGUAN **$$**
(Triangulo, 1km S; mains US$5-12; P ❄) Across from the Villas at Apoyo, this restaurant has a nice dock for day use (US$4).

ℹ Getting There & Around

You can walk here from Granada: take the dirt road northeast of the cemetery for about two hours through a poor but pretty region, and bring everything you'll need to eat and drink, as there are no services at this end of the lake. Once you reach the crater rim, ask local farmers for permission to cross their land. Steep trails also begin at the *miradores* (viewpoints) in Catarina and Diriá, more or less a 1½-hour round-trip.

The main entrance is from a road off the Carretera a Masaya at Km 37.5. Buses run every half-hour between the crater rim and Masaya (US$0.30, 6am to 6pm). Only three buses, which read 'El Valle de la Laguna,' descend all the way to the waterfront (US$0.70, 6:30am, 11:30am and 4:30pm), returning from Masaya at 5:30am, 10:30am and 3:30pm. The half-hour, 2km descent isn't a bad walk, but going uphill is hard work.

Hitchhiking is common on this stretch, but taxis are not (except on Sunday). Taxis from Granada (US$10) and Masaya (US$6) may charge less to drop you off at the top. The Bearded Monkey Hostel runs shuttles here from Granada.

LOS PUEBLOS BLANCOS

Originally built from the chalky, pale volcanic tuff upon which this pastoral scene is spread, this series of rural communities, often called the White Villages or Pueblos Blancos, once shimmered a blinding white, amid the pale-green patchwork of pasture and jungle.

Today the centuries-old buildings have been painted, and the shady roads are paved. Most days the roads between the villages are lined with stands selling vividly painted *artesanías* (handicrafts). Each town has its specialty: handcrafted ceramics or homemade sweets, wooden furniture or freshly cut flowers, and the region is famous for its *curanderos* (folk healers). The villages are most often visited as a day trip from Granada, but take the time to explore more and the inner workings of life in rural Nicaragua may reveal itself.

Catarina

POP 5700

At the crossroads of Los Pueblos Blancos, Catarina is known for its *viveros* (nurseries) that supply ornamental plants for households across Nicaragua

It's easy to visit Catarina, and almost any regional tour from Masaya or Granada includes a quick stop at the lookout over the Laguna de Apoyo.

👁 Sights & Activities

Mirador LOOKOUT
(car parking US$1) Catarina's real claim to fame offers views across the startling blue waters of Laguna de Apoyo to Granada and Lago de Nicaragua all the way to Ometepe. Today lined with inexpensive restaurants and sou-

FESTIVALS & EVENTS OF THE MESETA

With a pantheon of saints and virgins celebrated with an almost pagan vigor, the Masaya *meseta* claims some of the most colorful fiestas in the country. Here's some top events.

- **San Silvestre Papa** (Catarina; Dec 31–Jan 1) Hey, you've got to do New Year's somewhere, and this parade is famous for its bouquets of flowers.
- **Virgen de la Candelaria** (Diriomo; Feb 2–8) Wake up early – the fireworks will help – to see the Virgin off on her annual trip to nearby Los Jirones.
- **Domingo de Trinidad** (Masatepe; mid-May) Forty days after Semana Santa, this is the biggest *hipica* (horse parade) in Nicaragua; festivities peak on May 23.
- **María Auxiliadora** (Pío XII; May 24) There's rarely much reason to visit Pío XII, unless you want to see the Baile del Viejo y Vieja (Dance of the Old Couple) done right.
- **San Pedro** (Diriá; Jun 17–Jul) Diría celebrates its patron saint with some dances celebrating Cacique Diriangén, and with others involving dried bull penises.
- **San Juan Bautista** (Catarina; Jun 24) Coincidentally falling on the summer solstice, this wild festival features dances, ceremonial fights and music.
- **Santa Ana** (Niquinohomo; Jul 26) Folk dances, fireworks and parades make this one of the country's biggest celebrations for this popular saint.
- **Santa Catalina de Alejandría** (Catarina; Nov 25-26) Folk dances and a parade.

venir shops connected by windy walkways, this spot is rumored to have been youthful Augusto C Sandino's favorite place to meditate, and appropriately so, for this is also the gravesite of Benjamín Zeledón, whose burial Sandino witnessed. There's a half-hour trail to the water, with excellent views.

Horse Rides HORSEBACK RIDING
(Mirador; per 30min/1hr US$3.50/5) Rides can be arranged at the small farmyard to the right of the *mirador*.

Sleeping & Eating

Hotel Jaaris HOTEL $
(8640-5427; Iglesia, 1c O, 20m N; s/d/tr US$12/16/19; P) This is a decent-enough budget deal – rooms sleep four. There is a cool tiled porch with rocking chairs, hammocks and a veritable pack of dogs of all sizes.

Casa Catarina HOTEL $$$
(2558-0261; www.hotelcasacatarina.com; parque central, 1c O; d/ste incl breakfast US$70/80; P) The best digs in town are well overpriced. But you get big business-hotel-style rooms and a central garden evergreened by a million and one ferns.

Los Faroles NICARAGUAN $$
(Mirador; dishes US$5-8) Make your way up to the *mirador*, where the best restaurants – including Los Faroles – are scattered around the parking lot, some with excellent views. If you want to party *meseta* style, there are a couple of discos up here, too.

Getting There & Away

There are microbuses for destinations throughout the *meseta*, while buses run regularly between the *mirador* and destinations including the following:

Granada (US$0.50, 30 minutes, 6am to 6pm, at least hourly)

Managua (US$0.60, 50 minutes, 6am to 6pm, half-hourly) Arrives/departs Mercado Roberto Huembes.

Masaya (US$0.50, 30 minutes, 6am to 6pm, half-hourly)

San Juan de Oriente

POP 2600

Also known as San Juan de los Platos, this attractive colonial town has been in the pottery business since before the Spanish conquest. While production of inexpensive and functional pottery for local consumption is still important, most of the shops lining the hilly cobblestone roads are selling decorative pieces (vases, wind chimes, wall hangings, that sort of thing), which probably wouldn't fare too well in your backpack.

The town's most famous workshop, **Cooperativa Quetzalcóatl**, is found at the entrance to town, but there are dozens of places where you can find your masterpiece, and probably watch the artisans at work.

Buses leave hourly from Granada (US$0.50, one hour) from the parque central, or you can make your way out onto the highway and flag down any passing bus making the Granada-Rivas run.

Diriá & Diriomo

POP 12,300

These twin towns are located right across the road from one another (a US$0.50 *moto* ride) and both are well worth visiting.

Diriá boasts Mirador el Boquete, the mellower, less-touristed overlook of Laguna de Apoyo, where views include a handful of **bar-restaurants** (dishes US$4 to US$6), which get packed with *festejeros* (party people) on weekends.

From the lookout, there's a steep, half-hour trail to the bottom, where a muddy little beach offers access to the bright-blue water for swimming. This viewpoint is no more difficult to visit than Catarina's: from Granada, take any Niquinohomo-bound bus (US$0.50, every 30 minutes), which will stop in front of 1650 Parroquia San Pedro, in the city center. It's a 2km walk or US$0.30 *moto* ride to the lookout.

This unassuming **church**, by the way, marks the spot where Cacique Diriangén, chief of the Dirian peoples at the time of the Spanish conquest, first met conquistador Gil González Dávila, on April 17, 1523. Unlike Nicarao, Diriangén didn't trust the newcomers and opted to ignore their three-day deadline to become a Christian. Diriangén attacked, which in retrospect was the best course of action, and today both of these towns – as well as Diriamba in Carazo – are named for the indomitable *cacique* (chief). Dotted around town are sculptures of the man, always ready.

Enchanting **Diriomo** has long been known as the **Witch Capital of the Meseta**.

Most healers work out of their homes, which are unsigned. Ask at the alcaldía (mayor's office).

Diriomo is also famous for its *cajetas,* rich fruit-flavored sweets most famously available at **Casa de Cajetas** (cajetas US$1-2); the day's flavors are posted on the wall. They're also sold elsewhere in town and along the highway. The town is also known for its *chicha bruja* (an alcoholic corn beverage) and even stiffer *calavera del gato* ('skull of the cat'; drink at your own risk). **Iglesia Nuestra Señora de Candelaria** is the perfect centerpiece for this witchy place, with rather Gothic stone walls and an extra-interesting collection of saints.

There's no lodging in either town. The best eating in Diriá is at the *mirador* restaurants.

Buses leave almost hourly from the parque central for Mercado Huembes in Managua (US$0.80) and every 40 minutes for Masaya (US$0.50). If you're in a rush (or heading south), make your way out onto the highway and flag down any passing bus.

Niquinohomo

POP 7500

This quiet, 16th-century Spanish-colonial village is the birthplace of General Augusto César Sandino, who did indeed appreciate the fact that the name is Náhuatl for 'Valley of the Warriors.' The church is lovely and there's all sorts of attractive architecture all over town, but you're probably here to see the man's birthplace, now **Augusto C Sandino Library** (9am-noon & 1:30am-5pm Mon-Sat), a very basic museum with some simple exhibits.

If you've worked up an appetite after all that sightseeing, drop into **Estancia El Bosquecillo** (frente parque central; meals US$2-6) for some good, honest, home-style Nica eating.

Nandasmo

POP 3300

On a spur road, the small village of Nandasmo is best known for its tiny arts and crafts – itsy-bitsy wooden furniture and tableware, dollhouse scale. Unlike in the other towns in the region, adorable shops aren't really in evidence – the best place to shop is at the roadside stalls out on the highway at the entrance to town.

There's also an undeveloped **overlook of Laguna de Masaya** several kilometers north of town along a rough dirt road.

Masatepe

POP 15,500

Photogenic and fabulous, this growing colonial town has a wonderfully well-kept downtown, great food, better views of the volcano than Masaya and one truly marvelous guesthouse in the countryside.

There's not a whole lot to do, although Masatepe's old train station has been reincarnated as one of the better **artisan markets** (9am-6pm) in the country. While it probably won't make it home in your backpack, the town's hallmark cane-woven rocking chairs and brightly colored cabinets are worth checking out.

Towering over Masatepe's attractive central plaza, **Iglesia San Juan Bautista** is home to El Cristo Negro de La Santísima Trinidad, whose feast days mean a month of parties between mid-May and mid-June, and features nationally famous folkloric dances like La Nueva Milpa, Racimo de Sacuanjoche and Masatepetl. The sweeping adobe makes a fine colonial centerpiece, but it's the views from its gates, of fuming Volcán Masaya, that add depth to your prayers.

Sleeping & Eating

Centro Ecoturístico Flor de Pochote ECOLODGE **$$**
(8885-7576; www.flordepochote.com; dm/cabins US$10/35; P) A 4km downhill walk or US$2 *moto* ride from town, this beautiful ecolodge lies within the Reserva Natural Laguna de Apoyo, perched right on the crater rim. Cabins sleeping two to four are scattered around the 10-hectare finca and are made from natural materials. You can access the lodge's trails for US$1.

Meals (US$4) are served to guests in an upstairs dining room in the main house with even better views. Walking trails crisscross the property, where scores of bird species, including falcons, vultures and hummingbirds, can be seen.

Mondongo Veracruz NICARAGUAN **$**
(Iglesia, 3c N; dishes US$2-6) Masatepe is best known for delicious, steaming bowls of *mondongo* (tripe soup marinated with bitter oranges and fresh herbs, then simmered with garden vegetables for hours). This is the best place in town to sample the stew (and a traditional side of Flor de Cana Rum).

Leónor Barquero Tamugas/ Nacatamales NICARAGUAN **$**
(Parque central, ½c O; large/larger tamagus US$1/ 1.20) This spot specializes in a local favorite, the *tamagus*. It is like a *nacatamale* (banana-leaf-wrapped bundle of cornmeal, meat, vegetables and herbs), but made with sticky rice instead of cornmeal.

Dulcería Chepita NICARAGUAN **$**
(Antiguo Estación Ferrocarril, ½c O) A favorite sweets shop.

Getting There & Away

Buses leave the parque central half-hourly for Masaya (US$0.50) and Mercado Roberto Huembes in Managua (US$1.30, one hour), while minivans make the run to Jinotepe (US$0.50, 15 minutes) when full.

San Marcos

POP 18,900 / ELEV 600M

On the site of what's thought to be the oldest human settlement in Nicaragua, San Marcos has a pronounced and festive student presence thanks to bilingual **Ave Maria College** (www.avemaria.edu.ni), which also offers Spanish courses. San Marcos' *fiestas patronales* (April 24 to 25) are some of the most impressive in the country.

There's no statue for San Marcos' most famous native son: Anastasio Somoza García, the original dictator.

Sleeping & Eating

There are a few food kiosks on the main plaza.

Casa Blanca HOTEL **$$**
(2535-2717; parque central, 3c E; r with fan/aircon US$40/50;) Your best bet in the town proper, this hotel has big, cool rooms with institutional tile floors, flatscreen TV, firm beds and a leafy garden area.

La Mariposa Spanish School & Eco Hotel LODGE **$$$**
(8669-9455; www.mariposaspanishschool.com; El Cruce, 50m E, San Juan de la Concepción; r per week all inclusive US$250-450; @) Just out of San Marcos, on the road to Ticuantepe, this is one of the country's prettiest Spanish schools. Set out in the rolling hillside at the base of Volcán Masaya, this wonderful school-hotel minimizes impact through the use of solar electricity, grey-water recycling and regular reforestation campaigns. The setting is lush, and afternoon activities include hikes and horseback rides through the local area. During the high season, one-week minimum stays are mandatory, and include accommodation in comfy rooms with private bathroom (and awesome views), three meals a day, plus 20 hours of classes.

Cafetería Paladar NICARAGUAN $
(dishes US$2-4) This is a basic *comedor* at the corner of the park, with a good *fritanga* (grill) that sets up at dusk in front of Farmacia Inmaculada, also by the park.

Sabor Azteca MEXICAN $
(parque central; dishes US$3-4) A friendly little bar and Mexican restaurant right on the plaza.

★**Café Casona** NICARAGUAN $$
(Enitel, 1c N; dishes US$4-8; ⌚10am-midnight Tue-Sun, 4pm-midnight Mon) With great atmosphere, this is the best restaurant in town. It has huge burgers and sandwiches, and lots of other excellent coffee-shop grub, and an espresso machine that staff know how to use. There's live *trova* (folk) music on the weekend.

Information

BanCentro, on the main road just west of the park, has a 24-hour ATM (Visa/Plus only). If you're on the MasterCard system, go south two blocks for the BAC ATM.

Getting There & Away

San Marcos lies at the border of the Masaya and Carazo departments, and you'll probably have to changes buses or minivans here to get between them. Minibuses leave when full from the parque central to Managua (US$1, one hour), Jinotepe (US$0.30, 20 minutes), Masaya (US$0.60, 45 minutes) and other destinations all day long.

Carazo

This department, blessed with beautiful mountains reaching 870m (bring a sweater) and wide, sandy beaches (bring your swimsuit) – separated by only 35 steep kilometers – is central in Nicaraguan history and myth. It is not only where the first Nicaraguan coffee was sown but also where the nation's most famous burlesque, *El Güegüense,* was anonymously penned in the late 17th century. The comedy, which pits Nicaraguan ingenuity against Spanish power, always gets a laugh. It was written (and is still performed) in Náhuatl, Spanish and Mayangna.

Regional relations apparently predate the Spanish conquest, as Carazo's four major towns still celebrate an interesting ritual called the **Fiesta de Toro Guaco**. In it La Concepción brings out her patron saint, the Black Virgin of Montserrat, to meet Santiago, patron of Jinotepe, the old Nicarao capital; San Sebastián emerges from Diriamba, Jinotepe's ancient Chorotegan rival, and San Marcos appears from the university town of the same name. Four times throughout the year – the saints' feast days – the saints pay ceremonial visits to each other, an event livened up with striking costumes and masks displayed in dances, mock battles and plays that satirize their Spanish invaders. The biggest bash is on April 24 to 25, in San Marcos.

Diriamba

POP 35,200 / ELEV 576M

Already a bustling Chorotega settlement when the Spanish arrived, Diriamba has a pleasant central plaza and some good neighboring ecolodges. But on the whole, most will find little to do in town other than bop around checking out the European-style architecture that dates back to the coffee boom in the late 19th and early 20th centuries; the remains of the region's revolutionary roots as seen in the statue of Cacique Diriangén that welcomes you to town; and a small museum that leaves a lot to be desired.

Sights

Museo Ecológico Trópico Seco MUSEUM
(☎8422 2129; parque central, 4c S; admission US$2; ⌚8am-noon & 1-4pm Mon-Fri) This was Nicaragua's first natural-history museum (sort of), with informative, if low-budget, displays that focus primarily on the ecosystem of the Río Grande de Corazo and turtles of the Refugio de Vida Silvestre Río Escalante Chacocente. The admission fee includes a Spanish-language tour, which really brings the rainforest mural to life.

Sleeping & Eating

There are several simple *comedores* clustered close to the market.

Hospedaje Diriangén GUESTHOUSE $
(☎2534-2428; Shell station, 1c O; s/d US$6.50/10) On the road to Managua – rooms are a bit more cramped and slightly cleaner than other budget digs in town, but with older beds.

Abundance Farm LODGE $
(☎8217-8873; www.abundancefarm.com; dm all inclusive US$10) This organic farm about an hour out of Diriamba offers inexpensive lodging in simple dorm rooms. Ask about volunteering on the farm or in the local

school. There's a very cool waterfall here. Reservations are generally not accepted, so you are running a bit of a risk in coming all this way. To get here, catch the bus to El Aguacate, then walk 15 minutes to the farm or call to get picked up (US$10).

Jardín y Vivera Tortuga Verde LODGE **$$**
(☎2534-2948; www.ecolodgecarazo.com; Carretera a Managua, salida del pueblo; dm/s/d US$12/40/50;) While we aren't certain how happy the monkey tied up out front feels, this verdant spot on a coffee finca has around two acres of beautiful gardens, simple cabin-style rooms and a laid-back groovy feel, making it your top pick around Diriamba. The dorm room sleeps up to five people. The hotel's on the edge of town, on the way to Managua – look for the yellow columns on your right.

Hotel Mi Bohio HOTEL **$$**
(☎2534-3300; hotelmibohio@gmail.com; frente Museo Ecológico; s/d/tr/q with fan US$35/45/55/65, with air-con US$40/50/60/70;) Your best bet in the town proper, this new Colonial-style hotel is located just across from the museum, and has a cozy central garden. There is a spa, Jacuzzi and sauna on-site, and the rooms are as clean and cheery as you can get. In case you were wondering, Bohio is Cuban slang for a small house.

Café-Restaurante Iztatl NICARAGUAN **$$**
(Reloj, 1c N; dishes US$4-8) Go upscale here with a standard menu of grilled meat, fish and chicken. The *comida corriente* (set meal) is a bargain at US$1.50 and you can check your email at the adjacent internet cafe (US$0.70 per hour).

Getting There & Away

Jinotepe is the main transportation hub, and you can get a Jinotepe microbus (US$0.30, 15 minutes) any time at the market in front of the clock tower. A few buses and microbuses do leave from this station, including the following services. Mototaxis in town cost around US$0.25 per person.

La Boquita (microbus; US$0.80, 45 minutes, half-hourly, 6am to 6pm)

La Boquita/Casares (US$0.40, 1½ hours, hourly, 5am to 5pm)

Managua (US$1.25, 1¼ hours, every 20 minutes, 5am to 6pm)

Jinotepe

POP 31,300 / ELEV 600M

Historically separated from its eternal rival by the Río Grande de Carazo (which is, predictably, too polluted for swimming, but worth a wander if you're here), proudly Nicarao Jinotepe is the capital of Carazo and the closest to a city of any town this side of Masaya.

Sights & Activities

The Spanish colonial-style city is centered on the impressive church, **La Iglesia Parroquial de Santiago**, with excellent stained glass, and perpetually bustling **Parque Los Chocoyitos**.

Hertylandia AMUSEMENT PARK
(☎2532-3081; admission US$5;) Nicaragua's first and only theme park was built by perpetual optimist and popular former Managua mayor Herty Lewites. It's definitely a half-assed affair, with signs pointing to things that don't exist any more, and walkways that end abruptly in gaping precipices without guard rails. But the attached water park (included in admission) is worth the visit if you are passing through, and offers a big, clean pool and four vaguely thrilling waterslides. The park is a 1km, US$0.50 cab ride from Jinotepe.

Sleeping & Eating

The parque central is packed with food stands and *fritangas* all day long. A block away is an enormous Super Palí, which is the best grocery store in the region.

Casa Mateo HOTEL **$$**
(☎2532-3284; ministeriomateo516.org; BDF, 1½c O; s/d with fan US$15/40, with air-con US$60/70;) The friendliest hotel in town comes with a baffling array of options – with/without balcony or TV; 1st, 2nd or 3rd floor; air-con, fan etc – each varying the price. The average room is spacious and clean, balconies overlook a quiet pedestrian walkway and the downstairs restaurant serves up a decent meal.

Buen Provecho INTERNATIONAL **$**
(Plaza Güegüense; dishes US$3-6) Right around the corner from Casa Mateo, this popular eatery is the best in town. It serves up a cheap buffet lunch and plenty of international favorites from burgers to tacos. Across the

BUS SERVICES FROM JINOTEPE

DESTINATION	COST (US$)	DURATION (hr)	DEPARTURES	FREQUENCY
Granada	$0.80	1½	-	hourly
La Boquita (Carazo beaches; microbus)	$0.30	5min	-	every 10min
Managua (bus)	$1	1¼	5am-6pm	every 20min
Managua(microbus)	$1.15	1	6am-6pm	hourly
Masaya (via San Marcos, Masatepe & Catarina)	$0.40	1¼	5am to 5pm	every 30min
Rivas (via Santa Teresa & Nandaime)	$2	2	6am-3pm	hourly
Ticuantepe	$1	1	-	daily

small plaza from here is a good cafe and internet spot.

El Colisseo NICARAGUAN **$$**
(frente BDF; pizzas US$6-9; ⏲ Tue-Sun) One block north of the church, this is the local go-to spot for not-too-greasy pizza.

Information

BAC (frente parque central) Has a Visa/Plus ATM.
Intur (☎8412-0298; carazo@intur.gob.ni; frente Palí) Conveniently located inside a tiny arts-and-crafts market, it can recommend hotels and offer information for all of Carazo.

Getting There & Around

Jinotepe is a transportation hub, and the big, messy bus station is just north of the parque central, on the Interamericana (Pan-American Hwy).

Reserva Ecólogica La Maquina

About halfway between Diriamba and the beaches, take a break from dodging potholes at this excellent, respected private **reserve** (☎8887-9141; Carretera a La Boquita, Km 58; admission US$1.50, restaurant meals US$3-6, campsites per person US$3; ⏲ daylight hoursTue-Sun) that's a fine place for a swim.

There's an on-site **restaurant**, or you're welcome to have a picnic at the spectacular waterfalls just a few minutes from the road. Displays note that, according to an ancient legend, the water has Viagra-like properties.

There's also **camping** and three trails that explore the 154-hectare property, mainly primary dry tropical forest and a few bonus waterfalls and big trees, including huge strangler figs. Buses between the beaches and Diriamba pass every 40 minutes.

La Boquita

Make a right when you hit the T intersection on the coast to get to this scruffy beach village. Passing through the big, concrete archway means you've entered the **Centro Turistico La Boquita** (car US$1.25). The seafood in the seaside restaurants is excellent; they all serve basically the same thing. Fish and shrimp dishes are US$6 to US$15, or if you're feeling extravagant, go for the shrimp-stuffed lobster (US$18). There are a handful of basic hotels here, none especially worth recommending.

This is more of a swimming than a surfing beach, but if swells are big, waves can get a nice peak; some restaurants rent boards (US$10 per day).

Casares

If Boquita seems too synthetic, head south to Casares, a real fishing village, with a few simple seafood restaurants. South of here on an often impassable road is **Playa Huehuete**, where you'll find the best surf in the area. The 4WD-only road south from here to El Astillero is often overgrown and impassable. Check with locals before committing.

Buses stop at the *empalme* above the beach. For Hotel Casino, head straight downhill toward the water.

Sleeping

Hotel Casino HOTEL **$$**
(☎2532-8002; www.nicaraguabeachhotel.com; d with fan/air-con US$25/35; ❄) The only hotel actually in town is in the most modern building around. There are good sea views from the top front rooms, and the dining room even has a touch of elegance. This place closes outside of high season; call ahead to see if it's open.

Granada

POP 123,000 / ELEV 40M

Includes ➡

Best Places to Eat

- ➡ Tercer Ojo (p98)
- ➡ El Pizzaiol (p98)
- ➡ Encuentros (p99)

Best Places to Stay

- ➡ Hotel Con Corazón (p96)
- ➡ Hotel Casa del Consulado (p96)
- ➡ Hotel Los Patios (p96)

Why Go?

Granada drips with photogenic elegance, a picture postcard at every turn. It's no wonder many travelers use the city as a base, spending at least a day bopping along cobblestone roads from church to church in the city center, then venturing out into the countryside for trips to nearby attractions.

Just out of town half-day adventures take you to an evocative archipelago waterworld at Las Isletas and fun beaches at the Peninsula de Asese. Volcán Mombacho has walking trails, a canopy tour and a butterfly sanctuary, not to mention a few hot springs dotted around its foothills.

Culturally curious travelers may consider a trip to community-tourism operations in nearby villages like Nicaragua Libre, or out to Parque Nacional Archipiélago Zapatera, home to one of the most impressive collections of petroglyphs and statues in the country. Also worth your time is a trip to Reserva Silvestre Privada Domitila, a dry tropical forest home to birds, monkeys and butterflies.

When to Go

November 28 to December 7 is the celebration of La Inmaculada Concepción, or Purísimas as it is known in Nicaragua. It is celebrated throughout the country, but is especially vibrant in Granada, with parades, dances and, yes, plenty of fireworks.

During February the international poetry festival brings bards and wannabes from across Latin America to celebrate the word and wax poetic. Expect a city of magic surrealism with just a touch of pretension.

The December to May high season brings more people, higher prices and better weather. Book at least a week in advance during these times, especially during Christmas and Easter weeks, and during the mid-August festivals.

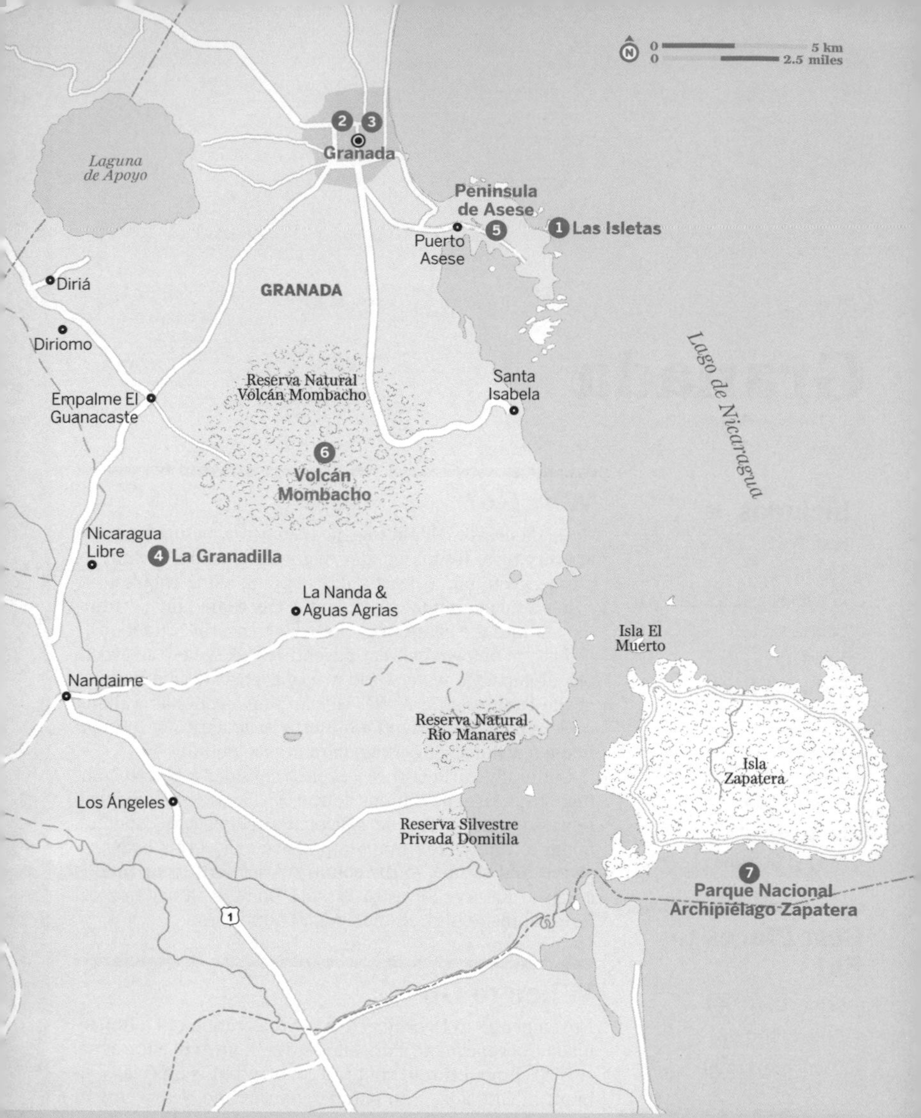

Granada Highlights

1. Cruise the narrow waterways of **Las Isletas** (p88), where luxury holiday mansions cast shadows on humble fishing shacks
2. Giddy-up on a horse-drawn **Granada city tour** (p92)
3. Feast on some of Nicaragua's most innovative cuisine in Granada's **restaurants** (p97)
4. Shift down a few gears and visit small villages offering community-based tourism, such as **La Granadilla** (p103)
5. Bike out along the **Peninsula de Asese** (p97) to secluded swimming beaches
6. Hike below the imposing summit of **Volcán Mombacho** (p102)
7. Dig the petroglyphs at **Parque Nacional Archipiélago Zapatera** (p104)

History

Nicknamed 'the Great Sultan,' in honor of its Moorish namesake across the Atlantic, Granada was founded in 1524 by Francisco Fernández de Córdoba, and is one of the oldest cities in the New World. It was constructed as a showcase city, the first chance that the Spanish had to prove they had more to offer than bizarre religions and advanced military technology. The city still retains an almost regal beauty, each thick-walled architectural masterpiece faithfully resurrected to original specifications after every trial and tribulation.

A trade center almost from its inception, Granada's position on the Lago de Nicaragua became even more important when the Spanish realized that the Río San Juan was navigable from the lake to the sea. This made Granada rich – and vulnerable. Between 1665 and 1670, pirates sacked the city three times.

Undaunted, Granada rebuilt and grew richer and more powerful, a conservative cornerstone of the Central American economy. After independence from Spain, the city challenged the colonial capital and longtime Liberal bastion León for leadership of the new nation.

Tensions erupted into full-blown civil war in the 1850s, when desperate León contracted the services of American mercenary William Walker and his band of 'filibusterers.' Walker defeated Granada, declared himself president and launched a conquest of Central America – and failed. Walker was forced into a retreat after a series of embarrassing defeats, and as he fell back to his old capital city, he set it afire and left in its ashes the infamous placard: 'Here was Granada.'

The city rebuilt – again. And while its power has waned, its importance as a tourist center and quick escape from bustling Managua keeps Granada the city vibrant.

GRANADA IN...

One Day

Hit the **Garden Café** for a light breakfast, then duck around the corner to see what's on at the **Fundación Casa de los Tres Mundos**. Once you've finished checking out the art, make your way back out to the Parque Central (central park) and jump into a waiting horse-drawn carriage for a two- to three-hour tour of the town's main churches and sights (or follow the walking tour route). From here it's down to the lake and out on a boat tour of **Las Isletas**. Grab a cab back into town and recharge the batteries with a coffee overlooking the plaza, and then get ready for dinner in the city center. From there, head down Granada's bustling bar strip, Calle La Calzada, for drinks and people-watching. Still going? Hit **El Club** for international dance tunes and a mixed crowd of locals and foreigners. If you're still up for it, make your way to **Inuit Bar**, everybody's favorite 24-hour lakeside bar, to watch the sunrise.

Three Days

On the first day, follow the one-day plan. On the second day, grab a healthy breakfast at **Euro Café**, then head out to **Doña Elba Cigars**, where a worker will happily take you through the entire cigar-making process. Head over to the **Mercado Municipal** to grab the ingredients for a picnic at **Fortaleza La Polvora**, or hire a bike and ride for an hour or two out along the Peninsula de Asese, its wild, largely untouched forest teeming with animal and bird life. Cabbing it back to town, take a turn around the shady Parque Central, stopping at the small snack stands. For dinner, take your pick from the excellent restaurants that line Calle La Calzada – you've got Mediterranean, Mexican, Spanish, Italian and probably the best steakhouse in the country to choose from.

Day three, it's time to get out of town. Book a tour (or DIY) out to **Volcán Mombacho**, where short hiking trails and a zipline canopy tour await, go further afield to the artisan villages around **Masaya** known as the **Pueblos Blancos** or have a day of swimming and lazing at nearby **Laguna de Apoyo**. Back in town, get some relief for those aching bones with an excellent massage at **Pure**.

PIRATES OF LAKE NICARAGUA!

The sacking of Central America's crown jewel, Granada, was one of the most daring exploits in pirate history, a career coup for dashing up-and-coming buccaneer Henry Morgan and his band of rum-soaked merry men.

It couldn't have been done in a full-sized sailing vessel – if you follow Morgan's path up the Río San Juan you'll see how those rapids would tear a regular ship apart. But this crafty band of quick thinkers appropriated six 12m wooden canoes (after their regular pirate ships were impounded by Spanish authorities) following an equally spectacular sacking of Villahermosa, Mexico. The atypical craft proved more than adequate for further pillaging along the Caribbean coast, which gave the 30-year-old Morgan an idea.

The crew battled the currents of the Río San Juan at night and hid their canoes during the day, then made their way across the great lake. The June 1665 attack caught complacent *granadinos* completely off guard: the pirates occupied the city for 16 hours – just like the Disney ride, but more violent – then stole all the ammunition, sank all the boats and sailed off to a warm welcome as heroes and legends in Port Royal, Jamaica... Eat your heart out Jack Sparrow.

Between 1665 and 1670, Granada was sacked three times, even as Morgan took more pirate canoes up the Río Coco, where he made powerful allies of the Miskitos. With their help, pirates sacked Ciudad Antigua and Estelí, where Morgan himself stayed for a while, and founded several of the surrounding towns.

Pirates actually founded more cities in Nicaragua than they ever sacked, including Pueblo Viejo and several surrounding towns in the Segovias; Bilwi, on the Caribbean coast; and, most famously, Bluefields, named for founder Abraham Blewfeldt, a Dutch pirate who worked the waters from Rhode Island to Panama.

Although the 1697 Treaty of Ryswick guaranteed that England, Spain, France and Holland would respect each other's property in the New World, the pirates continued to try for Granada. In 1769, 17-year-old Rafaela Herrera commanded Spanish forces at El Castillo against pirates trying to sack Granada yet again. She won, signalling the beginning of the end for the pirates of the Caribbean.

Sights

★Convento y Museo San Francisco CHURCH

(Map p90; admission US$2; 8:30am-5:30pm Mon-Fri, 9am-4pm Sat & Sun) The oldest church in Central America and the most striking building in Granada, **Iglesia San Francisco** boasts a robin's-egg-blue birthday-cake facade and houses one of the best museums in the region. Originally constructed in 1585, it was subsequently burned to the ground by pirates and later William Walker, rebuilt in 1868 and restored in 1989.

The museum is through the small door on the left, where guides (some of whom speak English) are available for tours; tips are appreciated. Museum highlights include top-notch Primitivist art, a scale model of the city and a group of papier-mâché indigenous people cooking, relaxing in hammocks and swinging on *comelazatoaztegams,* a sort of 360-degree seesaw.

The reason you're here, however, is the Zapatera statuary, two solemn regiments of black-basalt statues looming above large men and possessed of 10 times their gravity, carved between AD 800 and 1200, then left behind on the ritual island of Zapatera. Most were discovered in the late 1880s and gathered in Granada in the 1920s.

★Iglesia de La Merced CHURCH

(Map p90; Calle Real Xalteva; bell tower admission US$1) Arguably the most beautiful church in the city, this landmark is fronted by a plaza popular with young lovers. The caretaker usually takes people up to the **bell tower** at 11am, but you can ask to go up any time.

Originally completed in 1539, it was razed by pirates in 1655 and rebuilt with its current baroque facade between 1781 and 1783. Damaged by William Walker's forces in 1854, it was restored with the current elaborate interior in 1862. Today Catholics come here to see an important image of the Virgen de Fatima.

Casa de los Leones & Fundación Casa de los Tres Mundos CULTURAL BUILDING
(Map p90; Parque Central, 50m N; adult/child US$0.40/0.25; 8am-7pm Mon-Fri, to 6pm Sat & Sun) Founded in 1986 by Ernesto Cardenal, the Fundación Casa de los Tres Mundos moved to elegant 1720 Casa de los Leones in 1992. At the entrance, a board lists special events: poetry readings, classical ballet, folkloric dance and free movies. During regular business hours, your entrance fee buys you a look at a beautiful mansion and a few art displays.

Mi Museo MUSEUM
(Map p90; Calle Atravesada, Cine Karawala, ½c N; 8am-5pm) FREE This museum displays an incredible private collection of ceramics dating from at least 2000 BC to the present. Hundreds of beautifully crafted pieces were chosen with as much an eye for their artistic merit as their archaeological significance. They are displayed in the grand old adobe with the same aesthetic awareness. Guided tours are worth it.

Nicaragua Butterfly Reserve PARK
(www.backyardnature.net/nbr; admission US$7; 8am-4pm Mon-Sat) About 4km from Granada on the dirt road that leads from the cemetery to Laguna de Apoyo, this *mariposario* (butterfly farm) offers interesting tours. It's about a 45-minute walk; take Calle de las Comedias where it branches off to the right of the cemetery at the western edge of town.

Fortaleza La Polvora FORT
(Map p88; donations appreciated; 8am-5pm) Originally called the Fortaleza de Armas when it was constructed in 1748, this lavishly turreted Spanish fortress still has the best view in town, over ancient, water-stained church domes all the way to Lago de Nicaragua. You can also check out a roomful of paintings and a couple of artifacts. It was undergoing renovations at press time.

Antigüa Estación del Ferrocarril LANDMARK
(Map p88) Nine long blocks north of town along Calle Atravesada you'll find **Parque Sandino**, next to the Antigüa Estación del Ferrocarril (old train station), now a technical vocational school. It was built in 1882 and operational in 1886; the US Marines remodeled it in 1912. A few well-preserved railroad cars are on display. Out front is the **Parque de los Poetas**, dedicated to Nicaragua's literary giants.

Granada Cemetery CEMETERY
(Map p88; Nandame s/n) Used between 1876 and 1922, this beautiful cemetery has lots

STATUARIES OF NICARAGUA

Of all the archaeological sites currently under investigation (and the scores more waiting for funding to be adequately explored), four statuary sites stand out. The figurative pieces found here range from 1m to 4m tall and are probably between 1200 and 1400 years old. The best guess for construction methods is that they were carved using obsidian tools, sanded smooth, then possibly painted. While there are stylistic overlaps, work at each site displays its own distinguishing characteristics.

Isla de Ometepe

The squat, realistic figures here are thought to represent chiefs and other dignitaries. Only a few examples are on display, beside the church in Altagracia. It's thought that there are many more, buried over the years beneath the ashes of Volcán Concepción's eruptions.

Isla Zapatera Statuary

While the best examples from this site are on display at Granada's Convento y Museo San Francisco, there are various remaining pieces on the island – mostly at Pensacola, Zonzapote, Punta de las Figuras and Las Cañas. These figures show advanced workmanship and feature human-animal hybrids, probably referring to myths that humankind emerged from beneath the earth.

León Statuary

Including the Isla de Momotombito, this is the least known of the four. In 1854 there were a reported 50 statues in this collection – today, sadly, most of them have mysteriously disappeared.

Granada

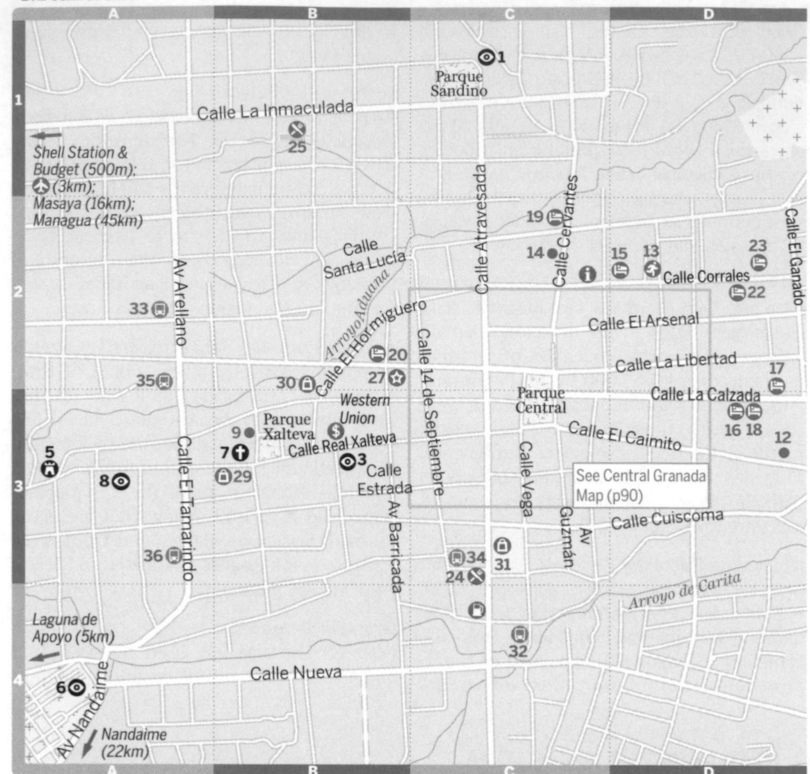

of picturesque mausoleums and tombs, including those of six Nicaraguan presidents. Most people come to see the 1880 neoclassical stone **Capilla de Animas** (Chapel of Spirits), a scale model of the French chapel of the same name. Close by is another scale model, this time of Notre Dame cathedral.

Centro Turístico BEACH
(Map p88) FREE This tourist center has restaurants, discos, sandy beaches, kids' play areas, picnic spots, and is the place to go to hire a launch or kayak for a Las Isletas excursion (hire boats at Cabinas Amarillas, 3km south from the park's entrance gate, or through Inuit Kayak). Use cabs here after dark.

Mercado Municipal MARKET
(Map p88; Calle Atravesada) Head to the overflowing and fun (if not particularly good for souvenir shopping) Mercado Municipal, a neoclassical building constructed in1892 that may be beautiful, though there's really no way of knowing until somebody gets up there and scrubs down the facade.

Las Isletas

An easy morning or afternoon trip from Granada takes you by boat to this miniature archipelago of 365 (OK, maybe fewer) tiny tropical islands. Along the way you'll spot rare birds, colorful flowers and some interesting indigenous fauna – keep your eye out for osprey, kingfishers, caimans and howler monkeys (along the mainland). Another highlight are the privately owned islands that would make tremendous evil lair, and lunch at the handful of island hotels and restaurants.

There's even a Spanish fortress. **Castillo San Pablo** was built in 1784 and has great views of Granada and Volcán Mombacho, plus a fine swimming hole nearby.

Most tours also pass **Isla de los Monos** (Monkey Island), where the spider and

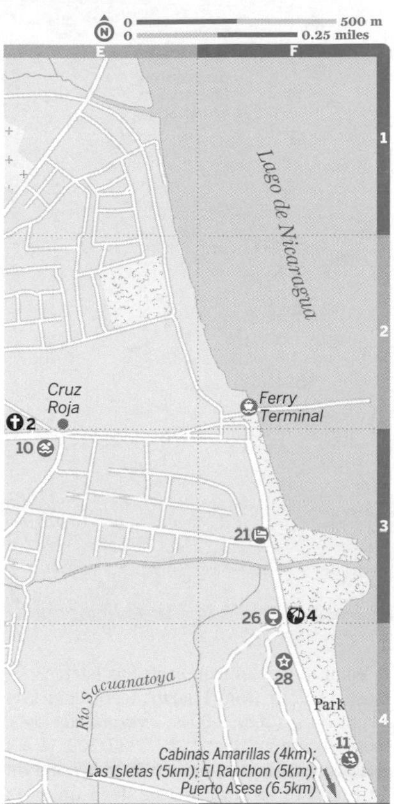

Granada

Sights

1 Antigüa Estación del Ferrocarril C1
2 Capilla del Sagrado Corazón E2
3 Casa Natal Sor María Romero Meneses B3
4 Centro Turístico F3
5 Fortaleza La Polvora A3
6 Granada Cemetery A4
7 Iglesia de Xalteva B3
8 La Capilla María Auxiliadora A3
Old Train Station .... (see 1)

Activities, Courses & Tours

9 Casa Xalteva B3
Corazón Tours .... (see 19)
10 Hotel Granada E3
11 Inuit Kayaks F4
12 Nicaragua Mia Spanish School D3
13 Pure D2
14 Xpress Spanish School C2

Sleeping

15 Casa San Francisco D2
16 Estancia Mar Dulce D3
17 Hospedaje La Calzada D2
18 Hospedaje Ruiz D3
19 Hotel Con Corazón C2
20 Hotel El Club B2
21 Hotel El Maltese F3
22 Hotel Limón D2
23 Hotel Los Patios D2

Eating

El Club .... (see 20)
24 Palí C3
25 Supermercado Colonia B1

Drinking & Nightlife

26 Bar César F3
Inuit Bar .... (see 11)

Entertainment

27 Café Nuit B2
El Club .... (see 20)
28 Heaven by the Lake F4

Shopping

29 Doña Elba Cigars B3
30 El Recodo B2
31 Mercado Municipal C3

Transport

32 Buses to Destinations South C4
33 Buses to Managua A2
34 Buses to Masaya C3
35 Tica Bus A2
36 Transnica A3

Capuchin monkey residents brought here by a veterinarian living on a nearby island are friendly but may run off with your picnic lunch.

Formed 10,000 years ago when very visible Volcán Mombacho exploded into its current ragged silhouette, these islands were once one of the poorest neighborhoods in Granada, and some are still home to impoverished families, who in general have no official property rights. They are being gradually supplanted by the beautiful homes of folks like the Pellas family (Flor de Caña owners), former president Chamorro and lots of expats in paradise. Want to join them? There are plenty of 'For Sale' signs, and your guide knows all the prices.

Most tour companies run trips to Las Isletas, or DIY with **Inuit Kayaks** (Map p88; ☎2552-6695; marielo_q75@hotmail.com; Centro Turístico, 1.5km S), which runs several guided kayak tours (from US$10 per hour). Touts

Central Granada

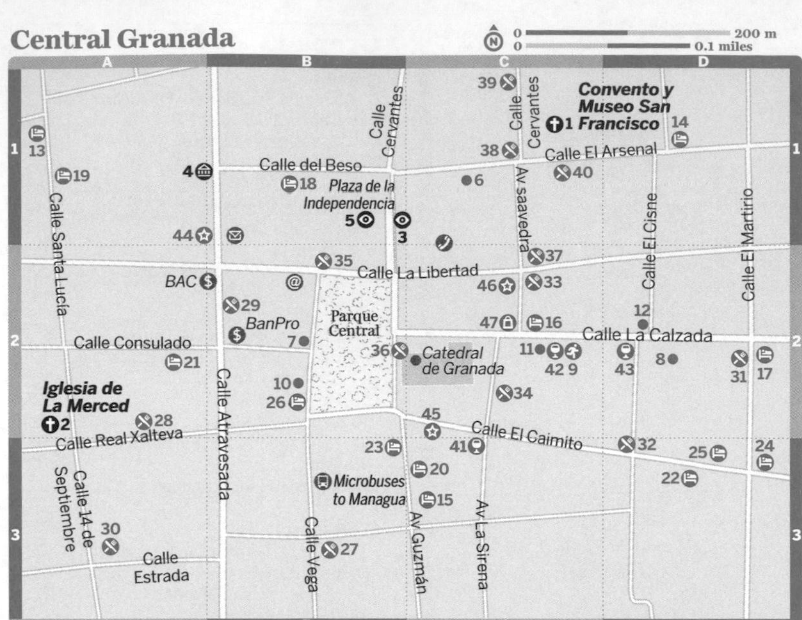

will offer to hook you up with a boat tour from pretty much the moment you enter the Centro Turístico. If you're on your own or in a small group, wait around until a larger group forms (unless you want to pay for the whole boat yourself – around US$20 for a one-hour tour) and the boat operators start offering discount seats just to fill their boat up. For the best bird-watching, you'll want to arrange your trip the day before to get out at dawn. Sunset is also quite nice, though the tour is quicker, with less exploration of further afield corners of the island group. You may be able to arrange a short sunset cruise to Castillo San Pedro for around US$5 per boat.

Taking a turnoff to the right just after Inuit Kayaks (look for the sign saying 'Marina Cocibolca') takes you out onto the other side of the Peninsula de Asese to **Puerto Asese**, where you can also hire boats to tour the *isletas* over this side. This is a less-popular option, so chances of forming an impromptu group are slimmer. The advantage of tours on this side is that there are fewer power lines and other boats, so it's a more tranquil experience, but it involves a fair bit of time in open water. Leaving from Cabinas Amarillas is good because you get straight in among the *isletas*.

Want to stay overnight in Las Isletas? Almost an hour from Puerto Asese, **Isla Los Españoles** (☎8759-0049; www.granada-isleta.com; d/house incl breakfast US$80/300; ❄🏊) is a beautiful home converted to a hotel on an island of its own. It can sleep up to 12 in three bedrooms. There's a small pool out front on your little castaway spot. Bring your own food to cook in the fully equipped kitchen or buy your meals out at US$15 a pop.

There are numerous restaurants in the island chain. Ask your boat operator to include a stop at one, where a large meal of locally caught fish will cost around US$7.50.

Activities

Aside from bopping through town and swimming at the Centro Turístico, most people end up using Granada as a base to take day trips to nearby attractions like Laguna de Apoyo, Volcán Mombacho and the Pueblos Blancos.

Pure DAY SPA

(Map p88; ☎8481-3264; www.purenica.com; Calle Corrales, Convento San Francisco, 1½c E) Sign up for yoga classes (US$5), daily, weekly or monthly gym memberships (US$5/13/29) or massages (US$24) at this Zenned-out day spa and gym.

Central Granada

Top Sights

1 Convento y Museo San Francisco........C1
2 Iglesia de La Merced........A2

Sights

3 Casa de los Leones & Fundación Casa de los Tres Mundos........B1
Iglesia San Francisco........(see 1)
4 Mi Museo........A1
5 Plaza de la Independencia........B1

Activities, Courses & Tours

6 Alliance Française........C1
7 APC Spanish School........B2
8 Calzada Spanish School........D2
9 Erick Tours........C2
10 Horse-drawn Carriage........B2
La Calzada Art Center........(see 47)
11 Leo Tours........C2
Seeing Hands Blind Massage........(see 35)
12 Tierra Tour........D2

Sleeping

13 Bearded Monkey........A1
14 Casa Capricho........D1
15 Casa del Agua........C3
16 Casa San Martín........C2
17 Hospedaje Cocibolca........D2
18 Hostal El Momento........B1
19 Hostal La Libertad........A1
20 Hostal San Angel........C3
21 Hotel Casa del Consulado........A2
22 Hotel Cocibolca........D3
23 Hotel Gran Francia........B3
24 Hotel La Pérgola........D3
25 Hotel Patio del Malinche........D3
26 Hotel Plaza Colón........B2

Eating

27 Café Blue........B3
28 Café de las Sonrisas........A2
Café Don Simon........(see 26)
29 Cafetín El Condor........B2
30 Cafetín El Volcán........A3
Comidas Tipicas y Más........(see 11)
31 Don Luca's........D2
32 El Camello........D3
33 El Pizzaiol........C2
34 El Zaguán........C2
35 Euro Café........B2
36 Fritangas........B2
37 Garden Café........C2
38 Kathy's Waffle House........C1
39 La Hacienda........C1
40 Tercer Ojo........C1

Drinking & Nightlife

41 Kelly's Bar........C3
42 Nectar........C2
43 O'Sheas........D2

Entertainment

44 Cine Karawala........A1
45 Encuentros........C2
46 Imagine........C2

Shopping

Lucho Libro Books........(see 46)
47 Olé........C2

Seeing Hands Blind Massage MASSAGE
(Map p90; Euro Café, Calle La Libertad; 9am-6pm Mon-Sat) Check inside Euro Café to learn more about this nonprofit project that offers massages (US$3 to US$10) by vision-impaired locals.

Hotel Granada SWIMMING
(Map p88; 2552-2974; www.hotelgranadanicaragua.com; Calle La Calzada, frente Iglesia de Guadalupe; pool admission US$7) While the hotel ain't worth the expense, it does offer day passes to the big, beautiful pool.

Courses

APC Spanish School LANGUAGE COURSE
(Map p90; 2552 4203; www.spanishgranada.com; frente Parque Central; 20hr with/without homestay US$185/100) Set in a gorgeous mansion right on Parque Central. Classes are generally held in the morning.

Casa Xalteva LANGUAGE COURSE
(Map p88; 2552-2436; www.casaxalteva.com; Calle Real Xalteva, Iglesia Xalteva, 25m N; 20hr without homestay US$135) Next to the church of the same name, Casa Xalteva also runs a program providing breakfast and education for street kids. If the school fills up, you may be placed in classes of up to three students (no discount).

Alliance Française LANGUAGE COURSE
(Map p90; www.alianzafrancesa.org.ni; Calle El Arsenal s/n) French and Spanish courses, plus franco-o-fantastic cultural events.

Calzada Spanish School LANGUAGE COURSE
(Map p90; 8402-7820; www.spanishonlinenicaragua.com; Galería Calzada, Calle La Calzada) Online or one-on-one tutoring for US$5.50 to US$7 per hour.

Nicaragua Mia Spanish School LANGUAGE COURSE
(Map p88; ☎2552 8193; www.nicaraguamiaspanish.com; Calle El Caimito, alcaldía, 3½c E; 20hr with/without homestay US$200/100) Run by a women's co-op, with a range of teaching methods and 11 years' experience.

Xpress Spanish School LANGUAGE COURSE
(Map p88; ☎2552-8577; www.nicaspanishschool.com; Calle Cervantes, Parque Central, 2½c N; 20hr with/without homestay US$210/120) Centrally located, with a young and dynamic staff.

La Calzada Art Center ART COURSE
(Map p90; ☎2552-6461; Calle La Calzada, Parque Central, 1c E) Out the back of handicrafts boutique Olé, this center offers classes in English and Spanish in the whole gamut of arts and crafts, including painting, mosaics, sketching, ceramics and glassblowing. Classes are available for adults and kids.

Tours

You can arrange trips all over the country from Granada, with recommended splurges including the Granada city tour (per person US$20 to US$25), Reserva Natural Volcán Mombacho (with/without canopy tour US$70/35), Masaya's Mercado Artesanías (US$30), and Volcán Masaya (US$25 to US$40, including Catarina).

Most operators also rent bikes (per hour US$1) and kayaks (per hour US$9), and can arrange Las Isletas tours.

Prices are lower for larger groups, so solo travelers should shop around to see who is already going or hook up with groups at your hostel.

Horse-drawn carriage TOUR
(Map p90; up to 5 people US$15) This classic Granada tour takes you from parque central on an hour-long whirl past churches, the cemetery, the *malecón* and more with your Spanish-speaking guide. They'll also wait while you take the other classic Granada trip, a boat ride through Las Isletas.

Corazón Tours TOUR
(Map p88; www.hotelconcorazon.com; Calle Cervantes, Parque Central, 3c N) Located inside the Hotel Con Corazón, this nonprofit tour operator offers well-organized trips including a two-hour bike tour (US$14), horse-drawn carriage tours (US$20), and a four-hour cooking class (US$25), along with trips to Mombacho (six hours, US$30 to US$40), Las Isletas (US$20 to US$30) and the Pueblos Blancos

City Walk
Colonial Explorer

START PARQUE CENTRAL
END FORTALEZA LA POLVERA
LENGTH 5KM; FOUR HOURS

Too tired to walk? Take a horse-drawn carriage, about the same price as a taxi, to any of these locations (at least between the city center and the lake), or ask for a city tour, around US$10 for a 35-minute tour for a maximum of five people.

Begin at the fine **1 Parque Central**, also called Parque Colón, pleasantly shaded by mango and malinche trees. The **2 Catedral de Granada**, on the eastern side of the plaza, was originally built in 1583 but has been destroyed countless times since. This most recent version was built in 1915.

On the park's southeastern corner, the beautifully restored **3 Hotel Gran Francia** (p96) was formerly the home of William Walker, and is now a fine place for a drink. Head north to **4 Plaza de la Independencia**, also known as the 'Plaza de los Leones.' The obelisk is dedicated to the heroes of the 1821 struggle for independence, while the Cruz de Siglo was erected in 1900 to mark the new century.

On the eastern side of this plaza is the **5 Casa de los Leones** (p87), named for the carved lions on the stone portal, the only part of the original structure that survived Walker's 1856 retreat. Rebuilt as a stately private home in 1920, it is currently home to the Fundación Casa de los Tres Mundos.

Head one block east on Calle El Arsenal to check out the awesome facade of **6 Convento y Museo San Francisco** (p86), best captured on film close to sunset. From here, head south on Calle Cervantes until you get to Calle La Calzada. This is where the carriage would be handy – it's a hot kilometer through featureless new neighborhoods to Lago de Nicaragua, passing the **7 Capilla del Sagrado Corazón**, originally built as a fort.

The ferry terminal is on your left, but make a right through the green Spanish fortress for the **8 Centro Turístico** (p88), a lazy lakeside park with restaurants, bars, playgrounds, beaches, kayaks and docks

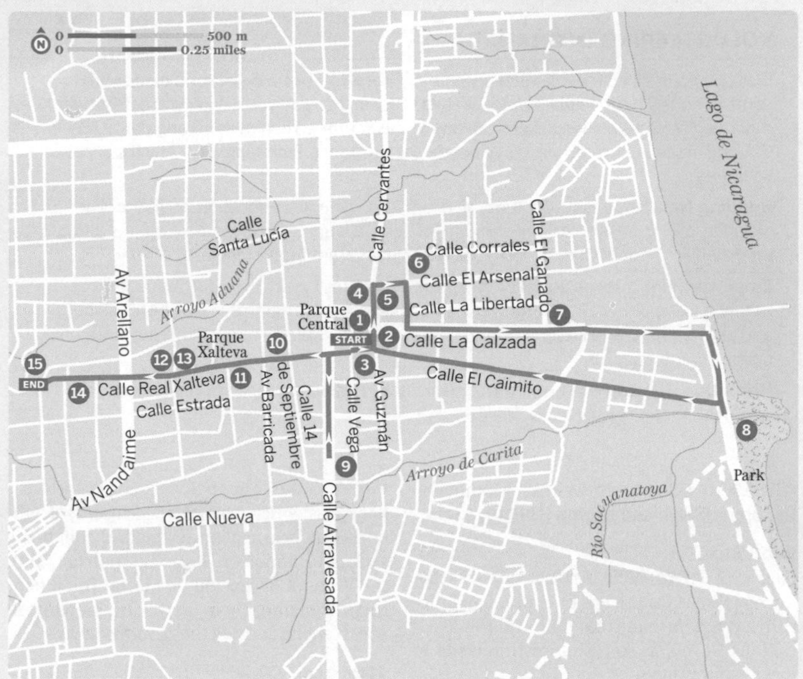

where you can catch boats to explore the Las Isletas volcanic lake archipelago.

Grab a cab – unless you're enjoying the heat – back to the Parque Central, where you can fortify yourself with a plate of *vigorón* (a pile of mashed yucca topped with a tangy cabbage salad and a big pork rind served up on a washed banana leaf) and a tall glass of *chicha* (a creamy, bright-pink corn-based drink). From here, you could head four blocks south on Calle Atravesada to the overflowing and fun (if not particularly souvenir-oriented) 9 **Mercado Municipal** (p88).

Or head west on Calle Real Xalteva, which once connected the Spanish town of Granada to its much older indigenous neighbor, Xalteva. Four blocks west of the Parque Central, you'll pass 10 **Iglesia de La Merced** (p86), considered the most beautiful of Granada's churches. Just south of the main road is the poorly signed 11 **Casa Natal Sor María Romero Meneses**, where a small collection of artifacts and original writings mark the birthplace of Central America's first official saint.

The old indigenous neighborhood, now wholly assimilated, is marked by 12 **Iglesia de Xalteva**, the attractive 19th-century church that houses La Virgen de la Asunción. Across the street is shady 13 **Parque Xalteva**, with rough stone columns and overgrown ambience. Continuing west, you'll pass another gorgeous little church, 14 **La Capilla María Auxiliadora**, worth a look for its beautiful pastel interior and a statue of a particularly stern-looking nun with a pair of tacked-on eyeglasses.

If you've come this far, it's only four more blocks to 15 **Fortaleza La Polvora** (p87), where you can climb to the top of the guard tower for the best view in town.

VOLUNTEERING IN GRANADA

Don't let yourself be fooled – just outside of Granada's beautiful historic center are some seriously poor neighborhoods. Go a little further and you'll find rural settlements that need services as desperately as any in the country. Thankfully, a range of NGOs is working in the area and trying to alleviate the problems. Following are a few that accept volunteers.

Building New Hope Runs a variety of programs, including education and school assistance, music classes for underprivileged kids, a lending library and an animal clinic. Intermediate Spanish a must, no minimum time commitment required.

Empowerment International Works mainly with rural youth providing education assistance to keep them in school. Also runs after-school programs in computer skills and photography, and baseball camps. Intermediate Spanish a must, three-month time commitment required.

Hotel Con Corazón The hotel with a heart is a good place to learn more about volunteer ops.

(US$30 to US$45), as well as Mombacho Canopy (US$35) and fishing (US$40) tours.

Leo Tours TOUR
(Map p90; ☎8422-7905; www.leotourscomunitarios.com; Parque Central, 1½c E) Enthusiastic locally owned business that offers all the usual options as well as some interesting visits to local communities.

Tierra Tour TOUR
(Map p90; ☎2552 8723; www.tierratour.com; Calle La Calzada, catedral, 2c E) A recommended company that offers all the usual, plus camping and day trips to Finca La Calera.

Erick Tours TOUR
(Map p90; ☎8974-5575; ericktour@hotmail.com; Calle La Calzada s/n) All the standard tours, plus airport transfers for two people for US$35.

Festivals & Events

Granada hosts a variety of interesting events and festivals throughout the year; check out the website **Casa de los Tres Mundos** (www.c3mundos.org) for what's on during your visit. There are bullfights here in August.

International Poetry Festival CULTURAL
(www.festivalpoesianicaragua.com; ⏲February) This festival brings together wordsmiths from all around the country and Latin America.

Fiestas de Agosto RELIGIOUS
(⏲third week of August) Granada celebrates the Assumption of Mary with fireworks, concerts in the park, bullfights (although it's illegal to kill the bull in Nicaragua), horse parades and major revelry by the lakefront.

Inmaculada Concepción RELIGIOUS
(Purísimas; ⏲November 28 to December 7) Neighborhoods bear elaborate floats through the streets in honor of Granada's patron saint, the Virgen Concepción de María. You'll hear them signaling their arrival by blowing in conch shells to drive the demons away.

Sleeping

The prices indicated in this section are for high season (December to May); at pricier hotels rates may drop around 15% outside of the peak. Make reservations and expect to pay more around Christmas, Semana Santa (Holy Week; Thursday, Friday and Saturday before Easter Sunday), the mid-August *fiestas* and Independence Day (September 15).

Bearded Monkey HOSTEL $
(Map p90; ☎2552-4028; bearded@yahoomail.com; Calle 14 de Septiembre, Parque Central, 2c O, ½c N; dm/d/tr without bathroom US$5/15/18; @📶) A backpackers' favorite and Granada institution, the Monkey is a rambling colonial monster, partially renovated in the grunge-chic style that backpackers will be familiar with. The bar is always hopping at this party-forward hostel. The dorm rooms have decent mattresses and are a little bigger than neighboring hostels, and of course you get hammocks, shared kitchen, book exchange and more.

Hostal El Momento HOSTEL $
(Map p90; ☎2552-7811; www.hostelgranadanicaragua.com; Calle del Beso; dm/s/d/tr/q US$8/14/38/34/40; @📶) Catering to the mature

backpacker set, this hip new offering has cool chill areas throughout, iPads in the lobby, a book exchange and a shared kitchen. The dorm room sleeps 11 and has great firm mattresses and lockers. Bring your earplugs. Private rooms are a good bet, some maintaining the historic character of the building.

Hostal La Libertad HOSTEL **$**
(Map p90; www.hostallalibertad.com.ni; Calle 14 de Septiembre; s/d US$15/20, dm/s/d without bathroom US$5/10/12; @ 📶) This hostel caters to a younger party set, with massive 16-bed dorms, a shared kitchen and a brightly painted courtyard framed by hammocks. The rooms are clean, but the mattresses can be a bit shoddy. There's a girls-only dorm.

Hospedaje Ruiz HOTEL **$**
(Map p88; ☎2552-2346; hospedajeycaferuiz@gmail.com; Calle La Calzada s/n; s/d US$18/22, d with air-con US$35; 📶) Walk through the friendly family's restaurant and kitchen area to find this excellent little budget choice. The freshly painted rooms are simple and spacious, with good, firm beds. Bathrooms are on the small side but spotless and recently renovated.

Hostal San Angel HOTEL **$**
(Map p90; ☎2552-6373; mariacampos118@hotmail.com; Av Guzmán s/n; s/d US$12/22; 📶) Half a block from parque central, this superfriendly colonial-style hotel is a good budget buy. The rooms are slightly cramped with hard beds and cold-water showers, but you get a shared kitchen, easy access to everything in town and a warm family atmosphere.

Hospedaje La Calzada GUESTHOUSE **$**
(Map p88; ☎9617-128; Calle La Calzada, Parque Central, 3½c E; s/d US$11/17, without bathroom US$7/13) A back-to-basics budget hotel – rooms are smallish and the beds have a definite sag to them – but the price is right (for some) and the location's a killer.

Hospedaje Cocibolca GUESTHOUSE **$**
(Map p90; ☎2552-7223; hospedaje_@hotmail.com; Calle La Calzada, Parque Central, 3c E; s/d with fan US$16/19, with air-con US$35/40; ❄ @ 📶) For the price you can probably do better, but this decent and centrally located budget spot does have some sweet 1980s headboards with inlaid mirrors. The common areas are dominated by giant water tanks, hardly an aesthetes dream.

Hotel El Club HOTEL **$$**
(Map p88; ☎2552-4245; www.elclub.com; Calle La Libertad; s/d/tr incl breakfast US$28/40/60; ❄ 📶 🏊) Decorated in an impeccable minimalist groove, with beds on platforms that rise from the floor, this is one of the coolest options in town. Fresh flowers daily, attention to lighting and a great courtyard for lounging are even better if you stay in the upstairs rooms. Party poopers take note: the patio turns into a dance club on weekends.

Casa del Agua HOTEL **$$**
(Map p90; ☎8872-4627; www.casadelaguagranada.com; Av Guzmán s/n; r US$50; @ 📶 🏊) Big rooms surround a small pool in a prize location just off Parque Central, making this a good pick for older travelers with an indie streak. Furnishings are all new and tastefully selected, and bathrooms are big, with serious showerheads. There's a fully stocked kitchen for guest use and free bike rentals.

Hotel Cocibolca HOTEL **$$**
(Map p90; ☎2552-8519; www.hotelcocibolca.net; Calle El Caimito, alcaldía, 2½c E; s/d/tr/q US$35/45/55/65; ❄ @ 🏊) A bit low on character, this central option has a gorgeous patio and lobby, but the rooms are less than

GRANADA FOR CHILDREN

Granada's a fairly kid-friendly city: wide footpaths, little traffic, a couple of pedestrian areas, a sizable Parque Central (central park) to chase pigeons in, and a good number of highchair-equipped restaurants – some high-end hotels even have portable cribs. Added to that, a couple of Granada's must-dos are well suited to junior travelers – it would be a world-weary kid indeed who didn't get a kick out of a ride in a horse-drawn carriage, or a tour of Las Isletas with their mixture of boat rides, swimming, monkeys and island lunches.

The old train station has a decent playground and an old steam engine out front. The Centro Turístico is a couple of kilometers of grassy lakefront with some surprisingly modern play equipment. The Volcán Masaya night tour takes you past glowing red lava before strapping on helmet and headlamp and descending into a bat cave – they'll love you forever.

spacious and heavily frangranced. There's a small dip pool to cool off.

Casa San Martín HOTEL **$$**
(Map p90; ☎2552-6185; www.hcasasanmartin.com; Calle La Calzada, Parque Central, 1c E; s/d incl breakfast US$41/46; ❄📶) In a reasonably quiet section of Granada's nightlife strip, the San Martín has an understated charm flowing through it. Rooms vary, but each is special, either for spaciousness, views, furnishings or atmosphere, making this a solid midrange bet.

Hotel La Pérgola HOTEL **$$**
(Map p90; ☎2552-4221; www.lapergola.com.ni; Calle El Caimito, alcaldía, 3c E; s/d incl breakfast US$49/50; P❄📶) Throw down 20 more bucks and you can get a much better hotel elsewhere, but for people on a pint-sized budget, this cozy hotel with its little center courtyard, spacious rooms and big, firm beds is a decent bet. Note: there's no hot water.

Estancia Mar Dulce HOTEL **$$**
(Map p88; ☎2552-3732; hotellagosyvolcanoes@hotmail.com; Calle La Calzada, Parque Central, 3½c E; s with/without air-con US$30/20, d with/without air-con US$45/40, all incl breakfast; P❄@📶🏊) Relax – the frantic decoration stops in the lobby and the slightly faded rooms have a pleasing simplicity and electric showers. There's a big pool out back!

Hotel El Maltese HOTEL **$$**
(Map p88; ☎2552-7641; www.nicatour.net; Centro Turístico entrance; s/d US$25/35; P❄) Right in front of the beach, this simple spot has heavy wooden ceiling beams and just enough *típico* (regional) decoration to make things homey. There's a restaurant onsite, and bikes and canoes for rent, but this area is seedy at night.

★**Hotel Con Corazón** HOTEL **$$$**
(Map p88; ☎2552-8852; www.hotelconcorazon.com; Calle Cervantes, Parque Central, 3c N; s/d/tr/q US$62/73/94/121; ❄@📶🏊) An elegant nonprofit hotel that directs earnings to the development of local educational programs. The rooms are simple and pleasing, spacious enough without being luxurious. The building itself blends modern and traditional styles to perfection, with much of the decoration coming from recycled materials made by local craftspeople. Ask about volunteer ops here.

It has salsa classes on Monday nights that are open to the public.

Hotel Casa del Consulado HISTORIC HOTEL **$$$**
(Map p90; ☎2552-2709; www.hconsulado.com; Calle Consulado, BanPro 30m O; r US$100; P❄@📶🏊) This elegant boutique hotel in an immaculately preserved *casona* (historic home) is the best high-end option in town. The large pool in the immaculate central garden is the focus of the cane-roofed patio areas. The tony-hued rooms have high ceilings, cane roofs and massive bathrooms with river-rock showers.

Hotel Los Patios BOUTIQUE HOTEL **$$$**
(Map p88; ☎2552-0641; www.lospatiosgranada.com; Calle Corrales 525; d/ste incl breakfast US$135/170; P❄📶🏊) New contemporary digs mix in interesting syncopation with the colonial layout of this five-room super boutique. Scandanavian design sensibilities, including low-slung beds, modern fixtures and space-age Zen gardens add to the modern allure.

Hotel Plaza Colón HISTORIC HOTEL **$$$**
(Map p90; ☎2552-8489; www.hotelplazacolon.com; Parque Central, costado O; d US$99-109, ste US$209; P❄📶🏊) The last word in plaza-side luxury, this chart-topper contends for the best high-end spot in town. Rooms are large and airy, with serious dark wood and wrought-iron trimmings, and come equipped with all the modern conveniences. If you're paying these prices, it's worth splashing out the extra US$20 to get a room with a deep, wide balcony overlooking the plaza.

Hotel Gran Francia HISTORIC HOTEL **$$$**
(Map p90; ☎2552-6000; www.lagranfrancia.com; Av Guzmán s/n; s/d US$80/100; P❄@📶🏊) The Gran Francia's elegance is slightly diminished by a touch of overdecoration. It's a gorgeous building, though, and the attention to detail is exquisite. Across the road, the restaurant, bar and lounge (set in William Walker's former home) are equally impressive, and well worth a wander for those interested to see just how lovingly an old building can be restored.

Casa Capricho GUESTHOUSE **$$$**
(Map p90; ☎2552-8422; www.casacapricho.com; Calle El Arsenal; s US$45, d US$55-60, q US$60-80, all incl breakfast; P❄@📶🏊) One of Granada's more eccentric offerings, the Casa Capricho (House of Whimsy in English, more or less) manages to be sprawling and cozy at the same time. Rooms are extremely comfortable, with hardwood and wrought-iron

furniture, and look out onto small balconies, themselves overlooking the dip pool and lush patio area.

Hotel Patio del Malinche HISTORIC HOTEL **$$$**
(Map p90; ☎2552-2235; www.patiodelmalinche.com; Calle El Caimito, alcaldía, 2½c E; s/d incl breakfast US$67/85; ❄📶🏊) The lovely smell of wood hits you on entering the lobby, and things only get better – the house has been lovingly restored and fitted out with authentic features like cane inlaid ceilings. The patio of the name is not one but two, both comfortably appointed with wicker furniture, the back one featuring a pool and bar area.

Rooms are moderately sized and stylish in a minimalist way.

Casa San Francisco HISTORIC HOTEL **$$$**
(Map p88; ☎2552-8235; www.casasanfrancisco.com; Calle Corrales, Convento San Francisco, ½c O; s US$65, d US$85-95; P❄@📶🏊) We love the ivy-covered walls, mosaic tiles, Turkish lamps, cute little balcony sitting areas and stylish decorations in this lovely colonial house turned nine-bedroom boutique hotel. Mosquito nets add a touch of romance to the rooms, but the beds are too bowed for this price point. The attached restaurant comes highly recommended, and specializes in Mexican cuisine.

Hotel Limón HOTEL **$$$**
(Map p88; ☎2552-2115; www.hotellimongranada.com; Calle Corrales, Convento San Francisco, 2c E; s/d incl breakfast US$50/60; ❄📶) Broad, clean and airy, this cheap boutique has modern rooms with hand-painted walls and a cozy garden area with a burbling fountain. It lacks a bit of the soul you get at other historic hotels, but self-caterers will be happy that you get use of the shared kitchen.

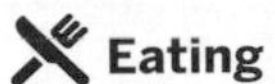

Eating

The classic Granada dining experience is relaxing over a light meal in a shady corner of the Parque Central. Four cute **kiosks** (vigorón US$2) anchoring the plaza serve *vigorón* (yucca with fried pork skin and slaw), best washed down with *chicha*. In many other restaurants, you should be aware that listed prices don't include either the 15% tax or the 10% 'voluntary' tip, which, combined, can boost your bill substantially.

There are two grocery stores: **Supermercado Colonia** (Map p88; Calle La Inmaculada, Parque Sandino, 4c O), out on the road to Managua, has slightly more 'gourmet' offerings and a good cheese selection; **Palí** (Map p88; Calle Atravesada, frente mercado), across from

WORTH A TRIP

BIKING THE PENINSULA DE ASESE

The Peninsula de Asese, jutting out into Lago de Nicaragua and surrounded by the famous *isletas* is a chunk of largely untouched wilderness – a world away, but only a few kilometers from downtown Granada.

It would make for a long walk but is perfect biking distance. There are a few bike-rental places in Granada. For a bit less pedaling, you can catch a cab to Puerto Asese and ride from there. There have been a few reported assaults here, so it's best to go in a large group or with a guided tour, and allow plenty of daylight to get back.

From downtown Granada, zip downhill toward the lake and take a right, entering the Centro Turístico. This is a good little ride in itself, along the waterfront under the trees. After a couple of kilometers, you'll pass Inuit Kayaks on your left. Shortly after, there's a turnoff to Puerto Asese on your right. Take that road, heading toward the lake. From here it's simple – follow the signs for Puerto Asese (turning left at the T intersection), then be on the lookout for a road veering to the left, with some hand-painted signs for Balneario El Rayo. Take that left – this road goes out along the peninsula, all the way to the end. The condition of the road deteriorates pretty quickly – be alert for monster-sized potholes but also keep an eye out for wildlife. Depending on the time of day, you may spot anything from a variety of birds to iguanas and maybe even a rattlesnake. The forest here is also full of orchids and some very exotic-looking mushrooms.

Where the road ends at Punto Ceiba look for the dirt track leading down to the beach: this is one of the cleanest swimming spots around, with views of Mombacho and – on a clear day – all the way to Isla de Ometepe. There's nothing out here, so bring everything you need – water, sunblock and a packed lunch. We recommend sandwiches from the Garden Café.

the Mercado Municipal, has better prices, a narrower selection and a tiny on-site bakery.

Granada has excellent street food, with bags of fruit salad (with fork US$0.30) and other goodies on sale between the Parque Central and the Mercado Municipal (p88) in the morning. Just before sunset, **fritangas** (sidewalk barbecues; Map p90; snacks US$1-3) set up in the Parque Central and Calle La Calzada, dishing up barbecue, *gallo pinto* (rice and beans) and all things fried onto washed banana leaves for you to enjoy.

Garden Café SANDWICHES **$**
(Map p90; Calle La Libertad, Parque Central, 1c E; sandwiches US$4-5; ⏲7am-9pm; ❄✍) Offering the best salads and sandwiches in town, this tranquil little spot also does excellent coffee and a range of breakfasts.

Don Luca's PIZZERIA **$**
(Map p90; Calle La Calzada s/n; pizzas US$2.50-4, mains US$5-10) While the pizza is on the bland side of scrumdiddlyumptious, this friendly outdoor eatery offers a great vantage for people-watching and a wide selection of Italian faves.

Café de las Sonrisas NICARAGUAN **$**
(Map p90; www.tioantonio.org; Calle Real Xalteva; dishes US$2.50-4; ⏲7am-5pm Mon-Fri, to 2pm Sat & Sun) Practice your international communication at this nonprofit cafe run by staff who are deaf. There's a picture-gram menu, sign charts and basic Nicaraguan fare that's hearty and wholesome. It also sells hammocks made by blind people.

Euro Café CAFE **$**
(Map p90; Calle La Libertad, Parque Central, 10m O; dishes US$3-4) One of the better cafes in town serves up a huge range of hot and iced coffees, juices, sandwiches, bagels, wraps and more in a plant-filled courtyard.

Café Don Simon SANDWICHES **$**
(Map p90; Parque Central, costado O; breakfast & sandwiches US$2.50-5) A surprisingly moderately priced cafe, considering its five-star location, with tables overlooking the plaza. There's a wide range of breakfasts (including bagels) and a good selection of hot and cold drinks.

Kathy's Waffle House BREAKFAST **$**
(Map p90; Calle El Arsenal, frente Convento San Francisco; dishes US$3-5; ⏲7am-2pm) Anybody doubting the rejuvenating qualities of *gallo pinto* and bacon and eggs should drop into this cute little cafe with a steaming hangover. Zing! Problem solved. There are all sorts of waffles, snacks and pancakes on offer, along with bottomless coffee and great views of the convent from the front balcony.

Cafetín El Volcán NICARAGUAN **$**
(Map p90; Calle 14 de Septiembre, Iglesia de La Merced, 1c S; quesillos US$0.50-2) You could come for the good-value set lunches (US$3), but pretty much everyone in town agrees that the real draw here are the *quesillos*, some of the tastiest around. Also a good range of traditional drinks including *tiste* (a toasted corn beverage; US$0.50), *grama* (wheatgrass) and carrot juice.

Café Blue SNACKS **$**
(Map p90; Calle Vega, Parque Central, 1c S; dishes US$2-4; Ⓟ) A refreshingly simple little cafe serving up good American and Nicaraguan breakfasts, some spicy huevos rancheros, pancakes and a range of sandwiches under a cane ceiling.

Cafetín El Condor BAKERY **$**
(Map p90; Calle Atravesada, frente Centro Comercial Granada; slices US$0.30) There's nothing fancy going on here – the chairs are ripped vinyl, the cracked formica tables are bolted to the floor, and the owner...well, she's not so cheery. But she sure knows how to bake a pie. Wash it down with a *cebada* (malted barley) or *coyolito* (palm fruit) drink.

★ **Tercer Ojo** FUSION **$$**
(Map p90; ☎2552 6451; Calle El Arsenal, frente Convento San Francisco; meals US$5-14; ⏲11am-11pm; 📶) Specializing in Asian cuisine (but taking you across at least three-quarters of the world with its expansive menu and wine list), the Third Eye is your go-to for tofu, Indian, sushi and Thai food.

El Pizzaiol ITALIAN **$$**
(Map p90; Calle La Libertad s/n; mains US$7-12.50; ⏲noon-10pm) You'll love the ambience in this lilting Italian trattoria. The food is pretty authentic – with a few regional variations – and the dessert list is to die for. The thin-crust pizza tops the menu, though you will do equally well with the savory pasta and meat dishes.

El Zaguán STEAKHOUSE **$$**
(Map p90; ☎2552-2522; Calle La Sirena s/n; meals US$7-13; ⏲noon-11pm; 👪) Scoring consistent props for the best steak in town, this large yet somehow cozy restaurant just behind the cathedral specializes in melt-in-your-mouth locally grown steaks, flame grilled right before your very eyes. Some solid chicken and fish dishes and a good wine list

round out the menu. Make reservations in the high season.

El Camello MIDDLE EASTERN **$$**
(Map p90; Calle El Caimito s/n; mains US$6-8) This affordable, friendly eatery takes you on a tour of the Middle East, featuring lamb stews, falafel and hummus... It offers a couple of pastas too.

Comidas Tipicas y Más NICARAGUAN **$$**
(Map p90; Calle La Calzada, Iglesia, 1c E; dishes US$4-6; ⏲Thu-Tue) An excellent place to embark on your typical Nicaraguan food adventure. Dishes here cost more than at your local *comedor* (basic eatery), but it's a sweet patio setting and the food is carefully prepared. The adventurous should go for the house combo (US$8), featuring sausage, fried cheese, pork rinds and *mondongo* (tripe stew).

There are more relaxed options, though – *indio viejo* (beef stew; US$2.50), *nacatamales* (banana-leaf-wrapped bundles of cornmeal, meat, vegetables and herbs; US$2) and quesadillas (US$2.50).

El Club INTERNATIONAL **$$**
(Map p88; Calle La Libertad, Parque Central, 3c O; mains US$4-8) This attractive restaurant-bar does excellent international cuisine, from Italian lasagna to Indonesian satay, in cool Euro styling.

La Hacienda STEAKHOUSE **$$**
(Map p90; Av Saavedra, frente Convento San Francisco; dishes US$6-9; ⏲breakfast, lunch & dinner) Good, if slightly pricey, imported steaks and Tex-Mex favorites. The undercover outside seats have a great view of the convent across the road.

El Ranchón NICARAGUAN **$$**
(Centro Turístico; fish US$7-15) There are probably a dozen restaurants, most of the 'fried fish and cold beer' variety, in the Centro Turístico, but the standout is right at the end. El Ranchón is a big, open-walled structure built on a point jutting out into the lake. Choose your fish from four sizes – small (US$7), medium (US$10), large (US$12) or gluttonous (US$15).

Drinking & Nightlife

Granada hops most nights, but Thursday to Saturday is when the real action takes place. Most people start the night off at one of the bars along Calle La Calzada (and some end it there too) before moving off to dance the night away.

O'Sheas IRISH PUB
(Map p90; Calle La Calzada s/n) One of the most popular pubs along the Calzada pedestrian strip, with friendly service and good pub grub.

Nectar LOUNGE
(Map p90; Calle La Calzada, Parque Central, 1½c E; dishes US$4-6) A seductive little lounge-bar with a good list of cocktails and some cozy sitting areas. In high season it often gets visiting DJs and live bands to liven the place up. Some delicious light meals and snacks make up the small, creative menu.

Kelly's Bar IRISH PUB
(Map p90; cnr Av La Serena & Calle El Caimito) Belfast meets Granada in this friendly pub that sports an excellent patio out back, sports on the TV and good times.

The Centro Turístico is home to several discos, including **Bar César** (Map p88; entrada Centro Turístico, 200m S; cover US$2) and **Heaven by the Lake** (Map p88; entrada Centro Turístico, 250m S; cover US$2-4), both close to the entrance. Another kilometer further in, **Inuit Bar** (Map p88; entrada Centro Turístico, 1km S; ⏲24hr Fri & Sat) is the late-night favorite and attracts a very mixed crowd with some sketchy characters thrown in. Watching the sun come up here can either be a very memorable or a very regrettable experience. Always use cabs between the Centro Turístico and central Granada at night.

Entertainment

Everyone's favorite hostel, the Bearded Monkey, screens indie and foreign films at 6pm and 8pm nightly.

Café Nuit DANCE
(Map p88; Calle La Libertad, Parque Central, 2½c O; Sat & Sun cover US$0.50; ⏲Tue-Sat) One of the most consistent and atmospheric live-music venues in town, set in a leafy courtyard. There's a small dance floor in front of the stage that gets packed when the band starts cooking.

Encuentros LOUNGE
(Map p90; Calle El Caimito s/n; meals US$7-12; ⏲5pm-2am) This studied lounge and restaurant has bee-bop-tastic atmosphere, made even groovier by the fedora-sporting waiters, acid jazz, and the modern menu that features contemporary cuisine like chicken in plum sauce and an assortment of tapas.

OFF THE GRID IN GRANADA

Tired of bumping into tour groups? Here are some places that might help you feel just that little bit special...

Antigüo Hospital (Av Arellano, Iglesia Xalteva 1c O, 1½c N) It is currently contemplating a renovation, so you aren't allowed to enter. But from the main street, photographers will love the crumbling colonial feel of this hospital in ruins.

Doña Elba Cigars (Calle Real Xalteva, Iglesia Xalteva, ½c O) We've all been nauseated by the overwhelming stench of a 'fine cigar,' but when was the last time you actually rolled one? Fascinating free tours at this cigar factory take you through the whole process and end with the opportunity to twist one up. Make sure you tip your worker-guide – their wages are nearly as pungent as the product.

La Piedra Bocona (cnr Calles La Libertad & 14 de Septiembre) Embedded into the cornerstone of an otherwise unremarkable building, the 'Big Mouth Stone' is as much local legend as it is landmark. Local belief is that it has the power to grant wishes. Give it a rub and see how you go.

El Club LOUNGE
(Map p88; www.elclub-nicaragua.com; Calle La Libertad, Parque Central, 3c O; cover US$2-5; ⏲Thu-Sat) A stylish and sophisticated venue hosting visiting DJs on a regular basis. This seems to be the preferred venue for the visiting A-list crowd from Managua – dress to impress. It has a US$8 open bar some nights.

Imagine LIVE MUSIC
(Map p90; Calle La Libertad s/n) Just like John Lennon would have liked it (before Yoko got into the picture), this chilled-out bar and well-overpriced restaurant features live music most of those days (based of course on an eight-day week).

Cine Karawala CINEMA
(Map p90; Calle Atravesada; tickets US$1.50) Granada's popular cinema shows mostly Western films on one of its two screens.

Shopping

Fundación Casa de los Tres Mundos BOOKS
(www.c3mundos.org; Casa de los Leones, Parque Central, 50m N) Sells a very good lefty selection of books, magazines and other souvenirs.

El Recodo CRAFT
(Map p88; www.casaelrecodo.com; Calle Consulado, Parque Central, 4c O; ⏲10am-5:30pm Mon-Sat) The oldest house in Granada has been faithfully restored and converted into a high-end souvenir shop. Far more interesting, though, is the exhibition space of artist Pablo Antonio Cuadra, also on the premises.

Doña Elba Cigars CRAFT
(Map p88; ☎2552-3217; Calle Real Xalteva, Iglesia Xalteva, ½c O) If you aren't getting up to Estelí this trip, stop by here for a cognac-cured taste of Nicaragua and a peek at the cigar-manufacturing process. You can even practice rolling a cigar.

Olé HANDICRAFTS
(Map p90; Calle La Calzada, Parque Central, 1c E; ⏲Wed-Mon) A clothing boutique and handicrafts store specializing in produce from local cooperatives. The emphasis is on rare and unique items not available elsewhere.

Bookstores

Lucho Libro Books BOOKS
(Map p90; Av Saavedra s/n) Swing in to this friendly store with a good selection of English-language books and maps.

Orientation

Granada is not actually on the Interamericana (Pan-American Hwy), but instead is linked to the Costa Rican border and Managua by two spur roads. The town's layout is a logical Spanish grid, centered on the cathedral and the Parque Central. Calle La Calzada runs eastward from the park about 1km to Lago de Nicaragua and the ferry terminal. South of the dock, a lakefront park extends toward the docks where day cruises depart for Las Isletas.

Calle Real Xalteva is the principal road heading west of the Parque Central, past three important churches to the old Spanish fortress. Calle Atravesada, one block west of the Parque Central, is the main north–south artery, connecting the Mercado Municipal (close to the Rivas- and

Masaya-bound buses) at the southern end of town with Parque Sandino, the old train station and the main highway to Managua, just north of the city.

Information

DANGERS & ANNOYANCES

There have been some reports of robberies on the road leading down to the lake and south into the Centro Turístico – take a cab after dark. Assaults have been reported on the bike to the Peninsula de Asese (take a tour to avoid problems).

EMERGENCY

Ambulance (Cruz Roja; ☎2552-2711) Red Cross.

Police (☎2552-2929)

INTERNET ACCESS

Those colonial adobes are packed with internet cafes, most charging about US$0.70 to US$1 a minute. Most hotels and some restaurants and cafes have wi-fi.

Alhambra Internet C@fe (Calle La Libertad, frente Hotel Colonial; per hour US$0.80) Very air-conditioned, with some of the fastest machines in town.

LAUNDRY

Your hotel will almost definitely offer laundry services, and may just send your clothes to one of the following:

Fernanda's Laundry Service (Galeria La Calzada, Calle La Calzada; per 1-2kg pounds US$3.75) Fast and friendly.

Laundry (Calle Consulado, Parque Central, 1½c O; per 450g US$0.75) Convenient for those staying out west.

MEDICAL SERVICES

Hospital Amistad Japonés (☎2552-2719; Calle La Inmaculada, Esso station, 2km O) The most frequently recommended private hospital is out of town, on the road to Managua.

MONEY

Several banks are within a block of Parque Central.

BAC (Calle La Libertad, Parque Central, 1c O)

BanPro (Calle Consulado, Parque Central, 1c O)

Western Union (Calle Real Xalteva) International money transfers.

TELEPHONE

Claro (Parque Central)

POST

Post Office (Calle Atravesada, BanCentro, ½c S) Opposite the Cine Karawala.

TOURIST INFORMATION

Check at hostels and tour operators for the latest tourist info.

Intur (www.visitanicaragua.com/ingles; Calle Corrales) The Granada branch of the national tourist office has up-to-date transportation schedules, a reasonable city map, and lots of information and flyers.

UCA (Union of Agricultural Cooperatives; www.ucatierrayagua.org) Organizes community-based rural tourism in the nearby townships of Nicaragua Libre, La Granadilla, Sonzapote and La Nanda. Check online, it didn't have a physical office as of press time.

USEFUL WEBSITES

Find It Granada (www.finditgranada.com) A somewhat complete guide to the city's business, restaurants and hotels.

Lonely Planet (www.lonelyplanet.com/nicaragua/granada-and-the-masaya-region/granada) For planning advice, author recommendations, traveler reviews and insider tips.

Getting There & Around

BICYCLE

While bicycling in town might require nerves of steel, there are several mellow bike rides from town, including Laguna de Apoyo, Peninsula de Asese, north of the Centro Turístico, and for strong bikers any of the Pueblos Blancos. Most tour operators and some hotels rent bikes for around US$1 per hour.

BOAT

Ferries leave the **ferry terminal** (Calle La Calzada, final; ⏰8am-1:30pm) at 2pm Monday and Thursday, stopping at Altagracia (Isla de Ometepe; lower/upper deck US$2/5, three hours), San Miguelito (lower/upper deck US$3/7.50, nine hours) and San Carlos (lower/upper deck US$4/9, 14 hours). First-class seats, on the upper deck, have padded chairs and access to the TV, which will be on all night. Stake out a sleeping spot early and don't forget your seasickness medication. If you're thinking about doing the Granada–Altagracia run one way only, it's best to leave from Granada – you travel in the day, get some views and arrive late afternoon. Leaving Altagracia for Granada, you travel at night and arrive in the early hours of the morning.

Puerto Asese about 2km southeast of town, has boats for the Las Isletas and Parque Nacional Archipiélago Zapatera.

BUS

Transnica (Map p88; www.transnica.com; Calle El Tamarindo, Iglesia Xalteva, 1c O, 1½c S) has buses to Costa Rica (US$29, eight hours) at 6am, 8am (express to San José) and 11am. **Tica Bus** (Map p88; www.ticabus.com; Av Arellano,

Antigüo Hospital, ½c S) leaves for San José (US$29 to US$40, eight hours) at 7am and 1pm. For other international services, you'll need to go to Rivas or Managua.

Granada doesn't have one central bus terminal. Buses to Managua (Map p88; US$.075, one hour, 4am to 7pm, every 20 minutes), arriving at Managua's Mercado Roberto Huembes, depart from the lot just north of the old hospital on the western edge of town. Microbuses to Managua (US$1, one hour, 5am to 7.30pm, every 15 minutes), arriving at UCA in Managua, leave from the convenient lot just south of the Parque Central on Calle Vega. Buses to Masaya (Map p88; US$0.50, 30 minutes, 5am to 6pm, every 20 minutes) leave from two blocks west of the Mercado Municipal, around the corner from Palí.

Buses to destinations south (Map p88) leave from a block south of the market, across from the Shell station.

Carazo (US$0.70, 50 minutes, 6am to 5:05pm, every 20 minutes) For San Marcos, Diriamba (with connections to the Carazo beaches) and Jinotepe.

Catarina and San Juan de Oriente (US$0.50, 30 minutes, 5am to 5:50pm, every 20 minutes) Also serves Niquinohomo.

Nandaime (Reserva Natural Volcán Mombacho; US$0.45, 20 minutes, 5am to 6pm, half-hourly)

Pueblos Blancos/Carazo (US$0.40 to US$0.70, 5:50am, 8:30am, 2:10pm and 5:10pm) For Diriomo, Diría, Catarina, Niquinohomo, Masatepe, San Marcos and Jinotepe.

Rivas (US$1.25, 1½ hours, 5:45am to 3:10pm, nearly hourly) Catch the 1:30pm bus to make the last boat to Isla de Ometepe.

Shuttle Bus

Considering that Managua is a one-hour, one-dollar hop in a minibus (and that León buses leave from the spot where you arrive) and that other destinations are nearly equally accessible, shuttle service is not so popular here. If you've got your heart set on shuttle travel, try to get a group together or you may find yourself paying for the entire trip (and in either case a taxi may work out way better). Erick Tours (p94) has airport transfers for US$35 for two people. The following are also recommended:

Bearded Monkey (bearded@yahoomail.com; Calle 14 de Septiembre, Parque Central, 2c O, ½c N) Has shuttles at 10:30am Monday, Wednesday and Friday to the Laguna de Apoyo (US$4/10 guests/nonguests at the Monkey Hut).

Casa San Francisco (www.casasanfrancisco.com; Calle Corrales, Convento San Francisco, ½c O) Shuttles leave Tuesday to Sunday at 8am to Laguna de Apoyo (US$10 return).

CAR & MOTORCYCLE

It's generally cheaper to rent cars in Managua, where your rental is probably parked right now – so be sure to allow a couple of hours for it to arrive. This region has good roads, and many attractions, including the Pueblos Blancos. With some forward planning, you can take cars to Isla de Ometepe.

Budget (www.budget.com.ni) At the Shell station.

Dollar (www.dollar.com.ni) At Hotel Plaza Colón.

Nicaragua's (relative) lack of traffic and decent roads make motorbiking an enjoyable way of getting around, particularly if you're planning a day trip to the Laguna de Apoyo or a tour of the Pueblos Blancos. Ask at tour operators around town.

TAXI

Taxis are plentiful. Always agree on a fare before getting into the taxi, which should be US$0.50 per person during the day and US$0.70 at night in the city. Always take a taxi between the beach bars and downtown.

It's inexpensive and convenient to take taxis to other destinations, including Masaya (US$12/17 market/volcano), Laguna de Apoyo (US$12), Rivas (US$24), San Juan del Sur (US$30) and Managua (US$24), keeping in mind that fares vary according to gas prices and your bargaining skills.

AROUND GRANADA

Reserva Natural Volcán Mombacho

It's been a few decades since this 1345m **volcano** (☎2552-5858; www.mombacho.org; park entrance US$15, mariposario adult US$1; ⏰8am-5pm Thu-Sun), the defining feature of the Granada skyline, has acted up, but it is still most certainly active and sends up the periodic puff of smoke, just to keep locals on their toes. It's easy to get to the crown of cloud forest, steamed up with fumaroles and other volcanic bubblings beneath the misty vines and orchids.

Reserva Natural Volcán Mombacho is managed by the Fundación Cocibolca, which since 1999 has been building trails and running an ecomobile (think refurbished military jeeps seating 25) on the 40% grade up to 1100m. Get there early to take the short trail through the **organic coffee farm**, or check out the **mariposario** (butterfly garden) and **orchid garden** (free with entrance) close to the parking lot.

Once you get to the top, where three species of monkey, 168 species of bird and over 100 types of orchids are just part of the jungle canopy this park is intent on preserving, you have a choice of three trails: **Sendero del Cráter**, a 1.5km jaunt to the fumaroles, plus great views of Granada and Las Isletas; **Sendero la Puma**, a steeper 4km trek around the lip of the crater, with even better views (guides, many of whom speak English, are available at the entrance and cost US$5 per group, six maximum, for Sendero del Cráter, which you can also do on a self-guided tour, and US$10 for Sendero la Puma, for which guides are mandatory); and **Sendero el Tigrillo**, a heart-pumping two-hour tromp up to two overlooks (guides are required for this one).

You can make reservations to sleep dorm-style in the biological station, with 10 beds and latrines outside, for US$30 per person. This seems steep but includes your entrance fee, transportation, a night tour, breakfast and dinner. Anyone can grab a simple meal at the cafeteria for US$5.

Although the park is only open Thursday to Sunday, groups can make arrangements to visit on Tuesday or Wednesday, when it's less crowded. Time your arrival to coincide with an ecomobile departure, at 8:30am, 10am, 1pm and 3pm. If you have a 4WD, you can drive for an extra US$15 – plus US$2 for every adult and US$1 for every child in the car (it's discouraged). Public transportation is inconvenient. Take any Nandaime bus from Granada and ask to be let off at the entrance. From here, you'll walk two steep kilometers (stay left where the road splits) to where the jeep picks you up.

Several operators in Granada arrange tours to Mombacho. There are two **Canopy Tours** on-site that take you across more than 1.5km of platforms and cables each for US$28.75 per person.

The beautifully maintained 45°C (113°F) **Aguas Termales La Calera** (☎2552-6330; osorio@invernic.com) hot springs replete with sulfur, calcium and other minerals quasi-scientifically proven to keep you radiant and healthy, are hidden away on Finca Calera, inside the reserve and right by the lake. They're easiest to visit on a day trip from Granada (about US$15 per person, including transport and entry). You can also call or write ahead, then arrange the boat trip yourself.

Nicaragua Libre

This small rural **community** (☎2552-0238; www.ucatierrayagua.org) at the base of Volcán Mombacho is part of the UCA community-tourism project. It offers guided trips through organic coffee farms, horseback rides to San Juan de Oriente and walks to Mombacho. A concerted effort has been made to rescue the art of traditional handicrafts here, and no doubt you'll be offered some of the results by the young artisans at some point during your visit. A basic, community-run **lodge** (☎8880-5848; r with/without 3 meals US$15/5) serves for accommodation and meals are available for around US$3. Arriving is easy – it's a 1km walk from where the bus drops you on the Granada–Nandaime road, or you can contact UCA's Granada office by phone for more details.

La Granadilla

A bit further down the road from Nicaragua Libre, La Granadilla (a member of the UCA project) is quite rustic and its electricity is iffy, but you're only 20 minutes from the entrance to Volcán Mombacho. You can arrange guided hikes up the mountain, visits to farms in the area, oxcart rides and bicycle tours. A basic, community-run **lodge** (r with/without 3 meals US$15/5) has accommodation; meals are around US$3.

La Nanda & Aguas Agrias

There's no lodging at this place (a member of the UCA scheme), but there is a restaurant (meals US$2 to US$4). The reason to come is for the three-hour hike to otherwise inaccessible **Reserva Natural Lagunetas de Mecatepe** (US$8 per group of five), which has five cute lagoons with plenty of river swims along the way. Transport here is tricky; contact UCA's Granada office for details.

Reserva Silvestre Privada Domitila

A great place to take a break from the Granada scene and get back to nature is this private **wildlife reserve** (☎8881-1786; www.domitila.org; r per person incl 3 meals US$90), which borders the Reserva Natural Volcán Mombacho.

It's pricey for what you get (no fans, composting toilets, but all the free fruit juice you can drink), but this protected patch of dry tropical forest is home to lots of howler monkeys, 165 species of bird and thousands of butterflies, which take over the place right at the end of rainy season (December or so). As dry season wears on, trees lose their leaves and you'll be able to see even more wildlife from the 20km of trails; bring sunscreen.

The reserve is 35km from Granada and not accessible via public transportation. Most Granada tour outfits run day trips (around US$30 per person, including lunch). Or drive here yourself (head east at Km 71½ on the Interamericana), then pay the US$5 entry fee and the mandatory guide fee (US$5 per hour).

Parque Nacional Archipiélago Zapatera

Isla Zapatera, a dormant volcano rising to 629m from the shallow waters of Lago de Nicaragua, is an ancient ceremonial island of the Chorotega and male counterpart to more buxom Isla de Ometepe, whose smoking cone can be seen after you take the three-hour hike to the top. The 45-sq-km island and surrounding archipelago of 13 islands are part of Parque Nacional Archipiélago Zapatera, designated to protect not only the remaining swaths of virgin tropical dry and wet forest but also the unparalleled collection of **petroglyphs** and **statues** left here between 500 and 1500 years ago.

A handful of archaeologists have worked these sites, including Ephraim Squier, who shipped several of the 15 statues he discovered here in 1849 to the US, where they are displayed at the Smithsonian Museum, and Swedish scientist Carl Bollivius, who discovered more statues, many of which are displayed at Granada's Convento y Museo San Francisco.

Perhaps the most impressive expanse of petroglyphs is carved into a 95m by 25m expanse of bedrock at the center of **Isla El Muerto**, where many statues have also been found. Several of the other islands also have petroglyphs and potential archaeological sites.

About 500 people live here quasi-legally, fishing and subsistence farming and hoping that no one puts pressure on Marena to do anything about it. Fortunately for them, the government isn't doing much of anything with these islands, which also means that infrastructure is basic and access is inconvenient. You can camp for US$3 per person on the island, but bring your own food and water; there's one restaurant, as well as a simple lodge, both run by the **community** (☎8899-2927; www.sonzapote.org). Community boats (one way US$5) leave Puerto Asese on Tuesday, Friday and Sunday, or you can hire a private boat from there for US$38/75 one way/return. Contact UCA in Granada for more information.

Otherwise, you'll need to sign up for a pricey day-long tour, offered by almost every operator in Granada.

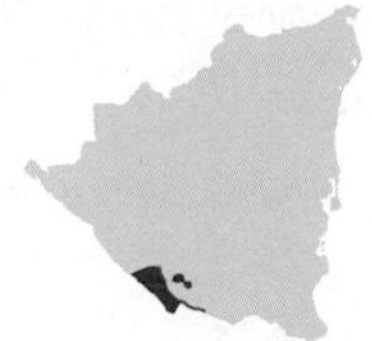

Southwestern Nicaragua

Includes ➡

Best Surfing

- Playa Hermosa (p136)
- Playa Maderas (p135)
- Bahía Majagual (p135)
- Playa Gigante (p125)

Best Places to Stay

- Playa Hermosa Beach Hotel (p136)
- La Posada Azul (p131)
- Morgan's Rock (p135)

Why Go?

Packed with attractions, the southwest offers up some of Nicaragua's hallmark vistas and adventures. Surfers have been hitting this coastline for years, drawn by perfect, uncrowded waves and chilled-out surfing encampments. Most start their trip through the region in San Juan del Sur, where you'll find better accommodations, high-octane parties and a solid selection of restaurants catering to international appetites. Beyond this there are spirited fishing villages, sea-turtle nesting grounds and tough-and-true inland towns.

No trip to the southwest would be complete without a few days on Isla de Ometepe. The island itself is shaped like an infinity symbol, with bookend volcanoes dominating either side of a secluded universe where you'll discover waterfalls, wildlife, lost coves and enchanted forests. There's kayaking, swimming, hiking and biking, and many travelers extend their stay as they dive into paradise lost in the quiet spots and friendly traveler encampments that define this island escape.

When to Go

November through May is the dry season. It means less verdant foliage, slightly longer days, plenty of adventure opportunities and remarkable sunsets over the curving Pacific Ocean.

April to December is surf season and you get big barrels and double-overhead exposure. Book ahead for surf camps during this time. Beginners may consider other times of the year to avoid the wave traffic.

September to October is the peak season for sea turtle arrivals at Refugio de Vida Silvestre La Flor. You could see over 3000 turtles arrive on the same day!

Southwestern Nicaragua Highlights

❶ Explore **Isla de Ometepe** (p112) – climb a volcano, kayak the wetlands or swim in a lagoon…or do all three

❷ Welcome the thousands of nesting turtles that arrive at **Refugio de Vida Silvestre La Flor** (p137) – a not-to-be-missed experience

❸ Ride giants at the world-class surfing (and sunbaking) spots north and south of **San Juan del Sur** (p127)

❹ Watch a sunset. There are few places better on earth to say goodbye to the day than one of San Juan del Sur's **beachside bars** (p133)

❺ Get to know the real pace of village life with community-based tourism in tiny **El Ostional** (p137)

❻ Charge the waves and sip the surfer's never-ending summer at **Playa Gigante** (p125)

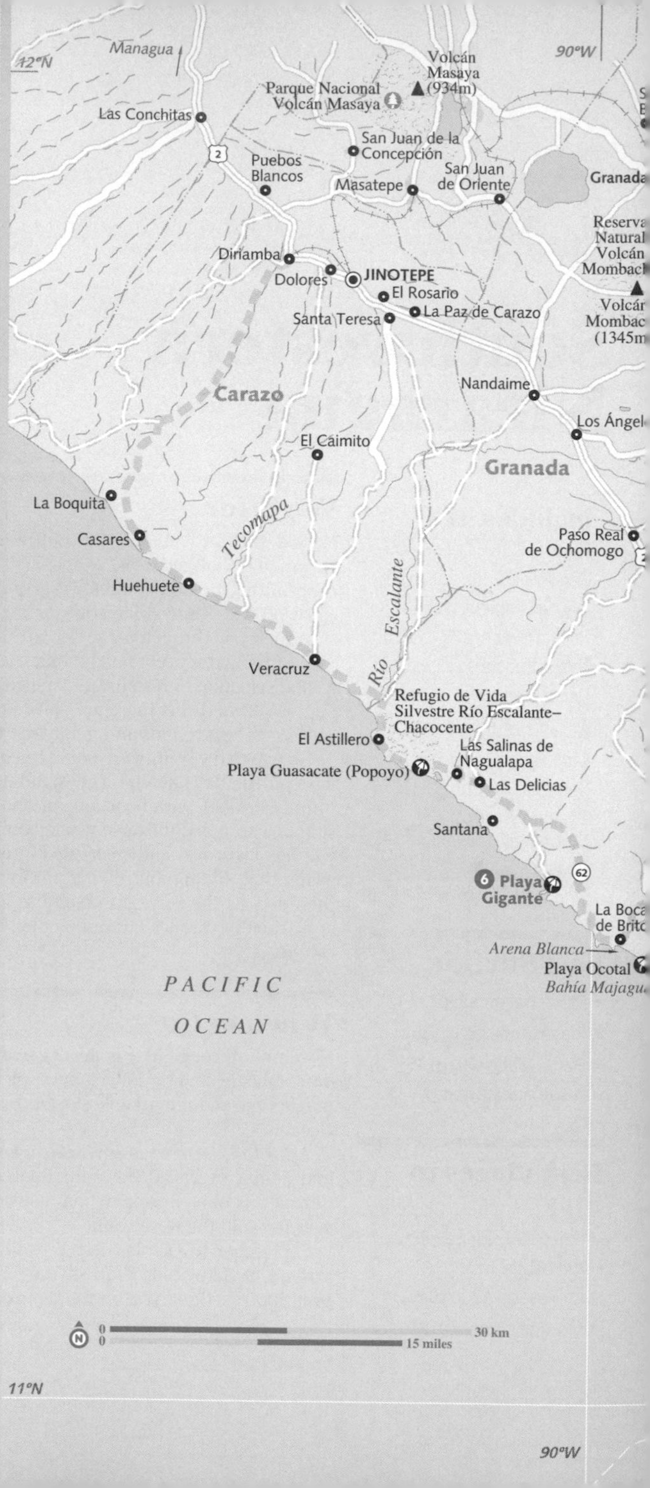

12°N
Managua
90°W
Volcán Masaya (934m)
Parque Nacional Volcán Masaya
Las Conchitas
2
San Juan de la Concepción
Puebos Blancos
Masatepe
San Juan de Oriente
Granada
Reserva Natural Volcán Mombacho
Diriamba
Dolores
JINOTEPE
El Rosario
Santa Teresa
La Paz de Carazo
Volcán Mombacho (1345m)
Carazo
Nandaime
Los Ángeles
El Caimito
Granada
La Boquita
Casares
Tecomapa
Paso Real de Ochomogo
Huehuete
Río Escalante
Veracruz
Refugio de Vida Silvestre Río Escalante–Chacocente
El Astillero
Las Salinas de Nagualapa
Playa Guasacate (Popoyo)
Las Delicias
Santana
62
❻ Playa Gigante
La Boca de Brito
Arena Blanca
Playa Ocotal
Bahía Majagual
PACIFIC OCEAN

11°N
90°W

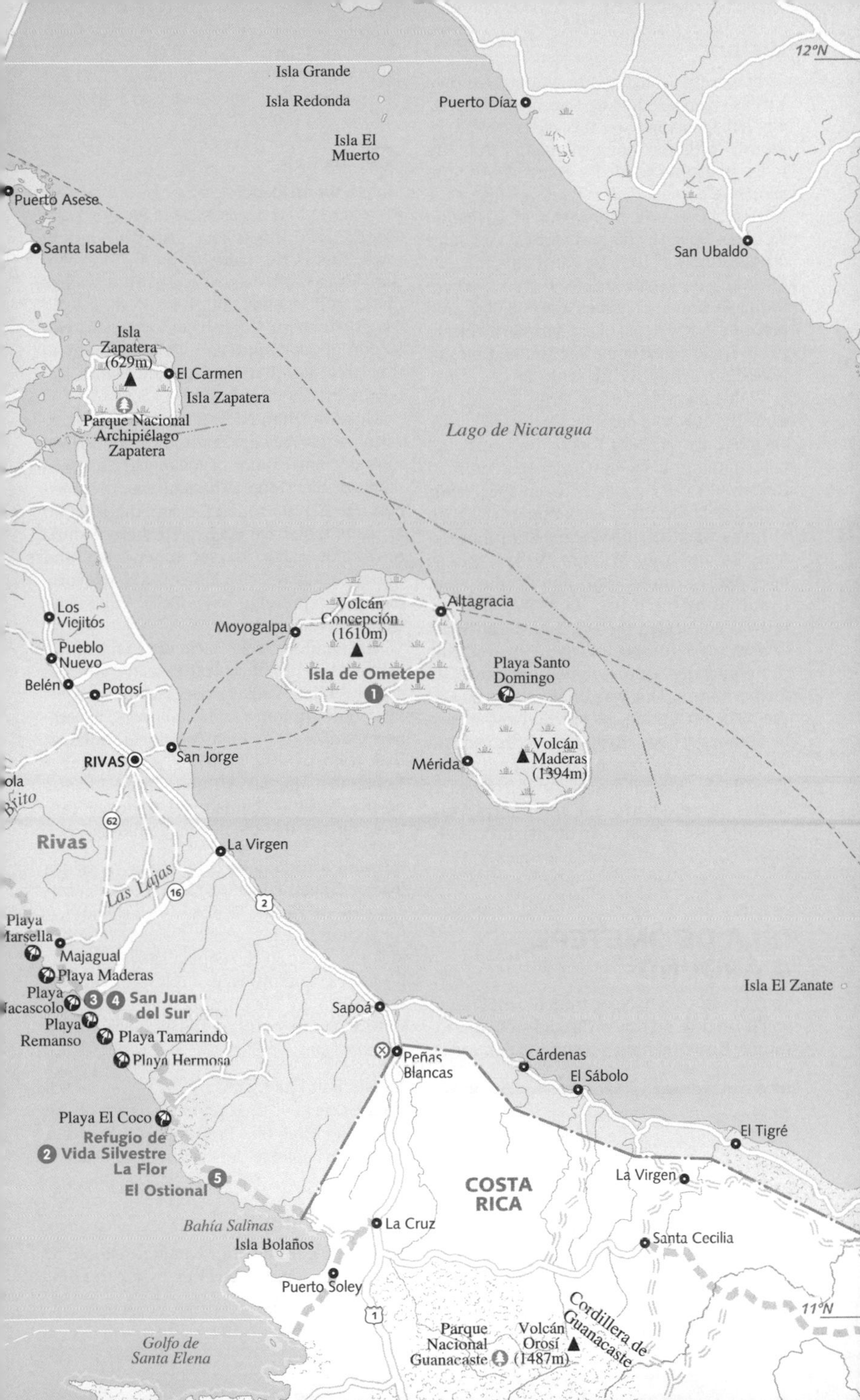
12°N
Isla Grande
Isla Redonda
Isla El Muerto
Puerto Díaz
Puerto Asese
Santa Isabela
San Ubaldo
Isla Zapatera (629m)
El Carmen
Isla Zapatera
Parque Nacional Archipiélago Zapatera
Lago de Nicaragua
Los Vicjitos
Pueblo Nuevo
Belén
Potosí
Moyogalpa
Volcán Concepción (1610m)
Altagracia
Isla de Ometepe
Playa Santo Domingo
Volcán Maderas (1394m)
Mérida
RIVAS
San Jorge
Brito
Rivas
62
La Virgen
Las Lajas
16
2
Playa Marsella
Majagual
Playa Maderas
Playa Nacascolo
San Juan del Sur
Playa Remanso
Playa Tamarindo
Playa Hermosa
Sapoá
Peñas Blancas
Cárdenas
El Sábolo
Isla El Zanate
Playa El Coco
Refugio de Vida Silvestre La Flor
El Ostional
El Tigré
COSTA RICA
La Virgen
Bahía Salinas
Isla Bolaños
La Cruz
Santa Cecilia
Puerto Soley
1
11°N
Cordillera de Guanacaste
Golfo de Santa Elena
Parque Nacional Guanacaste
Volcán Orosí (1487m)

History

Although first inhabited by the little-known Kiribisis peoples, it's the Chorotega who really left their mark on this region, most famously with the stone monoliths that are today on display beside the church in Altagracia. The Chorotega were soon overrun by the Nicarao, however, and it was Cacique Nicarao who met Spanish conquistador Gil González on the shores of Lago de Nicaragua in 1523. The Cruz de España marks the spot where the chief famously traded over 18,000 gold pesos for a few items of the Spaniard's clothing, a trade which some say set the tone for Nica–Euro commerce for centuries to come.

With time, this narrow strip of earth became the only land crossing for the gold rushers traveling from New York to California, and talk continues today of a 'dry canal' railroad that would carry goods between the Pacific and Lago de Nicaragua to continue on by boat.

Rivas was the site of some stunning defeats for filibuster William Walker, whose later plans to attack San Juan del Sur were thwarted by the British in 1858. Once the railway connected the USA's East and West Coasts, gold prospectors gave up on this route and the region slipped back into its former torpor. This was briefly disturbed in the 1979 revolution, as spirited resistance to Somoza troops turned the hills behind San Juan del Sur into bloody battlegrounds. The Isla de Ometepe was spared from such scenes and the horrors of the Contra War, possibly one reason that the island's nickname, 'the oasis of peace,' has stuck.

ISLA DE OMETEPE & AROUND

To get to Isla de Ometepe from the mainland, you'll need to first pass through rough-and-tumble Rivas, then get a boat from San Jorge.

Rivas

POP 50,600

Rivas has its fans – people say it's authentic and lively with some wonderful buildings downtown. Maybe. But with the beaches, lake and Ometepe beckoning, few travelers pause here long enough to find out.

Rivas' strategic position on the only sliver of land between the Pacific and Atlantic Oceans made it an important spot back in the colonial days. Now, with all the development on the southwestern beaches and Isla de Ometepe, it is once again an important trading and transport hub.

Sights

Museo de Antropología MUSEUM

(Mercado, 1c S, 1c E; admission US$1; 8:30am-noon & 2-5pm) If you have just two hours in town, this is the place to go. Inside you'll find some moth-eaten taxidermy, a wall of myths and legends and, best of all, a well-signed (in both English and Spanish) collection of pre-Columbian artifacts, many of them recently discovered by the Santa Isabela Archaeological Project.

This Canadian-Nicaraguan team is excavating what it believes to be Cacique Nicarao's ancient capital of Quauhcapolca, just north of San Jorge. The site was occupied between AD 1000 and 1250, and the 400,000 artifacts they have uncovered there include tools, blow guns, jewelry, funeral jars and cookware, as well as a fertility-goddess complex and representations of the Aztec deity Quetzalcoatl.

The building itself, Hacienda Ursula, is an 18th-century architectural treasure and the site of William Walker's decisive defeat. After his troops, limping home following an embarrassing rout by the Costa Rican military, took control of the hacienda, school teacher Emmanuel Mongalo y Rubio set the fortress on fire. Most of the men were shot or captured as they fled the burning building.

Iglesia Parroquial de San Pedro CHURCH

(Parque Central) This 1863 church on the eastern side of Parque Central is worth a look for its attractive classical facade. There's a kick-ass fresco in the cupola showing a battle at sea. Communism, Protestantism and secularism are the burning hulks, while the victorious ship entering the harbor is the SS Catholicism.

Iglesia San Francisco CHURCH

(Parque Central, 4c O) Four blocks west of the Parque Central this beautiful 1778 wooden church is notable for several well-carved saints.

Sleeping

Most people heading for Ometepe choose to stay in San Jorge to be close by for the first ferry.

Rivas

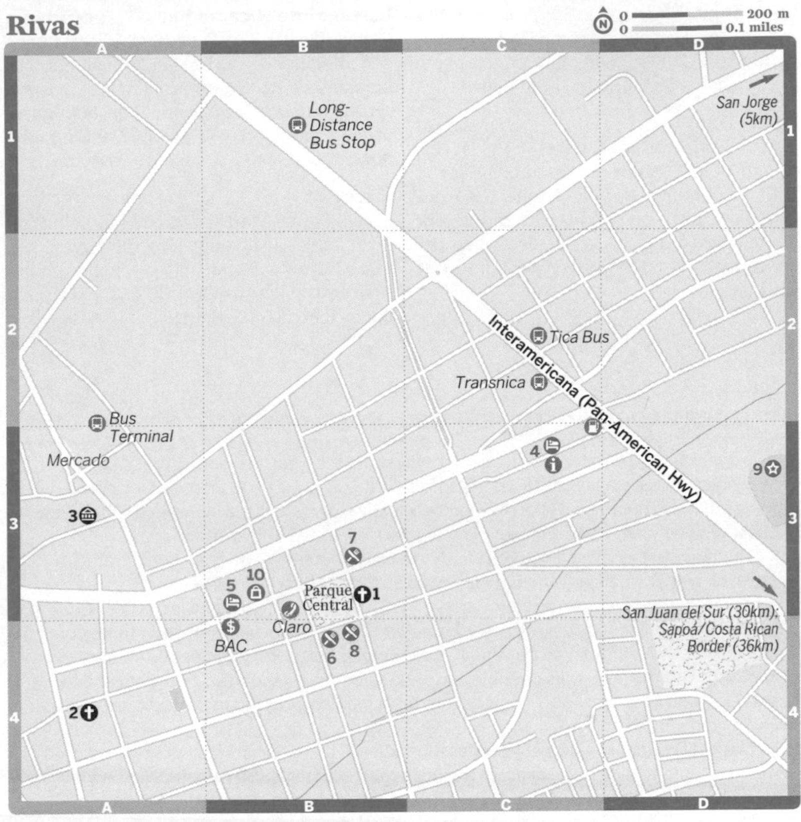

Hospedaje Lidia GUESTHOUSE $
(☎2563-3477; Uno, ½c O; s/d US$15/22, without bathroom US$10/18; 📶) Opposite Intur, this amiable, family-run operation offers great budget lodging, with well-scrubbed rooms, decent mattresses and a better-than-average room-to-bathroom ratio.

Hotel Nicarao Inn BUSINESS HOTEL $$$
(☎2563-3234; www.hotelnicaraoinn.com.ni; Parque Central, 1½c O; s/d US$58/70; P ❄ @ 📶) The best hotel in town has button-down business-style rooms, mustard-colored bedspreads and cable TV in a quasi-hacienda-style setting. The restaurant out front is a good deal, but the lack of a swimming pool is puzzling.

Eating

Rivas has plenty of cheap eats, with the very cheapest clinging to the outside of the chaotic *mercado* (market). The biggest grocery store is **Palí** (Parque Central, 1½c O).

Rivas

Sights
1 Iglesia Parroquial de San Pedro....B3
2 Iglesia San Francisco....A4
3 Museo de Antropología....A3

Sleeping
4 Hospedaje Lidia....C3
5 Hotel Nicarao Inn....B3

Eating
6 Chop Suey....B4
7 Pizza Hot....B3
Restaurante Nicarao Inn....(see 5)
8 Rosti-Pizza....B4

Entertainment
9 Baseball Stadium....D3

Shopping
10 Palí....B3

Chop Suey CHINESE $

(Parque Central, costado S; dishes US$3-6; [wifi]) Fairly standard Chinese food, right on the plaza. The seafood selection is the best in town.

Rosti-Pizza PARRILLA $$

(Parque Central, costado S; dishes US$5-10) This is one of the better restaurants in town, with good ambience. Grab a table out front and chow down on good steaks and decent burgers and watch as what seems like the entire town crosses the Parque Central at least once.

Restaurante Nicarao Inn NICARAGUAN $$

(Parque Central, 1½c O; dishesUS$5-10) Lunch and dinner are fairly standard affairs, but breakfasts here are some of the best in town, served out on the balcony. The bottomless coffee should get you going if nothing else does.

Pizza Hot PIZZERIA $$

(Parque Central, 10m N; pizzas US$4-6) Think you love cheese? Test yourself on the pizzas here, served up steaming hot on outside tables right by the Parque Central. There *is* a pizza under there, somewhere...

BORDER CROSSING: TO PEÑAS BLANCAS, COSTA RICA

If you've booked an international bus from Rivas or Managua, the border crossing between Sapoá, Nicaragua, and Peñas Blancas, Costa Rica, will be a snap, as they do everything but hold your hand. Make reservations in advance during the high season. It's often cheaper and more convenient, however, to take local buses and cross on your own.

The 1km-long, enclosed border is fairly simple, although the sudden (and strategic) crush of 'helpers' can be intimidating. Pedicabs (US$1) not only roll you through, they also protect you from the masses. Banks on either side exchange local currency for US dollars, while money changers (called *coyotes* for a reason) exchange all three currencies freely but may try to rip you off; look for folks wearing identification badges. Exchange as little money as possible here, know about how much you're supposed to get back, and note that 1000-córdoba bills from the Sandinista administration are out of circulation and worthless.

On the Nicaraguan side, get your passport stamped at a window in the large, poorly marked cement building just east of the main road. It costs US$5 to enter Nicaragua, US$2 to exit, payable in córdobas. The Municipality of Sapoá charges US$1 extra to enter or exit the border zone. There are three duty-free shops on the Nicaraguan side, but no restaurant or bathroom.

Leaving or entering Costa Rica is free. Immigration has a good restaurant, clean restrooms and a bank with an ATM. Everyone entering Costa Rica technically needs a ticket leaving the country, which is rarely asked for. If it's your unlucky day, Dendu Transport and Transnica, both located right outside, sell US$10 tickets from San José to Managua.

Sapoá has no real lodging, other than a few dodgy, unsigned guesthouses, and Peñas Blancas has none at all, so don't plan on spending the night. Although the border is open 24 hours, buses only run between 6am and 6pm, after which taxis triple their fares.

Buses from Sapoá run at least hourly to Rivas (US$10, one hour) between 6am and 5:30pm, where you can make connections throughout Nicaragua. *Taxistas* (taxi drivers) may tell you Nicaraguan buses aren't running, or are unsafe, but that is incorrect.

Transnica runs buses from Peñas Blancas to San José (US$10, five hours) at 5:15am, 7:30am, 9am (direct), 10:45am, noon, 1:30pm, 3:30pm and 6pm. Pulmitan de Liberia goes to Liberia (US$2, two hours) at 6:30am, 8:30am, 9:30am, 12:30pm, 2:30pm and 5:30pm.

It's always faster and easier to take a taxi, which may be prohibitively expensive on the Costa Rican side (US$50 to Liberia), but much more reasonable from Sapoá to Rivas (US$12), San Jorge (US$15), San Juan del Sur (US$20) and Granada (US$50). Find other tourists to share your taxi while you are still inside the border zone, and bargain hard.

Note: there are plans to pave the Pacific Coast road from El Ostional south to Costa Rica, opening a new international border crossing here, but it's still several years out.

★ Entertainment

Baseball Stadium STADIUM

This stadium, just south of town on the Interamericana (Pan-American Hwy), hosts one of the most competitive leagues in Nicaragua.

ℹ Information

Rivas has the biggest *mercado*, best groceries and widest choice of banks and businesses in southwestern Nicaragua. Stock up!

BAC (frente Hotel Cacique Nicarao)

Claro (Parque Central, costado O)

Intur (rivas@intur.gob.ni; Texaco station, ½c O; ⏲Mon-Fri) There's a decent selection of flyers on Rivas, San Juan del Sur and Ometepe.

ℹ Getting There & Around

BUS

Rivas is the regional transport hub. Both **Transnica** (www.transnica.com; Uno, ½c N) and **Tica Bus** (www.ticabus.com; Uno, 1½c N) have offices in town and daily buses to San José, Costa Rica (US$29 to US$40). For services north, you'll need to route through Managua.

The bus terminal is adjacent to the *mercado*, about 10 blocks west of the Interamericana. You can catch more luxurious long-distance buses (most headed to Managua, not Granada) at the long-distance bus stop just north of the exit to San Jorge. Bus services include the following:

Granada (US$1.25, 1½ hours, hourly) Alternatively, take any Managua-bound bus and change at Nandaime.

Managua (US$2, 2½ hours, 4:30am to 6pm, every 25 minutes)

Refugio de Vida Silvestre La Flor & El Ostional (US$1.80, two to three hours, 5am, 7:30am and noon)

Salinas and Tola beaches (US$1.70, two hours, 5:30am, 6am and 8:30am) Returns at noon and 2pm.

San Jorge (US$0.30, 20 minutes, half-hourly)

San Juan del Sur (US$0.75, 45 minutes, 6am to 6pm, half-hourly) With continuing service to La Flor and El Ostional at 11:30am, 3pm and possibly 4pm.

Sapoá/Peñas Blancas, Costa Rica (US$0.75, 45 minutes, 5am to 6pm, half-hourly)

Southern beaches (US$2.50, two to three hours, 11am, 3pm, 4:30pm) Service to San Juan del Sur, Playa el Coco, La Flor and El Ostional.

TAXI

Colectivos (shared taxis or minibuses) run regularly to San Jorge (US$0.50) and San Juan del Sur (US$1.75), but you'll have to charter your own for the Costa Rican border (US$10), Granada (US$35) or the Tola beaches. Pedicabs are usually less expensive (and more fun) for shorter trips; the usual cost is US$0.60 anywhere in town.

San Jorge

POP 8600

Just 15 minutes from the bustle of Rivas are the beaches of San Jorge, lined with inexpensive seafood restaurants and rollicking bars, not to mention the country's best views of Isla de Ometepe. It gets packed during Semana Santa (Holy Week; Thursday, Friday, Saturday before Easter Sunday) and on sunny summer weekends with revelers from all over the region.

International tourists, however, tend to just roll through en route to the island, stopping at the ferry terminal just long enough to wonder if those delicious breezes might be worth enjoying a moment more.

◉ Sights & Activities

The breezy, volcano-gray beach, **Playa San Jorge**, stretches 20m into the water during high season, when it boasts a busy boardwalk feel. During rainy season (June to November), lake levels rise and reduce the beach to a slender strand, and many of the restaurants keep limited hours.

Cruz de España MONUMENT

Ask your taxi driver to point out this monument, suspended from a gleaming half-arch above the traffic, which marks the spot where conquistador Gil González Dávila and Cacique Nicarao first met on October 12, 1523. Brightly colored statues of both men flank the monument.

Nuestra Señor de Rescate CHURCH

The most striking church in town, repainted a brilliant purple with a mix that uses *huevos de amor* (fertilized chicken eggs) donated by parishioners. It's a national historic landmark, and the destination of an annual caravan of some 150 *carretas* (wooden oxcarts) from Masaya each year. They arrive April 23, the anniversary of San Jorge's miraculous appearance on the coast of Lago de Nicaragua. The ensuing **fiestas patronales** include parades, rodeos and several ceremonial dances, including a much-celebrated dance between the city's two images of San Jorge.

Tours

Ometepe Tours GUIDED TOUR
(2563-4779) Part of Bar El Navigante, right at the ferry terminal, this guide service offers island tours, hotel reservations and more.

Travel Tours Nicaragua GUIDED TOUR
(Island Tours; 8607-3010; travel.tour.nicaragua@gmail.com; Ferry Terminal) Confused about how to get to Ometepe (or beyond)? Try this friendly operator on the ferry dock.

Sleeping

You can camp at the beach, close to the restaurants and bars, for free, although there's not much beach during rainy season. Restaurants offer showers for a small fee. The best (and most logical) place to stay is down by the ferry terminal.

Hotel Dalinky HOTEL $
(8912-1205; www.hoteldalinky.com; ferry terminal, 100m E; dm/s/d without air-con US$10/20/25, r with air-con US$50; P) Gleaming tiled rooms a stone's throw from the ferry entrance make this a top pick. Upstairs there's a balcony with island views, downstairs there's a lush little breakfast area out back.

Hotel Hamacas HOTEL $$
(2563-0048; www.hotelhamacas.com; ferry terminal, 100m E; s/d with fan US$25/30, with air-con US$35/40; P) Cute little brick rooms painted in cheerful colors make this hacienda-style hotel the most atmospheric offering in town. Rooms surround a leafy courtyard area, and the requisite hammocks are strung up around the porch areas.

Eating

The restaurants lining the beach are convenient if you're waiting on your ferry. *Sopa de mojarra* (fish soup made with coconut milk) is the local specialty.

Fritanga NICARAGUAN $
(Parque Central; dishes US$2-3; evenings) In town, there's a great *fritanga* (grill) that sets up in the kiosk in the Parque Central, satisfying your barbecued-chicken and people-watching cravings at the same time.

Bar-Restaurant Ivania NICARAGUAN $
(Parque Central, 2c O; dishes US$2-4; 6am-11pm) In the center of town, Bar-Restaurant Ivania does good fish soup and *típico* (Nicaraguan fare), and has a rollicking bar scene at night.

Orientation

San Jorge is convenient to stroll around, but the beachfront – with the ferry terminal, several restaurants and most of the bars – is a featureless 1km walk past a faux Spanish fortress on the main road. Take taxis after dark between the town and the waterfront.

Information

Cybercafé San Jorge (Parque Central, ½c E; per hour US$0.70) One of the few internet cafes in town.

Getting There & Around

Buses (US$0.25) leave for Rivas almost hourly from the ferry terminal, passing by the Parque Central. *Colectivos* (US$0.50 to Rivas) roam the streets.

The road ends at the ferry terminal, where there's guarded parking (US$3) for your car and a regular boat service to Moyogalpa and San José del Sur on Isla de Ometepe.

Isla de Ometepe

POP 29,800

Ometepe never fails to impress. Its twin volcanic peaks, rising up out of Lago de Nicaragua, have captured the imagination of everyone from precolonial Aztec descendents (who thought they'd found the promised land) to Mark Twain (who waxed lyrical about it in his book *Travels with Mr Brown*) to the surprisingly few travelers who make it out here.

The island's fertile volcanic soil, clean waters, wide beaches, wildlife population, archaeological sites and dramatic profile are quickly propelling it up traveler tick lists.

More than 1700 petroglyphs have been found on Ometepe, making this a DIY-ers fantasy island.

Activities

Many of the island's tourist attractions are hard to find or even a bit dangerous – take that active volcano, for example. Sometimes it's just worth hiring a guide.

The island's two volcanoes can be ascended from Moyogalpa or Altagracia for Volcán Concepción, and Fincas Magdelena, El Porvenir and Hacienda Mérida for Volcán Maderas. The uphill slog to Cascada San Ramón, more a walk than a hike, also makes for an excellent day trip. Relatively less challenging hikes abound, including to the halfway point up Maderas on the Finca

Magdalena trail, and **Tour al Floral** (guide per person US$10), a five-hour round trip to a viewpoint about 1000m up Concepción.

Swimming off Ometepe's beaches is excellent. Keep in mind that Lago de Nicaragua rises dramatically in the rainy season (and, if the rains are particularly heavy, the couple of months afterwards), shrinking the beaches to thin strands. By the end of the dry season in April, however, some 20m of gray volcanic sand may stretch out to the water. The most popular beaches are Playa Santo Domingo, Playa Balcón and the other beaches around Charco Verde and Punta Jesús María. If you're just looking for a dip, the mineral-rich rock pools at La Presa Ojo de Agua (p122) make a fine day trip.

Kayaking is also big on the island, with Isla del Congo, Isla de Quiste and the Río Istiam being the most popular destinations. Most hotels near these places rent kayaks.

Biking is a fun way to get around (and, with the sketchy bus service, sometimes the *only* way). Bikes can be rented in Moyogalpa, Altagracia, Playa Santo Domingo and most hotels. **Horseback riding** is another popular local transportation choice, and any tour operator or hotel can set you up with a ride.

Volunteering options abound. Check around at the hostels.

A growing number of farms on the island are signing up to the **Fincas Verdes agro-tourism program** (www.fincasverdes.com), offering farmstays, horseback-riding expeditions and tours of farm facilities explaining traditional, often organic farming techniques.

 Tours

The majority of tour operators are based in Moyogalpa. Just about any hotel can organize **horseback riding** (per hour US$4-6, guides

BULL SHARKS: A TALE OF OVERFISHING

There was a time when the people of Lago de Nicaragua, then called Cocibolca ('Sweet Sea' in Náhuatl), did not learn how to swim. From the gulf of the Río San Juan to Granada's shores, the bull shark ruled these waters, and had a taste for human flesh.

Carcharhinus leucus is among the Caribbean's most ferocious sharks, not enormous but strong, with an appetite for anything terrestrial that might fall into its realm. Its small eyes, adapted to the silty water of the river mouth, are useless, but it can smell blood from 100m away. Its flattened tail fin is perfect for the punishingly shallow rapids of rivers which it, unlike any other shark, can penetrate well inland.

All sharks can modify salts in their bloodstream, to sink and float at will, but the bull shark alone can urinate these salts away as it heads upstream, and find equilibrium in places where they are not expected.

The shark, always itself hunted, became a major cash earner as the 20th century began. By the 1930s Chinese buyers were paying as much as US$70 a kilogram for the fins, a legendary 'restorative.' As the market grew, Nicaraguans found buyers for the shark's liver, rich in vitamin A, and the skin, which can be prepared as fine leather. This shark's meat, however, rotted too quickly to export – the bulk of this brutal catch was ground into fertilizer or dog food, or simply thrown away.

In 1969 the Somoza family decided to take full advantage of this 'renewable' natural resource, and built a shark-processing plant in Granada. By some estimates, 20,000 sharks flowed through it during its decade of operation. More than 100 boats fed the facilities, even as the sharks became rarer, perhaps endangered, and ever more difficult to catch. The revolution coincided with this unprofitable decline, and the entire operation was shut down in 1979. It has never recovered.

These days, bull-shark sightings are a rare occurrence. Some locals say that they lurk out in the deep waters, far from the shoreline, others say that the only colonies left are around the entrance to the Río San Juan.

Now that the shark has no natural predators, it's possible that the population will make a comeback. And you have to wonder, as you swim these once-forbidden waters, if they remember the taste of what was once their favorite meal.

A great book about Nicaraguan bull sharks is the page-turner *Savage Shore: Life and Death with Nicaragua's Last Shark Hunters*, by the amazing Edward Marriot.

Isla de Ometepe

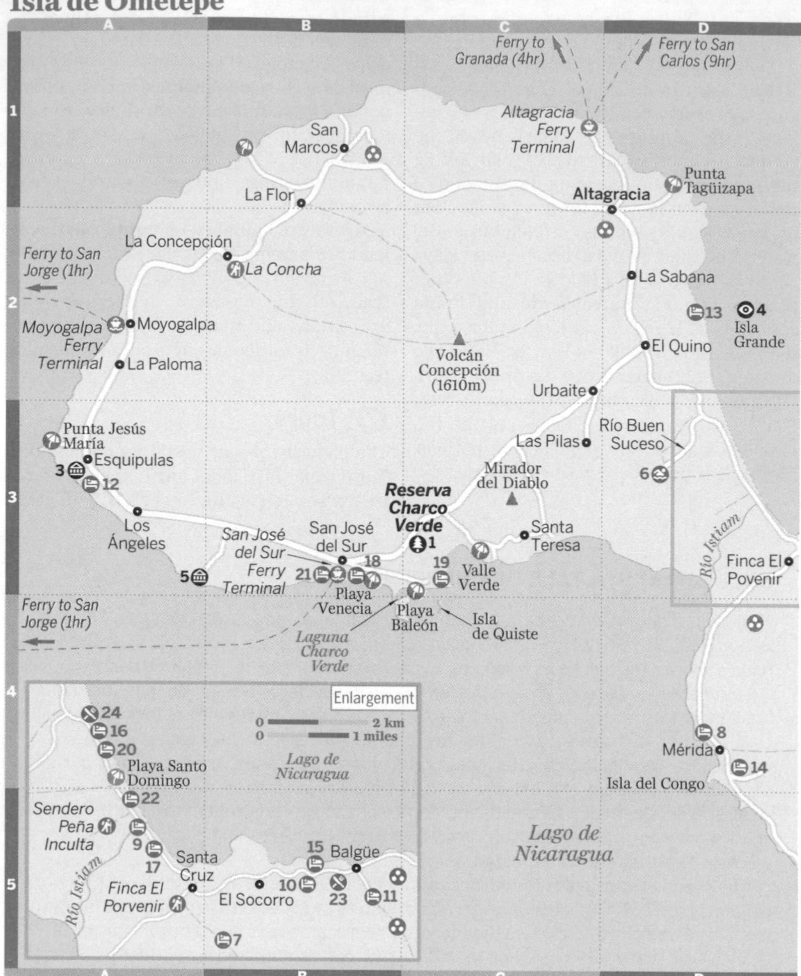

per group from US$10-20) and tours. Guides are not really necessary for San Ramón waterfall, La Presa Ojo de Agua or Reserva Charco Verde, although it's always easier to have someone else arrange transportation. Air-conditioned **island tours** (per person US$20-30) are much easier, but also more expensive than doing the scenic figure eight on a public Bluebird school bus (US$2 to US$4).

After various tourists got lost and died climbing volcanoes solo, it's now illegal to climb the volcanoes without a guide. Guides are available at or near the major trailheads in Altagracia, Moyogalpa, Balgüe and Mérida. Another place where it's worth having a guide along is on a kayak cruise of the Río Istiam – they know where all the animals are, and can call up a caiman for you.

Orientation

Isla de Ometepe's 78km main road runs in a rough barbell shape, circling each volcano and running along the northern shore of the isthmus between them. The Concepción side of the island is more developed, and the major port towns of Moyogalpa and Altagracia are connected by a paved road.

Isla de Ometepe

Moyogalpa is the major town on the island, and you'll find the majority of services for tourists here. Altagracia is the only other real population center and is a smaller, much more laid-back and less-touristed spot. This said, there's not much reason to come here, except to check out the statues and museums, or catch a boat to Granada or San Carlos.

Playa Santo Domingo is the most popular lodging spot on the isthmus; the road splits upon arriving on the less-developed Volcán Maderas side of the island, going right to Mérida and the San Ramón waterfall, left to Balgüe and Finca Magdelena.

Information

Lonely Planet (www.lonelyplanet.com/nicaragua/isla-de-ometepe) For planning advice, author recommendations, traveler reviews and insider tips.

Getting There & Away

The most convenient way to get to Isla de Ometepe is the one-hour, 17km boat ride from San Jorge to Moyogalpa or San José del Sur. There are two classes of boat: smaller, less stable *lanchas* (small motorboats) and larger, less frequent ferries, which can also transport bicycles, motorcycles and cars. Note that only *lanchas* (not ferries) serve San José and that between November and February winds can make the sea rough, particularly in the afternoon; consider taking the ferry. Fewer boats make the run on Sunday.

Ferries also run from Altagracia to Granada and San Carlos. If you're thinking about doing the Granada–Altagracia run one way only, it's best to leave from Granada – you travel in the day, get some views and arrive late afternoon. Leaving Altagracia for Granada you travel at night and arrive in the early hours of the morning.

The **Hacienda Mérida** (www.hmerida.com) does sailboat tours and transfers. You'll need a minimum of four (and a maximum of six) people for the following prices: San Jorge (US$25 per person, one hour), San Carlos (US$80 per person, nine to 11 hours) and Granada (US$60 per person, eight to nine hours).

Getting Around

The southern loop between Moyogalpa and Altagracia, the island's two major towns, is a beautifully paved road. All other roads vary between regular and atrocious. Remember when asking for directions that most locals have a very skewed idea of distances – it's better to ask how many minutes' walk than how many kilometers it is to your destination. The island is bigger than it looks and very few destinations are really walkable. The lack of traffic makes hitching a problem (although any passing pickup will almost certainly give you a ride). Bicycling is a breeze.

BICYCLE, CAR & MOTORCYCLE

Moyogalpa is the place to go to rent cars and motorbikes, although a couple of places in Playa Santo Domingo rent motorbikes. Car rentals run as much as US$90 per day (check at Hotel Ometepetl). Motorcycles cost US$25 per day (US$5 per hour), and bikes will run around US$5 per day.

If you have your own car, consider leaving it in the parking lot by the San Jorge ferry terminal, particularly in the wet season if you don't have a 4WD. Ferries can transport your car; make reservations well in advance.

BUS

Bus service is solid, but the southern island's terrible roads take their toll on buses and schedules change frequently. Fewer buses run on Sunday. Between Moyogalpa and Altagracia there are hourly buses. All buses from Moyogalpa to the Maderas side of the island stop in Altagracia about one hour later, then head down the isthmus past Playa Santo Domingo.

At Santa Cruz, buses go right (south) to Mérida and San Ramón, and left (east) to Balgüe, perhaps continuing to La Palma. Buses do not serve the southeastern portion of the island, between San Ramón and La Palma, at all.

TAXI

Taxis are rare and expensive, and they're all minivans, jeeps or pickups with 4WD. They meet all ferries, but otherwise you should have your hotel make arrangements with a driver at least a few hours in advance. From Moyogalpa, expect to pay at least US$20 to Altagracia, US$20 to Playa Santo Domingo, US$25 to Balgüe, US$30 to Mérida and US$45 to San Ramón.

Moyogalpa

POP 10,000

Not just the ferry terminal for hourly boats from the mainland, Moyogalpa is the nerve center for Ometepe's nascent tourist industry, with several hotels and restaurants and most of the island's tour companies. It's also base camp for the climb up Volcán Concepción. It's a bit of a tourist ghetto, and those looking for chillaxed island days should hightail it outta here.

Sights & Activities

Moyogalpa is very light on for sights of its own, but there are some rippers just out of town. The most obvious is the trek up Volcán Concepción. People based in Moyogalpa quite often take a bus or bike ride out to

GETTING YOUR WHEELS ONTO OMETEPE

Taking a car to Ometepe involves a bit of forward planning, some runaround and cash. Since rental cars on the island can cost upward of US$90 per day (when available) and public transport is patchy at best, it may just be worth the hassle. Four-wheel drives are best for the spiky volcanic roads.

To do it, get here for the first ferry from San Jorge to Moyagalpa by 7am. Ferries leave about every hour. You should be able to make it by noon with a little luck. There are a handful of ferry companies at the Moyagalpa terminal, but the central **Empresa Milton Garcia** (☎8966-4983; Ferry Terminal) is best to help you buy your tickets and arrange passage. With the port tax, mysterious 'car tax' and ferry transit fee, you'll pay about US$20 each way. Passengers buy separate tickets. While the companies say you can arrive that day and get on a ferry with a car, you're better off calling ahead.

Punta Jesús María, which makes a good day trip. There are numerous tour guides operating on the main drag, charging around US$20 per day for excursions.

Sala Arqueológica & Cyber Ometepe MUSEUM
(Muelle, 4½c E; museum US$1; ⏲8am-9pm) The past meets the future...well, the present, anyway, at this combination internet cafe and family-operated museum. Your fee includes a Spanish-language guided tour of *metates* (flat stones on which corn is ground) and lots of beautiful ceramics, including what may be the best collection of ceramic funeral jars in Nicaragua, emblazoned with bats, snakes and other emblems.

Fundación Entre Volcánes VOLUNTEERING
(☎2569-4118; www.fundacionentrevolcanes.org; frente Enitel) A grassroots, locally founded NGO involved in education, health, nutrition and environmental projects on the island. It accepts volunteers with an intermediate level of Spanish and a two-month minimum commitment. For more on volunteering in Southwestern Nicaragua see p128.

Festivals & Events

Moyogalpa's **fiestas patronales** (⏲July 23 to 26) are famous for the Baile de las Inditas, a celebration of both Spanish and indigenous culture, as well as several ceremonies timed with the solar calendar that have nothing at all to do with Catholicism. Patron Santa Ana leads a long walk to Punta Jesús María, where there are fireworks and drinking.

Sleeping

The most atmospheric sleeping options are elsewhere, but there are a few perfectly acceptable hotels in town.

Hotel Escuela Teosintal HOTEL $
(☎2569-4105; Muelle, 2c E, 1½c S; s/d US$12/18; 📶) Run by an agricultural cooperative, these are by far the sweetest rooms for the price. They're spacious and spotless, with cable TV, modern bathrooms and a lush little garden out back. Organic preserves and coffee beans are for sale at reception.

Hospedaje Central HOTEL $
(El Indio Viejo; ☎2569-4262; www.hostelometepe.com; Muelle, 3c E, 1c S; dm US$5.50-7.50, r US$10.50, d with air-con US$25; ❄📶) About as hippy-trippy as things get in town, the Central is all murals and hammocks. There's a tame deer and monkeys wandering the grounds out back – kind of sad to see, but staff promised us they are looking for a new spot for them. Rooms are definitely basic, but OK for the price. Bikes are available for rent.

Hotelito Aly HOTEL $
(☎2569-4196; www.hotelitoaly.com; Muelle, 2½c E; r per person US$10, without bathroom US$7; ❄📶) While the downstairs restaurant is cheery enough, the rooms surrounding it may be a bit grim for some. Upstairs, the situation improves, with spacious, airy rooms and good beds. Bathrooms can be a little gross.

Hotel Ometepetl HOTEL $$
(☎2569-4276; ometepetlng@hotmail.com; Muelle, 100m E; s with fan/air-con US$15/25, d with fan/air-con US$20/30; ❄📶) A favorite with tour groups, the Ometepetl has smallish, colorful rooms that can be a bit stale and feature cable TV, a pleasant garden area with hammocks, and excellent service.

Eating & Drinking

Almost everything grown on Ometepe is organically farmed, simply because fertilizers are unnecessary in the rich volcanic soil, and pesticides prohibitively expensive. Its rice and beans are considered the country's best, and the papayas are certainly among the largest.

Café Bistro Cocibolca NICARAGUAN $
(Muelle, 3c E, 1c S; dishes US$2-4) Serves up a great range of international foods and some really yummy sandwiches. The music is chilled most of the week, and the place converts into the town's biggest disco on weekends.

Yogi's Bar BURGERS $
(Hospedaje Central, ½c S; burgers US$4) Ground zero for comfort food, Yogi's offers US-style burgers and sandwiches, yummy homemade brownies, big breakfasts and movies on the big screen every night.

Los Ranchitos INTERNATIONAL $
(Muelle, 3c E, ½c S; mains US$4-6) One of the better-looking restaurants in town, with open walls, thatched roofs and a pressed-dirt floor. The menu's your fairly standard range of meat, chicken and seafood, with some good pizza and pasta options thrown in.

Pizzeria Buon Appetito PIZZERIA $$
(Muelle, 100m E; mains US$6-12; 🍸) Grab a table out front to watch the action on the main drag at the island's best pizza-pie place. There's a

wide menu featuring seafood dishes like snapper in shellfish sauce or shrimp cocktails, but the standard assortment of pasta dishes. Eggplant with pesto is a great veggie option.

Timbo al Tambo BAR
(Muelle, 2½c E; ⏲3pm-late Tue-Sat) A cozy bar that's popular with locals and travelers alike for a couple of drinks and some sports on the big screen. Judging by the school kids grinding it out to reggaeton hits on the small dance floor, your chances of getting asked for ID are slim.

Orientation

The ferry terminal is at the bottom of Moyogalpa's main street; almost all services are within one block of this street. Buses and taxis stop at the dock after 8:30am; before 8:30am they leave from the Catholic church at the top of the street. Go left for the dirt road to La Flor and San Marcos, right for the paved road to Charco Verde, Playa Santo Domingo and Volcán Maderas.

Information

@rcia Cyber Café (Muelle, 2½c E; per hour US$1) Not great, but the best in town.

Banco Lafise (Muelle, 200m E)

BanPro Credit (Muelle, 3c E) Accepts Visa. Not always operational.

Hospital (☎2569 4247; Parque Central, 3c S) Offers basic emergency services. For anything serious it's best to get off the island, to Rivas at least.

Police station (☎2569-4231; muelle, 3c E, 1c S)

Getting there & Around

BOAT

One-way fares from San Jorge to Moyogalpa are US$3, and you'll need to pay a US$0.40 dock fee. Departure times follow:

Moyogalpa to San Jorge 6am, 7:45am, 11am, 12:30pm, 4pm, 5:30pm

San Jorge to Moyogalpa 7am, 7:45am, 10:30am, noon, 2:30pm, 4pm, 5:30pm

BUS

Bus departures are more frequent here than anywhere else on the island. Timetables change rapidly – if you're going out for the day, ask your driver what time the last bus returns. Bear in mind that all buses pass Altagracia, stopping for half an hour, and that it can take three hours (on a good day) to get from Moyogalpa to San Ramón. Bus services:

Altagracia (US$0.75, one hour, 5:30am to 6:45pm, hourly)

Balgüe (US$1.10, two hours, 2:40pm)

Mérida (US$1.25, 2½ hours, 8:30am, 2:40pm and 4:30pm)

San Ramón (US$1.10, three hours, 8:30am and 2:30pm)

Volcán Concepción

The 10- to 12-hour **hike** (guides per person US$12-20) up loose volcanic stone to the summit of this looming peak can be tough, so be in good physical condition and bring water, snacks and real hiking shoes. Most hikes leave from either Moyogalpa or Altagracia. Remember that there's no shade above the tree line, it's even steeper than it looks, and it can get windy and cold, particularly if it's cloudy, at the top. It's almost always cloudy at the top, which means your chances of seeing the fuming craters and awesome views over the lake and across Central America's volcanic spine are slim, even during dry season. There are three main trails to the top: La Concha and La Flor (the most popular trail), both close to Moyogalpa, and La Sabana, a short distance from Altagracia.

Around Volcán Concepción

This has been the more populous side of the island (despite the looming, active volcano overhead) since the Chorotega arrived, and remains so today.

ALTAGRACIA VIA SAN MARCOS

There are no real tourist facilities along the northern route between Moyogalpa and Altagracia, although the trailheads for both La Concha and La Flor, which summit Concepción, leave from the towns of the same name. La Flor also has a nice beach. Several archaeological sites are rumored to be located near San Marcos.

PUNTA JESÚS MARÍA

About half an hour by bicycle from Moyogalpa, this well-signed sand spit stretches out into the lake for more than 1km at the height of the dry season, when lake levels drop and reveal what was once a natural dock for indigenous fishermen. It's still used the same way today, with the addition of a few ramshackle restaurants that may or may not be open.

ESQUIPULAS

A kilometer or so down the road from the turnoff to Punta Jesús María, this little town is unremarkable, except that it is home to the **Galería de Arte Carlos Vargas** (9am-6pm Mon-Sat, to noon Sun). On the southern edge of town, Ometepe's most prolific artist-photographer has his studio-gallery open to the public. The work draws heavily on island influences in the Primitivist style. If you can't afford a painting, postcard versions are on sale. A little further out of town, past the cemetery, is the turnoff to **Finca Samaria** (8695-5215; http://samariahotelrestaurante.wordpress.com; r per person US$7, breakfast US$2), a beautiful little farmstay option a 500m walk down a dirt road – take a left just before you hit the water. Rooms are fairly basic, but the farm is lovely, with hammocks and *ranchos* (small houses or houselike buildings) galore in the shady garden that backs onto a tree-lined beach with some of the best sunset views on the island. The family serves up simple, hearty meals, and rents bikes (US$5 per day) and horses (US$5 per hour) to guests.

MUSEOS EL CEIBO

About halfway between Esquipulas and San José del Sur, look for the turnoff to the island's best **museums** (www.elceibomuseos.com; admission per museum US$3; 8am-5pm), 2km down a shady lane off the main road. The **Museo Numinástico** (Coin Museum) documents the troubled history of the Nicaraguan economy through its coins and banknotes. Across the road, the **Museo Arqueológico** displays an excellent collection of more than 1000 pieces of ceramics, *metates,* funeral urns and jewelry, all collected from around the island. There's even what is claimed to be a pre-Columbian dildo on display. Women may not wish to hear the explanation for the little hole at the end.

SAN JOSÉ DEL SUR

The other arrival point for *lanchas* from San Jorge is this sizable workaday village. At the northern end of town, opposite the football field, is the turnoff to **Hotel Playa Santa Martha** (2569-4733; www.hotelsantamarthaometepe.com; cabins with fan/air-con US$30/35;), featuring some decent work-a-day little *cabinas* (cabins) down on the waterfront. They could do with a bit of decoration and a good airing but are still a good deal, particularly if you can get one that fronts onto the beach.

Lanchas for the 40-minute trip to San Jorge depart from the dock just off the main road in the center of town at 7:20am and 3:20pm and leave San Jorge for San José del Sur at 9:30am and 5pm. Southbound buses meet the *lanchas* at the dock.

CHARCO VERDE & ISLA DE QUISTE

On the southern side of Concepción lies a lush, less-windblown clutch of beaches, centered on **Reserva Charco Verde** (www.fincasverdes.com; admission US$0.75). The fine green Laguna Charco Verde is accessible from a short hiking trail that begins at Hotel Charco Verde. Not only is this a lovely spot for swimming, hiking and wildlife-watching, but it's also it's the home of Chico Largo, a tall, thin and ancient witch who often appears swimming or fishing in the lagoon. His primary duty is to protect the tomb and solid-gold throne of Cacique Nicarao, buried nearby.

VOLCÁN CONCEPCIÓN'S EXPLOSIVE MOOD SWINGS

She knows she's special: Volcán Concepción is Central America's most symmetrical and arguably loveliest volcano, not to mention one of its most active and dangerous. Concepción roared back to life the same year that Krakatoa blew, in 1883, after centuries of hosting gentle cloud forests around her now gray and smoking craters.

The fiery flow seems cyclical. In 1921 ash gave way to glowing red, and the following year lava and boulders were tossed out with explosions heard in Granada. In 1944 ash falls as far as Rivas were just a warning; six months later lava flows consumed hectares of crops. In 1957 tongues of flame 15m high leapt from the summit following months of ashy exhalation. President Somoza sent boats to evacuate the island – not one person left, and not one person died. And although no lava burst forth, ash inaugurated another two years of activity between 1983 and 1985.

In late 2005, in her first tantrum since the revolution, Concepción showered ash over Rivas, and guides were excitedly explaining that it 'smelled like lava' at the top. Volcano treks were cut short and everybody looked up a lot more than usual, but in the end there was no grand spectacle. In the 2007, 2009 and 2012 explosions there was more rumbling, smoke and ash, but again, no real drama. That said, you can bet that we haven't heard the last from this fiery madam yet.

Just offshore, Isla de Quiste is within swimming distance of the beach, or any of the area's hotels can arrange boat service and perhaps rental tents, as it's a prime camping, fishing and birding spot.

Sleeping

Hotel Finca Playa Venecia CABIN **$$**
(☎8887-0191; www.fincavenecia.com; cabins with fan/air-con US$30/45; P❄📶) A decent bet on this side of the island, this grouping of 20 *cabinas* and four basic rooms sits near the beach, and has a grassy play area for the tots. Unfortunately, not many of the *cabinas* have lake-front views, and they can be slightly stale, but air out quickly.

Hotel El Tesoro de Pirata HOTEL **$$**
(☎8927-2831; tesoroelpirata@gmail.com; d US$35; ❄🏊) Two kilometers to the south of Charco Verde is the turnoff to Valle Verde (Green Valley). It's another 2km walk from the bus stop down to the Pirate's Treasure Hotel. This is the best beach around, a private lagoon all of your own. The rooms aren't anything to write home about, but for the price, this is an excellent option on this side of the island.

Hotel Charco Verde CABIN **$$$**
(☎8887-9302; www.charcoverde.com.ni; cabins US$60; ❄📶) This hotel occupies a fabulous beach, and has a growing collection of large, modern *cabinas*, only some of which have a beach view.

EL QUINO

All buses headed to Playa Santo Domingo and Volcán Maderas stop in Altagracia, adding perhaps half an hour to your trip. If you're headed to Playa Santo Domingo, consider getting off at El Quino; it's a downhill, 4km walk to the beach, but you wouldn't want to do it in the blazing sun with luggage.

Sleeping

Finca San Juan de la Isla LODGE **$$$**
(☎8886-0734; sanjuandelaisla.com; El Quino, 500m N; r from US$100; ❄📶) 🌿 This top-end choice is accessed just north of the village of El Quino. Set on a working farm right on the beach, the hacienda-style hotel has a private beach, remarkable volcano views from the well-tended grounds, and a friendly common area where you can eat dinner or laze out in a hammock. The rooms are well appointed, though slightly stiff.

Altagracia

POP 7000

With more natural protection from Concepción's occasional lava flow than Moyogalpa, this is the original indigenous capital of Ometepe, and still the island's most important town.

Sights & Activities

This is base camp for the other trailhead to Concepción, called La Sabana, which begins about 2km from town. Both Hotel Central and Hotel Castillo can arrange guides.

The town's Parque Central is the center of the action, and features a sweet relief map of the island. Hotel Castillo rents mountain bikes (for US$1 per hour).

Museo de Ometepe MUSEUM
(Parque Central, 1c O; admission US$2; ⏲8am-noon & 1-4pm Mon-Fri, 9am-3pm Sat, 9am-1pm Sun) The village's main attraction is this museum packed with information (in Spanish) about the island. You'll find a much more comprehensive collection at the Museos El Ceibo. Non-Spanish speakers will still appreciate the amazing scale model of the volcanoes, as well as a few stone sculptures, petroglyphs and lots of pottery thoughtfully displayed as part of a timeline.

Monoliths ARCHAEOLOGICAL SITE
(admission US$0.50) A place to see some of the finest remaining ancient excavated statues on Ometepe is beside the Altagracia church, close to the Parque Central, where a handful of softly eroding monoliths still stand sentry.

Isla Grande ISLAND
Close to Altagracia, this island, basically a plantain *finca* (farm) gone feral, is rarely visited despite being a fantastic place for bird-watching. If you're interested, you could certainly arrange a custom trip; ask at Hotel Castillo or at the artisan cooperative in the Parque Central.

Artesanías Altagracia GUIDED TOUR
(Parque Central) Check at this artisan cooperative for guided tours (US$15 to US$30 depending on the size of your group).

Manuel Hamilton Silva Monje GUIDED TOUR
(☎8939-9911; manuelhamilton2000@yahoo.com; Museo Ometepe; workshops or tours US$35) Enquire at the museum for this local historian, who offers workshops on the island's history and town tours.

Festivals & Events

Altagracia's **fiestas patronales** (November 12 to 18) honor San Diego, whose feast day is coincidentally the same as that of Xolotl, the ancient city's original patron deity. The party's most famous dance, Baile del Zompopo (Dance of the Leaf Cutter Ant), was clearly choreographed long before the Christians got here.

Sleeping & Eating

All the hotels have restaurants. The cheapest eats are served up at the Parque Central – during the day a couple of kiosks serve snacks, and starting at dusk several *fritanga* setups offer roast chicken and more, until 9pm or so.

Hotel Central HOTEL $
(2569 4420; www.hotelcentraldeometepe.com; Iglesia, 2c S; r per person US$9.30, cabin per person US$12, cabin with air-con US$45;) The best-looking rooms in town are a simple affair but a good deal. Rooms out front are arranged around a pretty garden and have bathrooms with river-pebble accents. The *cabinas* out back are supercute, and the hotel restaurant serves good, cheap Nicaraguan food.

Hotel Castillo HOTEL $
(2569-4403; www.hotelcastillo-ometepe.blogspot.com; Iglesia, 1c S, ½c O; dm/s US$6/10, r with air-con US$20; @) Nothing fancy going on here, but it's fairly clean and brightly painted, with a couple of good hangout areas. The rooms can be a bit stale and the pillows are a lumpy porridge consistency. The restaurant (dishes US$3 to US$5) is excellent, and serves real coffee. You can arrange tours here.

Hospedaje Kencho HOTEL $
(8944-4087; www.hotelkencho.com; Iglesia, ½c S; r per person without bathroom US$3, s/d with fan US$5/7, r with air-con US$30;) This is a bargain-basement option with slightly rundown rooms. Everything is clean, however, and the owners are friendly. The high-end rooms out back with air-con aren't worth it.

Entertainment

Estadio Municipal BASEBALL
(Iglesia, 500m N) FREE Baseball games here are generally free!

Orientation

Buses stop at the attractive Parque Central. The museum and all services are within three blocks of here. To get to the ferry terminal, head north along the road in front of Chido's Pizza and Comedor Nicarao for another 2km. Pickup trucks (US$0.80) begin appearing around the park a couple of hours before ferry departures.

Information

Hotel Castillo offers reasonable internet access (US$1.50 per hour). The small artisan cooperative in the Parque Central can dispense basic tourist information but has no maps and few brochures.

BanPro (Iglesia, 2c S) ATM.

Getting There & Away

BOAT

Ferries cross the lake between Granada and San Carlos twice weekly, stopping in Altagracia (unless the weather is really bad) en route. Schedules change frequently. Ferry services include the following:

Altagracia to Granada (US$4.25, four hours, 3pm Tuesday)

Altagracia to San Carlos (US$6, nine hours, 6pm Monday and Thursday) Also serves San Miguelito.

Granada to Altagracia (US$4.25, four hours, 2:30pm Monday, 2pm Thursday)

San Carlos to Altagracia (US$6, nine hours, 2pm Tuesday and Friday)

BUS

Buses heading south from Moyogalpa all pass by here one hour after leaving before continuing south. Services include the following:

Balgüe (US$1.10, two hours, 11:30am, noon, 4:30pm and 6pm)

Mérida (US$1.25, 2½ hours, 9:30am, 3:30pm and 5:30pm)

Moyogalpa (US$0.75, one hour, 5:30am to 6:45pm, every hour)

San Ramón (US$1.10, three hours, 9:30am and 3:30pm)

Playa Santo Domingo

Windswept (sometimes a little too windswept) beaches and the island's finest accommodations lie southeast of Altagracia, on the long and lovely lava isthmus that cradles Playa Santo Domingo.

Sights & Activities

The main attraction is the **beach**, a 30m to 70m (depending on lake levels) expanse of gray volcanic sand that retreats almost to the sea wall at the height of the rainy season.

You can hire bikes (US$8 per day) and horses (US$4 per hour) from Hotel Finca Santo Domingo, or if you want to spread the money around, look for signs at roadside stores that rent out bikes and motorbikes.

Río Istiam RIVER
On the south side of the isthmus, this river shimmers as it snakes through the island's lava valley. The best way to explore the river (which is really a swamp) is by kayak – you're pretty much guaranteed to see turtles, caimans and howler monkeys. Enquire at nearby hotels.

La Presa Ojo de Agua SWIMMING
(admission US$2; comedor daylight hours) On the isthmus take a pleasant stroll through banana plantations to the well-signed shady swimming hole about 1.5km north of Playa Santo Domingo. The mineral-infused water here bubbles up from 35 small underground springs and, with an average temperature of 22°C to 28°C (71°F to 82°F), makes for a refreshing dip. There are two entrances, one at the northern end and one at the southern.

Sendero Peña Inculta HIKING
(admission US$2.50) This is a 1.5km interpretative trail meandering through the forest on the outskirts of Playa Santo Domingo. The trail starts just north of the village and ends opposite Villa Paraíso. At least 63 species of bird inhabit these parts, so walk quietly and look up every now and then. And make sure you wear good shoes – the loose volcanic-rock path can get very spiky!

Canopy Sendero Los Monos CANOPY TOUR
(per person US$10) If you're in the mood for more modern ecotourism, across from Hotel Finca Santo Domingo, Canopy Sendero Los Monos offers six platforms and 500m of zip lines constructed by a reputable company.

Sleeping & Eating

Make reservations for Hotel Finca Santo Domingo and Villa Paraíso well in advance during the high season.

Hospedaje Buena Vista HOTEL $
(2569-4864; s/d US$15/20; wi-fi) The best (well, only) budget spot along this stretch, with a tidy garden, good hangout areas and plenty of waterfront hammock action. The brick rooms are on the small side but spotless, with very thin mattresses (room 1 is best).

Hotel Finca Santo Domingo RESORT $$
(2569-4862; www.hotelfincasantodomingo.org; s/d US$25/30, cabins US$45-55; P air-con wi-fi) More like a resort than anywhere else on the island, this class act sprawls out along the beachfront. Rooms upstairs have a pleasant nautical feel to them and unfortunate slumping beds. Rooms 3 and 4 have the best views. The cement *cabinas* across the road are air-conditioned but further from the water. The restaurant is excellent, and staff arrange tours.

Villa Paraíso CABIN $$$
(2569-4859; www.ometepevillaparaiso.com.ni; cabins US$85; P air-con @ wi-fi) The nicest rooms in Santo Domingo are found at this friendly beachfront hotel. The elegant *cabinas* have air-con, Direct TV and private terraces. The excellent staff will arrange tours and there's a fantastic restaurant.

Natural Restaurant Vegetariano VEGETARIAN $
(juices US$2, dishes US$3-4; vegetarian) Right at the northern entrance to Santo Domingo, this little beachside beauty serves up some tasty vegetarian curries, healthy breakfasts (with wholemeal bread!) and delicious organic fruit juices.

South to Santa Cruz

Between Playa Santo Domingo and Santa Cruz are a collection of smaller hotels. The beach here (which is really the same one) is just as good as the one to the north, but far less crowded.

Sleeping

Casa Istiam HOTEL $
(2569-4879; r with fan/air-con US$15/30; air-con) About halfway between Playa Santo Domingo and Santa Cruz, with the beach right across the road and the Río Istiam out back, this is one classy location. Rooms are basic but cute, with fresh, bright paint jobs and cool stone floors.

Hostal Espirales HOSTEL $
(8573-4998; www.hostalespirales.com; dm/s/d US$7/15/20, r with air-con US$25) Across the road from the beach, this farm/hotel has simple rooms and a basic dormitory.

El Encanto HOTEL **$$**
(☎8867-7128; www.goelencanto.com; s/d US$20/25) Set on a 4-hectare banana farm, rooms here are simply but pleasantly decorated, with big, screened windows and clean, modern bathrooms. Hammocks out front of your room have great lake views. The restaurant gets raves for its mix of Nicaraguan classics and international food, including curries, wholemeal bread and several vegetarian options.

Volcán Maderas

Climbing this 1394m **volcano** (guides per person US$5-20) involves a muddy seven- to eight-hour slog (with four to five hours of climbing). Eventually, you'll reach a misty cloud forest ending with a steep crater descent to a chilly jade green lake. The halfway point of the Finca Magdalena trail, with benches, offers the money shot of Concepción.

There are three trails to the top: the original at Finca Magdelena (US$15 per group of three) and two slightly longer trails beginning at Hacienda Mérida (US$20 per group of three) and Finca El Porvenir (US$15/20 for one/two people).

Around Volcán Maderas

This is the lusher, wilder side of the island. It's even less developed than Concepción's side, and petroglyphs are much more common. Any hotel can arrange guided hikes (US$10 to US$20 per group) to different groups of petroglyphs, or you can go on horseback for a few dollars more.

A great day trip is walking (or biking) some or all of the circumference of Maderas (35km) on the rough dirt road (note that there are no stores, restaurants or bus service between San Ramón and La Palma).

SANTA CRUZ TO BALGÜE

The split in the road at Santa Cruz is marked by a small store. It's a pleasant, 3km, downhill walk to Balgüe from here, if you're on a Mérida-bound bus.

El Zopilote offers horse rentals (per hour US$5), massages (US$20), apiculture classes (US$10), Spanish-language classes (per hour US$2) and a variety of free cultural courses.

Buses leave Balgüe for Altagracia (US$1.10, one hour) at 10am, 1:30pm (continuing to Moyogalpa) and 4pm.

Sleeping & Eating

El Zopilote Finca Ecológica HOSTEL **$**
(☎8961-8742; www.ometepezopilote.com; 200m up trail from road; hammocks US$3, tents per person US$3, dm US$6, cabins US$14-18;) To reach this place on the inland side of the road, follow the trail to the left of the converted school bus/organic market, then 200m right to the clutch of traditionally constructed thatched-roof huts on the grassy hillside. By far the most laid-back hippy option on the island, this organic farm offers a range of accommodations scattered around a lush hillside on a sizable working farm.

The accomodations are pretty basic, but there's a cool common area and restaurant that sells organic products. There are a few petroglyphs scattered around and 'Japanese' showers (outdoor setups with bamboo plants for walls). If you really like it here, ask about volunteer or work opportunities.

Finca Magdalena HOSTEL **$**
(☎8498-1683; www.fincamagdalena.com; hammocks or campsites per person US$3, dm/tr/q US$3.50/15/24, cabins US$40; @) This Ometepe mainstay setup on the slopes of Volcán Maderas is a classic backpacking spot. Rooms and dorms on this working coffee *finca* are set in a rickety old wooden farmhouse and could be prettied up a bit, but really – who cares?

With sweeping views of the lake and Volcán Concepción, lush surrounds and yummy meals made from organic produce grown on the spot, you can probably rough it for a few days. And if you can't, the *cabinas* are several steps up in comfort. Note that it's a 1.5km climb to the *finca* from the bus stop.

Hospedaje Así es Mi Tierra GUESTHOUSE **$**
(☎8493-0506; www.mitierraometepe.com; r US$18, without bathroom US$12) At the southern end of town is a sweet little family-run affair offering basic but functional rooms. The best part is the 50m jungle trail that leads down to a pebble beach, complete with *rancho* (thatched-roof open-air bungalow), just waiting for you to string your hammock and pop your *cerveza* (beer).

Café Campestre HOSTEL **$**
(☎8571-5930; fincacampestre@gmail.com; dm US$10;) This good-vibes hostel has basic dorm rooms with mosquito-net-covered beds. The cafe is worth a look come dinner time, and staff offer kayak and hiking tours.

★**Totoco Ecolodge** LODGE $$$
(☎8358-7718; www.totoco.com.ni; 1.5km inland from main road; cabins/houses US$100/220; P 📶 🏊) The Totoco has seven *cabinas* perched high above the beach on a large 6.5-hectare organic farm (where you can volunteer). It works on solar power, recycles grey water and even has composting toilets. And while some lux-set travelers may miss air-con, the romantic rooms with spectacular views of Volcán Concepción and Tarzan-meet-Jane stylings are the best on the island.

Profits go to local initiatives, and there's a beautiful pool with views from here to eternity. We only wish it was closer to the beach. The restaurant is a worthwhile stop for nonguests.

Café Isabel NICARAGUAN $
(dishes US$3-4.50) Balgüe has a cluster of cafes just to the north of town, including this place which features a huge fixed plate with your choice of meat and freshly made *nacatamales* (banana-leaf-wrapped bundles of cornmeal, meat, vegetables and herbs; US$1.50).

SANTA CRUZ TO MÉRIDA & SAN RAMÓN

Although more heavily populated than the rest of the southern part of the island, this stretch of road still feels wild and untamed. As with the rest of the island, road conditions are laughable (except in the wet season, when they're no joke) and bus service is patchy at best.

Sights & Activities

Some of Ometepe's must-see attractions are accessed from this part of the island, including the **petroglyphs** at Albergue Ecológico El Porvenir, where a well-marked trail (US$1) meanders past approximately 20 of these rock carvings.

Being relatively sheltered, this side of the island is perfect for **kayaking**. An obvious destination is **Isla del Congo**, now called Isla de los Monos or Monkey Island, home to the descendants of four spider monkeys. Spider monkeys aren't present anywhere else on the island (howler and white face monkeys are), so these guys are pretty much alone. Don't get too close – these little guys bite. Hacienda Mérida is the closest place to the island that rents kayaks. The other classic kayaking trip is to the **Río Istiam**, a swampy inlet that's home to turtles, caimans, the occasional howler monkey and an array of birdlife. Caballito's Mar is the closest kayak-rental place to the entrance of the river and it has guides who know where all the wild things are.

Cascada San Ramón WATERFALL
(admission US$3, station guests free) This stunning 40m waterfall is one of the jewels of the island. The trail begins at the Estación Biológica de Ometepe. It's a steep four-hour round trip on an easy-to-follow trail that's lost some of its charm since lots of trees were cut down. But it's still mossy and beautiful at the top. If you've got a motorbike or 4WD, you can drive up the nasty uphill part of the hike and walk the remaining, relatively flat 2km.

Sleeping & Eating

★**Hacienda Mérida** HOTEL $
(☎8868-8973; www.hmerida.com; campsites or hammocks per person US$3, dm US$7, r downstairs/upstairs US$23/32; P @) On the south side of Mérida, this is by far the lushest budget option around (with some very nice midrange rooms thrown in), offering every activity you could possibly want – volcano hikes, kayaking, excellent mountain bikes, sailing, swimming etc. Dorms and 'standard' rooms are a good deal, but the superstars here are upstairs, with awesome lake views from a shared balcony featuring king-sized hammocks.

Albergue Ecológico El Porvenir LODGE $
(☎2569-4420; www.hotelkabanas.com/bienvenidosporvenir.html; r per person US$8; P) A kilometer past where the road splits is the entrance to this sunny hilltop lodge and restaurant that has it all – great volcano views and petroglyphs amid attractive gardens, a restaurant serving good-value meals, plus excellent, spacious rooms with funky, river stone–embedded bathrooms. Check here for nearby trails.

Caballito's Mar HOSTEL $
(☎8842-6120; www.caballitosmar.com; dm US$5) About 1km before Mérida, look for a sign to a simple little Spanish-Nica-run place right on the beach, with great lake views from the waterfront bar-restaurant. Dorms are simple brick constructions with corrugated-iron roofs, but the beds are good and the vibe is mellow. This is the best place to start kayak tours of the Río Istiam (US$15 per person) or DIY trips to nearby Isla del Congo.

Getting There & Away

Buses leave Mérida for Altagracia (US$1, 1½ hours) at 4am, 8:45am, 10:30am, 2pm, 3pm and 5pm, and San Ramón for Altagracia (US$1.50, 2½ hours) at 1pm and 2pm.

If you have got the cash, and a bit of a group together, by far the most romantic option for traveling to or from the island is on the 8m sailboat belonging to Hacienda Mérida. You'll need a minimum of four (and a maximum of six) people for the following prices: San Jorge (US$25 per person, one hour), San Carlos (US$80 per person, nine to 11 hours) and Granada (US$60 per person, eight to nine hours).

PACIFIC BEACHES

Southwestern Nicaragua's Pacific beaches offer amazing surf, sand and sun. To get to the Tola beaches – El Astillero down to Playa Gigante – you'll need to pass through Rivas and Tola, then head toward the beach. There is only extremely rough 4WD access on the coast between Veracruz and El Asillero. San Juan del Sur seves as the access point for the beaches between Playa Marsella in the north downward to El Ostional.

Tola & the Tola Beaches

The Tola beaches, once almost inaccessible and totally wild, are slowly coming into their own as a fabulous resort holiday-retirement village option. They still retain some of that lost-beach paradise feel, with top-notch surf and good vibes, but the pace of life is speeding up, thanks to new roads going in and new development dollars.

There are no banks or real grocery stores, and internet and cell-phone coverage is patchy at best. Do what you need to do before you hit the trail.

Getting There & Around

Bus access is reliable but inconvenient, though it is improving along with the atrocious roads. The road is paved to Tola, and the road from Tola to Playa Gigante is currently being paved.

Buses leave Rivas for Las Salinas de Nagualapa at 5:30am, 6am and 8:30am, and return at noon and 2pm. Note that Playa Gigante is a 7km walk from the bus stop.

Refugio de Vida Silvestre Río Escalante-Chacocente is hard to access without your own vehicle, but you could catch a US$30 cab from Las Salinas de Nagualapa or walk the 4km from El Astillero.

Taxis from Rivas make the gante (US$20), Santana (US$ de Nagualapa (US$45) and El As If you take the bus to Tola, cabs co US$5 less.

Tola

POP 5800

Tola, whose name means 'the land of the Toltecs', is rapidly developing into a service town for the big resort communities. The main reason to come here is to save a few dollars and catch a taxi to the beaches. There are no signed hotels, although you could arrange homestays.

Playa Gigante

This glorious white crescent of sand snuggled into the wildly forested mountains is almost worth the 7km hike from the bus stop. There are no taxis (and little traffic), but anyone with a pickup will no doubt give you a ride. Consider taking a taxi from Rivas or Tola. If you have reservations, your hotel may be able to arrange transport.

The popular sandy beach break right in front of 'town' gets hollow and fun when conditions are perfect, but it isn't really a surf beach. There's an endless tube about 45 minutes north. Special-name waves include Chiggers and Outer Chiggers, close to a rocky reef, and Hemorrhoids – this tube is for serious surfers, as it dumps you right onto gravel.

You'll need to hire a boat to most of the breaks, including the point break at Punta Manzanillo, just south, also called Punta Reloj. Ask the driver to take you past the 2m-long 'footprint' left in the rocky headlands.

Sights & Activities

From the beachfront restaurants, you can hire boards (US$10 per day) or bikes (US$10/50 per day/week) and get surfing lessons (www.costanica.com; US$10 per two-hour class).

Enquire at the Hostel Camino del Gigante (p126) for US$15 three-hour sailboat trips.

Reserva Ecológica Zacatan PARK

This is a 12-hectare swath of secondary tropical dry forest 2km back from the beach. There are interpretive trails and a swimming hole and plenty of monkeys, iguanas and morpho butterflies in residence.

BOAT TOUR
…rs.com; from US$25 … chartered boat …

…g

…camps offer all- …erything from …nks and boat …ne low season …ghtly room rates and you pay extra for everything else.

There are a handful of ramshackle restaurants on the beach. **Bar y Comedor La Gaviota** (dishes US$5-8) is by far the more popular (despite maddeningly slow cooking times), but **Margarita's** (dishes US$3-9) next door serves up food that's just as good, slightly quicker.

Hospedaje y Restaurante Blue Sol HOTEL **$**
(☎8508-2727; bluesol@yahoo.com; 100m inland from beach; r US$10) This last-ditch spot offers some seriously basic concrete rooms that are cheap, dark and dirty... But you're just 100m from the beach.

Hostel Camino del Gigante HOTEL **$$**
(☎8712-8888; www.gigantebay.com; 300m south of town entrance on beach; r without bath US$26, r with fan/air-con US$33/60; ❄) With basic rooms, mosquito nets, and fans that can get a little out of control, plus a totally kick-ass lounge area, this is a smart midrange bet. The rooms without bathroom are actually nicer than the rooms that have them, and there's a fun peaced-out vibe.

Dale Dagger's Surf Lodge LODGE **$$$**
(www.nicasurf.com; per week per person from US$1240; ❄@) Surf legend Dale Dagger's setup is a sweet little oceanfront beach house in the middle of the village. It's got three boats on call, so getting to the break you want won't be a drama. Rates include a weekly boat trip to San Juan del Sur (if you're that way inclined), and if the surf isn't up, they take you on fishing trips.

Giant's Foot Surf Camp LODGE **$$$**
(www.giantsfoot.com; per week per person Mar-Sep US$1000, yoga/surfing Nov-Feb US$900; ⏲closed Oct; ❄) Set on the southern end of the beach, this is the largest surf camp in town. Most come here on a set tour, with surfing, boat, transfers, meals and even beer included in the price. The rooms are comfy enough and the beachfront backyard features some good hammocking opportunities.

Aqua Wellness Resort RESORT **$$$**
(☎8739-2426; www.aquanicaragua.com; 1km inland from Playa Gigante; r/penthouse US$170/375; ❄📶🏊) If Tarzan flew a G6, this is how he'd roll. Thirty simple and elegant jungle *cabinas* bathed in hardwoods are built over this large rolling spa and resort. They have tremendous ocean views, a private beach and lush forest on all sides.

Party Wave Gigante CAFE **$**
(100m south of town entrance) This little surf cafe has internet and yummy baked goods.

Santana

The only way to walk to three of the prettiest beaches around – Playa Dorada, Playa Escondida and Playa Rosada – is if you're a guest or resident of plush **Rancho Santana** (☎8882-2885; www.ranchosantana.com; vacation rentals US$100-300; ❄📶🏊). Easily the most successful resort village on the block, it's got clubhouses, rental homes, pools, horses, tennis courts, a helipad and more.

The most famous of the three beaches is Playa Rosada, with pretty pink sand, great surfing and the **Jaro de Leche blowhole**, an odd hydro-geological formation that shoots ocean water several meters into the waves. You'll only see it if you stay here or come in a boat.

Playa Popoyo & Around

Home to one of the most storied waves in Nicaragua, the little town of **Las Salinas de Nagualapa**, named for the salt evaporation ponds you'll pass on the way in, is beginning to feel a bit like a beach town.

Most people continue past town to Playa Guasacate, where a shallow lagoon and slow river shift through the long, sandy beach. It's often called Playa Popoyo in honor of the famed beach break, with right and left point breaks that break huge and hollow over the outer reef when conditions are right. Other named waves include Bus Stop – fast, powerful and unpredictable, it ends in shallow water with a rocky bottom. Cobra, nearby, is another fast wave, breaking left on more rocks. Emergencias, considered the best wave in the region, has a long, smooth left for longboarders and a short, fast, hollow right for shortboarders.

Boards can be rented from La Tiendita, across the road from El Club del Surf, for US$10 per day. It also offers ding repair. You can check www.popoyo.com or www.guasacatesurf.com for surf conditions, beach-house rentals and other area info.

Sleeping

Sunset Villas Hostel HOSTEL $

(☎8464-9428; 5km toward beach from Tola Road; r without bathroom US$10; P wifi) This is the best budget spot in town. There's a beachfront restaurant with plenty of hammocks. The rooms are set in airy bungalows with firm beds, mosquito nets and fun beach vibes.

Hotel Magnific Rock HOTEL $

(☎8916-6916; www.magnificrockpopoyo.com; on top of big rock outcrop on Popoyo Beach; dm/d US$20/70; ❄ wifi) Built on what truly is a magnficient rock, this friendly surfer's hotel has amazing views on all sides of Popoyo beach. The dorm rooms are simple, but good enough, and the doubles have incredible beach views. The restaurant is recommended.

Casa Maur HOSTEL $

(☎8959-0300; www.popoyobeachhostel.com; dm US$10; wifi) The hippest hostel in town, about 1km from the entrance, this friendly beachfront hostel in a converted home has turbo-charged ceiling fans, four-bed dorms, a chillaxed beachfront patio, plenty of hammocks, table tennis and foosball.

Hotel Ola Verde HOTEL $$

(8574-2003; beach; s/d US$24/45; ❄) At the entrance to town on the beach, this simple line of rooms in a boring hotel block is basic but does the trick.

El Club del Surf HOTEL $$

(www.clubdelsurf.com; s/d US$30/40; ❄) Just past Casa Maur, this has spotless and spacious rooms. You're not quite on the beach (which lies about 100m away), but you do get air-con-cooled rooms and a friendly restaurant area, and good beach access at a decent price.

Hotel Punta Teonoste RESORT $$$

(☎2563-9001; www.puntateonoste.com; s/d US$159/193; ❄) If you're a dedicated surfer, and don't mind splashing out every once in a while, try this spot about 4km further on from the turnoff to Guasacate. Bamboo-accented, thatch-roofed *cabinas* have playfully plush interiors and overlook a fierce spire of rock jutting past Playa Conejo's pink-sand beaches.

El Astillero

This picture-per… village, fronting… sand beach, has… **Hamacas** (☎88… com; s/d with fan US… ❄), and it's a go… with wide beachf… ed marine blue r… and spacious bath… of here when turt… …arriving. There's a tourist information center at the center of town.

Refugio de Vida Silvestre Río Escalante-Chacocente

Much less visited than Refugio de Vida Silvestre La Flor, this **wildlife refuge** (☎2532-3293; admission US$5, guide US$3) also gets *arribadas* (flotillas) of more than 3000 nesting olive ridley turtles at one time, as well as more solitary leatherback turtles, which make their nests here between July and December (peaking in August and September). The refuge protects five species of turtle, as well as 48 sq km of dry tropical forests and mangrove swamps.

There's currently no public transportation, and no regularly offered organized tours to the refuge, but if you have a 4WD, you can take a signed rough track 7km north of town here. Or you could walk along the shore 7km from El Astillero.

San Juan del Sur

POP 15,500

This is the hub for exploration of Nicaragua's toned-and-tanned southern Pacific beaches. And while the once sleepy fishing village doesn't have an amazing beach – you need to head either 30 minutes north or south for that – it does have the best restaurants and nightlife around.

The town itself, with its clapboard Victorian houses and steady influx of young and beautiful international travelers and scenesters, is quite fun. The half-moon brown-sugar beach provides splendid sunset views. Top it all off with a towering statue of Christ on a neighboring hillside and you have all the workings to kick off an amazing adventure in paradise.

ING IN SAN JUAN DEL SUR

pportunities abound here. Some require several months commitment. nline.

lioteca Móvil (☎2568-2338; www.sjdsbiblioteca.org; Calle Iglesia, frente Parque Central) olunteers are needed to distribute books, teach English and work in the library.

Comunidad Connect (☎2568-2731; www.comunidadconnect.org) Can arrange all-inclusive 'voluntourism' packages (including placement, Spanish-language classes, homestays, transport etc).

Fundación A Jean Brugger (www.fundacionajbrugger.org) Runs a variety of programs – time commitments and language requirements vary.

Newton-San Juan del Sur Sister City Project (www.newtonsanjuan.org) Help build ecofriendly toilets and water systems.

Sights

SJDS' several square blocks of souvenir shops and businesses are worth a wander; drop by **Iglesia San Juan Bautista** (Calle Central), with a shady park right out front, for your cultural pit stop.

Christ of Mercy Statue MONUMENT
(2km north of San Juan del Sur; admission US$2; ⏲8am-5pm) This 25m statue of Jesus – one of the tallest in the world – overlooks the town. Take the one-hour hike up to catch a great bird's-eye (or son of God's eye) view of the harbor and ocean.

Activities

Surfing

The best surfing is generally April to December, but waves are less crowded in the low season. There's a beach break on bigger swells at the northern end of the beach, but most surfers hire boats or stay at the beaches north and south of town. Casa Oro Hostel runs a daily shuttle out to Playa Maderas.

Arena Caliente SURFING
(☎8815-3247; www.arenacaliente.com; Mercado, ½c N) Everyone loves this locally owned and operated shop, which rents boards and arranges group transportation to the best breaks.

Good Times Surf Shop SURFING
(☎8980-2951; Gato Negro, 100m S) Organizes half-/full-day trips to less-crowded, outlying beaches such as Hermosa and Yanqui for US$25/45 per person, shuttles to nearby spots (US$5 to US$10), rentals (US$10 per day) and lessons (US$30 per hour).

Swimming & Diving

The beach in town is OK; head to the northern end for the best swimming – and watch for boat traffic.

Neptune Watersports DIVING
(www.neptunewsn.com; Mercado 1c O, 10m N; 2-tank dive US$85) Check here for dives and boat excursions.

Hiking

The **Old Lighthouse Hike** takes you up an obvious trail that begins at the fishing port. It crosses private property, so you'll need to request access on the trail, and possibly pay for the use.

Sound like too much work? Try the **antennas trail**: ask the driver of any Rivas-bound bus to let you off at 'Bocas de las Montañas.' Follow the dirt road through jungle and pasture up to the radio antennas, from where you have similarly stunning views. This is a serious, all-day proposition – take plenty of water, a sun hat and snacks.

A slightly less hard-core expedition starts at the north of town, heading for the spectacular lookout at the Christ of Mercy Statue. Cross the pedestrian bridge north of town and follow signs up.

There's a spectacular **petroglyph** not far from town. Walk toward Rivas, passing the Texaco station, and make a left after the bridge. Pass a school and then a gate on your right. Continue to the old farmhouse; if anyone's around, you should ask permission to cross the land. Follow the irrigation pipes to the river, where you'll find the stone, showing an enormous and elaborate hunting scene.

Biking

Mountain-bike hire (per day US$6) is available from Hospedaje Elizabeth, perfect for the dirt roads heading to the northern and southern beaches. You can take your bike on buses that run between SJDS and El Ostional, as well as the little river ferry at the northern end of the SJDS beach.

Turtle-Watching

Between July and December – peaking in August and September – some 30,000 female olive ridley turtles and a few hundred very endangered leatherback turtles visit nearby Refugio de Vida Silvestre La Flor to nest. Several San Juan del Sur hotels, including Casa Oro Hostel, run nighttime tours, including transportation, entry fees and guide, for around US$25 per person.

Fishing

If you look south, you'll see an enormous peninsula jutting out into the sea, a wall of rock that hems in currents and the critters that ride them, including sailfish and dorado (best June through October), yellow-fin tuna (April and May) and marlin (August and September). In addition to the pricier professional operations at the surf and dive shops in town, you can always book a trip with local fishers more cheaply.

Courses

Check bulletin boards at hostels for cheaper private Spanish-language instruction.

Zen Yoga YOGA
(☎8465-1846; www.zenyoganicaragua.com; frente Parque Central; yoga US$8, massage US$35) Zen out at this urban yoga retreat.

Casa de Cultura COURSE
(Av del Mar s/n) Check this arts center for classes, arts exhibits and more.

Escuela Español San Juan del Sur COURSE
(☎8639-7377; int Casa de Cultura; 20hr with/without homestay US$165/100) Activities, which cost an extra US$30 per week, include beach trips and tours to Ometepe, Granada and Rivas. There are also free activities like city tours, and dance and cooking classes.

APC Spanish School LANGUAGE COURSE
(☎8450-8990; www.apcspanishschoolsjs.com; int Restaurante Lago Azul; 20hr with/without homestay US$195/120, per hour US$8) This fun operation offers tours, a cultural center and volunteer opportunities.

Spanish Corner School LANGUAGE COURSE
(☎2568-2142; chrisrodriguez80@gmail.com; Calle Iglesia, Parque Central, ½c O; class per 1hr/20hr US$8/100) Lessons here are more focused on history and culture.

Tours

Casa Oro Hostel TOUR
(☎2568-2415; www.casaeloro.com; Av del Cine, Parque Central, 1c O, 50m N) Offers budget excursions, including sailing tours and fishing trips, turtle-watching tours and more.

Da Flying Frog CANOPY TOUR
(☎8613-4460; daflyingfrog@hotmail.com; per person US$30; ⊙8am-4pm Mon-Sat) This canopy tour has 17 platforms and 2.5km of cables, making it one of the biggest ziplines in the country. The longest single zip is 328m and the fastest clocked time here is a cool 70km/h. The horseback ride up includes a peek at one of the more impressive petroglyphs in the area.

Rana Tours BOAT TOUR
(☎2568-2066; ranatours@gmail.com; Av del Mar s/n) Offers water-taxi services out to Bahía Majagual and Playas Maderas, Marcella and Hermosa (per person US$15 to US$20). Can also arrange private surfing (full day US$250), fishing (three hours US$120) or snorkeling expeditions (three hours US$120).

Festivals & Events

St John the Baptist RELIGIOUS
(⊙June 24) SJDS's patron offers another excuse to party.

Procession of the Virgin of Carmen RELIGIOUS
(⊙July 16) The Virgin – patron saint of fishers – is taken aboard a local ship at 2pm, placed on an altar decorated with fishing nets and poles, and taken on a sailing trip around the bay to bless the boats; seafood and mariachi music are involved.

Sleeping

This is one of the few destinations in Nicaragua with pronounced seasonal rates: prices rise dramatically during the December to March high season and double for Semana Santa and Christmas. Bargain for deals during the rainy season.

San Juan del Sur

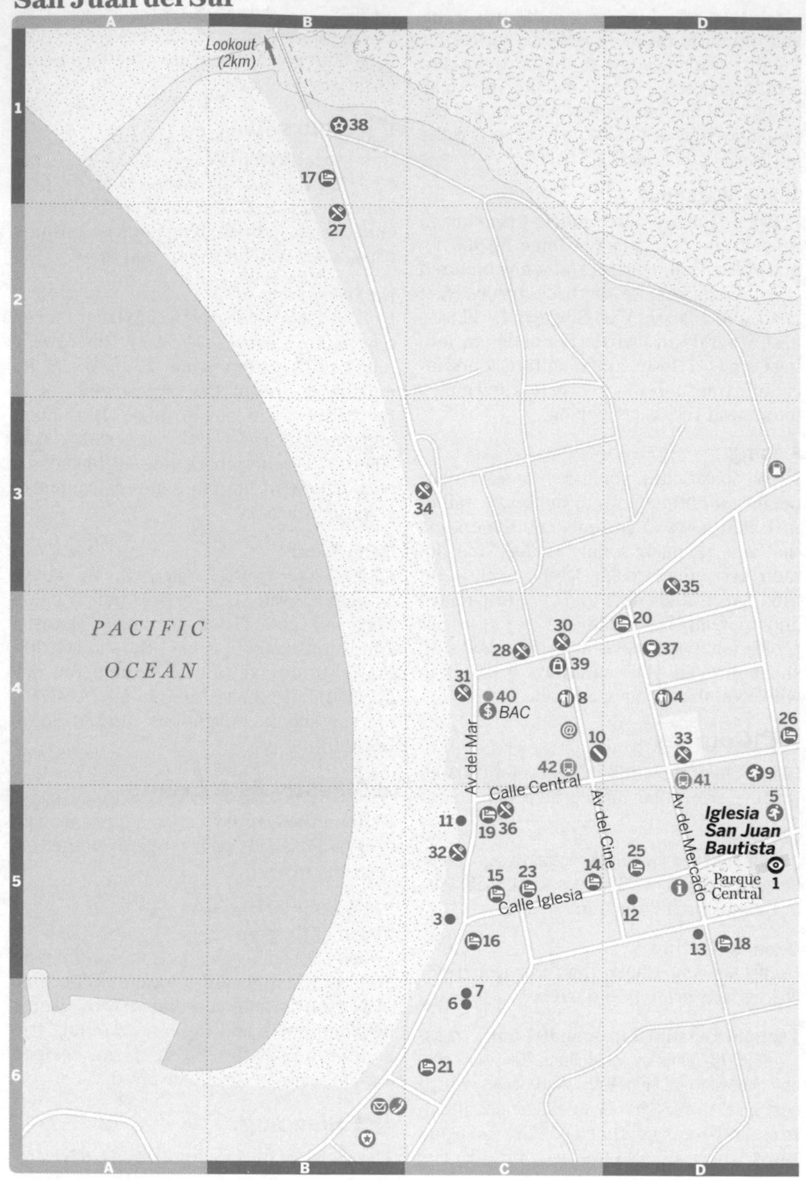

Casa Oro Hostel HOSTEL $
(2568-2415; www.casaeloro.com; Av del Cine, Parque Central, 1c O, 50m N; dm US$8-9, d with fan/air-con US$28/35, all incl breakfast;) This backpacker standby has all the amenities – great info center, discount internet, kitchen, and lounge areas. Rooftop bar (party ends at 11pm), and good vibes 24/7.

Hostel Esperanza HOSTEL $
(8754-6816; www.hostelesperanza.com; Av del Mar s/n; dm US$8-9, d with/without bathroom US$25/18;

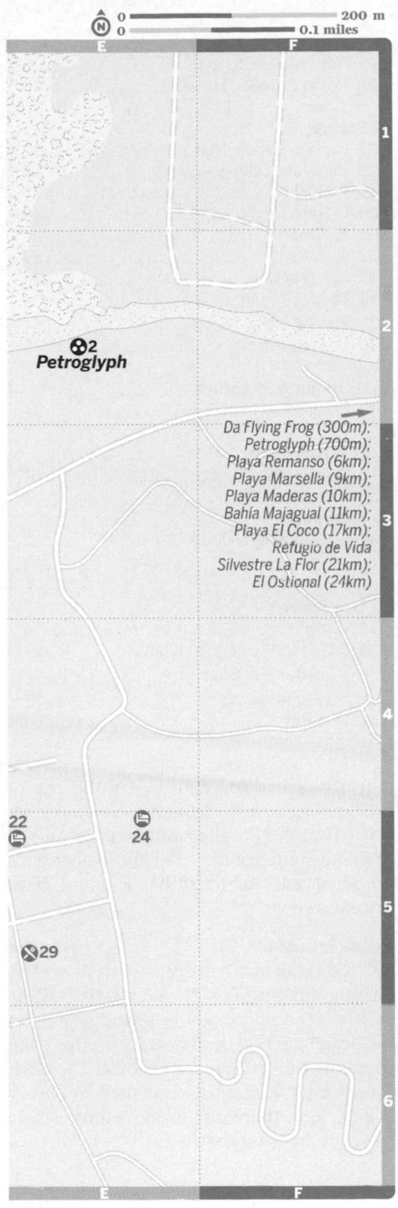

) This up-and-coming hostel has a great location right across the street from the beach. It also has clean, simple rooms, a fun central garden area and a shared kitchen. You won't go wrong staying here. The dorms are pretty big (14 and nine beds each) so bring your earplugs.

Posada Puesto del Sol GUESTHOUSE **$**
(2568-2532; lalacard98@yahoo.com; Calle Iglesia, Iglesia, 1½c O; r per person US$10;) Smallish but lovingly decorated rooms in a family home. Some share a bathroom with one other – ask to look around if this is a problem. It can get hot here.

Hotel Estrella HOTEL **$**
(2568-2210; infosanjuan10@gmail.com; Av del Mar, Mercado, 2c O; r per person without bathroom US$8-10) This high-ceilinged century-old landmark is a basic, atavistic beauty with run-down rooms and wonderful balconies with some of the best views in town. Bathrooms are downstairs in the backyard.

El Coco Azul HOTEL **$$**
(2568-2697; www.elcocoazul.com; Calle Iglesia s/n; d US$58, without bathroom US$46;) Run by the folks at Posada Azul, this young and affordable sister boutique has detail-oriented service, colorful common areas, and clean and airy rooms in a contemporary-style setting just 30m from the beach.

Hotel La Dolce Vita HOTEL **$$**
(2568-2649; ladolcevitahotel.sjs@gmail.com; Texaco station, 1c O; d/tr US$30/45;) Brightly painted in attractive shades of blue and yellow, this is one of the better-looking hotels in town. Rooms are on the small side but face onto a cheery courtyard that converts into a good Italian restaurant at night. Service drops when the bosses are away.

Royal Chateau Hotel HOTEL **$$**
(2568-2551; www.hotelroyalchateau.com; Texaco station, 3c S; s/d with fan US$44/50, with air-con US$50/57;) Bright and spacious modern rooms set around a palm-studded parking area. If your legs can take the climb, go for a top-floor room, highlighted by naive art, for sweeping bay views.

Hotel Encanto del Sur HOTEL **$$**
(2568-2222; www.hotelencantodelsur.com; Av del Mercado, Parque Central ½c S; r with fan/air-con US$25/40;) Not a bad deal, this basic cement hotel block is a short walk from all the action. Downstairs rooms can be a bit dark, but get one upstairs at the front and you'll be happy with the clean, spacious layout, cable TV and spotless bathrooms.

★**La Posada Azul** HISTORIC HOTEL **$$$**
(2568-2698; www.laposadazul.com; Calle Iglesia s/n; d US$105;) This classy converted Victorian boutique is located just a half

San Juan del Sur

Top Sights

1 Iglesia San Juan Bautista ... D5
2 Petroglyph ... E2

Activities, Courses & Tours

3 APC Spanish School ... C5
4 Arena Caliente ... D4
5 Biblioteca Móvil ... D5
6 Casa de Cultura ... C6
Casa Oro Hostel ... (see 14)
7 Escuela Español San Juan del Sur ... C6
8 Good Times Surf Shop ... C4
9 Mountain Bike Hire ... D4
10 Neptune Watersports ... C4
11 Rana Tours ... C5
12 Spanish Corner School ... D5
13 Zen Yoga ... D5

Sleeping

14 Casa Oro Hostel ... C5
15 El Coco Azul ... C5
16 Hostel Esperanza ... C5
17 Hotel Ana Mar ... B1
18 Hotel Encanto del Sur ... D5
19 Hotel Estrella ... C5
20 Hotel La Dolce Vita ... D4
21 Hotel Victoriano ... C6
22 Hotel Villa Isabella ... E5
23 La Posada Azul ... C5
24 Pelican Eyes ... E5
25 Posada Puesto del Sol ... D5
26 Royal Chateau Hotel ... D4

Eating

27 Bambu Beach Club ... B2
28 Big Wave Dave's ... C4
29 El Colibrí ... E5
30 El Gato Negro ... C4
31 El Timón Bar ... C4
32 Josselin's ... C5
33 Mercado ... D4
34 Mesón Español ... C3
35 Pan de Vida ... D3
36 Super Frutto ... C5

Drinking & Nightlife

37 Traditional Irish Bar ... D4

Entertainment

38 Crazy Crab Disco ... B1

Shopping

39 El Gato Negro Coffee Shop & Book Store ... C4

Transport

40 Alamo ... C4
41 Buses to Rivas, Managua & Northern & Southern Beaches ... D4
42 Tica Bus ... C4

block from the beach. In the rooms, vaulted ceilings, tasteful island decorations and whimsical artwork make for good sleeps, and the gardens and pool area out back provide a lush retreat in the heart of the city. To top it off, the breakfast is quite simply amazing.

Pelican Eyes RESORT **$$$**
(2563-7000, ext 310; www.pelicaneyesresort.com; d US$180-200, houses US$320-360;) With sweeping bay views and fairly fabulous *casas* (houses) featuring hacienda-style furnishings, kitchens, terraces and satellite TV, this resort is the best in town. For the price, we only wish you were beachside. It has three pools, bookstores, a spa, two restaurants and plenty to keep you busy, along with a nearby nature reserve.

Hotel Victoriano HISTORIC HOTEL **$$$**
(2568-2005; www.hotelvictoriano.com; Enitel, 20m N; s with/without view US$150/130, d with/without view US$160/140;) Looking more like something out of a fairy tale than a real building, this wooden classic dates back to 1902 and used to be one of the Somoza family's fabulous weekend getaways. If you've got the cash, splash it on one of the upstairs rooms – the four-poster beds are plush and the small bay windows have priceless views.

Hotel Ana Mar HOTEL **$$$**
(2568-2096; www.hotelanamar.com; Av del Mar, Hotel Casa Blanca, 700m N; r incl breakfast US$70;) The only hotel in town actually on the beach offers a good deal for groups – the rooms can sleep up to four people! The brick rooms are OK-sized and painted in cheery colors, and there are some sandy, shady hangout areas out back. The beachside pool is sweet.

Hotel Villa Isabella HOTEL **$$$**
(2568-2568; www.villaisabellasjds.com; Iglesia, ½c E; d US$85;) Spacious, comfortably decorated island-style rooms in a classic old house at the top of town. The pool is for dipping purposes only, but the cool tranquility of the place makes it one of the better options in town.

Eating

★Super Frutto ICE CREAM $
(Calle Central s/n; ice cream US$2-3) The best gelato in all of Nicaragua is served up at this after-dinner favorite. Note: in the heat, you are better off avoiding cones.

El Gato Negro SANDWICHES $
(Texaco station, 2c O; sandwiches & light meals US$4-6) The coolest cafe around has a great selection of espresso-based drinks, yummy cakes, comfy lounges, and a large selection of new and used books for sale.

Pan de Vida BAKERY $
(Entrance Rd; baked items US$1-3; 8am-6pm) Stop by this bakery for the best breads in town.

Mercado MARKET
(Dishes US$2-4) For the cheapest meals in town.

El Colibrí INTERNATIONAL $$
(Texaco station, 5c S; dishes US$7-10; dinner Tue-Sun;) One of the best menus in town can be found at this relaxed indoor-outdoor Mediterranean restaurant. The regular dishes are good and the specials board is always full of winners – try the stuffed bell peppers (US$7.50) or the succulent filet mignon with gorgonzola cream sauce (US$10). Also on offer is a small but good selection of vegetarian dishes.

Mesón Español SPANISH $$
(Av del Mar s/n; mains US$6-13; 11am-10:30pm) One of the more upscale beachfront eateries, this tapas joint also has a good selection of beef and seafood on offer. Try the paella or *tortilla española*.

Josselin's SEAFOOD $$
(Av del Mar, frente Hotel Estrella; dishes US$5-10) This beachfront joint has great *arroz marinero* (seafood rice), a riot of shrimp, lobster, fish and squid.

Big Wave Dave's BURGERS $$
(Texaco station, 2½c O; dishes US$5-8; Tue-Sun) A looong-time expat favorite, Dave serves up all sorts of comfort food including excellent burgers and big breakfasts. A healthy mix of foreigners and locals gather here at night to knock back beers till the wee hours.

El Timón Bar SEAFOOD $$$
(Av del Mar, frente Landmark Inn; dishes US$5-16) This excellent beach restaurant is the place to go for an upmarket seafood dinner.

Bambu Beach Club FUSION $$$
(Av del Mar, Hotel Casa Blanca, 600m N; dishes US$7-12) Mixing Asian, Italian and Nicaraguan influences, this superhip beachside hangout has some of the best food and coolest tunes in town. There's also a book exchange (two for one) and a tiny swimming pool.

Drinking & Nightlife

Most of the beachfront restaurants double as bars and lounges.

Traditional Irish Bar IRISH PUB
(Av del Mercado s/n) Don't think you would find this one in Dublin, but it does its best.

Entertainment

Crazy Crab Disco DANCE
(final, Av del Mar; Fri-Sun) The original SJDS disco. The mirrored balls and colored lights start spinning at 9pm, but the in-crowd doesn't show up until at least 11pm, primed for an all-night party. This area's a bit desolate – it's best to get a cab home.

Shopping

El Gato Negro Coffee Shop & Book Store BOOKS
(Texaco station, 2c O) New and some used books in English and other languages.

Information

Don't walk alone on the beach at night you're just asking for trouble. And when you head home from the bar, walk in a large group and ask for a cab.

Casa Oro Hostel (p130) is a good spot for information.

BAC (Av del Mar, Hotel Casa Blanca) There's a MasterCard-friendly ATM at Hotel Casa Blanca.

Claro (Av del Mar s/n) Telephone.

Cyber Leo's (Av del Cine, Gato Negro, ½c S; per hour US$1)

Intur (Calle Iglesia, frente Parque Central) Well stocked with brochures and willing (if not always able) to answer questions about the town and surrounds.

Police (2453-3732, 8453-3732; final, Av del Mar)

San Juan del Sur Info (www.sanjuandelsur.org.ni) English-language, traveler-savvy site that has links to several area businesses.

Santini Lavandería (Calle Iglesia s/n) Laundry priced by the eye.

Getting There & Around

Getting to the beaches north and south of town can be expensive, so ask at the surf shops if they have a boat going with extra space for you. Casa Oro Hostel's regular beach shuttle to Playa Maderas (return US$5) leaves at 8:15am, 10:45am, 1pm and 5pm.

Work is underway to open an international border to Costa Rica on the road south of El Ostional – keep your ears open.

BUS

Tica Bus (www.ticabus.com; Calle Central s/n) has an office here to buy tickets from Rivas to Costa Rica.

Bus service to the beaches depends very much on road conditions – if you're here in the wet season, you may find it drastically reduced (or even cancelled). There is regular bus service from the bus stop in front of the market to destinations including the following:

Managua (*expreso* US$3.30, three hours, 4:30am, 5am, 5:30am, 6am and 7am; *ordinario* US$2.50, four hours, 8am to 6:15pm, at least hourly)

Northern beaches (US$1, two hours, 10:30am and 1pm) Service to Toro Mixcal, Playa Nacascolo, Playa Marsella, Playa Maderas (Los Playones), Majagual, Playa Ocotal and Rivas.

Rivas (US$1, 40 minutes, 5am to 5pm, every 25 minutes)

Southern beaches (US$1, two hours, 1:10pm, 3pm and 4:30pm) Service to Empalme de Remanso, Playa El Coco, Refugio de Vida Silvestre La Flor and El Ostional; returning buses leave El Ostional at 5am, 6am and 4pm.

Shuttle Bus

Big Wave Dave's offers shuttles to Managua, Granada and Masaya (US$25) leaving at 7am. Casa Oro Hostel has shuttles to Granada (US$15), Rivas (US$5), Managua (US$30) and San Jorge (US$7). Book well in advance for either of these options.

CAR

Alamo (www.alamonicaragua.com; Av del Mar) rents sedans/4WDs for US$45/80 per day. It would be hard not to get a better deal in Managua or Granada.

TAXI

The Taxi Cooperative of San Juan del Sur charges US$0.70 to anywhere in town, US$1.50 for *colectivos* to Rivas. Each driver has a list of set rates for other destinations, including Morgan's Rock (US$20), Playa El Coco or Refugio de Vida Silvestre La Flor (US$40), El Ostional (US$50), the Costa Rican border (US$25), Masaya or Granada (US$50) and Managua (US$80). Taxis congregate close to the market.

Beaches North of San Juan del Sur

If you're taking the bus out to these beaches, bear in mind that there'll be at least a 2km walk from the bus stop to the water. Hitching is common (but traffic isn't), though you can always put a bike on top of the bus and do it that way.

Playa Nacascolo

Although access to Playa Nacascolo is privately owned, cooler than average **Nicaragua Properties** (www.realestatenicaragua.com) actually allows visitors onto the property to cross (for now); ask at the entrance and guards will give you directions to Las Miradores waterfall.

Playa Marsella

This beautiful beach lies about 9km north of San Juan del Sur. The water is calm and it makes for a good swimming spot. Although the best surfing is just north, at Playa Maderas (go back out to the road; you can't walk around the point), there's a good estuary break right here.

Sleeping & Eating

Hotel Villa Mar HOTEL **$$$**
(8392-1225; hotel.villamar@hotmail.com; r US$80;) This is across the road from the estuary, close enough to the beach for you to get rocked to sleep by the sound of crashing waves – ask for a room out front. Rooms are plain but comfortable with cool tiled floors. Check at the restaurant for area tours.

Pacific Bay Hotel HOTEL **$$$**
(8251-5728; www.pacificbayhotel.com; entrance to town; d US$87-150, apt US$315; P) As you descend into town, this resort-style hotel on the hillside is hard to miss. It has excellent views of the bay below from most of the hotel (though only a few rooms actually give you wake-up calls of rolling waves). The cozy, well-appointed rooms have all the conveniences you could ask for, and the pool is incredible!

Rancho Marsella NICARAGUAN **$**
(dishes US$3-5; 8am-8pm) Rancho Marsella serves simple meals and cool drinks beachfront.

Playa Maderas

A good-time-vibes backpacker and surfer hangout, this stunning beach, with rocky expanses that offer excellent tide pooling and wide, wonderful sandy stretches for sunbathing, is famed for having one of the best beach breaks in the country. Yes, you should expect some crowds.

Activities

Sometimes called Los Playones, it's a slow wave in fairly deep (2m) water, good for beginners, with two right and two left breaks that get hollow on a rising tide.

If the swell is really big on a low to medium tide, there's a faster, intermediate-level reef break between Madera and Majagual called Panga Drops, accessible by boat only, that offers an awesome ride before dumping you onto the rocky shallows. It gets choppy and you can be caught in the shore break, so watch the wind. Waves get big – as do crowds, and it doesn't hold a crowd well.

Many surf shops and hostels in San Juan del Sur offer shuttles here.

Rebelde Surf Schools SURFING
(200m inland from beach) Rents surfboards (per day US$10) and gives instruction.

Sleeping & Eating

Casa Maderas Ecolodge LODGE **$**
(☎8786-4897; www.casamaderas.com; dm/d/tr/q/ste US$13.50/39/49/60/69;) This place, about 800m before you hit the beach, is worth a look. Set on 3 hectares of lush jungle and terraced permaculture, it does rustic-modern to perfection. Six-bed dorms are spacious, with double beds, mossie nets and stylish bathrooms. The cabin-style private huts on the hillside are some of the best in town.

There's also a shared kitchen, yoga classes and free beach shuttle.

Hotel 3 Hermanos HOSTEL **$**
(☎8879-5272; los3hermanosarena@hotmail.com; beachfront; dm US$10) Shoestringing surfers love this rasta-bar restaurant and hostel, just steps away from one of the country's best breaks. The break-down basic upstairs dorm rooms have balconies overlooking the beach and catch the ocean breeze.

Café Revolución CAMPGROUND **$**
(100m inland from beach; campsites per person US$2;) This catch-all restaurant offers wi-fi (US$2), yoga (US$10), pizza (US$6 to US$10) and cheap camping spots that include use of the restaurant's bathrooms.

Buena Vista Surf Club GUESTHOUSE **$$$**
(☎8863-4180; www.buenavistasurfclub.com; rates on application) Where the road dips after Parque Maderas, take a right to get to this spot with awesome views over the bay. It's a small, upscale lodge offering just three rooms – two of them 'treehouses' (stilted *cabinas* snuggled into the forest, and decked out with beautiful woods, huge mirrors and great beds) and one room in the main house.

Tacos Locos MEXICAN **$$**
(beachfront; dishes US$6-14) Great fish-taco shop overlooking the beach. Look who's getting crazy now, ese!

Bahía Majagual

This beautiful bay with its steep white-sand beach is perfect for swimming (watch the rip current, though), but only has OK surfing – you'll need to walk all of 10 minutes to the big breaks. Tourist services are severely limited here

A beloved family-run option, the smurf-village **Matilda's** (☎8456-3461; permatents per person US$6-7, s/d US$15/25) rents concrete 1.2m-high surfer huts and basic rooms. Traditional Nicaraguan food is available for US$3.50 and there's kitchen access for guests.

Playa Ocotal

The best way to visit this shady cove beach is by booking a cabin at the very best hotel in Nicaragua, **Morgan's Rock** (☎2254-7989; www.morgansrock.com; s/d from US$224/360). Yes, it's ridiculously expensive, but you're staying in the poshest dream cabin ever, gleaming with precious woods and dappled with the forest light, which filters through the parrot- and monkey-filled jungle canopy right into your screened-in porch.

Follow the signs to Majagual and turn right after passing a black-and-yellow gate; continue until you get to the beach.

Arena Blanca

With some of the clearest water and whitest sand on the Pacific coast, this little inlet is only accessible by rented boat or along a very rough dirt road across very private property – ask permission. At the northern end of the beach is Punta Manzanillo, also called Punta Reloj, a point break that may work around midtide if swells are big enough.

Beaches South of San Juan del Sur

Although there is regular bus service between San Juan del Sur and El Ostional, you'll still need to walk several kilometers from the bus stop to most of the beaches; only Playa El Coco and La Flor are close to the road. The road is being paved with the hopes of opening an international border here.

Playa Remanso

The most accessible in a cluster of pretty beaches, this crescent of white sand has OK surfing, interesting caves, and good swimming and tide pooling. The smallish beach break would be good for beginners if it weren't so crowded. Word is you can camp on the beach for free (but watch your belongings). There are no hotels here, but you can check online for a **private beach house rental** (remansobeach@gmail.com).

Playa Tamarindo

The next beach south, Playa Tamarindo, a half-hour walk from Playa Remanso, is generally less crowded; surfers come with the rising tide to try for a long wave with right and left breaks, which can get hollow coming off the rock wall when swells are under 1m.

Playa Hermosa

This **beach** (admission US$3) with it's own surf camp has some dope-ass surfing (with five breaks on the beach alone), a cool lost-beach-in-paradise vibe and plenty of toned surfers running around. Check at the Playa Hermosa Beach Hotel for surf rentals (US$10) and horseback-riding trips (US$12).

Sleeping

★Playa Hermosa Beach Hotel HOSTEL **$$**
(8671-3327; www.playahermosabeachhotel.com; dm/d incl breakfast US$21/52) This is the best beach hostel on the southern Pacific coast of Nicaragua. The open-air six-bed dorm rooms in this rustic paradise catch the breeze to stay cool at night. Private rooms upstairs have giant mosquito nets (ask for the oceanfront room). There's a great vibe and surf scene here, with a chilled-out open-air restaurant.

Transfers to and from San Juan del Sur are included in the price.

Playa El Coco

This is a world-class beach, a spectacular stretch of sparkling sand punctuated by cliffs so pretty that they grace about half of the country's tourist literature. Prices here are steep (and the accommodations aren't actually as nice as the price tag would have you think).

Sleeping & Eating

Lug's Place HOTEL **$$**
(8381-6976; www.lugsplace.com; r without bathroom US$25, with air-con US$75;) Your best option in town is located on the southern section of the beach. The rooms are really simple – a brick room with a ceiling fan and clean sheets – with two new upper-scale options on the way. The bar and lounge are a good bet, with cheap(ish) international fare (US$6 to US$18). Check here for private house rentals and camping.

Parque Maritimo El Coco CABINS **$$$**
(8999-8069; www.playaelcoco.com.ni; bungalows US$80, cabins US$115-200; P) This place sprawls along a shallow ravine at the northern end of the beach, with around 20 rustic bungalows dotted through the trees. The beachfront bungalows have sofa sleepers, great views and are worth the price. Otherwise look elsewhere. Groups note: bungalows sleep four, you can put five to 10 (very small) people in a cabin.

Coco Cabañas CABINS **$$$**
(2276-5229; across street from beach; cabins US$90-150;) These simple *cabinas* are way overpriced, but give you another option in town. Most *cabinas* can sleep up to four people and include use of a kitchen.

Puesto del Sol SEAFOOD **$$$**
(lunch special US$5, dishes US$15-30) This is a casual beachfront eatery with lackadasical service, cheap lunch specials and specialty items like lobster tails that are not worth the price.

Refugio de Vida Silvestre La Flor

One of the principal laying grounds for endangered olive ridley and leatherback turtles, this **wildlife refuge** (☎8419-1014; admission US$8, campsites per tent US$20) is 20km south of San Juan del Sur. It's easy to visit on a guided tour from San Juan del Sur, or you can stay in the attractive campground. Park guards sell water and soft drinks, but there's no food or insect repellent, so come prepared.

Turtles lay their eggs here, usually between 9pm and 2am, between July and January, peaking in September and October. Leatherbacks usually arrive solo, but olive ridleys generally come in *arribadas,* when more than 3000 of them pack the beaches at a time. Some people time these arrivals by moon cycles, but no one really knows for sure until the ladies arrive; call the ranger station if you want to be sure.

When there aren't any turtles around, the park still has an attractive, undeveloped beach, a couple of monkeys on-site and a few short trails; there's a decent beach break (right and left) at the northern end. It's off-limits during turtle season.

El Ostional

This fishing village, practically a stone's throw from the Costa Rican border, has an attractive brown-sugar beach with a well-known point break called 'Los Senos' (the Breasts) that's best at midtide, with decent-sized swells. You can arrange accommodations and tours here with **Coopertur** (☎8353-7091; communitytours@yahoo.es; north end of beach; homestay per person per night US$10), a homegrown, community-based ecotourism initiative, but if you just turn up you should be able to find a place to stay.

Coopertur also offers kayak tours (US$10, 2.5 hours), guides (US$10 per tour – required), hiking (US$10, two hours), turtle tours (US$35) and boat trips (per hour US$40).

The rooms at **Manta Raya** (☎8353-7091; north end of beach; s/d/tr US$15/25/35) are quite basic (a bed, fan and lamp), but some come with ocean views (and a slight breeze).

Buses go from the Parque Central to San Juan del Sur (US$1.50, one hour, 5:30am, 7am, noon and 3:20pm).

León & Northwestern Nicaragua

Includes ➡

Best Places to Eat

- ➡ Mesón Real (p153)
- ➡ Fritanga La Parrillada (p162)
- ➡ El Mediterraneo (p153)

Best Places to Stay

- ➡ Tortuga Booluda (p149)
- ➡ Surfing Turtle Lodge (p155)
- ➡ Rancho Tranquilo (p167)

Why Go?

This is Nicaragua at its fieriest and most passionate. The regional capital of León is – and will always be – a hotbed of intellectualism and independence. The city has nourished some of Nicaragua's most important political and artistic moments. Less polished but somehow more profound than its age-old rival Granada, the city is beloved for its grand cathedral, breathtaking art museum, hopping nightlife and spirited revolutionary air.

Just out of León, more than a dozen volcanic peaks wait to be climbed (or surfed). This region has some of the best beach accommodation – and gnarliest surfing – in the country. And the virgin wetlands of the Reserva Natural Isla Juan Venado are not to be missed.

Further afield, you'll find the biggest mangrove forest in Central America, awe-inspiring beauty at Reserva Natural Volcán Cosigüina and unique windows into everyday Nicaraguan life in the little towns along the way.

When to Go

December is good for cool temperatures. This is the hottest part of the country, with daytime temperatures just above 30°C (86°F) almost year-round, spiking in sweltering April and dipping into the relatively cool mid-20s (mid-70s) in December.

October and November are the peak months to see nesting turtles at the Reserva Natural Estero Padre Ramos – the whole season lasts between July and December. This is also a good time to think about volunteering as a beach warden or visiting Reserva Natural Isla Juan Venado.

Semana Santa (Holy Week) is held in late March to early April, and Easter week is a Technicolor dreamscape in León. There are sawdust 'carpets' in colonial suburbs, and a sandcastle competition at a nearby beach.

History

The Maribios people were the first inhabitants of what is now León, in the township/suburb of Subtiava. After a series of volcanic eruptions led to the evacuation of the original city of León (now called León Viejo), this site was chosen. It turned out to be a good choice – Subtiava provided plenty of indigenous labor, it was far enough from the ocean to prevent the pirate attacks that had plagued Granada, and the volcanoes were distant and dormant enough not to threaten the city.

León has produced various heroes, most famously poet Rubén Darío, but also independence fighter Miguel Larreynaga (look for him on the 10-córdoba note) and Luisa Amanda Espinoza, the first female Frente Sandinista de Liberación Nacional (Sandinista National Liberation Front; FSLN) member to die in combat. A Sandinista stronghold, the city saw some of the toughest battles during the revolution, documented in the city's murals, museums and bullet-pocked walls.

Despite León's status as a religious and academic center (and the fact that it had been the nation's capital for 242 years), it was Chinandega, to the north, that was chosen as the meeting place for the ill-fated Confederation of American States in the 19th century. Chinandega's claim to fame as the 'city of oranges' waned in the 20th century, as cotton became the principal crop. This in turn changed as world cotton prices plummeted and farmers turned to sugarcane and peanuts, the region's main crops to this day.

El Corinto – these days Nicaragua's busiest commercial port – has entered the history books in a big way twice: first when it was the landing site for William Dampier and a band of French and British pirates in the only recorded pirate attack on León, and second when US president Ronald Reagan ordered the illegal mining of the bay, which set in motion a series of machinations that would eventually lead to the Iran-Contra affair.

LEÓN

POP 201,100 / ELEV 110M

Intensely political, buzzing with energy and, at times, drop-dead gorgeous (in a crumbling, colonial kind of way), León is what Managua should be – a city of awe-inspiring churches, fabulous art collections, stunning streetscapes, cosmopolitan eateries, fiery intellectualism, and all-week, walk-everywhere, happening nightlife. Many people fall in love with Granada, but most of them leave their heart in León.

History

Originally located on the slopes of Volcán Momotombo, León committed some of the Spanish conquest's cruelest excesses; even other conquistadors suggested that León's punishment was divine retribution. When the mighty volcano reduced León to rubble

THE CITY OF CHURCHES

With more than 16 places to pray, including several more in Barrio Subtiava, the city tourist board is lobbying to have León officially declared 'The City of Churches.'

The 1639 **Iglesia de San Francisco** is one of the oldest in the city, a national heritage site with lots of gold, a gorgeous nave and a rather rococo interior. It was abandoned between 1830 and 1881, then refurbished with two elaborate altarpieces for San Antonio and Nuestra Señora de La Merced (Our Lady of Mercy). The attached **Convent San Francisco**, founded in 1639, was badly damaged during the 1979 battle for León. Check out what used to be the convent at Hotel El Convento.

Nuestra Señora de Guadalupe, built in 1743, is León's only church oriented north–south, and it's historically connected to the city by the 1850 **Puente Guadalupe**, built across the Río Chiquito. And don't let the dumpy, modernist, neoclassic exterior of 1625 **Capilla San Juan de Dios** (1a Calle SO) fool you – when it's open, the interior is one of the city's prettiest, with lots of precious wood and a very human scale.

For something completely different, swing by ultra-Gothic 1884 **Iglesia Zaragoza**, one of the best spots for film students to stage a vampire flick. They could also use one of the several ruined churches around town, including **Ruinas Veracruz** and Iglesia Santiago (p146) in Barrio Subtiava, and **Ruinas San Sebastian**, near La XXI (the 21st Garrison).

León & Northwestern Nicaragua Highlights

1. Climb one of the spectacular volcanic peaks of the **Maribios chain** (p158) and sandboard back down again
2. Get away from it all in a beachside cabin at **Playa Jiquilillo** (p166) or **Mechapa** (p167)
3. Take in some street art in mural-infested **León** (p139)
4. Kayak through Central America's largest mangrove forest in **Reserva Natural Estero Padre Ramos** (p167)
5. Soak those aching bones in Potosí hot springs after climbing **Volcán Cosigüina** (p168)
6. Give back with a day or year of **volunteering** (p152) in the many nonprofits based in León

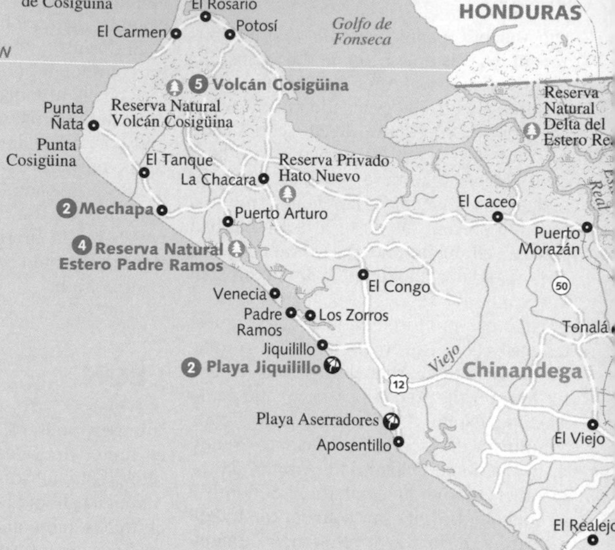

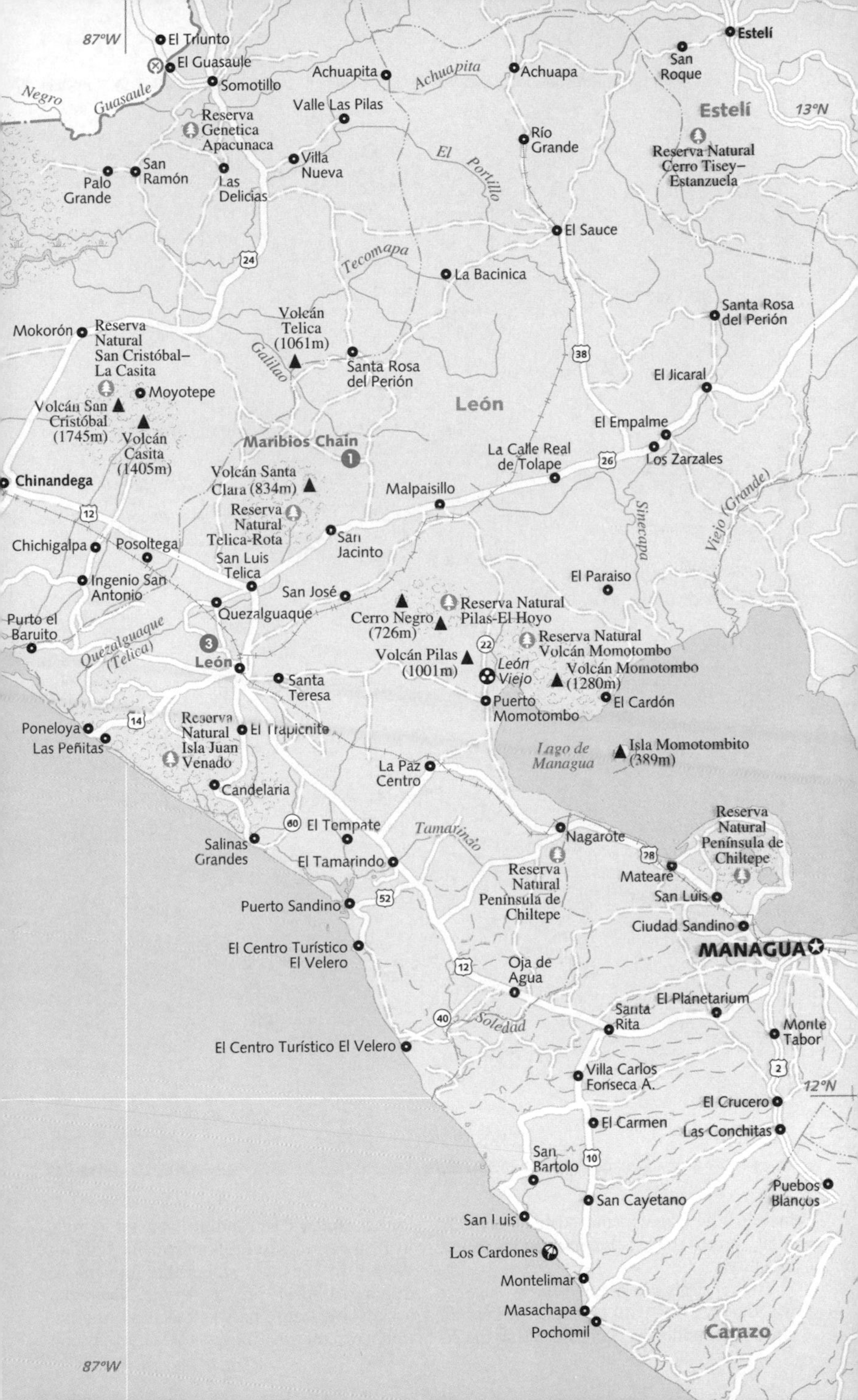
87°W
El Triunto
El Guasaule
Somotillo
Negro
Guasaule
Achuapita
Achuapita
Achuapa
Estelí
San Roque
Valle Las Pilas
Reserva Genetica Apacunaca
Estelí
13°N
Río Grande
El Portillo
Reserva Natural Cerro Tisey–Estanzuela
Villa Nueva
Palo Grande
San Ramón
Las Delicias
El Sauce
24
Tecomapa
La Bacinica
Santa Rosa del Perión
Volcán Telica (1061m)
Mokorón
Reserva Natural San Cristóbal–La Casita
Galilao
Santa Rosa del Perión
38
El Jicaral
Moyotepe
Volcán San Cristóbal (1745m)
León
Volcán Casita (1405m)
El Empalme
Maribios Chain
1
La Calle Real de Tolape
26
Los Zarzales
Chinandega
Volcán Santa Clara (834m)
Malpaisillo
Sinecapa
Viejo (Grande)
12
Reserva Natural Telica-Rota
San Jacinto
Chichigalpa
Posoltega
San Luis Telica
El Paraiso
Ingenio San Antonio
San José
Reserva Natural Pilas-El Hoyo
Quezalguaque
Cerro Negro (726m)
Purto el Baruito
Quezalguaque (Telica)
3
Reserva Natural Volcán Momotombo
22
León
Volcán Pilas (1001m)
León Viejo
Volcán Momotombo (1280m)
Santa Teresa
Puerto Momotombo
El Cardón
Reserva Natural Isla Juan Venado
El Trapichito
14
Poneloya
Las Peñitas
Lago de Managua
Isla Momotombito (389m)
La Paz Centro
Candelaria
60
El Tempate
Tamarindo
Nagarote
Reserva Natural Península de Chiltepe
Salinas Grandes
El Tamarindo
28
Mateare
Reserva Natural Península de Chiltepe
Puerto Sandino
52
San Luis
Ciudad Sandino
El Centro Turístico El Velero
MANAGUA
12
Oja de Agua
El Planetarium
40
Soledad
Santa Rita
Monte Tabor
El Centro Turístico El Velero
2
Villa Carlos Fonseca A.
12°N
El Crucero
El Carmen
Las Conchitas
San Bartolo
10
San Cayetano
Puebos Blancos
San Luis
Los Cardones
Montelimar
Masachapa
Pochomil
Carazo
87°W

León

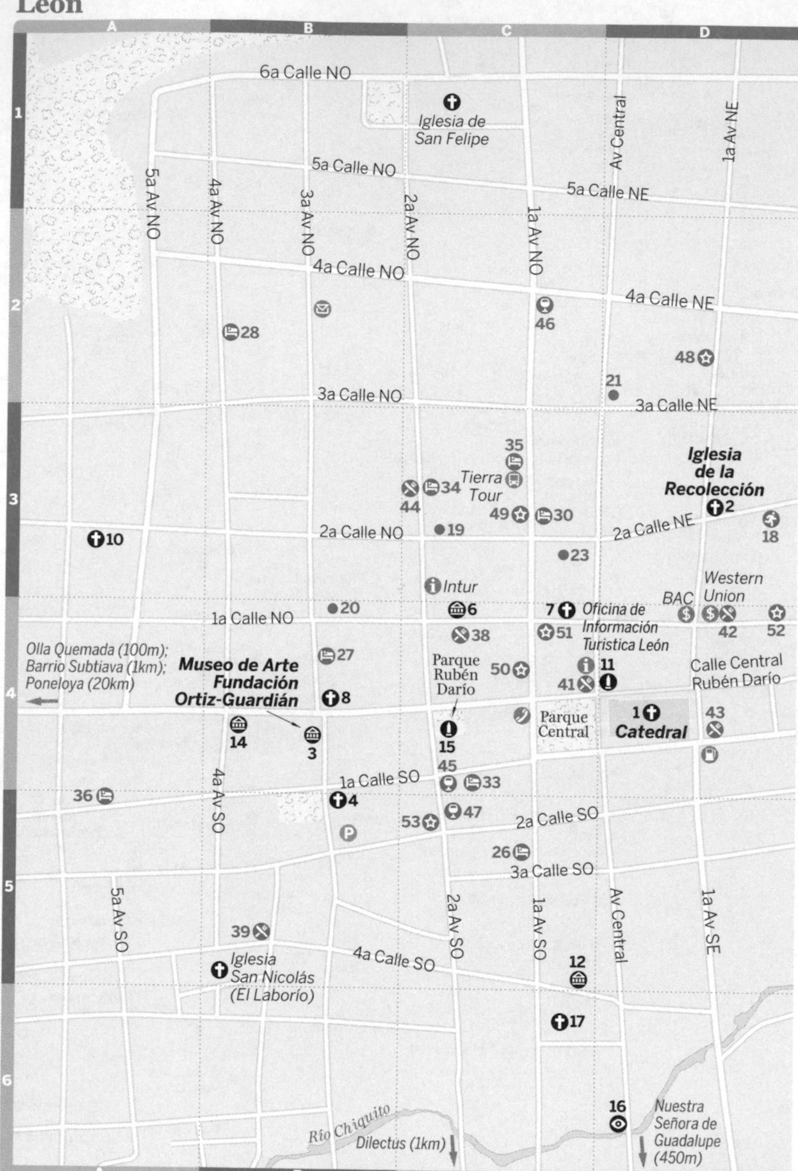

in 1610, the city was moved here, saint by saint, next to the existing indigenous capital of Subtiava.

The reprisals did not end there. Eager to win the civil war with Granada, which had, since independence, been contesting the colonial capital's continuing leadership role, in 1853 León invited US mercenary William Walker to the fight. After the Tennessean declared himself president (and Nicaragua a US slave state), he was executed; the nation's capital was moved to Managua, and

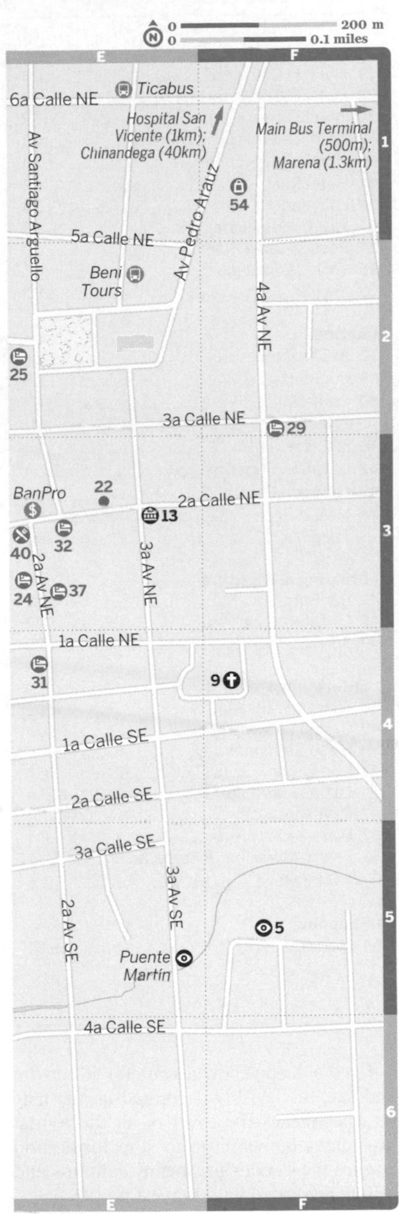

Granada's Conservatives ran the country for the next three decades.

Finally, in 1956, Anastasio Somoza García (the original dictator) was assassinated in León by Rigoberto López, a poet in a waiter's clothing. The ruling family never forgot, and when the revolution came, their wrath fell on this city in a hail of bullets and bombs, the scars of which have still not been erased.

León has remained proudly Liberal, even a bit aloof, through it all, a Sandinista stronghold and political power player that has never once doubted its grand destiny.

Sights

León is the most culturally rich of Nicaragua's cities; architecture and museum buffs will want to spend a few days exploring.

Central León

★Catedral CATHEDRAL

(Roof tour admission US$1; roof tours 8am-noon & 2-4pm Mon-Sat) Officially known as the Basílica de la Asunción, León's cathedral is the largest in Central America, its expansive design famously, and perhaps apocryphally, approved for construction in much more important Lima, Peru.

Leónese leaders originally submitted a more modest but bogus set of plans, and then architect Diego José de Porres Esquivel, the Capitan General of Guatemala (also responsible for San Juan Bautista de Subtiava, La Recolección and La Merced churches, among others), pulled the switcheroo and built this beauty right here.

This is the cathedral's fourth incarnation. The 1610 original was replaced in 1624 with a wood-and-adobe structure that pirate William Dampier burned to the ground in 1685. Another adobe was used until work began on this enormous 'Antigüeño,' Central American baroque-style masterpiece in 1747. Construction, done primarily by indigenous laborers from Subtiava and Posoltega, went on for more than 100 years.

The cathedral is a sort of pantheon of Nicaraguan culture. The tomb of Rubén Darío, León's favorite son, is on one side of the altar, guarded by a sorrowful lion and the inscription 'Nicaragua is created of vigor and glory, Nicaragua is made for freedom.' Nearby rest the tombs of lesser-known Leónese poets Alfonso Cortés and Salomón de la Selva, as well as Miguel Larreynaga.

Among the magnificent works of art within are the *Stations of the Cross* by Antonio Sarria, considered masterpieces, and *El Cristo Negro de Pedrarias*, possibly the oldest Catholic image in the Americas, brought here in 1528. Marble statues inside are beautifully crafted, most notably the elaborate *Inmaculada Concepción de María*.

León

Top Sights

1 Catedral ... D4
2 Iglesia de la Recolección ... D3
3 Museo de Arte Fundación Ortiz-Guardián ... B4

Sights

4 Capilla San Juan de Dios ... B5
5 Cimac ... F5
Convent San Francisco ... (see 8)
6 Galería de Héroes y Mártires ... C4
7 Iglesia de La Merced ... C4
8 Iglesia de San Francisco ... B4
9 Iglesia Dulce Nombre de Jesús el Calvario ... F4
10 Iglesia Zaragoza ... A3
11 Mausoleo de los Héroes y Mártires ... D4
12 Museo de Leyendas y Tradiciones ... C5
13 Museo Entomológico ... E3
14 Museo-Archivo Rubén Darío ... B4
15 Parque Rubén Darío ... C4
16 Puente Guadalupe ... D6
17 Ruinas San Sebastián ... C6

Activities, Courses & Tours

18 Asociación Mary Barreda ... D3
19 Eco-Camp Expeditions ... C3
Escuela de Español León ... (see 20)
Green Pathways ... (see 24)
20 La Casa de Cultura ... B4
21 La Isla Foundation ... D2
Nica Así Tours ... (see 33)
Pure Earth Project ... (see 24)
22 Quetzaltrekkers ... E3
Tierra Tour ... (see 35)
23 UNAN ... C3

Sleeping

24 Bigfoot Hostel ... E3
25 Casona Colonial ... E2
26 Hostel La Clínica ... C5
27 Hotel El Convento ... B4
28 Hotel El Sueño de Meme ... B2
29 Hotel Europeo ... F2
30 Hotel La Perla ... C3
31 Hotel Los Balcones ... E4
32 Hotel Real ... E3
33 La Siesta Perdida ... C4
34 Lazybones Hostel ... C3
35 Posada Doña Blanca ... C3
36 Tortuga Booluda ... A5
37 Vía Vía ... E3

Eating

38 Al Carbón ... C4
39 CocinArte ... B5
40 Comedor Lucia ... E3
El Mediterraneo ... (see 44)
41 El Sesteo ... C4
42 La Unión Supermercado ... D4
43 Mercado Central ... D4
44 Mesón Real ... C3
Taquezal ... (see 33)

Drinking & Nightlife

45 Bar Baro ... C4
46 La Taberna de Mau ... C2
47 Solero ... C5

Entertainment

48 Alianza Francesa ... D2
49 Casino La Perla ... C3
50 Disco Bohemios ... C4
51 Don Señor ... C4
La Casa de Cultura ... (see 20)
Oxygene ... (see 45)
52 Plaza Siglo Nuevo ... D4
53 Teatro Municipal José de la Cruz Mena ... C5

Shopping

54 Mercado San Juan ... F1

If it's clear, take the roof tour, with a spectacular view of the city and smoking volcanoes beyond. The cathedral was having a face-lift at press time but should be completed by the time you read this. Regardless it will still be open to the public.

★Iglesia de la Recolección CHURCH
(1a Av NE) Three blocks north of the cathedral, the 1786 Iglesia de La Recolección is considered the city's most beautiful church, a Mexican-style baroque confection of swirling columns and bas-relief medallions that portray the life of Christ.

Dyed a deep yellow accented with cream and age, the lavishly decorated facade may be what makes the cover of all the tourist brochures, but be sure to stop inside and admire the slender mahogany columns and ceiling decorated with harvest motifs.

Iglesia de La Merced CHURCH
Home to León's patron saint, La Virgen de La Merced, this not-so-immediately enchanting gray edifice is considered the city's second-most-important church.

The image, originally from Barcelona, was brought to León's original church in

1528. After Volcán Momotombo erupted and forced the city's evacuation, the Léonese built a new church here in 1615, replaced with the current building in the early 1700s.

Iglesia Dulce Nombre de Jesús el Calvario CHURCH

(Calle Central Rubén Darío) A hodgepodge of neoclassical and baroque styles, 18th-century El Calvario stands at the top of Calle Central Rubén Darío. The interior is nice, with predictably gory, full-sized statues of Jesus and the thieves being crucified, but you're here for the vividly painted facade between the red-brick bell towers, with brightly colored bas-relief biblical scenes that resemble comic-strip panels.

★Museo de Arte Fundación Ortiz-Guardián MUSEUM

(3a Av SO, Iglesia San Francisco, ½c S; admission US$0.80; ⏲10am-6pm Tue-Sat, 8am-4pm Sun) Probably the finest contemporary-art museum in all of Central America, the Ortiz-Guardián Collection has spilled over from its original home in Casa Don Norberto Ramiréz, refurbished in 2000 to its original Creole Civil style, with Arabic tiles and impressive flagstones. It and another beautiful old home across the street are now packed with artwork, a Spanish-speaking guide costs an extra US$1.25, which is well worth it.

Begin surrounded by the luxurious realism of the Renaissance and spare beauty of the colonial period, then wander through romanticism, modernism, postmodernism and actually modern pieces by Cuban, Peruvian and other Latin American schools. Rubens, Picasso, Chagall and other big names make an appearance, but it's the work by Latin American masters – Diego Rivera, Rufino Tamayo, Fernando Botero, Roberto Matta and more – that define the collection.

Museo de Leyendas y Tradiciones MUSEUM

(4a Calle SO, frente Ruinas San Sebastián; admission US$2; ⏲8am-noon & 1-5pm) León's most entertaining and eclectic museum, the Museum of Myths & Traditions is now housed in La XXI (the 21st Garrison). What makes this museum unmissable is the striking contrast of its main subjects: a quirky collection of life-sized papier-mâché figures from Leónese history and legend, handmade by founder Señora Toruña (also represented in glorious papier-mâché), and murals graphically depicting methods the Guardia Nacional used to torture prisoners.

You're led from room to room, each dedicated to a different aspect of Leónese folklore, from La Gigantona – the giant woman who represents an original colonist, still ridiculed by a popular ballet *folklórico* – to La Carreta Nagua (Chariot of Death), which picks up the souls of those foolish enough to cross intersections catercorner.

And between each rundown of local legends, your Spanish-speaking guide will cheerfully shift gears to describe the gory human-rights abuses – stretching on racks, beatings, water tortures etc – that took place here regularly until June 13, 1979, when Commander Dora María Téllez successfully breached Somoza's defenses and secured La XXI for the Sandinistas, releasing all prisoners. Signage is in English and Spanish.

Museo-Archivo Rubén Darío MUSEUM

(cnr Calles Central & 4a Av; admission US$1; ⏲8am-noon & 2-5pm Tue-Sat, 8am-noon Sun) Of all the museums and monuments dedicated to the poet that are scattered across his doting homeland, Museo-Archivo Rubén Darío seems like the one where you'd be most likely to run into his ghost.

Exhibits are displayed throughout the house where he lived until he was a teenager, ranging from everyday items – more a window into well-to-do Nicaragua in the late 1800s – to handwritten manuscripts of Darío's famous works.

Darío's final resting place is the León cathedral.

His bible, the bed where he died 'an agonizing death' and the fancy duds he wore as the ambassador to Spain are just highlights among the historic bric-a-brac.

Museo Entomológico MUSEUM

(www.bio-nica.info; cnr 3a Av NE & 2a Calle NE; admission US$0.50; ⏲9am-noon & 2-4pm) For a truly comprehensive collection of creepy crawlies, butterflies, scorpions and other critters from all over Central America, drop into this museum. The specialty is *Lucanidae,* a genus of beetles where males usually display ferocious-looking pincers. Anyone for a mosquito net?

Galería de Héroes y Mártires MUSEUM

(1a Calle NO, Iglesia de la Merced, ½c O; donation US$1; ⏲10am-5pm) A homage to León's more recent history is found at the Galería de Héroes y Mártires, run by mothers of FSLN veterans and fallen heroes.

There's some signage in English and Spanish, but you're here to look into the eyes of more than 300 revolutionaries, mostly pimply faced teens with feathered disco haircuts, and wonder if you would be willing to make the ultimate sacrifice to free your country from dictatorship.

Cimac GARDENS

(Puente Martín, ½c E, 1c N; admission US$1; ⏲ 8am-noon & 2-5pm) These excellent botanic gardens occupy 9 sq km on the edge of downtown, displaying four types of forest typical to Nicaragua. Groups of 10 or more get a guided tour; smaller groups get a self-guiding booklet (in Spanish).

Be on the lookout for tame deer, *guardabarrancos* (Nicaragua's national bird) and, rumor has it, a boa constrictor that inhabits the grounds. There's also a small orchid exhibit and plenty of information about environmental issues in the region and the country.

El Fortín de Acososco FORT

The Guardia Nacional's last holdout in León, El Fortín can be reached by the 2.5km dirt road that begins on the western side of Guadalupe cemetery, on the southern border of Barrio Subtiava. The fortress is next to a smelly garbage dump; you'll need to ask for permission to enter.

Muggings are common on this stretch, so go in a group and leave your camera and other valuables at the hotel.

The large, squat, gray building was originally constructed in 1889 to take advantage of the great city views. It was abandoned until the 1950s, when the Somozas realized that they needed to keep an eye on León itself. They lost the fort on July 7, 1979, and the Sandinistas still have a parade every July to celebrate.

Parque Rubén Darío MONUMENT

This quaint park has a statue of the poet master and busts of other, lesser Léonese poets, including Alfonso Cortés (1893–1969), Azarias H Pallais (1884–1954) and Salomon de la Selva (1893–1959). They are accompanied by a few choice verses.

Mausoleo de los Héroes y Mártires MONUMENT

A monument to the local heroes, the eternal flame of the Mausoleum of Heroes & Martyrs rests within a small plaza just north of the Parque Central, surrounded by the city's best murals.

Barrio Subtiava

A regional capital long before León moved in, the *barrio* (district) of Subtiava takes its name from a local tribe who still count themselves apart from León, and Nicaragua, as a whole. After refugees from León Viejo arrived in 1610, the two separate towns coexisted as equals until 1680. Flexing their rebuilt military muscle, the Spanish forced 12,000 indigenous inhabitants of Subtiava to become part of León, basically relegating them to slave labor. Tensions simmered for two generations, until a police crackdown in 1725 inspired a revolt. Although the insurrection was violently shut down by the Spaniards, Barrio Subtiava was able to remain a separate entity until 1902, when it was finally, officially, annexed to the city. The key word being 'officially.'

It's a solid 20-minute walk or US$0.70 taxi ride to Subtiava from the León cathedral, or you can take one of the covered trucks (US$0.18) plying the streets. Catch a Subtiava-bound truck at the southwest corner of the Parque Central (in front of Sandinista headquarters) and yell 'Catedral Subtiava' as they haul you inside, probably while the truck is still moving. Hang on!

Iglesia Parroquial de San Juan Bautista de Subtiava CHURCH

(13 Av SO) The Subtiava neighborhood is centered at this church, located about 1km west of the León cathedral. It's better known as 'Catedral Subtiava,' and is the oldest intact church in the city. Built in the 1530s and reconstructed in 1710, its relatively plain beige facade and precious wood interior is largely unadorned; even the struts are there to stabilize the structure during earthquakes.

There are two exceptions: spirals outside, and an extraordinary sun icon mounted to the typical arched timber roof, pay homage to deities far older than the Spanish conquest.

Ermita de San Pedro CHURCH

This church, two blocks east and one block south of San Juan Bautista, was constructed between 1706 and 1718, and is considered one of the best examples of primitive baroque style in Nicaragua. This means that it's almost unadorned, save for three brick crosses inlaid into the adobe.

Ruinas Iglesia Santiago CHURCH

Well signed 1½ blocks away from San Juan Bautista, this church was (according to local legend) cursed by *duendes* (fairies), and by the looks of it the curse worked. Enter through the corrugated-tin gate and ask the family there if it's OK to cross their front yard; they may ask for a few córdobas. The architecture is still obvious – and the bell tower still standing – and makes for an interesting wander.

Iglesia Veracruz CHURCH

A few blocks west of the Iglesia Santiago are the ruins of this 16th-century church destroyed by a volcanic eruption in 1835. It remains a spiritual center and, as the indigenous counterpoint to La Gritería, on December 7 people gather here for a pre-Columbian festival involving torches and the sun deity on the roof of San Juan Bautista.

Museo de Arte Sacre MUSEUM

(☎2311-8288; frente Iglesia San Juan Bautista; admission US$0.70; ⏰8am-noon & 2-5pm Mon-Fri, 8am-noon Sat) Call ahead to make sure this intriguing museum is open. You've probably noticed this neighborhood's churches are in some disrepair, a situation that inspired locals to preserve the region's absolutely beautiful 16th- and 17th-century religious art right here, where it would be safe.

Art ranging from faithfully detailed wooden saints (including one of the first Virgins of Guadalupe) to more ostentatious examples of baroque overkill, including lots of gold and silver artifacts, have been packed

WORTH A TRIP

LEÓN VIEJO

Buried and lost for over 300 years, this was Nicaragua's first **capital** (entrance US$5; ⏰8am-5pm) – a rough-and-ready settlement that some say was doomed from the start. Founded in 1824, the town was governed by a series of unusually cruel and money-hungry tyrants, whose public spectacles included beheadings and setting wild dogs on captured natives in the central plaza.

All of which gives some weight to the theory that divine intervention played at least a part in the series of earthquakes that shook the town from 1580 to 1609, culminating in the eruption of nearby Volcán Momotombo that buried the city under ash in 1610.

The Spanish fled, carrying whatever they could with them (including La Virgen de La Merced), and settled in present-day León, and the old city began to fade from memory.

Fast forward to 1967. After years of searching and theorizing, archaeologists from León's UNAN university finally locate the old town, unearthing its chapel and central plaza (and the headless remains of Francisco Fernández de Córdoba, founder of both León and Granada, beneath it).

In 2000 it was declared a Unesco World Heritage site – Nicaragua's first – and (funds allowing) excavations have continued. This is not Machu Picchu – most walls are about 1m high and you need a fair bit of imagination to see that there was once a city here – but it makes for an interesting day trip, more than anything for the evocative commentary provided by local guides.

Admission includes a Spanish-language guided tour, but detailed signs are also in English. The best time to visit is the second Sunday in November, when La Virgen de La Merced leaves her comfortable new church and, leading a procession of the faithful from La Paz Centro, revisits her first home in the New World.

Almost every tour outfit in León (as well as several in Managua and Granada) arranges visits to León Viejo (US$45 from León), which can be combined with a hike to the top of Cerro Negro and/or a cool swim in Laguna de Asososca, both nearby. But it's easy to visit on your own. Buses run every 50 minutes between León and La Paz Centro (US$0.80, 45 minutes), meeting buses to Puerto Momotombo (US$0.50), less than 1km from the site. Driving, the turnoff is 3km east of La Paz Centro on the new León–Managua highway. From there it's a 15km drive along a cobblestone road; make the poorly signed right to the ruins when you get into town.

If you continue straight through Puerto Momotombo, however, you'll quickly come to a less-than-appealing beach scene on Lago de Managua, where a handful of disposable-looking restaurants and a playground enjoy a truly awesome view of Volcán Momotombo, the hydroelectric plant steaming eerily against its naked red and black slopes, and Isla Momotombito; you could rent a boat for US$30 per hour and paddle around.

into the original Casa Cultural de Subtiava, built in 1544.

Museo Adiáct MUSEUM
(Iglesia San Juan Bautista, 2c N, Calle Central Rubén Darío; admission US$0.70; ⏲8am-noon & 2-5pm Mon-Fri, 8am-noon Sat) This interesting little museum, which also houses the neighborhood's government and present-day Casa Cultural de Subtiava, is a beautifully muraled building; you may need to ask that it be opened. You're likely to get a tour that's as much political as it is historical, detailing how Subtiava has been getting shafted since time immemorial, even by its former allies.

Funeral urns, ceramic tableware, stone statues and more are on display, with very little signage or attempt at a timeline.

Casa Cultural de Subtiava CULTURAL BUILDING
(Iglesia San Juan Bautista, 2c N, Calle Central Rubén Darío; ⏲8am-noon & 2-5pm Mon-Fri) Look for the faded mural at the headquarters and home to Museo Adiáct.

Museo Insurreccional Luís Manuel Toruño MUSEUM
(Casa El Buzón; Iglesia San Juan Bautista, 2c E, 1½c S; donations accepted; ⏲Sat) This fine museum was relocated from León proper to this smaller Subtiava Sandinista stronghold. Also called El Buzón (The Mailbox), this building was a secret weapons depot during the revolution.

Curator 'El Chanclazo' has kept the faith and displays his enormous collection of revolutionary mementos, newspaper clippings and communist memorabilia; if it's not open, ask around.

El Tamarindón LANDMARK
(Iglesia San Juan Bautista, 3c S, 2c O) This is a huge tree where Adiáct, *cacique* (chief) of the Subtiava tribe during the Spanish conquest, was unceremoniously hanged so his people would see him as weak. Today 'The Big Tamarindo' is a rallying point for indigenous locals, who placed a plaque there in 2003 that declares 'This tree was the cross of he who is our light.'

UCAN UNIVERSITY
(Universidad Cristiana Autónima de Nicaragua; www.ucan.edu.ni) Pricey private school worth checking out for a look into León's university scene.

UCC UNIVERSITY
(Universidad de Ciencias Comerciales; www.ucc.edu.ni) This university specializes in architecture and tourism-related degrees. Cruising around here makes for a good afternoon.

Courses

Hostels Vía Vía, Tortuga Booluda and Bigfoot are all good places to inquire about private Spanish tutors (about US$7 per hour).

UNAN COURSE
(Universidad Nacional Autónoma de Nicaragua León; www.unanleon.edu.ni/centrodeidiomas; continguo Iglesia de la Merced) Nicaragua's first and most important university was founded in 1812, and today has six separate León schools with more than 6000 students; the main campus is considered one of the city's loveliest collections of buildings. Wander around or drop in for some guerrilla learning. It also offers top-notch language learning programs and homestays.

La Isla Foundation COURSE
(☎2315-1261; www.laislafoundation.org; 3a Calle NE) Stop by to learn about Spanish, yoga and salsa classes, and volunteer opportunities.

La Casa de Cultura COURSE
Ask here about art, dance and music classes.

Escuela de Español León COURSE
(☎2315-5540; www.leonspanishschool.org; int La Casa de Cultura; 20hr with/without homestay US$200/135) Based in La Casa de Cultura, this is a professional operation with plenty of cultural activities and out-of-town excursions.

Tours

Volcano surfing, just so you know, involves hauling yourself to the top of steaming Cerro Negro, then riding a 'sandboard' (something like a modified snowboard) or toboggan down its black-gravel 45-degree slopes. The standard tour offerings from most agencies include Cerro Negro (US$28), Laguna Verde (US$65), León Viejo (US$45) and Volcán Cosigüina (US$90, two days).

Quetzaltrekkers ADVENTURE TOUR
(☎2311-6695; www.quetzaltrekkers.com; 2a Calle NE, Iglesia de La Recolección, 1½c E) Profits from this outstanding operator go to Las Tias, a charity that helps problem kids learn to build their own lives, and other worthy causes; volunteers are very welcome.

Green Pathways ADVENTURE TOUR
(☎2315-0964; www.greenpathways.com; opposite Bigfoot Hostel) Socially conscientious operator with a focus on rural tourism.

Eco-Camp Expeditions ADVENTURE TOUR
(☎2311-1828; www.ecocampexpeditions.com; Parque Rubén Darío 2c N, 10m E) A solid operation for camping and other adventure activities outside León.

Tierra Tour ADVENTURE TOUR
(☎2315-4278; www.tierratour.com; 1a Av NO, Iglesia de La Merced, 1½c N) A well-established operator offering trips to San Jacinto (US$18) and León Viejo (US$35), and five-hour mangrove and lagoon tours in Reserva Natural Isla Juan Venado (US$55).

Nica Así Tours TOUR
(www.nicaitours.com; inside La Siesta Perdida) Offers standard tours, plus a cooking class with a trip to the market (US$12).

Festivals & Events

Every Saturday, from early afternoon till midnight, the Parque Central comes alive for the Tertulia Leónesa, inviting everyone outside to eat, drink and dance to music played by local combos. Following are some of León's annual celebrations.

Semana Santa RELIGIOUS
(late March or early April) The Leónese Semana Santa is something special, with Barrio Subtiava's colorful sawdust 'carpets,' temporary and beautiful images that the funeral procession for Jesus walks over, and a sandcastle competition in Poncloya.

Masacre del 23 Julio 1959 HISTORIC
(July 23) One afternoon in 1959, local school children staged a demonstration against Somoza. As they chanted 'Freedom! Freedom!,' the Guardia Nacional fired into the crowd, killing four students and wounding several others. Those wounded, some in wheelchairs, still lead a parade, right after every single marching band from the area has announced that their generation will not forget.

La Gritería Chiquita HISTORIC
(August 14) This celebration began in 1947, as an erupting Cerro Negro threatened to bury the city in ashes. The volcano suddenly halted its activity after an innovative priest, Monseñor Isidro Augusto Oviedo, vowed to initiate a preliminary *gritería* (shouting), similar to December's but changing the response to *¡La asunción de María!* ('The ascension of Mary!').

Día de la Virgen de Merced RELIGIOUS
(September 24) León's saint's day is solemnly observed, but the preceding day is more festive: revelers don a bull-shaped armature lined with fireworks, called the *toro encohetado,* then charge at panic-stricken onlookers as the rockets fly.

Carnaval Mitos y Leyendas CULTURAL
(November 1) See the papier-mâché crew from the Museo de Leyendas y Tradiciones on a parade from the cathedral and Barrio Subtiava, for this Halloweenesque fiesta.

Día de la Purísima Concepción RELIGIOUS
(December 7) Observed throughout the country, this celebration of Nicaragua's patron saint is the occasion for the *gritería,* enjoyed here with unusual vigor.

Sleeping

León probably packs in more hotels and hostels per square meter than any other place in the country – it's hard to imagine them all filling up, although it may happen around the Christmas or Easter high season.

Tortuga Booluda HOSTEL $
(☎2311-4653; www.tortugabooluda.com; 1a Calle SO, Catedral, 4½c O; dm/r US$7/22; @) More small hotel than hostel, the 'Lazy Turtle' does, however, offer all the hostel amenities, namely a great kitchen, book exchange, free coffee, pool table, some good chill-out areas and a sociable atmosphere. Rooms are simple but stylish; dorms are spacious enough; and the one upstairs room is a real winner, with big windows and plenty of air and light.

Lazybones Hostel HOSTEL $
(☎2311-3472; www.lazyboneshostelnicaragua.com; 2a Av NO, Parque Rubén Darío, 2½c N; dm US$8, r with/without bathroom US$30/20; P @) Part of the new wave of hostels, this quiet, less party-oriented spot has trim grounds, excellent rooms and dorms, and a very laidback atmosphere. The age-old patio and sitting areas are every bit as lovely as those in some midrange hotels, and the bar, good-sized pool and yummy breakfasts make this a good deal.

Bigfoot Hostel HOSTEL $
(☎8505-1284; www.bigfootnicaragua.com; 2 Av NE; dm US$6, r without bathroom US$18, q US$33;

(❄📶🏊) With kitchen access, a miniature swimming pool and freshly made mojitos on offer, it wouldn't really matter what the rooms were like, but they're a good deal. There's a good travelers' vibe at this party hostel – staff swear the party shuts down at 10pm – and a sweet little cafe-bar out front.

Vía Vía HOSTEL **$**
(☎2311-6142; www.viaviacafe.com; 2a Av NE, Iglesia de La Recolección, 1c E, ½c S; dm/s/d US$7/19/29; 📶) The Vía Vía chain of hostels, which stretches from Katmandu to Buenos Aires, consistently comes up with the goods. This is no exception, offering beautiful, colonial-style rooms with great bathrooms, and spacious six-bed dorms with their own bathroom! The patio area is lush and there's an atmospheric bar-restaurant area out front.

Hostel La Clínica HOSTEL **$**
(☎2311-2031; 1a Av SO, Parque Central, 1½c S; dm US$5, r with/without bathroom US$12/8; 📶) A good location and friendly owners make up (kind of) for small rooms, SpongeBob beds and rough bathrooms that sit around a cramped and unkempt courtyard.

La Siesta Perdida HOSTEL **$**
(☎2311-2289; www.siestaperdida.com; Parque Central, 50m O; dm/d US$5/12; 📶) You are likely to lose sleep here, as the bar out front is one of the most popular in town. But it's a fun place all in all, with a large book exchange, shared kitchen and rougher edge than other hostels in town.

Casona Colonial HISTORIC HOTEL **$$**
(☎2311-3178; www.casonacolonialguest.com; 4a Calle NE, Parque San Juan, ½c O; s/d with fan US$17/22, r with air-con US$42; ❄📶) With more character than many in this price range, the medium-sized rooms here are long on colonial atmosphere without all the costly little extras. Beds are big, with lavish bedheads, and the occasional chip in the paintwork or tear in the wallpaper adds to rather than detracts from the charm.

Hotel Real HOTEL **$$**
(☎2311-2606; www.hotelrealdeleon.net; 2a Calle NE, Iglesia de La Recolección, 1½c E; s/d incl breakfast US$38/48; ❄📶) The 'Royal Hotel' has a quaint front sitting area and an old-style *casona* (historic mansion) feel, but with relatively modern rooms bedecked with flatscreen TVs and Flintstone-firm beds. Rooms are big and comfortable, and the rooftop terrace

City Walk
Following León's Revolutionary & Cultural Trail

START PARQUE CENTRAL
END MUSEO-ARCHIVO RUBÉN DARÍO
LENGTH 3KM–5KM; FOUR TO SIX HOURS

Begin at ① **Parque Central**, a fine place for people-watching and enjoying that most Léonese of treats, *raspado* (shaved ice flavored with fruit).

Enjoy your treat in front of the eternal (more or less) flame at ② **Mausoleo de los Héroes y Mártires** (p146), on the northern side of the park, where a phenomenal and heartbreaking mural traces Nicaraguan history from the Spanish conquest to the most recent revolution, complete with smoking volcanoes.

Dominating the plaza is ③ **Basílica de la Asunción** (p143), Central America's largest cathedral; take a rooftop tour early for the clearest views of the Volcáns Maribios.

On the southern side of the cathedral is 1679 ④ **Colegio La Asunción**, the first theological college in Nicaragua. It was partially destroyed by fire in 1935 and rebuilt in its current Gothic style. Next door is ⑤ **Palacio Episcopal** (Bishop's Palace), designed by Marcelo Targa and one of the first buildings to display Léonese neoclassical architecture. In this group of buildings, ⑥ **Archivo Histórico Dicesano de León** has documents dating back to 1674.

Continuing around the cathedral is the 1680 ⑦ **Colegio de San Ramón**. Revolutionary hero Miguel Larreynaga, who drafted the first Central American constitution, was educated here. The college was rebuilt in 1752, and housed the Universidad Autónoma, Nicaragua's first university. Though it's been a high school since 1945, paintings of all León's bishops are still on display.

Head south on 1a Ave SE, then west on 3a Calle SO one block, then south one block on Av Central to visit ⑧ **La XXI** (p145), an old military garrison that's today home to the truly fabulous ⑨ **Museo de Leyendas y Tradiciones** (p145); check out the mosaic tile work at the entrance. Across the street are the photogenic ⑩ **Ruinas San Sebastián**; the church was bombed almost into oblivion in 1979.

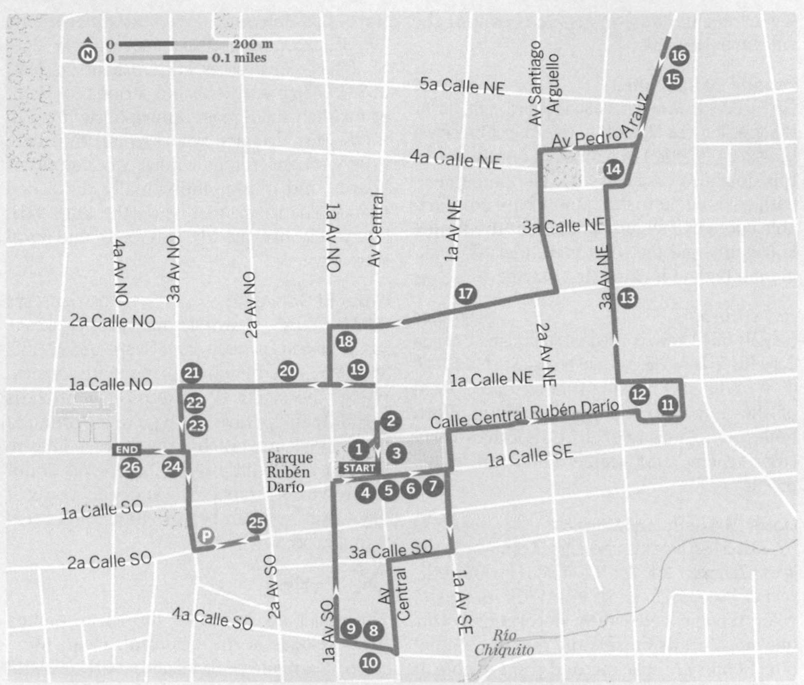

Backtrack through pleasant Mercado Central, then make a right on Calle Central Rubén Darío to the early-18th-century ⓫ **Iglesia El Calvario** (p161), famed for its comic book–style facade. Close by, ⓬ **Antiguo Reformatorio de Menores** (Old Reform School) is a rare, almost all original *casa pinariega*–style building.

Head north on 3a Av NE, stopping in to bug out at ⓭ **Museo Entomológico** (p145). Then it's on to somewhat scruffy 1625 ⓮ **Iglesia San Juan de Dios**, rebuilt in 1860 in the modernist neoclassical style. Close by is ⓯ **Mercado San Juan** and the ⓰ **old train station**, constructed in 1882 with austere lines and simple, utilitarian design.

Backtrack two blocks along 4a Av NE to 2a Calle NE and make a right to reach the unmissable 1786 ⓱ **Iglesia de La Recolección** (p144) after three blocks. This ornate, ultra-baroque masterpiece was described by one critic as 'the most important monument to passion in Nicaragua.'

Two blocks west on 2a Calle NE is the flagship campus of ⓲ **UNAN** (p148), with several beautiful buildings, and a collection of cheap restaurants and festive bars.

From the UNAN campus, head south on 1a Av NO for the 1615 ⓳ **Iglesia de La Merced** (p144), another of León's signature churches, then head west on 1a Calle NO to ⓴ **Galería de Héroes y Mártires** (p145), with photos of the revolution's fallen. Continue west, stopping at ㉑ **La Casa de Cultura** (p154), with its excellent art collection (including a portrait of former US president Ronald Reagan that you'll want to photograph), then head south on 3a Av NO.

Tired? Fortify yourself at ㉒ **Hotel El Convento** (p152), with an amazing collection of colonial-era religious art and a good, if pricey, restaurant. Attached ㉓ **Iglesia de San Francisco** (p139) was badly damaged during the revolution but is slowly being restored to its former glory.

Allow at least two hours to appreciate the best art museum in Central America, ㉔ **Museo de Arte Fundación Ortiz-Guardián** (p145), south of Calle Central Rubén Darío, then head two blocks further south and one block east to see if anything's on later that night at 1885 **Teatro Municipal José de la Cruz Mena** (p154). Finally, backtrack to the corner of Calle Central Rubén Darío and 4a Av SO for the poet's home and national museum, **Museo-Archivo Rubén Darío** (p145).

has excellent views of steeple tops and the volcanoes beyond.

Posada Doña Blanca HOTEL **$$**
(☎2311-2521; www.posadadonablanca.com; 1a Av NO, Iglesia de La Merced, 1c N; s/d incl breakfast US$42/54; P ❄ @) In a modern family home, this downtown oasis is all cool open spaces with colonial flourishes. Rooms are comfortable enough, if slightly bland, but the family is friendly and the service wonderful, making it a budget-busting first starter.

Hotel Europeo HOTEL **$$**
(☎2311-6040; www.hoteleuropaleon.com.ni; cnr 3a Calle NE & 4a Av NE; s/d incl breakfast US$40/47; P ❄) While it's missing that *casona* appeal of the area's historic hotels, this modern hotel block does offer an out-of-this-world color scheme and simple, fairly affordable rooms.

Hotel El Sueño de Meme HOTEL **$$**
(☎2311-5462; hotelmeme@hotmail.com; 4a Av NO, Iglesia Zaragoza, 1c E, 1½c N; s/d with fan US$16/26, with air-con US$25/36; ❄ 📶) With its pastel color scheme and cutesy decorations, this one steps firmly outside the quaint colonial box. Rooms are spacious and comfortable, if a little soulless, and you are a bit removed from the action in the city center.

Hotel La Perla HISTORIC HOTEL **$$$**
(☎2311-3125; www.laperlaleon.com; 1a Av NO, Iglesia de La Merced, 1½c N; s/d/ste incl breakfast US$94/111/181; P ❄ 📶 🏊) A pearl indeed. Set in one of León's most impressive mansions, the Perla has everything you would expect for the price, done with exquisite taste in a great location. There's an on-site restaurant, stately rooms with hardwood furnishings and a decent-sized swimming pool, making this the best high-end option in town.

Hotel Los Balcones HISTORIC HOTEL **$$$**
(☎2311-0250; www.hotelbalcones.com; 1a Calle NE, esquina de los bancos, 1c E; s/d/tr incl breakfast US$47/64/66; ❄ 📶) This is a serious contender for the title of most atmospheric hotel in town. Stay upstairs, where you'll find cute little wrought-iron balconies, wooden floorboards and quirky, individually decorated rooms. The rooms can be on the dark side, but you'll love the big soft beds and local artwork.

Hotel El Convento HISTORIC HOTEL **$$$**
(☎2311-7053; www.elconventonicaragua.com; Iglesia de San Francisco, 20m N; s/d US$90/180; P ❄ 📶) The building drips with atmosphere, the sculpted centerpiece garden is certainly impressive and you're surrounded by precious artwork, but the rooms? They're OK but still a little plain Jane – no doubt a throwback from the Franciscan convent days. Still, you can bet the nuns never had it this good.

Eating

The best place to eat on the cheap or buy fresh veggies is the beautiful, clean **Mercado Central** (⏲6am-5pm), with several inexpensive eateries serving *comidas corrientes* (set meals). After hours, two of the best *fritangas* (grills) in town set up right outside, on the street behind the cathedral, where you can enjoy a huge meal for around US$2. **La Unión Supermercado** (1a Calle NE) is your best super-sized market option.

Many hotels and hostels also have decent restaurant/bars/cafes.

Comedor Lucia NICARAGUAN **$**
(2a Av NE, Bigfoot Hostel, 10m N; mains US$2-4; ⏲Mon-Sat) In 'backpacker alley'; gets a predictable mix of locals and travelers.

VOLUNTEERING IN LEÓN

León is home to a range of grassroots, Nicaraguan-run NGOs. You'll probably need a higher level of Spanish than if you were volunteering in Granada or San Juan del Sur, but chances are it will be a more rewarding process too. Following are some of the many NGOs at work in and around the city. Hostels are a good starting point for information, and Quetzaltrekkers (p148) uses volunteer guides to lead volcano treks.

Asociación Mary Barreda (☎2311-2254; marybarreda@cablenet.com.ni; Iglesia de La Recolección, ½c E) Runs a variety of education programs focusing on women's rights, sex education and STD prevention. Intermediate Spanish and a two-month commitment required.

Pure Earth Project (☎2315-0964; www.greenpathways.com; opposite Bigfoot Hostel) Drop by to see about volunteer ops in nearby turtle-protection initiatives.

El Mediterraneo MEDITERRANEAN **$$**
(☎8895-9392; 2a Av NO, Parque Rubén Darío, 2½c N; dishes US$6-10; ⊙dinner) Date night? Check out the most frequently recommended fine-dining option in town. The decor is gorgeous yet casual, and the music soft and inviting. Diners feast happily on carefully prepared seafood, pasta, meats and curries. The reasonable wine list boasts Argentinean and Chilean wines.

CocinArte VEGETARIAN **$$**
(4a Calle SO, frente El Laborío; mains US$4-7; ✎) This cute little restaurant offers vegetarian versions of dishes from around the world in relaxed and arty surrounds. There are a few meat dishes (cooked in separate pans and served with separate cutlery) to keep the carnivores happy. Friday night is for romantics, with candlelight and soft live music.

Taquezal NICARAGUAN **$$**
(1a Calle SO, Parque Central, ½c O; dishes US$4-7; ⊙4pm-late) With a grand, high-ceilinged dining room kept cool by a battalion of ceiling fans, this is one of León's most atmospheric eating spots. The menu's not outrageously innovative, but the food is good and there's a cozy, candlelit patio out back.

El Sesteo NICARAGUAN **$$**
(Calle Central Rubén Darío, frente Parque Central; dishes US$5-13; ⊙11am-10pm) You can't beat the location (although you can beat the prices) of this pleasant plazaside cafe, with spectacular people-watching, fresh-brewed espresso beverages, a very full bar and a long menu of carefully prepared Nica classics.

★Mesón Real CONTEMPORARY **$$$**
(www.elmesonreal.com; Parque Rubén Dario, 220m N; mains US$6-15; ⊙dinner Mon-Sat, lunch Fri-Sat) Travel your way through the tapas menu, including an eyeball popping crab bisque, bull's balls and clams in garlic sauce, or check out the grilled grouper or other well-conceived mains, before settling into an obligatory romp through the dessert menu at this chart-busting high-end restaurant.

The friendly chef/owner Gustavo comes out of the open kitchen midmeal to check on his guests, adding a touch of humanity to the unique culinary adventure.

Al Carbón STEAKHOUSE **$$$**
(Iglesia La Merced, 25m O; mains US$5-15) León's best steakhouse has a long menu that takes you from pepper steak to special sauce. There's fish and chicken from the grill to choose from. And the sumptious patio dining in a well-preserved *casona* is delightful.

Drinking & Nightlife

León's university students fuel the diesel-charged party. Check out **La Taberna de Mau** (cnr 1a Av NO & 4a Calle NO), a cozy little bar with occasional live music. There are plenty of other places to get your drink on – 1a Calle west of the park is a particularly good area to go bar-hopping. La Siesta Perdida, Bigfoot Hostel and Vía Vía all have good bars out front.

There are some rather snooty discos just out of town on the bypass road, but also a few good dance floors right in the center of town.

Bar Baro BAR
(cnr 1 Calle SO & 2 Av SO) The corner bar offers a wide selection of international dishes (mains US$2 to US$8) and is a popular drink spot.

Olla Quemada BAR
(Calle Central Rubén Darío, Iglesia de San Francisco, 3c O) The hot bar at the time of writing, with live music (Wednesday), independent films (Sunday), Latin dance nights, and a good mix of locals and travelers all week.

Solero BAR
(2a Av SO, frente Teatro; ⊙7pm-late) Attracting a slightly older crowd, this is a great place to go for a few drinks if you actually want to hear what the other person is saying. Live music on Tuesday and some Thursdays.

Oxygene DANCE
(1a Calle SE, Parque Central, ½c O; ⊙8pm-late Wed-Sat) The hottest dance club in the city center with plenty of sleek, modern styling, bright young things, a pool table and occasional live bands.

Don Señor DANCE
(1a Calle NO, frente Iglesia de La Merced; cover US$1-3) This place is more than just a hot nightspot – it's three. It has a disco upstairs, a relaxed bar (with dance floor) downstairs, and the restaurant-pub El Alamo around the corner.

Disco Bohemios DANCE
(1a Av NO, Parque Central, ½c N; ⊙8pm-late Fri & Sat) In the unsigned orange building in front of the basketball court, this is your classic Latin disco – plenty of rum, reggaetón and *bacchata* (romantic Dominican dance music).

Casino La Perla CASINO
(1a Av NO, Iglesia de La Merced, 1½c N) It's not Vegas, baby.

☆ Entertainment

La Casa de Cultura (1a Calle NO, Iglesia de La Merced, 2c O; ⏲Mon-Fri) often has folk music and other events, while **Plaza Siglo Nuevo** (1a Calle NE, La Unión, 20m E; tickets US$3), León's cinema, shows mostly big-budget American films. The **Alianza Francesa** (☎2311-0126; 1a Av NE, Iglesia de la Recolección, 1½c N; ⏲8am-noon & 2-5pm Mon-Fri) hosts a range of cultural events – drop in for this month's program.

Teatro Municipal José de la Cruz Mena PERFORMING ARTS
(2a Av SO, Parque Central, 1c O, 1c S) Check the board in front of this attractive 1885 theater to see what's on during your visit. It's been impressively restored, and for less than US$2 you may be able to catch anything from Salvadorian rock groups to art films to the national ballet on the very accessible stage. The board often lists other cultural events going on in the city.

Shopping

Enterprising area teens sell poems (US$0.70 each) on the street, often illustrated with hearts and unicorns, the perfect gift for the nonmaterialist in your life.

Most museums have good selections of postcards and revolutionary memorabilia.

Orientation

León actually has a system of clearly signed and logically numbered *calles* (streets) and *avenidas* (avenues), allowing anyone to pinpoint any address. Unfortunately, no one actually uses it, preferring the old reliable '2½ blocks east of the Shell station' method instead.

Just for kicks, this is how it works: Av Central and Calle Central Rubén Darío intersect at the northeast corner of the Parque Central, forming the city's northeast, northwest, southeast and southwest quadrants. Calles running parallel to Rubén Darío are numbered NE (Calle 1 NE, Calle 2 NE) north of the cathedral, SE to the south. Av 1 SO (*suroeste;* southwest), one block from Av Central, forms the park's western boundary, paralleling Av 2 SO and so on.

Calle Central Rubén Darío is the city's backbone, and runs east from the cathedral to striking Iglesia El Calvario, and west almost 1km to Barrio Subtiava, continuing another 20km to the Pacific. The majority of tourist services are within a few blocks of the cathedral, with another cluster of museums and churches in Barrio Subtiava.

Information

EMERGENCY

Ambulance (Cruz Roja; ☎2311-2627) Red Cross.

Fire (☎2311-2323)

Police (☎2311-3137)

INTERNET ACCESS & RESOURCES

Internet cafes are all over town. and nearly every hotel has wi-fi.

León Online (www.leononline.net) Useful Spanish-language portal to all things Léonese, including hotels and attractions.

Lonely Planet (www.lonelyplanet.com/nicaragua/leon-and-northwestern-nicaragua/leon) For planning advice, author recommendations, traveler reviews and insider tips.

LAUNDRY

Clean Express Lavandería (cnr Av Central & 4a Calle NE; ⏲7am-7pm) DIY machine wash (US$2) and dry (US$1.25 per 20 minutes) your clothes, or pay a little extra to have it done for you.

MEDICAL SERVICES

Hospital San Vicente (☎2311-6990) Out past the main bus terminal, the region's largest hospital is a 1918 neoclassical beauty that attracts architecture buffs as well as sick tourists.

MONEY

Several banks have ATMs that accept Visa/Plus debit cards.

BAC (1a Calle NE, La Unión, 10m E)

BanPro (Bigfoot Hostel, 20m N) Twenty-four-hour Visa and MasterCard action.

Western Union (1 Calle NE) International cash transfers.

POST & TELEPHONE

Claro (cnr Parque Central & Calle Central Rubén Darío) Sells cell-phone cards.

Post Office (3 Av NO)

TOURIST INFORMATION

Check the hostels for information first, then head to the tour agencies. The tourist info offices are a last line of defense.

Intur (www.intur.gob.ni; 2a Av NO, Parque Rubén Darío, 1½c N) Helpful (if they're not too busy) staff have lots of flyers and a reasonable city map. For really tricky questions, the hostels are often better informed.

Ministry of the Environment & Natural Resources (Marena; mareleon@ibw.com) Inconveniently located across from the Shell station at the southern entrance to the León bypass road, it administers three volcanic national reserves – Telica-Rota, Pilas-El Hoyo and Momotombo – and nonvolcanic Isla Juan Venado. It offers general information. Your best bet is going directly to the Isla Juan Venado ranger station in Las Peñitas or with a private tour.

Oficina de Información Turistica León (Av Central, Parque Central, 25m N; ⏲8:30am-noon & 2-6pm Mon-Fri, 9am-5pm Sat & Sun) This place closes down a lot, but when it's open, it's a good source for local info.

Getting There & Away

BUS

International Buses

There are several international-bus agencies. Buses headed south stop first in Managua, with an often lengthy wait between connections – it's better to make your own way there.

Beni Tours (3a Av NE, Iglesia de San Juan, 25m N) You can buy your tickets for TransNica buses to San José, Costa Rica (US$35) and Tegucigalpa, Honduras (US$35) here. It also offers school-bus service to San Salvador, El Salvador (US$30) and Guatemala City (US$40) leaving at 10am daily.

Ticabus (www.ticabus.com; 6a Calle NE, Palí, 1c O) Has departures for Guatemala City (US$70); San Salvador (US$50); Tegucigalpa (US$23); and Tapachula (US$92).

Shuttle Buses

For shuttles book early and find out when a group is leaving (most shuttles don't leave without at least four passengers).

Tierra Tour (☎2315-4278; www.tierratour.com; 1a Av NO, Iglesia de La Merced, 1½c N) has departures for Granada and Managua. Bigfoot Hostel has departures for Antigua, Guatemala (US$75), Managua (US$10), Granada (US$15), San Juan del Sur (US$25) and Poneloya (US$2), leaving most days.

Buses to Beaches

Buses to Poneloya and Las Peñitas (US$0.75, 40 minutes) depart hourly 6am to 7pm from El Mercadito in Subtiava. Day-trippers take note: the last bus returns at 6:40pm.

Getting Around

The city is strollable, but big enough that you may want to take taxis (per person day/night US$0.70/1), particularly at night. The one-way streets and (relative) lack of traffic make León a good bicycling city. You can rent bikes for around US$5 per day from hostels Bigfoot, Lazybones and Tortuga Booluda. Good rides include Cimac, El Fortín de Acososco and Barrio Subtiava.

Pacific Beaches Near León

The most accessible beaches from León are Poneloya and Las Peñitas, both an easy 20-minute bus ride from Mercadito Subtiava in León. The road splits at the sea: go right for Poneloya proper, left for more-developed Las Peñitas and Reserva Natural Isla Juan Venado.

Several wilder, less-accessible beaches further south are a bit more difficult to reach, including Salinas Grandes, with regular bus service from León and its own access to Reserva Natural Isla Juan Venado. A group of three even less-explored beaches can be reached from the fractured but passable Carretera Vieja to Managua: Puerto Sandino, El Velero and El Tránsito.

Poneloya

Although this beach has the famous name – it's highly praised in the *Viva León Jodido* theme song – it's actually less developed than its twin (Las Peñitas). Be sure to visit during Semana Santa for the annual **Sand Castle & Sculpture Building Contest**.

From La Bocanita (p156), you can hire a private *panga* (small motorboat) seating four (US$70 to US$100) up to El Corinto, over to the Surfing Turtle Lodge on neighboring Isla Brasiles (US$0.75), or just out and back to explore the coastline.

Meet buses to León (US$0.75, 40 minutes, 5:40am to 6:40pm, every 50 minutes) at the *empalme* (three-way junction).

Sleeping & Eating

★ **Surfing Turtle Lodge** LODGE $$
(☎8640-0644; www.surfingturtlelodge.com; Isla los Brasiles, across estuary from La Bocanita; tent, US$5, dm US$10-12, r without bathroom US$32, cabins with bathroom US$40-60; 📶) Getting to this Utopian-like beach paradise is half the fun. From La Bocanita, you catch a small launch (US$0.75 each way), then take a 15-minute walk (or US$0.50 horse-carriage ride) to this beachfront lodge and hippie hideout on the 7km-long Isla Los Brasiles. There's good surf right out front (mostly lefts), bonfires at night, and a good chance you'll stay here…like forever.

The 2nd-story dorm is one of the coolest spots in all of Central America with a giant view to the ocean. The beds are pretty thin, but hey, what can you do? Camping in pre-set-up tents will save a few bucks, or you can go for it with a cabin all of your own. Electricity starts here at 6pm, and there's an on-site restaurant and turtle-protection program. Day visitors are welcome as are long-term volunteers.

Posada de Poneloya HOTEL **$$**
(☎2317-0378; empalme, 400m N; r US$40; P ❄) You're probably better off in Las Peñitas, but if you wanna stay in Poneloya, this clean, fresh, bright and overpriced spot at the entrance to Poneloya is a decent option. Unfortunately, the beach is still a good way from this spot.

La Bocanita NICARAGUAN **$**
About 1km north from the *empalme,* this offers a collection of thatched-roof seafood shacks at the edge of an estuary.

Las Peñitas

When people say they're headed to Poneloya, they usually mean the lazy beach town of Las Peñitas, a wide, sandy stretch fronted by a fine collection of hotels and restaurants. It offers the easiest access to the turtles and mangroves of Reserva Natural Isla Juan Venado, and there's also good, if not spectacular, surfing here, with smallish regular waves that are perfect for beginners.

Check at Hotelito Oasis for Isla Juan Venado tours (US$15), surf lessons (US$15) and board rentals (per half-/full day US$5/9).

NATIONAL BUS SERVICES FROM LEÓN

Most buses leave from León's chaotic **main bus terminal** (☎2311-3909; 6a Calle NE, Palí, 1½km E), which has a fun market area nearby. Watch your wallet. For trips to Rota (Cerro Negro) note that Rota is 5km from the base of the volcano. The San Isidro bus has connections to frequent Matagalpa and Estelí buses.

DESTINATION	COST (US$)	DURATION (hr)	DEPARTURES	FREQUENCY
Chinandega bus	1	1½	4:30am-6pm	every 20min
Chinandega microbus	1.25	50min	4:30am-8pm	depart when full
El Corinto	1.25	1½	4:30am-6pm	half-hourly
El Sauce	2.50	2½	6am-4pm	hourly
Estelí	2.50	2½	5:20am, 12:45pm, 2:15pm & 3:30pm	4 daily
Granada microbus	3	2-3	-	hourly
Hervideros de San Jacinto	0.75	40min	4am-5:30pm	half-hourly
La Paz Centro	0.75	40min	-	every 45min
Managua microbus	2	1¼	4:30am-7pm	depart when full
Managua (Carr Nueva, via La Paz Centro) ***expreso***	1.70	1¼	5am-4pm	almost hourly
Managua (Carr Vieja, via Puerto Sandino) ***ordinario***	1.50	1¾	5am-6:30pm	every 20min
Masaya	2.75	2½	-	hourly
Matagalpa	3	2½	4:20am, 7:30am & 2:45pm	3 daily
Nagarote	1	1hr		every 45min
Rota (Cerro Negro)	0.75	2¼	5:50am, 11am & 3:30pm	3 daily
Salinas Grandes	0.80	2	5:15am, 8:30am, 1:30pm & 4pm	4 daily
San Isidro	2.25	2½	6am-5:30pm	half-hourly

Sleeping & Eating

All the hotels mentioned here have restaurants serving Nicaraguan staples as well as fresh seafood. Las Peñita has quite a few hotels, but few make the cut.

Olazul HOSTEL $
(☎8435-7936; www.hotelolazul.com; empalme, 1km S; dm US$10, r with fan/air-con US$45/50; P ❄ ≋) Set on a wide stretch of open beach, these are the best digs in town. The restaurant overlooks the waves, and out back are five cute little cabins, minimally but stylishly decorated and quite comfortable considering their compact size. There's a six-bed dorm and a dirty pool here too.

Hotelito Oasis HOSTEL $
(☎8839-5344; www.oasislaspenitas.com; empalme, 3km S; dm/s/d US$7/18/20; ☎) A longtime surfer favorite, the Oasis definitely has that lazy backpacker vibe, helped along by its absolute beachfront location. Rooms are big and plain – save for the cool shell lampshades. Luckily, they catch some ocean breezes at night. The four-bed dorm is a bit dark and cramped.

Playa Roca HOTEL $$
(☎8428-8903; www.playaroca.com; empalme, 2km S; r with/without bathroom US$35/25; ☎) Looking out onto a rocky outcrop with a sweet patch of sand either side, this is the most scenic setting on the beach. Rooms are OK – big and bare, with cool tiled floors. None have beach views and some are missing some fundamentals (um...toilet seats?), but overall they're a good deal. This is a popular spot for day-trippers.

Getting There & Around

Buses leave for León (US$0.75, 5:40am to 6:40pm, every 50 minutes) from the clutch of restaurant-bars just north of Barco de Oro. You can also arrange private boats seating at least four to Salinas Grandes (US$60, three hours), including a tour of the reserve.

Reserva Natural Isla Juan Venado

This 18km-long, sandy barrier island (in some places only 300m wide) has swimming holes and lots of wildlife, including nesting turtles and mosquitoes galore. On one side of the island you'll find long, wild, sandy beaches facing the Pacific, on the other, red and black mangroves reflected in emerald lagoons. Best of all, it's very easy to visit.

Several hotels set up guided boat tours of the reserve, but it's generally cheaper to go through the reserve itself. You can get here by boat from less-developed Salinas Grandes, where you'll need to ask around for park rangers who organize three-hour **guided boat tours** (15 people US$50-60). Make reservations, if possible, or just show up at the **ranger station** (☎8861-9099, in León 2311-3776; infocomap@apcomanejo.com; admission US$2.50-4). It's actually much easier to go through Las Peñitas, which has a ranger station and is closer to the turtle nesting sites.

During turtle laying season, which runs July through January, peaking in September and October, thousands of olive ridleys, careys and leatherbacks lay their eggs in El Vivero, close to the Las Peñitas entrance; nighttime turtle tours (August to December, US$15 per person) can be arranged. You can also go fishing here, in Casa de las Peñas.

Puerto Sandino

This is a hard-working port town with 'Hawaii-sized waves.' There is reliable and rocky-bottomed 'Poneloya,' which is not actually in Poneloya (look for it at Playa Diamante). The most photogenic break is at the mouth of the port but isn't always working. The best wave around, sometimes called Miramar (although it's not actually in Miramar), is about 6km south of Puerto Sandino. At low tide, there's a reliable reef break just south.

Buses leave for León (US$0.75, 30 minutes) and Managua (US$1.75, one hour) at least hourly.

Sleeping & Eating

Miramar Surfcamp LODGE $
(☎8945-1785; www.miramarsurfcamp.com; dm US$19, s/d US$56/80, without bathroom US$35/56) Check out the basic rooms at this surf lodge outside of town that also offers weekly packages.

Hotel Yeland HOTEL $$
(☎2312-2256; hotelyelandpto@yahoo.es; s/d US$35/50; P ❄ @ ☎) For the one place to stay in town, this is actually pretty good, with big, clean rooms in a modern house. A great restaurant is attached. Surfing,

snorkeling and (with plenty of notice) dive trips can be organized here.

Restaurante Chango NICARAGUAN **$$**
(opposite Yeland Hotel; mains US$4-12; ⏲ lunch & dinner) This humble eatery serves all your faves, including fresh fish, shrimp and, if you're lucky, *rondon,* a slow-cooked seafood stew.

El Centro Turístico El Velero

This early Sandanista tourist compound with a wonderful beach, broken-down and abandoned buildings, and no one for miles makes for a fun day-trip from León or Puerto Sandino. From the entrance to Puerto Sandino, you get here on a dirt road heading south for a couple of kilometers. Occasionally buses or trucks ply this route for around US$0.50. Once you get to the gate, just ask for permission to go in – it generally allows day visitors.

Currently, all of the restaurants and corrugated-roof cabins here have been abandoned, but you never know, this may be the next Mc-Disney-Sandinista-Land.

El Tránsito

This little fishing village on the coast between León and Managua sits on a near-perfect crescent bay. The sand is blacker here, due to volcanic residue. The beach, while not exactly dirty, could certainly be cleaner and there's a strong undertow, but to the south, near the lava flows, there are protected swimming holes. You may be able to arrange a homestay in the village, and there are a few basic beachfront restaurants.

The arts center, **El Transito Centro de Artes** (ETCA; www.eltransitoarts.com), has ongoing volunteer ops. Directions here are online.

Sleeping

Solid Surf Tours HOTEL **$$$**
(El Transito beach, 100m N of village center; r US$60, 7 days all-inclusive US$945) This is about the only place to stay in El Transito. It runs all-inclusive surf and yoga camps. The owners promise us that the surf near El Transito is good for beginners. The rooms are pretty basic (with dorms underway), but you have a cool beachfront patio for hanging out and are miles away from the crowded waves of the southern beaches.

Getting There & Away

Buses to Managua (US$1, 1½ hours) leave at 5am, 6am and 7am, and return from Managua's Mercado Oriental at 1pm, 2pm and 3pm daily. You can always catch a ride in a pickup (US$0.50) from out the front of the church up the hill; they leave hourly from 8am to 5pm for the 30-minute ride out to the Carretera Vieja a León, where buses pass en route to Managua, León and points in between.

Volcanoes

The Maribios chain is the epicenter of one of the most active volcanic regions on earth. Park management is split between two Marena offices: **Marena León** (☎2311-3776; mareleon@ibw.com) manages Reserva Natural Volcán Momotombo, Reserva Natural Telica-Rota and Reserva Natural Pilas–El Hoyo, which includes Cerro Negro; **Marena Chinandega** (☎2344-2443; lider@ibw.com.ni) keeps tabs on Reserva Natural San Cristóbal–La Casita and Reserva Natural Volcán Cosigüina.

The easiest and safest way to visit the volcanoes is a guided hike, arranged by several outfitters in León and elsewhere, but there's always a way to get there on your own.

Reserva Natural Volcán Momotombo

The perfect cone of **Volcán Momotombo**, destroyer of León Viejo and inspiration for its own Rubén Darío poem, rises red and black 1280m above Lago de Managua, and is the country's most beautiful threat. It is a symbol of Nicaragua, and has furnished at its base itself in miniature – the lake **Isla Momotombito** (389m), sometimes called Isla Rosa or just 'The Child.'

There are several other structures worth seeing in the reserve, including the 4km-diameter, 200m-deep **Caldera Monte Galán**, tiled with five little lagoons (alligators included) reflecting theoretically extinct **Cerro Montoso** (500m), but you'd need to arrange a custom tour to see them.

Most people come to climb Momotombo, a serious eight-hour excursion that can be done in one day, though most outfitters offer an overnight involving hot springs at a nearby farm. Because of access issues, it's best to go with a guided tour.

Isla Momotombito is accessible from Puerto Momotombo (easier), just around the corner from the ruins of León Viejo, and Mateare (cheaper), both on the shores of Lago de Managua. The basaltic cone has long been a ceremonial site, and a few petroglyphs and statues are still visible on it.

Coming from Puerto Momotombo, a private boat seating four costs at least US$100 to make the 9km trip, over sometimes very choppy water. Boat operators hang around the handful of lakeshore restaurants, which all serve beer and *comidas corrientes*.

Reserva Natural Pilas-El Hoyo

Most people come to this reserve to see the volcano that doesn't even get second billing: **Cerro Negro** (726m...and growing), one of the youngest volcanoes in the world. It first erupted from a quiet cornfield in 1850, and its pitch-black, loose-gravel cone has been growing in spurts ever since.

Almost every guide in León offers a guided hike to the top, a shadeless, two- to three-hour climb into the eye-watering fumes of the yellow-streaked crater. Then your outfitter will offer a faster way down. **Volcano surfing** has come a long way as a sport – it used to be done on surfboards, old mattresses, cardboard boxes etc, but now there are people custom-designing boards. Gnarly.

Other peaks worth climbing include the dormant **Volcán Pilas** (1001m), which last had gas in 1954; and **El Hoyo** (1088m), the park's second-most active peak, basically a collapsed crater with fumaroles. Then it's time to relax in deliciously cool **Laguna de Asososca**, a jungle-wrapped crater lake that's poorly signed and on private property, and therefore difficult to visit on your own. If you book a tour climbing Cerro Negro (or are visiting León Viejo, nearby), definitely try to get this as an add-on.

Reserva Natural San Cristóbal-La Casita

This is the one that probably caught your eye: **Volcán San Cristóbal** (1745m), the tallest volcano in Nicaragua, streaming gray smoke from its smooth cone. Summiting this beauty is a serious hike: six to eight hours up, three hours down. A guide is highly recommended, as access is difficult and dangerous and requires crossing private property. The volcano is very active, with two large eruptions at the end of 2012.

There are several other volcanic structures worth seeing, including **El Chonco** (715m), an inactive volcanic plug contiguous with San Cristóbal, and **Moyotepe**, close by, a small crater lake at 917m, accessible from the Chinandega-Somotillo road.

Reserva Natural Telica-Rota

This very active, 90.52 sq-km complex peaks at **Volcán Telica** (1061m), the twin craters of which are a mere 30km north of León. Also called the 'Volcano of León,' Telica is active in four- to five-year cycles; the last really big eruption was in 1765. Most eruptions these days involve gases and a few pyroclastic belches.

There are several 'extinct' cones around the base, including **Cerro Agüero** (744m), **Loma Los Portillos** (721m) and **Volcán Rota** (832m), which still has constant fumaroles. There are big plans for this park, which is considered a potential ecotourism gold mine due to its easy access from San Jacinto.

San Jacinto

The only town of any size on this stretch of the Ring of Fire, San Jacinto is base camp for climbs up Volcán Telica (1061m; six to eight hours), Volcán Rota (832m; three to five hours), with great views of Telica, and **Volcán Santa Clara** (834m; three to five hours). If you're up for it, you can walk to Cerro Negro from here.

Organized tours invariably stop at the famous **Hervideros de San Jacinto** (admission US$2; 7am-5pm), an expanse of bubbling mud puddles. They shift in size and location after a good rain, so put more faith in your pint-sized **guide** (per child US$0.50 to $1) than the rickety fence. You can wash it off about six blocks away at the luke-warm **Aguas Termales San Jacinto** (San Jacinto Hot Springs).

Buses leave for León (US$0.75, 40 minutes) every half-hour between 4am and 5:30pm.

Tours

Safari Nicarao TOUR
(2266-1018; entrance to Hervidores San Jacinto)
This basic operator could take you to some of the nearby attractions, but you are probably better off with a León-based operation.

Sleeping

Turismo de Aventura HOTEL $
(entrance to San Jacinto; s without bathroom US$10) This bargain-basement spot is the only horse in town, and that horse won't pull.

El Sauce

POP 7600

Once a bustling and important link on the national railway, today scenic El Sauce is just a sleepy mountain town cut straight from an Old West movie. The town bursts to life on the third Sunday in January, when pilgrims from all over Nicaragua, Guatemala and beyond make their way here to pay their respects to **El Señor de Esquipulas** (The Black Christ).

The image, to which all manner of miracles have been attributed, arrived in El Sauce in 1723 from Esquipulas, Guatemala, and refused to move another centimeter upon arriving at this lovely spot. The beautiful, if not flashy, 1828 **Templo de El Sauce** was declared a national sanctuary in 1984, but burned in 1999. The Black Christ, however, was saved, and all of El Sauce pitched in to rebuild the sanctuary.

The gateway to the Cordillera Dariense, El Sauce is surrounded by cool green mountains strewn with waterfalls, and several **hiking trails** begin in town.

Ask around for directions to the trailhead through the year-round green of the forest to **La Piedra de San Ramón**, which starts about 3km north of town. If you're looking for more excuses to stay, you could take a taxi 6km from town to **Río Grande**, with a swimming hole.

Walking distance from town, **Finca Campestre Cárdenas** (☎2319-2329; Alcaldía, 1km S) has a small petting zoo and a swimming pool. It's also a *vivero* (plant nursery), and brings in a local crowd for its Sunday afternoon barbecue.

Sleeping & Eating

Hotel Blanco HOTEL $
(☎2319-2403; hotelblancoelsauce1@gmail.com; Alcaldía, 1c S, 1c O; s/d with fan US$12/15, with air-con US$20/25; ❄) The best rooms in town are found at this cement-block building. They have cable TV and look onto the central courtyard/parking garage. The service is friendly.

Bar-Hotel El Viajero HOTEL $
(☎2319-2325; Enitel, 1c N, ½c E; s/d air-con US$25/35, without bathroom US$5/10; ❄) This place isn't very friendly, and the rooms are pretty beat down (but clean!). The common areas in the historic building almost make up for it.

Comedor Falkis NICARAGUAN $
(Enitel, 2c E, ½c S; dishes US$3-5) Located near the sanctuary, this place serves Nicaraguan standards.

Getting There & Away

Buses to León (US$2.50, 2½ hours, 5am to 4:30pm, six daily) leave from the market, downhill from the sanctuary. Note that although the 28km road from the León–San Isidro Hwy is beautifully paved, the El Sauce–Estelí road (shown as the same 'level' of road on most maps) is 4WD only in the dry season, if you're lucky.

Chinandega

POP 133,000

Sultry Chinandega's never going to end up on anyone's Top 10 list. Sorry. It's just not. It isn't that the town's ugly (it's OK) or that there's nothing to do (there's some stuff), it's because Chinandega's the gateway to some of the most breathtaking spots in the entire northwest. And by the time you get there, your memories of this little workaday town will be well overshadowed by the glory before you.

Sights & Activities

In town, Chinandega has some seriously striking churches, including 1878 **Iglesia Guadalupe** (Santuario de Nuestra Señora de Guadalupe), which, despite the radiant and rather grandiose colonial-style facade, has a simple, precious wood interior with an exceptionally lovely Virgin. Three blocks to the north and two blocks west, **Iglesia San Antonio**, its dramatic facade steeped in a more sedate pastel yellow, has delightful Easter egg–blue and yellow columns and arches inside.

Next, it's 1586 **Parroquia Santa Ana**, three and a half blocks north, Chinandega's most important church, with a splendid Stations of the Cross, lots of gilt and some Russian Orthodox styling that earn this one 'Best Interior in Town.' A richer yellow with white trim, it stands watch over the festive Parque Central, crammed full of play equipment, canoodling teenagers, fast-food stands and, at the time of writing, a few rather

Chinandega

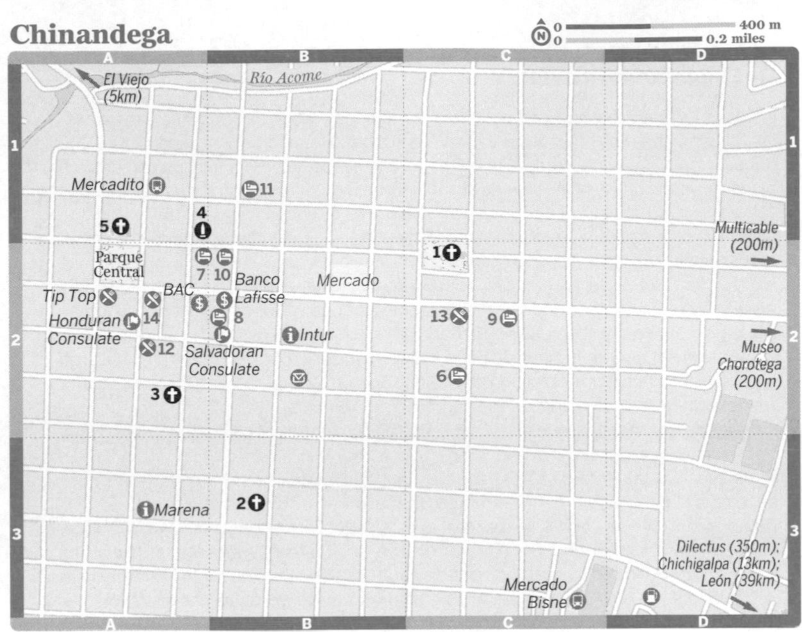

out-of-place-looking emos. There's sometimes ballet *folklorico* and live music in the central kiosk. The **mausoleum of Rubén Darío's mother** is just one block east.

It's seven blocks east of Santa Ana to **Iglesia El Calvario**, with a rust red, rather art deco exterior and a very nice bell tower, its otherwise simple interior hung with chandeliers.

Museo Chorotega MUSEUM

(☎2341-4291; Multicable, 1c S, Reparto los Angeles; admission US$5; ⊙7am-1pm & 3-6pm Mon-Fri) Anyone with even a passing interest in archaeology should stop in at the one of the finest museums in the country. The collection focuses on pre-Columbian ceramics and is presented in a logical timeline, from the early inhabitants up until the arrival of the Spanish.

There are about 1500 pieces in the collection, of which about 400 are on display. Of particular interest is the small collection on burial rituals, where the guide will no doubt put forward the theory that the flesh of human sacrifices was sometimes eaten as a religious practice. If your taxi driver doesn't know it, tell them it's in the compound of Fundación Chinandega, the NGO that acts as caretaker.

Chinandega

Sights

1 Iglesia El Calvario ... C2
2 Iglesia Guadalupe ... B3
3 Iglesia San Antonio ... A2
4 Mausoleum of Rubén Darío's Mother ... A1
5 Parroquia Santa Ana ... A1

Sleeping

6 Hotel California ... C2
7 Hotel Casa Grande ... A2
8 Hotel Cosigüina ... B2
9 Hotel El Chinandegano ... C2
10 Hotel los Balcones ... B2
11 Hotel San José ... B1

Eating

12 Fritanga La Parrillada ... A2
13 Fritanga Las Tejitas ... C2
14 Palí ... A2

Drinking & Nightlife

Bar La Bohemia ... (see 9)

WORTH A TRIP

DIY EXPLORATION IN NAGAROTE & LA PAZ CENTRO: QUESILLO CONTROVERSY

The towns of Nagarote and La Paz Centro don't receive much tourist traffic – there just ain't that much to see or do. Sure, La Paz Centro has a few monuments and a lovely 1600s adobe church, El Templo Parroquial Santiago, and Nagarote has its Mercado de Artesania across from the bus terminal, fun swims in nearby Río Tamarindo, and a tranquil plaza and cultural center, but really, it isn't enough to hold your attention for very long.

But, if you are passing through, you won't want to miss trying Nicaragua's most famous national dish, the *quesillo* (a thick, steaming corn tortilla topped with a pancake of mozzarella-like cheese, then loosely rolled into a cylinder and fitted into a special plastic bag). They cost just US$1 and normally include an optional topping like onion chutney (do it!) or sour cream (think twice!).

Two towns have a legitimate claim as the *cuña* (cradle) of *quesillo* culture: Nagarote, birthplace of innovator and originator Señora Socorro Munguía Madriz; and La Paz Centro, where she came up with the culinary triumph. In 1912, along with the Rueda sisters, she began selling *quesillos* – at both the Nagarote and La Paz Centro train stations, further confusing the issue.

As *quesillos* proliferated across the country, this original crew opened what's now an almost pilgrimage-worthy destination, **Quesillos Guiligüiste** (quesillos US$1-1.50), pronounced kay-*see*-yos wil-ee-*wee*-stay. It's so popular that it has its own freelance car-parking personnel out front. This, of course, is in La Paz Centro. But, as Nagarote natives note, Doña Dalila Lara, another early *quesillo* adherent, moved to Nagarote in the 1970s, where she opened Quesillos Acacia, also pilgrimage worthy, especially if you're still hungry.

Sleeping

Even Managuans complain that Chinandega is hot. Consider paying extra for air-con.

Hotel California HOTEL **$**
(☎2341-0936; Las Tejitas, 1½c S; r per person US$9) The slightly out-of-the way location is made up for by tidy medium-sized rooms with great bathrooms and cable TV. Rooms surround a big covered patio set out with comfy lounge furniture.

Hotel Casa Grande HOTEL **$**
(☎8266-0184; atiserino@spectrum.com.gt; Parroquia Santa Ana, 1½c E; r with fan/air-con US$15/25; ❄) Rooms are big and kind of grungy, but the location just off the Parque Central is unbeatable. The friendly owner speaks a bit of English and can organize trips up Volcán San Cristóbal, with a farmstay halfway up the slope for US$25 per person or birding tours (US$25).

Hotel los Balcones HOTEL **$$**
(☎2341-8994; www.hotellosbalcones.com; esquina de los bancos, 1c N; s/d incl breakfast US$41/53; P❄📶) The newest hotel in town is full of tasteful colonial style. There are, in fact, balconies, but you may choose to spend your time on the tiny roof terrace instead.

Hotel Cosigüina HOTEL **$$**
(☎2341-3636; www.hotelcosiguina.net; esquina de los bancos, ½c S; d incl breakfast US$40; P❄@📶) The hodgepodge blend of modern, motel-like stylings with hip 1960s accents may not win it any design awards, but the comfort factor's definitely here and the location is a winner.

Hotel San José HOTEL **$$**
(☎2341-2723; esquina de los bancos, 2½c N; s/d US$28/35; ❄📶) Heavy dark-wood furniture and an overload of religious-themed decoration give this place a somewhat somber feel, but the rooms are spacious enough, with big TVs.

Hotel El Chinandegano HOTEL **$$**
(☎2341-4800; chinandegoanohotel@yahoo.es; Mercado 3c E; r US$25; P❄📶🏊) Once one of the finest in town, this one's slipping a bit. The dark rooms get a bit depressing. Lucky it has cable TV.

Eating

The best cheap eats set up at dusk in the Parque Central, lined with hamburger stands. There are two great *fritangas* beside the basketball court just beyond. For basics, check out **Palí** (frente Parque Central).

★Fritanga La Parrillada STEAKHOUSE $
(Palí, 1c S; mains US$4-8) This is part steakhouse, part pizzeria, part *fritanga;* if you can't find something you want to eat here, chances are you're not hungry.

Fritanga Las Tejitas GRILL $
(Mercado, 2c E; mains US$2) An institution, this *fritanga* gets packed breakfast, lunch and dinner – and mariachis could show up at any time. It's a solid steam-table buffet with a nationwide reputation.

Drinking & Nightlife

Bar La Bohemia BAR
(⊙5pm-midnight) In Hotel El Chinandegano, La Bohemia serves quality food and 'the coldest beer in town,' which is a draw. It's also air-conditioned to the point where you'll want a sweater.

Dilectus DANCE
(Carretera a León; cover US$2-5; ⊙Wed-Sat) The most popular disco in town isn't in town, instead it's out on the highway to León. It's even more opulent than its sister disco in León and attracts a slightly more mature crowd. Thursday is mariachi night.

Orientation

Chinandega is on a logical Spanish grid, but note that the *alcaldía* (mayor's office) is actually five blocks east of the natural city center at Parroquia Santa Ana. Most of the development here is going on outside the historic city center, with new malls springing up along the highways.

Information

BAC (Parque Central, 1c E, ½c S) ATM.

Banco Lafisse (Parque Central 3c E)

Intur (chinandega@intur.gob.ni; Mercado, 1c O, ½c S) The local tourist office has a good collection of flyers and handy, information-packed scrapbooks.

Marena (Iglesia Guadelupe, 1½c O; ⊙9am-4:30pm Mon-Fri) This office keeps tabs on Reserva Natural San Cristóbal–La Casita, Reserva Natural Volcán Cosigüina and Reserva Natural Estero Padre Ramos, all with reasonable access; and Reserva Natural Delta del Estero Real, where you're on your own. Staff also keep an eye on Reserva Genetica Apacunaca (Apacunaca Genetic Resource Reserve).

Post office (Mercado, 2cE)

Getting There & Around

Taxis charge US$0.50 in town, and also make the runs to El Viejo (US$3) and El Corinto (US$6).

BUS

There are two places to catch a bus: the big and relatively well-organized Mercado Bisne, and the more chaotic Mercadito, close to Parroquia Santa Ana.

Tica Bus has departures for Guatemala City, Guatemala (US$52); San Salvador, El Salvador (US$35); Tapachula, Mexico (US$69); Tegucigalpa, Honduras (US$23); and San Pedro Sula, Honduras (US$37).

Bus Services from Mercado Bisne

Chichigalpa (microbus US$0.20, 15 minutes, 5am to 6pm, depart when full)

El Corinto (bus US$0.50, 40 minutes, 4:30am to 6pm, every 15 minutes;microbus US$0.75, 25 minutes, 4:30am to 7pm, depart when full)

El Guasaule (Honduran border) (bus US$1.50, 1¾ hours, 4am to 5pm, every 25 minutes; microbus US$2, one hour, 4:30am to 7pm, depart when full)

León (bus US$0.75, 1½ hours, 4am to 7pm, every 15 minutes; microbus US$1, one hour, 4:30am to 7pm, depart when full)

Managua (bus US$2.50, three hours, 4am to 5:20pm, hourly; microbus US$3, two hours, 4:30am to 7pm, depart when full)

Bus Services from Mercadito

El Viejo (bus US$0.80, 20 minutes, 5am to 6pm, every 15 minutes; microbus US$0.60, 10 minutes, 5am to 6pm, depart when full)

Mechapa (US$1.30, three hours, 2pm) Buses continue to Punta Ñata (US$1.75, 4½ hours).

Playa Jiquilillo & Reserva Natural Estero Padre Ramos (US$1, 1½ hours, 6:30am, 10am, 11:30am, 3pm and 4:30pm) The 6:30am bus meets collective boats to Venecia Wednesday, Thursday and Saturday.

Potosí (Reserva Natural Volcán Cosigüina) (US$1.50, 3½ hours, 9:30am and 10:30am)

Around Chinandega

El Viejo

Just 5km from Chinandega is the ancient indigenous capital of Tezoatega, today called El Viejo. This is the site of **Basílica de Nuestra Señora de la Inmaculada Concepción de la Virgen María**, home of Nicaragua's patron saint and mistress of its biggest national religious event, La Gritería, when troupes of *festejeros* shout the question *¿Quién causa tanta alegría?* ('Who causes so much joy?')

WORTH A TRIP

DIY: PUERTO MORAZÁN & DELTA DEL ESTERO REAL

If you love wetlands, you're going to be disappointed: there's no tourist infrastructure at all for enormous Reserva Natural Delta del Estero Real, about 20km – two hours by bus on this terrible road – north of Chinandega in the desperately poor town of Puerto Morazán.

The worst part is that this monumental river delta, luxuriating along the Honduran border, is beautiful, with alligators lounging alongside the lush, mangrove-lined shores, views to Volcán Cosigüina and natural lagoons all aflutter with migratory birds. Unfortunately, it is also threatened: its inaccessibility has emboldened poachers, loggers and dirty shrimping operations. These wetlands need tourists.

Should you choose to accept this mission, head out early for a day trip to Puerto Morazán, or pack your mosquito net and ask at the **alcaldía** (☎2342-2580) if anyone is renting rooms or hammock space in town. Fishing boats holding four, plus your Spanish-speaking guide, ask about US$25 for a four-hour tour of the reserve. There are seven buses daily from the Chinandega Mercadito (US$1, two hours).

to receive the response, *¡La concepción de María!* ('The conception of Mary!').

The most dedicated pilgrims show up to her beautiful church a few days early for the **Lavada de la Plata** (Polishing of the Silver) on December 5 and 6. The work is meditative but fun, with mariachis serenading the faithful at their brilliant task.

Tours

There's not much to do here, but El Viejo is home to two organizations that work together to arrange recommended guided trips to Reserva Natural Estero Padre Ramos and Reserva Natural Volcán Cosigüina.

Fundación Lider GUIDED TOUR
(☎2344-2381; Portón Inatec, 1c N, 1c O) This caters primarily to larger groups, and offers two-day (per person US$80) and three-day (per person US$100) trips to the volcano, including transportation, food and lodging. Prices are very dependent on group size – try to get some friends together.

Selva GUIDED TOUR
(www.selvanic.org) This is a nifty little acronym for Somos Ecologistas en la Lucha por la Vida y Ambiente; We Are Ecologists Fighting for Nature (*selva* is Spanish for 'forest'). It offers recommended package tours to Reserva Natural Estero Padre Ramos and Reserva Natural Volcán Cosigüina. It has no official office – ask at the *alcaldía* if a representative is around.

Eating

As with most of small-town Nicaragua, the best, most fun eating to be had is at the *fritanga* stands in the Parque Central.

Getting There & Away

Drivers should note that this is the last chance for gas on the peninsula. All buses headed north from Chinandega to Potosí or the Cosigüina beaches stop at the El Viejo *empalme* about 20 minutes after leaving Chinandega. To Chinandega, you can get buses (US$0.60, 20 minutes, every 15 minutes) and minivans (US$0.80, 10 minutes, leaving when full) from in front of the basilica. A taxi to Chinandega costs US$3.

Chichigalpa

The town with the cutest name in Nicaragua is best known as the source from which all **Flor de Caña rum** flows, in seven beloved shades running from crystal clear to deepest amber. Chichigalpa is also home to **Ingenio San Antonio**, the largest sugar refinery in the country, and cane fields carpet the skirts of **Volcán San Cristóbal**, which rises from the sweaty lowlands a mere 15km from the city center.

There's no Intur, but the **Chichigalpa alcaldía** (☎2343-2456; alchichi@ibw.com.ni), about two blocks from the charming Parque Central, has a Commission of Culture that can arrange guided tours of **Flor de Caña** (not open to the general public), city tours that take in the ruins of **Iglesia El Pueblito**, and guided hikes to the top of San Cristóbal via **Parque Ecológico Municipal**. This smoking city park, about 10km from town and accessible by 4WD only, preserves 50 *manzanas* (city blocks) of mostly primary forest, including a trailhead to the top of the volcano. Guides cost US$15 per group.

Other than the automotels at the *empalme*, there's the reasonable **Hospedaje Friends** (frente licoreria; s/d US$7.50/10), just west of the entrance to the rum factory in an unsigned building. These are decent budget rooms, but solo female travelers may feel uncomfortable here. Right at the other end of the scale is **Hotel La Vista** (☎2343-2035; Alcaldía, 1c E, 75m N; s/d incl breakfast US$40/60; P❄@), with good-sized rooms stocked with wrought-iron and hardwood furniture. The breakfast is big, and the balcony does indeed have a vista.

Microbuses to Chinandega (US$0.20, 15 minutes) depart from the market when full, 5am to 6pm.

Cosigüina Peninsula Beaches

The Cosigüina peninsula is well on its way to becoming an island, worn away on two sides by brilliant estuaries and fringed with sandy beaches, ranging from the pearl grays of Jiquilillo to coal black at Playa Carbón.

These aren't the easiest beaches to visit, but you'll be rewarded with impressive stretches of sand interrupted only by fishing villages, sea turtles and mangrove swamps. The surfing is great but largely unexplored, and hotels are few and far between.

El Corinto

POP 18,000 / ELEV 10M

Nicaragua's only deep-water port, El Corinto actually inherited the job from a much older town, Puerto El Realejo, founded on February 26, 1522, and subsequently attacked by such famous pirates as William Dampier and John Davis. As the centuries passed and sand filled in the estuary, the barrier island of Punto Icaco became the port, where El Corinto was founded in 1858.

This was the port that US president Ronald Reagan mined in 1983, after which Congress passed a law specifically forbidding the use of taxpayer dollars for overthrowing the Nicaraguan government. Thus began the Iran-Contra affair.

Today, just 19km from Chinandega, El Corinto's 19th-century wooden row houses, narrow streets and broad beaches score high on the 'adorability potential' scale, although actual adorability ratings are much lower. It's sort of sad; although some 65% of the nation's imports and exports flow through, very little of the money stays here. Cruise ships arrive throughout the year, but passengers are whisked away to more scenic spots.

The **Parque Central** is downright audacious: a concrete confection of fountains and turtles with a very Jetsons-esque clock tower. **Alfonso Cortes-Corinto History Museum, Library & Auditorium** (admission by donation; ⏲7:30am-noon & 1:30-6pm), in the bright-blue former train station, has a handful of informative displays about Corinto's once and future greatness arranged around a few railroad artifacts, gathering dust in the grinding reality of the present.

Across the street, a squat, green Catholic church is the final resting place of poet **Azarías H Pallais**, although most literature ignores him, noting instead that **Isla El Cardón**, just offshore, inspired Rubén Darío's poem 'A Magarita Debayle.'

The **beaches** close to town are dirty, but walk just a few minutes north to find cleaner **Paso Caballos**, with a string of thatched restaurant-bars, a terrible rip current and good **surfing**. Between El Corinto and Paso Caballos, a big, hollow left is supposed to be one of the best waves in the country, but it's boat access only. North of Paso Caballos is a river-mouth break and some peaks break left. The protected bay also offers world-class **windsurfing**, if you've brought your own equipment – big swells roll in toward the estuary when the tide changes, good for jumps.

El Corinto actually does get packed the first weekend in May for the **Fiesta Gastronomica del Mar**. It begins with a fishing competition and ends with every chef in the department turning out top-quality seafood dishes for the crowd. Cultural activities, parades, beauty contests and lots of dancing help you work it off.

Stay a while at downscale **Hospedaje Luvy** (☎2342-2637; Eskimo, 1½c E; s/d US$10/13, without bathroom US$5/8), which is a model for budget hotels worldwide – no frills, but freshly painted, with good beds, clean bathrooms and new, nonrattling fans. **Hotel Central** (☎2342-2380; frente Puerto; s/d US$30/40; P❄), the best hotel in town, scrapes in ahead of the *hospedaje* by adding air-con and TV. It may seem overpriced unless you're a ship's captain or customs agent on an expense account.

Most restaurants are on the water. **Costa Azul** (Eskimo, 6c N; dishes US$5-9) is a pleasant outdoor affair serving truly gringo-sized portions of chicken, beef and seafood. Next door, **El Peruano** (mains US$2-5) serves cheaper, smaller plates and attracts a bigger drinking crowd. At either one, you can arrange boats for about US$35 to take you on a sightseeing tour of the islands, some of them

TO SOMOTILLO & EL GUASAULE (HONDURAN BORDER)

It's a smooth, paved 80km through mostly empty grazing land to the border town of Somotillo, though you will see signs for **Reserva Genetica Apacunaca** (Apacunaca Genetic Resource Reserve). There's no tourist infrastructure, which is sort of the point. It protects one of four known caches of *teosinte* (wild corn) in the world, only discovered here in the late 1990s.

Corn, long a Nicaraguan staple food, has rather mysterious origins. *Teosinte* has a very hard outer shell, rendering it almost inedible except as popcorn – an odd choice for domestication. It, like modern maize, employs a type of photosynthesis most common in cacti and other dry-weather plants, but its roots are actually modified branches, an adaptation more common in swamps.

However, both adaptations are common in epiphytes – tree-dwelling plants usually associated with cloud forest. But there are also tropical dry-forest epiphytes, such as *pithaya* (also known as dragonfruit), which is closely related to prickly pear cactus; perhaps corn started up in the trees. But no one knows, and the cache at Apacunaca is key to this genetic sleuthing: while other *teosinte* stocks grow in dry, high-altitude areas, fast-growing *Zea luxurians* thrives at an elevation of 10m, surviving in standing water during the six-month rainy season.

If you're not deeply interested in corn, however, it's on to sunny Somotillo, more a place to get stuck than to visit. If this happens to you, hire one of the 7000 pedicabs to take you on a grand tour, perhaps of the two **churches**.

A cluster of hotels on the main road is the real attraction, however. **Hotel Fronteras** (☎2346-2264; d with fan/air-con US$12/18; P ❄) is the most comfortable, with attractive furniture, cable TV and a nice restaurant.

For further information, head to shop.lonelyplanet.com to purchase a downloadable PDF of the Honduras chapter from Lonely Planet's *Central America on a Shoestring* guide.

(including Isla El Cardón – sorry, Darío fans) private and off-limits.

Buses (US$0.50, 40 minutes) and microbuses (US$0.75, 25 minutes) depart the Parque Central every 15 minutes or so for Chinandega.

Playa Aserradores

Worth the bumpy ride from the well-signed exit off the Chinandega–Potosí Hwy, this long, smooth stretch of sand has two good lodging options and excellent surfing. The name of the wave is Boom-wavos, and it's worth checking Hotel Chancletas' website to see it for yourself. There's also a left five minutes offshore and a few other good breaks around. Chancletas offers fishing tours (US$120, four hours), kayak tours (US$30, six hours), surfboard rentals (per day US$15), and horses (US$20) and bikes (US$6).

Hotel Chancletas (☎8868-5036; www.hotelchancletas.com; Asseradores; r with air-con US$80, without bathroom & with fan US$35; P ❄ ᯤ), perched up on a grassy hillside overlooking the famed Boom-wavos break is a surfers' spot with shared rooms that may have some mysterious animal droppings on the sheets, and nice upscale rooms.

Marina Puesta del Sol (☎8880-0019; www.marinapuestadelsol.com; r incl breakfast from US$200; P ❄ ᯤ 🏊), at the end of the road before the estuary, is a very upmarket yacht club offering great views of smoking San Cristóbal from the infinity pool, and even better ones from the enormous, fully equipped rooms. It has a beach basically all to itself on the other side of the hill.

Buses here from Chinandega depart at 2:30pm and 4pm, and leave for Chinandega at 5am and 7:45am (US$1, 1½ hours).

Playa Jiquilillo

This endless pale-gray beach (pronounced *heekeeleeyo*) frames what you thought existed only in tales that begin 'You should have seen it back when I was first here...' The picture-perfect fishing village fronts a dramatic rocky point, where tide pools reflect the reds and golds of a huge setting sun, Cosigüina's ragged bulk rising hazy and postapocalyptic to the north. The region remains largely undeveloped, despite its beauty and accessibility, because a devastating 1992 tsunami wiped this village out completely.

And the beach is perfect. There's no real rip current in the calm cove. Just beyond is a good river-mouth break, with regular peaks where you can almost always carve out a few turns; bring your own board. Most people are here to see Reserva Natural Estero Padre Ramos, where you can also arrange lodging.

Check at the Rancho Tranquilo or online for information on the area's turtle-rescue program, **Sea Turtle Rescue** (www.seaturtlerescue-nicaragua.org), which occasionally looks for volunteers.

Sleeping & Eating

★ Rancho Tranquilo HOSTEL $
(☎8968-2290; www.rancho-tranquilo-nicaragua.com; dm US$7, cabins without bathroom US$20; P) The best budget spot in town, this collection of bungalows and a small dorm on its private stretch of beach is great. There's a cool bar and common area, and vegetarian dinners (US$3 to US$5) are served family style. Nobody gets out of Rancho Tranquilo without giving the dazed-and-dazzling owner Tina a hug.

Hospedaje Rancho Esperanza GUESTHOUSE $
(☎8879-1795; www.rancho-esperanza.com; dm US$6, cabañas s/d US$10/16) Let staff know you're on your way to this quiet collection of simple bamboo huts scattered across a grassy field a bit back from the beach. The dorm is on stilts above the common area, where meals (US$1.50 to US$3.50) and hammocks are available. Tours are available.

Finca Ecológica Trinchera FARM $
(☎8382-8560; www.fincatrinchera.com; Los Zorros, 500m E of Y Junction; dm US$8, r per person without bathroom US$12) Don't want to be on the beach? This inland option on a 2-hectare fruit farm has plenty of hammocks to spread out, and offers unique tours in the reserve. It's clean and friendly.

Monty's Surf Camp LODGE $$
(☎8949-1952; www.nicaraguasurfbeach.com; dm US$20, s/d US$65/70, without bathroom US$35/40; @) The most upscale option here, this hotel–surf camp is set right on the waterfront. The lounge and common areas are sweet with a wasting-away-in-paradise feel par excellance. The rooms are just above average, but nicer than anything else around. Check the website for all-inclusive package deals.

Getting There & Away

Buses to Chinandega (US$1, 1½ hours) leave at 6am, 7:30am, 9:30am, 1:15pm and 3:30pm, returning from the Chinandega Mercadito at 6:30am, 10am, 11:30am, 3pm and 4:30pm.

Reserva Natural Estero Padre Ramos

A few minutes north of Los Zorros is the community of Padre Ramos, one of 16 small towns inside the federally protected wetlands of Reserva Natural Estero Padre Ramos. The river delta is part of the largest remaining mangrove forests in Central America, and is key in the proposed Reserva Biologica Golfo de Fonseca (Gulf of Fonseca Biological Corridor), a wetlands conservation agreement between Nicaragua, Honduras and El Salvador.

There is a **visitors center** (Los Zorros, 500m E of Y-Junction) in the community of Los Zorros, next to Finca Ecolólica Trinchera with some basic info. **Finca Ecológica Trinchera** and Jiquilillo hostels offer boat tours (US$35 to US$40), two-hour birding tours (US$10) and an interesting nightime shrimping tour (US$10 to US$20) where locals show you both the commercial and ecological sides of the reserve. Boat tour prices vary according to the type of boat, running from US$30 for a motorized canoe to US$90 for a plush 10-person *lancha* (small boat). Bargain hard. There are collective boats (US$2) from Padre Ramos to Venecia and other inland villages on Wednesday, Thursday and Saturday only.

The ranger station in Padre Ramos offers access to a boats-only system. Rent boats with local guides or DIY in a dugout canoe, and explore these 88 sq km of mangroves inhabited by alligators, ocelots, all manner of birds and an epic number of mosquitoes. You can visit Isleta Champerico; Isla La Tigre, with swimming beaches; or La Loma Chichihualtepec, a good spot for bird-watching.

GETTING TO EL SALVADOR

There are plans to open a ferry port in Potosí (some say as early as 2015) for transfers to La Unión in El Salvador and perhaps to Honduras. For now, you can do it by hiring a boat (1½ hours) with Ecodetur (p168) for US$35 per person, with a six-person minimum. There's a passport checkpoint in both Potosí and La Unión (open daily 8am to 5:30pm).

Olive ridleys and other sea turtles lay their eggs here between July and December, peaking in October and November, when Sclva arranges turtle tours and accepts volunteers. It also offers package tours of Estero Padre Ramos year-round, including comfortable bamboo huts with real beds (and mosquito nets!) in paradise, all transportation and food. Huts are in three picturesque spots: Padre Ramos, where the bus drops you off; Mechapa, with bus access from Chinandega; and Venecia, with boat access only. Packages run US$90 for two days, including food, transportation and guides, or you can just show up and stay at any of its outposts for US$10 per person, with meals available for US$3 to US$5 each.

Sleeping

Redwood Beach Resort LODGE **$$$**
(☎8996-0328; www.rbrmechapa.com; d with fan US$79, with air-con US$89-109, all incl breakfast; P ❄ ☮) Across the estuary in Mechapa there is a sweet little spot nestled among the coconut trees right on the beach. Accommodation is in comfy little stilted guanacaste-wood cabins, each with balconies overlooking the waves.

Access is tricky – there's the three-hour bus ride from Chinandega, or if you call ahead, staff can come pick you up from Jiquilillo or Padre Ramos. Adventurous souls could try to hire a launch here from Playa Jiquilillo.

Getting There & Away

Buses to Chinandega (US$1, two hours) leave Padre Ramos at 5:50am, 7am, 9am, 1pm and 3:30pm, returning from the Chinandega Mercadito at 7am, 10am, noon, 3pm and 4:30pm. There's one bus to Mechapa from Chinandega daily, leaving the Mercadito at 2pm.

Reserva Privada Hato Nuevo

Just near the turnoff to Mechapa, is the newly established **private reserve** (☎in Chinandega 2341-4245; www.hatonuevo.com; Carretera El Viejo–Potosí, Km 177.5; s/d incl breakfast US$40/50). Rooms in the old farmhouse are a careful blend of rustic charm and modern amenity, and the dining area, bar and gardens are all beautifully designed. It offers trekking, horseback riding and boat tours.

Reserva Natural Volcán Cosigüina

It was once the tallest volcano in Central America, perhaps more than 3000m high, but all that changed on January 20, 1835. In what's considered the Americas' most violent eruption since colonization, this hot-blooded peninsular beauty blew half her height in a single blast that left three countries in stifling darkness for days and scattered ash from Mexico to Colombia. Today what remains of Volcán Cosigüina reclines, as if spent, the broad and jagged 872m heart of the peninsula. It's now a very manageable (if blisteringly hot) three-hour climb up one of two trails to the top: **Sendero La Guacamaya**, which starts at the ranger's station near El Rosario; and **Sendero el Jovo**, which descends to more developed Potosí.

And beyond all that lies the **Golfo de Fonseca**, bordered by the largest mangrove stand left in the Americas. In the other direction, around the volcano's back, Punta Ñata overlooks cliffs that plunge 250m into the Farallones-studded sea.

Sore muscles? Head to the **hot springs**; in Potosí, Centro Ecoturistico Potosí offers hot springs with shade and food service, or go wild at one of several undeveloped springs that locals will happily point out.

Tours

Ecodetur GUIDED TOUR
(☎8320-3481; www.ecodetour.com; entrance to Potosí) This homegrown tour operator does volcano tours (US$15 per person, five hours), birding trips to the neighboring Los Islotes islands (US$45 per person, four-person minimum) and fun shrimping tours (US$15 per person).

Sleeping

Hotel Brisas del Golfo HOTEL **$$**
(☎8774-4356; Potosí; s/d US$20/25) This friendly hotel has clean beds, Pepto-pink rooms and a laid-back restaurant – it's also the only place to stay in town, unless you can arrange a homestay.

Getting There & Away

There are at least three buses daily to Chinandega (US$1.50, 3½ hours). One bus leaves Chinandega daily for Punta Ñata (US$1.50, 3½ hours) at 1pm, returning in the early morning.

Northern Highlands

Includes ➡

Best Places to Eat

- El Pullaso (p199)
- La Vita é Bella (p199)
- El Pescamar (p199)
- Café-Arte Tipiscayán (p176)

Best Places to Stay

- La Bastilla Ecolodge (p193)
- La Sombra Ecolodge (p202)
- Selva Negra (p201)
- Hotel Café (p190)

Why Go?

You've officially escaped Central America's backpacker superhighway and arrived in a place where colorful quetzals nest in misty cloud forests, and Nicaragua's best coffee and tobacco are cultivated with both capitalist zeal and collective spirit. With a little time and commitment you'll duck into ancient, crumbling cathedrals, get pounded by countless waterfalls, explore recently discovered canyons, and pay tribute to the pirates, colonists, revolutionaries, artists and poets who were inspired by these fertile mountains and mingled with the humble, open-hearted people who've lived here for generations.

On either end of the region are two up-and-coming cities; hardworking Estelí buzzes with students, farmers and cigar moguls, while Matagalpa is slightly hipper, and better funded, thanks to nearly a century of successful coffee cultivation. All around and in between are granite peaks and lush valleys dotted with dozens of small towns and infinite caffeine-fueled adventures.

When to Go

The northern highlands stunning landscapes are at their best from May to October when the wet season brings out vibrant shades of green and the many waterfalls are at their best. If you plan on hiking, consider visiting from November to February when the weather is fairly dry yet mild and the scenery is still lush. This is also the height of the coffee harvest, which gives visitors the chance to not only drink endless cups of the stuff but also pick and sort your own beans. The region's other cash crop, tobacco, is harvested from March to April and cigar fans are able to follow the leaves from the fields to the rolling tables.

Northern Highlands Highlights

1. Pick coffee beans beneath the towering cloud forest of **Reserva Natural Cerro Datanlí–El Diablo** (p192)
2. Scramble, swim and float through the magnificent **Cañon de Somoto** (p182)
3. Hike through the **Área Protegida Miraflor** (p177) to secluded swimming holes
4. Visit the cigar factories of **Estelí** (p173)
5. Scramble up Cerro la Cruz in **Jinotega** (p189) for breathtaking mountain views
6. Get civilized and overcaffeinated in **Matagalpa** (p194)
7. Rappel down spectacular waterfalls shrouded in old-growth forest in **Reserva Natural Macizos de Peñas Blancas** (p201)
8. Cruise the high-altitude waters of **Lago de Apanás** (p193) with local fishermen
9. Explore the cavernous abandoned gold mines around **San Ramón** (p200)

86°W
Cordillera Entre Ríos
Champigny
Jalapa
Aguas Calientes
Salto El Rosario
Valle Cangjas
Murra
30 km
15 miles
14°N
Río Bocay
Reserva de Biosfera Bosawás
Ayapal
Jinotega
Río Cuco
Plan de Grama
Wiwilí
Wiwili de Jinotega
Quilalí
Reserva Natural Cerro Kilambé
San José de Bocay
La Rica
Zinica
Las Walices
El Cuá
Pantasma
Reserva Natural Macizos de Peñas Blancas
Cordillera Isabelia
Waslala
Yaoska
San Rafael del Norte
Asturias
Caratero
Lago Asturias
Mancotal
Lago de Apanás
Sisle
San Pedro de Buculmay
San Antonio de Kuskawas
La Dalia
Reserva Natural Cerro Datanlí–El Diablo
El Quebracon
Río Tuma
Jinotega
Wanawas
Reserva Natural Cerro El Arenal
El Tuma
El Arenal
Selva Negra
Matagalpa
13°N
Monte Grande
Santa Elsa
La Rosa
Reserva Genetica Yacúl
Reserva Natural Cerro Apante
Garita
Reserva Natural Cerro Musun
Matagalpa
San Ramón
Pancasán
Chagüitillo
San Pablo
Sébaco
El Chile
Matiguás
Río Grande de Matagalpa
San Dionisio
Muy Muy
86°W
Pineda

History

Originally home to Náhuatl refugees from the Aztec empire, the northern highlands were off the radar until gold was discovered here in 1850, attracting an influx of Spanish, *mestizos* (persons of mixed ancestry; usually Spanish and indigenous people) and the first wave of German immigrants to Matagalpa. The Europeans married local, planted the region's first coffee bushes, and then sold their berries in Berlin.

When the revolution bloomed in 1977, many of the region's impoverished farmers became armed Sandinistas. Some of the heaviest fighting took place in the mountains in and around Jinotega. When the Frente Sandinista de Liberación Nacional (Sandinista National Liberation Front; FSLN) seized power, they made the area a priority, nationalizing and redistributing much of the highlands' arable land into community farming cooperatives. Some have since been divided up among the cooperative members, but the spirit of collective farming remains strong throughout the region.

ESTELÍ

POP 122,900 / ELEV 844M

A Sandinista stronghold, a university town, a market center for the thousands of farmers that populate its surrounding hills, Estelí has a multifaceted soul. On weekdays you can wake up with sunrise yoga before Spanish class, and on Saturday you can mingle with farmers at the massive produce market, then see them again at midnight, dancing like mad in a *ranchero* bar. And we haven't even mentioned the world-class cigars or the zeal with which a city with socialist roots has taken to slot machines. Yes, you don't have to be a Che Guevara devotee to dig this town.

Set on the Pan-American Hwy close to the Honduran border, it was a strategic stronghold that saw heavy fighting and helped turn the revolution and, later, the Contra War. Makes sense, then, that Estelí has remained one of the Sandinistas' strongest support bases. You'll see the murals and probably take in a political rally or three, and you won't want to miss the nearby collective farms in the cloud forests.

Sights & Activities

Although Estelí's most impressive attractions are in the surrounding mountains, the 1823 **Catedral** has a wonderful facade, and is worth a wander. Keep an eye out for the interesting **murals** that crop up about town, many of which were painted by participants in the **Funarte** (www.funarte.org.ni) children's mural workshop.

★Galería de Héroes y Mártires MUSEUM
(☎8419-3519, 2714-0942; galleryofheroesandmartyrs.blogspot.com; Av 1a NE, Calle Transversal, ½c N; donations appreciated; ⏲9:30am-4pm Tue-Fri) Be sure to stop by this moving gallery devoted to fallen revolutionaries, with displays of faded photos, clothes and weaponry. Check out the exhibit (with English signage) on Leonel Rugama, the warrior-poet whose last line was his best. When he and Carlos Fonseca were surrounded by 300 Guardia Nacional troops, supported by tanks and planes, they were told to surrender. 'Surrender, your mother!' he famously replied. Which proves a 'your mama!' retort is always a solid plan B.

Museo de Historia y Arqueología MUSEUM
(☎2713-3753; Catedral, 2c E, 3c N; ⏲8am-noon & 2pm-5pm Mon-Fri) In a large concrete faux indigenous pyramid on the north side of town, Estelí's museum has a small but interesting collection of pottery and petroglyphs from local pre-Hispanic cultures, fossils of extinct megafauna and items from the revolution.

Casa de Cultura Leonel Rugama CULTURAL BUILDING
(☎2713-3021; esq Av 1a NE & Calle Transversal; ⏲8am-8pm) In the bullet-hole marked former home of a high-ranking Somoza official, the Casa de Cultura offers a range of art, dance and music classes to locals, even as the building seemingly falls apart around them.

Courses

Ananda Yoga YOGA
(⏲6am Mon-Fri, 6:40pm Mon-Wed & Fri) Yoga classes are offered at the Licuados Ananda health-food restaurant next to the Casa de Cultura.

Escuela de Héroes y Mártires LANGUAGE
(☎8419-3519; inside Galería de Héroes y Mártires; per week with/without homestay US$180/100) More low-key than the competition and

frequently recommended, the Escuela de Héroes y Mártires offers Spanish classes right in the middle of town.

CENAC Spanish School LANGUAGE
(2713-5437; www.spanishschoolcenac.com; Panamericana, btwn Calles 5a SE & 6a SE; per week with/without homestay US$180/110) Professionally run Spanish school with classes for all levels.

Horizonte Nica LANGUAGE
(2713-4117; www.escuelahorizonte.edu.ni; Av 2a SE, Calle 9a SE ½c S; per week with/without homestay US$220/150) This well-established program uses its extensive contacts with local development groups to get students involved in the community.

Tours

★Tree Huggers GUIDED TOUR
(8496-7449; treehuggersnicaragua.wordpress.com; Av 2a NE & Calle 3a NE; 8am-8pm) This friendly and vibrant tour office is the specialist in trips to Miraflor but also offers other interesting community tourism trips around town and a great-value cigar tour. It also has a wealth of information for independent travelers. Profits support local social projects.

Cigar Tours

Estelí produces and rolls some of the world's finest tobacco. Seeds are original Cuban stock, as are the curing and rolling techniques you can witness firsthand in the warehouse-like factories. Fumes can get intense, but you'll acclimatize. Tobacco is harvested March through April and *puros* (cigars) are rolled always and forever.

While the tobacco industry is a massive employer in the region and a major contributor to the local economy, conditions for workers vary dramatically. Some factories have airy and spacious rolling areas while others are your classic sweatshop.

Many of the major producers have special tax status and are unable to sell cigars from their factories. It is not possible to send cigars home via the postal service in Nicaragua.

Local tour guide **Leo Flores** (8415-2428; leoafl@yahoo.es) is well connected in the industry and can get you access to a wide variety of factories and plantations.

Alternatively organize a tour to watch the rolling process at Cuban-owned **Tabacalera Santiago** with Tree Huggers for US$5 including transport and a local guide. The tour offers insights into the entire cigar-making process and visitors are free to talk to the staff as they roll 60 varieties of stogie. Cigars are available for purchase at the end of the tour.

The following producers also organize tours with advance notice.

Tabacalera Cubanica CIGAR TOUR
(2713-2383; Panamericana & Calle 7a SE) This pioneering factory produces Padrón cigars, Nicaraguás most prestigious (and costly) brand.

Drew Estate CIGAR TOUR
(www.cigarsafari.com; Barrio Oscar Gamez 2) Estelí's most innovative cigar company offers all inclusive multiday 'Cigar Safari' tours aimed at serious cigar enthusiasts.

Plasencia Cigars CIGAR TOUR
(2713-4074; Escuela Normal, 200m N) Large company that produces over 30 brands of *puros* including a selection of organic cigars. It is one of the most socially responsible factories.

Festivals & Events

Virgen del Carmen RELIGIOUS
(Jul 16) *Fiestas patronales* with fireworks, fiestas and Masses.

Virgen de Rosario RELIGIOUS
(Oct 7) An annual event since 1521, this was originally celebrated in Villa de San Antonio Pavía de Estelí, too close to the river and those pesky pirates, and moved here with the Virgin in the late 1600s.

Sleeping

Hotel Nicarao GUESTHOUSE $
(2713-2490; hotelnicarao79@yahoo.es; Av Central, Calle Transversal, ½c S; r per person US$19, without bathroom US$12;) This charming garden gem looks grubby from the street, but inside you'll find pleasant rooms at exceptional value set around a spacious courtyard with sofas and rocking chairs.

Hostal Miraflor GUESTHOUSE $
(2713-2003; Av Central, Calle 2a NE, ½c N; s/d/t US$12/17/25;) Friendly family-run place offering basic rooms with new tiled bathrooms and hot water. Sure, the beds sag and there are stains on the walls, but the price is comfy. Cheap meals are available.

Hospedaje Luna HOSTEL $$
(8441-8466; www.cafeluzyluna.com; esq Av 2a NE & Calle 3a NE; dm/s/d/t US$7/15/25/30;) With

Estelí

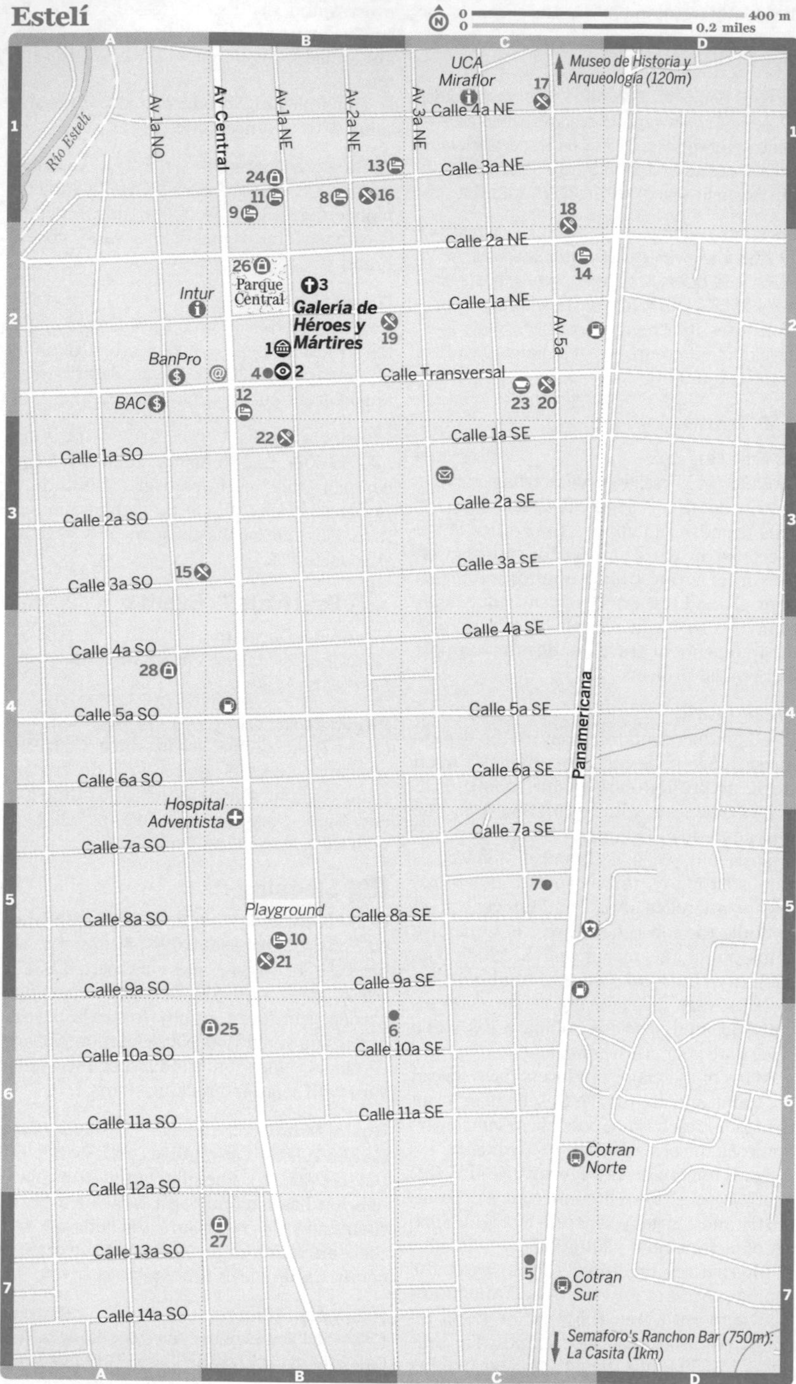

0 400 m
0 0.2 miles
UCA Miraflor
Museo de Historia y Arqueología (120m)
Río Estelí
Av 1a NO
Av Central
Av 1a NE
Av 2a NE
Av 3a NE
Av 5a
Calle 4a NE
Calle 3a NE
Calle 2a NE
Calle 1a NE
Calle Transversal
Parque Central
Intur
BanPro
BAC
Galería de Héroes y Mártires
Calle 1a SE
Calle 2a SE
Calle 3a SE
Calle 4a SE
Calle 5a SE
Calle 6a SE
Calle 7a SE
Calle 8a SE
Calle 9a SE
Calle 10a SE
Calle 11a SE
Calle 1a SO
Calle 2a SO
Calle 3a SO
Calle 4a SO
Calle 5a SO
Calle 6a SO
Calle 7a SO
Calle 8a SO
Calle 9a SO
Calle 10a SO
Calle 11a SO
Calle 12a SO
Calle 13a SO
Calle 14a SO
Hospital Adventista
Playground
Panamericana
Cotran Norte
Cotran Sur
Semaforo's Ranchon Bar (750m); La Casita (1km)

Estelí

Top Sights
1 Galería de Héroes y Mártires ... B2

Sights
2 Casa de Cultura Leonel Rugama ... B2
3 Catedral ... B2

Activities, Courses & Tours
4 Ananda Yoga ... B2
5 CENAC Spanish School ... C7
Escuela de Héroes y Mártires ... (see 1)
6 Horizonte Nica ... B6
7 Tabacalera Cubanica ... C5

Sleeping
8 Hospedaje Luna ... B1
9 Hostal Miraflor ... B1
10 Hostal Tomabú ... B5
11 Hotel Los Arcos ... B1
12 Hotel Nicarao ... B2
13 Hotel Puro Esteli ... B1
14 Sonati ... C2

Eating
15 Buffet Castillo ... A3
16 Café Luz ... B1
17 Café-Arte Tipiscayán ... C1
18 El Quesito ... C1
19 Koma Rico ... B2
Licuados Ananda ... (see 4)
20 Pullaso's Ole ... C2
21 Repostería Gutiérrez ... B5
22 Rincón Pinareño ... B3

Drinking & Nightlife
23 Mocha Nana Café ... C2

Shopping
24 Artesanías La Esquina ... B1
25 Calzado Figueroa ... B6
26 Farmers' Market ... B2
27 Mercado ... B7
28 Supermercado Las Segovias ... A4

a central location, spotless rooms, courtyard common area and a wealth of information on Estelí and the surrounding area, this nonprofit hostel is the budget traveler's favorite. Profits are donated to community projects in Miraflor which also welcome volunteers.

Sonati HOSTEL $$
(2713-6043; sonati.esteli@gmail.com; Catedral, 3½c E; dm US$6-7, s/d/t US$15/25/40;) This chilled hostel feels a lot like a houseshare with plenty of communal space, a spacious shared kitchen and a pleasant rear garden. The rooms are neat and you could get lost in some of the huge bathrooms. The management offers tours and hikes in the area and organizes volunteer placements with local organizations. Profits go toward local environmental education projects.

Hotel Puro Esteli HOTEL $$
(2713-6404; www.hotelpuroesteli.com; Catedral, 1c N, ½c E; s/d/t US$15/25/30;) You feel the Esteliano culture in this small cigar-themed hotel. There is work from local artists on the walls throughout and a selection of cigars for sale in the reception area. The smallish rooms set around a sunny internal garden are not flash but are comfortable and quiet with fast wi-fi and cable TV.

Hostal Tomabú HOTEL $$
(2713-3783; hostaltomabu.esteli@gmail.com; costado sur Parque Infantil; s/d US$14/23; P) Friendly and welcoming, this unpretentious hotel on the south side of the Parque Infantil offers brightly painted rooms, some offering mountain views, with hot water and cable TV.

★ **Hotel Los Arcos** HOTEL $$
(2713-3830; hotelosarcos@hotmail.com; esq Av 1a NE & Calle 3a NE; s/d with fan US$45/50, with aircon US$55/60, all incl breakfast; P) Run by a nonprofit organization, Los Arcos remains the best hotel in town, with a dream location one block north of the cathedral, a roof deck with kick-ass mountain and city views, and spotless rooms with soft sheets, Spanish tiles and high ceilings. The rooms at the rear get more natural light.

Eating

Self-caterers can visit **Supermercado Las Segovias** (cnr Calle 4a SO & Av 1a NO), a solid supermarket with great deals on gourmet coffee. Estelí's municipal **market** (cnr Calle 12a SO & Av 1a SO) is always stocked with amazingly fresh produce.

Buffet Castillo NICARAGUAN $
(2713-0337; Parque Central, 4c S, ½c O; meals US$2-3.50; 7am-3pm Mon-Sat) Often packed at lunchtime, this neat diner offers up restaurant-quality meals, including ribs, fried fish and jalapeño chicken, at a budget price.

El Quesito NICARAGUAN $
(cnr Calle 2a NE & Av 4a NE, Del Asoganor, 1c N; items US$1-2, meals US$3-4; 6:30am-8pm) Pull up a handmade wooden chair at this rustic

corner diner and enjoy homemade yogurt flavored with local fruits, *quesillos* and *leche agria* (sour milk) – yes, what most of us pour down the sink is a delicacy in Nicaragua! It also prepares excellent, nongreasy Nica breakfasts and set meals.

La Casita CAFE **$**
(Panamericana; snacks US$1-2; ⌚9am-7pm Tue-Sun) Hidden about 1km south of town (US$1 in a cab), La Casita is surrounded by gardens shading a trickling stream. Sip coffee or chai, munch muesli with homemade yogurt, or snack on rustic loaves of brown bread served with spreads or chunks of cheese.

Koma Rico NICARAGUAN **$**
(cine, 2c E; dishes US$2-3; ⌚6pm-10pm, closed Fri) Stack your plate high at this popular *fritanga* (grill) that's based upon the tried-and-tested marriage of tasty barbecued meats and ice-cold beer.

Repostería Gutiérrez BAKERY **$**
(☎2714-1774; Av Central, entre Calles 8a SE & 9a SE; pastries US$0.20-1; ⌚7am-8pm) Nestle into one of the wooden tables in the cozy tiled dining area and sip coffee or hot chocolate as you down delicious cookies, cakes, donuts or local pastries stuffed with fruit and cream.

Licuados Ananda VEGETARIAN **$**
(esq Calle Transversal & Av 1a NE, contiguo Casa de la Cultura; dishes US$2, drinks US$0.75-1; ⌚8am-7pm Mon-Fri, to 4pm Sat; ✎) Disregard the empty pool (although that graffiti lotus is pretty cool), sit beneath the dangling vines, and sip your post-namaste juice or *licuado* (blended fruit, milk and water drink), which is made fresh before your eyes. Vegetarian fast food is also available.

★**Café-Arte Tipiscayán** NICARAGUAN **$$**
(☎2713-7303; Calle 4a NE, Av 4a NE, 10m E; snacks US$2-4, mains US$6-8; ⌚noon-10pm Thu-Tue) The family of San Juan de Limay soapstone sculptor Freddy Moreno serves ultra-traditional fare such as *güirílas* (corn pancakes) and cheese curd, *montucas* (Nicaraguan *tamales*) and grilled meats, as well as excellent coffee.

Café Luz INTERNATIONAL **$$**
(☎8405-8919; www.cafeluzyluna.com; esq Av 2a NE & Calle 3a NE; mains US$6-7; ⌚8am-11pm; 📶✎) Bored of Nica grub? Pop into this hip coffee house where the burritos and fajitas have some kick, and the organic salads arrive on your table direct from the growers in Miraflor.

Pullaso's Ole STEAKHOUSE **$$**
(☎2713-4583; esq Av 5a SE & Calle Transversal; dishes US$12-20; ⌚noon-10pm) Named for an Argentine cut of beef (the *pullaso*), this sweet, family-owned grill serves beef, pork, chicken and chorizo on its front porch and in a quaint dining room crowded with racks of South American red.

Rincón Pinareño CUBAN **$$**
(☎2713-4369; Av 1a SE & Calle 1a SE; mains US$7-9, sandwiches US$2.50-4; ⌚noon-10pm) A tasty Cuban diner with a lovely 2nd-floor veranda, deliciously messy pressed sandwiches, tasty grilled chicken and pork chops.

Drinking & Nightlife

Being a university town teeming with students, and an ag-town surrounded by farmers and ranchers, Estelí throws a good party. Most nightlife is out on the Panamericana.

★**Semaforo's Ranchon Bar** BAR, RESTAURANT
(Panamericana, Hospital 300m S; ⌚8pm-5am Thu-Sun) Get down with the good working people of Estelí, Tisey and Miraflor at a proper *ranchero* bar. This indoor-outdoor club with the *palapa* (thatched) roof and bandstand brings terrific live music to a crowd that is here to dance in their boots and cowboy hats. You will see asses (aged 18 to 60) shimmy and shake.

Cigarszone CLUB
(Panamericana, Petronic Sur, 75m S; ⌚9pm-3am) Expansive club big on bling and high-tech lights that is popular with a young crowd and is the venue of choice for concerts by visiting artists.

Mocha Nana Café CAFE
(☎2713-3164; Calle Transversal, Av 4a SE, ½c E; drinks US$1.50; ⌚11am-9pm) Where Estelí intellectuals gather to sip caffeine, debate politics and culture, and munch tasty waffles. On Friday evenings there is usually live music by local bands (cover US$1.50).

Shopping

The must-have souvenir of Estelí is a box of cigars, best purchased after a cigar tour. The region is also known for reasonably priced custom leather – think: saddles, boots and wallets, with many workshops located along Av 1a SO.

Farmers' Market MARKET
(Parque Central; ⌚7am-noon) Every Friday morning farmers from the surrounding hills

come down to Estelí and set up stalls on the north side of the park selling fresh organic vegetables, cheeses and typical foods.

Calzado Figueroa SHOES
(☎8946-4341; Av 1a SO, Calle 9a SO, 30m S; boots US$80-100; ⏲8am-7pm Mon-Sat, 8am-noon Sun) Get in touch with your inner cowboy with some genuine handcrafted Cuban-heel riding boots at this high-quality leather workshop. Peruse the large selection or order a tailor-made pair and watch the boot-making entire process.

Artesanías La Esquina HANDICRAFTS
(☎2713-3239; cnr Av 1a NE & Calle 3a NE; ⏲8am-noon & 2-6pm) An artisans cooperative with an extensive inventory that blends tourist kitsch with an array of excellent pottery and sculpted wood bowls.

ℹ Orientation

Atypically, Estelí utilizes a street-numbering system, and most blocks are clearly signed. Avenidas run north–south; calles are east–west. Both ascend in number the further they get from the city center. Streets and avenues are also suffixed NE (northeast), SO (southwest) etc, according to their town quadrant. The intersection of Av Central and Calle Transversal is the center of the grid and is steps away from the lovely parque central.

ℹ Information

BAC (cnr Calle Transversal & Av 1a NO) MasterCard/Cirrus/Visa/Plus ATM.

BanPro (cnr Calle Transversal & Av 1a NO) Reliable ATM.

Correos de Nicaragua (Av 3a SE, Calle 2a SE, 50m S; ⏲8am-4pm Mon-Fri, 8am-noon Sat)

Estelí@Net (Calle Transversal, Av Central 20m O; per hr US$0.50; ⏲8am-8pm) Also offers international calls.

Hospital Adventista (☎2713-3827; Av Central, Calle 6a SO, ½c S, Petronic, 1½c S) Private clinic with a variety of specialists.

Intur (☎2713-6799; Plaza Plator, Parque Central, ½c O; ⏲8am-1pm) Official tourist office with an abundance of regional brochures, but not a lot of expertise.

Lavanderia Express (☎2714-1297; Av 3a SE, Calle 1a SE, 30m S, Migracion, ½c N; per pound US$1 ; ⏲9am-5pm) Economical wash and dry service.

Police (☎118; Panamericana)

UCA Miraflor (Unión de Cooperativas Agropecuarias de Miraflor; ☎2713-2971; www.ucamiraflor.com; cnr Av 4a NE & Calle 4a NE; ⏲8am-noon & 12:30pm-5:30pm Mon-Sat) Arranges tours to Área Protegida Miraflor.

ℹ Getting There & Away

BUS

Estelí has two bus terminals – blue collar **Cotran Norte** (☎2713-2529), with plenty of slot machines and a soft-rock soundtrack, and the more refined **Cotran Sur** (☎2713-6162). Both are located at the southern end of the city on the Panamericana.

Buses departing from Cotran Norte:

Jalapa (US$3.50, 2¾ hours, 4:10am and noon)

Jinotega (via Concordia, San Rafael) (US$1.80, 2½ hours, 5:45am, 8:15am, 9:15am, 2:15pm, 3:45pm and 4:45pm)

León (bus US$2.80, 2½ hours, 3:10pm; microbus US$3, two hours, depart when full) Alternatively, take the Matagalpa bus and change at San Isidro.

Managua (*expreso* US$3, 2½ hours, 5:15am, 6:15am, 7:45am and 11:15am) First three buses don't run on Sunday.

Masaya (US$3, three hours, 2pm and 3pm)

Ocotal (US$1.25, 1½ hours, 6am to 11am, hourly)

San Juan de Limay (US$1.80, two hours, 5:30am, 7am, 10am, 12:15pm, 2pm, 3pm and 5pm)

Somoto (US$1.15, 1½ hours, 5:30am to 6:10pm, hourly)

Buses departing from Cotran Sur:

León (US$2.80, 2½ hours, 5am, 5:45am and 6:45am) First two buses don't run on Sunday.

Managua (*expreso* US$3, 2½ hours, 4:45am to 3:15pm, hourly; *ordinario* US$2.25, 3½ hours, 3:30am to 6pm, half-hourly) First two express buses don't run on Sunday.

Matagalpa (*ordinario* US$1.25, 1¾ hours, 5:15am to 5:40pm, half-hourly)

Área Protegida Miraflor

Miraflor is not your average tourist destination. Part nature reserve, part rural farming community, its challenging to get to and even more difficult to define. There are no big hotels or restaurants here, just a loose collection of like-minded farmers with an interest in tourism and the environment.

Its namesake is a small mountain lake around which the Área Protegida Miraflor (declared a reserve in 1999) unfurls with waterfalls, blooming orchids, coffee plantations, swatches of remnant cloud forest home to hold-out monkey troops, hiking trails and dozens of collective-farming communities that welcome tourists. Yes, nature is glorious here, but the chance to participate in rural Nicaraguan life – making fresh tortillas, milking cows, harvesting coffee, riding horses through the hills with living, breathing *caballeros* (horsemen) – is unforgettable.

Miraflor played an integral role in Nicaragua's revolutionary struggle. When the Contras snuck over the Honduran border with a plan to march into Managua and seize political power, a large contingent came through these mountains, planning to sack nearby Estelí. But the farmers here rose up in resistance and helped turn the Contra War toward the Sandinistas. Afterward, Ortega nationalized this farmland and gave it back to the people who organized themselves into *colectivos*. This population may look and act humble, but it has war stories and ambitious, utopian dreams of economic equality burned into its collective brain.

These days most of the cooperatives have been dissolved and the lands distributed among their former members. And while many locals now own their lands, poverty remains widespread and sustainable tourism is just one of the ways local residents eke out a living. Advanced reservations are essential to ensure visitor income is distributed evenly among participating farmers and your hosts are prepared for your arrival.

UCA Miraflor (p177) in Estelí manages the reserve and can help you plan a visit, hook you up with an English-speaking guide and book family homestays. Alternatively, Tree Huggers (p173) provides detailed, impartial advice on planning a trip and also makes reservations.

Sights & Activities

Miraflor has three climate zones (ranging from 800m to 1400m), home to over 200 species of orchid and 307 bird species, linked by 20km of trails and rutted roads. The *zona bajo* (low zone), around Coyolito, is a tropical oak savannah ecosystem; the *zona intermedia* (intermediate zone), which includes Sontule, has some remnant cloud forests and tons of orchid varieties; in the *zona alta* (high zone), you'll find coffee farms, more swatches of cloud forest, and some excellent quetzal and monkey viewing near Cebollal in Los Volcancitos.

Local **guides** (per day US$15, horses per person US$10) usually meet incoming buses and are both inexpensive and a great resource. They know all the best hikes and climbs, and can share insights into Miraflor's unique history and local daily life.

Specialty coffee (with/without tasting session US$70/30, up to 10 participants), orchid (US$30, up to 10 participants) and bird tours (US$60, up to six participants) are held seasonally and should be arranged via UCA Miraflor in advance.

Some landowners charge admission to visit sights or pass through their property; bring plenty of change.

Coyolito VILLAGE

The lowest in elevation, this is the warmest and closest settlement to Estelí. It offers magnificent views, especially from the **Mirador La Meseta** (admission US$0.40), and access to several waterfalls that range from trickling to thundering depending upon the season.

Check out **Las Tres Cascadas** (admission US$1), a series of cascades and swimming holes, and **La Chorrera**, a towering 65m-high waterfall that was used as en execution site by Somoza's troops. There's also brilliant bird-watching in the forest that lines the river here.

Sontule VILLAGE

This friendly community is surrounded by coffee farms managed by three working cooperatives. Sontule families once worked for just four prominent landowners who owned Miraflor and compensated their workforce with only room and board. When the Sandinistas took power and nationalized the land, it was the women of Sontule who started Miraflor's first farming collective. Stay here and you can learn all about it, join in the coffee harvest, or hike or horseback ride up to cloud forests. The community has English-speaking guides and a bird-watching specialist.

Cebollal VILLAGE

The first settlement to cater to tourists, and it remains the most popular. You can stay with families or in more comfortable *cabañas* (cabin) and enjoy miles of trails that reach up to 1400m with pockets of cloud forest that draw colorful quetzals to their canopy in May and June.

La Perla VILLAGE

A fine place to immerse yourself in the collective-farming universe that is Miraflor, this small village is in the high zone, which means there are hundreds of orchid varieties here. The village is home to a women's farming cooperative and guests are encouraged to wake up with the smacking rhythm of fresh, handmade tortillas, milk the cow, collect the eggs and work the farm before hiking into the nearby forests. La Perla is also a convenient spot from which to visit the **Laguna Miraflor**.

Los Volcancitos FOREST

The wildlife-lovers' destination. This is where you'll find the best remaining patch of virgin cloud forest, although deforestation is a serious issue. It is home to technicolor quetzals in April and May, as well as troops of spider and howler monkeys. There are homestays nearby, but it's also quite easily accessible from Cebollal. Walk 45-minutes to the La Rampla bus stop on the Estelí–Yali road, from where it's a further one-hour walk south to the jungled, volcano-shaped mountain (which, despite the name, isn't actually a volcano).

La Pita VILLAGE

There are not many activities for visitors in this dynamic village, but it has some fine homestay options and it's only a 30-minute walk from Cebollal. It is also the most convenient departure point for **Pozo la Pila** (admission US$0.40), a refreshing waterfall-fed swimming hole surrounded by high rock walls.

Sleeping & Eating

There are several choices of accommodations within the reserve, all of which should be booked through UCA Miraflor or Tree Huggers in Estelí.

Farmhouse rooms (per person with/without meals US$19/8) allow the most interaction with local families; **cabañas** (per person with/without meals US$24/10) have more privacy. Both options are rustic and some accommodations have pit latrines.

If creature comforts are important, **Finca Neblina del Bosque** (8701-1460; www.visitamiraflor.com; Cebollal; dm with/without meals US$19/7, cabañas per person incl meals US$25-38), owned by a Nica-German couple, is the most comfortable option in Miraflor but it has decidedly less rural farming flavor.

Note that the entire reserve is a dry zone and no alcoholic beverages are sold.

Getting There & Away

For Coyolito (US$0.70, one hour) and La Pita (US$1, 1¾ hours) buses leave Estelí from the Pulpería Miraflor near the Uno gas station on the Panamericana north of town at 5:45am and 1pm daily, returning from La Pita at 9am and 3pm.

There is one direct bus daily, except Sunday, from Estelí to Sontule (US$1.50, three hours) via Cebollal (US$1, two hours) and La Perla (US$1.20, 2¼ hours) leaving from Cotran Norte at 1:30pm and returning at 7:30am.

Alternatively for Cebollal take the Estelí–Yali (via Miraflor) bus at 6am, noon or 3:45pm from Cotran Norte to La Rampla (US$1, two hours), from where it's a 1km walk uphill to the beginning of the accommodations. The bus continues onto Puertas Azules, from where its a 20-minute walk to La Perla and 1¾ hours to Sontule.

It is also possible to walk up the hill from La Pita to Cebollal in around 45 minutes but it's a steep climb. Tree Huggers (p173) in Estelí has plans to offer mountain-bike hire within Miraflor – check to see if the service is up and running.

Área Protegida Cerro Tisey–Estanzuela

Smaller, drier, less populated but every bit as gorgeous as Área Protegida Miraflor, the *other* protected area, just 10km south of Estelí, has also jumped on the tourism bandwagon. You won't see the same species diversity in Tisey (which is what locals call the region), but those rugged pine-draped mountains, red-clay bat caves, waterfalls and marvelous vistas that stretch to Lago de Managua and even El Salvador on clear days are worth the trip.

It's possible to visit Tisey on a day trip from Estelí; however, the park's attractions are spread out all over its 9344 hectares and public transportation is limited so you'll see more if you spend the night.

The main entrance is accessed from the dirt road beside Hospital San Juan de Dios in Estelí. In the park's lower elevations, just 5km from Estelí, is the inspiring **Salto Estanzuela** (admission US$1), a gushing 36m waterfall that careens over a bromeliad-studded cliff, and breaks into a half-dozen foaming threads that feed a perfect swimming hole. Locals descend in hordes during Semana Santa. There have been reports of robberies recently on the path to the Falls from the main Tisey road – travel in a group and don't take any valuables.

After the Falls, the road begins to climb high into the mountains before arriving at the Eco-Posada (p180), where you'll find a handful of Spanish-speaking guides (US$20 to US$25 per day).

The nearby, 2km **Mirador de Tisey Trail** is absolutely spectacular. After meandering up an oak- and pine-draped hillside, you'll reach a peak with 360-degree views that encompass a dozen volcanoes, including mighty San Cristóbal, and the blue outline of a Salvadorian peak.

A short walk further along the road is the entrance to Alberto Gutiérrez's singular **Galería del Arte el Jalacate** (entry by donation). Gutiérrez is an artist, a naturalist and, some might say, a bit of a hermit. But he's a welcoming one who loves showing off his property, studded with orchids, carpeted with coffee and accented with a dozen kinds of fruit tree. But his pride and joy is a 40m stretch of cliff that he's carved into an ever-evolving mural. You'll find animals from Africa, the Amazon and Nicaragua, an Aztec sun, Jesus on the cross, his vision of downtown USA, Christopher Columbus and Sandino. It is the work of a sweet and peaceful eccentric.

About 3km beyond the *galería* is the cute hamlet of **La Garnacha**, known for a chapel that housed huddled refugees of a Contra invasion during the war, and a **dairy cooperative** (☎8658-1054; garnachaturistica@yahoo.es; Comunidad La Garnacha) that produces artisanal Italian-style goat cheese.

The progressive cooperative organizes several interesting activities, including organic agriculture tours (US$5 per person) and tortilla-making and soapstone-carving classes (US$2 per person). It also rents horses (US$5 per hour) and organizes guides (US$10 per person) for the rugged five-hour trail to the Cuevas de Cerro Apaguaji, three caves at 1580m teeming with bats. You'll also find the best beds in Tisey in this little town.

Sleeping & Eating

The one *comedor* (basic eatery) in La Garnacha serves excellent *comida típica* (regional specialties; dishes US$3 to US$5) made from local ingredients, including organic salads and, of course, cheese.

Cabañas La Garnacha LODGE $

(☎8658-1054; garnchaturistica@yahoo.es; La Garnacha; r US$15, cabañas US$20-40) These cute *cabañas* with hot water are run by the community and overlook a small lake. There are also cheaper, hotel-style rooms with tiled bathrooms by the entrance. Reserve in advance.

Homestay Reynaldo HOMESTAY $

(☎8524-4764; La Garnacha; r per person incl meals US$20) For full cultural immersion, check out this family homestay in the house of an energetic local farmer that is surrounded by lovely gardens. Meals are prepared using organic produce fresh from the host's farm.

Eco-Posada LODGE $

(☎2713-6213, 8386-1427; r per person US$6, cabañas US$14) This place offers comfortable *cabañas* with flush toilets, and front porches slung with hammocks overlooking a small creek lined with flowers and fruit trees and spartan tin-roofed rooms with shared bathrooms. Cheap meals are available in the attached *comedor*.

Getting There & Away

Tisey is served by two buses a day (US$1, 1½ hours), which are marked 'La Tejera' and leave from Estelí Cotran Sur at 6:30am and 1:30pm. The buses pass Salto Estanzuela and Eco-Posada before arriving at the La Garnacha turnoff, a 1.5km walk from the community. Buses return to Estelí from the La Garnacha turnoff at 8:30am and 3:30pm. On Wednesday there is no service.

In the dry season, you can also charter a taxi from Estelí (about US$40 to US$50 for five to six hours), which is a good idea for day-trippers.

Salto Estanzuela is about a 90-minute walk or 40-minute bicycle ride from the Hospital San Juan de Dios in Estelí. Expect to pay around US$8 to US$10 in a taxi.

Condega

POP 9900 / ELEV 560M

Dyed a deep terra-cotta, scarred proudly by revolution and surrounded by gorgeous, forested hills, Condega translates from the indigenous Náhuatl as 'the place of the potters.' You'll see their wares in a museum and at a famed factory shop on the outskirts, but if terra-cotta doesn't get you going, then check out that Somoza-era bomber shot down here in 1979 and reassembled on a hilltop. Talk about spoils of war.

Sights & Activities

Condega's parque central is actually at its extreme southern end, opposite **El Templo Parroquial de Condega**. The church gets packed December 11 and 12 for the **Virgin of Guadalupe festival**. Come a few days later for the **Feria del Patio**, when local women dress up as Mother Nature – in dresses made of corn husks and medicinal plants – and throw a huge party.

Across from the park, the **Museo Arqueológico Julio César Salgado** (☎2715-2330; Parque Central; admission US$0.30; ⏲8am-4pm Mon-Fri, 8am-noon Sat) is packed with ceramic bowls, studded incense burners, and stone tools dating back to AD 300. A map in the corner marks some 60 unexcavated or partially excavated archaeological sites in the area.

The best new stuff can be found at the **Taller de Cerámica Ducualí Grande** (2715-2418; Restaurante Guanacaste, 1km O; 9am-5pm), a collective of women who sell their fine work all over Nicaragua. It's located in the community of Ducualí Grande, 3km northwest of town. Any northbound bus will drop you at the intersection on the Panamericana, from where it's a 1km walk to the community. In the village, take a left at the basketball court and look for the small sign.

Condega's most unique attraction is the riveted twin-engine bomber used by the FAN (Nicaraguan Air Force) to bomb the region. It was shot down on April 7, 1979. Now it sits, tagged in lovers' scrawl, at **Airplane Park**, the local make-out point overlooking mountain mesas. Alongside the aircraft is a faux control tower **mirador** (admission US$0.20) which offers fantastic views of the town with its tiled roofs and palm trees jutting out of a canopy of green. To get to the park, climb the steep dirt trail across the street from the museum.

Sleeping & Eating

Several cheap and tasty *carne asada* (barbecued meat) stalls are located on the northeast corner of the park.

★Hospedaje Baldovinos GUESTHOUSE $
(2715-2222; Parque Central; s/d/t US$10/15/20; P) Set in a lovely colonial house with a vibrant internal courtyard, this family-run *hospedaje* (guesthouse) offers simple, cool brick rooms with tiled bathrooms. The most comfortable and atmospheric choice in Condega.

Hospedaje Framar GUESTHOUSE $
(8353-4647; Parque Central; r US$6) Very basic rooms with shared bathrooms.

Getting There & Away

Buses depart from Condega's new bus terminal on the Panamericana for the following destinations:

Estelí (US$0.60, 45 minutes, 6am to 7pm, every 20 minutes)

Ocotal (US$1, one hour, 7am to 7pm, every 45 minutes)

Somoto (US$0.80, one hour, 4:15am to 5:45pm, every 40 minutes)

OFF THE BEATEN TRACK

SAN JUAN DE LIMAY

San Juan de Limay's cobblestone and brick streets seemingly appear from the dust 44km west of Estelí to form a precious country town, known for its stone carvers and surrounded by soaring peaks. Look for the enlightened *gorda* (pudgy lady); she's the town's signature symbol. Most often she's carved from *marmolina* (soapstone), a heavy rock that is mined in nearby Cerro Tipiscayán and carved and sanded in home workshops until it shines. The best gallery, **Taller Casco Dablia** (8842-5162, 2719-5228; 8am-6pm), is located behind the school opposite the town square.

The road to Limay branches off the Panamericana north of Estelí near the community of La Sirena. Buses leave the Cotran Norte in Estelí for Limay (US$2, two hours) five times daily.

Somoto

POP 37,000 / ELEV 705M

Diminutive Somoto has not always been a shoe-in on the itineraries of visitors to northern Nicaragua. In fact, until 2003 this was just another sleepy colonial town in the Honduran shadow famed for its donkeys and *rosquillas* (crusty cornbread rings). Then two Czech scientists stumbled onto a rift in the rugged, overgrown clay earth outside town and, just 75 million years after these charcoal granite cliffs pierced the earth's surface, Europeans 'discovered' Cañon de Somoto (Somoto Canyon), where the Río Coco is born.

Of course, the locals living nearby have known about it all along and formerly referred to the site as 'La Estrechura,' while it is said that the area's original inhabitants, the Chorotegas, referred to the region as Tepezonate (Mountain of Water).

Sights

Iglesia Santiago CHURCH
This wonderfully understated adobe church fronting the shady parque central was constructed in 1661, making it one of the oldest places of worship in Nicaragua.

Outside Town

Monumento Nacional Cañon de Somoto PARK

(admission US$2) Central America's longest river, the Coco (or Wangki), runs all the way to the Caribbean, but her first impression may be her most spectacular. Gushing from underground, she has carved solid rock into this 3km-long gorge that drops 160m, and at times is just a hair under 10m wide.

Protected as Monumento Nacional Cañon de Somoto, the canyon is an unmissable experience. There are three routes to explore the canyon. You won't always have comfortable footing, so reef shoes or sandals help a lot, and you'll have more fun if you're fit.

The full six-hour, 12km circuit will take you to two bat caves well above the rim before you hike down to the river, boulder hop, swim through (small) rapids and leap off 8m rocks into deep swimming holes.

The most popular option is the four-hour, 6km classic loop that will get you straight into the canyon, where you'll swim, hike and leap beneath slate-rock faces and jagged peaks.

For those that are adverse to exercise, there is also a three-hour 'lite' tour where you are paddled up the gorge in a small boat and float back down in an inflatable tube.

Guides (half-/full day up to five people US$15 to US$20) are not technically mandatory if you just want to hang around the lower reaches, but are absolutely essential if you want to venture into the canyon.

In addition to having expert knowledge of river conditions – which may become dangerous during the wet season – guides also blend local insight with adventure and create a richer experience.

Guides from the local community of Sonis at the entrance to the reserve have formed a **cooperative** (☎8676-5883; Carretera Somoto–El Espino, Km 229.5) and work on a rotation basis. They offer a fantastic package including taxi transportation from Somoto, life vest and water shoes, a dry bag, entrance fee, guide, lunch and a boat trip for US$25 per visitor. They also offer horseback-riding tours to the surrounding mountains to get a birds-eye view of the area and organize homestays in the community so you are able to spend more time exploring. Another option is to visit the site with one of the professional guides from **Cosermuturma** (☎8630-0704, 2722-2340; reymen2008@hotmail.com; Enitel, 7½c S) in Somoto.

To visit the canyon take any El Espino bound bus (US$0.40, 30 minutes) from the bus terminal to the trail head at Km 231 near the community of Sonis. A taxi will cost around (US$5). From here it's a 3km hike to the canyon including a river crossing that may be over a meter deep. The last bus back to Somoto passes at around 5:30pm.

The canyon often closes in October, when the water is too high. Call the guides to check on conditions.

Reserva Natural Tepesomoto-Pataste NATURE RESERVE

Somoto's 'other' natural reserve, to the southwest of town, is rarely visited but has a hiking trail and is a popular spot for horseback-riding tours.

Sleeping

If you are just in Somoto to see the canyon, consider staying with one of the local families as part of their community-based tourism project in the village of Sonis, right at the canyon entrance. Accommodations (US$5 to US$7 per person) are basic and sleeping right next to the canyon will give you plenty of time to get out and explore. You can eat simple, inexpensive meals with your hosts. Contact coordinator **Henry Soriano** (☎8610-7642; Carretera Somoto–El Espino, Km 229.5) to reserve a room.

Hotel El Rosario HOTEL $

(Enitel 1c E, ½c S; s/d/t US$10/17/25, r with aircon US$35; wi-fi) Next to one of Somoto's oldest houses, this brightly painted new hotel has comfortable rooms with flatscreen TV, strong wi-fi and shiny private bathrooms. Best value in town.

Hotel Colonial HOTEL $$

(☎2722-2040; Parque Central, 1c S; s/d/t US$20/25/30; P air-con) Clean, comfortable rooms with tiled floors and thin walls. Some rooms are (much!) bigger than others, so look before you sign.

Eating

Before the canyon, Somoto was famous for *rosquillas*, crusty cornbread rings, baked with cheese and herbs, and served with black coffee (go ahead, dunk 'em). You can buy a bag anywhere, but those in the know say the best are found at **Rosquillas Vílchez-Tinoco** (☎2722-0745; Enitel 1c E, 7½c S).

Carne Asada El Buen Gusto NICARAGUAN $
(Frente Intae; mains US$3; ⌚noon-10pm, closed Sun) Pull up a handcrafted wooden stool and dine under the traditional pottery hanging from the ceiling in this popular grill restaurant west of parque central. There are your standard *fritanga* options as well as a variety of typical regional plates and great *refrescos naturales* (made from local fruits, herbs and seeds blended with water and sugar and poured over ice).

Bar y Restaurant El Almendro NICARAGUAN $$
(☎2722-2152; Parque Central, 2c S; mains US$7-9; ⌚noon-10pm) This bar-room restaurant feels like something from the Wild West, but the food is actually pretty good. Choose from fish, chicken or beef in a variety of sauces served with all the usual extras.

Information

BDF (Parque Central, 1c S, 20m E) The only ATM in town is unreliable. Arrive with sufficient cash.

Hospital (☎2722-2247; Panamericana)

Marena (☎2722-2431; INSS ½c N; ⌚8am-2pm Mon-Fri) It has limited information on Cañon de Somoto, and can source guides, but not as efficiently as your hotel.

Police (☎2359-2169, 118)

Getting There & Away

The bus terminal is on the Panamericana, six blocks from the town center.

El Espino (Honduran border) (US$0.50, 40 minutes, 5:15am to 5:15pm, hourly)

Estelí (US$1.30, 1¾ hours, 5:20am to 5pm, every 40 minutes)

Managua (*ordinario* US$3, 4½ hours, 4am to 5pm, almost hourly; *expreso* US$4, four hours, 5am, 6:15am, 7:30am, 2pm, 3:15pm)

Ocotal (US$0.60, one hour, 5:15am to 4:30pm, every 45 minutes)

Ocotal

POP 41,900 / ELEV 612M

Sunken into a boulder-strewn valley sprinkled with Ocote pines and wildflowers and ringed with gorgeous Segovias, Ocotal is the commercial center of the mythic Segovias.

These mountains once baited gold-hungry pirates up the Río Coco from the Caribbean Sea. Then, in 1927, Sandino and his 'Crazy Little Army,' seized control of Ocotal from federal forces for his first big victory. This action won him some extra attention from the US White House, who soon made humble Ocotal the first city in history to be bombed by fighter planes.

Today, Ocotal is just a peaceful market town that serves farmers and families who live in the dozens of surrounding pueblos.

Sights

With mossy columns, twin bell towers (although one was technically built in 2003) and a faded, chipped facade, the baroque-neoclassical **El Templo Parroquial de Ocotal** (1803–69) is transporting, especially in the late-day sun. But the star of the town center is Nicaragua's finest **parque central**. Former mayor Fausto Sánchez was a botanist, and he planted hundreds of tropical plants, including magnolias, roses, orchids and birds of paradise, between soaring cypress and pine trees that are more than 100 years old.

Around the corner, **Casa de Cultura** (c 1890) was once a US Marine base, and is now the public library. Continue west three more blocks to the 1945 **Monument to San Francisco**, which is a popular teenage hangout at night, but remains a vessel for many an *abuelita*'s (grandmother's) humble prayers. The views from here are magical.

Festivals & Events

Festival de La Virgen de la Asunción PARADE
(⌚Aug) Festival de La Virgen de la Asunción is held in mid-August, when area ranchers parade through Ocotal showing off their riding skills.

OFF THE BEATEN TRACK

CERRO MOGOTÓN

Nicaragua's highest peak, **Cerro Mogotón**, towers over the coffee fields of Nueva Segovia close to the Honduran border. Once off-limits due to land mines, it is now safe to climb with a local guide. The easiest access is from the Ocotal–Jalapa road near the village of Achuapa. It's a seven-hour round-trip hike to the peak, which is covered in dense cloud forest. Independent guide **Mayerlin Ruiz** (☎8842-1515) runs trips to Mogotón (US$50 per person, minimim two people) departing from Ocotal.

Sleeping

Hotel El Viajero HOTEL $
(☎2732-2040; cotran, 1c N; d/tr US$14/18) The rooms are a little dark but are clean and have big TVs and huge bathrooms. Not all rooms share the same standards, but choose wisely and you'll snag terrific value.

Hotel Llamarada del Bosque HOTEL $$
(☎2733-3469; Parque Central; s/d/t US$20/35/45;) With an unbeatable location in front of the lush parque central, the small but tidy rooms at this popular hotel fill up fast. Don't plan on watching any movies over the weak wi-fi.

Hotel Frontera HOTEL $$$
(☎2732-2668; hofrosa@turbonett.com.ni; Panamericana, contiguo a Shell Ramos; s/d with fan US$23/34, with air-con US$55/73; P) Yes, it's a highway hotel nestled behind an abandoned gas station and removed a bit from town. But the rooms are huge and come with creature comforts like hot water, air-con and a pool.

Eating & Drinking

★Llamarada Cafetín del Bosque NICARAGUAN $
(Parque Central; meals US$2-3; 7am-3pm) This steam-table buffet deluxe is your breakfast and lunch destination, where trays of fluffy pancakes, *gallo pinto* (a common meal of blended rice and beans) and scrambled eggs rotate with barbecued chicken and plantains. Devour some or all of the above in a shady courtyard.

La Yunta NICARAGUAN $$
(☎2732-2180; Parque Central, 2c O, 1c S; mains US$7.50-10; noon-11pm Tue-Thu, to 1am Fri-Sun) Ocotal's succulent staple has been serving up big portions to hungry locals for well over a decade. Munch tasty mixed grills on a leafy patio with two bars and warmth to spare. It draws a bar crowd on weekends.

★Casa Vieja BAR
(Supermercado San Juan, ½c N; noon-midnight) Step through the majestic wooden doors of this lovely old adobe house and enjoy cold beer and typical snacks in a wonderful social atmosphere accompanied by a *trova* (Latin folk music) soundtrack that complements rather than dominates the conversation.

Information

BanPro (frente Mercado) Has a Visa/Plus ATM.

Hospital (☎2732-2491; Panamericana) Ocotal has the region's biggest hospital.

Intur (☎2732-3429; ocotol@intur.gob.ni; Parque Central, 3c S, 1c O; 8am-2pm Mon-Fri) Helpful tourist office that offers advice on visiting coffee farms in the region and arranges guides to climb Cerro Mogotón.

Police (☎2732-2580)

Xiam Cyber Café (Parque Central, 3c S, 3c O; per hr US$0.60; 10am-9pm) The best connection in town.

Getting There & Away

Buses depart from the **main bus terminal** (☎2732-3304), 1km south of the parque central. Border-bound buses stop to pick up passengers by the Shell station at the northern end of town.

Ciudad Antigua (US$0.85, 40 minutes, 5am and noon)

Estelí (US$1.25, 2¼ hours, 4:45am to 6pm, hourly)

Jalapa (US$1.85, 2½ hours, 5:45am to 4:30pm, every 1¼ hours)

Jícaro (Ciudad Sandino) (US$1.40, 2½ hours, 6:15am, 10:45am, 3:20pm and 5pm)

Las Manos (Honduran border) (US$0.60, one hour, 5am to 4:40pm, half-hourly)

Managua (US$4.30, 3½ hours, 4am to 3:30pm, every 90 minutes)

Murra (US$2.10, 3½ hours, 5:15am, 7am, 8:45am, 12:30pm and 1:25pm)

Somoto (US$0.60, 1¼ hours, 5:45am to 6:30pm, every 45 minutes)

Dipilto

POP 200 / ELEV 880M

It would be hard to dream up a sweeter setting than what you'll find in this tiny mountain pueblo 20km north of Ocotal, and just a 30-minute drive from Honduras. Think: narrow, cobbled streets, surrounded by the pine-studded, coffee-shaded Segovias, carved by a rushing, cascading river. The principal site is the **Santuario de la Virgen de la Piedra**, where the radiant Virgin of Guadalupe blesses a kneeling pilgrim surrounded by fragrant gardens that attract butterflies. Her faithful arrive on Saturday and Sunday to light candles and voice their prayers. And if you land here on December 12, the Día del Virgen de Guadalupe, you can be a part of the festive love mob, which descends from all corners of the northern highlands.

The majestic mountains around Dipilto are known for producing some of the best coffee in Nicaragua. The brand-new **Oficina de Turismo** (☎2737-9047, 8925-5002; inside Alcadía) in the *alcadía* organizes hikes through 15 of Dipilto's stunning shade-grown plantations with especially trained local guides. Several of the farms offer rustic accommodations, including **Finca San Isidro** (r per person incl dinner & breakfast US$20), a charming old hacienda with great views. The tourist office also organizes guided treks to quetzal nesting grounds in the cloud forest on the 1867m **El Volcán**.

Dipilto is divided into two communities, Dipilto Nuevo and Dipilto Viejo, a further 3km along the highway toward the Honduran border. The *alcadía* and access to the *santuario* is from Dipilto Nuevo. Take any bus bound for the Las Manos border crossing and ask the driver to let you out in Dipilto Nuevo ($0.45, 30 minutes). Buses run south to Ocotal and beyond every half-hour or so until around 5pm.

MOUNTAIN HIKES

To explore more of the mountains of Nueva Segovia, download the free ebook of self-guided hikes at **Hiking Nicaragua** (www.hikingnicaragua.org) – a nonprofit tourism initiative.

Ocotal to Jalapa

North of Ocotal a sinuous 65km (mostly) brick road branches into the Segovian pine forests and leads to beautiful Jalapa. From ceramic factories to ancient cities with Captain Morgan ties, there's a lot to see here. It helps to have your own vehicle, though Ocotal buses serve most of these locations several times daily. Remember, when it rains, dirt spur roads get messy, so if you're planning deep off-road adventures make sure to rent a 4WD.

The town of **Mozonte**, just 5km from Ocotal, is located on the site of a pre-Hispanic Chorotega community and still retains strong indigenous roots. It is home to ceramics collective **Colectivo de Artesanías de Mozonte** (☎8858-8704; Carretera Jalapa, entrada Mozonte; ⏲8:30am-4:30pm Mon-Sat, 9am-4pm Sun), where you can watch artisans work a variety of ceramic materials and techniques in a hacienda that abuts a small vineyard surrounded by mountains. It's a fascinating spectacle and you can buy your vases, candleholders, windchimes and wall ornaments here on the cheap.

Looming above town is **Hermita de la Virgen de Guadalupe**, a rock-top shrine to divine femininity with spectacular views. And take a stroll up the forested hill overlooking town to **Capilla Los Pozos**, where locals gather in the afternoon to play music. Along the way, keep an eye out for the golden warbler, an endangered bird species that migrates between here and Texas.

There's a well-signed turnoff to **Ciudad Antigua** down a very good 4.5km dirt road to a cute old Spanish town famous for an ambitious Brit. Founded in 1536 and under almost constant attack from local indigenous groups for the next century, it was sacked in 1654 by pirate Henry Morgan, who had come up the nearby Río Coco in a canoe, thirsty for gold. The city's jewel is the sensational **Santuario de los Milagros**, with its gorgeous brick arches, enormous wooden doors and candlelit altar. Check out the Christ figure brought from Austria. Local legend has it that any time pirates entered the sanctuary, the sculpture grew to enormous proportions and the pillaging parties could not get it out the doors. Attached, the small but fun **Museo Segoviano** (contiguo Iglesia; ⏲8am-4pm Mon-Fri) has a few pre-Columbian ceramics, 500-year-old Spanish-colonial fashion, ancient wine goblets and the original stone altar from the church.

Back on the main road, continue to the speed bumps of **San Fernando**, which has a great parque central and is famous for its *cheles* (individuals with white skin), which many trace to the presence of US marines in the area from 1927 to 1931. Cerro Mogotón is less than 20km from town.

About 10km past San Fernando, you can make a right onto the sketchy dirt road to **El Jícaro (Ciudad Sandino)** where Sandino's military mined for gold at **Las Minas San Albino**. It's possible to visit the ruins of the mine and check out Sandino's rusted old mining gear. The town itself is attractive and friendly, and makes a good base from which to explore the attractions in the surrounding countryside or just soak up the rural mountain vibe.

Local agronomist **Rúrico Castellón** (☎8643-0339; Oficina UNAG) knows the mountains surrounding El Jícaro better than anyone and offers horseback-riding tours through the lush countryside. There are several cheap *hospedajes* including **El Segoviano** (☎2735-2293; salida a Murra; s/d US$6/12) and the basic but affable **Maryfer** (☎2735-2243; Parque, 4c E, 2c N; s/d without bathroom US$4/6.50, r US$8). The best place to eat is **Comedor Kenia** (Petronic station, 1c S; meals US$2; 11am-9pm), which serves delicious typical meals in a large bamboo walled hut.

If you have a 4WD, stay on this road and you'll eventually come to the community of **Murra**, where the surrounding countryside undulates between 820m and 1300m and hides **Salto El Rosario**, one of the highest and quite possibly the most spectacular waterfalls in the country. The water falls for nearly 200m in three sections close to gorgeous **Finca Santa Rita**, which sits on 200 hectares of land outside Murra.

Returning to the main highway, about 30km south of Jalapa you'll reach las **Termales de Aranjuez**, where mineral-rich waters gush out of the ground and form a stream that locals say has medicinal properties. Bring some raw eggs to cook in the boiling puddles.

Another 12km further on is the turnoff to **El Limón**, where sulfuric thermal springs seep out of the mountains forming small caves alongside a river. Somoza once had private thermal baths here, but the pools were destroyed by Hurrican Mitch.

To the north of El Limón, there are two sustainable farms in the Las Nubarrones area. **Finca Ecológica Sonzapote** (☎8644-0830) grows organic shade-grown coffee and is in the transition zone between the pines and cloud forest. It has a 'tobaggon' – a butt-bruising but fun concrete slide and large swimming pool. **Finca Ecológica La Reforma** (☎8653-3082; Los Nubarrones, El Limón) is set in the pines, laced with trails and split by a crystalline river flush with swimming holes. It offers accomodations in a pair of rustic *cabañas*.

Jalapa

POP 25,400 / ELEV 687M

In a region freckled with remote mountain towns, Jalapa is one where the emerald hills are so close you can see their dips and grooves, their texture and shadows.

While the town itself is not likely to win any beauty contests, the surrounding countryside boasts such dramatic natural beauty and so many adventure opportunities that the utter lack of tourism here is difficult to fathom.

Sights & Activities

Agua Termales Porvenir THERMAL BATHS
(Comunidad El Porvenir) Located in the community of Porvenir near the border with Honduras, these natural thermal baths are populated by a colony of turtles. The mineral-rich water is lukewarm at best but is said to cure all kinds of ailments and it's a pleasant place for a swim.

Finca San Ramón COFFEE FARM
(☎2737-2046; admission US$3.50) At one of the closest coffee farms to town you can hike trails to vistas overlooking Jalapa, and see over 40 varieties of tropical flower. Expect butterflies and hummingbirds en masse. Private round-trip transport costs about US$10.

Finca Cerro de Jesús COFFEE FARM
(☎2737-2474; www.jesusmountaincoffee.com) In the community of El Escambray is perhaps the most spectacular of all the Jalapa sites. This 630-hectare property is set on Jalapa's largest mountain, Cerro de Jesús (1885m). There are 600 *manzanas* of organic coffee, intact primary forest, a gushing 8m waterfall and, if you're up to it, you can hike the peak.

Tours

Hotel El Pantano TOUR
(☎2737-2231; www.hotelelpantano.com; Parque Central, 6c O; 8am-4pm) This is by far the best resource for tourists in the area. It hosts and/or arranges 18 guided treks and trips spanning from one to four days. If you wish to organize your own adventure yourself, helpful English-, Dutch- and Spanish-speaking owner, Wim Van der Donk, can suggest local guides and offer directions.

Festivals & Events

Feria del Maíz AGRICULTURE
(Sep) The Feria del Maíz (Corn Festival) blooms around the September harvest, when farmers converge in corn clothing to erect corn altars, enjoy a week of corn contests, and take part in theater and dances that shed a local light on corn history.

Sleeping & Eating

Hospedaje Jonathan GUESTHOUSE $
(☎2737-2451; Parque Central, 2c N, 1c O; s/d/t US$8/14/18; P) The rooms at this sunny courtyard hotel are a little grubby, but its cheap, centrally located and has hot water and cable TV.

El Pantano HOTEL $$
(☎2737-2031; www.hotelelpantano.com; Parque Central, 6c O; s/d/t US$17.50/22.50/27.50) Set on lovely lush grounds by a creek up a short walk from town you'll find these spare but comfy brick rooms with cable TV and hot water. Campers are welcome to pitch their tent (US$3.50 per night) and warm up in the morning over amazing coffee at the restaurant (meals US$3.50 to US$8).

Comedor Sandra NICARAGUAN $
(costado sur Mercado; meals US$2.50; ⊙7am-3pm) This humble *comedor* by the market serves cheap, filling Nica meals from a steam table buffet.

Luz de Luna NICARAGUAN $$
(Parque Central, 1c S; mains US$6.50-7.50; ⊙11am-10pm) Order another plate of *típica* served on plastic tables that can be easily jettisoned when this sleepy *comedor* in a garish purple restaurant becomes the closest thing to a happening nightclub in Jalapa.

Shopping

Flor de Pino HANDICRAFTS
(☎8704-0532; frente Plazoleta, Champigny; ⊙9am-6pm) Members of this small womens' cooperative weave elegant baskets from pine needles. It's in the community of Champigny, 4km north of town.

Information

There are two banks in town, both with Visa-only ATMs. For internet access and phone calls visit **Megacyber** (opposite Bancentro; per hr $0.50).

Getting There & Away

The bus terminal is just south of town, near the cemetery. Services include the following:

El Jícaro (Ciudad Sandino) (US$1.75, 1½ hours, noon and 4pm) Meets buses to Murra.

El Porvenir (US$1.50, 30 minutes, hourly until 6pm)

Estelí (US$4, four hours, 4am and 10:50am)

Managua (US$6.50, 5½ hours, 3am, 4am, 5:30am, 9am, 9:40am and 1:45pm)

Ocotal (US$1.85, 1½ hours, 5am to 4pm, hourly)

Estelí–Jinotega Road

The gorgeous back-country drive between Estelí and Jinotega – two hubs of the expanded Ruta de Café – has multiple personalities depending on your chosen path.

The most direct route is a smooth drive over new paving stones and recently tarred roads through oak-studded rangeland and spectacular mountain vistas. Leaving from Estelí, take the road toward Miraflor Veer right at each of the first two Y intersections, and from there it's a straight shot to **La Concordia** (899m), almost exactly 33km from both Jinotega and Estelí.

Once you arrive in sleepy La Concordia, you can stroll through the lovely peach-tinted **Iglesia Nuestra Señora de Lourdes**, built in 1851 and crowned with Gothic crosses on its white-domed facade. From La Concordia it's a steep climb up a narrow but good mountain road to San Rafael del Norte.

The alternative (and much longer) route is reserved for those that fancy themselves as rally drivers and took out the no-excess policy on their rental. Don't even think about attempting it without 4WD. Take the same road out of Estelí, but keep to the left, climbing through the heart of Miraflor before reaching the small town of **San Sebastián de Yali**, which has petroglyphs in the parque central. Consider taking a detour 10km further north to **La Pavona**, where you'll find a huge petroglyph storyboard carved into the rocks near Cerro la Cruz.

The 'road' from Yali to San Rafael del Norte skirts the edge of the Reserva Natural Volcan Yali and is deeply rutted in some parts and can get thick with deep, sticky mud in the wet season. Go slow and you'll be rewarded with fresh mountain air and splendid landscapes known to few travelers. There are plans to pave this stretch so by the time you read this it may be possible to complete the loop without rearranging your internal organs.

San Rafael del Norte

POP 5400 / ELEV 1085M

One of the highest towns in Nicaragua, charming San Rafael del Norte is surrounded by soaring, fissured peaks with coffee *fincas* on their shoulders. Founded in the 1660s, it is rich in culture and a great jumping-off point for hikes and outdoor activities high in the mountains.

Sights & Activities

★Templo Parroquial de San Rafael Arcángel CHURCH

Beginning in 1955, the revered Father Odorico D'Andrea turned this antiquated cathedral into a labor of divine love. It's impeccably restored, with a soaring interior flooded with light streaming through stained-glass skylights that illuminate a wonderful altar and a series of inspiring murals painted by Austrian artist Juan Fuchs Holl in 1967 and 1968.

It's no wonder it was made a National Artistic Monument in 2000.

Santuario Cerro Tepeyac CHURCH

Climb the staircase that disappears into the trees at the northern end of town to find the final resting place of Father Odorico D'Andrea at this hillside church modeled after the Shrine of the Virgin of Guadalupe in Mexico. You can pay your respects at the popular priest's grave out the back.

Museo Sandino MUSEUM

(Parque, 30m N; admission by donation; ⏲9am-4pm) Closed for a major facelift at the time of research, the Museo Sandino honors Nicaragua's national hero, Augusto César Sandino, who married local girl Blanca Aráuz in 1927. The museum is set in her parents' former home, later used as a telegraph house.

Inside are a rack of Sandino's old rifles, his typewriter, newspaper articles and political posters, and just about every existing photo of Sandino with his 'Crazy Little Army.' The anniversary of the Sandinos' wedding day, which took place here on May 18, 1927, is still one of the best parties of the year.

El Jaguar PARK

(☎8886-1016, 2279-9219; www.jaguarreserve.org) Both coffee enthusiasts and nature lovers will be enamored with this fantastic private reserve with comfortable *cabañas* (dorm/room per person including three meals US$35/75) and family-friendly trails (read: nothing too long or too steep) as well as strenuous ones through primary cloud forest and past coffee stands to spectacular *miradores* (lookout points). It's outside town on the road to Lago Apanas. Advance reservations are essential.

Finca Kilimanjaro FARM

(☎8838-9418, 2782-2113; fincakilimanjaro@hotmail.com) This working farm at 1300m near San Rafael offers a wide variety of activities including horseback riding, hiking, cow milking, swimming, and harvesting during coffee season. Day trips (US$35 per person) include lunch, transportation from Jinotega and a short tour of San Rafael. If you want to stay longer, overnight packages (per person including all meals with/without transport US$50/45) are also available. Reserve at least two days in advance and bring warm clothes.

La Brellera Canopy Tour ADVENTURE TOUR

(☎2784-2356; labrelleranatural@yahoo.es; per person US$18; ⏲9am-4:30pm) Tired of coffee? Head just 4km from San Rafael to La Brellera to traverse 1500m through pine forest via nine platforms, eight cables and two hanging bridges. For an extra US$7 you make the return trip on horseback.

Sleeping & Eating

Casita San Payo GUESTHOUSE $$

(☎2784-2327; casitasanpayo@gmail.com; Parque Central, 2½c N; s/d/t US$15/20/27.50) This is a terrific budget hotel with sunny upstairs rooms wired for cable TV, and it has an even better restaurant (meals US$2 to US$4). The fabulous owner, Naraya Zelaya, is beyond helpful; she rents a 4WD car (US$100 per day with driver) and can arrange guides (US$10/20 per half/full day) to the **Cascadas Verdes** and **Salto Santa María** waterfalls, the **Cuevas del Hermitanio** caves and pine-blanketed **Volcán Yalí** (1542m).

Getting There & Away

Buses (US$0.80, 45 minutes) and minibuses (US$1, 30 minutes) to Jinotega leave at regular intervals from the parque central. Buses for Estelí (US$1.50, 90 minutes, every two hours) travel via La Concordia.

Jinotega

POP 46,000 / ELEV 985M

Hidden in a cat's eye of a valley, the City of Mists is enclosed on all sides by mountains dappled in cloud forests, crowned with granite ridges and pocked with deep gorges.

While coffee tourism percolates in Matagalpa, Jinotega, which brims with adventure and promise, still sees far more foreign-aid workers than tourists. So walk these cobbled streets, visit nearby Lago de Apanás and hike into the misty mountains, where you can harvest coffee with locals and stroll through primary forest. Just make sure

Jinotega

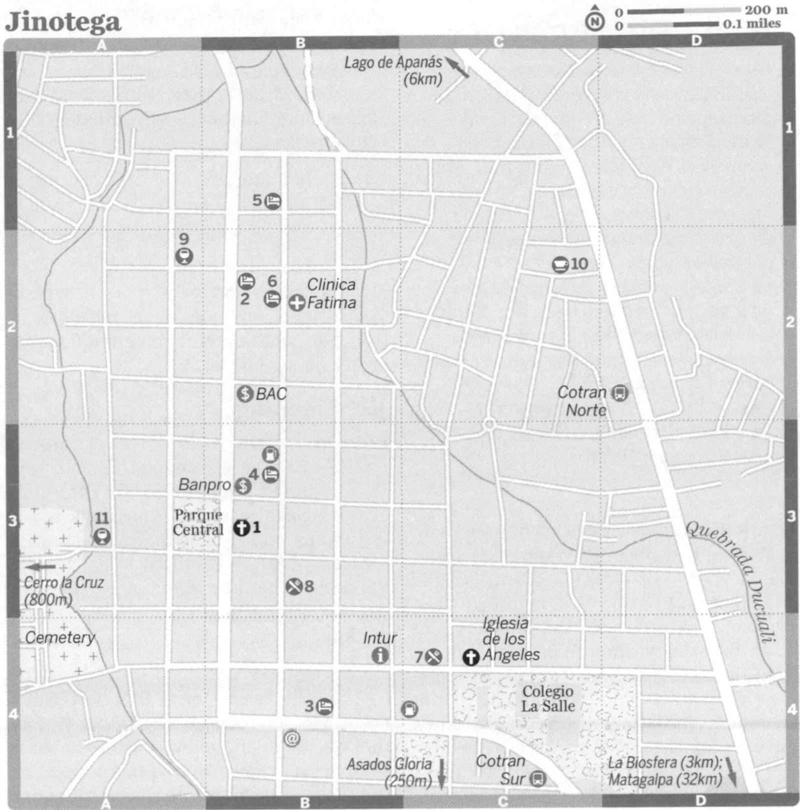

to get to Cerro La Cruz on a clear day to glimpse the cat's eye in all her jade glory.

That City of Mists moniker is no joke. The average temperature is just 20°C (68°F) and the town can get 2600mm of rain annually. Bring rain gear and a fleece for the cool evenings.

Sights & Activities

The beauty of Jinotega's **Catedral San Juan** (c 1805) is in the sanctuary, where you'll marvel at the chestnut and gold-leaf altar, pristine white arches and rows of heavenly saints, sculpted with so much life and light they make spiritual peace contagious. Opposite the church is a terrific, split-level **parque central** shaded by palms and towering laurel trees.

★Cerro La Cruz RELIGIOUS

A steep yet worthwhile hour's hike from the cemetery and embedded in a boulder-crusted

Jinotega

Sights

1 Catedral San Juan B3

Sleeping

2 Hotel Bosawás B2
3 Hotel Café B4
4 Hotel Central B3
5 Hotel Primavera B1
6 Hotel Sollentuna Hem B2

Eating

7 La Casa de Don Colocho C4
La Terraza .... (see 8)
8 Soda El Tico B3

Drinking & Nightlife

9 Bar Jinocuba A2
10 Café Flor de Jinotega C2
11 La Taverna A3

FATHER ODORICO D'ANDREA

Father Odorico D'Andrea was born in Italy in 1916, and annointed as a Franciscan friar in 1942. He found his way to San Rafael del Norte 12 years later, where he not only constructed the magnificent temple but also got the first roads, running water, schools and clinic into the region. His efforts never sat well with the government; in 1959 he had to flee Somoza's forces, and he later became an outspoken critic of the Sandinistas, though he always worked for peace. And he lived to see it, just barely. On May 3, 1989, in La Naranja, he gave the Eucharist to Sandinistas and Contras together. He would die peacefully a year later.

ridge is the town's cross, originally placed here in 1703 by Franciscan Fray Margíl de Jesús. The view of the layered Cordillera Isabelía and Jinotega from up here is unreal. Take the center path through the cemetery and begin the sweaty climb. When you emerge from the trees and come to a plateau, hug the ridge tightly and keep climbing. If you land here during Jinotega's biggest party, the **Fiestas de la Cruz** (April 30 to May 16), which peaks on May 3, you can follow the *abuelas* (grandmothers) as they ascend, ever so gingerly, en masse.

La Biosfera FARM
(☎8427-8414, 8698-1439; www.hijuela.com/labiosferaretreat; Carretera vieja Matagalpa) This American-run permaculture farm just 3km outside town has fantastic views and 7 hectares of forest to explore. It offers subsidized accommodation for those that want to volunteer on the farm.

Tours

Cuculmeca CULTURAL
(☎2782-3579; www.cuculmeca.org; Barrio Daniel Teller, Salida al Guayacán; ⏲9am-5pm Mon-Fri) This dynamic NGO arranges accommodation and guides for visits to farms and sustainable tourism projects in the Reserva Natural Cerro Datanlí–El Diablo and around San Rafael del Norte. Among the farms involved is **Finca La Estrella**, 20km from Jinotega, where you can tour organic coffee plots, hike through trails of intact forest or take part in the harvest.

Festivals & Events

Festival de la Cruz RELIGIOUS
(⏲May 3) One of Nicaragua's most athletic *fiestas*; since 1703 visitors have been shamed into climbing to the cross by area octogenarians. Breathe...

San Isidro Laborador RELIGIOUS
(⏲May 15) Locals honor the patron saint of farmers by building altars out of fruit and veggies.

Fiestas Patronales RELIGIOUS
(⏲Jun 24) Solemn processions, rodeos, beauty queens and more celebrate the feast day of San Juan Bautista.

Sleeping

Hotel Primavera GUESTHOUSE $
(☎2782-2400;ParqueCentral,5cN,1cE;s/dUS$8.50/12.50, without bathroom US$5/10) The sunniest and cleanest cheapie has new tile in the rooms and decent mattresses, and is owned by a lovely family who hang out in the lobby. The door shuts at 10pm sharp, so make arrangements if you intend to stay out late.

Hotel Bosawás HOTEL $
(☎2782-6689; Parque Central, 4c N; s/d US$10.50/14.50, without bathroom US$6.50/8.50; 📶) Pass through the bright lobby to access the basic but excellent-value rooms at this budget classic. Those at the front with shared bathrooms and windows onto the street are actually nicer than the more expensive ones with private bathrooms at the rear.

Hotel Central HOTEL $$
(☎2782-2063; Parque Central, 1c E, ½c N; s/d/t US$10.50/19/25.20; P) The friendly staff rents comfy rooms with hot water and cable, although the walls are somewhat thin. The rooms on the north side are brighter as they have outside facing windows.

Hotel Sollentuna Hem HOTEL $$
(☎2782 2334; solentunahem@gmail.com; Parque Central, 4c N; s/d US$16.50/29.50; P 📶) A favorite among travelers, this small hotel has a variety of rooms with cable TV and hot water. Choose carefully as some are better than others.

★**Hotel Café** HOTEL $$$
(☎2782-2710; www.cafehoteljinotega.com; Gasolinera Uno, 1c O, ½c N; s/d/t incl breakfast US$47/57/67; P ❄ 📶) The most comfy sleep in Jinotega is located at this three-star property. Most

(but not all) of the rooms are flooded with natural light, which reflects pastel paint jobs. The marble baths and hyper-speed laundry service are nice too.

Eating

★ La Casa de Don Colocho BAKERY $
(☎2782-2584; Parque Central, 3c E, 3c S; pastries US$0.60-1.10; ⏰7am-8pm; 👪) A bakery every town would love. The cinnamon rolls are dense and sugary, the pineapple triangles are addictive, and those are just two of the dozens of items this place turns out twice daily. The ovens open at 8am and 4pm. Plan your visit accordingly.

Soda El Tico NICARAGUAN $
(☎2782-2059; Parque Central, 1c E, ½c S; buffet meals US$4, mains US$6; ⏰7:30am-10pm) By far the most appetizing restaurant in town, Soda El Tico is a classic steam-table buffet with steak, pork loin and grilled chicken served with a tasty salad bar. You can also order a variety of snacks and specialties from the menu.

Asados Gloria BARBECUE $
(Hospital ½c O; meals US$2-2.50; ⏰noon-9pm) At last a cheap *fritanga* with inviting ambience and real salad. The stock standard fluorescent lights and plastic chairs have been replaced with wooden furniture and a *trova* (folk) soundtrack, and the meats are tangy and delicious.

La Terraza CAFE $$
(contiguo Banco Procredit; mains US$6-7; ⏰noon-10pm) This flash new cafe-restaurant above Soda El Tico feels just a tad too stylish for hard-working Jinotega with attractive wrought-iron tables, big sofas, hanging lamps and huge glass windows. It has a full range of caffeinated beverages and a small but diverse menu including salads and gourmet sandwiches.

Drinking & Nightlife

Café Flor de Jinotega CAFE
(☎2782-2617; www.soppexcca.org; Cotran Norte, 1½c N; espresso drinks US$0.50-0.75; ⏰8am-6pm) Quite simply the best cup of coffee in town, and possibly on all of the Ruta de Café. Relax at one of the see-through tables filled with three kinds of coffee beans and get to know what good is.

Bar Jinocuba BAR
(Alcadía 5c N; ⏰noon-midnight, closed Tue) Groovy alternative rock bar (and guaranteed *ranchero*-free zone) with hip live music performances and cultural events. The young owners are very knowledgeable about tourism in the region and are able to hook you up with independent English- and German-speaking guides to explore the surrounding mountains.

La Taverna BAR
(Parque Central, 2c O; ⏰noon-midnight) The coolest dive in the northern highlands has timber tables, a dark wood interior, a lively late-night crowd and tasty beef fajitas (US$5).

Orientation & Information

BanPro (Catedral San Juan, ½c S) and **BAC** (Parque Central, 2c N) both have ATMs that accept Visa and MasterCard credit and debit cards.

Clinica Fatima (☎2782-6577; Esso Central, 2½c N) Private clinic with a range of specialists.

Cyber Xtreme (Gasolinera Uno, 2c O; per hr US$0.60; ⏰9am-9pm) Large internet facility with plenty of machines.

Intur (☎2782-4552; Parque Central, 2c S, 3c E; ⏰8am-2pm) Stop in to pick up the latest brochures.

Police (☎2782-2398, emergency 118)

Getting There & Around

There are two bus terminals. **Cotran Norte** is on the highway east of town, while **Cotran Sur** sits near the town's southern entrance.

Buses departing from Cotran Norte:

Estelí (US$2, 1¾ hours, 5:15am, 7am, 9am, 1pm, 2:45pm and 3:30pm)

Pantasma (Asturias) (US$2, 1½ hours, 4am to 4:30pm, hourly)

Pantasma (San Gabriel) (US$1.80, 1½ hours, 5:30am to 4:30pm, hourly)

San Rafael del Norte (*ordinario* US$0.80, 40 minutes; *expreso* US$1, 30 minutes; 6am to 6pm, half-hourly)

Yalí (US$2, two hours, 6am, 8:30am, 10am, noon and 2:30pm)

Buses departing from Cotran Sur:

Managua (US$3.40, 3½ hours, 4am to 4pm, 10 daily) Via new road, does not enter Matagalpa.

Matagalpa (US$1, 1¼ hours, 5am to 6pm, half-hourly)

SANDINO: PROPHET OF THE SEGOVIAS

Born in 1895 to a wealthy Niquinohomo landowner, Gregorio Sandino, and an indigenous servant girl, Margarita Calderón, Augusto César Sandino was always painfully aware of class differences. He spent his childhood in poverty until his mother abandoned him and the Sandinos unenthusiastically took him in.

The family eventually entrusted him with overseeing the farm, but after he almost killed the son of a prominent local Conservative politician in a gun duel, Sandino had to leave that life and flee the country. He traveled and worked in Guatemala, Honduras and Mexico, discovering yoga, communism and Seventh Day Adventism along the way, even becoming a Freemason. For seven years he primed himself for a higher path, and when the statute of limitations ran out on his attempted-murder charges, he returned to Nicaragua, which was by then embroiled in civil war.

Sandino offered his services to the Liberal forces, which refused to arm the untried newcomer. A group of prostitutes loaned Sandino the money instead, and he began a tireless guerrilla campaign, attracting mostly *campesino* (farmer) and indigenous followers.

In 1927 more than 2000 US Marines arrived with a treaty and orders to enforce it. 'All my men surrender,' said the Liberal commander during the formalities, tired of war and now hopelessly outgunned. 'Except one.'

On July 15, 1927, Sandino attacked the marines in Ocotal; the US responded with aerial bombing. Sandino retreated to the mountains and began a six-year, low-intensity war with US occupiers and the Guardia Nacional. Throughout the early 1930s Sandino's ragged army collected a series of hit-and-run victories. He declared himself the incarnation of Caesar, saying that a horrific Managua earthquake was proof of his divinity, and delivering the *Manifesto of Light and Truth,* which revealed that Nicaragua would be the final staging ground in the battle between good and evil. Things had gone way beyond ridding Nicaragua of US imperialism.

By 1933, despite Sandino's position as the de facto president of a large chunk of Nicaragua, the writing was on the wall: international support was gone and popular moderate Juan B Sacasa had just been elected president.

In exchange for peace, Sacasa gave Sandino 36,000 sq km of homestead near Jinotega, which they operated as a commune, and Sandino seemed to settle down. But the US military, which had to pull out due to domestic pressures, suspected he still had a secret cache of weapons.

As an insurance policy, the US began providing substantial military support to Anastazio Somoza García, a former water-company official married to a niece of President Sacasa, who spoke fluent English. He was among the guests at an official dinner party celebrating the big peace treaty with Sandino's forces on February 20, 1934.

After dinner, as they left the presidential palace, Sandino and his supporters were abducted and shot by Somozás men. Their bodies were never found.

Reserva Natural Cerro Datanlí–El Diablo

The mountains towering over and buffering the eastern end of Jinotega are part of this stunning 10,000-hectare reserve, which climbs well into the quetzal zone at 1650m. It is a magical place with butterflies dancing around coffee bushes that cling to impossibly steep mountainsides in the shade of lush cloud forest. Cuculmeca (p190) has organized tourist routes through the reserve and can arrange guides. For more on the park's attractions check out the website, **Explore Datanlí** (www.exploredatanli.com).

The main southern entrance to the reserve is 12.5km down yet another lousy dirt road from the signed turnoff 'Km146' on the Matagalpa–Jinotega road. Stay straight until you reach the village of **La Fundadora**, where you'll find the incredibly peaceful community-run **Eco-Albergue** (☎2782-3579, 8929-7439; La Fundadora; r per person US$10). It consists of half-a-dozen cute brick huts with tiled roofs overlooking farmland about 1km outside the village. If there is no-one around, ask at **Comedor Nilita** (La Fundadora; meals

US$1.50-2.50; 7am-8pm), which also serves a great typical rural meal.

From La Fundadora, it's another rough 30-minute drive to the impressive **La Bujona** waterfall in the community of **La Esmeralda**. Surrounded by ethereal cloud forest, La Bujona is a wide wall of water that crashes over the rock face in various streams. It feels far from civilization and receives very few visitors, a fact certified by the lack of rubbish and the rotten planks you walk over on the trail. The path begins by two small posts just before the wooden bridge. In La Esmeralda there are two *comedores* serving hearty meals.

One daily bus leaves Cotran Norte in Matagalpa at 1:45pm for Las Nubes, passing through La Fundadora and La Esmeralda, returning at 6am. It gets full, so arrive early or you may be riding on the roof. There are plans for a new bus service from Jinotega, which should be running by the time this book is published.

Heading north from Jinotega, there are a number of coffee farms inside the reserve that welcome visitors. Set on a dramatic forested mountainside at 1200m with views all the way down to Lago Apanas, **La Bastilla Ecolodge** (8654-6235, 2782-4335; www.bastillaecolodge.com; Reserva Natural Datanlí–El Diablo; dm/s/d/t incl breakfast US$15/40/60/90) has easily the most comfortable accommodations in the reserve. The spacious, solar-powered brick *cabañas* have red floor tiles and sparkling bathrooms with solar hot water. But the best part are the sensational views over the coffee plantations full of birds from the rocking chairs on the wide wooden balconies. There are also classy tent platforms with private bathrooms and a comfortable dormitory. But 1st-class comfort and service is only half the story here. The ecolodge is an entirely nonprofit initiative that funds the nearby technical training center. Many students from the center work as guides and can take you along the 450 *manzana* farm's three hiking trails. Or you can try your hand picking your own coffee.

To reach here take any Pantasma via Asturias bus from Jinotega and jump out at the 'empalme La Bastilla,' from where it's a tough 5km hike uphill. If you call in advance, staff will pick you up at the turnoff.

A short distance north of La Bastilla (a walking trail was under construction at the time of research) in the heart of the reserve is the community-run **Cabañas El Gobiado** (Cooperativa Lina Herrera; 8844-0024, 8507-2750; Reserva Natural Datanlí–El Diablo; s/d/t US$10/15/22.50). The coffee clumps you'll see on your way here bear beans destined for market and are the only source of income in a deeply impoverished corner of Nicaragua. A local family runs the lodge on a plateau between jungled mountains that rise like jagged teeth into the sky. There's a nature trail (guides US$5 per visitor) that winds through them for three hours, connecting waterfalls to bird towers that peak above the canopy. You can visit as a day trip, camp here or stay in one of the recently refurbished *cabañas*. Waking up here, when the mist clings to those peaks, pays off.

El Gobiado is 3km down a rough spur road from the village of Venencia on the Jinotega–Asturias road. It is a one-hour walk or phone ahead to organize horses.

Lago de Apanás

The third-largest body of water in Nicaragua came into being in 1964 when the Mancotal dam was built on the Río El Tuma, just 6km north of Jinotega. It's actually two lakes, the much larger Lago de Apanás (54 sq km) and Lago Asturias (3 sq km), just north. If you like freshwater bass, try the *guapote*, on sale at lots of rickety-looking *ranchos* lining the lakeshore in the town of Asturias. If you'd prefer to catch your own, fishermen will take you out on the lake for around US$5 per hour in a rowboat, US$10 per hour with a small outboard.

On the western lakeshore in the village of Sisle, the community-run **Cooperativa El Conejo** (8917-0072; Sisle; 8am-6pm) will take you out on boat tours to nearby islands including Isla Ave (US$2) and Isla Conejo (US$5). It also organizes fishing trips (US$5 to US$10) and prepares fresh fish meals at the brand-new Malecón Turistica de Sisle (Sisle Tourist Dock) overlooking the water. It's possible to spend the night here in the simple community lodge (US$7 per person).

There are two bus routes to Pantasma from the Cotran Norte in Jinotega: via Asturias on the eastern shore of the lake and via San Gabriel on the western side. To get to Sisle, take any San Gabriel bus and ask to be let off at the Pulpería Emilio Gomez, from where it's a 800m walk downhill to the dock.

Matagalpa

POP 89,100 / ELEV 902M

If you love coffee, mountains and urbanity, then have your cake and eat it in Matagalpa, a town where for decades an ever-increasing number of Liberal coffee patriarchs and subsistence Sandinista farmers have rubbed shoulders during city festivals and at market. Growth has sent Matagalpa sprawling into the foothills, up crumbling streets lined with shacks and onto graded plateaus laid out in tony subdivisions. Don't worry, the mountains rise so high and layer so deep, Mother Nature doesn't look the least bit threatened. Just glance skyward from nearly every city street and you'll see pristine boulder-strewn peaks.

Besides, this kind of rampant growth, commerce and social tension does a city good. It keeps it moving with enough noise, speed and pointlessness to make you feel like you're performing a cameo in some caffeine-addled existential comedy. Lucky for you, it's one with good catering from established restaurants, upstart hipster cafes and local juice bars.

And when you've sipped your last cup of city, head for the hills, where you can hike through primary forest to gushing waterfalls, pick coffee, explore mineshafts and listen to *ranchero* troubadours jam under a harvest moon.

LA RUTA DE CAFÉ

The Ruta de Café is a loose association of coffee *fincas* that welcome tourists to their fields (which range from *colectivos* of small subsistence growers to 100-year-old plantations). You can spend the night, hike through neighboring cloud forests, join in harvests (October to March) and sip plenty of local joe. There are four branches to the ever-expanding Ruta de Café, which spans the entirety of the northern highlands.

Estelí & Nueva Segovia

Near Estelí, the Área Protegida Miraflor is a tapestry of family coffee *fincas* that formed in the wake of the Sandinista revolution. Further north, the lush, layered and shady coffee fields of Dipilto produce some of the most acclaimed beans in Nicaragua, and Finca Cerro de Jesús grows terrific coffee among large tracts of cloud forest in the rocky peaks surrounding Jalapa.

San Rafael del Norte

Accessed from San Rafael del Norte, El Jaguar is a family farm and model of sustainability with 14 hectares of organic coffee parcels surrounded by 53 hectares of tropical cloud forest. Nearby Finca Kilimanjaro also arranges tours and overnight stays. In addition to joining the harvest, you can ride trails to glorious *miradores* (lookout points), plunge into swimming holes and milk the family cows.

Jinotega

When German coffee growers and their families first arrived in Nicaragua in the early 20th century, they came to the mountains that soar above Jinotega. It is here that you'll find La Bastilla Ecolodge, a nonprofit initiative within a nature reserve that offers full coffee tours including tasting sessions.

Also in the reserve are Finca La Estrella, where you can harvest berries with family farmers, and Cooperativa Lina Herrera, a shade-grown cooperative surrounded by thick forest.

Matagalpa

The big draw here are two very different coffee-farm experiences. Selva Negra, an 850-hectare estate, was founded by German immigrants in the 1880s and is still managed by their heirs. It offers sustainable coffee and wildlife tours.

For a more rustic experience, head to the communities surrounding San Ramon where you can join the locals in the harvest and follow the beans to a community roasting plant.

Sights

★Casa Museo Comandante Carlos Fonseca — MUSEUM

(Parque Rubén Darío, 1c E; donations appreciated; ⌚9am-5pm) Commander Carlos Fonseca, the Sandinista equivalent of Malcolm X (read: bespectacled, goateed, intense, highly intelligent and charismatic), grew up desperately poor in this humble abode with his single mother and four siblings, despite the fact that his father was a coffee magnate. Now it's a tiny but enthralling museum that follows his evolution as a leader from childhood until his death.

Iglesia Catedral San Pedro — CHURCH

(Parque Morazán) Built in 1874, Matagalpa's glorious whitewashed neoclassical cathedral is flooded with light. Inside the sanctuary are a natural wood altar, gorgeous domes, arches and crown moldings. It fronts Parque Morazán, a reasonably shady hangout with outstanding people-watching.

Museo de Café — MUSEUM

(Av José Beníto Escobar, Parque Morazán, 1c S; ⌚8am-12:30pm & 2-5pm Mon-Fri) FREE Recently overhauled, this absorbing museum features large, glossy printed displays in Spanish and English on the roots of regional *café* and modern coffee production in the region, as well as old coffee processing machinery. Particularly interesting are the panels on the hardy immigrants who set up the first plantations in the region. Well worth a visit before any trip into the surrounding countryside.

Iglesia San José — CHURCH

Originally constructed in 1751 and used as a jail for indigenous rebels in the late 1800s, this church was rebuilt in 1917 by Franciscan friars. She shows her age, but her baroque gold-leaf altar and arched ceilings are lovely, and she fronts leafy Parque Rubén Darío.

Foreigners Cemetery — CEMETERY

If you 'dig' graveyards, check out both the Foreigners Cemetery (and nearby National Cemetery) on the eastern edge of town, where you'll find great views and the headstone of Benjamin Linder, an American hydroelectric engineer and unicycle clown who was killed by Contra forces.

El Castillo del Cacao — FACTORY

(☎2772-2002; www.elcastillodelcacao.com; admission US$6; ⌚9am-4pm Mon-Sat) On the road to San Ramón is Matagalpa's sweetest site. You've seen the chocolate bars by now, and if you know what's good for you, you've also tasted Castillo de Cacao. Now tour the 'castle' where they mix the cacao with sugar, cashews and coffee beans. A taxi from town costs US$1 per person.

Activities

Local hiking opportunities abound. The gorgeous boulder fields and red-rock faces of El Ocote are sensational. You can access the trail from behind El Castillo del Cacao and hike two to three hours before rejoining the highway to San Ramón at Finca La Praya. It's just a US$0.50 bus ride back to town.

For more hiking options, pop into nonprofit **Café Girasol** (☎2772-6030; www.familiasespeciales.org; ⌚6:30am-10pm) for detailed leaflets (US$1.30 to US$1.80) explaining a number of self-guided walks in the Matagalpa area that vary in length from four to eight hours. While you're there, make sure to sample the excellent coffee – profits support projects for children with disabilities.

Reserva Natural Cerro Apante — PARK

(admission US$1.50) Matagalpa's most popular hiking trail leads from Finca San Luis, a 20-minute walk (or US$1 taxi ride) south of Parque Rubén Dario, into this reserve. It's a two-hour round-trip hike to the *mirador*. If you're aiming for the misty 1442m peak, it's best to hire a guide. There are two other entrances to different sectors of the park: one is just north of town on the road to El Tuma; the other is on the road to Guadalupe-Samulali, off the Matagalpa–Muy Muy road.

Tours

★Matagalpa Tours — ADVENTURE

(☎8647-4680, 2772-0108; www.matagalpatours.com; ⌚8am-12:30pm & 2-6pm Mon-Fri, 8am-4pm Sat) Matagalpa Tours offers nearly a dozen interesting and enriching ways to get into this city and the surrounding countryside. In Matagalpa proper it offers urban walking tours and rents bicycles (US$10 for two hours, additional hour US$2), but its best work is done around the local mountains where it offers both day trips and multiday excursions, including an informative tour of local coffee farms.

Cecosemac — COFFEE

(☎2772-0654; Parque Rubén Darío, 4c E, ½c N; per person incl all meals US$20-30; ⌚8am-5pm) This small-scale coffee growers cooperative represents farmers in La Dalia, Jinotega, San

Matagalpa

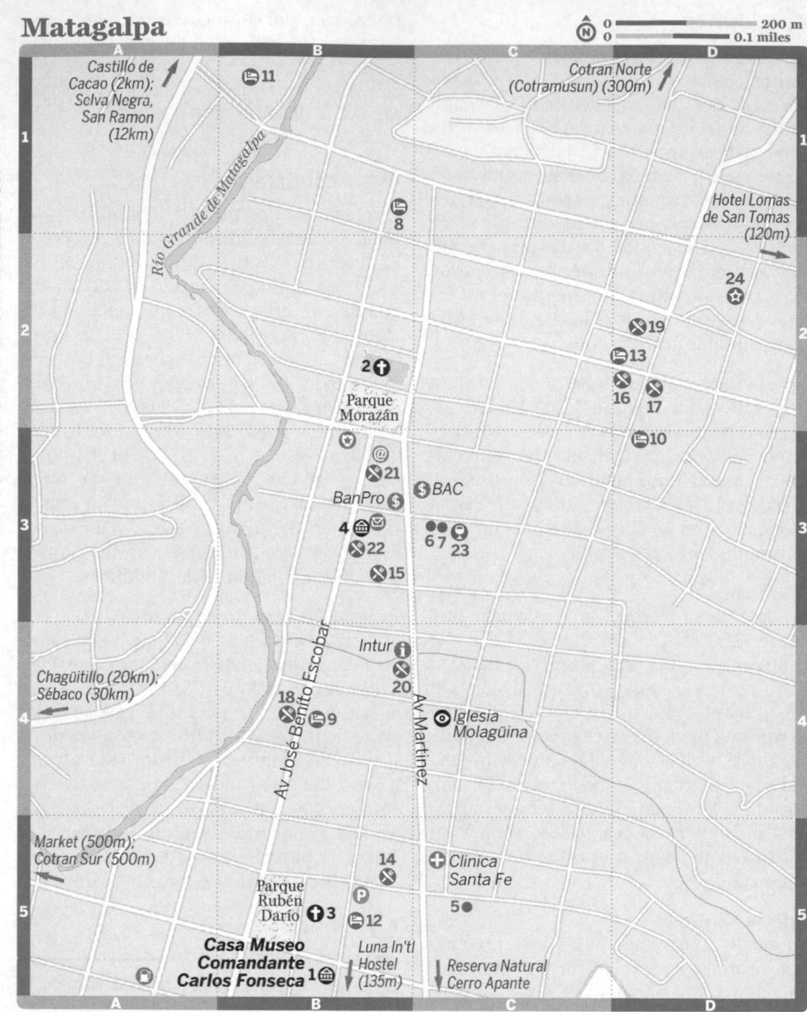

Ramon and Matagalpa and arranges harvest tours with homestays similar to those you'll find in Miraflor. It's also a great place to purchase local shade-grown beans.

Courses

Escuela de Español Colibri LANGUAGE COURSE
(www.spanishnicaragua.net; Parque Morazán, 1c S, ½c E; per hr US$10) This popular school inside Matagalpa Tours offers one-on-one Spanish classes, plenty of cultural activities and volunteer placements for students. Packages including 20 hours of classes per week plus homestay and all meals cost US$308.

Festivals & Events

Anniversary Party CULTURAL
(Feb 14) A fireworks-splashed extravaganza with live music, parades, beauty contests and lots of *chicha bruja* (fermented corn liquor).

Fiestas Patronales CULTURAL
(mid-Sep) Even more beloved than the Anniversary bash, this is a weekend party of old-school horse shows, promenades and the all-night Fiesta Huipil. At daybreak, lingerers converge on the social club for tamales.

Matagalpa

Top Sights
1 Casa Museo Comandante Carlos Fonseca ... B5

Sights
2 Iglesia Catedral San Pedro ... B2
3 Iglesia San José ... B5
4 Museo de Café ... B3

Activities, Courses & Tours
5 Cecosemac ... C5
6 Escuela de Español Colibri ... C3
7 Matagalpa Tours ... C3

Sleeping
8 Hospedaje Vic Pal ... B1
9 Hotel Central ... B4
10 Hotel El Castillo ... D3
11 Hotel Fuente Azul ... B1
Hotel Mana Del Cielo ... (see 20)
12 Hotel San José ... B5
13 La Buena Onda ... D2

Eating
14 Buffet Oasis ... B5
15 El Cafeto ... B3
16 El Mexicano ... D2
17 El Pescamar ... D2
18 La Matagalpa ... B4
19 La Vita é Bella ... D2
20 Maná de Cielo ... B4
21 Repostería Gutiérrez ... B3
22 Rincón Don Chato ... B3

Drinking & Nightlife
23 Artesanos ... C3

Entertainment
24 Centro Cultural Guanuca ... D2

Shopping
Telares de Nicaragua ... (see 7)

Festival of Polkas, Mazurcas and Jamaquellos DANCE
(28-30 Sep) A wink at coffee country's German roots. Think: Oktoberfest, but with *chicha bruja* instead of beer and *güirílas* instead of sausages.

Sleeping

Hotel El Castillo HOTEL $
(2772-0034; hotelelcastillomt@gmail.com; Parque Morazán, 3c E; s/d/t US$15/17/24;) This excellent-value new hotel set on a hillside has great views but is only three blocks from the park. All of the rooms are bright and modern, but those at the front have small private balconies overlooking the cathedral.

Hotel Central HOTEL $
(2712-3140; Av José Benito Escobar, Parque Rubén Darío, 2½c N; s/d/t US$11.50/15.50/21;) Vacillates between dumpy and bright depending upon the rooms, which all come with cable TV, plump pillows and new spring mattresses regardless of the paint job. It's surprisingly quiet considering the central location.

Hospedaje Vic Pal GUESTHOUSE $
(2772-6735; Parque Morazán, 3½c N; r US$8, s/d without bathroom US$3/6) Really cheap and basic, it's also clean, quiet and friendly, with big beds, and cathedral and mountain views over courtyard laundry lines.

Luna International Hostel HOSTEL $
(8496-3408; www.cafeluzyluna.com; Gasolinera Uno, 3½c E; dm/r US$7/20) This new branch of the popular Estelí hostel was just finding its feet when we passed through, but has clean and spacious rooms, a large kitchen and plenty of information for travelers. Best of all, like the Estelí version, all profits go to worthy social projects.

La Buena Onda HOSTEL $$
(2772-2135; www.hostelmatagalpa.com; cancha Brigadista, 2½c E; dm/s/d US$8/25/30;) Clean, centrally located and with a chilled vibe, this fine hostel ticks all the boxes. It's located in a cozy converted house with well-furnished rooms, spacious dorms with private bathrooms and big lockers, and a balcony overlooking the street. There is a kitchen for guest use, a sizable book exchange and plenty of information on local attractions.

Hotel Mana Del Cielo HOTEL $$
(2772-0150; mana01@turbonett.com.ni; Av Martínez, Parque Morazán, 3½c S; s/d/t US$15/20/35, r with air-con US$40;) The rooms aren't huge and are bright pink, but they are also super clean with ceramic-tiled baths, hot water and wi-fi. They don't live up to the elegant stone lobby, but if you go without air-con, it's a terrific deal.

Hotel San José HOTEL $$
(2772-2544; www.hotelsanjosematagalpa.com; detras Iglesia San José; s/d US$25/35, r with air-con

US$45; ❄ 📶) This fine new hotel is already popular with travelers thanks to its spotless rooms, central location and professional service.

Hotel Lomas de San Tomas HOTEL **$$**
(☎2772-4189; snthomas2006@yahoo.com; Escuela Guanuca, 350m E; s/d/t US$35/45/60; P 📶) This three-story hilltop hacienda property has huge rooms with ceramic-tiled floors, a pastel paint job and wrought-iron beds. Each has a balcony overlooking the city and surrounding mountains. It's a US$1.50 taxi ride from downtown.

Hotel Fuente Azul HOTEL **$$**
(☎2772-2733; Parque Morazán, 4c N, 3c O; s/d US$15/30, without bathroom US$10/20; P 📶) Just across the creek in the northwestern end of town is a converted home with super-clean, freshly painted rooms dressed with crisp bedding, new bathrooms and ceiling fans. A superb-value option.

Eating

Matagalpa has a few good restaurants, but you'll need to look to the smoky booths that set up at sunset just north of Palí supermarket and the cathedral for the regional specialty, *güirílas*. Made with a fresh corn *masa*, they are sweeter and thicker than your average tortilla; a *servicio* includes a hunk of crumbly, salty *cuajada* cheese and *crema*, and costs about US$0.60.

Repostería Gutiérrez CAFE **$**
(☎2772-2502; Parque Morazán, ½c S; pastries US$0.50-1.50; ⏲7am-8pm) With a great 1st-floor terrace overlooking busy Av José Beníto Escobar and the hillside barrios beyond, this satellite branch of an Estelí classic serves tasty fresh pastries and excellent local coffee to a dedicated clientele.

El Mexicano MEXICAN **$**
(Parque Morazon, 1c N, 2½c E; mains US$3; ⏲noon-10pm; ✍) It looks posh from the outside, but

FAIR TRADE & CAFFEINE DREAMS

More fiercely traded than any global commodity other than oil, black coffee makes up half of Nicaragua's exports and is the jittery engine upon which the economy turns. Until 1989 coffee prices were regulated by the International Coffee Organization (ICO), after a drought in Brazil doubled prices several years before. But the USA pulled out of the ICO about the same time that Vietnam and other new producers were beginning to flood the market with beans. By 1999 coffee prices had dropped from a spike of more than US$3 to only US$0.42 per pound, less than it costs to produce.

In Nicaragua, small farmers abandoned their land; of Matagalpa's 25 major haciendas, 20 of them closed, putting 36,000 people out of work. Some went to Costa Rica or other parts of the country to work; most were stuck here, begging for change by the sides of the road. A union, Rural Workers Association (ATC) formed, and former coffee workers shut down the highway four times until the government fell back on an old Sandinista tactic and agreed to give each family a plot of land, for which they would need to pay half.

Some farmers, with the help of international organizations, began growing organic coffee. It was relatively easy to become certified in Nicaragua, as agriculture has never relied on fertilizers and pesticides (because farmers couldn't afford them). It was expensive, however. No single organization certifies coffee 'organic' or 'fair trade.' Starbucks, for example, has its own certification program, but there are dozens of others, including Rainforest Alliance and Utz Kapeh. A cooperative of 150 farmers pays around US$2500 per year to be certified, which is still a good deal considering how much more the coffee earns.

Despite the fact that fair trade basically asks consumers to voluntarily pay extra (who thought that would work?), it's now the fastest-growing segment of the coffee market. Some 800,000 farmers in 40 countries are working fair-trade plots. In Nicaragua, communities often still work together as Sandinista-style cooperatives, making group decisions and encouraging women to participate.

It's not as though these growers are getting fat off fair trade – most make around US$2 per day. But in a desperately poor region where electricity and running water are luxuries, a better and more reliable price for their coffee means three meals a day – plus the chance to plan for the future.

go in to enjoy cheap authentic Mexican food prepared by the owner/chef from Guadalajara and served in a casual dining area.

Maná de Cielo NICARAGUAN $

(Av Martínez, Parque Morazán, 3c S; meals US$3-5; 7am-9pm) The best-loved steam table in Matagalpa. Take your choice from dozens of options including chorizo and eggs in the morning, and perfectly caramelized grilled chicken at lunch. Whatever you pick, it's all top notch.

Buffet Oasis NICARAGUAN $

(Parque Rubén Darío, 1½c E; meals US$4-5; 7am-9pm; P) A great Matagalpa steam table buffet with all your Nica favorites and excellent *frescos*. High turnover means it is always fresh.

Rincón Don Chato NICARAGUAN $

(Av José Benito Escobar, Parque Morazán, 2c S; batidos US$1.20-1.80, mains US$4; 7:30am-6pm Sun-Thu, to 5pm Fri) A fresh-pressed, formica diner with amazing *batidos* (fruit shakes made with milk or water). The pineapple and celery in orange juice is an instant classic, while the broccoli smoothie is way better than it sounds. It also has a rather indulgent pound cake dripping with simple syrup.

La Matagalpa SUPERMARKET $

(Av José Benito Escobar, Parque Rubén Darío, 3c N; 8am-8pm) Matagalpa's go-to all-purpose supermarket is an essential haven for self-caterers. It carries locally produced coffee and cheeses, and its own brand of hot sauce.

El Cafeto CAFE $

(Parque Morazán, 2c S, ½c E; coffees US$0.75-1.75, mains US$3.50; 9am-9pm Tue-Sat, to 2pm Sun, 5:30am-9pm Mon) A cute and sunny coffee bar with flowers on the tables, salads and pressed panini on the menu. The coffee is fantastic and it even has ice cream!

★**La Vita é Bella** ITALIAN $$

(2772-5476; Parque Morazán, 2½c E, 1½c N; pastas US$3-4, mains US$5-8; noon-10pm) This local institution serves up flavorful authentic Italian dishes at low prices in a relaxed bistro atmosphere. The thin-crust pizza is some of the best in Nicaragua and vegetarians can take their pick from a wide selection of menu items. Carnivores can get theirs too. Try the scaloppini. Come early to get a table.

El Pullaso STEAKHOUSE $$

(Carretera Managua; dishes US$4-9; 11am-11pm) Matagalpinos love beef and it's no surprise that their steakhouse of choice is El Pullaso, which serves big portions of tender cuts of meat at bargain prices. Come with an appetite. It's a US$1.50 to US$2 taxi ride from town.

La Pradera de San Francisco STEAKHOUSE $$

(2772-2543; empalme San Ramón; mains US$6.50-10; 11am-11pm) Just a US$2 cab ride from the city center, this snazzy dining room is where Matagalpa's business elite take their long lunch hour. You'll be forgiven if you pass on the bull-testicle ceviche; just know that the sizzling skillets of tender steak and shrimp deliver. There is another, less atmospheric branch, on the highway in town.

El Pescamar SEAFOOD $$

(Parque Morazán, 3c E, 1c N; dishes US$7-11; noon-10pm) Join the local business crowd for some damn good seafood. It smells like a fish market at first, but that's because it receives a daily supply of fresh fish, shrimp, crab and lobster.

Drinking & Nightlife

For events around town, check out **Aguali** (www.aguali.net).

Artesanos BAR

(27722444; www.artesanoscafebar.blogspot.com; Parque Morazán, 1c S, ½c E; 9am-midnight) Hands down the grooviest bar-cafe in town. There's an all-dark-wood dining room, a large patio, great coffee, and a young, hipster crowd who drink and groove to electronica and latin rhythms till closing time.

Entertainment

Centro Cultural Guanuca CULTURAL CENTER

(2772-3562; Guadalupe 1½c S; 10am-10pm) Run by a nonprofit women's organization, this great venue shows art-house movies and hosts concerts and live events ranging from theater to dance competitions.

Shopping

Telares de Nicaragua HANDICRAFTS

(2772-0108; Parque Morazán, 1c S, ½c E; 8am-5pm Mon-Fri, 8am-2pm Sat) In the Matagalpa Tours building, this fair-trade outlet sells brightly colored fiber arts from El Chile, corn-husk dolls, beaded jewelry, baskets and a selection of the smooth, black local pottery, which is mixed with volcanic ash and fired at extreme temperatures.

Information

Most banks are located on Av Martínez, a couple of blocks south of Parque Morazán.

BAC (Parque Morazán, ½c S) ATM serves Visa and MasterCard networks.

BanPro Reliable Visa/MasterCard ATM.

Clinica Santa Fe (2772-5113; Silais, 1c S) Professional private clinic. It plans to move to a new, bigger location. Ask around.

Copymat Cyber (Parque Morazán, 20m S; per hr US$0.40; 9am-9pm) Cheap and speedy internet access.

Correos de Nicaragua (Parque Morazán, 1c S; 8am-1pm)

Intur (2772-7060; Av Martínez, Parque Morazán, 3c S; 8am-2pm) Big on fliers, low on useful tips.

Lavanderia Cuenta Conmigo (2772-6713; Parque Morazán, 2c E, 3½c N; small/large load US$2.50/5; 9am-6pm Mon-Fri) Wash your clothes and support mental-health programs at this pioneering nonprofit laundry service.

Police (2772-3870; Parque Morazán)

Getting There & Around

There are two main bus terminals in Matagalpa. Clean, well-organized **Cotran Sur** (2772-4659), about 800m west of Parque Rubén Darío, generally serves Managua and points south. Buses departing from Coltran Sur:

Chinandega (US$3.40, 3½ hours, 5am and 2pm)

Ciudad Darío (US$0.85, one hour, 5:30am, 7:30am, 10:25am, 11am, 11:25am and 12:55pm)

Estelí (US$1.20, 2¼ hours, 5:20am to 5:40pm, half-hourly)

Jinotega (US$1, 1½ hours, 5am to 6pm, half-hourly)

León (US$3, 2½ hours, 6am, 9:30am, 3pm and 4pm)

Managua (*ordinario* US$2.10, 2¾ hours, 3:35am to 6:05pm, half-hourly; *expreso* US$3, 2¼ hours, 5:20am to 5:20pm, hourly)

Masaya (US$3, three hours, 2pm and 3:30pm)

Chaotic and disorienting by comparison, **Cotran Norte** (Cotramusun) goes to the following destinations:

El Cuá (US$3.20, four hours, 6am, 7am, 9am, 10:30am, noon and 1:30pm)

Esquipulas (US$1.75, 1½ hours, 5:40am, 7am, 8am, 9am, noon, 1:30pm, 3pm, 4:30pm and 5:30pm)

San Ramón (US$0.45, half hour, 5am to 7pm, half-hourly)

San Ramón

Only 12km from Matagalpa, the small town of San Ramon feels a world away with small-town pleasantries and a relaxed vibe.

But the real reason to come here is to get an authentic taste for rural life with the hardworking farmers in the surrounding hills.

Activities

Local agricultural cooperative, **UCA San Ramón** (2772-5247; www.tourism.ucasanramon.com; frente Parque Municipal, San Ramón; 8am-5pm Mon-Fri, 8am-noon Sat) has developed a tempting menu of fascinating activities in four nearby villages: La Pita, El Roblar, La Corona and La Reina.

All of the communities offer hikes through the countryside and classes in preparing traditional foods, and during the harvest (November to February) visitors can try their hand picking and sorting organic coffee.

It's possible to visit the attractions on a day trip from Matagalpa, but it's highly recommended to spend the night in one of the villages for the full cultural experience. Homestay accommodations (around US$10) and hearty country meals (US$3 to US$4.50) are available in all villages, while La Pita has a comfortable community-run guesthouse (US$15 per person) with amazing views.

Make reservations in advance by email with the UCA. If you want to stay longer, the UCA also organizes volunteer placements.

Tours

La Pita CULTURAL

This small, relaxed community has extensive coffee and cacao plantations. There is also excellent hiking in the nearby mountains, a swimming pool and a waterfall to climb. It's a 40-minute walk (or US$4 in taxi) from San Ramón.

La Reina CULTURAL

La Reina was once one of the main mining communities in Nicaragua and local guides can take you deep into an abandoned mine (US$1). Other activities include spotting howler monkeys and toucans in the forest and learning to make handicrafts with local artisans. It's a 45-minute walk (or US$4 taxi) from San Ramón or take the Matiguas bus (hourly departures) from Cotran Norte in Matagalpa.

La Corona CULTURAL

This community is located near the Yasica Sur waterfall, which is surrounded by forest and has a deep swimming hole. It is also home to a large organic coffee cooperative where visitors can learn about the entire coffee cultivation process. There are four buses a day from Cotran Norte in Matagalpa to Yasica Sur.

El Roblar CULTURAL

Located 32km from San Ramón, this community has great hiking and horseback-riding opportunities, including a trek up into the mountains to three spectacular *miradores*. It is also home to Cooperativa El Privilegio, a women's farming cooperative that grows and roasts its own brand of coffee. There are six buses a day from Cotran Norte in Matagalpa to El Roblar.

Selva Negra

If you're looking for comfort with your virgin cloud forest experience, then **Selva Negra** (2772-3883; www.selvanegra.com; admission US$2.50), part family resort, part coffee farm and part rainforest preserve, could be for you. The 850-hectare estate, founded in the 1880s by German immigrants, is named after Germany's Black Forest. The founders were part of the original German coffee invasion that created the industry. Their descendants still manage the reserve, which is webbed with several kilometers of lush jungle trails. The forest blooms with bromeliads and rare orchids year-round and is home to nesting quetzals in April and May.

Visitors can do **wildlife tours** (per hr US$10 ; 7am), **coffee tours** (regular/during harvest US$20/30), **sustainable agriculture tours** (per person US$14; 10am & 1pm) and **horseback riding** (per hr US$10). Or simply hike the 20km of trails at your leisure or relax at the restaurant, which overlooks a swan lake backed by cloud forest. Given the setting and abundance of activities, it's no surprise that North American families and package tourists flock here. If you want to stay, there's a variety of **accommodation** (budget r US$15 per person, superior r/cabañas US$45/85) options. The cute brick *cabañas* with fireplaces, and roofs sprouting bromeliads, are sprinkled in a magical fern gulley while the superior rooms have lovely lake views.

Take the Matagalpa–Jinotega bus and get off 12km north of town at the signed turnoff marked by an old tank from the revolution. From there it's a pleasant 1.5km walk to the lodge.

La Dalia & Peñas Blancas

Heading east from Matagalpa, no sooner than you have left the city, you will begin driving through gorgeous green hills typical of the hinterland of the department.

Take a break at the **Puente Las Cañas** (Km147) – about 25 minutes out of Matagalpa, where a community-based tourism project has constructed 2km of walking trails through coffee, banana and cacao plantations and over a rickety old suspension bridge. The highlight is **Salto Santa Emilia**, a 15m waterfall and cave a short walk from the highway. Don't swim here during the coffee harvest when the water is often polluted.

Continuing on the highway, you'll arrive at the town of La Dalia, a busy agricultural center surrounded mostly by cleared farmland but with some tracts of cloud forest to the northwest. If you keep heading north, eventually you'll spot the breathtaking sheer white cliffs draped in forest of the **Reserva Natural Macizos de Peñas Blancas**, one of the six nuclear areas of the Reserva Natural Bosawás and possibly the most enchanting nature reserve in Northern Nicaragua. Here you'll find the mossy, misty, life-altering primary cloud forest scenery you've been waiting for. In addition to the massive cathedral trees draped in orchids and bromeliads, you'll find as many as 48 waterfalls, some of which pour into crystalline swimming holes; at least one of them is over 120m tall. And we haven't even got to the wildlife – the 116 sq km reserve is home to an incredible array of fauna, including pumas, jaguars, large troops of monkeys and many rare bird species. The reserve has only rustic accommodations, but don't even consider not spending the night – unless you want to miss out on gazing in awe at those cliffs in the late evening and early morning light.

Activities

★**Centro Entiendemiento con la Naturaleza** ECOTOUR

(CEN; 8852-6214,8852-6213; http://www.cenaturaleza.org; Empalme la Manzana, 800m E, Peñas Blancas) If you really want to delve deep into the reserve, pay a visit to this grassroots environmental education and conservation project. In addition to reforesting and managing vast swathes of the reserve, the center also serves as a scientific research post. It organizes guides for the trek to the magnificent Arco Iris waterfall (US$13 including lunch) and wildlife zones high in the mountains.

The center rents some pretty basic rooms (US$30 per person including all meals and guide service) catering mainly to visiting scientists and students, but upmarket bamboo huts for travelers are in the pipeline.

Guardianes del Bosque ECOTOUR
(☎8428-6208, 8641-3638; nahadi30@hotmail.com; Empalme la Manzana, 400m E, Peñas Blancas) This environmentally focused farming cooperative offers a variety of activities around the reserve including guided treks to the Cascada La Niña waterfall and Mirador del Sol lookout. It also organizes coffee tours and horseback riding.

Sleeping

Eco-Albergue Guardianes del Bosque LODGE $
(☎8428-6208, 8641-3638; nahadi30@hotmail.com; Empalme la Manzana, 400m E, Peñas Blancas; dm US$6, r US$17) It's possible to stay in the village of Peñas Blancas, at this charming but basic place run by the Guardianes del Bosque. Rooms are basic wooden boxes with soft mattresses, but there is hot water and the staff are super friendly. Meals are available (US$2 to US$3) on-site.

La Sombra Ecolodge LODGE $$$
(☎8445-3732; www.lasombraecolodge.com; Carretera Waslala, La Dalia; r per person incl 3 meals US$40-50; P) You really ought to splurge here at this a 220-*manzana* coffee *finca* set among tracts of cloud forest. In addition to tours of the coffee plantations, there is excellent bird-watching, a fine *mariposario* (butterfly enclosure) and a *ranario* (frog enclosure). Day-trippers (admission US$15 including lunch) are welcome to use the 3km of trails past several waterfalls. Advance reservations are recommended.

HACIENDA SAN JACINTO

It will take a history buff to appreciate this **national monument** (admission US$0.50; 8am-4pm Tue-Sun), a shadeless 3km walk from the closest bus stop. It commemorates the Battle of San Jacinto, when William Walker's filibusters and León Liberals were met by stiff resistance from the southern Conservatives. At one point Andrés Castro, a 23-year-old Granadino with an arm cannon, ran out of ammunition and began throwing rocks instead, killing a filibusterer. Walker lost the battle, and ultimately the war. This recently renovated early-1800s Spanish hacienda has a couple of murals and a few busts depicting the event.

It's about 25km south of Ciudad Darío. Managua-bound *ordinario* buses can drop you off at the spur, which leads to the hacienda.

Getting There & Away

Buses leave Matagalpa for La Dalia (US$1.25, 1½ hours) almost hourly from 6am to 6pm. To get to Peñas Blancas, take any bus leaving Matagalpa for El Cuá and get off at 'Empalme la Manzana' – the Peñas Blancas turnoff (US$2.25, three hours). There are also two buses a day from Jinotega to Peñas Blancas. The village is 600m off the main road.

South to Managua

The smooth, paved road from Matagalpa to Managua slithers down the shoulders of stunning peaks into prairies framed by distant volcanoes. It also passes an excellent museum, among other intriguing diversions.

Chagüitillo

You may miss the right turn into tiny Chagüitillo, just 20km south of Matagalpa and 4km north of Sébaco. There's no Spanish grid or parque central, just a single brick road where all pueblo life blooms. The main reason to visit is to check out the pre-Columbian museum and petroglyphs around town.

Sights

Museo Precolombino de Chagüitillo MUSEUM
(☎8837-7535; Puente, 1c N, 2c O, 1c S; admission US$1; 8am-5pm Mon-Fri, 8am-noon Sat) This worthwhile museum has lots of Chorotegan pottery, and an exhibit on local hero Domingo Sánchez Salgado, aka 'Chagüitillo,' one of the leaders of the early resistance against the Somozas. Museum staff arrange guides (US$4) to visit the petroglyph sites.

★Santuario Salto El Mico ARCHAEOLOGICAL SITE
Dońt miss this incredible petroglyph site, 1.5km outside town, with a swirl of moons, snakes and dancers 3m long and 2m high carved into rocks alongside a river.

Santuario de los Venados ARCHAEOLOGICAL SITE
This archaeological site in town features more than 60 zoomorphic petroglyphs including many depicting deer.

Ciudad Darío

POP 20,200 / ELEV 433M

About 5km down a paved turnoff from the highway, and tucked back into the chaparral-speckled Cordillera Dariense is cute, hilly Ciudad Darío. Follow the spur all the way and you'll wind up at the leafy parque central.

Buses leave for Managua and Matagalpa every half-hour so there's no reason to spend the night.

Sights

Casa Natal Rubén Darío MUSEUM
(2776-3846; admission US$4; 8am 4:30pm Tue-Fri, 9am-4pm Sat & Sun) Two blocks east of the parque central you'll find the town's primary roadside attraction, where Rubén Darío was born. Although the baby poet didn't spend more than a few weeks in this sweet 19th-century adobe (this was his aunt's house), the museum is quite cool, with a mid-1880s kitchen, a Rubén Darío timeline, and a wonderful amphitheater on the grounds where the museum hosts the rare poetry reading or theater production.

Caribbean Coast

Includes ➡

Best Beaches

- Long Bay (p232)
- Wild Cane Key (p230)
- Monkey Point (p227)
- Otto Beach (p237)
- Maroon Key (p231)

Best Places to Eat

- Cevicheria El Chino (p224)
- Habana Libre (p238)
- Casa Ulrich (p228)
- Queen Lobster (p228)
- Restaurante Faramhi (p210)

Why Go?

An overland ramble to Nicaragua's Caribbean coast would be the perfect terrain for an epic novel. Your settings would include wide, muddy rivers surrounded by thick jungle, a fascinating tropical port town and an expanse of mangrove-shrouded black water home to more than a dozen ethnic fishing enclaves. And we haven't even got to the pristine offshore islands ringed by white sand with a turquoise trim.

Your cast will feature tough and insightful characters from English-speaking Creole towns and indigenous Miskito, Mayangna, Rama and Garifuna communities. And there will be plenty of action too, with scuba diving, epic treks through dense rainforest, beachcombing, and fishing in the mangroves.

But even the most skilled author would struggle to capture the essence of the region, a vibrant mix of indigenous, African and European cultures that you'll only really get a feel for if you check it out for yourself.

When to Go

From February to April visitors are greeted by clear skies and perfect beach weather, although you may be sharing your patch of paradise and accommodation prices tend to increase.

The region's strong winds drop off significantly from March to April, bringing the best conditions for diving around the Corn Islands and snorkeling in the Pearl Keys.

While technically in the middle of the wet season, during September and October the heavy rains ease off, prices are low and beaches are empty.

For a high-energy full-color carnival experience, head to Maypole in Bluefields in May for a full month of partying, culminating in the colorful Carnival and Tulululu.

History

Christopher Columbus landed on Nicaragua's Caribbean coast in 1502, during his fourth voyage, but with the Spanish focused on settling the Pacific coast, their hold on the Caribbean was tenuous. Portuguese, Dutch and British pirates patrolled these seas (Bluefields was named for the Dutch pirate Blewfeldt), attacking and robbing Spanish vessels full of South American gold. Meanwhile, the British crown cultivated relations with the indigenous Miskito people, who had battled Mayangna and Rama communities for regional supremacy long before Columbus came calling. In 1687 they created the puppet kingdom of Mosquitia, which ruled until the mid-19th century.

During this period British colonists moved with their African slaves from Jamaica to the Corn Islands, which until then had belonged to the Kukra and Sumu people. They also arrived in Bluefields, where slaves worked banana groves and mingled with free West Indian laborers of mixed ethnicity to form English-speaking Creole communities that are still thriving.

English-speaking Nicaraguans have never fully bought into Spanish-speaking rule. During the Contra war, many took up arms against the Frente Sandinista de Liberación Nacional (Sandinista National Liberation Front; FSLN) while many more fled to neighboring Costa Rica to avoid the conflict, emptying villages that have still not recovered. Although the region was eventually granted special autonomy status by the Sandinistas with the rights to have a say in the exploitation of its natural resources, it remains the poorest and least developed part of the country.

Dangers & Annoyances

Nicaragua's Atlantic coast is as poor and underserved as Nicaragua gets. Expect dodgy infrastructure, bring a flashlight (torch) and enjoy those occasional bucket showers.

Local agents for Colombian coke impresarios have often done more to develop area infrastructure than the sitting government, but the cocaine traffic in Región Autónoma Atlántico Norte (North Atlantic Autonomous Region; RAAN) and Región Autónoma Atlántico Sur (South Atlantic Autonomous Region; RAAS) isn't bloodless. However, tourists won't have any problems as long as they refrain from purchasing and partaking.

But, given the poverty, even in seemingly innocuous small towns sober travelers should stick to big-city rules: stay alert, don't wander alone, take taxis at night and watch your valuables.

Getting There & Away

You can travel overland from Managua to the Caribbean coast, but most visitors take the frequent, inexpensive La Costeña flights. There are active commercial airstrips in Bilwi, Waspám, Bluefields, Great Corn Island and two of the three Las Minas towns. Still, if you have more time than cash and enjoy the (really) slow lane, there are two overland routes into the region.

There are irregular passenger-boat services between Bluefields and Bilwi via Corn Island, but don't count on it if your schedule is tight.

BILWI (PUERTO CABEZAS)–WASPÁM & RÍO COCO

We won't sugarcoat this. You're in for a grueling ride on a beat-up old school bus packed to the gills. It begins with a 10- to 12-hour bus ride from Managua to Siuna in Las Minas, where you can access the Reserva de Biosfera Bosawás (Bosawás Biosphere Reserve). From Siuna it's another 10 to 12 hours on a horrendous road to Bilwi. Waspám and the Río Coco are a smoothish six hours north from there.

JUIGALPA–EL RAMA–BLUEFIELDS–CORN ISLANDS

The (much!) preferred trip to the crystalline Caribbean Sea unfurls on the smooth, paved road to El Rama, with rejuvenating side trips to the mountain towns of Boaco and Juigalpa. From El Rama, you can hop on a testing five-hour bus along the rutted dirt road to Pearl Lagoon or take a convenient two-hour fast boat ride down the Río Escondido to Bluefields, from where there are twice-weekly boat services to the Corn Islands and daily speedboats to Pearl Lagoon.

Getting Around

Most local travel within the region is by *panga* – an open speedboat with outboard motor. Tickets are much more expensive than a comparable distance by bus.

BILWI (PUERTO CABEZAS)

POP 48,500

This impoverished Caribbean port town and ethnic melting pot sprawls along the coast and back into the scrubby pines on wide brick streets and red-earth roads, full of people and music, smiles and sideways glances. Old wooden churches, antique craftsman homes and ramshackle slums are knitted together with rusted sheet-metal fencing, coconut palms and mango trees. In a single stroll you'll eavesdrop on loud, jagged Miskito banter, rapid-fire español and lovely,

Caribbean Coast Highlights

1 Dive with hammerheads and explore the underwater caves off **Little Corn Island** (p237)

2 Experience true Caribbean food and culture in laid-back **Pearl Lagoon** (p226)

3 Charter a speedboat to the luscious, snow-white **Pearl Keys** (p230) and snorkel with magnificent sea turtles

4 Groove to classic reggae in a lobster warehouse by the water on **Great Corn Island** (p236)

5 Sip spiced rum, eat fresh fish and dance to Garifuna drummers in **Orinoco** (p230) during National Garifuna Week

6 Dance through the streets then party all night during Maypole in **Bluefields** (p224)

7 Feel like a rock star as you are greeted by scores of barefoot children in tiny Miskito villages around **Waspám** (p215)

8 Hire an indigenous guide in **Kakabila** (p229) and trek deep into the dense jungle

Bilwi (Puerto Cabezas)

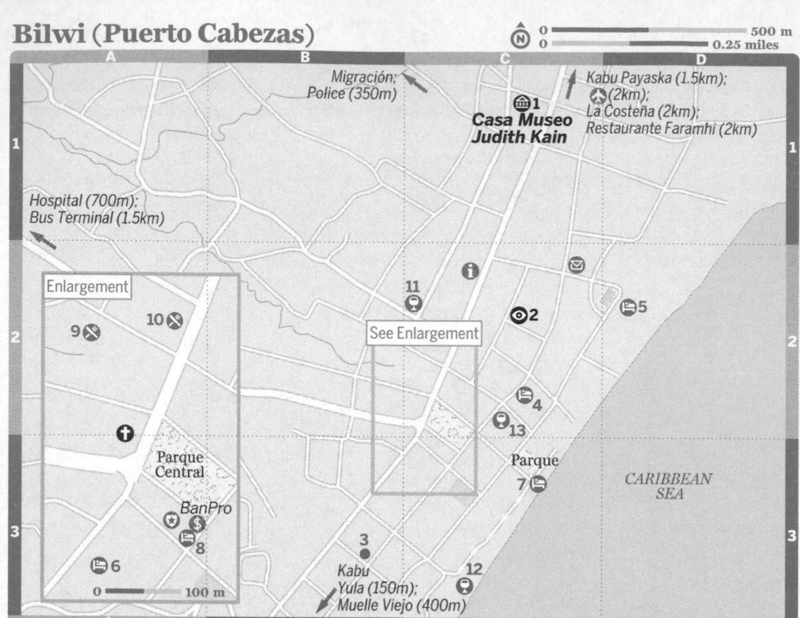

lilting Caribbean English. Sure, this city has systemic problems (poverty, decay, crime), and it's never good when international aid is a town's biggest source of income. But with tasty seafood, great-value historic lodging options, and seaside indigenous communities a boat ride away, it can also be as alluring as a sweet, yet slightly sketchy, new friend.

History

Founded in 1690 by three English pirates who called it Bragman's Bluff, the port was always referred to by indigenous Miskito and Mayangna people as Bilwi (Mayangna for 'Snake Leaf'). Then, in 1894, General Rigoberto Cabezas invaded and flew the Nicaraguan flag over an area ruled by an English-indigenous alliance for two centuries. In 1925 the Nicaraguan government honored Cabezas by naming the port after him. Spanish-speaking locals still refer to the capital of Nicaragua's enormous RAAN as Puerto Cabezas, or just Puerto.

Yet even after the English were forced out, English-speaking companies like the banana giant Standard Fruit, which built the dock, helped keep federal interference in the region minimal as it siphoned fruit, fish and timber from the Caribbean coast. It wasn't all bad for the locals. Old-timers still reminisce about the good old days of high-paying jobs and a thriving middle class. Which is why it was such a tragedy when Standard Fruit pulled out just before its dock was used in the 1960s to launch Kennedy's Bay of Pigs invasion of Cuba.

There are still plenty of international pirates and profiteers. They hail from Colombia and trade in a certain ego-boosting powdery substance, some of which is off-loaded here and heads north to Mexico and the US.

Mother Nature has roughed up Bilwi too. Her most recent assault came in the form of Hurricane Felix in 2007. In fact, hurricane-relief efforts sparked the current wave of NGO involvement, and aid workers and missionaries still far outnumber tourists here.

Sights

Beaches around Bilwi are nobody's idea of the Caribbean dream. **La Bocana**, an old pirate hangout at the river mouth north of town, has a stretch of decent beach, but crooks still dig it here. Come with a local.

★**Casa Museo Judith Kain** MUSEUM
(2792-2225; Parque Central, 4c N, 1c O; 8am-3pm Mon-Fri) FREE Set in the former home of a prolific local painter, this museum provides a window into what it was like to live in Bilwi

Bilwi (Puerto Cabezas)

Top Sights
1 Casa Museo Judith Kain C1

Sights
2 Mercado Municipal C2

Activities, Courses & Tours
3 Amica B3

Sleeping
Casa Museo Judith Kain ..... (see 1)
4 El Cortijo C2
5 El Cortijo II D2
6 Hospedaje Rivera A3
7 Hotel Liwa Mairin C3
8 Hotel Monter A3

Eating
9 Bar y Restaurante Crisfa A2
10 Comedor Alka A2
Wachi's Pizza ..... (see 7)

Drinking & Nightlife
11 Bar Titi C2
12 Bar-Restaurant El Malecón C3
13 Karibbean Sol C2

in the good old days. There are B&W photos, old dugout canoes, terrific local handicrafts and an antique collection (the sewing machines are especially cool); dozens of Kain's paintings are also on display. It's attached to one of the best hotels in town.

Muelle Viejo PORT
Take a stroll along the wooden boards of the historic Muelle Viejo (Old Pier), where both Sandino and the Contras received arms smuggled in from abroad, the former with the assistance of the town's prostitutes. But the 420m-long pier's biggest moment in the spotlight was in 1961, when Somoza lent the facility to US-funded Cuban exiles to launch the failed Bay of Pigs invasion.

There is a security gate halfway down the pier, but if you ask permission it's possible to walk all the way to the end. As you walk back, check out the *panga* graveyard in front of the military base on your right where large fiberglass skiffs seized from narcotics traffickers lie half-buried in the sand – a testament to the not-so-legal shipping lanes that pass in front of the town.

Seventh-Day Adventist Church CHURCH
The most beautiful church in town, it was getting its lovely whitewashed wooden boards replaced by concrete at the time of writing, but it's still worth a look. Come for Saturday-morning services and listen to the Creole gospel choir.

Mercado Municipal MARKET
(7am-3pm) This ramshackle collection of stalls selling ripe produce, traditional fried-fish breakfasts and sweet, savory *rundown* (seasoned fish or meat cooked in coconut milk with root vegetables) is a popular place to pass the morning.

Activities

Amica CULTURAL TOUR
(Association of Indigenous Women on the Atlantic Coast; 2792-2219; asociacionamica@yahoo; Parque Central, 3c S; 8am-noon Mon & 2-5:30pm Mon-Fri, 8am-noon Sat) Your ticket into the area's natural reserves and indigenous communities is through Amica. In addition to working to stop domestic violence and promote family planning and indigenous rights, it can arrange forest treks, canoe tours and fishing trips in the mangroves. It also offers overnight visits to the Miskito Keys (US$500, eight visitors) and guides (US$6.30) for the turtle-nesting sites in Tuapí 8km north of town.

Festivals & Events

Dance of King Pulanka CULTURAL, DANCE
(Jan 6–mid-Feb) First performed in the late 1800s, the dance of El Rey and La Reina is still performed throughout the Mosquitia. Two groups of dancers wearing 18th-century costumes represent the king's allies and enemies, and stage a mock battle using arrows, machetes and *triki trakas* (firearms). The good guys win and there's traditional food and drink to keep the party going. Many local communities host their own events before the grand finale in Bilwi.

Día de la Autonomía CULTURAL
(Oct 30) Celebrates the day the RAAN was finally rid of those Spaniards in Managua! Well, sort of.

Sleeping

Lodging is high in comfort, charm and value. But even with a dearth of tourism it helps to reserve ahead as the NGO brigade often snaps up the best rooms.

OFF THE BEATEN TRACK

ALAMIKANGBAN & PRINZAPOLKA

The isolated towns of Alamikangban, about 70km southeast of Rosita, and Prinzapolka, another two hours by boat along the Río Prinzapolka to the Caribbean coast, don't get many visitors. They both have a couple of *hospedajes* (guesthouses) and simple *comedores* (basic eateries), but the real reason to go is the river. It marks the southern boundary of natural pine forest that phases into tropical rainforest, with wetlands that are a haven for all sorts of birds. The fishing is also top-notch.

Buses leave Rosita (US$4, four hours) twice daily for Alamikangban, where you can hire a private boat to Prinzapolka. Both towns, as well as the smaller communities lining the river, have indigenous government structures, so ask for the *wihta* (judge) or *síndico* (resource manager) when trying to find guides or lodging.

Casa Museo Judith Kain HOTEL **$**
(2792-2225; casamuseojudithkain@hotmail.com; Parque Central, 4c N, 1c O; s/d/tr with fan US$12/15/20, with air-con US$23/27/30;) In a town with an abundance of great-value lodging, this may be the best of the bunch. Rooms set in two superb old craftsman gems are superclean and charming with high, beamed ceilings, hot water, porches and balconies sprinkled with wooden rockers overlooking gardens full of birds. No wonder it's always booked up.

Hospedaje Rivera GUESTHOUSE **$**
(2792-2471; Parque Central, 1½c S; r US$11) The clean rooms on the 2nd story of this fine, centrally located family home are a terrific budget choice. They come with cable TV and views of nearby swaying palms and rusted tin roofs.

Hotel Liwa Mairin HOTEL **$**
(2792-2315; Parque Central, 2c E, 1c S; s/d US$15/20, with air-con US$25/30;) This centrally located hotel right by the Caribbean Sea offers large air-con rooms with firm mattresses and high ceilings. Just watch out for the leak-prone electric-shock showers.

El Cortijo II GUESTHOUSE **$$**
(2792-2340; cortijoarguello@yahoo.com; Parque Central, 3c N, 1c E; s/d/tr US$22/26.50/29) This 60-year-old craftsman gem is your Caribbean grandma's house. Rooms are spotless with worn wooden floors and high ceilings. The common living room is filled with gorgeous antiques – including old handblown glass buoys – and if you reserve ahead, you may be able to snag a room with a private sea view, steps from a creaky wooden walk that leads to the rolling sea. Nice!

El Cortijo GUESTHOUSE **$$**
(2792-2340; cortijoarguello@yahoo.com; Parque Central, 1½c N; s/d/tr downstairs US$20/24/26.50, upstairs US$22/26.50/29;) This beautiful wooden home is so nice the Sandinistas once used it as their east-coast base. Grab one of the more attractively furnished rooms upstairs in the original house; they have the wooden fixtures and high ceilings. Downstairs rooms are less charming, but cheaper. Fabulous breakfasts (US$3) with terrific coffee are served on the wide deck overlooking a rambling garden.

Hotel Monter HOTEL **$$**
(2792-2669; hotelmonter@gmail.com; Parque Central, 1c S; s/d/tw incl breakfast US$29/35/46) The newest and shiniest hotel in town is adjacent to the *supermercado* of the same name. You'll find two stories of superclean rooms with firm beds and all the amenities, although there are few external windows and it lacks the charm of many of the other lodgings.

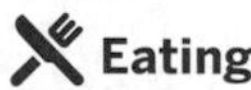

Eating

Most local lobster is exported, but when it's in season you'll find it at around US$7.50 a plate – often the same price as chicken or fish! If you're pinching pennies, head to the market, where you'll find some stalls selling tasty fried fish.

Comedor Alka NICARAGUAN **$**
(frente Parque Central; meals US$2.75-3; 11am-9pm) Stop here for savory and cheap eats where barbecued beef and chicken are served with a bit of attitude.

Restaurante Faramhi SEAFOOD **$$**
(2792-1611; frente Aeropuerto; mains US$7.50; 11am-10pm) Close to the airport, this popular restaurant serves some of the best seafood in town including an awesome mixed-seafood soup, a local specialty. The dining

area is a little crowded, but the food is most definitely worth it.

Kabu Payaska SEAFOOD **$$**
(Parque Central, 1.5km N; seafood dishes US$7.50-8.50; ⏲noon-10pm) Bilwi's best-loved seafood house is set on one large concrete patio overlooking the swirling Caribbean. Order fish, shrimp or (occasionally) lobster, sauced, steamed and fried. You will leave satisfied. This neighborhood is considered unsafe, so take a taxi (US$.70) at night.

Wachi's Pizza PIZZA **$$**
(Parque Central, 2c E; pizzas from US$4-12; ⏲noon-9pm) Being the only real pizzeria within a 200km radius, this place would run a brisk trade even if it wasn't up to scratch – fortunately it is with crispy crusts and tasty toppings served on a pleasant porch overlooking the Caribbean.

Bar y Restaurante Crisfa NICARAGUAN **$$**
(☎2792-2318; Parque Central, 1c N, 1c O; mains US$5-8; ⏲noon-10pm) It has all the typical shrimp, beef and chicken dishes you've come to expect, plus a fish in garlic sauce that tastes like it came from your favorite Chinese kitchen.

Drinking

Drinking is a popular pastime in Port and it often begins early in the morning. You should get an early start too, as things sometimes get a little rough later on.

Bar Titi BAR
(⏲noon-late) Sounds like a strip club but it's actually one of Port's most chilled bars with two large open-air huts and a mixed crowd striking up plenty of conversation without a nipple in sight. Music ranges from reggae to *ranchero* depending on who's controlling the jukebox.

Kabu Yula BAR
(Parque Central, 5c S; ⏲2pm-2am) A two-story *palapa* (thatched, palm-leaf-roofed shelter with open sides) with unbroken sea views. Perfect for an afternoon tipple.

Bar-Restaurant El Malecón CLUB
(Parque Central, 2c E, 1c S; ⏲6pm-2am Thu-Sat) This large air-con disco space by the water plays mix of dancehall, reggae and Latin pop to keep the young crowd moving.

Karibbean Sol CLUB
(⏲8pm-3am) Sooner or later anyone out on a big night ends up here at this rustic dancehall half a block from Parque Central. It's a little sketchy but has plenty of atmosphere.

Information

There are numerous internet cafes around Parque Central charging around US$0.50 per hour.

BanPro Changes dollars and has a Visa/MasterCard ATM.

Correos de Nicaragua (Post Office; adentro Alcaldía; ⏲8am-1pm Mon-Fri)

Hospital (☎2792-2259/43)

Migración (Immigration Office; contiguo a la Policia; ⏲8am-2pm Mon-Fri) Visa extensions and entry/exit stamps for the Honduran border.

Intur (puertocabezas@intur.gob.ni; Parque Central, 2c N; ⏲8am-2pm) Dedicated staff know the area in detail and facilitate trips to local communities.

Police (☎2792-2256)

Getting There & Away

AIR

Although you can hop on a super-long-distance (and rather painful) bus from Managua or (occasionally) catch a boat from Corn Island, most people come by plane. **La Costeña** (Aeropuerto; ⏲8am-noon & 3-6pm) offers regular flights to Managua and Bluefields. Book tickets in advance. Departure tax is US$2. Flights include the following:

Bluefields (one way/return US$96/148, 50 minutes, 11:20am Monday, Wednesday and Friday)

Managua (one way/return US$97/149, 1½ hours, 7:40am, noon and 3:40pm Monday to Saturday, 7:40am and noon Sunday)

BUS

Buses depart from the bus terminal, 2km west of town, to the following destinations:

Managua (US$25.20, 20 to 24 hours, 10am and 1pm)

Rosita (US$7.50, six to to 10 hours, 6am and 7pm)

Siuna (US$10, eight to 12 hours, 7am)

Waspám (US$6, six hours, 5:30am and 7pm)

BOAT

The only regular boat service to/from Bilwi is the **Captain D** (☎8850-2767), which runs between Corn Island and Bilwi (US$22, 10 to 12 hours) about once a month depending on demand. Call to check the schedule.

THE MOSQUITIA

Some legends say that the Miskito nation originated in the Miskito Keys, then took control of the Miskito Coast of Nicaragua and Honduras, more properly known as the Mosquitia. The keys first appeared on a European map in 1630, labeled the Musquitu Islands, '14 leagues from Cabo de Gracias,' where the Miskitos first made contact with pirate captain Sussex Camock in 1633.

The Miskitos quickly grasped the potential of firearms and, in return for the new technology, aided in the sacking of Spanish strongholds up and down the Río San Juan and Río Coco. In 1687 the English monarchy was pleased enough to help found the Miskito monarchy, and by the mid-1800s most of the Caribbean territory between central Honduras and Limón, Costa Rica, was under Miskito and British control. When the crown hosted King Jeremy in England, his tutors were surprised that he looked more African than Indian.

Miskito culture has historically embraced outsiders, and not always figuratively. Most trace their African roots to a Portuguese slave ship that wrecked on the keys in 1640, though waves of escaped slaves and West Indian banana workers are almost certainly part of the mix.

The Miskitos did not submit willingly to Nicaraguan rule in 1894, and their discontent at domination by the 'Spaniards' in Managua was brought to a head by one of the most horrific chapters of Sandinista rule. President Somoza had been somewhat popular in the region mainly because he left the Miskito to get along with their business. However, being off the radar meant the region was also seriously neglected and did not share in the profits from the exploitation of Nicaragua's natural resources.

Thus the Miskitos' loyalty was split, and when the revolution triumphed, some joined the Frente Sandinista de Liberación Nacional (Sandinista National Liberation Front; FSLN)–backed group Misurasata (MIskito, SUmo, RAma, SAndinista & AslaTAlanka), hoping to help with the literacy campaign. Volunteers were soon informed, however, that the Sandinista-led government had decreed Spanish the official language, which few people spoke, much less read. The FSLN then declared the Mosquitia's natural resources to be public property, 'to be exploited efficiently and reasonably.' Tensions simmered.

At the same time, Somoza's Guardia Nacional regrouped in the Mosquitia. The Sandinistas got intelligence that they would be meeting in San Carlos on December 23, 1981, and sent 7000 troops to evacuate the people, burn the houses, kill the animals and destroy the wells. Every single town on the Río Coco was burned to the ground, and no one knows how many civilians died. It is remembered as Red Christmas.

Some 20,000 people became refugees, moving to Honduras, Bilwi, San José de Bocay and what's now known as Tasba Pri ('Free Land'), the impoverished string of roadside towns that stretches from Rosita to Bilwi.

The Sandinistas backpedaled and apologies were issued, but it was too late. In 1987 the National Autonomy Law granted the Región Autónoma Atlántico Norte (North Atlantic Autonomous Region; RAAN) and Región Autónoma Atlántico Sur (South Atlantic Autonomous Region; RAAS) official independence in response to local pressure. The major international gold mine in Las Minas is not part of the autonomous zone, however, even though it is in the center of the region. Anomalies such as this have led some locals to believe that the central government legislated provisions so it could continue to exploit the region's natural resources, and not be held responsible for providing much-needed infrastructure.

After the war, former Contras and Misurasata members formed Yapti Tasba Masraka Nanih Asla takanka (Yatama; 'Descendants of Mother Earth'), a political party that gets the vast majority of the indigenous vote in every election. With the return of the FSLN to power, Yatama leaders, many of whom are former Contras, have divided their supporters by aligning themselves with the Sandinistas. Whether this is another example of a cunning Miskito strategic alliance to exercise power in the region or a sellout for personal gain depends on which side of the divide you sit.

And even though there are now Miskito leaders sitting in parliament in Managua, this indigenous pueblo remains as feisty and independent as ever, evidenced by the not uncommon street protests and occupation of government offices and airports in the region.

Around Bilwi

Arrange trips and accommodations in these and other communities at the Amica office in Bilwi.

Haulover

The first Moravian missionaries arrived here, 30km south of Bilwi, in 1860, and named it in honor of the sandbar that boats had to cross to enter the lagoon. Protected by Reserva Natural Laguna Kukalaya and Reserva Natural Layasiksa, the town has comfortable *cabañas* (cabins; US$5 per person), seafood meals (US$3) and beautiful views.

There's a pristine, palm-dappled beach, and it's possible to organize performances of the King Pulanka dance. Collective *pangas* leave Lamlaya (5km south of Bilwi) around noon (US$9), and return at 5am daily. A private charter will set you back around US$150.

Wawa

Wawa is a scenic Miskito village 17km south of Bilwi, at the mouth of the Río Wawa. There's a beautiful lagoon packed with migratory birds and alligators, plus a sandy oceanfront beach. Hiking, fishing and canoeing options abound and you can spend the night in a simple homestay. Further upriver in **Karatá**, where you can rent pastel-tinted *cabañas* (US$4 per person). Transportation is by collective *panga* (Wawa/Karatá US$2.20/3.30), which leave from Lamlaya, 5km south of Bilwi.

Krukira

About 20km north of Bilwi, this is the gateway to the Reserva Natural Laguna Pahara, with lots of wildlife, including huge tarpon. Although homestay accommodations and meals can be arranged with local families, there are currently few services for visitors other than canoe tours (US$3 per hour). Buses leave Bilwi for Krukira daily at 1pm (US$1.50, one hour).

Miskito Keys

Sitting 50km offshore, the Miskito Keys are a group of rocky isles rimmed with stilted Miskito fishing villages. Their thatched over-water bungalows loom over crystalline turquoise coves that double as an ideal lobster habitat. The historic first meeting between the British pirate Captain Sussex Camock and his future Miskito allies took place here in 1633. It's still a haven for seafaring bad guys, so if you see any boats with Colombian plates, look the other way.

Unlike the Pearl Keys further south, this is a cultural rather than beach destination – very few of the islands have any sand at all. Most are pure rock with the odd bit of vegetation. But a visit to this isolated community sticking out of the ocean is an absolutely remarkable experience. It's possible to rent traditional wooden canoes from the fishers to explore the area.

There are no hotels or restaurants in the keys, and just one part-time guesthouse, at the Acopio Knight, affectionately known as 'Mirkiki' (Miskito for 'American') for the owner's gringolike appearance. Make reservations at Intur in Bilwi. You can also rent a hammock in a private home. Either way you should bring your own food, water and plenty of insect repellent.

Amica in Bilwi arranges overnight visits for US$500 for six visitors, a large chunk of which goes toward transportation costs. Transport in a large, fast *panga* for up to 12 will cost you around US$800 round trip; Intur is able to recommend responsible captains. Otherwise, you'll need to make arrangements with a lobster fisher: do-able, but your return could take days. It's two hours to the keys on a fast boat, up to five on a lobster vessel, and the ride is often rough.

Waspám & the Río Coco

POP 7800

Waspám feels different from the rest of RAAN. Yes, it's just as poor and has the same development issues and jagged-edge feel as Bilwi and Las Minas, but there's also a simple beauty: children at play, twittering flocks of parakeets in the trees, and dugout canoes plying the edges of Waspám's biggest attraction, the lazy, mocha Río Coco.

Known as Wangki in Miskito, the Río Coco, the longest river in Central America, links 116 Miskito communities that run from the rainforested interior to the Atlantic coastal marshlands. This makes Waspám, its epicenter, the cultural, geographic and economic heart of the Mosquitia. It also forms a natural border with Honduras, a fact most Miskitos prefer to ignore. You shouldn't. If you plan on crossing into Honduras, get your passport stamped at Bilwi Migración.

But even if you remain on the Nicaraguan side of things, you will probably spend plenty of time on the river. Upstream lies the Reserva de Biosfera Bosawás. Access isn't cheap and will require boat charters, but trips are easily organized and your memories will be well worth the investment.

Sights & Activities

The town is worth a wander. You'll see the oddly constructed **Iglesia San Rafael**, you can dangle your legs over the cinderblock outfield walls of the **baseball stadium** with the locals on weekends, and you can stroll **Parque Central**. Its **war monument** was erected for fallen Contras overrun by the Sandinistas, who then torched and occupied Waspám until the war was over.

Museo Auka Tangki MUSEUM
(☎8417-8128; brownmelgara@hotmail.com; Planta Electrica, 150m E; donations accepted; ⏲by appointment) Don't miss Dr Dionisio Melgara Brown's museum, a 10-minute walk along dirt roads curving away from the river. Brown, a retired teacher, built this museum

RESERVA DE BIOSFERA BOSAWÁS

Supported by three neighboring reserves in Honduras (Río Patuca National Park, Tawhaka Anthropological Reserve and Río Plátano Biosphere Reserve), Reserva de Biosfera Bosawás is the largest protected expanse of rainforest north of the Amazon, clocking in at 20,000 sq km, more than 14% of Nicaragua's national territory.

Named for three geographical features that delineate the reserve (the Río Bocay, Cerro Saslaya and Río Waspuk), enormous Bosawás is also home to more than 200,000 people, including 30,000 Mayangna and Miskito, who have some claim to this land. The reserve loses 120 to 175 hectares of forest per year to farms, and more to illegal lumber operations. A 12,000 sq-km, multi-use 'amortization area' aims to protect Bosawás by promoting sustainable economic development, such as collecting wild plants to sell, organic cacao and coffee *fincas* (farms), and, of course, tourism.

That's the trick. Access to the reserve's 8000 sq-km wild and undeveloped nucleus ranges from challenging to almost impossible, and is never cheap or risk-free. Come prepared: someone in your group (don't do this alone) should speak a fair amount of Spanish, and you should consider taking malaria pills for longer adventures. Water-purification technology is necessary for most of the reserve. But the real key to access is persistence – you can get in, just don't count on it happening on your timetable, and expect to be following leads like: 'find Jaguar José at the *pulpería* near the *empalme* of (something unpronounceable); he's got a truck that can get through.'

During the reserve's February to April dry season, rivers (read: the freeway system) may be too low to travel, unless you help carry the canoe around the rapids.

Luckily, it's usually raining, and some spots (for instance, the Río Waspuk region) get 3200mm of rain per year – regular roads may be impassable most of the year. Temperatures average a sweaty 26.5°C (80°F), but bring a fleece for Cerro Kilambé (1750m).

You can begin inquiries at the Bosawás office at **Marena Central** (Ministry of the Environment & Natural Resources; ☎2263-2830; www.marena.gob.ni; Carretera Norte, Km 12.5, Managua; ⏲8am-2pm) in Managua, or any of the satellite offices located in most large towns bordering the reserve, where they can arrange guides and transportation, or at least point you in the right direction. It's often easiest to access the reserve through lodges or private organizations, however, so ask around. Following are some points of entry (see the boxed text of p217 for more more):

- Peñas Blancas – take guided trips to waterfalls and the stunning cliff-top mesa.
- Siuna – park rangers guide you to campsites in Parque Nacional Saslaya.
- Waspám & the Río Coco – take a riverboat ride into the waterfall-strewn wilderness, spending the night in a jungle paradise.
- Musuwas – head from Bonanza into the heart of the Mayangna nation.
- Reserva Natural Cerro Cola Blanca – these waterfall-strewn highlands were named for the white-tailed deer teeming on its forested slopes. The Bonanza Intur office can get you there.

on the ground floor of his home with his own savings in order to preserve Miskito language, history and tradition.

Inside you'll peruse photos and artifacts including hammocks and a fishing net hand-woven from natural materials, cow-skin drums, shakers made from horse clavicles, wooden bowls, turtle shells, and huge mortar-and-pestle sets used for making *wabul*, a traditional Miskito power shake consisting of plantains mashed with coconut or cow's milk. Brown also sells the world's only Miskito-Spanish and Miskito-English dictionaries (US$25), which he wrote and published himself.

Sleeping & Eating

Although authentic Miskito cuisine is hard to find, keep an eye out for delicacies like *wabul*, *pihtu talla laya* (fermented pineapple-rind drink), *twalbí* (corn liquor), *takrú* (fish and yucca baked together in banana leaves) and *auhbi piakan* (Miskito for 'mixed together'), which involves plantains, meat and coconut.

Hotel Coco GUESTHOUSE $
(☎2792-9126, 8910-3435; Muelle, 100m O; r US$12.60, without bathroom US$6.30) Waspám's best budget choice, with simple varnished wooden rooms and flasher ones with cable TV and bathrooms. There's also a great rear porch overlooking the river.

Hotel Casa de la Rose HOTEL $
(☎2792-9112; frente la pista; s/d with fan US$10.50/14.50, with air-con US$17/21; ❄) Rooms are clean with fresh tiles, cable TV and a lovely wooden porch nestled in the banana palms. It has a terrific restaurant (meals US$2.50 to US$3.50), set in a sweet wooden *cabaña* patrolled by parrots.

★**Hotel El Piloto** HOTEL $$
(☎8331-1312, 8642-4405; hotelitoelpiloto@live.com; Muelle, 20m S; s/d US$25/35; ❄ 📶) Waspám's best all-round choice. Rooms have fresh paint and bathroom tiles, and a terrific location steps from the river. The friendly owners are a wealth of information and will happily arrange all manner of local excursions.

Comedor Milagros NICARAGUAN $
(Hospital, ½c S; meals incl drink US$3.50; ⏲7am-9pm) Sit at one of the five wooden tables on the neatly painted deck and enjoy well-prepared plates of chicken and beef while you observe the comings and goings on the main street in front. Gringos that smile may even get fries.

LOCAL KNOWLEDGE

GOLD FEVER

If you've arrived in Waspám and are wondering where all the people are, you've probably come during the gold rush. Every dry season, hordes of locals travel up the Río Coco to the rapids near Carizal to pan for gold, leaving the place feeling like a ghost town.

Information

Mosquitoes are the big drawback, particularly during rainy season (June to October). Wear long sleeves and pants at dusk, and be liberal with your repellent of choice.

There are no banks in Waspám, bring sufficient funds. If you run short, it's possible to receive transfers at **Western Union** (Muelle, 20m S; ⏲9am-5pm).

Hospital (☎8708-1647)

Marena (detras Mercado; ⏲8am-2pm) In the little green house behind the market. Staff can show you maps of the Bosawás, but they don't recommend guides or arrange boat charters.

Wangki Net (frente Pista; per hour US$1.20; ⏲8:15am-7pm Mon-Fri, 9am-6pm Sat) Waspám's only internet cafe offers surprisingly reliable access.

GETTING THERE & AWAY

La Costeña (Aeropuerto; ⏲9am-noon) planes only seat 12, so it's best to book in advance. Flights depart from Managua to Waspám (one way/return US$103/160, 90 minutes) at 11am and return at 12:40pm, though they are frequently late.

Buses leave for Bilwi (US$6, six hours) at 6am and 7am daily. Come early if you want a seat. There are also several direct buses a week to Managua (US$25, 25 hours), usually departing departing on Monday, Wednesday, Thursday and Saturday at around 8am.

Río Coco

Waspám's prime attractions are out of town and accessible by the Río Coco, which forms the northern boundary of the Bosawás. Access is pricey but easily organized. Expect to pay US$60 per day for boat hire plus fuel, which will make up most of the cost.

Transporte Castillo (☎8421-0826; Barrio Santa Ines; ⏲6am-8pm) has honest and experienced navigators who will take you wherever you want to go at the drop of a hat. You can also arrange trips through **Hotel El Piloto**

(☎8642-4405, 2792-9045), where owner Barry Watson speaks terrific English.

The classic trip (US$450 per boat) takes you 135km upriver to **Salto Yaho** (US$540, maximum 5 people), a spectacular waterfall on the Río Waspuk. After swimming in the falls, you'll spend the night in the small village downriver before returning home in the morning.

Or extend the trip two more days, continue upriver on day two and take a two-hour tour of a **Mayangna Pueblo** and the **Coco gold mines** on foot or horseback. Then shoot the **Los Raudales canyon** rapids in a canoe and sleep in a typical village *cabaña* overlooking large boulders, foaming water and narrow canyon walls. The extended four-day trips cost US$1000 and have a five-person maximum.

It's also possible to continue up the Waspuk and onto Bonanza where you jump on a flight or bus to Managua – but this requires travel in a long wooden boat rather than a *panga.*

Although most locals discourage trips downriver because of the inhospitable insect life, bird-watchers may consider a five-hour excursion eastward to **Cabo Viejo** (per person US$425, maximum 5 people), a haven for migratory birds, oysters and tarpon. There's also excellent tarpon-fishing in **Cabo Gracias a Dios** (per 5 people round trip US$2000), where the river mouth meanders into a lagoon dotted with colorful wooden homes. A two-day trip will cost around US$500. One problem: if there's no wind, you will feel like you're starring in a horror movie called *Attack of the Killer Sand Fleas.*

If you're short on time or money, consider a day trip to the local riverside Miskito communities of **Ulwas**, **Sowpuka**, **Bilwas Karma**, **Kisalia** or **Kum**, where the former Miskito royal family still resides. You can organize a private *panga* (US$40, two hours) at the main dock.

Managua–El Rama Road

If you plan on heading to and from the Costa Atlantica overland (and don't fancy the grueling 24-hour journey to Bilwi), then you will take the smooth paved roads from Managua to El Rama, a river-port town that is just a two-hour boat ride from Bluefields.

You can make the trip in six hours on a reasonably comfortable bus, but then you'll miss the rugged Serranía Amerrisque. In and around these muscular granite peaks are a number of cute ranching pueblos, and one worthwhile city (that would be Juigalpa), linked by twisting, rutted back roads that also connect to Matagalpa and the northern highlands. So, embrace that whole 'journey is the destination' cliché, take the slow road and enjoy a welcome blast of earthy Nicaraguan culture before or after diving into the Caribbean.

Boaco

POP 21,500 / ELEV 1020M

'The City with Two Floors' was once two separate ranching communities separated by a steep 400m slope. They've grown together from the hill and valley, and now this *ranchero* market town, a couple of hours' drive from Managua with easy access to Matagalpa, Juigalpa and El Rama, makes a decent overnight respite.

Sights & Activities

You can duck into two interesting churches. **Parroquia de Nuestra Señora del Perpetuo Socorro** (salida, 1c N, 2c E), downstairs, has fading onion domes that hint at a Russian heritage. But it's Catholic and always has been. The pale yellow and coral trimmed adobe-esque **La Parroquia de Santiago Apóstol**, on the upper floor, makes a nice picture with the Parque Central in the foreground. But the best views in town can be glimpsed from **Parque El Cerrito del Faro** (Parque Central, 2c N, 1½c O).

Aguas Claras THERMAL BATHS
(☎2244-2916; admission US$1.25; ⏲Tue-Sun) On Hwy 9, 15 minutes west of town, you'll find this ageing midlevel hot-springs resort. Water is mineral rich, if not steaming, and funneled into concrete pools. Rooms (US$29 per person) are nice enough. Midweek it's mostly deserted and feels like a good place to hide out after a bank heist, but according to management it gets a huge local crowd on weekends. Taxis charge US$4 from Boaco.

Sleeping & Eating

Hotel Sobalvarro HOTEL $
(☎2542-2515; frente Parque Central; r US$16.80, without bathroom US$8.40; ❄) You'll sacrifice some comfort and space here, but the budget rooms off the creaky deck come with patio access and absolutely spectacular mountain and valley views. The shared bathrooms are downstairs, next to the more expensive

rooms with newly tiled floors and private bathrooms.

Hotel Alma HOTEL **$**
(☎2542-2620; entre los dos pisos; r with/without air-con US$14.50/10.50, without bathroom US$9.50; P ❄) This place is superclean, and a few extra dollars buys a TV and/or air-con, but it's the cheaper, older rooms that are blessed with magnificent views.

★**Hotel Farolitos** HOTEL **$**
(☎2542-1938; Abajo, salida, 4c E; s/d US$14/20, with air-con US$19/25; ❄) Large, clean rooms with Spanish tiles, mosaic baths, cable TV and wi-fi. It's great value considering the amenities, and the upstairs terrace is a cozy spot to hang and peer down over the bustling main road.

Restaurante Maraita NICARAGUAN **$**
(Parque Central, 1c N, 1c E; meals US$4-6; ⏲8am-midnight) An inviting atmosphere, attentive service, a satisfactory jukebox and more cuts of steak than you knew existed.

Information

Banpro (Iglesia Santiago, 1c N) Visa/MasterCard ATM.

Cyber Space (frente Casa Pellas; per hour US$0.40; ⏲8am-9pm) The town's swiftest connection; international calls are available as well.

Hospital (☎2542-2542) This new hospital is one of the most modern in Nicaragua.

OFF THE BEATEN TRACK

LAS MINAS (THE MINING TRIANGLE)

During their heyday early last century, the towns of Las Minas bustled with immigrants from China, Europe, North America and the Caribbean looking to strike the mother lode. These days very few outsiders visit this wild and remote part of the country and its main towns, **Siuna**, **Rosita** and **Bonanza**, are most notable for their shocking infrastructure and abundance of armed, inebriated men.

While gold panning is still popular among villagers, the gold rush is well and truly over and the only real money being made here is in Bonanza, where a large foreign-owned mine continues to operate despite criticism from environmentalists. But Las Minas still has one jewel more valuable than any that has been dug out of these red soils, a place so remote and untouched that only the most dedicated tourist ever sets foot in it: the Reserva de Biosfera Bosawás.

The easiest access to the reserve is from Siuna via the **Parque Nacional Saslaya**. Head to the ranger station, 3.5km from the community of Rosa Grande, where you'll register and contract a guide for the trek to **Piedra Colorada**. You'll overnight by a pine-shaded lagoon and in the morning begin the three-day climb to **Cerro El Toro** (1652m), the park's highest point, or an overnight trip up **El Revenido**. A rolling trail circumnavigates both peaks, and can be done in one day. **Hormiguero** is another national-park gateway. From the ranger station at the trailhead it's a five-hour hike to **Camp Salto Labú**, with a stunning swimming hole that has a cave, canyons and petroglyphs. From here you can also begin a four-day trek to the top of **Cerro Saslaya** (1651m). Bring a sleeping bag, tent and water purification for both treks.

Siuna has a number of other worthwhile attractions. Locals love the nearby, crystalline **aguas calientes** (hot springs). Take a taxi to *la bomba*, then follow the trail for about an hour across private Finca Dorado to the springs. Also popular are the rocky beaches of the lazy **Río Wani**, a slow-motion, sinuous beast carving rocky sand bars and encroaching jungle with lazy grace about 11km from town.

Bonanza is the jumping-off point for **Reserva Natural Cerro Cola Blanca** and the Mayangna indigenous communities downriver on the **Río Waspuk** and **Río Pispis**. There are also a couple of great swimming holes and waterfalls around town.

If you plan to visit the mines, **Intur** (☎8655-6658, 8665-9534; adentro Alcaldia; ⏲8am-2pm) in Bonanza is able to recommend guides for hikes and activities throughout the region. La Costeña flies daily from Managua to Siuna and Bonanza at 9am. It's a long, hard slog in a bus from Managua to Siuna (10 to 12 hours) and an even more challenging journey to Bonanza (14 to 17 hours).

Getting There & Away

Boaco is 12km from the Empalme de Boaco, on the main Managua–El Rama Hwy. Local buses leave from the market. Managua-bound buses leave from the station, another 200m uphill. Matagalpa-bound folks need to take the bus to Muy Muy, from where there are frequent departures for Matagalpa. Bus services include the following:

Managua (*ordinario* US$1.50, three hours, 3:45am to 5:25pm, half-hourly; minivan US$1.90, two hours, every 1½ hours or so) Bus departs when full.

Muy Muy (US$1.25, one hour, 5am–5:30pm, every three hours)

Río Blanco (US$2.20, 2½ hours, 7am and 1pm)

San José de los Remates (US$1.25, 1½ hours, 2:30pm) Returns at 8:30am.

Santa Lucia (US$0.80, one hour, noon and 3pm)

Santa Lucia

POP 3000

Just 12km north of Boaco off a 4WD-only road, the picturesque, crumbling Spanish-colonial town of Santa Lucia is nestled in the heart of a 1000-year-old volcanic crater surrounded by rainforested peaks that are part of **Reserva Natural Cerro Cumaica-Cerro Alegre**.

From town it's a difficult 4km hike to **Cueva Santo Domingo**, an old Sandinista stronghold with many petroglyphs left by the previous indigenous residents. There are more petroglyphs at **Piedra de Sapo**, at the top of the volcanic rim, from where you can see Masaya, Managua and the lakes on a clear day.

Back Road to Matagalpa

If you're heading north from Boaco and not in any hurry, consider taking the scenic backcountry route to Matagalpa through peaceful pastoral lands at the foot of rugged and rarely visited mountains.

The first stop is the quiet farming town of **San José de Remates**, an hour north of the turnoff at Teustepe on the Boaco–Managua road. San José has relatively easy access to Reserva Natural Cerro Cumaica-Cerro Alegre, and it flaunts it through a municipal tourism program launched to help preserve its own clean water supply.

Several years ago, a Boaco-based cattle-ranching operation had polluted the watershed to the point that municipal ground water was threatened. The townspeople mobilized, convinced the rancher to grow sustainable organic coffee instead, and reforested much of the property themselves. The land is now protected as a municipal park, **Reserva Hídrica Municipal La Chorrera**, adjacent to the national reserve. Local tourism helps foot the bill.

Within the reserve, the four-hour Ruta de los Chorros trail takes you past three 50m waterfalls (one of which you can see from town) to a *mirador* (lookout point) with views clear to the Pacific Ocean.

From San José de los Remates the road continues north past a string of rural communities with strong Chorotega roots to scenic **Esquipulas**, where you can hike through the cloud forest to Cerro Santa Maria, which offers terrific views of Boaco; or head for the orchid show on El Cerro del Padre.

From Esquipulas, it's a long and rutted road past family *fincas* (farms) and forested volcanoes. **San Dionisio**, with two basic *hospedajes*, is the biggest town on this stretch of road. Continue onward to **El Chile**, which is known for its colorful textiles, handbags and dolls. You can visit any of the family workshops before navigating the final 12km to Matagalpa.

There are four buses a day from Teustepe (US$1, one hour) to San José los Remates. From San José, irregular buses ply the back road to Esquipulas, from where there are frequent services to Matagalpa; however, the journey is much easier in a private 4WD vehicle.

Juigalpa

POP 59,500 / ELEV 117M

Blessed with a wonderful setting, Juigalpa is nestled on a high plateau peering into a golden valley quilted with rangeland carved by a crystalline river, and enclosed on all sides by the looming Serranía Amerrisque, the sheer granite faces and layered peaks of which are ripe for contemplation and adventure. To the west is a series of smaller hills and dry valleys that crumble into marsh, which melts into Lago de Nicaragua. The town itself, sprinkled with well-preserved colonial buildings and peopled by ranchers, rambles along both sides of the Managua Hwy. Apart from a fascinating archaeological museum, there are not a lot of attractions here and the pulse of tourism is quite faint, which makes Juigalpa a particularly authentic destination.

Sights & Activities

★Museo Arqueológico Gregorio Aguilar Barea MUSEUM
(☎2512-0784; Parque Central, 2½c E; admission US$0.40; ⏰8am-noon & 2-4pm Mon-Fri, 8am-noon Sat) Mystical stone statues rise like ancient totems in the courtyard entrance here. It houses the most important collection of stelae in the country, with more than 120 basalt statues, carved between AD 800 and 1500, including *La Chinita*, known as 'The Mona Lisa of Chontales.' She too has appeared at the Louvre. Inside the museum are hundreds of pre-Columbian pots, incense burners, funeral jars, art objects and the largest *metate* (corn grinder) ever found.

Parque Central PLAZA
The central plaza is constantly buzzing with man gossip thanks to the steady stream of ranchers who come to get their boots shined next to *La Lustrador*, the beloved statue of a shoe-shine boy. **El Templo de Cultura**, the large gazebo in the center, occasionally hosts live music and poetry readings.

Palo Solo Park PARK
(Parque Central, 5c E) This shady park is where couples come to whisper, cuddle and kiss beneath palm and ficus trees, and absorb a truly magnificent view of the Serranía Amerrisque.

Pozo el Salto WATERFALL
This absolutely stunning, partially dammed swimming hole, 4km north of town on the road to Managua, is framed in cascades of water and has been popular with picnickers for generations; unfortunately it's often polluted so ask around before diving in. It's a US$2 taxi or US$0.30 bus ride away.

Festivals & Events

Juigalpa's **fiestas patronales**, held from August 11 to 18, are internationally known for their *hipícas* (horse parades and rodeos). This is the only time of year you'll need to book your room in advance. The party's beating heart is Juigalpa's **Plaza Taurina Chontales** (admission US$2.50-4), a rodeo venue that hosts events and shows throughout the year.

Sleeping

Hospedaje El Nuevo Milenio GUESTHOUSE $
(☎2512-0646; Iglesia, 1c E; s/d without bathroom US$4/8, r US$10; ❄) By far the best of the cheapies, this place has a sweet family atmosphere, and clean and basic rooms.

Hotel Casa Country HOTEL $
(☎2512-2546; frente Parque Palo Solo; r with fan/air-con US$12.50/17; ❄) With comfortable rooms, wooden furnishings, cable TV and a great location, this is excellent value.

★Hotel Los Arcangeles HOTEL $$
(☎2512-0847; hotellosarcangeles@cablenet.com.ni; detras Iglesia; d US$46; ❄) This large ranch-style hotel has huge rooms with high ceilings, Spanish-tile floors, plasma TV and wi-fi in a top location directly behind the cathedral.

Eating

Mercado MARKET $
(Parque Central, 1c E, ½c N; meals US$2; ⏰6am-6pm) For supercheap eats, hit the market, where local mothers bring home cooking to the masses. Come for full chicken meals (grilled and fried) served with *gallo pinto* (rice and beans) or refried beans and freshly made tortillas.

Palo Solo NICARAGUAN $$
(☎2512-2735; Parque Palo Solo; dishes US$7.50-10.50; ⏰noon-10pm) Set on a shady patio beneath a beamed bamboo roof at the western edge of Parque Palo Solo, this restaurant serves up tasty Nicaraguan mixed-grill plates. It might have been classy once, but the cigarette holes in the tablecloths and bubble-blowing waitresses limit its claim to fine-dining status. Still it's lively, the food is good and the view is fantastic.

La Cazuelita NICARAGUAN $$
(Gasolinera Uno, 2c E; dishes US$5.50-10.50; ⏰noon-10pm) About as posh as it gets in Juigalpa, this large air-con dining room with double tablecloths serves up expertly prepared Nicaraguan meat dishes and a massive, artery-busting mixed platter.

Information

BanPro (frente Parque Central) Reliable Visa/MasterCard ATM.

Cyber Palo Alto (Parque Palo Alto, 1½c O; per hour US$0.60; ⏰10:30am-9pm) New machines and cheap calls.

Hospital (Barrio Hector Ugarte)

Intur (Parque Central, 1c O, ½c N; ⏰9am-2pm Mon-Fri, to noon Sat) Friendly tourist office that is able to arrange guides to surrounding attractions.

Getting There & Away

Buses to Managua, El Rama and San Carlos all leave from the Cotran bus terminal across Hwy 7 from downtown, 500m south of the hospital (taxis US$0.60). Minivans for Managua (US$3.30) leave the Cotran when full. Passing *expreso* buses to Managua originating in San Carlos and El Rama do not enter the Cotran – hail them on the highway. Buses to Cuapa, La Libertad and Puerto Díaz leave from the Mercado.

El Rama (US$4, five hours, almost hourly from 4:30am to 2:45pm)

Managua (US$2.10, four hours, 4am to 6pm, hourly)

Puerto Díaz (US$1, one hour, 5:30am, 9:30am, 11:30am and 1pm)

San Carlos (US$4.50, four hours, 4am to 3:30pm, two hourly)

Puerto Díaz

Just 28km west of Juigalpa, the lakefront village of Puerto Díaz defines the term *tranquilo*. Aside from visiting some of the least-visited islets in the lake, eating fresh fish and contemplating the vast expanse of pale-blue water that is Lago de Nicaragua, there's not a whole lot to do here.

Absalon Rivera (8444-4976; contiguo El Pescadito) arranges boat trips (per day US$50, six to seven passengers) to the archipelago in front of town, where you can visit each of the three rocky islands with their array of birdlife and swimming beaches. There's a house on **Isla Redonda** where you may be able to sling your hammock for the night, but you'll need to bring food and water with you from the mainland. **Isla Grande** is home to a tiny farming community and **Isla El Muerte** is owned by an absent foreigner, but the guard will probably let you poke around.

In a breezy ranch by the water, **El Pescadito** (8639-6116; meals US$3-5; 6am-10pm) serves a terrific fried fish (so fresh the meat really does fall off the bones) with panoramic lake views. **Bar y Restaurant Lizayel** (meals US$3.50-4.20; 6am-10pm), right across the road, has a similar menu but less ambience. It also organizes boat trips (US$21 per hour) to the islands.

For a refreshing swim, head up to the cement pools and thatched bar of **Mirador Vista Linda** (2512-2699; adult/child US$0.80/0.40; 8am-7pm Sat & Sun), on the hill just above town. Even if you don't plan to jump in, its worth walking up here for the view, which is magnificent. It takes in the three islands and a stunning back view of Isla de Ometepe's smoldering crater. Order a cold beer and let the view work on you a while.

Buses and trucks (US$1, one hour) run to Juigalpa at 4am, 5:30am, 7am, 3:40pm and 4:30pm. Taxis from Juigalpa cost around US$25. It's also possible to travel from here to Isla de Ometepe (US$4, six hours) on one of the sailing boats that bring plantains to the mainland. They leave around four times a week, usually setting sail around 7pm. Call El Pescadito to check on departures.

Cuapa

POP 2200

This small, picturesque mountain town became a famous pilgrimage-worthy destination thanks to the **Virgin of Cuapa**, the porcelain goddess holding flowers in her angelic hands at the entrance to town. On April 15, 1980, when tailor Bernardo Martínez was walking home, the statue began to glow. The Virgin then appeared to him five times, three times as apparitions and twice in his dreams, over the next five months. Her message was that all Nicaragua would suffer without peace.

This, of course, turned out to be true, which is why pilgrims descend on the **Virgen de Cuapa Santuario** (www.cuapa.com; Parque Central, 2km N; 8am-5:30pm) for a week each May. The grounds, surrounded by magnolias, mango trees and boulder-strewn rangeland, include two shrines, a replica statue and a small amphitheater. Pilgrims are welcome to sleep here on May 8 to commemorate the first apparition. Sunday services are held at 11am weekly.

The leafy Parque Central is set on a hill just above downtown across from the Catholic church, where Martínez is now laid to rest beneath a marble stone in the chapel floor.

Cuapa's other big draw is **El Monolito de Cuapa**, a massive stone dome that rises from a hillside savanna. If you walk from town, it will take about two hours to reach the peak. Or you could drive to the base and scramble up the back side until you reach the top (10 to 20 minutes).

Villa Sandino

It doesn't get many visitors, but the tiny rural town of Villa Sandino on the Juigalpa–El Rama Hwy is the gateway to two of Nicaragua's most important archaeological sites.

The main attraction here is **Parque Arqueológico Piedras Pintadas** (admission US$1; ⌚8am-4pm), 8km north of town on a firm dirt road, where you'll find hundreds of petroglyphs carved into the mossy boulders, including deer, snakes, turtles, crocodiles and spirals, set among rolling green hills. There are also large stones with carved channels that are said to have been used for ritual sacrifice, and an impressive bathing pool carved out of a single massive boulder. The park is overgrown with thick scrub and high grass – bring sturdy footwear. There are no explanation panels, so it's best to go with a guide. Buy your entrance ticket and organize guides at the **Alcaldía** (☎2516-0058; www.villasandino.gob.ni; Iglesia Catolica, 1c O; ⌚8am-4pm) before leaving town. A round-trip taxi from town is around US$12.

If you are feeling particularly Dr Jones-ish, consider the three-hour horseback ride to the **pre-Columbian pyramids**, the largest ruins of their kind in Nicaragua. What you see are the partially buried bases of larger pyramids that once stood on the site. It's no Tikal, but it's interesting to sit and contemplate how the area looked when the pyramids were complete and the area was full of indigenous worshippers.

Villa Sandino is easy to visit as a detour between Juigalpa and El Rama, but if you want to stay, **Hotel Santa Clara** (maisalar@hotmail.com; frente Alcaldía; s/d/tr US$20/25/30; ❄) has comfortable air-con rooms and serves fine meals. Any Juigalpa–El Rama bus will drop you here.

El Rama

POP 13,900

The Río Rama and Río Escondido converge at El Rama, turning an otherwise lazy tropical river into an international thoroughfare that empties into Bahía de Bluefields. Roads between El Rama and Managua are some of the best in the country thanks to the commerce of Rama International Port, Nicaragua's only heavyweight Atlantic harbor.

While you are still 60km from the Caribbean sea, take a walk around town and you'll notice plenty of Creole influence with booming reggae, braided hair and a plethora of Bob Marley T-shirts. But even with big business, wide tree-shaded brick city streets, an attractive Catholic church and solid infrastructure, Rama is still a scruffy port town that does not generally inspire travelers to extend their layover on the way between Managua and Bluefields.

Sights & Activities

The **Catholic church**, about two blocks downriver from the dock, is outfitted with funky stained-glass picture windows and a neon cross. It opens onto a cheery, palm-shaded Parque Central. You can climb the big hill just east of town, **La Loma** (Cerro de Rama), but you'll need to navigate the port-town slums.

Sleeping & Eating

Hotel Rio Escondido HOTEL $
(☎2517-0287; rioescondidohotel@yahoo.es; Enitel, 1c E, 30m S; s/d/tr US$11/12.50/17.50, r with air-con US$17; ❄ wifi) This choice new hotel has spacious rooms with high ceilings, spotless tiled bathrooms, flatscreen TV and wooden beds with firm sprung mattresses.

Hotel Doña Luisa HOTEL $
(☎2517-0073; frente Muelle; d with/without TV US$8.50/7) Large, clean rooms with fans and cable TV convenient to buses and boats.

Oasis Hotel del Caribe HOTEL $
(☎2517 0264; Muelle, 2c E; s/d US$8.50/12.50, with air-con US$12.50/21; P ❄) Professionally run hotel offering comfortable rooms with cable TV in a quiet location. Second-floor rooms open onto a common terrace with leafy, sunset views.

Eco-Hotel El Vivero HOTEL $
(☎8535-1276; s/d US$8.50/12.50, with air-con US$14.50/25; ❄) Set in the woods 3km, and a US$1 taxi ride, west of town, these wooden *casitas* (cottages) are a little run-down but are still elegant with hardwood floors, beamed ceilings and rocking chairs on the front porch. It's a little complicated to get into town for the early *panga*.

Comedor Silvia NICARAGUAN $
(Muelle ½c E; meals US$2.50-5; ⌚6am-8pm) Pull up a chair at a plastic table next to the bustling street and enjoy delicious home-style Nicaraguan food at this great-value *comedor* (basic eatery) close to the dock. It's all prepared fresh to order.

Kingstown Ranch NICARAGUAN $
(Muelle, 4c E; meals US$2-4; ⌚11am-9pm) An outstanding local buffet sets up daily on the ground floor, with gorgeous pots of beans, *gallo pinto*, salad and chicken (grilled and fried). Follow the crowd.

El Expresso STEAKHOUSE, SEAFOOD **$$**
(Muelle, 4c E; meals US$6.50-10.50; ⌚noon-10pm) This modern, spacious dining room is known for its generous cuts of export-quality beef and seafood dishes, including lobster prepared in nine different ways.

Information

BanPro (Muelle, 3c E) Has an ATM that usually works, and changes US dollars.

Cyber Isis (Bancentro, 1c S; per hour US$0.50; ⌚9am-9pm) Reliable internet access.

Getting There & Around

El Rama is walkable, but you may choose to take a pedicab (US$0.30) the 1.5km to Rama International Port for large, slow boats to Bluefields. The *Río Escondido* (US$8, five hours) leaves at 9pm on Tuesday. The *Captain D* (US$4, seven hours) departs at 6pm on Tuesday, with continuing service to El Bluff and Corn Island (US$13).

At the Muelle Municipal, close to the *expreso* buses, **Transporte Vargas** (⌚24hr) and **Transporte Jipe** (⌚24hr) have a faster, more convenient collective *panga* service to Bluefields (US$10.50, 1½ hours). Boats leave at first light in the morning and then 'when full' throughout the day. There is usually always service around noon and another around 3pm.

Transporte Vargas also runs private *expreso* buses that are timed to leave once the morning *pangas* arrive from Bluefields.

Other *expreso* buses depart from outside the *muelle* throughout the day, while *ordinarios* park at the small square one block east and one block south.

Bus services include the following:

Juigalpa (US$4, four hours, 4:40am to 2:55pm, hourly)

Managua (*expreso* US$7, five hours, 2am, 3am, 9am, 10:30am, 4pm and 7pm; *ordinario* US$5, seven hours, 4:40am to 9:40am, hourly)

Pearl Lagoon (US$6.50, five hours, 4:20pm)

Bluefields

POP 54,900

With brick streets etched into a series of jade peninsulas, Bluefields (the city) stretches into Bluefields (the bay) like so many fingers. In between is a series of docks, floating restaurants, shipwrecks, and fish and produce markets. The city was once full of old wood Victorian charm before Category IV Hurricane Juana wiped it off the map in 1988. Today's Bluefields is rather overindulgent in new concrete boxes, especially in the loud knot of streets downtown that eventually gives way to poor tin-roof neighborhoods that ramble over nearby hillsides and inland along brackish creeks.

Named after the Dutch pirate Blewfeldt, who made his base here in the 1700s, the capital of the RAAS is the the beating heart of Creole culture, famed for its its distinctive music, colorful dances and delicious cuisine, considered by many as the best in the country. And while it is not your typical Caribbean dream destination, if you give it a chance and get to know some of the town's colorful locals, Bluefields' decaying tropical charm will definitely grow on you. Still, you probably won't linger too long. After all, you are just a boat ride away from the intriguing Pearl Lagoon basin, the spectacular Pearl Keys and those luscious Corn Islands.

Sights

★ **Museo Historico Cultural de la Costa Caribe** MUSEUM
(CIDCA; Iglesia Morava, 2c S; admission US$2; ⌚9am-noon & 2pm-5pm Mon-Fri) Learn about the Caribbean region's diverse cultures with a visit to this fascinating museum that contains an interesting mix of historical items from the pre-Columbian era and British rule, including a sword belonging to the last Miskito king and artifacts left by the Kukra indigenous group.

Moravian Church CHURCH
This large concrete church is Bluefield's most iconic building and was constructed to the exact specifications of the 1849 wooden original, destroyed in Hurricane Juana. Like all churches of the order it has a red tin roof and all-white exterior.

Mercado MARKET
(⌚7am-3pm) Spilling out from a dank warehouse perched on a public pier, the local market is packed with small stands brimming with pineapple, banana, citrus and casaba alongside others selling fresh fish, shrimp, prawns and crab. Fishing boats dock and unload right at the market's back doors. It's an especially cool scene early in the morning.

Parque Reyes PARK
Bluefields' best green space is a popular meeting point with impressive 25m trees sprouting bromeliads in the canopy and a monument to the six ethnic groups of the region.

Bluefields

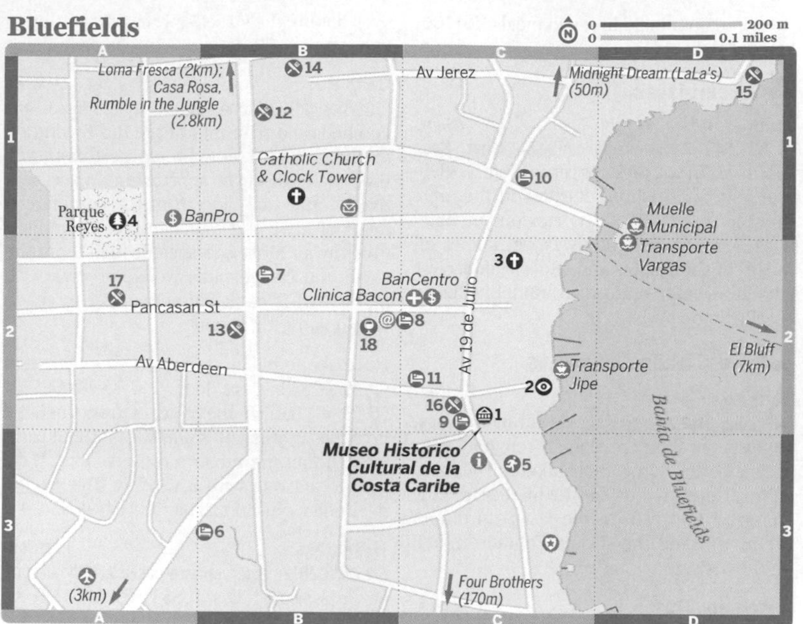

Bluefields

Top Sights
1 Museo Historico Cultural de la Costa Caribe C2

Sights
2 Mercado C2
3 Moravian Church C2
4 Parque Reyes A1

Activities, Courses & Tours
5 Fadcanic C3

Sleeping
6 Guesthouse Campbell B3
7 Hostal Doña Vero B2
8 Hotel Anabas C2
9 Hotel Caribbean Dream C2
10 Hotel Oasis C1
11 Los Pipitos C2

Eating
12 Cevicheria El Chino B1
13 Comedor de Las Platas B2
14 Maranatha Vineyard Bakery B1
15 Pelican Bay D1
16 Pesca Frito C2
17 Pizza Salmar A2

Drinking & Nightlife
18 Cima Club B2

El Bluff PORT, BEACH

Across the bay, the port of El Bluff is nestled at the point of a long sliver of land where the Caribbean Sea rushes into Bahía de Bluefields. There is not much to see in the town, but the enormous oil tanks and shipping tankers are cool if you like a certain industrialized tropical setting.

To the north of the town there is a long beach that, while not particularly attractive, is clean enough and sure beats plunging into the polluted lagoon. On weekends there are sometimes a couple of huts selling food and cold beer.

Reserva Silvestre Greenfields NATURE RESERVE

(☎2779-0589; www.greenfields.com.ni; r incl 2 meals US$100, day admission 1 2 visitors US$30; by appointment) This privately managed, 284-hectare wildlife reserve near Kukra Hill has tracts of both mangroves and jungle, and offers a variety of activities including canoeing, swimming and hiking. Advanced reservations essential. There's also a comfortable *cabaña* (room including two meals US$100) for overnight stays.

Activities

Rumble in the Jungle FISHING
(8832-4269; www.rumbleinthejungle.net; Casa Rosa, Loma Fresca; packages per day from US$325) The only sportfishing outfitter in the area, Rumble in the Jungle is run out of hotel Casa Rosa. Owner Randy Poteet knows all the best fishing spots and offers lagoon, river and blue-water options around Bluefields, Pearl Lagoon and beyond.

Festivals & Events

★**Palo de Mayo** CULTURAL
(Maypole Festival; May) Nicaragua's best street party simmers along throughout May with a series of neighborhood parties and cultural events, but the highlights are the energetic Carnival on the last Saturday of the month and the closing Tulululu march on the 31st.

Autonomy Day POLITICAL
(Oct 30) Celebrates the granting of autonomous status to the region with a parade and concert. There is often a counterrally by those that see autonomy as a farce.

Sleeping

Hostal Doña Vero GUESTHOUSE $
(2572-2166; Galileo, ½c N; r US$14, without bathroom US$11.50;) A great centrally located budget option with clean, comfortable rooms with unlimited coffee and filtered water.

Guesthouse Campbell GUESTHOUSE $
(8827-2221; Galileo, 2½c S; r with/without air-con US$11/20;) A bit out of the way but great value, this family-run guesthouse has clean, comfortable rooms with cable TV.

Los Pipitos GUESTHOUSE $
(2572-1590; Mercado, 1½c S; r with/without air-con US$20/15;) Walk through the diner to reach these simple, quiet rooms set around a small courtyard. Party animals will be given a key to the side gate so you won't have to rouse anyone in the early hours.

Hotel Caribbean Dream HOTEL $$
(2572-0107; Mercado, 1c O, ½c S; r US$27-32;) A sweet downtown hotel that strikes a good balance between price and amenities. Rooms are not particularly inspiring but are well maintained, with air-con and hot water, and there is a great balcony with rockers overlooking the street – perfect for getting to know some of Bluefields' colorful characters.

Casa Rosa LODGE $$
(8832-4269; Loma Fresca; d US$45-65;) Perched on a tributary of the Río Escondido in the breezy Loma Fresca neighborhood, this Nica-American sportfishing resort is a five-minute taxi ride from the commercial heart of town but looks and feels a million miles away. Most guests come to fish, but the clean and comfortable wooden rooms with air-con, wi-fi, cable TV and a river serenade would work for anyone.

Hotel Anabas HOTEL $$
(2572-2640; Iglesia, 1c S, ½c O; r/tw/tr US$35/50/75;) Bang in the center of town, this large hotel has rooms and suites with tasteful paint jobs and all the modern conveniences. Make sure to get one with a window. The rooftop deck offers sensational bay and city views.

Hotel Oasis HOTEL $$$
(2572-2812; reservations@oasiscasinohotel.com; Muelle Municpal, 1c O; s/d US$55/65, ste US$70/80, presidental ste US$160/180, all incl breakfast;) Easily the best hotel in town as long as you avoid the dark rooms downstairs. Up top there are ample modern rooms, some with bay views, boasting bright tiled floors, big comfortable beds and powerful air-con. The service is courteous and professional, and there is a free pickup service from the airport.

Eating

Bluefield's favourite snack is the *paty* – a savory spiced meat pastry sold for US$0.25 by roaming vendors all over town.

★**Cevicheria El Chino** SEAFOOD $
(frente Colegio Bautista; ceviche US$1.80; 7am-9pm) Don't leave Bluefields without trying El Chino's marvelous *ceviche* (seafood marinated in lemon or lime juice, garlic and seasonings) prepared fresh every day and served in small polystyrene cups at this unremarkable grocery shop. Choose from shrimp, fish, oyster or mixed and watch out for the outrageously spicy homemade 'Dos Bocas' chili sauce – made with pounds of habanero chillies.

Maranatha Vineyard Bakery BAKERY $
(items US$0.25-1; 8am-7pm) Traditional Creole bakery of local preacher and career politician Rayfield Hodgson that prepares the best coconut bread in town – but even

LOCAL KNOWLEDGE

PUTTING THE DANCE IN DANCEHALL

If you want to look the part in the dark dancehalls of the Caribbean, there are two basic routines you'll need to master.

For country and reggae soul numbers you'll need to employ the 'slow dance,' which involves selecting a partner (preferably several sizes larger than you) and hugging them like they are the lost love of your life while resting your head on their shoulders and slowly swaying to the music.

When the DJ drops in a fast dancehall tune it's time to *wine*, which is basically frenetically dry humping your partner either vertically or horizontally on the dance floor in a high-energy display of simulated lovemaking.

Be warned, you'll often be required to seamlessly move from one style to the other.

that is nothing compared to the delectable cinnamon-infused pineapple roll. The soda cakes (ginger cookies) ain't bad either.

Comedor de Las Platas NICARAGUAN $ (contiguo Galileo; meals US$2.50; ⊙noon-8pm) A quiet *comedor* serving budget lunches during the day, this local institution transforms into the best *fritanga* (grill) in town in the evenings, serving up delicious *fritos* – greasy fried chicken on piles of plantain chips with pickles. Come early.

Pesca Frito NICARAGUAN $$ (Mercado, 1c O; mains US$4-7.50; ⊙11am-10pm) If you don't mind (really) loud reggae and domino slamming, this lively bar serves great-value seafood including good fried fish and cheap lobster (US$7.50). Book in advance and they'll cook you up some *rundown* or any other Creole dish that you want to try.

Luna's Ranch NICARAGUAN $$ (Loma Fresca, frente Urracan; mains US$5-9; ⊙11am-10pm) There are many reasons to visit this impressive thatched restaurant on the Loma Fresca hill, such as occasional live concerts and the interesting collection of images of the old Bluefields including many of the devastation wrought by the hurricane, but the biggest attraction is the generous portions of mouthwatering seafood. It's a 10-minute taxi ride (US$0.50) from downtown.

Pelican Bay NICARAGUAN $$ (Barrio Pointeen; mains US$7-11.50; ⊙noon-10pm) At the end of the Pointeen peninsula, this flash restaurant has an elevated balcony with fantastic views across the bay to El Bluff. The house specialty is seafood and the mixed plate (US$10) featuring shrimp, fish and lobster sautéed with herbs is outstanding.

Pizza Salmar PIZZA $$ (Parque Reyes, 1c S; pizzas US$2.50-9, Mexican dishes US$3-4; ⊙4pm-10pm) Too much seafood? Head to this popular pizzeria for a selection of passable pizzas and surprisingly good quesadillas and burritos served by bow-tied waiters.

Drinking & Nightlife

★**Four Brothers** CLUB (Parque Reyes, 6c S; ⊙8pm-4am Thu-Sun) Dance up a storm to dancehall, country and reggae on the wooden dance floor at this legendary disco ranch, comfortable in the knowledge that your dignity is protected by the extremely low-wattage lighting. It doesn't get going until after midnight. Go in a group, it sometimes gets a little rough later on.

Midnight Dream (LaLa's) BAR (Iglesia, 2c N; ⊙11am-midnight) With an open-air deck that feels like it is floating on the bay and ridiculously loud reggae numbers, this atmospheric spot is undeniably the coolest bar on the coast.

Cima Club CLUB (☎2572-1410; Mercado, 2c O, 1c N; ⊙8pm-late) This popular, massive late-night venue has two very distinct zones. The open terrace bar downstairs is favored by hard-drinking seafarers and prostitutes while upstairs is one of the more upmarket clubs in town, playing an eclectic mix of Latin pop, rock and dancehall.

Information

BanCentro (Iglesia, ½c S) Has a Visa/Plus ATM.

BanPro (frente Iglesia) Reliable Visa/MasterCard ATM.

Ciber Central (Iglesia, 1c S, ½c O; per hour US$0.50; ⊙8am-8pm) The swiftest connection in town.

Clinica Bacon (Iglesia, 1c S, ½c O) Private clinic with a range of specialists and a laboratory.

Correos de Nicaragua (Post Office; Moravian College, 1c O; ⌚8am-2pm Mon-Sat)

Intur (Iglesia, 2c S; ⌚8am-2pm Mon-Fri) Tourist office with few practical recommendations

Police (☎2572-2448; Barrio Punta Fria)

Right Side Guide (www.rightsideguide.com) Informative website with cultural insights, off-the-beaten track attractions and transport schedules.

Getting There & Away

AIR

Take a taxi (US$0.50) to the Bluefields Airport, where **La Costeña** (Aeropuerto; ⌚6am-5pm) has daily flights to Managua and Great Corn Island, and flies to Bilwi three days a week.

Bilwi (one way/return US$96/148, 50 minutes, 10:10am Monday, Wednesday and Friday)

Corn Island (one way/return US$64/99, 20 minutes, 7:25am and 3:10pm)

Managua (one way/return US$82/127, 70 minutes, 8:35am, 10:10am and 4:20pm)

BOAT

There are several scheduled boat services to Corn Island. The government-run Rio Escondido (US$10, five hours) has the most reliable schedule, departing from the **Muelle Municipal** (Municipal Dock) at 9am on Wednesday. Larger and more comfortable but slightly slower, the **Captain D** (seat/bunk US$10/12) leaves an hour later, and occasionally has continuing service to Bilwi. The **Island Express** (per seat US$10) leaves from El Bluff between 3am and 5am on Friday. You'll need to take the *panga* from Bluefields the night before. There are also a number of cargo boats making the trip on irregular schedules.

Transporte Vargas (Muelle Municipal; ⌚5am-4pm) has collective *pangas* to El Rama (US$10, 1¾ hours, 5:30am, 1pm and 3pm) and Pearl Lagoon (US$7, one hour, 7am, 11am and 3pm). Service to El Bluff (US$1.60, 30 minutes) departs continually when full. **Transporte Jipe** (contiguo Mercado; ⌚5am-4pm) next to the market also runs *pangas* to El Rama (US$10, 1½ hours, 6am and 3pm).

Pearl Lagoon

POP 4900

At last, you've arrived in the real Caribbean. Here are dirt roads and palm trees, reggae music, and an English-speaking Creole community that fishes the local waters for shrimp, fish and lobster, and still refers to Spanish-speaking Nicaraguans as 'the Spaniards.' You can feel the stress roll off your shoulders as soon as you get off the boat from Bluefields. And the best part is that this town still sees just a few dozen tourists a month – which means you may well be the only foreigner buzzing through the mangroves and jungle that surround Pearl Lagoon (the bay), a timeless expanse of black water home to more than a dozen ethnic fishing villages.

If your Caribbean dream is tinted turquoise, you can easily arrange a tour of the nearby Pearl Keys, where you'll find sugar-white beaches that double as turtle hatcheries, and swaying coconut palms that lull you into inner peace. Of course, nothing tops off a day on the water like cold beer, lobster with coconut sauce and heavy doses of reggae music, all of which are available among Pearl Lagoon's collection of barefoot restaurants and bars sprinkled along the dirt roads patrolled by fishers, their families and free-roaming horses.

Sights & Activities

The town is laid out along two main north-south roads: Front Rd, on the water, and another road a block inland.

At the southern end of the inland road you'll find the **Moravian Church**, with its characteristic red tin roof. Take the path opposite the church due west and walk through town until you reach the savannah, a striking flat ecosystem with several freshwater creeks and interesting birdlife. Keep on the concrete path and after 30 minutes you will reach the humble Miskito fishing communities of **Raiti Pura** and **Awas**, where the grassy shore is perfect for a picnic. The water here is shallow and great for swimming.

You can also make the journey by bike; Queen Lobster Tours (p228) rents bikes for US$1 per hour.

Tours

Fuel costs make up the lion's share of any boat charter. Plan on paying around US$50 to US$60 per day for the boat and captain plus fuel. If you're on a budget, look for a captain with a small engine; it will take longer but you'll save plenty.

★**Captain Sodlan McCoy** BOAT TOUR

Anyone can take you to the Pearl Keys, but few know the area even half as well as Captain Sodlan McCoy, a colorful, no-nonsense fisherman who has been visiting the islands

OFF THE BEATEN TRACK

TERRITORIO RAMA-KRIOL

If you really want to get away from the crowds and discover the best the Caribbean coast has to offer, plan a trip into the little-visited Territorio Rama-Kriol. Jointly administered by the indigenous Rama and Creole peoples of the region, it stretches from the southern half of Bahía de Bluefields all the way to the Costa Rican border, and includes stunning solitary beaches, mysterious ruins cloaked in virgin rainforest and lazy mocha-colored rivers teeming with wildlife.

It's possible to visit the territory on a loop from Bluefields or continue all the way down to San Juan de Nicaragua near the mouth of the Río San Juan. Begin with a visit to **Rama Cay**, a tiny, rocky, barbell-shaped island in Bahía de Bluefields 15km southeast of the city and de facto capital of the Rama nation. The island is dotted with coconut and banana palms and mango and breadfruit trees and laced with earthen trails that link clusters of stilted thatched bungalows, home to over 1000 people, which accounts for over half of all remaining Rama. Check out the Moravian church or head up to the breezy point on the north side of the island to chill out under coconut trees. If you're feeling more active, learn to sail a traditional *dory* (dugout canoe) on the bay and head across to wild **Mission Cay** for a picnic.

Across the bay and up the Kukra River you'll find **Tiktik Kaanu**, a remote Rama community that's a great place to spend the night surrounded by the sounds of the jungle.

Heading out of Bahía de Bluefields through the Hone Sound passage (a turbulent gathering of breaking waves that is a true test of your captain's skills) you'll come to **Monkey Point**, a Rasta-influenced Creole community spread out on hillsides by the sea and surrounded by thick jungle. Here you'll find some of the best beaches on the Caribbean mainland and a fascinating yet unexplored indigenous burial site shrouded in thick foliage, which is said to be one of the oldest archaeological sites in the country.

A short boat ride further south is **Bankukuk**, a small Rama community with fine beaches and jungle-covered headlands jutting out into the calm Caribbean Sea.

Continuing south past Punta Gorda you'll arrive at **Corn River**, one of the most important waterways of the magnificent Reserva Natural Indio Maíz. At the river mouth you'll find a tiny Creole community, but the real attraction here is upriver where you'll be treated to some of the best wildlife-viewing in the country. The towering trees are awash with birds and monkeys and you may spot sloths or even a tapir.

Visit the **Gobierno Territorial Rama-Kriol** (GTRK; ☎2572-1765; www.rama-territory.com; Parque Reyes, 2c N; ⊙8am-5pm) in Bluefields to arrange transportation and accommodation. Most communities rent rooms in solar-powered communal houses, but homestays are also available. The GTRK is planning to launch a regular *panga* (small motorboat) service from Bluefields to San Juan with stops at all the communities, but until then you'll either have to charter a boat or hitch a ride with a traveling local – you'll be expected to contribute to fuel costs.

since he was a boy. A trip with Sodlan is much more than sightseeing, it's a cultural experience. He also offers bird-watching, fishing and community trips. Ask for him at Fry Fish.

George Fox Tours BOAT TOUR
(☎8944-3381; Front Rd, Muelle, 150m N) A true Pearl Lagoon gentleman, George not only provides transport to the keys and communities, he walks and talks you through the area's culture, history and cuisine.

Kabu Tours ECOTOUR
(www.kabutours.com) Just getting off the ground at the time of writing, this new community-run venture was set up by the Wildlife Conservation Society to offer an alternative source of income to turtle fishers from the community of Kakabila. It offers overnight and multiday trips to the Pearl Keys including turtle-spotting and snorkeling and community tours.

Queen Lobster Tours BOAT TOUR
(☎8499-4403, 8662-3393; www.queenlobster.com; Muelle, 200m N) Offers trips to the Pearl Keys

CARIBBEAN CUISINE

Nicaragua's best eating happens on the Caribbean coast. Fresh seafood, particularly lobster and shrimp, is inexpensive and exquisitely prepared, most famously as *rundown*, a one-pot meal in which seasoned fish is steamed atop plantains, cassava and other root vegetables, letting the flavor 'run down.' Coconut milk, the Caribbean coast's not-so-secret ingredient, is considered the key to good health and digestion, and is added to almost everything including bread, *gallo pinto* (rice and beans) and rich seafood soup.

and a number of other inventive activities around town including traditional cooking classes.

Sleeping

Comfort Zone GUESTHOUSE $
(Muelle, 2c S, ½c E; r US$12.50-14.50) Next to the family store, these brand-new tiled rooms with flatscreen TV, small desks, fans and private bathroom are the best value in town and the owners couldn't be more accommodating.

Green Lodge HOTEL $
(☎2572-0507; Front Rd, Muelle 75m S; s/d with air-con US$30/35, r without bathroom US$10-14; ❄) Half a block from the dock, this long-running hotel is a fine choice. The cheaper rooms upstairs in the family home are a little cramped, but those in the new wing are clean, spacious and comfortable. Owner Wesley Williams is a knowledgeable source of information on local history and culture.

Slilma Guesthouse GUESTHOUSE $
(☎2572-0523; slilma_gh1@yahoo.com; Enitel, 1c S, 1c E; r with/without air-con US$30/20, r without bathroom US$10; ❄) Take the first left after the cell tower to find this budget guesthouse offering small but very clean rooms with small TVs and the cleanest shared bathrooms in the Atlantic region. There are also excellent-value breezy and spacious rooms upstairs.

Casa Blanca HOTEL $$
(☎2572-0508; Enitel, 250m O; s/d with air-con US$35/40, s/d/tr without bathroom US$20/25/35; ❄) This lovely white house has wooden floors and furnishings made in the attached workshop. The small rooms upstairs have very low ceilings but those out the back are spacious and full of natural light. These ladies can cook too. Try the shrimp in coconut sauce.

Eating & Drinking

★**Casa Ulrich** INTERNATIONAL $$
(Up Point, Muelle 350m N; mains US$5.50-12.50; ⏲7am-10pm) Local boy and Swiss-trained chef Fred Ulrich has returned to Pearl Lagoon after a long absence working in resorts all over the Americas and invested in his own hotel and restaurant right by the water. Everything on the menu is top-notch, but make sure to try the tender filet steaks that arrive at your table on a sizzling platter or the delicate shrimp pasta.

There are also a range of rooms available and guests have private lagoon access via the lovely grassed yard.

Queen Lobster SEAFOOD $$
(☎8662 3393; www.queenlobster.com; Front Rd, Muelle, 200m N; mains US$3.50-8.50; ⏲noon-midnight) Some of the best seafood in town is served in this utterly picturesque thatched dining room jutting over the lagoon, which is also a great place for a drink. Fresh fish, shrimp and lobster is served fried, sautéed in coconut sauce and steamed with butter and garlic. It also offers two beautifully crafted bamboo and thatch huts (s/d/tr US$30/40/50) on stilts over the water with private bathrooms and hammocks on the porch.

Coconut Delight BAKERY $
(Miss Betty's; Muelle, 30m S; ⏲7am-8:30pm) Follow the sweet smells to this pink wooden hut to discover Caribbean baking at its finest. Tear into hot coconut bread, *toto* (sticky ginger bread), journey cakes, fluffy soda cakes and even vegetarian *paty* served with a smile by jolly giant and all-round-nice-guy Mr Byron. They also prepare cheap and delicious meals with advance notice.

Fry Fish BAR
(Point View; Up Point; ⏲11am-9pm) Follow the road from the dock all the way north to find this breezy thatched neighborhood bar with cold beers and great reggae. It also serves fantastic home-style seafood dishes.

Information

There are no banks in Pearl Lagoon, so come with ample cash and plan on staying longer than anticipated. You can receive emergency cash transfers at **Western Union** (frente Muelle; ⌚9am-5pm Mon-Fri). You can get online at **Taylor's Cyber** (contiguo Muelle; per hour US$0.80; ⌚8am-8pm).

Getting There & Away

Boats run to Bluefields (US$7) at 6:30am and 1pm. Sign up the day before for the early boat.

Every Monday, Wednesday, Thursday and Saturday a *panga* makes the run to Orinoco from Bluefields via Pearl Lagoon (US$12, two hours, 9am); it returns to Pearl Lagoon and Bluefields the following day. There are *pangas* from Bluefields to Tasbapauni (US$12, 2½ hours, 11am) that pass Pearl Lagoon every day except Sunday. Times are liable to shift depending upon the season, so you'll need to ask about departure times at the dock.

One bus (US$6.30, five hours) a day leaves Pearl Lagoon at 5am for El Rama.

Around Pearl Lagoon

With a dozen villages belonging to three distinct ethnic groups clinging to its shores and a similar number of jungle-lined rivers feeding it, a boat trip on Pearl Lagoon can make you feel like an 18th-century explorer venturing into an intriguing new world. This is authentic, off-the-beaten-track cultural tourism at its best and there is nothing like it anywhere else in the country.

Kakabila

Crossing the lagoon to the northwest from Pearl Lagoon town, you'll come to Kakabila, a welcoming Miskito village carpeted with soft grass and studded with mango, pear and breadfruit trees and coconut palms where the horses roam free. There's definitely some tropical country romance happening here. To the south of town is Tuba Creek, a narrow, jungle-lined river that is great for wildlife-spotting.

You can stay here at the community-run guesthouse, set on a grassy point to the north of town with a small sandy beach. The night sky here is spectacular. The lodge organizes interpretive treks through the thick jungle behind the village, where you'll learn about bush food and natural medicines.

Río Wawashang

This lazy, wide mocha-colored river surrounded by jungle flows into Pearl Lagoon just west of Orinoco. Its banks are home to two fascinating projects run by the **Fadcanic** (☎2572-2386; wawashang@fadcanic.org.ni; Mercado, 1c O, ½c S; ⌚9am-5pm Mon-Fri, to noon Sat) organization. Call or visit its office in Bluefields to arrange a trip.

Wawashang Education Center (☎2572-2386) is a vocational training school where youth from all over the RAAS learn about sustainable agriculture. You can tour the greenhouses, check out the cool coconut farm or sample artisanal chocolate made from locally grown cacao.

Continue upriver to arrive at the **Reserva Natural Kahka Creek** (☎8725-0766, 2570-0962; Pueblo Nuevo), a reforestation and ecotourism project set in lush gardens surrounded by jungle. There are a number of hiking trails and a lookout tower above the forest canopy. Visitors can also get involved in the reforestation process by planting trees. Accommodations are in a solar-powered wooden lodge (dorm/room US$7/13) and simple meals are available (US$3.50 to US$4). The project is a 30-minute walk or horseback ride from the town of Pueblo Nuevo.

Orinoco

When you can hear the call of the *djimbe* (wood and animal-skin drum) spilling out across the rippling water from the red-earth streets of Orinoco, you know you're approaching Garifuna country.

Orinoco is home to 2000 of Nicaragua's approximately 5000 Garifuna. Here you can learn to paddle dugout canoes, try artisanal fishing or take the 30-minute stroll northeast along the water to Marshall Point, a neighbouring Creole village.

There are a couple of cheap guesthouses in town, the best of which is **Hostal Garífuna** (☎8937 0123, 8648 4985; www.hostalgarifuna.net; Muelle, 50m inland; s/d/tr US$7.50/10/15), owned by anthropologist, activist and entrepreneur Kensy Sambola. It's a simple but very comfortable affair with spotless tiled rooms and shared bathrooms. It serves tremendous seafood meals (US$2.50 to US$3.50), and can arrange boat transportation to **La Fe**, a charming Garifuna village on a grassy peninsula surrounded by bush and famous for its troubadours.

Note that a number of robberies targeting tourists, including one very serious assault, have been reported recently in and around Orinoco. All visitors, but particularly female travelers, should exercise caution and not walk through remote areas without a trusted local guide. Ask at your hotel for a recommendation.

Pearl Keys

You would be hard-pressed to imagine a more beautiful and romantic tropical-island chain than the snow white, palm-shaded, turquoise-fringed Pearl Keys. Located in the Caribbean Sea 30km from Pearl Lagoon town, there were once 18 pearls, but rising tides have trimmed the number to 12.

Once communally owned by Miskito and Creole villagers, some of the keys have been bought – illegally according to locals – by foreign investors with dreams of tropical-island isolation.

You can certainly understand the appeal. Larger islands include lagoons and shady palm groves in the interior, while smaller islands seem to exist purely for their cotton-white sand beaches. Sheltered by reefs, and channeled into crystalline coves, the sea gets bathtub warm here.

Endangered hawksbill turtles nest from May to November in the Pearl Keys, peaking in August and September. Traditionally hunted by the locals for their shells, as opposed to the meat of the tastier green turtles, hawksbills are now also under pressure because of island development that has compromised their nesting grounds. The **Wildlife Conservation Society** (WCS; ☎2572-0506; www.wcs.org; Muelle, 20m S, Pearl Lagoon ; ⏰9am-5pm Mon-Fri) 🍃 has helped by hiring fishers to watch turtle nests and by educating them about the damaging effects of artificial light and egg poaching on the ecosystem. Before WCS arrived, 97% of hawksbill eggs were poached by fishers. Now they lose only 10% a year. The WCS also manages an extensive turtle-tagging program that has enabled international scientists to learn how vast the turtles' range actually is. It's worth dropping by the WCS office to learn more.

Arrange trips to the keys in Pearl Lagoon. A day trip will set you back US$200 to US$300 depending on the size of your group and how many islands you want to visit. There are no longer any hotels operating on the keys, but it's possible to stay in tents on one of the islands that remain in community hands.

In calm weather, it's just another hour (and another US$200) by *panga* from the keys to the Corn Islands. Considering the adventure quotient, the price and the time involved, it actually makes good sense to travel to the Corn Islands from Pearl Lagoon via the Pearl Keys rather than doubling back to Bluefields and flying to Great Corn from there.

Sights

Wild Cane Key ISLAND
(☎2572-1644) This large island with a spectacular long beach was once the family paradise of a young New Zealand millionaire. However, after the watchman up and left following a pay dispute, local fishers moved in, and like an army of leafcutter ants each taking what they could carry, stripped the once-opulent resort bare.

Visiting the island now is an eerie experience: the building looks like it was hit by a hurricane, but if you look carefully you'll spot traces of luxury like the busted chan-

THE GARIFUNA

The Garifuna people trace their origins to the Caribbean island of San Vicente, where the survivors of a wrecked slave ship intermarried with the indigenous population. The resulting ethnic group was referred to as the Black Caribs by the British, who, following repeated indigenous rebellions, forcibly moved them from San Vicente to the the island of Roatan in Honduras.

From Roatan, the Garifuna spread throughout Central America, founding their own free communities such as Orinoco, where they practiced their Yoruba religion in relative peace. Christianity eventually came calling in the 19th century, but traditional shamanic healing ceremonies, such as the three-day *walágayo* ritual, persist.

The best way to get a taste of Garifuna music, ritual, history and cuisine – such as *hudutu* or *fu fú* (a mash of plantains and fish flooded with coconut sauce and paired with home-distilled, clove-spiced rum), is to attend November's **National Garifuna Week**. Events include live music and dance performances, and historical and cultural symposiums that climax on November 19.

PEARL KEYS: PRIVATIZING PARADISE

For the fishers of the Pearl Lagoon basin, the Pearl Keys are like a second home, a place to rest and gather fresh water while out at sea for days. So when in 1997 a foreign land speculator, Peter Tsokas, purchased some old deeds to the islands – the legality of which are disputed – and proceeded to sell them off at huge profits to wealthy expat dreamers, things took a turn for the worse.

Soon the new 'owners' began raising foreign flags, constructing large houses and hotels and ordering the locals to keep off the islands, despite Nicaraguan laws guaranteeing public access to beaches.

In response, the local community hired a lawyer to take up the case. In addition to claiming to be the legitimate owners of the keys, the community also expressed concerns that the unregulated construction was destroying the sensitive ecosystem.

The Nicaraguan government has publicly stated its commitment to returning the islands to the community, but there has yet to be a definitive resolution.

delier and expensive furniture at the bottom of the pool.

Vincent Key ISLAND

This uninhabited island is easy to spot by the huge rusted metal buoy in its shallow waters. It has just a half-dozen palm trees so there's not much shade, but there's also no sand flies as the wind blows right through.

Crawl Key ISLAND

This is a slender crescent of white sand bunched with soaring coconut palms. It's also home to an unfinished three-story concrete monstrosity that was destined to be a private pad for a wealthy American until the community called in the authorities because the beach is a prime hawksbill nesting ground.

Maroon Key ISLAND

The closest key to the mainland, this tiny football-field-sized patch of white sand and coconut trees is completely uninhabited and the perfect place to indulge in your shipwreck fantasies.

Corn Islands

The Caribbean coast's biggest tourist draw is actually 70km offshore on a pair of enchanting islands with horseshoe bays, crystalline coves and underwater caves. Great Corn is larger and peopled by a Creole population that lives in colorful wooden houses, many of which are sprinkled along the main road that encircles the island. And though tourism is the second-largest industry, behind lobster fishing, you won't see megadevelopments here. Little Corn, a tiny, jungled, carless jewel, actually attracts more tourists, with most visitors heading for funky, creative beachside *cabañas* that are the perfect setting for Robinson Crusoe 2.0. The dive sites are more diverse on Little Corn, the jungle is thick and the food is outrageously good, which explains why so many ignore the larger island and indulge in car-free tranquility. But there is a catch. During high season there can be more foreigners than locals.

History

Christopher Columbus breezed through the Corn Islands in 1502, but it wasn't until 1660, when a French pirate by the name of Jean-David Nau arrived, that relations with the indigenous Kukras were cultivated. In the 1700s British pirates patrolled these waters, and African slaves were bought in to grow corn for export (hence the name). Both groups mingled with the Kukras. Although the British were asked to leave the islands in 1786, as part of their treaty with the Spanish, they returned in 1841 after Nicaragua's independence from Spain, which signified the end of slavery. The **Crab Soup Festival** celebrates freedom every August 27 with music, dance and, of course, crab soup.

Diving & Snorkeling

Both islands have excellent diving and snorkeling, with over 40 species of coral and migrating hammerhead sharks. Most dive sites are within 10 minutes of the shore and fairly shallow (9m to 18m), with 30m visibility on the best days. Dive sites can be inaccessible during high winds. Dive shops monitor long-term forecasts; call ahead to check on conditions. Popular dive sites:

Blowing Rock (10m to 30m) This pinnacle lies 26km from Little Corn and is arguably

SAFE & RESPONSIBLE DIVING

Exploring the coral reefs and underwater caves is one of the Corn Island's main attractions, but the scuba-diving industry is far more low-key here than in many other destinations in the region.

Most dives around the Corn Islands are in fairly shallow waters, which alleviates many safety concerns, but it's still vitally important that you choose a responsible dive center that you feel comfortable with.

When choosing an operator, find out the instructor-to-student ratio and ask to see the equipment before you dive to make sure it is well maintained. You may also want to test the air in the tanks (it should be taste and odor free) and make sure that the boats have sufficient life vests.

When the diving industry was in its infancy here, some divers returned from trips with environmental horror stories, including boat captains dropping their anchors on the reefs, disposing of rubbish at dive sites and manhandling the coral. Since then sustainable practices have come a long way and local dive operators now run pretty tight ships but visitors still play an important role in protecting the fragile ecosystem. Follow the instructions of your divemaster closely, fasten all your equipment tightly so nothing is flapping about, and resist the temptation to reach out and touch no matter how insignificant it may seem – small organisms are often the most fragile.

the best of the Corn Island dive sites. It attracts large pelagics year-round.

The Caves (9m) A swim-through flooded with light on Little Corn's east coast. Geographical set-piece diving at its finest.

Nautilus House Reef (9m to 19m) Just off the northwest shore of Great Corn is a patch of reef teeming with colorful fish and large fan corals.

Tarpon Channel (9m to 22m) When the water cools off, hammerheads cruise this channel regularly.

White Holes (9m) A favorite site on the northern side of Little Corn, thanks to the resident nurse sharks, eagle rays and barracuda.

Yellowtail (9m to 15m) Dolphins are sometimes seen here, at the southern corner of Little Corn.

Dangers & Annoyances

Bare-bones law enforcement and a growing tourist industry has seen theft become a problem on the Corn Islands, especially from hotel rooms. While muggings are uncommon, tourists on Great Corn are discouraged from walking around Bluff Point without a local chaperone.

The *panga* crossing between Great and Little Corn can get extremely rough, especially during the windy season (November to January). Squalls are common (on land and sea) and swells can grow as high as 3m, throwing walls of water over the boat and her passengers. It makes for one white-knuckle, and sometimes bruising, roller-coaster ride. The back seats bounce less, but you are more likely to get wet.

Great Corn Island

POP 7100

Large enough to get lost in humble hillside and beachfront neighborhoods that are poor but still so full of spirit, and small enough to find your way home again, Great Corn is on the shortlist for most authentic Caribbean island. Here are barefoot bars, commercial fishing wharfs, pickup baseball games on the beach, smiling young lobster divers catch-in-hand, an ever-present armada of elders sitting in rocking chairs on creaky front porches and elegant virgin beaches backed by picturesque headlands. It's a place where reggae and country music can coexist without irony. Where fresh lobster is a staple ingredient rather than a luxury. And the longer you stay, the less you want to leave.

Sights

Great Corn measures about 6 sq km and is looped by one main road – which has several spur roads that lead to various beaches and neighborhoods. **Long Bay** is where you'll find the island's best stretch of golden sand. It arcs from a pileup of local fishing *pangas* and lobster traps to a wild, jungle-covered headland. If you're looking for a place to snooze and swim in absolute tranquility, this is your destination. **Southwest**

Great Corn Island

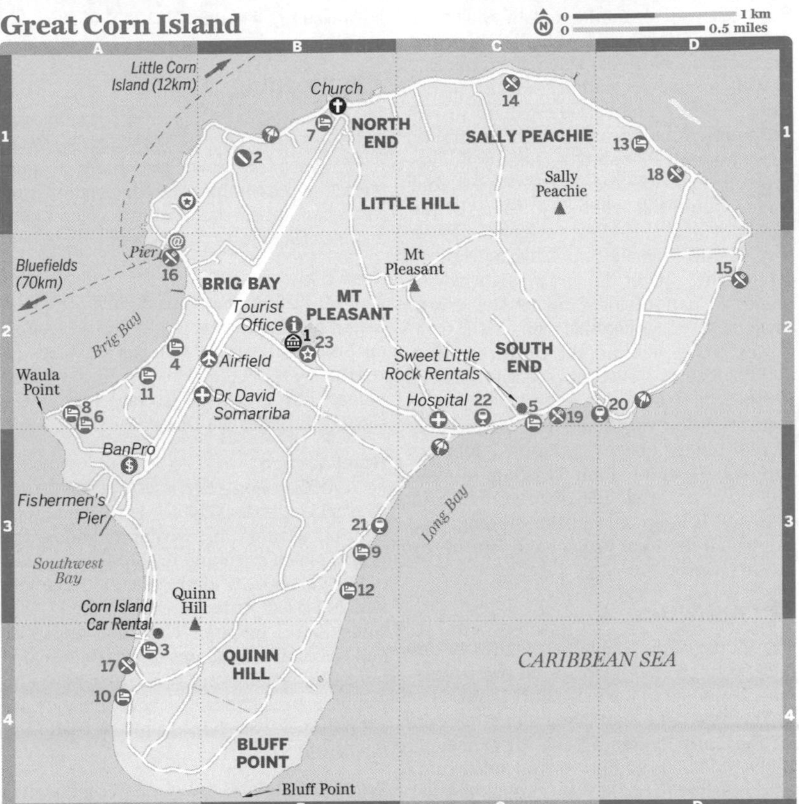

Great Corn Island

Sights
1 Culture House B2

Activities, Courses & Tours
2 Nautilus Dive Center B1

Sleeping
3 Arenas Beach Resort A4
4 Casa Blanca A2
5 Casa Canada C2
6 El Paraíso A2
7 Hotel Morgan B1
8 La Princesa de la Isla A2
9 Lodge at Long Bay B3
10 Martha's Bed & Breakfast A4
11 Mayflower A2
12 Sea Star Spa B3
13 Yellowtail D1

Eating
14 Comederia Mari C1
15 Doña Lola D2
16 Fisher's Cave A2
17 Picnic Center A4
18 Seva's D1
19 South End Pulpería C2

Drinking & Nightlife
20 Bambule D2
21 Island Style B3
22 Nico's C2

Entertainment
23 Estadio Municipal Karen Tucker B2

Bay beckons with another outstanding wide beach. The water here is usually calmer but the area is more developed and less rustic.

Walk up the dirt trail behind the Sunrise Hotel in South End past the banana groves and you will be rewarded with panoramic views from **Mt Pleasant** as the sun plunges beneath the Caribbean Sea. Or make your way to **Quinn Hill**, where Spanish artist Rafael Trénor has installed a cube (the lower half is buried to make it look like a pyramid) symbolizing one of the earth's eight vortex points as part of his **Soul of the World Project** (www.souloftheworld.com).

Next to the stadium, the **Culture House** (☎8702-8519; Mt Pleasant, contiguo Alcaldía; ⏲8am-8pm Mon-Fri) museum won't hold your attention very long with its pictures of old beauty queens, preserved lobsters and collection of John Grisham novels. But there are a couple of pre-Columbian pots and if you come in the evening, you can watch the local youth band jam in the music room.

Activities

The tourist office is able to organize guides (US$20 to US$50) for hikes all over the island, including to the wild **Bluff Point**.

There's terrific snorkeling along the reef off the **Sally Peachie** coast. Mr Dorsey at Yellow Tail offers highly recommended guided snorkeling tours. El Paraiso rents snorkel gear (US$10 per half-day) as well as arranging chartered snorkeling tours (US$30 per person) and fishing trips (US$40 per person).

Nautilus Dive Center DIVING
(☎2575-5077; www.nautilus-dive-nicaragua.com; Brig Bay, Muelle, 150m N; ⏲8am-6pm) Big Corn's only diving outfitter, Nautilus Dive Center, is run in true island style – relaxed to some, disorganized to others. It gets mixed reviews and some of the equipment is a bit worn. However, it is friendly and staff have good local knowledge.

English-speaking dive guides lead trips to the local reef (US$40 per dive), which has an abundance of hard and soft corals, and two-dive trips to Blowing Rock (US$95). It also offers a cool snorkel tour of a sunken Spanish galleon (US$25). What's left of the ancient vessel is immersed in 5m of water, but you can see several cannons, an anchor and chestlike structures. Dive packages (10 dives for US$300), and open-water (US$280) and advanced open-water (US$230) courses are available.

Sleeping

Mayflower GUESTHOUSE $
(Brig Bay, Pasenic, 600m S; r/tw US$15/25) Walking distance from town, but on a nice, quiet stretch of beach, this relaxed guesthouse offers a handful of neatly painted, clean rooms a stone's throw from the water.

Casa Blanca GUESTHOUSE $
(☎8629-4529; Brig Bay, Pasenic, 250m S; r US$10) Cheap and basic, this family-run *hospedaje* on Brig Bay beach is a budget traveler's favourite with six small rooms in a wooden house. It's a good deal, so take note of the sign on the gate: 'No Deals!'

Hotel Morgan HOTEL $
(☎2575-5502; North End; r with/without air-con US$25/15, cabañas US$40; ❄) Efficient hotel offering a range of accommodations, the best of which are found in split-level duplexes. Downstairs are pink concrete flats with two full-sized beds, air-con, cable TV, hot water and a minibar. The same amenities and layout are found upstairs in the wooden bungalow-style rooms, which also have ample deck space and ocean views. Smaller single rooms are set back from the road (and the beach).

Yellowtail GUESTHOUSE $$
(☎8659-3634; r US$25) Just east of Seva's restaurant, this relaxed place has just two cabins with fridge, cooker and private bathroom in a lovely part of the island.

Lodge at Long Bay GUESTHOUSE $$
(☎8339-7745, 8660-6785; lodgeatlongbay@gmail.com; Long Bay; r US$45-50) You won't find better value than these two small, comfortably furnished apartments alongside the best beach on the island. Both have bright tiled floors, wooden walls and ceilings, and are equipped with comfortable beds, a sofa and a kitchenette, which can really bring down the costs around here.

La Princesa de la Isla HOTEL $$$
(☎8854-2403; www.laprincesadelaisla.com; Waula Point; r/bungalows US$55/70) Set behind thick coral walls are a handful of large wooden bungalows and cheaper but spacious and attractive wooden rooms. All come with indoor-outdoor bathrooms, hammocks and sea views. There is also a large communal lounge

area with a great sun deck up top. The Italian owners make tremendous coffee and outstanding pastas (US$8) and three-course meals (US$25). Nonguests can eat here if they call in advance to make a reservation.

El Paraíso HOTEL **$$$**
(2575-5111; www.paraisoclub.com; Waula Point; cabañas s/d US$45/60, with fan US$35/50, bungalow d/tr US$70/80;) With a lively bar-restaurant and half a dozen attractive thatched duplexes, where hammocks are strung on mosaic and stone verandas scattered beneath the coconut palms, this is a popular midrange choice. There is one cheaper room without air-con.

★**Arenas Beach Resort** HOTEL **$$$**
(2575-5223; www.arenasbeachhotel.com; Southwest Bay; s/d US$77/104, ste s/d US$97/129;) Corn Island's most professionally managed resort. Choose from colorful wooden bungalows with sea views, or modern rooms with fantastic bathrooms (and hairdryers!) in the main building. The white-sand beach comes raked and dotted with cushy lounge chairs.

Martha's Bed & Breakfast HOTEL **$$$**
(8835-5884, 8835-5930; Southwest Bay; s/d incl breakfast US$45/57;) Tucked into the coconut palms at the end of the beach is this bright family-owned B&B. Rooms have newly tiled baths, cute paint jobs and cable TV.

Casa Canada HOTEL **$$$**
(2575 5878, 8644-0925; www.casa-canada.com; South End; r/cabañas US$99/139;) The resort unfurls amid tropical flower gardens on the rocks just above the sea. Long Bay glows to the south, palms sway above and waves crash endlessly. The rooms are just OK, but the huge, dark-wood *cabañas* with soaring ceilings, Spanish-tiled floor, ceiling fan, leather sofa and queen-sized bed are fabulous.

Sea Star Spa RESORT **$$$**
(8901-2410; www.seastarspa.net; Long Bay; ste per night US$150;) A work in progress at the time of writing, this elegant place on Long Bay promises to lift the luxury bar on the island. It offers spacious suites with 4m sliding glass doors, sofas, plasma screens and water views from the king-sized beds. The rooftop lounge is spectacular. It's all class – except for the monkey on a rope.

Eating

Most of the hotels listed also have restaurants.

South End Pulpería BAKERY **$**
(South End; items US$0.50-1; 8am-9pm) It sells fresh-baked coconut loaves and soda cakes. The bread comes out steaming at 4pm.

Doña Lola SEAFOOD **$$**
(8519-4332; btwn South End & Sally Peachie; mains US$6-12.50; noon-10pm) Perched on an isolated point on the east side of the island, this colorful and airy restaurant serves up delicious plates that you won't find on the seemingly photocopied menus of other local establishments. Try the *mofongo* – garlic-infused mashed plantains topped with seafood. It also has some great-value rooms upstairs.

Comedería Mari SEAFOOD **$$**
(8650-6811; Sally Peachie; mains US$7.50-10.50; noon-9pm) Eat at your Corn Island mom's house. You will sit right outside the mother chef's home, under the palms with a cricket serenade, and taste kingfish braised in tomato sauce, shrimp sautéed in garlic, and lobster *al gusto* (to your liking). She makes *rundown* upon request. Order it a day in advance.

Fisher's Cave SEAFOOD **$$**
(2575-1191; contiguo Muelle, Brig Bay; mains US$5-16; 7am-11pm) It's no wonder that this is the locals' preferred fish house. It's bright and clean, with tablecloths and wooden furniture, and great views of the action around the dock. The seafood soup is tasty when you mix in a dollop of the scalding chili sauce and wash it down with an icy Toña.

Seva's SEAFOOD **$$**
(Sally Peachie; dishes US$6.50-10-50; 7am-10pm) Lobster, shrimp and fish come grilled, garlic sautéed, fried and smothered in tomato sauce. It's served with ice-cold beers on the concrete porch or inside the dining room humming with fantastic reggae music. The food is just OK, but the ambience makes up for it.

Picnic Center NICARAGUAN **$$**
(Southwest Bay; dishes US$8-15; 8am-10pm) The first resort on the island is quickly losing its canary yellow, screened-porch luster, but its thatched pagodas set on a magnificent stretch of sand remain great spots to eat shrimp and lobster in coconut sauce and bob your head to reggae tunes.

Drinking & Nightlife

★Nico's BAR

(South End; ⏲noon-2am Thu-Sun) Part lobster cooperative, part rocking bar, Nico's is a truly authentic island experience. It's basically a warehouse by the water's edge with a couple of fridges and a booming sound system. It's no longer the wildly popular spot it once was, but it's still great for a beer. The biggest party is the Sunday session.

Island Style BAR

(Long Bay; ⏲10am-10pm) The only bar and restaurant on Long Bay is the barefoot, palm-thatched variety. It draws its biggest crowds on Sunday afternoons for a soulful reggae jam after the baseball games.

Bambule CLUB

(South End; ⏲9pm-3am Thu-Sun) Corn Island's hottest disco is an indoor/outdoor affair right by the water. There is a small dance floor with thumping dancehall music, but most hipsters just hang around outside. It's down a dark, bumpy road in South End – take a taxi.

Entertainment

Estadio Municipal Karen Tucker BASEBALL

(admission US$1-2) This large, well-manicured ballpark with cinderblock walls hosts regular games on Saturday and Sunday, weather permitting.

Information

There is only one ATM on Great Corn Island and it does run out of money occasionally, so you should still plan ahead and carry ample cash. Few businesses on the islands accept credit cards (although more expensive hotels do accept plastic).

BanPro (Brig Bay) ATM and currency conversion available on the main road, just southwest of the airport.

DRINKING WATER

Tap water on the Atlantic Coast generally comes from wells or rainwater collection tanks and is usually untreated. Often it is potable, but it may also contain bacteria; bring water-purification tablets if you don't want to take the risk. Bottled water is widely available and some hotels offer filtered water refills.

Big Corn Island (www.bigcornisland.com) Good English-language website with tips, listings and links for Great Corn.

Cyber Miss Normis (frente Muelle; per hour US$1; ⏲8am-8pm Mon-Fri, to noon Sat) Most reliable internet access.

Dr David Somarriba (☎8355-3140; Aeropuerto, 150m S) He's not cheap, but if you are sick or hurt, this fine doctor will make a hotel house call.

Hospital (Alcaldía, 500m E) This 24-hour public clinic offers emergency services.

Lonely Planet (www.lonelyplanet.com/nicaragua/caribbean-coast/corn-islands) For planning advice, author recommendations, traveler reviews and insider tips.

Police (☎8702-8780; Brig Bay)

Tourist Office (shereleeivel@gmail.com; contiguo estadio; ⏲8am-4pm Mon-Fri) At the time of writing a new tourist kiosk was under construction at the pier, but if it's closed, swing by this friendly office inside the Culture House.

Getting There & Away

Great Corn's small airport is served by La Costeña, which runs flights to Bluefields (one way/return US$64/99, 20 minutes), with continuing service to Managua (one way/return US$107/164, 70 minutes) at 8am and 4:10pm.

Several regular boats make the five- to six-hour trip to Bluefields via El Bluff. The government-run *Rio Escondido* (US$10) leaves on Thursday at 9am. More comfortable is the *Captain D* (seat/bunk US$10/12), a large cargo ship that leaves at 11pm on Saturday. It also runs once a month from Corn Island to Bilwi (US$22, 10 hours), usually leaving Thursday in the evening.

There are a number of other less-comfortable cargo boats that make the Bluefields run and there is usually always at least one departure on Sunday nights. Bring a hammock or you will be trying to get comfortable on the cold steel deck.

Getting Around

Taxis cost US$0.65 per person (US$0.85 at night) to anywhere on the island. During the day, there is one bus (US$0.20) that continuously runs the circuit, but you might wait a while until it passes.

Rentals are a great way to explore the island. Casa Canada rents bicycles for US$3 per hour. **Corn Island Car Rental** (☎8643-9881, 2575-5222; cornislandcarentals@hotmail.com) offers motorbike (US$45 to US$50 per day) and golf-cart (US$45 to US$55 per day) rentals. **Sweet Little Rock Rentals** (☎8942-1605; South End) has scooters for US$30 per day.

Little Corn Island

POP 500

This jade *isleta* is a dreamy escape with imaginative bungalow properties encamped on otherwise virgin beaches. Even if cars were allowed (which they aren't), they wouldn't be able to maneuver the thin concrete and muddy jungle paths that wind beneath the mango, coconut and breadfruit trees, and into the thick forest that buffers the northern and eastern coasts. The northern end of the island is the most secluded, has the best beaches and is the perfect setting for your Crusoe homage. Locals live, drink, dine, shoot pool and dance in the Village, which is set on a serene harbor sheltered from the north winds. The rugged, windy eastern coast makes for a transcendent afternoon of beachcombing: gorgeous white-sand beaches are framed by boulders, driftwood, headlands and coconut groves.

Sights

The island's best and most picturesque beaches are on opposite ends of the island. From Casa Iguana you can stroll south along the windward shore, scramble over the rocks and arrive on **Big Fowl House Beach**, then **Jimmy Lever Beach**. Or walk 20 minutes north from the Village through the jungle to **Otto Beach**. Then navigate the rugged northern shore until you find the spectacular **Goat Beach**, framed by two headlands.

On the way back, don't forget to climb the **lighthouse**, a steel tower jutting 6m above the mango trees, where you can glimpse the island's curves and coves, and catch an outrageous sunset.

Activities

There is great snorkeling on the east and north sides of the island. Many hotels in these areas rent snorkeling gear, as do the dive shops. If you want a guide, ask in the village for **Alfonso** (☎8434-2520; School, 300m N), who runs tours in his boat (US$20 per person) and also organizes fishing trips (US$40 per person).

Dolphin Dive DIVING
(☎8917-9717; www.dolphindivelittlecorn.com; 1/10 dives US$35/280; ⏲8am-6pm) Professional yet laid-back, this locally owned dive shop has good equipment and experienced instructors that really know these reefs. They visit over 20 different sites, and offer open-water (US$305), rescue-diver (US$230) and advanced open-water (US$240) courses. They also rent snorkel gear for US$5 per day.

Dive Little Corn DIVING
(☎8856-5888; www.divelittlecorn.net; Village; 1/10 dives US$35/280; ⏲8am-6pm) Little Corn's original dive shop is owned and managed by Casa Iguana and provides a high level of service. It offers open-water (US$309) and advanced open-water courses (US$249).

Kite Little Corn KITESURFING
(www.kitelittlecorn.com; inside Dolphin Dive; ⏲8am-6pm) Soar over the turquoise waters of Little Island with this new kitesurfing school run by Nacho, an affable Spaniard who is passionate about the sport. Located inside Dolphin Dive, it offers two-day intensive courses (US$270) and group tuition (US$30 per hour).

Sleeping & Eating

You can stay either in the Village, which is convenient and offers the most restaurant and nightlife options, or in one of the more secluded slices of paradise. Most businesses have signs in the Village telling you which path to take.

Village

Three Brothers GUESTHOUSE $
(☎8658-8736; Escuela, 50m S; s/d/tr US$12/15/25, r without bathroom US$10) A favorite among budget travelers, this guesthouse in the middle of the Village is run by the extremely laid-back Randy and has a communal, hostel-like vibe. It offers bright, simple rooms with big screened windows and self-caterers will dig the spacious guest kitchen.

Lobster Inn HOTEL $
(☎8847-1736; r with/without TV US$20/15) Sit back in the rocking chairs and admire the sea views from the balcony of this sweet hotel safe in the knowledge that you've snagged one of the best-value rooms on the island. Shoot for one of those at the front.

Hotel Los Delfines HOTEL $$
(☎8892-0186; s/d/tr US$40/50/60; ❄) These tiled bungalows scattered among the citrus trees could do with an overhaul, but if you desire air-con, hot water and cable TV, you'll find it here. Plus, it's locally owned and you can negotiate low-season discounts.

Sweet Oasis NICARAGUAN $$
(snacks US$1.80-4.20, meals US$6-8.50; ⏲7am-10pm; 📶) Sit in small kiosks or at the bar and tuck into tasty, if a little greasy, lobster, fish,

Little Corn Island

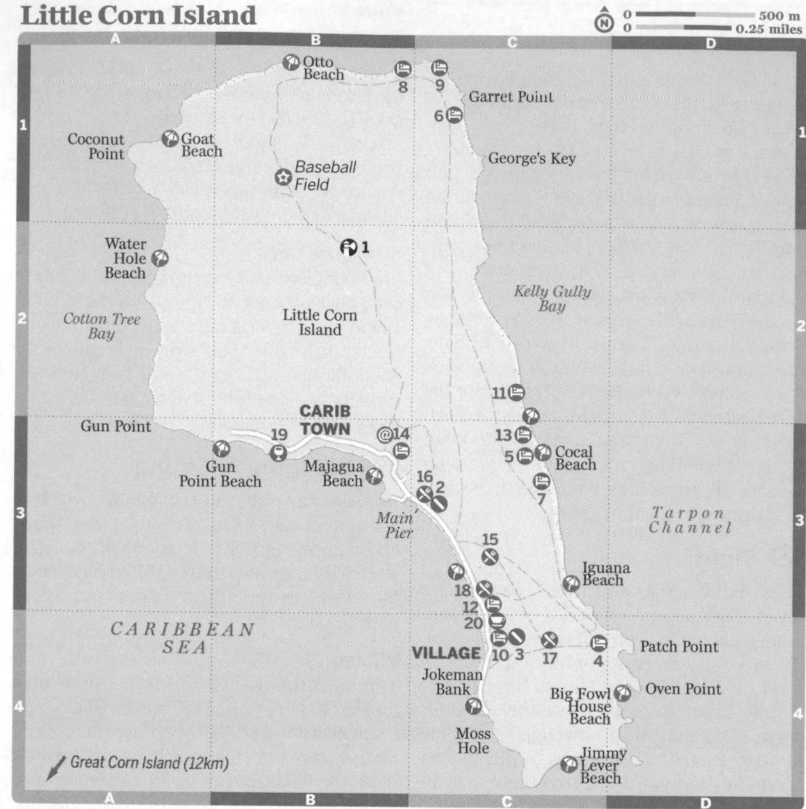

shrimp or chicken dishes at this popular pathside diner. There is also a snack menu including quesadillas, tacos and *fritos*.

Comedor Bridget NICARAGUAN $$
(☎8437-7295; meals US$7-8.50; ⏰7am-10pm) Order the superb salt-dusted, lightly fried fish at this local joint behind Dive Little Corn. It also serves great-value lobster, shrimp and fried-chicken dishes. If the music gets loud inside, pull up a chair on the large porch instead.

★**Habana Libre** CUBAN $$$
(☎2572-9086; mains US$10-14; ⏰noon-10pm) Long considered the Corn Islands' best restaurant, this Cuban-run kitchen serves up outstanding plates of fish, shrimp, roast pork and *ropa vieja* (a Cuban shredded-beef delicacy) in a swank dining patio. But the absolute star of the show is the lobster in jalapeño sauce – don't leave the island without trying it.

There's also Cohiba cigars and Cuban rum if you really want to live it up.

Garret Point

The northeastern corner of the island has a cluster of midrange accommodations, one of Little Corn's most beautiful beaches and great snorkeling just offshore. It's a solid 25-minute hike from the Village, which is a bit of a mission in the dark. All of these accommodations serve meals.

Ensueños BUNGALOW $$
(www.ensuenos-littlecornisland.com; cabañas without bathroom US$25, casas US$45-70) Surrounded by forest and fruit orchards, and perched on a golden crescent of sand and a sheltered turquoise cove, are three rustic candlelit *cabañas* made from rocks and driftwood and three delightful wind- and solar-powered *casas* with small kitchens.

It is run by Ramón, a Spanish artist/naturalist/bohemian madman (and we mean

Little Corn Island

Sights

1 Lighthouse B2

Activities, Courses & Tours

2 Dive Little Corn C3
3 Dolphin Dive C4
Kite Little Corn (see 3)

Sleeping

4 Casa Iguana C4
5 Cool Spot C3
6 Derek's Place C1
7 Elsa's Place C3
8 Ensueños B1
9 Farm Peace & Love C1
10 Hotel Los Delfines C4
11 Little Corn Beach and Bungalow C2
12 Lobster Inn C3
13 Sunrise Paradise C3
14 Three Brothers B3

Eating

15 Comedor Bridget C3
16 Habana Libre C3
17 Rose's C4
18 Sweet Oasis C3

Drinking & Nightlife

19 Aguila's B3
20 Tranquilo Cafe C4

that in the best way). If you come, Ramon has but one request: don't ask too many questions. Just go with the flow.

Derek's Place BUNGALOW **$$$**
(www.dereksplacelittlecorn.com; cabañas US$55-95) The funkiest beach bungalows on the island are found sprinkled over a lovely grassy promontory covered with coconut palms. The *cabañas* are thatched, geometrically inspired and fashioned from bamboo, wood, old bottles, recycled shipping line and other natural materials. There's dedicated hammock space, snorkel gear for rent and a small, friendly dive shop on-site.

Farm Peace & Love FARM **$$$**
(☎8847-9786; www.farmpeacelove.com; apt US$75-90) Set back from a gorgeous sheltered cove and nestled in the palms is this farm with just two accommodation options. The smaller one is joined to the main farmhouse and has one bedroom (but two beds) and a kitchenette, while the larger is a traditional white house with a kitchen and rockers on the front porch.

Cocal & Iguana Beaches

This side of the island gets a constant breeze which keeps the mosquitoes at bay. Budget travelers should head to Cocal Beach where there are several similar places side by side. Take a walk and see which of them appeals. Accommodations here are more basic, but with a beach like this on your doorstep, you won't be spending much time inside.

Elsa's Place BEACH HUT **$$**
(☎8437-5210, 2575-5014; r US$25-40, without bathroom US$12-20) Miss Elsa sticks to a winning formula: cheap, comfortable rooms right by the water. There are a variety of thatched wooden bungalows with private bathrooms and some basic cheapies out the back.

Cool Spot BEACH HUT **$$**
(Grace's Place; ☎8617-4491; r US$25, without bathroom US$10) This rocking backpacker haunt was destroyed by fire just after we passed through, but at press time rebuilding work was already underway. The location is fantastic and if it's anything like the last version, the new place is sure to have a great social vibe.

Sunrise Paradise BEACH HUT **$$**
(Carlito's Place; ☎8461-7395, 2570-0432; www.carlitosplacelittlecorn.com; huts US$30-40, apt US$60-80) A little quieter than its neighbors, Carlito's features spartan cabins right on the beach with firm beds and little porches that are kept cool by ocean-facing windows. The beach is cleaned regularly and the fine restaurant prepares some great juicy fried chicken, but the rooms are a little pricey for what you get.

Little Corn Beach and Bungalow BUNGALOW **$$$**
(☎8333-0956; www.littlecornbb.com; r U$89-129, without bathroom US$40; 📶) The most upmarket place on Cocal Beach has elegantly furnished bungalows with big doors opening onto a hammock-strewn beach with plenty of coconut palms. The downside: the rooms are fairly close together, detracting from any castaway fantasies. Even if you don't stay, make sure to eat at the restaurant, which prepares outstanding gourmet meals (US$9 to US$16).

Casa Iguana LODGE **$$$**
(www.casaiguana.net; s/d cabañas US$30/35, casitas US$60-85) This gathering of colorful wooden *cabañas* (smaller, with shared bathrooms) and *casitas* (larger, with private bathrooms) arranged on a rocky cliff

just above the beach is hugely popular. The location and views are tremendous and the restaurant serves first-class fare; however, the reliance on an endless stream of young expat workers doesn't give the place much local flavor.

Rose's NICARAGUAN, VEGETARIAN **$$**
(meals US$4-8.50; ⌚6:30am-9:30pm) This humble *comedor* on the trail to town has vegetarian pastas and coconut curries, as well as other dishes you won't find elsewhere.

Drinking & Nightlife

Tranquilo Cafe CAFE
(⌚8am-late; 📶) Feeling homesick? Head to this hip open-air cafe for great burgers, buffalo wings and bruschetta with an indie-rock soundtrack. It's popular among travelers for an evening drink and hosts bonfire parties.

Aguila's BAR
(⌚11am-1am) Little Corn Island's most popular after-hours hangout. The sweaty pool hall is a hotbed of hustling and competition, and the music thumps in the open-air dancehall just above the beach.

Information

A number of restaurants and hotels around the island have wi-fi and laptops for use by clients.

Little Island Radio (internet per hour US$1.25; ⌚noon-9pm) Tune in to Little Corn's community radio station (88.1 FM) for plenty of classic reggae or swing by to use the internet cafe.

Getting There & Around

Little Corn is only about 1.5 sq km. You can walk end to end in an hour. Which is just as well, because the only wheels on the island's jungle trails belong to wheelbarrows.

Collective *pangas* to Little Corn (US$6, 40 minutes) leave from the pier on Great Corn at 10am and 4:30pm; if you're staying on the northern end of Little Corn, you should take the morning boat. Boats leave Little Corn at 7am and 1:30pm from the main pier. If you're taking the morning flight to Managua, you need to travel the day before. It can get very rough and you may get soaked. Bring garbage bags to cover your luggage. For a smoother ride, it's possible to ride on the large cargo ships (US$2 to US$3, 1¼ hours) that supply the *islita*, but there are only a handful of departures each week.

San Carlos, Islas Solentiname & the Río San Juan

Includes ➡

Best Wildlife-Spotting

- Río Papaturro (p251)
- Aguas Frescas (p256)
- Islas Solentiname (p247)
- Río Indio (p257)
- San Miguelito (p246)

Best Places to Stay

- Sábalos Lodge (p253)
- Hotel La Comunidad (p249)
- Río Indio Lodge (p258)
- Refugio Bartola (p256)
- Hotel Sábalos (p253)

Why Go?

You could roam the globe for decades and it would be tough to top what you are about to experience here. This is a place where an enlightened priest once mingled with transcendent artists on forgotten island utopias. Where the beautiful teenage daughter of a Spanish conquistador stared down an on-rushing armada of British pirates. It's a haven for migratory birds, ranchers and fishermen where the monkeys howl, alligators cruise the black water, and enormous 500-year-old trees bangled in delicate orchids shelter fluorescent fingernail-sized tree frogs and carnivorous jaguars under one canopy.

It's also a place thousands of travelers simply pass through on their way to Costa Rica, ignoring the sweet Archipiélago de Solentiname, mythic Río San Juan and spectacular Reserva Biológica Indio-Maíz. Huge mistake. Spend some time and money. Explore. Take it all in. These are the places you imagined when you booked your ticket. This is why you travel.

When to Go

Dry season in the Rio San Juan runs from February to April with more sunshine and shrinking pools of water concentrating migratory waterfowl in Los Guatuzos. From mid-September to October it's possible to hook huge tarpon in the Caribbean Sea at the mouth of the Río Indio and there is the best bird-watching around San Miguelito. And in November, dancers and artists from all over the country descend on San Carlos for the Río San Juan's biggest party – the Carnival Acuático.

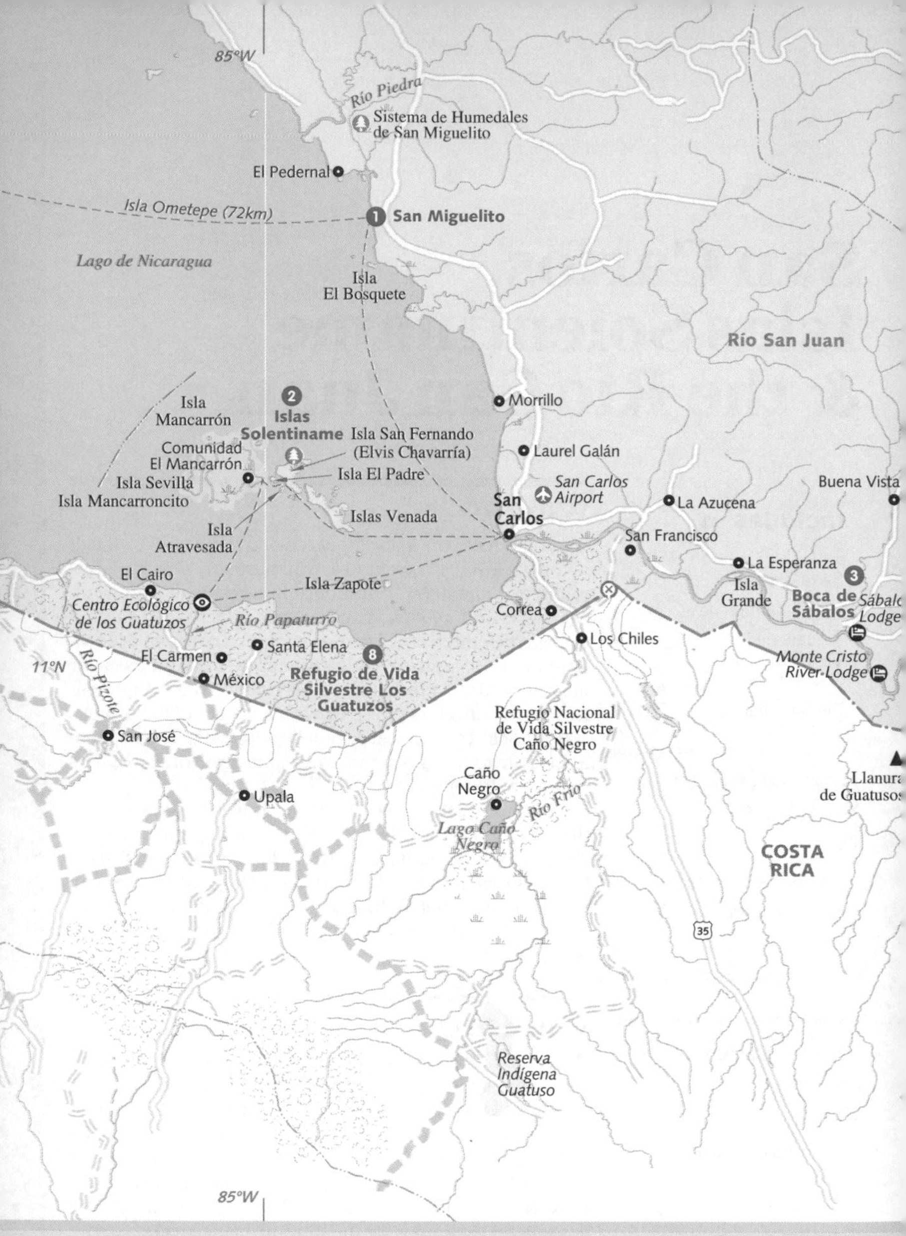

San Carlos, Islas Solentiname & the Río San Juan Highlights

1 Spot migratory birds on a tour through the wetlands and humid forests of **San Miguelito** (p246)

2 Hike, swim and stargaze in the peaceful **Islas Solentiname** (p247)

3 Dine on sweet and giant shrimp on a riverside balcony in **Boca de Sábalos** (p252)

4 Scale the imposing Spanish fortress in **El Castillo** (p254)

5 Trek through the spectacular **Reserva Biológica Indio-Maíz** (p256) beneath 500-year-old orchid-jeweled giants

6 Explore hidden, jungled lagoons by boat in **San Juan de Nicaragua** (p257)

7 Troll for tarpon in the mighty **Río San Juan** (p251)

8 Spot alligators in the **Refugio de Vida Silvestre Los Guatuzos** (p251) wetlands

History

Almost as soon as Columbus happened upon Nicaragua in 1502, the search was on for a passage that would link the Atlantic to the Pacific Ocean. In 1529 the Spanish finally navigated the rapids and reached the mouth of the river at the Caribbean Sea, where they established San Juan de las Perlas in 1539.

In the 17th and 18th centuries Granada was growing wealthier by the year, which attracted unwanted attention from English, French and Dutch pirates, who sacked the city three times in five years. A series of forts, including one in San Carlos and another in El Castillo, were built along the river and lake to ward them off.

When the gold fever took hold in North America in the 1800s, the Río San Juan became part of the fastest route between New York and San Francisco. American Cornelius Vanderbilt's ships sailed from New York to New Orleans and then steamed down to Greytown before continuing upriver to Lago de Nicaragua, where voyagers traveled overland to an awaiting steamship on the Pacific.

After the Panama Canal was built in 1914, dashing hopes for a local version, Greytown (by then reincorporated into Nicaragua as San Juan del Norte) reverted to a sleepy outpost at the end of a rarely transited jungle river.

SAN CARLOS

POP 12,200

The capital of the isolated Río San Juan department is the gateway to some of Nicaragua's most compelling countryside but is itself a curious place with a bit of an identity crisis. During the day it is a busy international port filled with herds of travelers in transit, which explains the bustling and festive *malecón* (waterfront) lined with restaurants. But when night falls, and the magnificent views disappear with the setting sun, it reverts to a rather lackluster small town where gossiping is the main form of entertainment.

Most travelers burn their San Carlos hours by exploring the old Spanish fortress, planning river and island adventures, stocking up on córdoba and checking emails one last time before they drop off-grid for a while.

Sights & Activities

San Carlos is less a tourist destination and more a place to wait for your ship, or *panga* (small motorboat), to come in, but there is beauty here – particularly on the grounds of **Centro Cultural Jose Coronel Urtecho**, which is set within the crumbling walls of **Fortaleza de San Carlos** (9am-5pm) FREE. It's no El Castillo, but it was built in 1724 and has amazing lake and Río San Juan views from several lookout points linked by garden trails. The cultural center has some interesting displays on local culture, biology and history. It even has a map of the Nicaraguan canal that never was, c 1791. There's another old **Spanish observation post**, with cannons, at Restaurant Mirador.

Festivals & Events

Carnival Acuático DANCE, FOOD

(Nov) The Río San Juańs biggest party features a colorful river parade, concerts and food festival on the *malecón*.

Sleeping

Hospedaje Peña GUESTHOUSE $

(2583-0298; Parque Central, 1c S; r per person without bathroom US$3) Don't expect many frills (or toilet seats) in this original San Carlos flophouse, but it's cheap and just a block from the *malecón*. The rooms are tiny wooden boxes but some have windows with river views.

Gran Lago Hotel HOTEL $$

(2583-0075; Parque Central, 1c O, 1c S; s/d incl breakfast US$35/40;) The four air-con rooms here are clean and comfortable but don't take advantage of the great lakeside location. However, the small rear deck offers great views across to the Archipiélago de Solentiname and a second floor under construction at the time of research is set to offer rooms with more natural light.

Hotel-Cabinas Leyko HOTEL $$

(2583-0354; leykou7@yahoo.es; Parque Central, 2c O; d with air-con US$50-65, without air-con US$20-24, all incl breakfast; P) The comfy wooden air-con rooms overlooking the wetlands at the rear of the hotel are a little overpriced but are the most charming accommodations in San Carlos. Avoid the dingy cheaper rooms above reception. The friendly owners speak English and arrange tours.

San Carlos

Hotel Carelhys HOTEL **$$**
(☎2583-0389; Parque Central, ½c S; r with/without air-con US$30/15) This budget favorite half-a-block from parque central has a selection of slightly shabby rooms with cable TV and private bathroom.

Eating & Drinking

The cheapest eats in town are at the cluster of bus-terminal *comedores* (basic eateries), the best of which is **Comedor Alondra** (meals US$2.50).

Soda La Fortaleza CAFE **$**
(Malecón; meals US$2-6; ⏲6am-10pm) This lively spot on the lakefront serves up filling breakfasts and cheap, tasty Nica dishes. In the evening it's a fantastic place from which to observe the frenetic football games, canoodling couples and dedicated drinkers on the *malecón.*

Parador Berlin BISTRO **$$**
(Mercado, 300m N; pizzas US$4-8, mains US$6-9; ⏲11am-10pm) Pull up a table under the whirring ceiling fans and tuck into the best European food in Río San Juan with excellent pizzas and great schnitzels all accompanied by a hip electronic soundtrack. A top choice before hitting the endless plates of *comida corriente* (a mixed plate of typical regional foods) downriver.

San Carlos

Sights
1 Fortaleza de San Carlos....B2

Sleeping
2 Gran Lago Hotel....A3
3 Hospedaje Peña....B3
4 Hotel Carelhys....B2
5 Hotel-Cabinas Leyko....A1

Eating
6 Comedor Alondra....C1
7 Restaurant Mirador....B3
8 Restaurante Kaoma....B3
9 Soda La Fortaleza....B3

Restaurante Kaoma NICARAGUAN **$$**
(☎2583-0293; Parque Central, 1½c S; mains US$7-11; ⏲8am-midnight) A beautiful terrace restaurant with old wooden floors, beamed ceilings and massive lake views. The extensive menu includes tender beef dishes and fish which comes sautéed in a buttery garlic sauce or stuffed with shrimp.

Restaurant Mirador NICARAGUAN $$
(Parque Central, 1½c S; mains US$5-7; ⌚11am-10pm) This sweet dining spot on the lake bluffs has a stone wall fringed with antique Spanish cannons. Tasty seafood is served on the breezy patio.

Information

Banpro (Malecón) ATM inside the second pavilion on the *malecón*.

Correos de Nicaragua (Post Office; ⌚8am-2pm)

Hospital Felipe Moncada (☎2583-0244) About 1km north of town.

Intur (☎2583-0301; riosanjuan@intur.gob.ni; contiguo a Migración; ⌚8am-1pm) Not visitor focused but offers some basic travel advice.

Marena (☎2583-0296; ⌚8am-1pm) Processes fishing licenses, technically required for all fishing on the Río San Juan, but unless you are in your own boat your captain/tour operator should organize these.

Police (☎2583-0397)

Telecentro (Parque Central; per hr US$0.40; ⌚8am-5:30pm Mon-Fri)

Getting There & Around

San Carlos is no longer the isolated corner of Nicaragua it once was thanks to the construction of a new smooth tarred road to Juigalpa. The highway still receives little traffic, but that is likely to change once the new bridge over the Río San Juan at Santa Fe is completed, linking the region by road with Las Tablillas in Costa Rica.

AIR

The San Carlos airport is a 3km, US$1 cab ride from downtown San Carlos. Buy tickets from **La Costeña** (☎2583-0048; frente Cementerio; ⌚8am-noon & 3-5pm) for flights from San Carlos and San Juan de Nicaragua. The compact, 12-seat planes leave for Managua (one way/return US$76/116, 45 minutes) at 2pm.

BOAT

Collective riverboat services to Boca de Sábalos (US$3.10, 2¼ hr) and El Castillo (US$3.40, 3½ hr) leave from the **Muelle Municipal** (Municipal Dock), half a block west of the mercado (market), at 8am, noon, 2:30pm and 3:30pm Monday through Saturday; 8am and 1:30pm on Sunday. Express boats to Sábalos (US$4.75, one hour) and El Castillo (US$5.70, 1½ hours) leave at 6:30am and 10am.

The government-run ferry leaves from the Muelle Municipal at 2pm Tuesday and Friday for San Miguelito (US$3, two to three hours), Altagracia (Isla de Ometepe; US$6.50, nine hours) and Granada (US$9.50, 12 to 14 hours). Stake out a sleeping spot early, bring extra layers, and don't forget your hammock or you may be sleeping on the cold, hard deck. The ferry returns from Granada at 2pm Monday and Thursday, stopping at the same ports and arriving in San Carlos at sunrise.

BUS

Buses leave from the **bus terminal** in San Carlos for the following destinations:

El Rama (US$6.50, seven hours, 9am)

Juigalpa (US$4, four hours, 10am, 11am, 12:40pm and 1:30pm)

Managua (US$6.50, six hours, eight daily)

San Miguelito (US$2, two to four hours) Direct buses leave at 12:20pm and 1pm, but you can hop on any Managua- or Juigalpa-bound bus and get off at the San Miguelito turnoff.

San Miguelito

Most travelers miss this mellow lakeside fishing community and gateway to the region's newest and least-visited reserve, the **Sistema de Humedales de San Miguelito** (San Miguelito Wetlands). A handful of rivers meander through the reserve, including the Río Tepenaguazapa, the Río Camastro, the Río Tule and the gorgeous Río Piedra, a glassy slice of black water framed by a dense tangle of jungle. Trees, hip-deep in water and sprouting with orchids and bromeliads in the canopy, stretch back as far as you can see. Occasionally the grasslands and lotus fields teeming with birds and butterflies intervene. The best time for bird-watching is at daybreak or dusk in September and October, when the migration peaks. If you're lucky, you may even see some alligators.

Hotel Cocibolca (☎2583-3260; hotelcocibolca@yahoo.com; frente Muelle; s/d/tr without bathroom US$6/12/18) is a fantastic budget choice with wooden rooms boasting high-beamed ceilings and French doors that open onto private balconies overlooking the lake. The staff arrange visits (US$20, four to six hours) to **Finca El Cacao**, a private family-run *finca* (farm), a 30-minute boat ride away where it's possible to observe iguanas, alligators and monkeys.

Getting There & Away

The most popular way to arrive in San Miguelito is on the boat from San Carlos or Altagracia in Isla de Ometepe, although the service from Ometepe arrives in the middle of the night. Direct buses to San Miguelito (US$2, two hours) leave San Carlos at 12.20pm and 1pm, but any San Carlos–Managua bus will drop you at the Empalme de San Miguelito, from where *colectivos* (shared taxis; US$1) make the 8km trip into town.

Islas Solentiname

POP 800 / ELEV 40M TO 250M

If you're the type who likes islands draped in jungle, surrounded by crystalline waters that reflect the forest, sun and sky, and populated by farmers and fishers who share their wealth and also happen to be terrific artists and craftsmen, you do not want to miss this oft-overlooked archipelago. And we haven't even mentioned the gators, monkeys, orchids and migratory waterfowl, the sensational offshore fishing, the mind-blowing sunsets and the spectacular starlight. Almost forgotten for 500 years, and nearly destroyed in a single day, the Archipiélago de Solentiname does not seem entirely of this world.

Getting There & Around

At the time of research, **Transol** (8555-4739, 8828-3243; www.transol.com.ni; 24hr) was running a new daily fast boat service (US$10, 90 minutes) between San Carlos and the islands, leaving San Carlos at 3pm and returning at 9am. However, the subsidies for the service were due to expire by the time this book goes to press; call ahead before planning your trip.

If the service is discontinued, you'll need either time or money to visit the archipelago. Slow and inexpensive public boats (US$4, two to three hours) run twice a week, leaving San Carlos at 1pm Tuesday and Friday, with stops at San Fernando and Mancarrón. They leave Mancarrón, stopping about 30 minutes later at San Fernando, at 4:30am Tuesday and Friday (US$4). If that doesn't work with your schedule, you can hire a private boat (seating at least six) for US$120 to US$150 between San Carlos and the islands.

Most visitors hire private *pangas* between the islands; it's at least US$20 round-trip between San Fernando and Mancarrón. A cheaper and more adventurous way to explore the archipelago is to paddle. Kayaks and canoes are available for rent on both Mancarrón and San Fernando.

Isla Mancarrón

This island feels small because residents, guests and commerce converge on a rather slender slice of land that includes the harbor and the village. But hike the muddy trails, which traverse these jungled hills, and you'll quickly notice that the island is deceptively large, sprawling into the azure lake and forming a succession of sheltered coves. The extreme western end seeps into an 800m-long stretch of wetlands that nurture fish and turtle hatcheries and are teeming with migratory waterfowl.

Internet access is available for a small fee in the **Biblioteca Ernesto Cardenal** (admission free; 8am-noon & 1-5pm Mon-Sat). This is the only public internet access in the archipelago.

BORDER CROSSING: TO LOS CHILES, COSTA RICA

The lush Río Frio in the Refugio de Vida Silvestre Los Guatuzos is one of the most scenic border crossings in Central America and the Río San Juan region's sole legal portal to Costa Rica. All this will change when the new Japanese-funded bridge over the Río San Juan at Santa Fe is completed, linking the department by road with Las Tablillas in Costa Rica, but until then, this is your only option. Not that you should complain, this laid-back crossing is really just a delightful river cruise through stunning wetlands.

Begin at friendly **San Carlos Immigration** (2583-0263; Malecón; 8am-5pm), 1½ blocks from the Muelle Municipal (Municipal Dock), where you'll have your passport stamped before being ushered onto collective boats (US$10, two hours, 10:30am, 1pm and 4pm Monday to Saturday, 12:30pm and 4pm Sunday), which leave from the dock behind Immigration. Come at least half-an-hour before your departure to complete immigration formalities.

It costs US$12 to enter Nicaragua, US$2 to exit. Entering or leaving Costa Rica is free. When you arrive in Los Chiles, go to customs, opposite the dock, to have your bags searched, then another building about two blocks away to have your passport stamped. Buses leave from the bus terminal, about five blocks east of the dock, to San José and Refugio Nacional de Vida Silvestre Caño Negro

For further information, head to shop.lonelyplanet.com to purchase a downloadable PDF of the Northwestern Costa Rica chapter from Lonely Planet's *Costa Rica* guide.

ERNESTO CARDENAL & REVOLUTIONARY CULTURE

As a poet, his subject matter ranges from theoretical physics to Marilyn Monroe; as a sculptor, from the creatures of the jungle to the life of Christ. A Trappist monk originally committed to nonviolence, Ernesto Cardenal (see www.ernestocardenal.org, in Spanish) came to fully support the Sandinista-led revolution, by any means necessary. He was Nicaragua's original liberation theologian, the revolutionary government's Minister of Culture, but has since fallen out with his former bosses.

When Cardenal arrived in Solentiname in 1966, he found a community all but forgotten by the modern world, impoverished and poorly educated, but where a special wisdom had been born. Cardenal helped erect the islands' first simple adobe church, where he gave Mass. Here, the people of Solentiname interpreted the scripture through their own eyes and lives, a living word of Christ, which Cardenal recorded and published as *El Evangelio de Solentiname* (Gospel of Solentiname). It would later be rendered in song by legendary artist Carlos Mejía Godoy as *La Misa Campesina* (Peasants' Mass).

One day, a grateful islander named Eduardo Arana presented Cardenal with an elaborately decorated jícara shell, which impressed the priest into giving the young man paints and a canvas. Those first few paintings launched Nicaragua's Primitivist art movement, internationally recognized for the vibrant colors and expert lines that capture this tropical paradise. One artist, Ufredo Argüello, began applying the same saturation of color to balsa-wood carvings, which also caught on.

Throughout the late 1960s and early 1970s, families worked together painting and sculpting, sending their work to market in Managua. There, trouble was brewing, and even this peaceful haven could not isolate itself. In October 1977, inspired by Cardenal, the islands rebelled; retribution by the Guardia Nacional was swift and complete. Solentiname was abandoned and Cardenal was denounced as an outlaw.

When the Sandinistas took power in 1979, however, they appointed Cardenal Minister of Culture, a position he used for almost a decade to successfully preserve and enrich Nicaraguan arts and folklore. These days he's even fallen out of favor with the Sandinistas, after he criticized front man Daniel Ortega's 'Stalinist' control of the party, but at 88, he still works and travels. And when he grows tired of his wandering, this is where he returns. Islanders point out the tidy wooden house with pride, saying simply 'that's where Ernesto Cardenal comes to write.'

Sights

★Nuestra Señora de Solentiname CHURCH

(admission US$1) Mancarrón's greatest human-made gift is Nuestra Señora de Solentiname, where populist priest Ernesto Cardenal ran a rather enlightened parish. Constructed by the community in 1979, it features a beautiful whitewashed nave from within which you can still hear the lake, and feel the trees. The altar spares the usual golden idolatry and instead is graced with a colorful yet humble mural depicting life in the archipelago.

El Refugio VILLAGE

(Comunidad El Mancarrón) The highest concentration of craft workshops on the islands are just inland from the dock in Comunidad El Mancarrón (also called El Refugio). Feel free to wander and watch as families carve balsa-wood figures in their homes and front yards. Children sand the pieces smooth, and the most talented adult paints. Wooden animals cost US$1 to US$50; prices rise with size and quality.

Museo Arqueológico MUSEO

(admission US$1; 8am-noon & 1-5pm) Recently renovated, this polished museum up the hill from the church houses a small but intriguing collection of pre-Columbian metates, pottery and idols unearthed in the archipelago.

Activities

The flash new **Centro Información Turística** (9am-noon & 2-5pm) to the left of the dock is able to organize guides for local treks.

Alianza de Solentiname KAYAKING

(8983-7289; www.solentiname.org; entrada El Refugio; 8am-5pm) This nonprofit education initiative rents out kayaks at the bargain price of US$5 per day. All profits go to local projects. Guides are available for US$15 per day.

Conoce Solentiname TOUR
(☎8963-2845, 8869-6619; hostalbuenamigo@gmail.com; inside Hospedaje Buen Amigo; tours US$20-100; ⏲6am-8pm) Energetic tour operator that offers a great variety of natural and cultural activities including fishing, birdwatching in the wetlands, hikes to petroglyphs and trips to Los Guatuzos.

Sleeping & Eating

Hostal Buen Amigo GUESTHOUSE **$**
(☎8869-6619; hostalbuenamigo@gmail.com; El Refugio; r per person with/without bathroom US$10/6) This popular cheapie has several neat, freshly painted rooms set in a pleasant garden. You can order cheap meals at the *comedor/tienda* (basic eatery/small shop), which doubles as a popular local watering hole.

★**Hotel La Comunidad** GUESTHOUSE **$$**
(☎2277-3495, 8966-7056; contiguo Muelle; r per person with/without meals US$35/15) This pair of charming solar-powered wooden houses overlooking the bay is easily the best deal on Mancarrón with breezy hammock-strung balconies, spacious rooms and huge bathrooms with outdoor showers and bidets (no joke!). Hotel profits support the local school. If there is no-one around, ask for Doña Esperanza at the library.

Hotel Mancarrón HOTEL **$$**
(☎2270-9981; www.hotelmancarron.com; r per person with/without meals US$55/25) This rambling whitewashed hotel surrounded by tropical gardens on a hillside above the southern shore was the archipelago's first. The rooms are large and comfortable but fairly spare. The restaurant, however, is exceptional, serving tasty, inventive meals in a large screened dining room.

Isla San Fernando (Elvis Chavarría)

With even fewer people, tranquil San Fernando has comfortable accommodation, delicious meals, and the islands' only gallery and museum. But the biggest attraction is the San Fernando sunset. First the lake loses its color before reflecting the deep jungle green of the surrounding forests. Then the sky pales, streaks pink and burns gold behind the neighbouring islands. When it gets dark, expect a black dome sky full of stars.

Sights & Activities

Located at the main dock, the **Oficina de Turismo** (Tourist Office; solentinamecantur@yahoo.com; ⏲9am-5pm) is able to provide guides (US$15 per group) and recommend captains for boat tours.

Some small **galleries** and **workshops** are strung along the strand of homes between Musas and Albergue Celentiname.

The **Sendero El Trogón** is a 45-minute walking trail that passes some impressive petroglyphs and a lookout point. Pay US$5 admission at your hotel or the tourist office to use the trail. Albergue Celentiname (p249) rents two-man canoes (US$4 per hour) to explore the surroundings, while Hostal Vanessa (p250) organizes sportfishing trips (US$100 per day for up to three participants).

Union de Pintores y Artesanos de Solentiname 'Elvis Chavarría' GALLERY
(⏲8am-noon & 2-5pm) Set in an old mahogany house uphill from the sheltered dock, this cooperative features the work of about 50 of the islands' top artists and artisans. Affordable balsa sculptures are in one room, and higher-end paintings (US$50 to US$1000) are in the other. The view from here is incredible. If it's closed, ask for the key at Hotel Cabañas Paraiso.

Museo Archipiélago Solentiname MUSEUM
(Musas; admission US$2; ⏲7am-noon & 2-5pm) Follow the trail to the right of the dock uphill through the avocado grove, and you'll find this museum. The view and surrounding gardens alone are worth the hike. And inside you'll find terrific natural-history exhibits and cultural exhibits including a collection of pre-Columbian pots and pestles.

Sleeping & Eating

There are no dedicated restaurants on San Fernando. If your accommodation does not offer meals, you'll need to order in advance at one of the other hotels.

Albergue Celentiname GUESTHOUSE **$$**
(☎8893-1977, in Costa Rica 506-8500-2119; hotelcelentiname.blogspot.com; r per person incl 3 meals US$35) Tucked into a flowering garden that feels like something out of a tropical utopia is this secluded guesthouse, a gorgeous 10-minute walk from the main dock on the extreme northern end of the west -coast trail. Basic but neat wooden *cabañas* (cabins) come with two beds and a terrace with lake

and garden views. Some rooms are better than others, so ask to look around – the larger *cabaña* familiar is the one you want.

Hospedaje Mire Estrellas GUESTHOUSE **$$**
(☎8561-4943; r per person with/without bathroom US$12/10) With tidy wooden rooms right by the water's edge, this simple *hospedaje* is a fine budget choice. The laid-back owner offers cheap tours around the islands in his small boat.

Hostal Vanessa GUESTHOUSE **$$**
(☎8680-8423; jose.sequeirapineda@gmail.com; Muelle, 10m O; r per person with/without bathroom US$15/10) The wooden rooms with shared bathrooms by the path are a little cramped and noisy but the spacious new rooms with private bathrooms up on the hill offer fantastic views and are a great deal.

Hotel Cabañas Paraíso HOTEL **$$**
(☎8894-7331; hcp.nicaragua-info.com; s/d/tr US$30/45/60, r per person incl meals US$45) These modern, concrete rooms have wooden shutters and new shower tiles but are a little basic considering the price. And while the dining area is lovely with 180-degree lake views, the food does not measure up to the magnificent setting.

Isla Mancarroncito

Across a narrow strait from Mancarrón's western shore is this small, rocky jewel thick with the last stands of primary forest in the archipelago. **Loma San Antonio**, a 15m boulder, protrudes from a hill on the eastern shore. Local legend has it that *brujas* (witches – not the good kind) once lived in the caves at the top of the cliff, which may explain why the island is still so wild. You can come for the day and explore the trails, or you can stay the night at the **Estación Biológica**, a biological research station that offers basic lodging in its wooden cabin. Call **Fundación del Rio** (☎in San Carlos 2583-0035) in advance to arrange your stay.

Isla Venada (Isla Donald Guevara)

Meet the Aurellanos. Three generations of the archipelago's most renowned artists come from the jumble of wooden homes overlooking a gorgeous, glassy strait on the northwestern shore of this wooded island.

Rodolfo Aurellano was the trailblazer. His works are dreamy, colorful reflections of Isla Venada and the surrounding islands, Islas Rosita, Carolina and El Padre. Take some time to talk with the elderly, barefoot artist and he might tell you about how he used to have to hide deep in the bush to paint to avoid being identified as a revolutionary by Somozás forces. Well into his 70s, Rodolfo still paints regularly and maintains a small collection of works for sale (US$30 to US$1000).

Rodolfo's daughter and granddaughter, **Clarissa and Jeyselle Aurellano** (☎8815-1761), have followed his example. In addition to selling truly remarkable work, some of which tours art galleries internationally, they also rent out simple rooms in the family home (US$8 per person). Typical meals are also available (US$2.50) and guides (US$7 per day) can be arranged to explore the island on foot. Call in advance to let them know you are coming; they don't get many visitors.

A system of **caves** at the waterline honeycombs the island's northern shore and are only visible in the dry season. You'll need a boat to explore them and see the many petrolgyphs carved into their walls.

Isla Atravesada

Named because it's the only one oriented north–south, rather than east–west like the rest of the archipelago, Atravesada (meaning 'to cross') is famed for its enormous 5m alligators and rich bird life. Flocks of ives, with their crab-cracking beaks, congregate in the north-shore canopy alongside trees full of the dangling nests of the resident black cormorants. Look for tiny colondrines in the marsh at sunset.

Other Islands

There are at least 36 islands in the archipelago, many privately owned and most without much to interest the casual visitor.

You will hear the residents of **Isla El Padre** before you see them. Set between Mancarrón and San Fernando and named for yet another priest who long ago sought solitude in these tranquil waters, it's inhabited by a troupe of howler monkeys.

Isla Sevilla, just west of Mancarroncito, is a haven for bird-watchers, with thousands of cormorants, tiger herons and pelicans here to enjoy some excellent fishing.

Avid birders won't want to miss tiny **Islas Zapote** and **Zapotillo**, with Nicaragua's highest concentration of birds, most famously flocks of roseate spoonbills that nest in February and March. Migratory birds of all kinds converge here between December and April – where more than 30,000 nests have been counted by visiting biologists. These islands are 12km from the rest of the archipelago, but a visit could easily be tacked on to a day trip to Refugio de Vida Silvestre Los Guatuzos, or a chartered cruise to or from San Carlos.

Refugio de Vida Silvestre Los Guatuzos

Like so many national treasures, Los Guatuzos wildlife reserve, a 44,000-hectare band of rich, river-streaked wilderness wedged between the Costa Rican border and Lago de Nicaragua, was conserved by accident. The earliest inhabitants, the Guatuzos, were sold into slavery, their lands co-opted by farmers whose crops (rubber and cacao) demanded shade. Just as foreign timber companies were poised to buy out the subsistence farmers, revolution and war hit hard along the border, leaving this region as pristine as only a minefield can be. (It was declared mine-free in 2001.)

By the time it was safe for people to return, the federal government had already taken pains to protect it. The **Río Pizote** (Long-Tailed Raccoon River) and **Río Medio Queso** (Half Cheese River) form the eastern and western boundaries of the preserve, home to 18 rivers, 2000 people, 81 amphibians, 42 mammals and almost 400 bird species. The wetlands are also a paradise for mosquitoes – bring plenty of repellent.

There are two excellent nature-focused accommodations on the Río Papaturro. **Cabañas Caiman** (☎8676-2958, 506-8704-3880; aillenm@hotmail.com; Río Papaturro; r per person incl breakfast US$14) is owned by Guatuzo's original crocodile man and nature-guide-extraordinaire Armando Gomez. It has two comfortable wooden rooms and serves tasty meals. Directly across the river, the **Centro Ecológico Los Guatuzos** (☎8877-5096, 2270-3561; www.losguatuzos.com; Río Papaturro; r per person with/without bathroom US$13/11) is a professionally run research station that welcomes tourists. It offers guided hikes and moonlight alligator tours (US$45 per person). Kayaks are also available to rent.

There are slow collective boats from San Carlos to Río Papaturro (US$4, four hours) at 9am Tuesday, Wednesday and Friday, returning to San Carlos from Río Papaturro at 8am Monday, Tuesday and Thursday. It costs around US$130/240 one way/round-trip from San Carlos in a private *panga*. It's cheaper to rent a boat (round-trip boat/*panga* US$70/100) in Solentiname.

Nestled on the Río Frio, **Reserva Esperanza Verde** (☎2583-0459; Río Frio; r per person incl 3 meals US$50) is a 5000-hectare humid tropical forest reserve. You can do it in a day trip from San Carlos (US$30 per person, two-person minimum), including private *panga* transport, guide and trail access, or spend the night in one of its simple, solar-powered rooms. Arrange visits through Hotel-Cabinas Leyko (p244) in San Carlos.

Río San Juan

You simply must see this river. It surges purposefully through rolling green hills, thick jungle and wetlands on its irrepressible march to the Caribbean.

Not that you'll be sitting around all day admiring its beauty. This river demands action. After all, it was once the domain of indigenous traders, Spanish conquistadors, British pirates, gold hunting travelers and even Mark Twain. Follow their example and visit the small towns of Boca de Sábalos and El Castillo, penetrate the vine-hung wilderness of jaguars and macaws that is the Reserva Biológica Indio-Maíz, troll for tarpon, search for alligators in the moonlight and dine on plump lobsteresque giant shrimp while overlooking the remains of a 16th-century Spanish fort. All of which will cost you. But it's worth it to fully experience this spectacular and unforgettable waterway.

La Esperanza

The first major settlement after passing under the La Fe bridge, La Esperanza is a typical Río San Juan rural community surrounded mostly by pasture but with some pockets of jungle and plenty of birdlife.

The community itself is set 2km from the river, but right by the dock yoúll find **Grand River Lodge** (☎8936-3919, 8366-6187; www.hotelgrandriverlodge.com; La Esperanza; tents or hammock US$3, dm/s/d US$7/10/20), one of the few backpacker-orientated places on the river. It is run by affable local boy and veteran cruise-ship employee Marvin, who has converted his family farm into a rural lodge. The 12 simple thatched-roof huts with private bath-

DREDGES, BULLDOZERS & CROSS-BORDER MUDSLINGING

The Río San Juan is no stranger to conflict. Ever since Spanish colonizers and pillaging pirates began battling it out at El Castillo, these strategic waters have been the source of many a conflict.

Well before the inauguration of the Panama Canal, the river had been identified as the keypiece in any interoceanic route through Nicaragua. After countless border disputes, in 1858 the US facilitated a treaty between Nicaragua and Costa Rica that defined the border along the southern bank of the river but awarded the river in its entirety to Nicaragua, making it clear that any future canal project would only have to negotiate with one government. Thus the Río San Juan became one of the few border rivers on the planet that belongs exclusively to one country, a fact that has been a constant source of friction between the two nations, especially over the extent of Costa Rica's navigation rights.

The long-running dispute hit the headlines again in 2010 when the government of Daniel Ortega began dredging the lower stretches of the Río San Juan in what they claimed was an attempt to restore the river's natural course that had been diverted by Costa Rican dredging in the Río Colorado in the 1960s.

Costa Rica immediately expressed concerns about the environmental impact of the dredging and soon afterward alleged Nicaragua was hacking a new channel through one of its islands, Isla Calero, in order to annexe part of the territory. Dredging boss, and former Contra leader, Eden Pastora rejected those claims, even famously pulling up Google maps to make the point that the island, which Nicaragua refers to as Harbour Head, had always been part of that country.

Tensions escalated and Costa Rica sent heavily armed police to the area. Amid fears of a military confrontation, Costa Rica took the issue to the International Court of Justice (ICJ) with the court ruling that all parties should abandon the disputed area in the absence of a definitive decision but that the main dredging project could continue.

While Pastora was pushing ahead with Lady Laura, the dredge named in honor of Costa Rican president Laura Chinchilla, Costa Rica began the construction of a 160km highway along the edge of the river to facilitate movement to and from the delta. This saw Nicaragua taking its turn to don the environmentalist hat, denouncing deforestation and erosion along the length of the new road.

The extent of the impact on the environment from both projects is open to debate but with the troops gone you'll have no problems visiting the lower reaches of the river to check it out for yourself. Just make sure to ask your boat captain to slow down as you approach San Juan de Nicaragua so you can get a good look at the small patch of insect-infested swampland that sparked the dispute and has galvanized nationalist sentiment in both nations.

rooms run along a ridge with river views and there are plenty of activities, including horseback riding and treks to forested hills inhabited by monkeys. Meals (US$3 to US$4) are served in the rustic bar-restaurant.

Any San Carlos–El Castillo boat will drop you here (US$3). It's also possible to arrive by bus from San Carlos (US$1.75), but it's a tough slog though thick mud from the highway when its raining.

Boca de Sábalos

POP 800

It feels like that thick jungle looming on its edges is about to reclaim this muddy, dusty town set at the confluence of the Río San Juan and Río Sábalos (Tarpon River). And therein lies its appeal. When you lounge on the terrace of your hotel, lodge or guesthouse at sunset, you'll watch birds fish, and ride end-of-the-day thermals as you hear that familiar, primordial roar of the howler monkeys.

Río Sábalos effectively splits the town in half, with the inexpensive *hospedajes* and main road on one side, and a smaller community, threaded by a slender footpath past rustic homes and gardens, on the other. It's two córdobas (US$0.10) to cross the canal in a dugout canoe.

Sights & Activities

Reserva Privada El Quebracho NATURE RESERVE
(2583-0035; www.fundaciondelrio.org; admission US$5) Administered by the Fundacíon

del Rio, this 90-hectare property borders the Reserva Biológica Indio-Maíz, and offers a peek at the region's very big trees, very small frogs, beautiful rivers and wealth of wildlife. Take a taxi to Buena Vista, and walk the last hour to the reserve, where you can hike and horseback ride along two trails through primary forest dangling with orchids. If it inspires you to stick around, accommodations are available in simple rooms with shared bathrooms.

Asociación de Guías Jacamar ADVENTURE TOUR
(☎8441-5958, 8970-0007; asociacionguiasjacamar@yahoo.com; frente Muelle; ⏲8am-5pm) This association of young nature guides is your one-stop ticket to adventure. In addition to offering a variety of kayaking trips along jungle-clad rivers, it also offers treks through private nature reserves and night alligator-spotting boat trips (US$15 per person, minimum four people).

Other interesting options include a full-day Chocolate Tour (from US$44 per person) to the Cooprocafuc cacao cooperative in the community of Buena Vista where visitors are able to observe the entire chocolate-making process.

It's also possible to hire a guide to follow your own itinerary for US$15 per day.

Sleeping & Eating

Basic budget lodging is located in town. Two more-comfortable ecolodges are just downstream. Tell the riverboat driver where you're staying and you'll be dropped in the right spot.

Hospedaje y Comedor Clarissa GUESTHOUSE $
(☎8364-3588; Muelle, ½c N; s/d without bathroom US$4/8, r US$10; ❄) Rooms in the nice wooden home are basic but clean. Pay the extra for the better rooms upstairs with private bathrooms. Its beef, chicken and pork plate lunches (US$2.50), served on a wide, leafy patio, are beloved locally.

★**Sábalos Lodge** LODGE $$
(☎2583-0046; www.sabaloslodge.com; Muelle, 1km E; d US$35-60) This collection of stilted thatched bungalows set in one meandering riverside row achieves the *Robinson Crusoe* ideal. Each one has an indoor-outdoor living room with two hammocks, a bed swathed in mosquito netting, and an outdoor shower. The best part: each bungalow has its own personalized view of the river and offshore island, which is alive with birds at sunset. Meals run around US$12.

Hotel Sábalos HOTEL $$
(☎2271-7424, 8659-0252; www.hotelsabalos.com.ni; frente Muelle; s/d US$20/30, with river view US$25/40, all incl breakfast) Perched on stilts over the water at the mouth of the Río Sábalos, this charming hotel has comfortable wooden rooms with hot water, and rocking chairs on the wide veranda. It also has the only real restaurant in Sábalos (mains US$6 to US$7), serving an exceptional plate of jumbo river shrimp (US$15) with tasty thick-cut steak fries.

Hospedaje y Comedor Kateana GUESTHOUSE $$
(☎2583-3838; Muelle, ½c N; r per person with/without bathroom US$10/8; ❄) A fine budget choice with clean, polished-wood rooms, a nice porch and, absolutely essential for vegetarians in Sábalos, kitchen access. The savvy management will also give you access to the washing machine to clean that bag of stinking clothes you've been hauling through the jungle.

Monte Cristo River Lodge LODGE $$$
(☎2583-0197, 8649-9012; www.montecristoriverlodge.com; Muelle, 2km E; r per person incl meals & activities US$75) This massive riverside resort started out as a tarpon fishing lodge, and it still is one of the best fishing outfitters. But this 120-*manzana* property also boasts 60 *manzanas* of primary forest with 300-plus cathedral ceibu and almendra trees, two to four hours of hiking and horseback-riding trails, a stable of free kayaks, a coffee plantation and a cacao grove.

The rooms are clean, comfortable and perfect for families. It also offers an excellent deal for day visits: for US$15 per person you get lunch and access to the trails, kayaks and horseback riding. Snook and tarpon expeditions cost from US$150 per day.

Getting There & Away

Boat services from Boca de Sábalos:

El Castillo (US$0.55, one hour, 10am, 2pm, 4:30pm and 5:30pm Monday to Saturday, 10am and 2:30pm Sunday; express US$1, 30 minutes, 7:30am and 11am)

San Carlos (US$3.50, 2½ hours, 6am, 7am, 8am and 3pm Monday to Saturday, 6am and 3pm Sunday; express US$4.75, one hour, 6am and noon)

Getting Around

Public transportation by road to communities surrounding Boca de Sábalos consists of 'taxis' – beat-up old 4WD vehicles that are filled to bursting point and make collective runs (US$2.50) to local communities. They have no fixed schedule, departing from the dock when full, usually coinciding with the arrival of river transport to the port.

It is far easier to hire a vehicle (up to eight passengers) for an express trip – expect to pay around US$50 to US60 to Buena Vista.

El Castillo

POP 1000

Cute, compact and crowned with its stunning 17th-century Spanish fortress, it's no surprise that diminutive El Castillo is the Río San Juan's showpiece destination. It's laced with pebbled-concrete walking paths that wind up, down and around the hill, shaded by mango, coconut, orange and almond trees, and cradled by the Río San Juan – wide and foaming with two sets of rapids that proved to be the bane of British pirates for centuries. A town this civilized means that the jungle has been tamed here. So don't expect the howlers to sing you to sleep. The good news is that you are just 15 minutes by boat from Nicaragua's best-preserved lowland rainforest, the Reserva Biológica Indio-Maíz.

Sights & Activities

La Fortaleza FORT

(admission US$2, camera fee US$1; ⏲8am-noon & 1-4:30pm) Properly known as La Fortaleza de la Limpia Pura e Inmaculada Concepción, this photogenic fortress was constructed between 1673 and 1675, commissioned after Granada was sacked three times in five years. The Raudal El Diablo rapids were key – they slowed the pirates down just long enough to aim enormous cannons their way. Still, it was attacked, rebuilt and fortified every other decade for 200 years.

The fort's cinematic moment arrived when proto-feminist folk hero Rafaela Herrera was only 19 years old. Her father, the fortress commander, was critically wounded in a 1762 battle with an on-rushing British fleet. Herrera, still the region's favorite heroine, stepped into command (evidently wearing a nightgown) and successfully repelled the pirates. In some versions of the story she fired the cannon that sank the lead ship.

Then, in 1780, 22-year-old Brit Horatio Nelson conquered the edifice. However, British control was short-lived, malarial mosquitoes ravaged the battle-depleted party and within a few months, the Spanish were able to walk back into the abandoned fort. Today the fortress houses a terrific museum, with informative Spanish-language displays. Your entry fee includes a tour by the enthusiastic staff.

El Mariposario BUTTERFLY ENCLOSURE

(Loma Nelson; admission US$3; ⏲10am-noon & 1-4pm) Flutter over for a tour of this butterfly garden, run by a local women's collective. It's located on Loma Nelson, the hill from where Horatio Nelson bombarded the Spanish fortress.

Tours

Conveniently located at the dock, El Castillo's **tourist office** (⏲8am-noon & 2-5pm) sources local guides for a variety of tours. It helps to make reservations a day in advance. Some menus of guided hikes and *panga* trips:

Reserva Biológica Indio-Maíz, Río Bartola (US$65; four hours, maximum four people) Take a private *panga* to the Río Bartola entrance of the Indio-Maíz reserve, then hike 3km though primary forest, where you'll be dwarfed by 500-year-old giants, taste medicinal plants, and spot tree frogs, green iguanas and three types of monkey (spider, white-faced and howler). After the hike you'll motor up Río Bartola, where you'll swim in a crystal-clear river surrounded by jungle.

Reserva Biológica Indio-Maíz, Aguas Frescas (US$75; five hours, maximum four people) Although this is virtually identical to the Bartola trip, less visitors hike this tract of forest, which means you are likely to see more wildlife.

Reserva Biológica Indio-Maíz, Caño Sarnoso (US$120, five hours, maximum four people) This boat-only trip (no trekking) travels further down the Río San Juan to observe the ruins of the old steamboats and abundant wildlife around the El Diamante rapids including crocodiles and abundant birdlife.

The tourist office also organizes a **Cacao Tour** (US$15 per person), where visitors observe the entire chocolate-making process, and a **Horseback-Riding Tour** (US$15) through a private reserve.

You don't have to go through the tourist office, which can seem less than helpful at times. There are several private operators with signs up around town offering similar tour rosters.

Nena Tour ADVENTURE TOUR
(☎8821-2135; www.nenalodge.com) A fantastic tour operator based at Nena Lodge offering all the standard tours plus canoe tours on the nearby Río Juana (US$15 per person, three hours) and a night alligator tour (US$45 for up to four passengers). Also rents an inflatable raft to run the rapids in front of town (US$10 per hour).

Angel Tapia HORSEBACK RIDING
(☎8431-2389) Offers half-day horseback-riding tours (US$15 per person) through lush countryside with fantastic bird-watching. Includes visits to cacao plantations and a chocolate workshop. Book at the grocery shop 30m before the bridge.

Basiliscus Tour RIVER TOUR
(☎8448-9170; darwing86@gmail.com) Specialists in canoe trips down the river, including a four-day, 160km trip all the way to Greytown (US$300 per person, minimum two people). Also offers overnight camping trips to the Río Bartola (US$65 per person, minimum two people).

Sleeping

There are a handful of very basic but pleasant *hospedajes* lining the waterfront close to the dock.

Some establishments offer 'internet access' via a USB modem but it is frustratingly slow even when it works.

★**Hotel Tropical** HOTEL $$
(☎8699-8886, 8447-8213; Muelle 130m E; r with/without air-con incl breakfast US$30/25; ❄) Lie back and listen to the rushing water of El Castillo outside your window at this fantastic small hotel above Restaurant Vanessa. While the spotless rooms with air-con, cable TV and tiled bathrooms are an excellent deal, the best thing is the breezy wooden porch perched right above the rapids.

Casa de Huesped Chinandegano GUESTHOUSE $$
(☎2583-3011; Muelle, 240m E; r per person with/without bathroom US$9/7; 📶) This creaky wooden house done up with potted tropical plants and a shabby-chic dining area is the best cheapie in town. The wooden and bamboo rooms have high ceilings and private bathrooms. Get the corner room if you can. Or just come for lunch or dinner.

Posada del Río GUESTHOUSE $$
(Muelle 300m E; s/d/tr incl breakfast US$20/40/60; ❄) Friendly family-run place at the end of the path with neat wooden rooms and a generous breakfast.

Hotel Albergue El Castillo GUESTHOUSE $$
(☎2583-3007; frente La Fortaleza; s/d without bathroom incl breakfast US$15/30) This two-story wooden house feels like a Swiss chalet. Fine hardwood rooms open onto a terrace with hammocks and commanding river views. Shame about the shared bathrooms, which look like they belong in a bus terminal.

Hotel Victoria HOTEL $$
(☎8697-2509, 2583-0188; hotelvictoria01@yahoo.es; Muelle, 250m E; s/d US$35/46) The rooms in the original construction are elegant but a little cramped; however, the spacious rooms in the new wing are easily the best in town with split-system air-con, shiny wooden floors, stylish modern bathrooms and private balconies.

Eating

★**Borders Coffee** CAFE $$
(☎8408-7688; detras Base Militar; meals US$3.50-13; ⏰7am-10pm) By the time you read this, this fun cafe should be settled into its expansive new open-air locale behind the military base, which was nearing completion at the time of research. There you'll find a full menu of burgers, pasta, river shrimp and several vegetarian options. It's also a great place for breakfast. The food is delicious, and the coffee (US$0.50 to $2) wins the unofficial title of 'best in region'.

Casa de Huesped Chinandegano NICARAGUAN $$
(☎2583-3011; Muelle, 240m E; meals US$6-8; ⏰7am-10pm) Locals come for tasty chicken plates, but giant shrimp is served here too. It comes perfectly grilled and glazed with garlic butter, garnished with a tomato salad dressed in vinegar and plated with golden *tostones* (fried green plantains) and a carved heart of lime. Service is just as superb as the food. Do not miss it.

Comedor Vanessa NICARAGUAN, SEAFOOD $$
(☎8447-8213; Muelle 2c E; meals US$6-7; ⏰11am-9pm) Perched over the roaring rapids is one of the river's best restaurants. It serves tasty giant river shrimp, claws and all, and a number of chicken, beef and pork dishes. It also pours a damn fine *michelada* (beer with bloody-mary and margarita fixings) if you're in the mood.

Getting There & Away

From El Castillo, collective boats leave for San Carlos (US$3.50, three hours) via Boca de Sábalos (US$0.50, 30 minutes) at 5am, 6am, 7am and 2pm. On Sunday there are only two services at 5am and 2pm.

Fast *pangas* to San Carlos (US$5.70, 1½ hours) via Boca de Sábalos (US$1, 15 minutes) leave at 6am and 10am.

Reserva Biológica Indio-Maíz & the River Eastward

About 15 minutes downriver from El Castillo, after Costa Rica's border tumbles down to the edge of the river's southern bank, you'll notice a smaller river flow into the jungle to the north. That's the **Río Bartola**, which marks the boundary of Nicaragua's second-largest tract of intact primary forest, the 2606-sq-km **Reserva Biológica Indio-Maíz**. For years 85% of the reserve's landmass belonged to Somoza. Thanks to geographic isolation and inaccessibility, followed by more than a decade of war, it was spared the chainsaw. Once the Sandinistas took power it was legislated as a reserve and for the next several years it was the domain of scientists and remained off-limits to tourists.

While the vast majority of the reserve remains restricted, it is now possible to visit some small designated sections of the reserve where you can hike among 50m-tall, 500-year-old cathedral trees, search for fingernail-sized tree frogs and watch monkeys perform death-defying leaps through the canopy.

At the confluence of Río Bartola and Río San Juan the park ranger's office administers a 3km walking trail that winds through the reserve's towering trees. In order to really experience the amazing rainforest ecosystem, a local guide is essential and most visitors come on a package from El Castillo. Another 20 minutes downriver by boat is a military post and reserve entrance at **Aguas Frescas**. While the plant life is virtually identical, it feels even more pristine here than the Bartola section, because it is less visited by tour groups from El Castillo, although the trail is gaining in popularity.

About an hour further along from the mouth of the Río Sarapiquí, the San Juan Delta begins to weave through the wetlands, meeting up with the almost-as-enormous Río Colorado. Birding becomes increasingly interesting, and fishing even better – but note that you have officially entered the bull sharks' territory, so no swimming.

When you finally enter the expansive Bahía de San Juan del Norte, you'll notice the rusted old dredger owned by Cornelius Vanderbilt's Transit Company, which kept the shipping lanes open for would-be gold prospectors en route to San Francisco. The dilapidated dock to the south marks the entrance to what's left of Greytown, founded on what was then the mouth of the Río San Juan, now a sandy extension of dry land. After you cross the bay to the mouth of the remarkable Río Indio, you'll reach San Juan de Nicaragua, where you can explore blackwater creeks, hidden lagoons and thick jungle within the wide reach of the Indio-Maíz.

Sleeping & Eating

The Indio-Maíz is a restricted area and there are no accomodations in this part of the reserve; however, there are a couple of excellent options just outside its boundaries on the other side of the Río Bartola.

Basecamp Bartola COMMUNITY LODGE **$$$**
(☎8913-8215; indio.maiz@gmail.com; Comunidad Bartola; per person incl meals & transport US$66) Run by the tiny community of Bartola, 6km up the Río Bartola, this groundbreaking new project is the future of sustainable tourism in the region. Visitors sleep in tents (complete with mattresses and towels folded into swans) on wooden platforms overlooking the thick canopy of the Indio Maíz across the river. Activities include fantastic guided treks through nearby virgin forest full of monkeys and trips in traditional boats. Prices vary depending on number of visitors.

★ **Refugio Bartola** NATURE RESERVE **$$$**
(☎8885-7386, 8376-6979; www.refugiobartola.com; r per person incl meals US$50, day-use fee US$5, guides per day US$20) Set at the confluence of Ríos San Juan and Bartola opposite the ranger post, this rustic wooden lodge and private reserve is the superlative option for true nature lovers in the region yet receives surprisingly few travelers.

The large tract of virgin forest is identical to the vegetation inside the reserve and the animals don't know the location of the boundaries; the only difference is here you are free to walk deep into the jungle along a network of trails.

Accommodations are in simple, breezy wooden rooms with high ceilings set around a lovely garden overlooking the river. Kayaks are available to explore the Río Bartola at your own pace.

San Juan de Nicaragua (San Juan del Norte)

POP 1100

Dripping wet and laid-back, one of the Americas' oldest European cities feels like it's on the edge of the world. There are wide streets but no cars; the restaurants have no signs. But it's certainly not lazy or joyless. Fishers and boat builders work from morning to night, and they do not want for food, shelter or activity. How could they, in a town surrounded by rivers teeming with fish, virgin rainforest and jungle-fringed lagoons. They are cash poor, however, which leads to spotty electricity (carry a flashlight) and water service (shower when you can), and the locals dream of a tourism gold rush. Considering the number of knowledgeable local guides and the nearby adventure-soaked terrain, a future ecotourism boom is definitely plausible. Today, however, it remains a dream destination for those comfortable on the edge.

Internet access is available in town at **Telecentro** (per hr US$1; ⌚9am-5pm Mon-Fri), a block inland from the dock.

Sights & Activities

San Juan de Nicaragua's traditional tourist attraction is the swampy remains of **Greytown**, a short boat ride (four people US$85, three to four hours) across the bay. Here you'll find a few solid building foundations and four very interesting cemeteries: one for the British (including those members of Horatio Nelson's doomed campaign who were not fed to the sharks), another for Catholics, a third for North Americans and the last allegedly for Freemasons from St John's Lodge. Unfortunately, the new airport has been constructed bang in the middle of the ruins, which torpedoes the atmosphere somewhat.

More and more visitors are coming to San Juan de Nicaragua to explore deeper into the mystical Reserva Biológica Indio-Maíz. There are few hiking trails – you will spend most of your time exploring the spectacular jungle in your boat.

You can spend a glorious six hours cruising between enormous yet hidden **Laguna Silica**, **Laguna de San Juanillo** and **Laguna La Barca** (four people US$150), which are surrounded by primary rainforest. You will occasionally hack through humid forests with machetes just to get from place to place and may spot manatees.

Or dedicate a day or two to the jungle and its original Rama inhabitants along the **Río Indio**, which runs parallel to the Caribbean Sea before turning inland and winding deep into the heart of the reserve.

On a typical one-day trip (up to six visitors, US$180) you'll cruise upriver through **Laguna Manatee** to **El Encanto**, where there is a hiking trail in the forest. On the way back you'll stop on the beach at El Cocal, where you'll sip fresh coconut water on the sand. The two-day version (US$400) continues upriver to **Makenge**, a Rama community where you'll spend the night in the solar-powered communal house. It's also possible to organize a homestay with a Rama family further upriver. The next morning hike four hours through primary forest to **Canta Gallo (Piedras Basálticas)**, a basalt outcrop that local Rama say is the foundation of an ancient pyramid. Others say the formation is geological in nature. Whatever. It's stunning, and the hike is tremendous.

Hotelito Evo SPORTFISHING, KAYAKING
(☎8350-5145, 2583-9019; evohotel@yahoo.es) In addition to being top jungle guides, Enrique Gutiérrez and his sons at Hotelito Evo offer kayaking trips (US$25 per person, minimum two people) and nocturnal alligator-spotting tours (US$25 per person, minimum two people) in the waters around town. They also offer half-day sportfishing trips (US$180 per boat).

Tours

Asociacíon de Guias de Greytown GUIDED TOUR
(☎8535-1898; guiasdegreytown@yahoo.com; contiguo Muelle) Located next to the dock, this cooperative of professional, accredited local guides offers tours to Old Greytown and into the Reserva Biológica Indio-Maíz. Prices are set and work is shared among all the guides.

Gobierno Rama-Kriol NATURE
(☎8549-3272; donde Alicia McRea, Barrio Rama) The official representatives of the Rama community are able to organize tours deep within the Reserva Biológica Indio-Maíz. Expect to pay around US$170 for round-trip transport to Makenge and US$15 per person per night for food and accommodation. Ask for Alicia McRea in the Rama neighbourhood at the edge of town.

If your budget doesn't stretch to a jungle trip, chat with Miss Alicia about Rama culture over a traditional Rama meal (US$8).

THE RAMA: GUARDIANS OF THE FOREST

For the indigenous Rama people the low jungle of the eastern Reserva Biológica Indio-Maíz is sacred. Rama ownership of these lands has been recognized by the Nicaraguan government and they are the only group permitted to live within the reserve.

Traditionally, tours into the magnificent forests of the Rama ancestral homeland have been run by *mestizo* tour operators based in San Juan de Nicaragua; however, the Rama are beginning to organize jungle tours themselves. Whether it proves to be a positive thing or not for the community depends on the attitude of their visitors.

You will probably have a more polished, professional experience going with the tour operators in town. The Rama are new to tourism and still learning the ropes. However, they know this vast jungle better than any professional guide and spending some time traversing the area with them is an immense cultural experience.

Whoever you choose to go with, make sure your tour operator obtains the Rama area entry permit (US$20 per person). The fee ensures tourism directly benefits the reserve's original inhabitants – a desperately poor indigenous community that is fighting to survive in modern Nicaragua.

Sleeping & Eating

★Hostal Familiar GUESTHOUSE **$**
(☎8446-2096; Muelle, 300m S; r with/without river view US$20/14) A fantastic budget choice offering two big, breezy wooden rooms right on the river and a couple of cheaper options upstairs. The attached restaurant serves outstanding fresh seafood (imagine river shrimp and snook steaks braised in coconut-tomato sauce).

Hotelito Evo HOTEL **$**
(☎8350-5145, 2583-9019; Muelle, 150m O, 20m S; r with/without bathroom US$15/12) Located a few blocks back from the river, this friendly hotel is cheap, clean and secure but the small rooms are a little worn and airless.

Cabañas Monkey HOTEL **$$**
(☎8330-1898; Muelle, 200m N; s/d/tr US$15/24/36) Turn right out of the dock to find these clean, spacious *cabañas* with private bathroom and TV set around a garden.

Río Indio Lodge LUXURY HOTEL **$$$**
(☎in Costa Rica 506-2231-4299, in the US 866-593-3168; www.therioindiolodge.com; r per person incl all meals & drinks US$193, sportfishing packages from US$2225; ❄) This enormous, and at times deserted, sportfishing lodge is surrounded by rainforest with views of Vanderbilt's dredge ruins. It offers opulence in the middle of the jungle with rooms linked by elevated walkways through the jungle. Don't expect to drop in, you'll need to reserve well in advance.

Soda El Tucán NICARAGUAN **$$**
(Muelle, 100m S; mains US$5-6.50; ⏲6:30am-9:30pm) Centrally located and easy to find, this cheery wooden diner will do just fine. The menu is simple: chicken or fish, grilled or fried, but the results are delicious. If you order a few hours in advance, you can have river shrimp (US$10) prepared *al gusto* (to your liking).

Getting There & Around

San Juan de Nicaragua's airport is located across the bay next to the Greytown ruins. La Costeña flies from Managua to San Juan (one way/return US$110/165) via San Carlos at noon on Thursday and Sunday, returning at 1:30pm. The airline has no office in San Juan town, so you'll need to purchase your return ticket before you arrive. There is also no public transport from the airport to San Juan, but Hotelito Evo offers a water taxi service for US$10 per person (minimum two people) – call before you arrive.

Slow boats leave from San Carlos for San Juan de Nicaragua (US$14, nine to 12 hours, 6am Tuesday, Thursday and Friday) stopping in Boca de Sábalos at 9:15am and El Castillo at 10am. Fast boats leave San Carlos for San Juan de Nicaragua (US$25, six hours) at 6am Tuesday and Friday and at 10am Wednesday and Sunday, stopping in Boca de Sábalos and El Castillo one hour or 90 minutes later respectively. Slow boats return from San Juan de Nicaragua at 5am Thursday, Saturday and Sunday. Fast boats return at 5:30am Thursday and Sunday and at 8:30am Monday and Friday.

At the time of research there was no regular transport from San Juan to Bluefields, but the Gobierno Rama Kriol (p227) had plans to introduce a regular *panga* service stopping at the communities of Corn River, Monkey Point and Rama Cay. Otherwise it is occasionally possible to pay for a ride on a local boat that is making the trip. Note that this is a long trip in a small boat on the open ocean that oscillates between uncomfortable and spine shattering depending on the swell. You'll probably also get soaked; bring plastic bags for your luggage.

Understand Nicaragua

Nicaragua Today

Like him or loathe him, President Daniel Ortega's re-election has delivered something that Nicaragua has lacked for a long time: a sense of stability. Gone are the transport strikes, debilitating power rationing and unpredictable rallies. And, after being devastated by the civil war, the country's economy and infrastructure are slowly being reconstructed. But all is not rosy, Nicaragua remains the poorest nation on the American continent and questions continue to be raised at home and abroad over perceived erosion of democracy.

Best in Film

La Yuma Portrays the challenges facing a female boxer from Managua.
Palabras Magicas The making of modern Nicaragua through the lens of a young filmmaker.
Walker Biopic of a megalomaniac with music by the late, great Joe Strummer.
Carla's Song British bus driver falls for Nicaraguan dancer in exile in romantic drama with a political edge.
Pictures from a Revolution The story behind the famous war images of Susan Meiselas.

Best in Print

Blood of Brothers (Stephen Kinzer) Fascinating account of revolution and war.
The Country Beneath My Skin (Gioconda Belli) Autobiography by revolutionary poet.
Selected Poems of Rubén Darío (translated by Lysander Kemp) Bilingual anthology of the master poet's best work.
The Jaguar Smile (Salman Rushdie) Accessible insider's look at the Sandinistas during the revolution.
Tycoon's War (Stephen Dando-Collins) Documents the epic battle between imperialists Vanderbilt and Walker.

Election Controversy

Prior to reclaiming the top job, President Daniel Ortega had appeared on the ballot paper in every one of the previous four Nicaraguan elections, so it was not a huge surprise when, as his return term was nearing its end, reports surfaced that the FSLN leader was not too hot on the idea of handing over the reigns to a successor.

Confirmation that Ortega was not yet ready to relinquish power surfaced in 2009 when the Frente Sandinista de Liberación Nacional (Sandinista National Liberation Front; FSLN)-dominated Supreme Court overturned a constitutional ban on consecutive presidential terms. The opposition launched legal challenges in an attempt to overturn the ruling without success.

Despite the controversy, the lead-up to the November 2011 election was somewhat subdued. Ortega's return to the presidency had not turned out to be the disaster that many on the right had predicted. During his five years in office, the economy had performed strongly with exports doubling and foreign direct investment increasing fivefold.

Polls leading up to the election showed Ortega well in front, confirming the suspicion that many in the once-rabidly anti-FSLN private sector had gotten over its distrust of the former rebel.

In the end, Ortega cruised to victory with 62.7% of the vote, more than twice that of his closest rival, conservative radio personality Fabio Gadea, who claimed fraud. Observers from the Organization of American States reported significant irregularities, but not sufficient to change the outcome.

Ortega's democratic credentials were further challenged in local elections in 2012, in which the FSLN won 127 of the 153 municipalities. Monitoring organization, Ética yTransparencia (Ethics and Transparency), identified irregularities in 70 municipalities it surveyed.

Redrawing the Map

Simmering tensions over the Río San Juan, Nicaragua and Costa Rica's favorite patriotic flash point, once again boiled over in late 2010 regarding Managua's dredging operations in the river's delta.

Costa Rica lodged a demand against Nicaragua before the International Court of Justice (ICJ) in the Hague claiming that Nicaragua was hacking a new canal through a Costa Rican island in order to annexe part of the territory. Nicaragua rebutted by claiming to simply be cleaning an existing channel (with dredging boss and former Contra leader Eden Pastora even pulling up Google Maps to prove a point) and launched a counterclaim suggesting that Costa Rica's construction of a new highway along the river was damaging the local environment.

While the two countries were still trading barbs, the ICJ handed down its final ruling in another case involving Nicaragua, the disputed maritime border with Colombia in a potentially mineral-rich area of the Caribbean Sea. In November 2012 the court awarded ownership of several small islands to Colombia, but 100,000 sq km of sea formerly within Colombia's boundaries was handed over to Nicaragua.

President Ortega sent a small flotilla of lightly armed ships and fishing boats to the disputed waters to exert sovereignty. However, shortly afterward, the Nicaraguan government was forced to admit that Colombia, which rejects the ruling, was still patrolling the zone.

Petroleum Economy

Since the FSLN's return to power, the government's economic and social programs have been bankrolled through aid, loans and subsidized fuel from its partner in the Alianza Bolivariano por Las Americas (ALBA), Venezuela.

And while the hunger eradication programs, new houses and other initiatives have been well received by FSLN supporters, the lack of transparency of their funding has caused controversy.

The issue was brought to the forefront by the death of Venezuelan president Hugo Chavez. Many analysts suggest the Nicaraguan economy is overly dependent on Venezuelan handouts and changes in policy by a new government in Caracas could have a devastating impact on the country's economy.

This uncertainty has left ordinary Nicaraguans following the political situation in the South American country almost as closely as Venezuelans themselves.

AREA: **129,494 SQ KM**

POPULATION: **5,869,859**

GDP: **US$7.18 BILLION**

GDP GROWTH: **4.7%**

INFLATION: **8.1%**

UNEMPLOYMENT: **7.3%**

if Nicaragua were 100 people

69 would identify as Mestizo
17 would identify as White
9 would identify as Black
5 would identify as Indigenous

belief systems

(% of population)

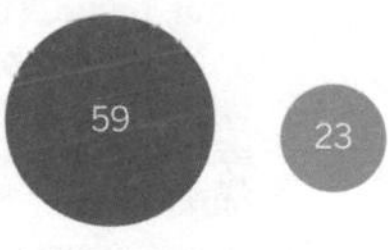

Roman Catholic
Protestant

15
None

3
Other

population per sq km

USA

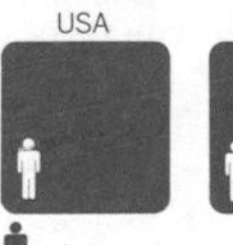

MEXICO

NICARAGUA

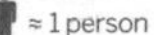
≈ 1 person

History

For such a small country, Nicaragua has played a disproportionate role in modern history. In the midst of cold-war tensions, the young Sandinista revolutionaries' reforms captured the attention of the most powerful governments on earth and unleashed scandals in the corridors of power. But when the bullets stopped flying, the world lost interest, leaving the clean-up, reconstruction and return to power of the Sandinistas like a captivating sequel that never made it to the big screen.

There were forgers even before coins were invented and the currency was cacao – they'd scoop the cacao out of the seed and replace it with mud.

Indigenous Nicaragua

Pre-Hispanic Nicaragua was home to several indigenous groups, including the ancestors of today's Rama, who live on the Caribbean coast, and the Chorotegas and Nicaraos, on the Pacific side. The latter spoke a form of Náhuatl, the language of the Aztecs. Many Nicaraguan places retain their Náhuatl names.

By 1500 BC Nicaragua was broadly settled, and though much of this history has been lost, at least one ancient treaty between the Nicarao capital of Jinotepe and its rival Chorotegan neighbor, Diriamba, is still celebrated as the Toro Guaco.

European Arrival

Although Columbus stopped briefly on the Caribbean coast in 1502, it was Gil González de Ávila, sailing north from Panama in 1522, who would really make his mark here. He found a chieftain, Cacique Nicarao, governing the southern shores of Lago de Nicaragua and the tribe of the same name. The Spaniards thus named the region Nicaragua.

Nicarao subjected González to hours of inquiry about science, technology and history. González famously gave Nicarao an ultimatum: convert to Christianity, or else. Nicarao's people complied, a move that in the end only delayed their massacre at the hands of the Spanish; other native groups were thus warned.

Six months later González made Cacique Diriangén the same offer; Diriangén went with 'or else.' His troops were outgunned and eventually destroyed but inspired further resistance. After conquering four Pacific

TIMELINE

6000 BC

Indigenous groups construct elaborate burial sites out of clam shells at Monkey Point on the Caribbean coast.

450 BC

The agricultural revolution arrives in the region, with the introduction of domesticated corn, yucca and beans. Soon after, trade links with modern-day Colombia and the USA are established.

AD 800

Petroglyph and statue fever sweeps across Nicaragua. Many designs, including an Aztec calendar and representations of the deity Quetzalcóatl, herald the arrival of one of Nicaragua's most important migrations.

tribes – 700,000 Chorotega, Nicarao, Maribios and Chontal were reduced to 35,000 in 25 years – the nations of the central highlands halted Spanish expansion at the mountains, with grim losses.

Colonial Settlement

The main Spanish colonizing force arrived the next year, founding the cities of León and Granada. Both were established near indigenous settlements, whose inhabitants were put to work.

The gold that had attracted the Spaniards soon gave out, but Granada and León remained. Granada became a comparatively rich colonial city, its wealth due to surrounding agriculture and its importance as a trading center. It was also a center for the Conservative Party, favoring traditional values of monarchy and ecclesiastical authority. Originally founded on Lago de Managua, León was destroyed by volcanic eruptions in 1610 and a new city established some 30km northwest. León in time became the center for radical clerics and intellectuals, who formed the Liberal Party and supported the unification of Central America and reforms based on the French and American Revolutions.

The difference in wealth between the two cities, and the political supremacy of León, led to conflicts that raged into the 1850s, at times erupting into civil war. The animosity stopped only when the capital was moved to the neutral location of Managua.

In Situ Petroglyphs

- *Isla Ometepe*
- *Chagüitillo*
- *Islas Solentiname*
- *Villa Sandino*

Enter the USA

In 1893 a Liberal general named José Santos Zelaya deposed the Conservative president and became dictator. Zelaya soon antagonized the US by seeking a canal deal with Germany and Japan. Encouraged by Washington, which sought to monopolize a transisthmian canal in Panama, the Conservatives rebelled in 1909.

After Zelaya ordered the execution of two US mercenaries accused of aiding the Conservatives, the American government forced his resignation, sending marines as a coercive measure. Thus began a period of two decades of US political intervention in Nicaragua – it installed presidents it favored and ousted those that it didn't, using the marines as persuasion, leading *Foreign Policy* magazine to label governments of this era 'US surrogate regimes'. In 1925 a new cycle of violence began with a Conservative coup.

The Conservative regime was opposed by a group of Liberal rebels including Augusto C Sandino, who recruited local peasants in the north of the country and eventually became leader of a long-term rebel campaign resisting US involvement.

1502

Christopher Columbus sails down the Caribbean coastline looking for a sailing route to the Pacific Ocean, landing briefly in the north. First recorded contact between indigenous inhabitants and Europeans.

1523

The main colonizing force arrives, led by Francisco Fernández de Córdoba. Cities of León (later moved after being buried by Volcán Momotombo) and Granada are founded soon after.

1635

The first European settlement on the Atlantic Coast is founded near Cabo Gracias a Dios by the grandly named British Providence Company.

1821

Nicaragua, along with the rest of Central America, becomes independent from Spain and briefly joins the Mexican Empire and then the United Provinces of Central America.

Somoza Era

When the marines headed home in 1933, the enemy became the new US-trained Guardia Nacional, whose aim was to put down resistance by Sandino's guerrillas, as is documented in Richard Millett's comprehensive

WILLIAM WALKER: SCOUNDREL, VAGABOND, PRESIDENT

In a country long accustomed to land grabs and mysterious foreigners with hidden agendas, none has managed to shine quite like Tennessee-born William Walker.

While Walker's name is pretty much unheard of outside Central America, you can bet that every Nicaraguan you meet will know exactly who he is.

A quiet, poetry-reading youth who had mastered several languages and earned various degrees by early adulthood, Walker first found work as a newspaper editor, publishing outspoken pieces condemning slavery and the interventionist policies of the US at the time (warning: irony approaching).

A different type of opportunity presented itself in 1848 when the Treaty of Guadalupe was signed, ceding half of Mexico to the US and leaving the other half dangling temptingly. Walker quickly jettisoned his liberal ideals, got a posse of thugs and crooks together, and embarked on a career that would etch his name into history books forever – filibustering.

Taken from a Dutch word meaning pirate, filibustering came to mean invading a country as a private citizen with unofficial aid from your home government.

Walker's foray into Mexico was as successful (he managed to take the Mexicans completely by surprise, raise his flag and name himself president before getting chased back over the border) as it was short-lived.

Word of Walker's derring-do spread, though, and it wasn't long before the city of León offered him the job of taking care of their pesky rivals in Granada.

With another rag-tag group of mercenaries at his command, Walker arrived in San Juan del Sur in September of 1855 and, aided by the element of surprise and the latest in US weaponry, easily took Granada.

Walker's Liberal Leónese employers must have felt a bit put out when he decided not to hand over Granada after all, but instead stayed around, got himself elected president, reinstituted slavery, confiscated huge tracts of land and led an ill-fated invasion attempt on Costa Rica.

These audacious actions, supported by then US president Franklin Pierce, inspired something that has been sadly lacking ever since – Central American unity. But even getting chased back to the US by every Central American army in existence (stopping long enough to burn Granada to the ground) didn't dampen Walker's imperial ambitions. He returned to Nicaragua once more (and was sent briskly packing) before trying his luck in Honduras, where the locals were much less lenient, and put him before a firing squad in September 1860.

1838

In abandoning the regional union, Nicaragua becomes the first modern Central American nation to declare independence.

1848

The British seize the Caribbean port of San Juan del Norte, renaming it Greytown.

1853

Filibuster William Walker arrives in San Juan del Sur, taking Granada quickly and installing himself as president soon after.

1857

In an effort to quell continued fighting between León and Granada, the small fishing village of Managua is named capital. The fighting stops, but the rivalry continues to this day.

study *Guardians of the Dynasty: A History of the US-Created Guardia Nacional de Nicaragua and the Somoza Family*. This military force was led by Anastasio Somoza García.

Somoza engineered the assassination of Sandino after the rebel leader was invited to Managua for a peace conference. National guardsmen gunned Sandino down on his way home. Somoza, with his main enemy out of the way, set his sights on supreme power.

Overthrowing Liberal president Sacasa a couple of years later, he established himself as president, founding a family dynasty that would rule for four decades.

After creating a new constitution to grant himself more power, Somoza García ruled Nicaragua for the next 20 years, sometimes as president, at other times as a puppet president, amassing huge personal wealth in the process (the Somoza landholdings attained were the size of El Salvador).

After his assassination in León, Somoza was succeeded by his elder son, Luis Somoza Debayle. In 1967 Luis died, and his younger brother, Anastasio Somoza Debayle, assumed control, following in his father's footsteps by expanding economic interests throughout Nicaragua.

Rising Opposition

In 1961 Carlos Fonseca Amador, a prominent figure in the student movement that had opposed the Somoza regime in the 1950s, joined forces with Colonel Santos López (an old fighting partner of Sandino's) and other activists to form the Frente Sandinista de Liberación Nacional (Sandinista National Liberation Front; FSLN). The FSLN's early guerrilla efforts against Somoza's forces ended in disaster for the fledgling group, but over the years it gained support and experience, turning it into a formidable opponent.

On December 23, 1972, at around midnight, an earthquake devastated Managua, leveling over 250 city blocks. The *Guardian* newspaper reported that, as international aid poured in, the money was diverted to Anastasio Somoza and his associates, while the people who needed it suffered and died, which dramatically increased opposition to Somoza among all classes of society.

By 1974 opposition was widespread. Two groups were widely recognized – the FSLN (Sandinistas) and the Unión Democrática de Liberación, led by Pedro Joaquín Chamorro, popular owner and editor of the Managua newspaper *La Prensa*, which had long printed articles critical of the Somozas.

In December 1974, the FSLN kidnapped several leading members of the Somoza regime. The government responded with a brutal crackdown in which Carlos Fonseca was killed in 1976.

Sandino's Daughters by Margaret Randall is a series of interviews that takes a look at the way that feminism was incorporated into the Sandinista revolution.

SANDINISTA

1912
The USA, in response to a rebellion against the corrupt Conservative administration, sends 2500 marines to Nicaragua, thus beginning two decades of US-dominated politics in Nicaragua.

1914
The Bryan-Chamorro Treaty is signed, granting the US exclusive canal rights in Nicaragua. It has no intention of building such a canal, but wants to ensure that no one else does.

1934
Guerrilla leader Augusto Sandino is killed by troops loyal to military strongman Anastasio Somoza García after being invited to Managua to discuss peace.

1937
Somoza overthrows Liberal President Juan Sacasa, thus beginning the Somoza dictat[illegible] 42 years in which the old man, then his sons, Luís and Anastasio, would rule the country.

Revolution & the FSLN

The last straw for the Nicaraguan public was the assassination of Chamorro. As street violence erupted and a general strike was called, business interests and moderate factions in the Frente Amplio Opositor (Broad Opposition Front; FAO) unsuccessfully attempted to negotiate an end to the Somoza dictatorship.

By mid-1978 many major towns were rising up against government forces. The Guardia Nacional's violent reprisals garnered further support for the Sandinistas.

The FAO threw in its lot with the Sandinistas, whom they now perceived as the only viable means with which to oust the dictatorship. This broad alliance formed a revolutionary government provisionally based in San José, Costa Rica, which gained recognition and arms from some Latin American and European governments.

The Death of Ben Linder by Joan Kruckewitt is a painstaking investigation (incorporating declassified CIA documents) into the assassination of Linder, the first US citizen to die at the hands of the Contras.

Thus the FSLN was well prepared to launch its final offensive in June 1979. The revolutionary forces took city after city, supported by thousands of civilians. On July 17, as the Sandinistas were preparing to enter Managua, Somoza fled the country. He was assassinated by Sandinista agents a year later in Asunción, Paraguay. The Sandinistas marched victorious into Managua on July 19, 1979.

They inherited a shambles. Poverty, homelessness, illiteracy and inadequate health care were just some of the problems. An estimated 50,000 people had been killed in the revolutionary struggle, and perhaps 150,000 more left homeless.

Trying to salvage what it could of its influence over the country, the USA (under President Jimmy Carter) authorized US$75 million in emergency aid to the Sandinista-led government.

However, by late 1980 it was becoming concerned about the increasing numbers of Soviet and Cuban advisers in Nicaragua and allegations that the Sandinistas were supplying arms to leftist rebels in El Salvador.

Contra War

After Ronald Reagan became US president in January 1981, relations between Nicaragua and the US began to sour. Reagan suspended all aid to Nicaragua and, according to the Report of the Congressional Committees Investigating the Iran-Contra Affair, by the end of the year had begun funding the counterrevolutionary military groups known as Contras, operating out of Honduras and Costa Rica, despite the US maintaining formal diplomatic relations with Managua.

Most of the original Contras were ex-soldiers of Somoza's Guardia Nacional, but as time passed, their ranks filled with disaffected local people.

1956

Somoza is assassinated in León by Rigoberto López Pérez, a poet disguised as a waiter. López Pérez is shot at the scene but becomes a national hero.

1961

Diverse guerrilla groups inspired by the Cuban revolution and united by their opposition to the Somozas combine to become the Frente Sandinista de Liberación Nacional (FSLN).

1967

Luis Somoza Debayle dies, and his younger brother, Anastasio Somoza Debayle, assumes control of the country.

1972

A devastating earthquake hits Managua, killing over 6000 people and leaving 300,000 homeless. Somoza embezzles international relief funds, fomenting support for the FSLN.

Honduras was heavily militarized, with large-scale US-Honduran maneuvers threatening an invasion of Nicaragua. The Sandinistas responded by instituting conscription and building an army that eventually numbered 95,000. Soviet and Cuban military and economic aid poured in, reaching US$700 million in 1987.

A CIA scheme to mine Nicaragua's harbors in 1984 resulted in a judgment against the US by the International Court of Justice. The court found that the US was in breach of its obligation under customary international law not to use force against another State and ordered it to pay repatriations to the Nicaraguan government; the Reagan administration rejected the findings and no payments were ever made.

TEN WHO SHAPED NICARAGUA

President Violeta Barrios de Chamorro (president 1990–96) The first female president in the hemisphere pulled together a fractured nation.

Cacique Nicarao Along with Cacique Nagrandano (for whom the Llanura Nagrandano, or northwestern plains, are named) and Cacique Diriangén (still remembered on La Meseta), wise Nicarao gave the nation his name.

President Daniel Ortega (president 1984–90, 2007–) Love him or hate him, you've got to admire the man's tenacity (and patience), waiting 17 years for another bite at the presidential apple.

Rubén Darío Began busting rhymes at age 12 and went on to become the favorite poet of a poetry-obsessed nation.

Carlos Fonseca Cofounder of the Frente Sandinista de Liberación Nacional (Sandinista National Liberation Front; FSLN). The martyred, intellectual hero of the Sandinista revolution, felt by many to represent its true ideals.

US President Ronald Reagan (president 1981–88) Together with political philosopher Jeanne Kirkpatrick, Secretary of State Alexander Haig Jr and Colonel Oliver North, Reagan masterminded the Iran-Contra debacle.

Augusto C Sandino His somber silhouette still dominates the Managua skyline, and his refusal to back down dominates the Nicaraguan collective consciousness.

Costa Rican President Oscar Arías Sánchez (president 1986–90, 2006–10) Architect of the 1987 peace accords that finally brought peace to Central America. Picked up a Nobel Prize for his efforts.

The Somozas A dynasty of Nicaraguan dictators, the first installed by the US military, and the last deposed more than four decades later by popular revolution.

William Walker The Tennessean who thought he could take on Central America but ended up in front of a Honduran firing squad.

1974

The FSLN kidnaps several members of the Somoza regime, exchanging the hostages for ransoms and the freeing of political prisoners.

1976

The government responds to FSLN kidnappings and attacks with a brutal crackdown in which FSLN co-founder Carlos Fonseca is killed.

January 1978

A general strike is declared following the assassination of newspaper editor and Somoza critic Pedro Joaquín Chamorro. Moderates unsuccessfully attempt to negotiate an end to the Somoza dictatorship.

August 1978

FSLN occupies the Palacio Nacional, taking over 2000 hostages and securing release for 60 imprisoned Sandinistas. There are uprisings in many major towns. The Guardia Nacional responds by shelling cities.

Shortly afterwards, the *New York Times* and *Washington Post* reported the existence of a CIA drafted Contra training manual promoting the assasination of Nicaraguan officials and other strategies illegal under US law, causing further embarrassment for the Reagan administration.

Nicaraguan elections in November 1984 were boycotted by leading non-Sandinistas, who complained of sweeping FSLN control of the nation's media. The Sandinistas rejected the claims, announcing that the media was being manipulated by contra supporters (*La Prensa* eventually acknowledged receiving CIA funding for publishing anti-Sandinista views). Daniel Ortega was elected president with 63% of the vote, and the FSLN controlled the National Assembly by a similar margin.

In May 1985 the USA initiated a trade embargo of Nicaragua and pressured other countries to do the same. The embargo lasted for five years, helping to strangle Nicaragua's economy.

With public opinion in the US growing wary of the war, the US Congress rejected further military aid for the Contras in 1985. According to the congressional report into the affair, the Reagan administration responded by continuing to fund the war through a scheme in which the CIA illegally sold weapons to Iran and diverted the proceeds to the Contras. When the details were leaked, the infamous Iran-Contra affair blew up.

After many failed peace initiatives, the Costa Rican president, Oscar Arías Sánchez, finally came up with an accord aimed at ending the war that was signed in Guatemala City in August 1987 by the leaders of Costa Rica, El Salvador, Nicaragua, Guatemala and Honduras. Less than a year later, the first ceasefire of the war was signed by representatives of the Contras and the Nicaraguan government at Sapoa, near the Costa Rican border.

Oliver North, co-architect of the Iran-Contra scheme and the man whom Ronald Reagan called 'an American hero,' is now a TV host and video game consultant.

Polls & Peace

By the late 1980s the Nicaraguan economy was again desperate. Civil war, the US trade embargo and the inefficiencies of a centralized economy had produced hyperinflation, falling production and rising unemployment. As it became clear that the US Congress was preparing to grant the Contras further aid, Daniel Ortega called elections that he expected would give the Sandinistas a popular mandate to govern.

The FSLN, however, underestimated the disillusionment and fatigue of the Nicaraguan people. Economic problems had eclipsed the dramatic accomplishments of the Sandinistas' early years: redistributing Somoza lands to small farming cooperatives, reducing illiteracy from 50% to 13%, eliminating polio through a massive immunization program and reducing the rate of infant mortality by a third.

The Unión Nacional Opositora (UNO), a broad coalition of 14 political parties opposing the Sandinistas, was formed in 1989. UNO presidential

1979

At the end of seven years of guerrilla warfare and 52 days of all-out battles, Sandinistas march on Managua. Anastasio Somoza flees the country on July 17 – the revolution is victorious.

1980

Ousted dictator Anastasio Somoza Debayle is assassinated by Sandinista agents in Asunción, Paraguay.

1980s

Opposition fighters known as the Contras carry out nationwide attacks. With US funding, the Contras grow in numbers to 15,000; the FSLN responds by implementing compulsory military service.

1984

Daniel Ortega is elected president with 63% of the vote. The FSLN controls the National Assembly by a similar margin.

candidate Violeta Barrios de Chamorro had the backing and financing of the USA, which had promised to lift the embargo and give hundreds of millions of dollars in economic aid to Nicaragua if UNO won. The UNO took the elections of February 25, 1990, gaining 55% of the presidential votes and 51 of the 110 seats in the National Assembly, compared with the FSLN's 39. Ortega had plenty of grounds for complaint, but in the end he went quietly, avoiding further conflict.

Politics in the 1990s

Chamorro took office in April 1990. The Contras called a heavily publicized ceasefire at the end of June. The US trade embargo was lifted, and foreign aid began to pour in.

Chamorro faced a tricky balancing act in trying to reunify the country and satisfy all interests. Economic recovery was slow; growth was sluggish and unemployment remained stubbornly high. Nevertheless, in 1996, when Nicaragua went to the polls again, the people rejected the FSLN's Ortega and opted for former Managua mayor Arnoldo Alemán of the PLC, a center-right liberal alliance.

Alemán invested heavily in infrastructure and reduced the size of the army by a factor of 10, but his administration was plagued by scandal, as corruption soared and Alemán amassed a personal fortune from the state's coffers, earning himself a place on Transparency International's list of the top 10 corrupt public officials of all time. Meanwhile, however, the Sandinistas had their own image problems, as the ever-present Ortega was accused by his stepdaughter of sexual abuse. In a gesture of mutual self-preservation, Ortega and Alemán struck a sordid little deal, popularly known as *el pacto* (the pact), which *Time* magazine reported was designed to nullify the threat of the opposition, pull the teeth of anti-corruption watchdogs and guarantee Alemán immunity from further investigation.

Sandinista diehards felt betrayed by Ortega's underhanded dealings, but many still believed in their party, and Ortega remained an important figure.

Hyperinflation played havoc with Nicaragua's currency during the war. Immediately prior to Somoza's fall, one US dollar would buy you 10 córdobas but it eventually peaked at 3.2 million to the dollar. The Sandinistas were unable to print money fast enough and resorted to stamping existing bills with new values.

Sandinista 2.0

After losing three successive elections, FSLN leader Ortega returned to power in the November 2006 elections, capitalizing on disillusionment with neoliberal policies that had failed to jump-start the country's economy and an *el pacto*-sponsored law that lowered the threshold for a first round victory to 35% of the votes (Ortega received 38%).

Taking office in January 2007, Ortega proclaimed a new era of leftist Latin American unity, leaving the USA and some international investors a little jumpy. The early days of Ortega's presidency were a flurry of activ-

1987

Central American Peace Accords signed. Ortega promises to lift press censorship, enforce a ceasefire and hold free elections as a sign of the Sandinistas' commitment to democracy.

1990

Violeta Barrios de Chamorro beats Daniel Ortega in presidential elections. The process of national reconciliation begins as the Contra War and US-led economic embargo end.

1996

Voters go to the polls again, once more rejecting the FSLN's Ortega, opting instead for former Managua mayor Arnoldo Alemán of the PLC, a center-right liberal alliance.

2001

Enrique Bolaños is elected president by a small margin. After 11 years of trying to make a comeback, it is Ortega's third defeat.

ity, with Nicaragua's energy crisis seemingly solved via a deal with Venezuela's Hugo Chávez, and Ortega pledging to maintain good relations with the USA while at the same time courting closer ties with US archrival Iran.

Daniel Ortegás presidential comeback featured its very own theme song – a Sandinista version of the John Lennon classic 'Give Peace a Chance'.

But as the Ortega government found its feet, there was no sign of radical land reforms or wave of nationalizations that the business sector had dreaded and some die-hard FSLN supporters had hoped for. Ortega for the most part followed the economic course set by the previous government and continued to honor Nicaragua's international financial obligations.

The first test for Nicaraguan democracy under the new Ortega government surfaced in 2008, with countrywide municipal elections. The FSLN claimed victory in over 70% of municipalities, when it had come to power with only 38% of the vote. Opposition forces claimed widespread voter fraud and *La Prensa* labeled the election 'the most fraudulent elections in Nicaraguan history.'

Nevertheless Ortega weathered the storm and by the end of his return term was able to point to solid economic growth alongside the reintroduction of free health care and education among the achievements of his government.

2006

After three failed bids, Ortega regains the presidency with 38% of the vote. He seeks closer ties with left-wing governments in Venezuela, Bolivia and Cuba.

2008

The Electoral Council bans two opposition parties. The FSLN sweeps countrywide municipal elections, which are widely denounced as fraudulent resulting in a reduction in foreign aid.

2010

Tensions flare at Harbour Head in the Río San Juan with Costa Rica responding to Nicaraguan dredging operations by sending heavily armed police to the border.

2011

After the FSLN-dominated Supreme Court overturns a constitutional ban on successive terms, Ortega wins reelection with an increased majority.

Nicaraguan Way of Life

When it comes to their country, Nicaraguans strike a wonderful balance of pride and humility. While many live in poverty and even the middle classes struggle to make ends meet, when asked about their country, most prefer to highlight its rich culture and natural beauty rather than dwell on the difficulties. And while the nation's distinct ethnic groups have their own particular cultures, one thing that unites all Nicaraguans is their laid-back style, great sense of humor and an openness that manifests itself in their love of socializing with whoever happens to be around.

The National Psyche

Nicaragua has a fierce cultural streak and prides itself on home-grown literature, dance, art, music and cuisine. This spiritual independence is a holdover not only from the revolution and Contra War, it goes back to Spanish colonization, when indigenous nations won limited autonomy at enormous personal cost.

Nicaragua also still suffers from a bit of post-traumatic stress disorder. Spanish-speakers will hear plenty of stories involving tanks, explosions and aerial bombings, not to mention 'the day the family cow wandered into the minefield' stories. Former Sandinistas and Contras work, play and take communion together, however, and any tensions you might expect seem to have been addressed and worked through. Opinions differ about the Sandinista years, but both sides will always agree to a good debate. Jump in and you'll learn more about the political scene than you ever would by reading a newspaper or guidebook.

It's not uncommon for Nica shopkeepers to engage in unbridled flattery and even declarations of love when trying to sell you something, especially in markets.

Of course, attitudes differ from place to place. Residents of the English- and Miskito-speaking Atlantic coast rarely consider themselves part of Nicaragua proper, and many would prefer to be returned to the British Empire than suffer further oppression by the 'Spaniards' on the other side of the country. The cattle ranchers of the central highlands resist interference from the federal government, while coffee pickers in Matagalpa or students in León are willing to walk to Managua to complain to the government if they perceive that an injustice has been done.

Lifestyle

Nicaragua is a country in motion. One in five Nicas live outside the country, most in the USA, Costa Rica and Honduras. Waves of migration to the cities, which began in the 1950s, have left more than 55% of the population urban. Most internal immigrants are young women, and most go to Managua; men tend to follow the harvest into rural areas and the surrounding countries. Regular jobs are difficult to find, and more than half of employed Nicaraguans are in the 'informal sector' – street vendors, maids, artisans – without benefits or job security.

Despite the country's Catholic background, couples often live together and have children without being married, especially in larger cities.

Nicaraguans are generally fairly accepting of the GLBT community, although the community is still fighting for full legal recognition.

Wealth is distributed unequally, with the moneyed elite living much as they would in Miami or elsewhere. For the vast majority of Nicaraguans, however, just putting food on the table is a daily struggle, with 46% living below the poverty line and perhaps a third of the country subsisting on two meals or fewer per day; almost one-fifth of children are at risk of problems relating to malnutrition, while in the Atlantic regions it is more than 30%.

However, when hitting the streets, even the poorest Nicaraguans will generally always appear in clean, freshly pressed clothes, which is why they find 'wealthy' backpackers in smelly rags so amusing.

Many of Managua's retired old school buses have been converted into *bus pelones* (bald buses) – open-air party buses that give residents without vehicles the chance to cruise the streets of the city in the evening.

Economy

Nicaragua's solid grounding as an agricultural nation is a blessing and a curse. While the average *campesino* (farmer) will generally have something to eat, the sector as a whole is vulnerable to a range of threats. Plunging world commodity prices, natural disasters and environmental factors like soil degradation and water shortages are all problems that Nicaraguan farmers face regularly. Coffee remains Nicaragua's main agricultural export, followed by beef, shrimp, dairy products and tobacco.

Industrial production, encouraged under the last of the Somozas, was all but destroyed by the war and is only now beginning to slowly pick up again. By far the biggest industry is textile and apparel production, but the cigar industry is growing rapidly. Gold mining is another important industry. Tourism plays an increasingly important role in the economy, and it is here more than anywhere else that many see a bright future for Nicaragua.

By the end of the war, Nicaragua was a heavily indebted nation. In 1979 the departing dictator Somoza emptied the country's coffers. The incoming Sandinista government engaged in some shaky economic policies (including massive public spending financed by foreign lending), while the economy was being slowly strangled by the US trade embargo. In 2000 Nicaragua was included on the Highly Indebted Poor Countries

FREE TRADE VS FAIR TRADE

In March 2006 Nicaragua ratified the Dominican Republic-Central America Free Trade Agreement (DR-CAFTA). An agreement between an economic superpower like the US and various struggling nations was always going to be controversial, and plenty of political mileage was made, but it's worth remembering that, in the end, the agreement was approved by liberals and Sandinistas alike.

The central question to any such agreement is this: who benefits? The US stood to gain from cheaper imports, wider markets, investment opportunities and access to cheap foreign labor, but what was in it for Nicaragua?

The short answer was exports, foreign investment and jobs. What *kinds* of exports, investment and jobs? Well, there's been a little spike in the export of primary products such as beef and sugar, but the biggest change to Nicaragua's economic landscape has been the spread of the *maquilladoras* (clothing assembly factories) across the country. These factories provide much-needed work (Nicaragua's underemployment rate runs at around 46%), but critics say the *maquilladoras* are no real solution – they set up in Free Trade Zones (Nicaragua has four), which aren't bound by Nicaraguan law, so they don't pay minimum wage or respect workers' rights. When exported, goods don't incur export duty, so Nicaragua ends up earning very little. It's a process that workers' rights and environmental activist Ralph Nader calls 'the race to the bottom,' where poor countries end up competing to see who can offer the most favorable deal to investor nations.

list, meaning that a large chunk of its massive foreign debt was canceled after it complied with a series of conditions set down by the World Bank and International Monetary Fund (IMF). These measures – which included privatizing public assets and opening the economy to foreign markets – are highly controversial and it remains to be seen whether Nicaragua's participation in the program will produce long-term gains for its ordinary residents.

Population

With 6.1 million people spread across 130,000 sq km, Nicaragua is the second-least densely populated country in Central America after Belize. The CIA World Factbook estimates that 69% of the population is *mestizo* (of mixed ancestry, usually Spanish and indigenous people), 17% white, 9% black and 5% indigenous. The most recent census reports that just over 440,000 people describe themselves as indigenous: the Miskito (121,000), Mayangna/Sumo (9800) and Garifuna (3300), all with some African heritage, occupy the Caribbean coast alongside the Rama (4200). In the central and northern highlands, the Cacaopoeras and Matagalpas (15,200) may be Maya in origin, while the Chorotegas (46,000), the Subtiavas (20,000) and the Nahoas (11,100) have similarities to the Aztecs.

European heritage is just as diverse. The Spanish settled the Pacific coast, while a wave of German immigrants in the 1800s has left the northern highlands surprisingly *chele* (white, from *leche,* or milk). And many of those blue eyes you see on the Atlantic coast can be traced back to British, French and Dutch pirates.

The original African immigrants were shipwrecked, escaped or freed slaves who began arriving soon after the Spanish. Another wave of Creoles and West Indians arrived in the late 1800s to work on banana and cacao plantations in the east. Mix all that together, simmer for a few hundred years and you get an uncommonly good-looking people who consider racism a bit silly.

Stunning Pearl Lagoon's handful of ethnic fishing villages are home to Miskito, Creole and Garifuna people who have lived and traded with one another for over 300 years.

Sports

It's just not a weekend in Nicaragua without the crack of a baseball bat, but there really are other sports in the country – you just have to look.

Football (soccer) is growing in popularity and is especially big in the north of the country. The National Futból League (www.fenifut.org.ni) has a website with schedules and stats. Boxing is also extremely popular and Nicaragua produces some champion pugilists, especially in the lower weight divisions.

While it is considered barbaric by many people, cockfighting is one of Nicaragua's most popular spectator sports, especially in rural areas. Beautiful alpha roosters with knives strapped to their feet slash each other apart in miniature bullrings while the crowd place bets and drink copious amounts of moonshine.

Rodeos and bullfights, which take place during *fiestas patronales* (saints days), are considerably less gory than their Spanish or South American counterparts as it's illegal to use any weapons or kill the bull (although the occasional town drunk does sometimes end up getting gouged or walloped). Even so they are pretty lowbrow affairs and there is no doubt the bull does not enjoy the spectacle.

Many towns have pickup soccer, baseball, volleyball and basketball games, and foreigners are usually more than welcome to join in. It's a fine opportunity to interact with the locals without worrying about the subjunctive tenses.

TAKE ME OUT TO THE BÉISBOL GAME

Every Sunday, all over the country, from abandoned lots to the national stadium, there's one game that's got Nicaraguans obsessed, and if you think it's football, you're dead wrong.

Despite popular belief, baseball was big here even before the marines arrived in 1909 – their presence just gave the sport a shot in the arm. The first recorded series was played in 1887, when two Bluefields teams – Four Roses and Southern – battled it out over seven games. Four years later, baseball fever hit the Pacific coast and by 1915 there was a national championship.

While major-league Nica players are generally treated like royalty here, very few of them don't dream of going to the US to play, joining a long list of their countrymen, including Tony Chevez, Albert Williams, David Green, Porfirio Altamirano, Vincent Padilla, Marvin Bernard and, of course, Hall of Famer Denis 'El Presidente' Martínez, who pitched more winning major-league games than any Latino and who had Nicaragua's national stadium, Estadio Denis Martínez, named after him.

Every town has some sort of baseball ground, from a dusty lot on the outskirts to some fairly fancy affairs in Managua, León, Granada and Chinandega (among others). These four towns, incidentally, compete in Nicaragua's major league.

Games are played on Sunday in villages, towns and cities all over the country, but if you'd like to catch some major-league action, log on to www.lnbp.com.ni (in Spanish) for schedules. For even better atmosphere, check out the biennial Atlantic Series, which features teams from all over the Caribbean region playing off for a cup. The tournament takes place in different cities and towns throughout the region, but is always a great party.

Media

International media-monitoring bodies have reported that freedom of the press in Nicaragua has deteriorated significantly under the Frente Sandinista de Liberación Nacional (Sandinista National Liberation Front; FSLN) government, although an independent media still operates in the country.

The current FSLN leadership are particularly media savvy and have made controlling the airwaves a priority. According to the *New York Times,* since returning to power, Daniel Ortega has invested heavily in media operations, while at the same time cutting government advertising in non-Sandinista outlets. The newspaper goes on to report that Ortega's children run television networks Multinoticias, Channel 8 and Channel 13, and that the FSLN leader now controls nearly half of Nicaragua's television outlets.

In Caribbean Nicaragua, domino tournaments are serious events, with neighborhood clubs decked out in team T-shirts slamming down tiles in front of noisy spectators.

According to the Committee to Protect Journalists (CPJ), Ortega uses these media outlets to launch 'character attacks against his critics' as part of an effort to marginalize independent media. In its 2010 Freedom of Press report, Freedom House notes that Ortega referred to the independent media in the country as 'terrorists, agents of the CIA,' and 'sons of Goebbels.'

The CPJ lists the 'most egregrious example of government intimidation' as that directed at television journalist Carlos Fernando Chamorro, son of former *La Prensa* editor Pedro Joaquín Chamorro whose assasination by Somoza was one of the sparks of the revolution. Following the airing of reports on an extortion scheme involving the Sandinista party, Chamorro was formally investigated for money laundering. After a wave of domestic and international criticism, the charges were later dropped.

Despite Nicaraguan law stating that officials must supply accurate information to the media upon request, local journalists have reported restrictions in accessing government press conferences and officials, while those working for government-linked news outlets are given free reign. The CPJ reports that First Lady Rosario Murillo is a 'virtual prime minister' who manages all of the government's communications, and officials in the executive branch are permitted to talk to the press only with her authorization.

While the government controls many of the radio and TV stations, Nicaragua's two national daily newspapers – *La Prensa* and *El Nuevo Diario* – remain highly critical of the Ortega government (a fact the FSLN repeatedly alludes to when confronted with claims of censorship and media control). The former is your classic conservative rag – understandably railing against all things Sandinista. The latter (more classically a blue-collar publication) seems to draw a distinction between the old-school Sandinistas (whom it still vaguely supports) and the new-breed Danielistas (for whom it has very little patience).

It remains to be seen if, as it consolidates its power and media empire, the Ortega government will continue to tolerate independent opinion. After Ortega's initial return to power, the *Nica Times* reported that Attorney General Hernán Estrada made the following statement, which some interpreted as a veiled threat: 'A call from [President] Daniel Ortega would leave nothing left of the opposition media...not a single radio station or channel. But thank God he hasn't done that because of our governor's wisdom and serene [sic].'

Most Nicaraguan TV stations have two types of news: a sensationalist ambulance-chasing edition featuring graphic portrayals of fights and accidents – usually displayed on the big screen at dinner time – followed by a far less popular political edition.

Religion

Although Nicaragua's majority religion is Catholic (about 59% of the population identifies as such), Nicaraguan Catholicism retains many indigenous elements, as the decor and ceremonies of churches such as San Juan Bautista de Subtiava and Masaya's María Magdelena make clear. Liberation theology also made its mark on Nicaraguan Catholicism, influencing priest and poet Ernesto Cardenal to advocate armed resistance to the Somoza dictatorship. Publicly chastised and later defrocked by Pope John Paul II, Cardenal remains a beloved religious leader. Nicaragua's incredible selection of Catholic churches and fascinating *fiestas patronales* remain highlights of the country.

On the Atlantic coast, Moravian missionaries from Germany began arriving in the early 1800s, and today their red-and-white wooden churches are the centerpieces of many Creole and Miskito towns. More recently, over 100 Protestant sects, most US-based and collectively referred to as *evangelistas,* have converted at least 21% of the population; in fact, many of the foreigners you'll meet in rural Nicaragua are missionaries, who may try to convert you too.

Perhaps most interesting, nearly 16% of Nicaraguans say they are atheist or agnostic, unusual in Latin America and a huge relief if you're one too.

Women in Nicaragua

Women, especially in rural sectors, are likely to work outside of the home, and do half of all agricultural labor. This stems in part from ideals espoused by the (original) Sandinistas, who considered women equal players in the remolding of the country, but also from necessity, as many men died or were maimed during the wars, or later emigrated to find work; after the Contra War, the country was more than 55% female. The strong women's movement is fascinating; check out Boletina at www.puntos.org.ni to learn more.

In traditional Miskito societies, women own the farmland and plant crops.

Despite loud protests by many organizations, in 2006 Nicaragua passed a controversial law declaring abortion illegal even when the life of the mother is at risk. Women's groups say the law has led to the deaths of dozens of women and mostly affects the poor, as the wealthy (including the daughters of politicians) are able to travel to other countries for medical attention without restrictions.

Arts & Architecture

Nicaragua, as any book will tell you, is the only country in the world that celebrates literature, particularly poetry, with appropriate passion, revering its writers with a fervor reserved, in more developed countries, for Hollywood stars. But it's not all about printed prose – Nicaragua also boasts a variety of homegrown musical genres, energetic dances and renowned painters all shaped by the nation's dominant themes of romance and rebellion.

Gioconda Belli's *The Inhabited Woman* is well worth tracking down. It's a loosely political tale based partly on true events, but the magic here is in Belli's sensual, poetic prose.

Nation of Poets

Poetry lies at the very heart of Nicaragua's cultural identity. Both major daily newspapers run a literary supplement in their Friday editions, high-school kids form poetry clubs, and any *campesino* (farmer) picking coffee in the isolated mountains can tell you who the greatest poet in history is: Rubén Darío, voice of the nation. They will then recite a poem by Darío, quite possibly followed by a few of their own.

Nicaragua is also home to the peculiar cultural archetype of 'warrior poets,' folks who choose to go with both the pen and the sword. Among the most famous are Leonel Rugama, who held off the Guardia Nacional while hero Carlos Fonseca escaped; Rigoberto López Pérez, who assassinated the original Somoza in León; liberation theologian Ernesto Cardenal; and former Sandinista undercover agent Gioconda Belli.

The nation's original epic composition, the Nicaraguan equivalent to *Beowulf* or *Chanson de Roland,* is *El Güegüense,* a burlesque dating from the 1600s. A morality play of sorts, it pits an indigenous Nicaraguan businessman against corrupt and inept Spanish authorities; using only his sly wit and a few multilingual double entendres, the Nica ends up on top.

León has been home to the nation's greatest poets, including Darío, Azarias H Pallais, Salomon de la Selva and Alfonso Cortés, the last of whom did his best work while going insane in Darío's childhood home. A Rubén Darío tribute site (www.dariana.com) has biographies and bibliographies of major Nicaraguan writers. The most important modern writers include Pablo Antonio Cuadra, a former editor of *La Prensa,* and Ernesto Cardenal.

One of the few Nicaraguan writers regularly translated into English is Gioconda Belli (www.giocondabelli.org), who was working undercover with the Sandinistas when she won the prestigious Casa de las Americas international poetry prize. Her internationally acclaimed work is both sexual and revolutionary, and is the best way to get a woman's-eye view of Nicaragua in the 1970s.

Music

Folkloric music and dance received a huge boost from the revolution, which sought to mine Nicaraguan culture for cultural resources rather than import more popular options, quite possibly at great cost. As a result, you'll probably be able to see a musical or dance performance during even a short visit, the most convenient being *Noches Verbenas,* held

RUBÉN DARÍO

To say that Rubén Darío is a famous poet is an outrageous understatement. The man is a national hero – his birthplace (Ciudad Darío), the national theater and the entire Cordillera Dariense mountain range are named after him.

Something of a child prodigy, Darío could read by age four (he'd polished off *Don Quixote* and various other classics by age 10) and had his first poetry published in León newspapers at age 12.

Deemed too 'antireligious' to be awarded a scholarship to Europe, Darío was sent to El Salvador at the age of 15. There he met and befriended Salvadorian poet Francisco Gavidia, whose work and teachings would have a profound influence on Darío's style.

Darío traveled extensively: to Chile, where he worked as a journalist and wrote his breakthrough piece, *Azul*; to Argentina, where he became a leading member of the modernist literary movement; and, last, to Europe, where he continued to write some of what Chilean poet Pablo Neruda called some of the most creative poetry in the Spanish language.

Darío was appointed Nicaragua's ambassador to France, then Spain, but such officialdom never slowed him down. His hard-drinking, womanizing lifestyle was by now legendary (and somewhat requisite for poets of the era), but it took its toll in 1914 when Darío contracted pneumonia. He recovered, but was left weak and bankrupt. Friends banded together and raised the money for him to return to Nicaragua. He died in León two years later, at the age of 49.

Poesía en Español (luis.salas.net/indexrd.htm) has most of Rubén Darío's poems available online, while English-language Dariana (www.dariana.com), a Rubén Darío tribute site, has 11 of his poems translated into English by fellow legendary Léonese poet Salomón de la Selva.

every Thursday evening at the Mercado Artesanías (National Artisans Market) in Masaya. Also check out cultural centers, close to the Parque Central in most larger towns, or at the municipal theaters in Granada, León and Managua, to see what's on. *Fiestas patronales* (patron saint parties) are a good time to catch a performance, which in the northern highlands will likely have a polka component.

Perhaps the most important musical form is marimba, usually played on xylophones made of precious wood with names like 'The Lovers,' 'Dance of the Black Woman,' and 'Fat Honey,' which you'll enjoy over a cold glass of *chicha* (mildly alcoholic corn beverage) at some shady Parque Central. The guardians of this and other traditional forms of Nicaraguan music are the Mejía Godoy brothers (see www.losmejiagodoy.com), whom you can (and should) catch live in Managua.

Marimba music was given a new sense of cool with the arrival on the scene of La Cuneta Son Machín (lacunetasonmachin.com), a cumbia-rock fusion group heavily influenced by traditional Nicaraguan sounds. If you get the chance, make sure to check out their energetic live performances.

On the Atlantic coast reggae and country are king but there are also homegrown sounds including upbeat Maypole music, which is often accompanied by spicy dance moves, and Miskito pop, heavily influenced by the electronic keyboard music of rural churches where many of the musicians learned to play.

Considering how few venues there are available for them to play, new talents are plentiful in Nicaragua. If you're looking for laid-back electronica, try Momotobo. Quirky bossa-pop fans should hunt down anything by Belén, while Division Urbana is probably the best of many groups doing the hard rock thing. Manu Chao fans will probably like Perrozompopo,

THE WRITING (PAINTING) ON THE WALL

Nothing quite captures Nicaraguans' spirit, creativity and political sentiment like their love for murals. Often strikingly beautiful pieces of art in their own right, murals served a practical and political end in the days before the Sandinistas' Literacy Crusade of broadcasting a message to an audience that was largely illiterate.

There are murals in all major cities, but the Sandinista strongholds of León and Estelí are standouts, where at one stage nearly every blank wall in the downtown was covered with colorful revolutionary messages. The area around the UCA university in Managua has some fine examples too.

However, with the modernization of the cities, some of the best examples have been painted over, often with propaganda from multinational cell-phone networks.

Estelí has its own NGO teaching mural painting to kids and teenagers, and is also home to a new movement of muralistas, who use more-recognizable graffiti techniques but continue to paint the walls of the city with images of a social slant.

For a look at murals from around the country, check out the gorgeous coffee-table book *The Murals of Revolutionary Nicaragua* by David Kunzle.

and for sheer lyrical beauty, floating melodies and electro-pop crossover, keep an eye out for discs by Clara Grun.

Painting & Sculpture

The oldest artistic tradition in Nicaragua is ceramics, dating from about 2000 BC with simple, functional vessels, developing into more sculptural representations by around AD 300. By the time the Spanish arrived, Nicaraguan ceramics were complex, artistic and often ceremonial, and indicate a pronounced Aztec influence in both design and decoration. Remember that it's illegal (and lame) to remove pre-Columbian ceramics from Nicaragua.

Today top-quality ceramics are most famously produced in San Juan de Oriente, which is known for colorfully painted fine white clays and heavier, carved pots; in Mozonte, near Ocotal; and at Matagalpa and Jinotega, which are renowned for their black ceramics.

Almost as ancient an art, stone carving probably became popular around AD 800, when someone realized that the soft volcanic basalt could be shaped with obsidian tools imported from Mexico and Guatemala. Petroglyphs, usually fairly simple, linear drawings carved into the surface of a stone, are all over the country, and it's easy to arrange tours from Isla de Ometepe, Granada and Matagalpa.

Stone statues, expressive and figurative, not to mention tall (one tops 5m) are rarer but also worth seeing; the best museums are in Granada and Juigalpa. Much finer stone statues are being produced today, using polished, translucent soapstone worked in the backyard workshops of San Juan de Limay, near Estelí.

Painting apparently arrived with the Spanish (though there's evidence that both statues and petroglyphs were once more vividly colored), the earliest works being mostly religious in nature; the best places to see paintings are in León, at the Museo de Arte Sacre and the Museo de Arte Fundación Ortiz-Guardián. The latter also traces Nicaraguan painting through to the present, including the Romantic and Impressionistic work of Rodrigo Peñalba, who founded the School of Beaux Arts; and the Praxis Group of the 1960s, led by Alejandro Arostegui and possessed of a heavy-handed social realism, depicting hunger, poverty and torture.

In the 1970s Ernesto Cardenal founded an art colony on the Islas Solentiname, an isolated group of islands in the southeast corner of Lago

MURALS

Selected Poems by Rubén Darío (translated by Lysander Kemp) has verses from Nicaragua's most famous poet in the original on one page and in English translation on the facing page.

de Nicaragua, today internationally renowned for the gem-toned paintings and balsa-wood sculptures that so colorfully (and accurately) capture the tropical landscape. If you can't get to the islands yourself, try the Masaya markets, or any of the art galleries in Managua or Granada.

A more venerable form of the art is on display every Semana Santa in the Subtiava neighborhood of León, when 'sawdust carpets,' scenes painstakingly rendered in colored sawdust, are created throughout the neighborhood, then swirled together as religious processions go by.

Theater & Dance

Traditional music, dance and theater are difficult to separate; all are mixed together with wild costumes to create spectacles that generally also have a religious component plus plenty of fireworks. Pieces you'll see performed by streetside beggars and professional troupes include *La Gigantona,* with an enormous Spanish woman and teeny-tiny Nicaraguan guy. Another common piece is *The Dance of the Old People,* in which an older gentleman woos a sexy grandma, but once she gives in, he starts chasing younger women in the audience.

Modern theater is not well developed in Nicaragua, and only major towns have performance spaces. There's a growing independent film scene, and you can catch very low-budget, usually documentary films, often with overtly feminist or progressive themes, at cultural centers – but never movie theaters, which show mostly Hollywood blockbusters.

To Bury Our Fathers by Sergio Ramírez – one of Nicaragua's most respected writers (and former Sandinista vice president) – is possibly the best fiction-based portrait of the Somoza years in print.

CHURCHES OF NICARAGUA

Nicaragua hasn't always been this poor – in the 1960s Costa Ricans were sneaking across the border to work here. From the first days of the Spanish conquest through to the late 1800s, when Nicaragua controlled the only warm-water route between the world's two great oceans, this little country was a major power broker.

With cash to spare and a Catholic population to impress, the authorities constructed churches even devout atheists will enjoy. León may be the nation's pinnacle of religious architecture, but here are a few other must-sees.

➡ **Cathedrals of Managua** (p47) The poignant, burnt-out husk of Managua's original cathedral is off-limits, but you're welcome to ponder the new cathedral's ultramodern domes: cooling towers for a divine nuclear reactor? Homage to Islam? Eggs hatching into a peaceful tomorrow?

➡ **Basílica de Nuestra Señora de la Inmaculada Concepción de la Virgen María** (p**163**) Even Pope John Paul II visited the beautiful Virgen del Trono, patron saint of Nicaragua and mistress of La Gritería, the nation's most important religious event.

➡ **Templo de El Sauce** (p160) Quite literally a pilgrimage-worthy destination; every January thousands come to see El Señor de Esquipulas, the Black Christ.

➡ **Moravian Church in Bluefields** (p222) Faithfully rebuilt to its Victorian-era specs after Bluefields' utter destruction during Hurricane Juana; it's not just lovely, it's a symbol of hope and perseverance.

➡ **Iglesia Catedral San Pedro** (p195) This baroque 1874 beauty, known for its twin bell towers, remains one of the country's most elegant churches despite a desperate need for renovation.

➡ **Templo Parroquial de San Rafael Arcángel** (p188) This is religion as sensory overload, with beautiful architecture and truly amazing murals.

➡ **Nuestra Señora de Solentiname** (p248) Ernesto Cardenal and the Solentiname community built this heartfelt and humble adobe church, its murals designed by children.

Architecture

Famous Nicaraguan musician Carlos Mejía Godoy, who wrote theme songs for the Sandinista revolution, went on to sue the FSLN for improper use of those very songs.

The success of the Spanish conquest let the motherland finally break free of French architectural forms, such as Gothic architecture, and experiment with homegrown styles both at home and in the Americas.

Some of the earliest New World churches are a Moorish-Spanish hybrid called *mujédar,* with squat silhouettes, wooden roofs and geometric configurations. Influenced by Islam as well as the Italian Renaissance are *plateresque* (elaborate silver filigree) on altars such as in El Viejo.

Baroque hit big in the mid-1600s, and was the most popular choice for major buildings over the next century. Primitivist baroque, featuring graceful but unadorned adobe and wood columns, and common in smaller colonial towns, was followed by full Spanish baroque style, with extravagant design (stone grapevines wending up massive pillars, for example), sometimes called *churriguera.*

The most famous examples of Spanish colonial architecture can be found in Granada and León, but colonial gems are scattered throughout the country.

Land & Wildlife

With over a million hectares of virgin forest, 19 active volcanoes and vibrant coral reefs, Nicaragua has been endowed with more than its share of natural beauty. Combine that with a low population density and very little industrialization and you'll discover that in Nicaragua, wilderness is never far away.

The Land

The formation of the Central American Isthmus began about 60 million years ago, connecting the two massive American continents for the first time three million years ago. Marking the volcanic crush of the Cocos and Caribbean tectonic plates, the Maribios Volcanic Chain is one of the most volcanic places in the world.

The Mesoamerican Biological Corridor was established in 2008 to protect 106 critically endangered species. It stretches from Panama to Mexico.

There are 40 major volcanic formations, including 28 volcanoes and eight crater lakes, among them Reserva Natural Laguna de Apoyo, with hotels and private homes, Laguna Tiscapa in downtown Managua, and Laguna Asososca, with no development at all.

The region's appeal to early colonists increased as they realized that the soil was further enriched by this striking geological feature. Earthquakes and volcanoes are a part of life along the borders of the Caribbean and Cocos plates, and you'll find very few authentic colonial buildings that haven't been touched up since the 1500s.

Nicaragua's highest mountains, however, are metamorphic, not volcanic. Running down the center of Nicaragua like an opening zipper, they rise to their greatest heights as a granite chain contiguous with the Rocky Mountains and the Andes. They go by several names, including Cordillera Dariense (after Rubén Darío). Topped with cool cloud forests above 1200m, these refreshing regions are home to some of the best national parks and protected areas. Two of the most accessible reserves up north are Área Protegida Miraflor, close to Estelí, and Reserva Natural Cerro Apante, a hike from Matagalpa. Or go deeper, to Reserva Natural Macizos de Peñas Blancas, actually part of Bosawás, the largest protected swathe of rainforest north of the Amazon. It's 730,000 hectares of humid tropical and subtropical forest, also accessible by the largest river in Central America, the Río Coco (560km).

Nicaragua also has the two largest lakes in Central America, Lago de Managua (1064 sq km) and Lago de Nicaragua (8264 sq km), with more than 500 islands, some protected, as well as wonderful wetlands, like Refugio de Vida Silvestre los Guatuzos.

The Atlantic coast is worlds apart, geologically as well as culturally, from the drier, more developed Pacific side. A vast eroding plain of rolling hills and ancient volcanic plugs, here's where around 90% of the country's rainfall ends up. This is the region with the wildest protected reserves and worst access – with very few exceptions, it's difficult and relatively expensive to travel here, as most transportation is by boat. The lowlands are remarkable for their dry pine savannas and countless wetlands and have four major river systems. The easiest way in is along the Río San Juan, a Unesco biosphere reserve.

DID THE EARTH MOVE FOR YOU?

Straddling two tectonic plates has had mixed results for Nicaragua. On the one hand, it's produced the spectacular Maribios chain and the rest of the 40 volcanoes that make up western Nicaragua's dramatic skyline, providing geothermal energy, poetic inspiration and hiking opportunities galore.

On the down side, volcanoes have, over the years, blackened skies, changed landscapes and buried entire villages, not to mention the entire original city of León.

Nicaragua's position between the stationary Caribbean plate and the eastward-moving Cocos plate (the two are colliding at a rate of about 10cm per year) has produced some other geologic excitement as well – most of it spelling bad news for the locals.

Tension builds between colliding plates and is released in the form of earthquakes. Nicaragua gets rocked on a regular basis – the 1972 quake all but flattened Managua, which had already been hit hard in 1931. In 2000, two major quakes in two days leveled villages in the southwest.

When earthquakes happen at sea they cause tsunamis. Tsunamis were registered in 1854 and 1902, but the biggest one in recent history was in 1992, when waves of up to 10m pummeled the Pacific coastline, killing 170 people and leaving 130,000 homeless.

Slower (but no less dramatic) plate movement produced the Lago de Nicaragua – the theory being that the Pacific and Atlantic were once joined, but the upward thrust of earth caused by plate collision cut them off. Volcanic sedimentation and erosion then created the Pacific and Atlantic coastlines.

Flora & Fauna

Nicaragua is home to about 1800 vertebrate species, including 250 mammals, and 30,000 species in total, including 688 bird species (around 500 resident and 150 migratory).

Animals are slowly working their way northward, a migration of densities that will one day be facilitated by the Mesoamerican Corridor, a proposed aisle of shady protected rainforest stretching from Panama to Mexico. Other countries in on the agreement are just getting started on the project, but Nicaragua's two enormous Unesco biosphere reserves, Bosawás and Southeast Nicaragua (Río San Juan), make a significant chunk.

Animals

Most people are looking for monkeys, and there are three natives: big howler monkeys, smaller spider monkeys and sneaky capuchins. Pizotes, elsewhere called coatis, are the long-tailed, toothy-smiled rodents that are particularly bold on the Rivas peninsula – feed them at your own risk. Several cats (pumas, jaguars and others) survive, but you probably won't see them. Baird's tapirs, 250kg herbivores, are another rare treat. At night you'll see hundreds of bats, including, maybe, vampire bats – which usually stick to livestock.

Birders are discovering Nicaragua, in particular the wild east-coast's estuaries, where migratory birds flock, starting in August and packing places like the Río San Juan and Islas Solentiname by September and October.

While Nicaragua has no endemic bird species of its own, 19 of Central America's 21 endemics are represented here. Nicaragua's spectacular national bird, the turquoise-browed mot-mot (*guardabarranco* in Spanish), has a distinctive notched tail.

Kingfishers, swallows, scarlet tanagers and Tennessee warblers are just a few of the birds that make their winter homes here. Local birds are

PARKS & RESERVES

About 18.2% of Nicaragua's land is federally protected as part of 76 wildlife areas. The system isn't even close to perfect, and problems with poaching and deforestation are rife. But the government has deemed it worth fighting for and is stepping up patrols in and around parks.

Nicaragua's national parks and reserves are unlike those in many other countries in that the majority have next to no facilities for visitors. Accommodations within park boundaries are rare, dedicated zones to pitch a tent even more so. There are very few marked trails, which makes hiring local guides even more important, and reliable maps of the reserves are also hard to come by.

Marena administers most wildlife areas, often through other public and private organizations. There's a Marena office in most major towns, and while tourism is not its main job, staff may be able to find guides, transportation and lodging for more-difficult-to-access parks. They can at least point you toward folks who can help, which could be, for example, a women's organic coffee collective. Have fun!

MAJOR PARK OR NATURAL AREA	FEATURES	ACTIVITIES
Parque Nacional Volcán Masaya	most heavily venting volcano in Central America, possible gateway to hell; lava tunnels; parakeets	driving to the edge of an active crater, bird-watching, hiking
Reserva Natural Volcán Concepción & Parque Nacional Volcán Maderas	1 island, 2 volcanoes: gently smoking Concepción & dormant Maderas, crowned in cloud forest	hiking, petroglyph hunting, swimming, kayaking
Reserva Biológica Indio-Maíz	epic riverboat rides, macaws, walking trees, frogs	canoeing, kayaking, hiking
Reserva de Biosfera Bosawás	largest reserve in Central America, indigenous villages	testing your limits, trail-less hikes
Reserva Natural Cerro Musún	quetzals, cloud forests, huge waterfalls, real trails	hiking, bird-watching, swimming
Área Protegida Miraflor	cloud-forest reserve innovatively managed by agricultural cooperative: its nature & culture!	milking cows, hiking, swimming in waterfalls, admiring orchids
Área Protegida Cerro Tisey-Estanzuela	cloud forests, views across the Maribios Volcanic Chain, goat cheese	hiking, swimming, eating cheese
Monumento Nacional Cañon de Somoto	the Río Coco is born – in the 'Grand Canyon' of Nicaragua	hiking, rock scrambles, swimming in freezing-cold water
Reserva Natural Isla Juan Venado	sandy Pacific barrier island; mangroves, sea turtles, lagoons	boating, surfing, camping, swimming
Parque Nacional Archipiélago Zapatera	isolated islands covered with petroglyphs, ancient statues, small volcano, rustic accommodations	climbing, hiking, boating, pretending you're an archaeologist
Refugio de Vida Silvestre La Flor	leatherback & olive ridley turtles, primary dry tropical forest, beaches	surfing, camping, sea-turtle ogling
Reserva Natural Volcán Mombacho	volcanic views of Granada & Cocibolca, dwarf cloud forest, 100 species of orchid, fumeroles, butterfly garden	hiking, camping, riding in military transport
Reserva Natural Volcán Cosigüina	volcanoes, hot springs, crater lakes, macaws, archaeological sites	hiking, camping, swimming, thermal baths

even more spectacular, including the red macaw, the yellow-chested oropendola (which hangs its ball-shaped nests from trees), the three-wattled bellbird of the cloud forests, with its distinctive call, and of course the resplendent quetzal.

Other winged attractions are the uracas, (huge blue jays) of Isla de Ometepe, the canaries living inside the fuming crater of Volcán Masaya and the waterfall of Reserva Natural Chocoyero–El Brujo, and the beautiful waterfowl of the Río San Juan.

Other visitors are more interested in the undersea wildlife, which on the Pacific side includes tuna, rooster fish and snook. Lago de Nicaragua and the Río San Juan have their own scaly menagerie, including sawfish, the toothy gaspar, mojarra, guapote and, most importantly, tarpon, as well as the extraordinary freshwater bull shark.

The tiny strawberry poison dart frog (*Dendrobates pumilio*) is famous for its color morphs, with around 30 different color combinations identified.

There are lots of reptiles, including five kinds of sea turtle, two kinds of iguana and several snakes. When walking in rainforests, keep your eyes peeled for the feared tercipelo (fer-de-lance, Bothrops Asper), the most dangerous snake in Central America. Unlike many snakes found in the region, it is aggressive and often chooses to attack rather than flee danger. It's common in the jungles of the Río San Juan. Other poisonous snakes to look out for include the coral snake and the cascabel, a danger mostly to cattle.

Nicaragua also has plenty of scorpions, yoúll find them living in dark corners (they love those atmospheric old houses), under rocks, in wood piles and on the beach. But while they look mean, their sting is not lethal and is more like a hardcore bee sting.

Insects, of course, make up the vast majority of species, including over 1000 species of butterflies. Tarantulas are common, but not deadly, and keep your eyes open for leaf-cutter ants, which raise fungus for snacks beneath massive anthills the size of VW Beetles. Acacia ants are hidden inside the hollow thorns of acacia trees – shake one of them and you'll see several hundred swarming reasons why the plant goes to all the trouble. And the weird-looking woody balls in the trees? Termites.

Endangered Species

Nicaragua has about 200 species on the endangered list, including sea turtles and iguanas, both traditional food sources, as well as boa constrictors and alligators. Golden frogs and blood frogs, like amphibians across the globe, are also dwindling. Endangered birds include quetzals, peregrine falcons and macaws, with two of Central America's last viable populations in Reserva Natural Volcán Cosigüina and Reserva Biologica Indio-Maíz. Several endangered or threatened mammals also make their homes here, including howler, white-face and spider monkeys; several kinds of cats, including jaguars and mountain lions; as well as aquatic species like manatees and dolphins. Offshore fisheries are being, or have been, depleted of oysters, lobsters, green turtles and all manner of fish.

Plants

Nicaragua has four major environment zones, each with very different ecosystems and plants. Dry tropical forests are the rarest, as their location – below 500m, often right by the beach – and seven-month dry season make them perfect places to plant crops and build resort hotels. These forests are home to more than 30 species of hardwood, including precious mahogany.

Some dramatic species found in the ecosystem include strangler figs, which start out as slender vines and end up entombing the host tree in a dramatically buttressed encasement; the wide-spreading guanacaste of the endless savannahs; and the pithaya, a branch-dwelling cactus with delicious edible fruit. Most plants lose their leaves by January, except in the largest remaining mangrove stand in Central America, partially preserved as Reserva Natural Isla Juan Venado and Reserva Natural Estero Padre Ramos, and crossing borders into El Salvador and Honduras.

Subtropical dry forests have sandy acidic soils and four species of pine tree (this is their southernmost natural border); they can be seen in the Región Autónoma Atlántico Norte (Northern Atlantic Autonomous Region; RAAN) and the Segovias.

Humid tropical forests are home to the multistory green canopies most people think of as classic rainforest. Conditions here are perfect for all plant life; almost no nutrients are stored in the soil, but there is a vast web just beneath the fallen leaves of enormous ceibas, formed of

SEE SEA TURTLES

At least five of the world's sea-turtle species nest on the shores of Nicaragua, all (theoretically) protected except for green turtles, present only on the Atlantic coast and legal to catch July to April.

The most common Pacific turtles, the olive ridley (Paslama), are only 45kg and at their most impressive when invading a nesting beach (July to December, peaking in September and August) in flotillas of 3000 or more that storm ashore at the same time to lay. Often using the same beaches from November to February, leatherbacks (*tora* or *baula)* are the largest (450kg) and rarest of the turtles; because they eat jellyfish they often accidentally consume plastic bags and bottles, which kill them. Both species have edible, illegal and widely available eggs, considered by locals to be an aphrodisiac. In this book we do not list establishments that serve them, but if you see them on the menu, make your distaste known to the proprietors.

Hawksbill (carey) turtles – which nest May to November, peaking in October and September – are inedible and have lousy-tasting eggs; they're generally caught only for their shells, which are made into graceful, beautiful jewelry that we hope you won't buy. Loggerhead (caguama) turtles are also inedible, but their 160kg bulk often gets caught in the green-turtle nets.

Most tours only take you to see the eggs being laid, usually between 9pm and 2am, except during olive ridley *arribadas* (arrivals), when the beaches are packed day and night. Babies usually hatch about 60 days later, just before sunrise, then make their run to the sea; it's worth camping to see this. If you want to get more involved, you can hook up with grassroots turtle-conservation initiatives once you arrive, or contact the Cocibolca Foundation (www.mombacho.org) or the Wildlife Conservation Society (p230).

Places to see the turtles:

Refugio de Vida Silvestre La Flor (p137) Easily accessible from San Juan del Sur, La Flor's wildlife reserve has the best infrastructure, access and protection for its collection of olive ridley and leatherback turtles – plus camping!

Refugio de Vida Silvestre Río Escalante Chacocente (p127) Access to this wildlife reserve is limited, but it's within walking distance of rapidly developing Playa El Astillero, so guided tours are just a matter of time.

Reserva Natural Isla Juan Venado Conveniently close to León, and olive ridleys show up right on time.

Reserva Natural Estero Padre Ramos Not much infrastructure, but there's a grassroots turtle-conservation program where you can volunteer.

Pearl Keys This group of expensive-to-access Caribbean islands hosts hawksbill turtles while green turtles feed on the seagrass just offshore.

Other nesting sites on the Atlantic coast include the Miskito Keys, even more difficult to get to, and Río San Juan Wildlife Preserve, where green, hawksbill and leatherback turtles nest, and which can only be reached via San Juan de Nicaragua, a challenge in itself.

tiny roots, fungus and other assorted symbiotes that devour every stray nutrient as soon as it hits the ground.

Cloud forests are found above 1200m and are easily the most impressive (and rarest) biome, with epiphytes, bromeliads (a variety of high-humidity plant that grows in the branches of other trees), mosses, lichens and lots of orchids, which you can see at Reserva Natural Cerro Datanlí–El Diablo, among many other places.

The central subtropical forests of Boaco and Chontales have been largely devoured by cattle ranches, and while there are a few reserves, including Reserva Natural Sierra Amerisque, access to these areas is limited. Just to the east are the Caribbean lowlands, where there are swamps and thick, dense foliage that you can see on the riverboat ride from El Rama.

Wildlife-watchers migrating to Central America should read L Irby Davis' *Field Guide to the Birds of Mexico & Central America* or Adrian Forsyth's *Tropical Nature: Life & Death in the Rainforests of Central & South America.*

Environmental Issues

With a developing economy, poor infrastructure and limited resources, Nicaragua faces a tough task in protecting the environment at the same time as lifting its citizens out of poverty.

While there has certainly been progress in recent times, the country still faces a variety of pressing environmental issues.

Deforestation

One of the biggest environmental issues facing Nicaragua is deforestation – the country has lost about 85% of its virgin forest cover since the Colonial period. Since the end of the war, overall forest cover has fallen from 63% to 42%, although the rate of deforestation has slowed somewhat since 2000.

Deforestation is a major issue because it affects the entire biosystem. Root systems prevent erosion, thus keeping water supplies clean of soil runoff. Foliage supplies habitat for wildlife. Trees also help maintain climatic conditions. With climate change, scientists are noticing that pollinating insects are migrating to more favorable environments, leaving plants unpollinated.

Part of the problem is commercial logging. With the national economy struggling after the war, environmental issues took a back seat and liberal governments granted a number of forest concessions that contributed significantly to deforestation.

Illegal logging is another contributing factor, particularly on the Caribbean coast, where the environment ministry has limited resources to patrol and manage vast reserves with difficult access.

Another major factor is the advance of the 'agricultural frontier' – the eastward migration by small farmers slashing and burning forest in the hope of carving out a subsistence livelihood. As the land often occupied is usually humid tropical forest, the soil generally only has enough oomph for two or three harvests, when the would-be farmer has to carve another farm from the jungle. Even more concerning are the wealthy land speculators who illegally clear large tracts of forest, then sell the land and move on.

The traditional dependence on firewood as a means of cooking and heating is another factor, especially affecting the dry tropical forests that surround densely populated regions.

The pine forests of Nueva Segovia took a huge hit from their natural enemy the pine bark beetle in late 1999, with an estimated 6000 hectares of forest destroyed by the time it had finished its rampage. While recent hurricanes, particularly Hurricane Felix in 2007, have felled large numbers of trees in the Caribbean region and caused erosion and landslides in areas that have been deforested.

Agricultural Chemicals

Another pressing issue is the use of agricultural chemicals, which is widespread in Nicaragua, although nowhere near the levels in its famously 'green' neighbour Costa Rica. Any time you travel in rural areas youll see farmers decked out with their pump backpacks ready to spray herbicides, fungicides, pesticides or fertlizers on their crops. Chemical use is poorly regulated and many of these products end up in the local river systems.

In 2010 there was a major fish kill in Pearl Lagoon that was unlike any that even older members of the community had seen. Many locals blamed agricultural run-off, either from the local palm oil plantations or farmlands up the Río Grande de Matagalpa, although a government-sponsored investigation found no evidence of this.

Whether or not it was connected to the fish kill, environmentalists maintain that large-scale African Palm plantations destroy critical habitat for endangered species and contribute to soil erosion.

Mining

While mining companies provide well-paid employment (even if profits do go straight out of the country), conservation groups maintain that cyanide, mercury and other industrial pollutants flow into the water table. The mines in Las Minas are of particular concern to environmentalists because they are located on the edge of the Reserva de Biosfera Bosawás, the largest nature reserve on the Central American isthmus. Small-scale mining in rural Chontales has lead to mercury contamination in local water supplies around La Libertad.

Sustainable Harvest International works with indigenous communities to help them move away from slash-and-burn agriculture and toward more sustainable methods. For more info go to www.sustainable-harvest.org.

MINING

Climate Change

Global warming is taking its toll in Nicaragua, too. Of the 18 original Pearl Keys, six have been swallowed by rising sea levels. A few are visible seasonally, but they are no longer the full islands they used to be. The smaller keys obviously remain at risk.

Nicaragua is also particularly at risk to both flooding and drought. The extended dry period is often followed by heavy downpours. Flooding is made worse by deforestation in catchment areas.

Erratic rains have severely effected small-scale farmers, many of whom have no access to irrigation systems. However, a new water harvesting project in the north of the country is dramatically increasing yields among farmers in that region.

NICARAGUA'S ECO-WARRIORS

If you see a large bunch of heavily armed men making their way through the canopy while you are in one of the country's nature reserves don't be alarmed, it's probably just the national armýs new Batallon Ecológico (Ecological Batallion).

And if you think Nicaragua is not serious about environmental protection, try telling these guys. Made up of 580 soldiers, the batallion was created in late 2011 to combat deforestation and the illegal lumber trade, and has an annual budget of 6.2 million dollars. It sounds like a reality TV show, but these guys take their job very seriously.

And they've already had some success. Only months after their inception, they seized 112,000 cubic meters of illegally felled lumber in the Wawashang reserve on the Atlantic Coast.

But the soldiers don't just carry guns, they also carry shovels so they are able to plant trees in their downtime. Together with the national forestry institute, they have created a network of 28 tree nurseries that will supply saplings for an ambitious reforestation plan in natural reserves affected by illegal logging.

NOT FOR SALE: NICARGUA'S NATURAL RESOURCES

It's not ecologists or politicians but Nicaragua's indigenous communities that are the most fundamental players in the conservation of the disappearing forests of the Caribbean lowlands.

In 2001 the indigenous Mayangna of Awas-Tingni won a landmark battle when the Inter-American court ruled that the Nicaraguan government had violated the rights of the community by signing a deal with an Asian company for lumber extraction on 62,000 hectares of the community's land.

Shortly afterward, the national government passed a new autonomy law giving the indigenous communities of the Atlantic autonomous regions free determination of the use of their territories and the management of all natural resources found on their land. Nicaragua has since issued land titles to Awas-Tingni and many other indigenous groups in both the Región Autónoma Atlántico Sur (South Atlantic Autonomous Region; RAAS) and Región Autónoma Atlántico Norte (North Atlantic Autonomous Region; RAAN).

However, the issuing of titles without providing support to reclaim the lands has created problems for some of the communities. Many indigenous groups don't have the resources to patrol and protect their lands, which are subject to land invasions by mestizo farmers. Particularly affected are the indigenous Rama, who number less than 5000, but administer a large territory stretching from the Río San Juan to Bluefields Bay. Many Rama have been displaced by armed farmers who refuse to respect the titles.

Sustainable tourism is one way these communities are able to exercise ownership and derive profits from their lands without destroying precious natural resources.

Positive Developments

It's not all doom and gloom, though. Environmental consciousness is growing within Nicaragua and there have recently been a variety of victories, both on small and large scales.

The government has declared the environment a national priority and has made a measurable commitment to fighting deforestation and other pressing environmental issues.

Each municipality now has a department devoted to natural resources and, in general, respect for conservation laws has grown, while practices such as wildlife hunting and trafficking are on the downturn.

The government has also mobilized the army to protect endangered sea turtles and created a special ecological battalion to fight the illegal lumber trade.

Another positive sign is than Nicaraguans are also starting to organize on a community level. Specific examples include the agreement between restaurant owners in San Juan del Sur not to offer menu items made from turtle eggs, and the communities in the Cordillera Volcanica who act as volunteer firefighters when wildfires threaten the endangered dry tropical forest. There has also been a significant move toward growing organic coffee and vegetables in the north of the country, with many farming cooperatives adopting chemical-free methods.

More Information

For an overview of Nicaragua's protected areas, the issues they are facing and some of the efforts being made to save them, start with the official Ministry of Natural Resources website, www.marena.gob.ni (in Spanish). For general activism (some of it related to the environment), check www.nicanet.org.

Survival Guide

Directory A–Z

Accommodations

Ranging from five-star resorts to windowless shacks with shared latrines, you really have your choice of accommodations in developed A-list destinations like Managua, Granada, León, San Juan del Sur and the Corn Islands. Top-end places start to thin out a bit as you head for the interior.

Hotels in this guide are divided into categories according to price, then arranged by author preference. Being that the majority of hotel rooms in Nicaragua have their own bathroom, we stipulate when the bathroom is shared, except of course in dorms where the bathroom is always shared.

Absolute peak season in Nicaragua is really only two weeks or so – Christmas and Easter, when entire towns book out and prices skyrocket. Outside that time, many hotels maintain prices year-round. If there is a high season, it's somewhere between November and March – outside the rainy months. Prices in this guide are for normal/high season, not absolute peak.

BOOK YOUR STAY ONLINE

For more accommodations reviews by Lonely Planet authors, check out http://hotels.lonelyplanet.com. You'll find independent reviews, as well as recommendations on the best places to stay. Best of all, you can book online.

ADDRESSES IN NICARAGUA

As few streets are named and fewer houses are numbered, Nicaraguans use a unique system for addresses. They take a landmark, then give the distance from it in blocks, using cardinal points for directions. Abbreviations we use in this guide:

N	north	*norte*
E	east	*este*
S	south	*sur*
O	west	*oeste*
c	block	*cuadra*

For example, 'De la universidad, 2c S, 1c E' would be two blocks south, then one block east from the university. Some locals use *arriba* (up) and *abajo* (down) to refer to east and west respectively, terminology derived from the rising and setting of the sun.

Other landmark-based addresses such as '*frente catedral*' (in front of the Cathedral) are also given in Spanish in the text, so that locals can point you in the right direction. To decipher some address terms yourself, see the Glossary.

Budget

Budget hotels, sometimes called *hospedajes*, are inexpensive compared to the rest of Central America. You can almost always get your own clean wooden room, with a window and a shared bathroom, for under US$6 per person per night. Double that and you get a bigger room and a private bathroom; prices are higher in A-list destinations, where there are always cheap dorm beds (US$8 to US$10) if you're travelling on a shoestring. In less-developed regions, you may be using bucket-flush toilets and bucket showers in this price range. Budget travelers should always bring candles and a flashlight (torch), just in case. If there's no mosquito net, just ask.

Midrange

There's a good midrange option, with clean, modern rooms, private bathroom,

24-hour electricity, running water and a nice setting or neighborhood, in every major town. It tends to cost US$20 to US$35 for a double; tack on US$10 to US$15 for an A-list destination. Solo travelers usually get a 20% discount, tops, in this category. A 15% tax applies to hotel rates in the midrange and top-end categories.

Top End

Luxury accommodations, where they exist, can be a good deal – the most expensive resort in the country clocks in at around US$250 per person, which certainly isn't for everyone, but is a steal compared to Costa Rica. Boutique hotels (with doubles going for US$80 to US$120), concentrated in Managua, generally have fewer than 10 rooms, and come with lots of little luxuries.

Other Accommodations

In rural areas, there may not be signed guesthouses, but almost all small towns have families who rent rooms. Ask at the *alcaldía* (mayor's office) for leads on weekdays, or any open business on weekends. Some communities have formalized homestays through Spanish schools (you don't need to be a student – just ask at the school) or as part of community-based alternative tourism, such as at Área Protegida Miraflor. Camping is available in a few private and natural reserves, and is also allowed for free on most less-developed beaches.

Children

Nicaragua, like all Latin American countries, is relatively easy to travel around with children, despite the lack of infrastructure. Parents rarely pay extra for hotels, transportation or other services for youngsters small enough to fit in a lap comfortably, and even complete strangers will make an effort to accommodate and entertain children.

Practicalities

- Some top-end (and very few midrange) hotels will be able to arrange a cot if you ask ahead. Otherwise the assumption is that the child will share your bed or use a single.
- Major car-rental companies can organize car seats. Car seats for Nicaraguan toddlers tend to be mom's lap.
- Breastfeeding in public is very common and should only really be avoided in places of worship.
- Baby formula is widely available, while disposable diapers are available in every *pulpería* (corner store) around the country.

Sights & Activities

Generally speaking, the major tourist towns of Granada, San Juan del Sur and León are best for kids – San Juan and Granada both have excellent libraries with scheduled activities. Kids tend to get a kick out of the Isla de Ometepe and other rural areas with a bit of comfort, and the Corn Islands are a guaranteed winner.

Climate

Bluefields

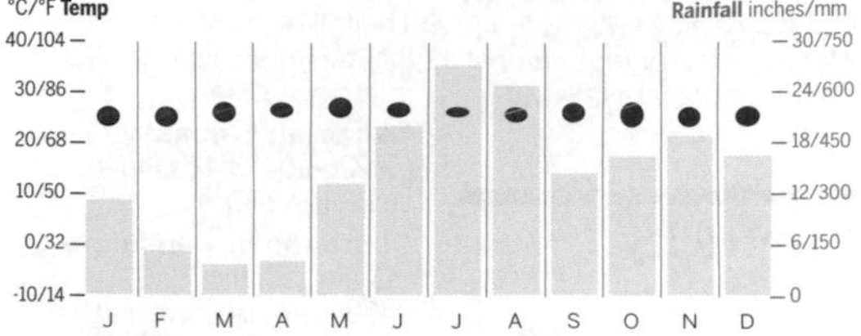

Managua

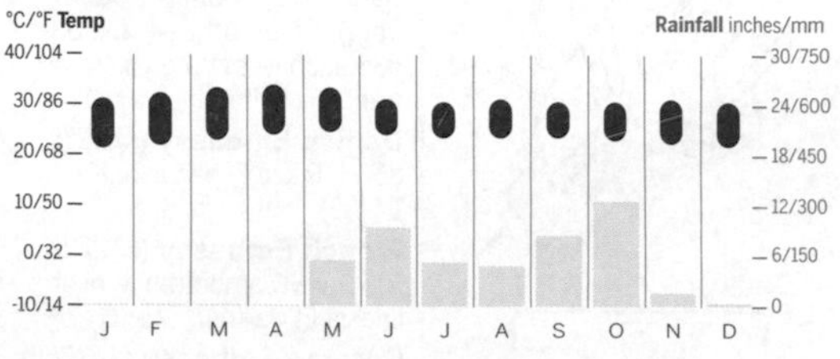

Customs Regulations

The only really unique addition to the list of things that shouldn't be in your backpack as you leave Nicaragua are pre-Columbian or early

ACCOMMODATION PRICES

Price indicators for sleeping options in this book denote the cost of a standard double room with private bathroom.

Price Indicator	US$
$	less than 20
$$	20-50
$$$	more than 50

colonial artifacts – you could end up in prison for trying to take these out of the country. Arriving, you can bring pretty much anything legal as long as it's obviously for personal use and not for resale within the country.

Electricity

Embassies & Consulates

The following offices are located in Managua unless otherwise noted.

Canadian Embassy (☎2268-0433; Los Pipitos, 2c abajo, Bolonia)

Costa Rican Consulate Managua office (☎2251-0429; consuladocrmanagua@yahoo.com; Rotonda Rubén Darío, 2c E, 500m N; ⏰8am-3pm); Rivas office (☎2563-5353; ichaves@rree.go.cr; frente Hospital)

Danish Embassy (☎2276-8630; Plaza España, 2c N, 1½c O)

French Embassy (☎2228-1056; www.ambafrance-ni.org; Iglesia El Carmen, 1½c O)

German Embassy (☎2266-7500; Rotonda El Güegüense, 1½c N)

Guatemalan Embassy (☎2279-9606; Carretera a Masaya, Km 11.5)

Honduran Embassy (☎2276-2406; Av del Campo 298, Las Colinas; ⏰9am-5pm Mon-Fri)

Honduran Consulate (☎2341-8974; consulhn@cablenet.com.ni; Palí, 20m S, Chinandega; ⏰9am-4pm Mon-Fri)

Mexican Embassy (☎2278-1859; http://embamex.sre.gob.mx/nicaragua; Altamira d'Este, frente Claro)

Panamanian Embassy (☎2266-8633; Cuartel General de Bomberos, 1c E)

Salvadoran Embassy (☎2276-2132; Av del Campo 142, Las Colinas)

Salvadoran Consulate (☎2341-2049; esquina de los bancos, ½c S, Chinandega)

US Embassy (☎2266-6010; Carretera Sur, Km 5.5)

Food

Eating establishments in this guide are separated into budget categories and then listed according to author preference.

Many Nicaraguans eat lunch on the go, but the majority eat dinner at home, so outside tourist areas you may find eating options are reduced in the evening. Budget eateries including *comedores* (basic eateries), where you choose from a variety of ready-prepared dishes, and market stalls serve a limited range of filling dishes and set meals from US$2 to US$5. Also in this price range are *fritangas* (grills), which serve grilled meats and fried sides. Mid-range eateries will have a decent-sized menu charging US$5 to US$10 per plate. Top-end establishments (mostly found in Granada, Managua and San Juan del Sur) will have an even better range, including dishes from around the world, costing more than US$10.

While both breakfast and dinner are often served with a big scoop of *gallo pinto* (a common meal of blended rice and beans), at lunch the rice and beans are usually separate – it's said to be more filling that way. Be sure to keep an eye out for local specialties including *nacatamales* (banana-leaf-wrapped bundles of cornmeal, meat, vegetables and herbs), *baho* (plantain and beef stew) and *rundown* (seasoned fish or meat cooked in coconut milk with root vegetables).

Nicaragua has a wonderful array of fresh fruits which are often sold cut up in small

EATING PRICES

Price indicators for eating options in this book denote the cost of a typical main course.

Price Indicator	US$
$	less than 5
$$	5-10
$$$	more than 10

bags on the side of the road or as *frescos naturales* (juices in water with sugar).

Gay & Lesbian Travelers

While consensual gay sex was recently decriminalized in Nicaragua, attitudes may take a bit longer to change. As in most of Latin America, gay and lesbian travelers will run into fewer problems if they avoid public displays of affection, and ask for two beds and then push them together. That said, lots of Nicaraguan gays and lesbians flaunt their sexuality, so you probably won't have much difficulty figuring out the scene.

Get started on the web at www.gaynicaragua.org, which has some listings. There are a small selection of gay and lesbian bars and clubs in Managua and a vaguely tolerant scene in Granada, but apart from that, it's a pretty straight (acting) country.

Health

Most visitors to Nicaragua travel without incident; however, as a developing nation with poor infrastructure and a tropical climate there are certain medical conditions to be aware of to avoid an unnecessary visit to the doctor.

Stomach problems and diarrhea are the result of bacteria, viruses and parasites which may be present in contaminated food and water. Many other illnesses affecting travelers, such as infected bug bites, rashes and heat exhaustion, are the result of Nicaragua's tropical climate.

Other more serious diseases are carried by infected mosquitoes. Bring clothes that provide protection against bites and repellent.

MEDICAL CHECKLIST

- antibiotics
- antidiarrheal drugs (eg loperamide)
- acetaminophen/paracetamol (Tylenol) or aspirin
- anti-inflammatory drugs (eg ibuprofen)
- antihistamines (for hay fever and allergic reactions)
- antibacterial ointment (eg Bactroban) for cuts and abrasions
- steroid cream or cortisone (for poison ivy and other allergic rashes)
- bandages, gauze, gauze rolls
- adhesive or paper tape
- scissors, safety pins, tweezers
- thermometer
- pocket knife
- DEET-containing insect repellent for the skin
- permethrin-containing insect spray for clothing, tents and bed nets
- sunblock
- oral rehydration salts
- iodine tablets (for water purification)
- syringes and sterile needles
- tampons
- preferred contraceptive pills

Drinking Water

Tap water is potable in cities and larger towns but should be avoided in rural areas and throughout the Región Autónoma Atlántico Sur (South Atlantic Autonomous Region; RAAS) and Región Autónoma Atlántico Norte (North Atlantic Autonomous Region; RAAN). In cheaper restaurants, ice and juices are usually made with untreated water.

Health Care

Medical attention in Nicaragua is cheap; however, apart from at the best clinics in the capital, it is probably not up to the standards you are used to at home.

In rural areas and small towns, English-speaking doctors are hard to find. Local clinics are fine for dealing with minor illnesses, cuts and sprains, but for anything more serious you should make your way to Managua, where there are several competent private hospitals. If you develop a life-threatening medical problem, you'll want to be evacuated to a country with advanced medical facilities.

Infectious Diseases

- Dengue fever is a mosquito-born viral infection transmitted by Aedes mosquitoes most commonly during the day and usually close to human habitations, often indoors.
- Malaria is also transmitted by mosquitoes, although those that carry the disease prefer to bite in the evening. It's more common in rural areas.

➡ Leptospirosis is a rare but serious bacterial infection transmitted through water contaminated with animal urine.

Recommended Vaccinations

There are no obligatory vaccinations for Nicaragua, with the exception of Yellow Fever for travelers arriving from affected areas. However, you may consider getting typhoid and hepatitis shots before you set out. Some travelers also choose to take anti-malaria medications.

Insurance

Nicaragua is an unpredictable kind of place and infrastructure is poor, so travel insurance is always a good idea. Health care is cheap, so you're really only going to need travel insurance in the case of hospitalization or a big emergency. Make sure your bill covers emergency helicopter evacuation, full coverage for lost luggage and, if you're into it, extreme sports.

Worldwide travel insurance is available at www.lonelyplanet.com/travel_services. You can buy, extend and claim online any time, even if you're already on the road.

Internet Access

Internet access on the Pacific coast is fast (US$0.70 to US$1 per hour), cheap and widely available even in small towns. The Caribbean coast has slightly slower, slightly more expensive internet service, which is not widely available. Top-end hotels mostly have 'business centers' and often connections for laptops, and wi-fi, in rooms. The computer icon used in hotel listings in this guide signifies that the hotel has a computer with internet access available to guests free of charge.

Public wi-fi networks in restaurants and cafes are becoming more common, but are still rare outside big cities. If you are going to be around for a while, consider purchasing a USB modem, which work well in larger cities but are often very slow in rural areas.

Legal Matters

Nicaragua's police force is professional and visible, and very approachable by Central American standards. Some people advocate slipping traffic cops a 100-córdoba (US$4) bill with your ID to smooth out minor traffic violations, but that could always backfire, and if you get caught with drugs or committing a more serious crime, it won't be that easy to get away from the law.

Maps

Detailed maps are hard to find inside Nicaragua, so consider purchasing before you arrive if you plan to get off the beaten track.

Intur (www.intur.gob.ni) Offices have tourist-oriented regional and city map.

Ineter (Nicaragua Institute for Territorial Studies; www.ineter.gob.ni; frente Dirección de Migración y Extranjeria, Managua) Has the best selection of detailed maps in the country. Many are out of print, but bring a flash drive and they'll upload the files.

International Travel Maps & Books (www.itmb.ca) Publishes a detailed road map (US$12.95), but don't trust it completely for secondary roads.

Mapas Naturismo (www.mapas-naturismo.com) Has the most current road map on the market (US$9).

Money

Nicaragua's currency is the córdoba (C$), sometimes called a 'peso' or 'real' by locals. Córdobas come in coins of C$0.25, C$0.50, C$1, C$5 and C$10, and bills of C$10, C$20, C$50, C$100, C$200 and C$500. The plastic bills are flimsy and tear easily. Bills of C$100 and larger can be difficult to change; try the gas station.

US dollars are accepted almost everywhere, but they will be rejected if they are even slightly marked, ripped or damaged. Córdobas are usually easier to use, particularly at smaller businesses and anywhere off the beaten track – always keep at least 200 córdoba on you, preferably in smaller bills.

The córdoba is devalued according to a fixed plan against the US dollar. All prices in this guide are given in US dollars (US$), as costs in córdoba are more likely to fluctuate with the exchange rate.

ATMs, Banks & Traveler's Checks

ATMs *(cajeros automatícos)* are the easiest way to access cash in Nicaragua. They are available in most major towns and tourist regions. Most ATMs charge around US$2.50 per transaction on top of whatever your bank charges. It's also possible to organize a cash advance over the counter in many banks. Traveler's checks are inconvenient and may be changed at only some banks, for a steep fee but it may be worth bringing a small amount for an emergency stash.

Branches of the following banks have reliable ATMs:

BAC Visa/Plus and MasterCard/Cirrus.

Bancentro Visa/Plus.

BanPro Visa/Plus and MasterCard/Cirrus.

Banco ProCredit Visa/Plus.

Black Market

Moneychangers *(coyotes)* are regularly used by locals to change córdobas for US dollars at about the same rates as the banks. *Coyotes* in cities and towns are generally honest, but you should know the exchange rate and how much to expect in the exchange. *Coyotes* may also exchange other currencies, including euros, UK pounds, Canadian dollars, Honduran lempira and Costa Rican colones, for a much larger fee.

Coyotes at border crossings are much less reputable. Stay on your toes and avoid changing large amounts.

Credit Cards

Visa and MasterCard are accepted throughout Nicaragua, and you can almost always count on midrange hotels and restaurants to accept them. In places where electricity is unreliable – for instance, most of the Caribbean coast – credit cards may not be widely accepted, so be prepared.

Tipping

Tipping is expected for table service in Nicaragua, and restaurants usually include a 10% 'voluntary' tip in the bill. Small and/or rural eateries may not include the tip, so leave behind a few coins. You should tip guides; that's often their only salary.

Opening Hours

General office hours are from 9am to 5pm Monday to Friday, and 9am to noon on weekends. Many offices, most museums and some shops take a lunch break from noon to 2pm.

Banks 8:30am to 4:30pm Monday through Friday, 8:30am to noon on Saturday.

Bars Open from around noon to midnight, and until 2am on weekends.

Discos Usually don't get going until at least 9pm, later in Managua.

Government Offices Most government departments, including Intur, Marena and Migración, officially attend the public from 8am to 1pm, although many stay open longer.

Restaurants Generally open from noon to 10pm, *comedores* are normally open from about 6am until 8pm while *fritangas* serve from 6pm to 10pm.

Shops Most shops open around 9am and close around 6pm, although they often stay open later in larger cities.

Post

Considering that there are no real addresses in Nicaragua, the mail service is surprisingly effective. It costs about US$0.80 to send a standard letter or postcard to the US, about US$1 to Europe. You can receive mail at any post office by having it addressed as follows:

(*your name*)
Lista de Correo
Correo Central
(*town name*)
Nicaragua

Make sure you bring your passport when you go to check your mail, and don't leave mail sitting there for more than two weeks.

Public Holidays

National holidays:

New Year's Day (January 1) Shops and offices start closing at noon on December 31.

Semana Santa (Holy Week; Thursday, Friday and Saturday before Easter Sunday) Beaches get packed, hotel rates skyrocket and everything is closed – make sure you have a place to be.

Labor Day (May 1)

Mother's Day (May 30) No one gets away with just a card – more places close than at Christmas.

Anniversary of the Revolution (July 19) No longer an official holiday, but many shops and government offices close anyway.

Battle of San Jacinto (September 14)

Independence Day (September 15)

Día de los Difuntos (November 2) All Souls' Day.

La Purísima (December 8) Immaculate Conception.

Navidad (December 25) Christmas.

Safe Travel

Despite the fact that Nicaragua has one of the lowest crime rates in Central America, as a 'wealthy' foreigner you will at least be considered a potential target by scam artists and thieves. Make sure they pick a different tourist by staying alert and taking precautions against theft and mugging. Several areas are considered

PRACTICALITIES

- *La Prensa* and *El Nuevo Diario* are Nicaragua's most respected, widely available daily newspapers.
- For English-language news and analysis, look out for *Envio* magazine.
- DVDs on sale use the NTSC image-registration system.
- Nicaragua officially uses the metric system, but *libras* (pounds) may still be used in markets. The archaic Spanish measurement of *varas* (0.70m or 33in) is often used in directions.
- Smoking is still permitted practically everywhere, although Nicaraguans are not heavy smokers.

dangerous enough to merit their own warnings, including Managua, with big-city problems; San Juan del Sur, with bohemian tourist-industry problems; and most of the Caribbean coast, with narco-inspired security problems.

Always play it extra safe in the rural Caribbean coast, undeveloped nature reserves, and anywhere that infrastructure is limited and communications are weak. Even if it's expensive or seems silly, consider taking precautions if recommended by a reliable source: hey, if they think two guides are better, maybe there's a reason.

Back-country hikers should be aware that while Nicaragua has been officially declared free of land mines, there still may be other kinds of unexploded ordinance in remote areas, particularly along the Honduran border in the northern highlands and RAAN. If in doubt, take a local guide.

Telephone

Nicaragua's calling code is 505. There are no area codes within Nicaragua. Many homes and businesses 'rent' their phone for a fee (usually around US$0.25 per minute) for national calls to landlines and cell phones. Direct calls abroad using the phone network or cell phones are expensive – any internet cafe will offer much cheaper rates.

Many travelers simply buy a phone upon arrival – prices start around US$15, and there are phone shops at the airport. You can also buy a SIM card (around US$3.50) and insert it into any unlocked North American phone. The two phone companies are Claro, which has better coverage, and Movistar. Electronic top-ups are available at *pulperías* and gas stations all over the country.

Toilets

In cities and towns, toilets are your regular sit-down flush variety. Public toilets are not common but most businesses will let you use their facilities. As you venture into rural areas you will come across dry latrines, which are little more than a hole in the ground covered by a wooden box.

There is often no toilet paper in public bathrooms. Always carry a spare roll. And when you've finished, throw it in the trash basket, don't flush it – the pipes get blocked easily.

Tourist Information

Intur (Nicaraguan Institute of Tourism; ☎2222-3333; www.visitanicaragua.com/ingles), the government tourism office, has branches in most major cities. It can always recommend hotels and activities (but not make reservations) and point you toward guides.

Alcaldías are your best bet in small towns without a real tourist office. Although tourism is not the mayor's primary function, most will help you find food, lodging, guides and whatever you might need. In indigenous communities, there may not be a mayor, as many still have councils of elders. Instead, ask for the president (or *wihta* in Miskito communities), who probably speaks Spanish and can help you out.

Travelers with Disabilities

While Nicaraguans are generally accommodating toward people with mobility issues, and will gladly give you a hand getting around, the combination of cobbled streets, cracked sidewalks and stairs in pretty much every building can make life tough.

There are few regular services for disabled travelers and because of difficulties in finding suitable transport, it's easiest to go through a tour company. **Kool Tour** (cmejia@kool-tour.com; Ciudad Jardin q-12, Managua) are specialists in arranging tours for travelers with disabilities.

There are very few wheelchair-accessible toilets and bathrooms in Nicaragua, so bringing toilet-seat extensions and wall-mountable mobility aids are highly recommended. For general mobility-impaired advice, go to www.able-travel.com.

Visas

Visitors from most countries can stay in Nicaragua for up to 90 days without a visa, as long as they have a passport valid for the next six months, proof of sufficient funds (US$200 or a credit card) and an onward ticket (rarely checked).

Citizens of some parts of Eastern Europe and Latin America and many African and Asian nations need visas to enter Nicaragua. Check the Nicaraguan Foreign Ministry website (www.cancilleria.gob.ni/servicios/visas.shtml) for the full lists.

Nicaragua is part of the CA-4, a regional agreement covering Nicaragua, Honduras, El Salvador and Guatemala. Officially, you can only stay for 90 days maximum in the *entire* CA-4, at which point you can get one extension of 90 days from the **Migración (Immigration) office** (Dirección de Migración y Extranjeria; ☎2244-3989; www.migob.gob.ni/dgme; semaf Tenderí, 200m N) in Managua for around US$10 per month. After those 90 days, you must leave the region (this means going to Costa Rica, basically) for 72 hours, which automatically renews your visa.

Don't bet on it, but flying between CA-4 countries tends to get you another 90 days on landing. Land border officials are stricter in adhering to the regulations.

Volunteering

Nicaragua has a very developed volunteer culture traceable to the influx of 'Sandalistas' (young foreign volunteers) during the revolution. Many hostels and Spanish schools maintain lists of organizations or check out **Volunteer South America** (www.volunteersouthamerica.net) and **Go Abroad** (www.goabroad.com).

Following are some organizations that accept foreign volunteers.

Local Organizations

Los Pipitos (www.lospipitos.org) Has offices throughout the country working with young Nicaraguans with disabilities. Accepts volunteers with training in medicine, education, sports and other associated fields.

UCA San Ramon (www.ucasanramon.com) Works with rural coffee-growing communities near Matagalpa.

International Organizations

Habitat for Humanity (www.habitatnicaragua.org) Construction brigades work on new housing in impoverished communities.

Seeds of Learning (www.seedsoflearning.org) Sends work brigades with an educational focus to Nicaragua.

Women Travelers

The biggest problems that many solo female travelers encounter in Nicaragua are the *pirópos* (catcalls) and general unwanted attention from men. Nicaragua is not particularly dangerous for women, but you know the drill: dress conservatively (knees should be covered, though shoulders are OK), especially when in transit; avoid drinking alone at night; and – this is the hard one – reconsider telling off the catcalling guy, as he might become violent. Sigh. The Caribbean coast is more dangerous in general, so all this goes double there.

Work

Nicaragua is one of the poorest countries in the hemisphere, with almost 50% of its adults unemployed or underemployed. Thus, finding a job in Nicaragua is difficult and taking one that a Nicaraguan could be doing is probably just plain wrong. Backpacker-oriented businesses may offer you under-the-table employment, usually in exchange for room and board, but this is mostly about extending your vacation. If you're a serious, qualified English teacher, you may be able to find a job in an international school or private-language center.

Transportation

GETTING THERE & AWAY

Nicaragua is accessible by air via the international airport in Managua, by road using five major border crossings with Honduras and Costa Rica, and by boat between El Salvador and Potosí.

Flights can be booked online at www.lonelyplanet.com/bookings.

Entering the Country

All visitors to Nicaragua are required to purchase a Tourist Card for US$10 and pay a US$2 migration processing fee.

Air

Nicaragua's main international hub is **Managua International Airport** (MGA; www.eaai.com.ni; Carretera Norte, Km 13), a small, manageable airport that doesn't receive many flights but does have connecting services to Miami, Fort Lauderdale, Atlanta and Houston in the US, and several major cities within Central America. It's worth checking fares to neighboring Costa Rica, which may be significantly cheaper.

Nicaragua has no national airline, but is served by the following carriers.

American Airlines (www.aa.com)

Copa (www.copaair.com)

Delta (www.delta.com)

Spirit (www.spirit.com)

Taca (www.taca.com)

United (www.united.com)

Land

Border Crossings

Nicaragua shares borders with Costa Rica and Honduras. Generally, Nicaraguan border crossings are chaotic (there are no signs anywhere) but the procedure is fairly straightforward provided you have your documents in order (p296).

Ocotal to Tegucigalpa, Honduras See the sunny Segovias and the Honduran capital at this major, businesslike border. The Las Manos crossing point is efficient, although sometimes crowded.

Somoto to Choluteca, Honduras A high-altitude crossing that comes with an amazing granite canyon. Crossing point El Espino is laid-back and easy.

El Guasaule to Choluteca, Honduras The fastest route from Nicaragua, an easy cruise north from lovely León. The El Guasaule crossing is hot, hectic and disorganized.

Sapoá to Peñas Blancas, Costa Rica The main border crossing is generally relatively easy unless your arrival coincides with an

CLIMATE CHANGE & TRAVEL

Every form of transport that relies on carbon-based fuel generates CO_2, the main cause of human-induced climate change. Modern travel is dependent on airplanes, which might use less fuel per kilometer per person than most cars but travel much greater distances. The altitude at which aircraft emit gases (including CO_2) and particles also contributes to their climate change impact. Many websites offer 'carbon calculators' that allow people to estimate the carbon emissions generated by their journey and, for those who wish to do so, to offset the impact of the greenhouse gases emitted with contributions to portfolios of climate-friendly initiatives throughout the world. Lonely Planet offsets the carbon footprint of all staff and author travel.

international bus or two, in which case it could take hours. The local municipality charges an additional US$1 fee at this crossing.

Bus

International buses have reclining seats, air-conditioning, TVs, bathrooms and sometimes even food service, and are definitely safer for travelers with luggage. Crossing borders on international buses is generally hassle-free. At many borders the helper will take your passport, collect your border fees, get your stamp and return your passport to you as you get back on the bus. At the Costa Rican border post at Peñas Blancas you must complete the formalities in person.

There are direct bus services (without changing buses) to Costa Rica, Honduras, El Salvador and Guatemala, and connecting services to Panama and Mexico.

Central Line (www.transportescentralline.com) Runs between Nicaragua and Costa Rica.

King Quality (www.kingqualityca.com) Luxury buses to Costa Rica, Honduras, El Salvador and Guatemala.

Nica Expreso (www.nicaexpreso.com) Runs from Chinandega (via León) to San José, Costa Rica.

Tica Bus (Map p44; www.ticabus.com) Travels to Costa Rica, Honduras and El Salvador with connecting services to Guatemala, Mexico and Panama.

Transnica (Map p48; www.transnica.com) Serves Costa Rica, Honduras and El Salvador.

Transporte del Sol (Map p44; www.busesdelsol.com) Same-day service to Guatemala and San Salvador.

COSTA RICA

There are several bus companies running direct services between San José and Managua. The journey usually takes around nine to 10 hours and costs around US$25.

EL SALVADOR

Although there is no common border, there are several direct buses a day to San Salvador passing through Choluteca in Honduras. The journey costs US$35 to US$50 and takes around 11 hours but may be significantly longer if there are delays at any of the two border crossings.

HONDURAS

There are two main bus routes between Honduras and Nicaragua. From Tegucigalpa it's around seven to 10 hours and costs US$23 to US$30, while from San Pedro Sula it's 11 hours and costs US$37.

Car & Motorcycle

To bring a vehicle into Nicaragua, you'll need the originals and several copies of the ownership papers (in your name), your passport and a driver's license.

You'll get a 30-day permit (lose it and you'll be fined US$100) and you will need to purchase obligatory accident insurance for US$12. You may also be required to pay US$4 for the fumigation of your vehicle. Your passport will be stamped saying you brought a vehicle into the country; if you try to leave without it, you'll have to pay import duty.

You can only drive across one border crossing to Costa Rica, at Sapoá–Peñas Blancas. You can drive across the Nicaragua–Honduras border at El Guasaule, Somoto–El Espino and Ocotal–Las Manos.

River

The one main river crossing into Costa Rica (from San Carlos to Los Chiles) is a breeze – a gorgeous boat ride down an egret-lined river. From Los Chiles there are regular bus services onto Ciudad Quesada and San José.

You can also cross into Honduras from Waspám to Puerto Lempira, but it's a serious jungle adventure.

Sea

It's now possible to travel directly between Nicaragua and El Salvador by boat through the Golfo de Fonseca. **Cruce del Golfo** (www.crucedelgolfo.com) runs a boat from Potosí on the Cosigüina peninsula to La Union (US$65, two hours) every Tuesday and Friday. It also runs connecting minibus shuttles to Leon (US$34) and San Salvador (US$34). Prices do not include *migración* (immigration) fees.

GETTING AROUND

Air

The hub for domestic flights is Managua International Airport. Other airports are simple affairs and many are little more than dirt strips outside of town (or in Siuna and Waspám, in the middle of town). The airport in San Juan de Nicaragua is located across the bay in Greytown and is one of the few airports in the Americas where you need to take a boat to get on your flight.

There is one domestic carrier, **La Costeña** (☎2263-2142; www.lacostena.com.ni; Managua International Airport), which offers regular services to Bluefields, the Corn Islands, Las Minas, San Carlos, San Juan de Nicaragua (Greytown), Bilwi and Waspám. Many domestic flights use tiny single-prop planes where weight is important and bags necessarily get left behind, so keep all necessities in your carry-on luggage.

Note La Costeña is one of the few airlines that actually charges more to book online – a US$15 surcharge.

Bicycle

Nicaragua gets praise from long-distance cyclists for its smooth, paved roads and wide shoulders. Apart from in the mountainous northern region, the main highways through the country are also fairly flat, which gives cyclists plenty of opportunities to enjoy the spectacular scenery.

Bicycles are the most common form of private transport in the country and most drivers are used to seeing them everywhere from main highways to country roads. However, while the infrastructure is designed to accommodate bicycles, the extremely limited enforcement of speed limits and drink-driving legislation is an issue and the hazards of riding on Nicaraguan roads are not negligible.

Rental

Renting bicycles is difficult outside Granada, San Juan del Sur, Ometepe and León, but your hotel can probably arrange it for you. Bikes rent for around US$5 per day – weekly discounts are easily arranged. Bike-rental places may require a few hundred córdobas or your passport as deposit.

Purchase

Buying a bike is easily done; even the smallest towns will have somewhere selling them. The price-to-quality ratio is not great – expect to pay a little under US$100 for a bottom-of-the-line model. Something fancy will probably cost more than it would back home. Selling your bike when you leave is a matter of luck; places like Granada, León and San Juan del Sur all have notice boards in travelers' cafes, which would be your best bet. As a last shot, try selling it to a bike-rental place, but don't expect to recoup much of your investment.

> **DEPARTURE TAX**
>
> Domestic departure tax is US$2, payable in córdobas or US dollars. It is not included in the price of your ticket.

Boat

Many destinations are accessible only, or most easily, by boat. Public *pangas* (small motorboat) with outboard motors are much more expensive than road transport – in general it costs around US$6 to US$8 per hour of travel. In places without regular service, you will need to hire your own private *panga*. Prices vary widely, but you'll spend about US$50 to US$100 per hour for four to six people; tour operators can usually find a better deal. It's easy, if not cheap, to hire boat transport up and down the Pacific coast. On the Atlantic side, it's much more difficult. While it's not common, boats *do* sink here – please wear your life jacket, or at least keep it handy.

Following are the major departure points with regular boat service.

Bluefields To Pearl Lagoon, El Rama and Corn Island. Regular boats run between Great Corn and Little Corn Islands.

El Rama To Bluefields.

Granada To Isla de Ometepe and San Carlos.

San Carlos To Granada, the Islas Solentiname, the Río San Juan, the scenic border crossing to Costa Rica and several natural reserves.

Waspám The gateway to the Río Coco.

Bus

Bus service in Nicaragua is excellent if basic. Public transport is usually on old Bluebird school buses, which means no luggage compartments. Try to avoid putting your backpack on top of the bus, and instead sit toward the back and put it with the sacks of rice and beans.

Pay your fare after the bus starts moving. You may be issued a paper 'ticket' on long-distance buses – don't lose it, or you may be charged again. Some bus terminals allow you to purchase tickets ahead of time, which should in theory guarantee you a seat. While buses generally cruise around town before getting underway, you're more likely to get a seat by boarding the bus at the station or terminal.

Bus terminals, often huge, chaotic lots next to markets, may seem difficult to navigate, particularly if you don't speak much Spanish. Fear not! If you can pronounce your destination, the guys yelling will help you find your bus – just make sure they put you on an *expreso* and not an *ordinario* or you'll be spending more time on the road than you planned.

Costs & Classes

Buses cost about US$1 per hour, 30km to 40km, a bit more for *expreso* buses, sometimes called *directos*, which only stop in major destinations. *Ordinarios* or *ruteados* stop everywhere and for everyone.

Faster microbuses cost about 25% more, and service most major routes, with vans leaving when full. Many rural destinations connected to large cities by really bad roads use covered military trucks with bench seats which cost about the same as a regular bus.

Shuttle buses are privately owned minibuses that zip between major tourist destinations. They're OK value if you're traveling alone and can't handle another public bus, but if there are two (or more) of you, a taxi often works out to be cheaper and more convenient.

Car & Motorcycle

Driving is a wonderful way to see Pacific and central Nicaragua, but it's best to use public transport on the Caribbean side as roads are, for the most part, terrible.

Fuel & Spare Parts

Gas stations are generally located on the outskirts of major towns and cities and can be rare in rural locations. The availability of spare parts depends on the make of your car. Toyota, Nissan and Hyundai are the most common, and parts are widely available. For other makes you may have a frustrating wait while parts arrive from Miami.

Driver's License

Your home driver's license is valid for driving in Nicaragua for the duration of the entry stamp in your passport.

Rental

To hire a car, you'll need a driver's license and major credit card. Most rental companies want you to be at least 25 years old. Renting a car at Managua International Airport costs 15% extra, so consider taking a taxi to an offsite office.

Following are some of the better rental-car agencies:

Budget (www.budget.com.ni)

Dollar (www.dollar.com.ni) Offers drivers for additional US$15 per day with rentals.

Hertz (☎Airport 2233 1237; www.hertz.com.ni)

Lugo (Map p44; ☎2266-4477; www.lugorentacar.com.ni; Canal 2, 2c N, 3c O, Managua)

Insurance

Whether renting or driving your own vehicle you must purchase obligatory third-party insurance. If arriving in Nicaragua in your own vehicle, you'll purchase this at the border. For rentals this usually costs around US$12 per day.

When renting, you'll also be recommended supplemental insurance, which ranges from US$10 to US$30 per day depending on the coverage and excess, but your credit card may already covers this; call to make sure.

Road Conditions

Road conditions vary wildly throughout the country. The Panamericana (Pan-American Hwy) is paved all the way from Honduras to Costa Rica. Some secondary roads are very good. Access to Pacific beaches is for the most part woeful, as is the majority of the road network on the Atlantic side.

There are no up-to-date maps showing real road conditions, which change every rainy season anyway. Always ask locals if you aren't sure. Older paved roads are often horribly pockmarked with axle-cracking potholes. One tactic is to get behind a local driver and follow them swerve for swerve. Keeping an eye on older tire tracks is also helpful.

You'll often see people with shovels pointing to a dirt-filled pothole, which they just fixed for free. They're asking for a couple of córdobas (US$0.10) from you for their efforts.

During rainy season, roads flood, wash away and close. Some roads are never recommended for casual drivers, including the Río Blanco–Bilwi road, easily the worst in the country.

Road Hazards

Driving in Managua (heck, driving period) is not recommended after dark; even if you've rented a car, consider taking taxis instead. Most sizable towns are mazes of unsigned one-way streets that prove a boon to police officers in search of a bribe.

Your biggest danger on Nicaragua's highways isn't other cars (although gas stations selling liquor is a worry), but rather everything else that uses the roads; from bicycle rickshaws to drunk, staggering pedestrians and wandering wildlife. It's best to keep an eagle eye out and keep speeding to a minimum.

NICARAGUA'S TRAVELING TRADERS

Who said travelling by bus is boring? In Nicaragua not only do you have awe-inspiring volcanic landscapes to gaze at through the windows, inside the bus is a whole world of entertainment.

And we're not talking about the soft-rock soundtrack or classic Steven Seagal marathon on the tiny TV. The real entertainment on Nicaragua's battle-scarred school buses comes from the traveling salesman, particularly those hawking cut-priced medicines and ointments.

Need to get smarter before arriving in Rivas? No problem. Hair loss issues? There's an elixir for that too. And you probably didn't even know that in addition to your backpack, you were carrying around all those parasites on the unnecessarily graphic images on the full-color poster.

While they are not doctors, not even pharmacists, these 'medicine men' must be on to something as they always do a brisk trade, although they seem to not yet have cracked the traveler market. Perhaps the lack of a hangover cure has something to do with it.

Road Rules

Nicaragua's traffic laws are pretty standard and universally ignored, although driving on the right, giving way to anything bigger than you, wearing a seat belt at all times and keeping speeds well below 50km/h in cities should keep you out of trouble.

There have been reports that traffic cops target foreigners, looking for a quick shakedown. Officers may wave drivers over and accuse them of something as vague as 'poor driving.' Drivers should never initiate a bribe – it may be an honest officer who just wants to give a warning. When a bribe is requested, prudent drivers pay it and are done with it.

In the event of a real ticket being issued, you'll need to surrender your license and then pay the fine at the bank before picking up your documents at the departmental police station (which may be a fair distance from where you were actually pulled over). The procedure may take several days and is more than a little inconvenient.

Hitchhiking

Hitchhiking is very common in Nicaragua, even by solo women – just stick out your thumb. Foreign women, particularly those carrying all their bags, should think twice before hitchhiking solo. Never hitchhike into or out of Managua.

In rural areas where bus service is rare, anyone driving a pickup truck will almost certainly stop for you. Climb into the back tray (unless specifically invited up front) and when you want to get off, tap on the cabin roof a couple of times.

You should always offer to pay the driver, which will almost always be refused.

Hitchhiking is never entirely safe, and we don't recommend it. Travellers who hitchhike should understand that they are taking a small but potentially serious risk.

Local Transportation

Bus

The only city really big enough to warrant catching local buses is Managua, where pickpockets and bag slashers may make you think twice. If you can keep your wits (and belongings) about you, though, there are some handy cross-town routes that could save you some coins on taxi fares.

Rickshaw & Tuk Tuk

In smaller towns there are fewer taxis and more tuk tuks (motorized three wheelers) and *triciclos* (bicycle rickshaws). They're inexpensive – around US$0.50 per person to go anywhere in town – and kinda fun (although the *triciclo* driver pedaling around Rivas wearing the 'I love my job' t-shirt was probably overstating the case slightly).

Taxi

Almost all taxis in Nicaragua are *colectivos*, which stop and pick up other clients en route to your destination.

Managua taxis are unmetered and notorious for ripping off tourists. Taxis at major border crossings may also overcharge, given the chance. Most other city taxis have set in-town fares, usually around US$0.50 to US$0.70, rising slightly at night. Ask a local how much a fare should cost before getting into the cab.

Hiring taxis between cities is a comfortable and reasonable option for midrange travelers. Prices vary widely, but expect to pay US$10 for every 20km.

Language

Spanish is the national language of Nicaragua. Latin American Spanish pronunciation is easy, as there's a clear and consistent relationship between what you see written and how it's pronounced. Also, most sounds have equivalents in English.

Note that kh is a throaty sound (like the 'ch' in the Scottish *loch*), v and b are like a soft English 'v' (between a 'v' and a 'b'), and r is strongly rolled. There are some variations in spoken Spanish across Latin America, the most notable being the pronunciation of the letters *ll* and *y*. In our pronunciation guides they are represented with y because they are pronounced as the 'y' in 'yes' in most of Latin America. Note, however, that in some parts of the continent they sound like the 'lli' in 'million'. Read our colored pronunciation guides as if they were English, and you'll be understood. The stressed syllables are indicated with italics in our pronunciation guides.

The polite form is used in this chapter; where both polite and informal options are given, they are indicated by the abbreviations 'pol' and 'inf'. Where necessary, both masculine and feminine forms of words are included, separated by a slash and with the masculine form first, eg *perdido/a* (m/f).

BASICS

Hello.	*Hola.*	*o*·la
Goodbye.	*Adiós.*	a·*dyos*

WANT MORE?

For in-depth language information and handy phrases, check out Lonely Planet's *Latin American Spanish Phrasebook*. You'll find it at **shop.lonely planet.com**, or you can buy Lonely Planet's iPhone phrasebooks at the Apple App Store.

How are you?	*¿Qué tal?*	ke tal
Fine, thanks.	*Bien, gracias.*	byen *gra*·syas
Excuse me.	*Perdón.*	per·*don*
Sorry.	*Lo siento.*	lo *syen*·to
Please.	*Por favor.*	por fa·*vor*
Thank you.	*Gracias.*	*gra*·syas
You are welcome.	*De nada.*	de *na*·da
Yes./No.	*Sí./No.*	see/no

My name is ...
Me llamo ... — me *ya*·mo ...

What's your name?
¿Cómo se llama Usted? — *ko*·mo se *ya*·ma oo·*ste* (pol)
¿Cómo te llamas? — *ko*·mo te *ya*·mas (inf)

Do you speak English?
¿Habla inglés? — *a*·bla een·*gles* (pol)
¿Hablas inglés? — *a*·blas een·*gles* (inf)

I don't understand.
Yo no entiendo. — yo no en·*tyen*·do

ACCOMMODATIONS

I'd like a single/double room.
Quisiera una habitación individual/doble. — kee·*sye*·ra *oo*·na a·bee·ta·*syon* een·dee·vee·*dwal*/*do*·ble

How much is it per night/person?
¿Cuánto cuesta por noche/persona? — *kwan*·to *kwes*·ta por *no*·che/per·*so*·na

Does it include breakfast?
¿Incluye el desayuno? — een·*kloo*·ye el de·sa·*yoo*·no

campsite	*terreno de cámping*	te·*re*·no de *kam*·peeng
guesthouse	*pensión*	pen·*syon*
hotel	*hotel*	o·*tel*
youth hostel	*albergue juvenil*	al·*ber*·ge khoo·ve·*neel*

EL VOSEO

Nicaragua differs from much of Latin America in its use of the informal 'you' form. Instead of *tuteo* (the use of *tú*), Nicaraguans commonly speak with *voseo* (the use of *vos*), a relic from 16th-century Spanish requiring a slightly different form of verbs. Examples of *-ar*, *-er* and *-ir* verbs are given below – the pronoun *tú* is only given for contrast. Imperative forms (commands) also differ, but negative imperatives are identical in *tuteo* and *voseo*.

The most common irregular verb you'll hear is *ser* (to be). In much of the Spanish-speaking world, you may be asked *¿De dónde eres?* (Where are you from?), but in Nicaragua, be prepared for *¿De dónde sos?*

This chapter uses the *tú* form in relevant phrases, as it's more useful throughout Latin America – Nicaraguans will have no trouble understanding if you only use the *tú* form.

A Nicaraguan inviting a foreigner to address him or her informally will say *Me podés tutear* (literally, 'you can address me with *tú*') even though they'll use the *vos* form in subsequent conversation.

Verb	Tuteo	Voseo
hablar (to speak): You speak./Speak!	*Tú hablas./¡Habla!*	*Vos hablás./¡Hablá!*
soñar (to dream): You dream./Dream!	*Tú sueñas./¡Sueña!*	*Vos soñás./¡Soña!*
comer (to eat): You eat./Eat!	*Tú comes./¡Come!*	*Vos comés./¡Comé!*
poner (to put): You put./Put!	*Tú pones./¡Pon!*	*Vos ponés./¡Poné!*
admitir (to admit): You admit./Admit!	*Tú admites./¡Admite!*	*Vos admitís./¡Admití!*
venir (to come): You come./Come!	*Tú vienes./¡Ven!*	*Vos venís./¡Vení!*

air-con	*aire acondicionado*	*ai*·re a·kon·dee·syo·*na*·do
bathroom	*baño*	*ba*·nyo
bed	*cama*	*ka*·ma
window	*ventana*	ven·*ta*·na

DIRECTIONS

Where's ...?
¿Dónde está ...? — *don*·de es·*ta* ...

What's the address?
¿Cuál es la dirección? — kwal es la dee·rek·*syon*

Could you please write it down?
¿Puede escribirlo, por favor? — *pwe*·de es·kree·*beer*·lo por fa·*vor*

Can you show me (on the map)?
¿Me lo puede indicar (en el mapa)? — me lo *pwe*·de een·dee·*kar* (en el *ma*·pa)

at the corner	*en la esquina*	en la es·*kee*·na
at the traffic lights	*en el semáforo*	en el se·*ma*·fo·ro
behind ...	*detrás de ...*	de·*tras* de ...
in front of ...	*enfrente de ...*	en·*fren*·te de ...
left	*izquierda*	ees·*kyer*·da
next to ...	*al lado de ...*	al *la*·do de ...
opposite ...	*frente a ...*	*fren*·te a ...
right	*derecha*	de·*re*·cha
straight ahead	*todo recto*	*to*·do *rek*·to

EATING & DRINKING

Can I see the menu, please?
¿Puedo ver el menú, por favor? — *pwe*·do ver el me·*noo* por fa·*vor*

What would you recommend?
¿Qué recomienda? — ke re·ko·*myen*·da

Do you have vegetarian food?
¿Tienen comida vegetariana? — *tye*·nen ko·*mee*·da ve·khe·ta·*rya*·na

I don't eat (red meat).
No como (carne roja). — no *ko*·mo (*kar*·ne *ro*·kha)

That was delicious!
¡Estaba buenísimo! — es·*ta*·ba bwe·*nee*·see·mo

Cheers!
¡Salud! — sa·*loo*

The bill, please.
La cuenta, por favor. — la *kwen*·ta por fa·*vor*

I'd like a table for ...	*Quisiera una mesa para ...*	kee·*sye*·ra *oo*·na *me*·sa *pa*·ra ...
(eight) o'clock	*las (ocho)*	las (*o*·cho)
(two) people	*(dos) personas*	(dos) per·*so*·nas

Key Words

bottle	*botella*	bo·*te*·ya
breakfast	*desayuno*	de·sa·*yoo*·no
(too) cold	*(muy) frío*	(mooy) *free*·o

Question Words

How?	*¿Cómo?*	ko·mo
What?	*¿Qué?*	ke
When?	*¿Cuándo?*	*kwan*·do
Where?	*¿Dónde?*	*don*·de
Who?	*¿Quién?*	kyen
Why?	*¿Por qué?*	por ke

dinner	*cena*	*se*·na
fork	*tenedor*	te·ne·*dor*
glass	*vaso*	*va*·so
hot (warm)	*caliente*	kal·*yen*·te
knife	*cuchillo*	koo·*chee*·yo
lunch	*comida*	ko·*mee*·da
plate	*plato*	*pla*·to
restaurant	*restaurante*	res·tow·*ran*·te
spoon	*cuchara*	koo·*cha*·ra

Meat & Fish

beef	*carne de vaca*	*kar*·ne de *va*·ka
chicken	*pollo*	*po*·yo
duck	*pato*	*pa*·to
lamb	*cordero*	kor·*de*·ro
pork	*cerdo*	*ser*·do
prawn	*langostino*	lan·gos·*tee*·no
salmon	*salmón*	sal·*mon*
tuna	*atún*	a·*toon*
turkey	*pavo*	*pa*·vo
veal	*ternera*	ter·*ne*·ra

Fruit & Vegetables

apple	*manzana*	man·*sa*·na
apricot	*albaricoque*	al·ba·ree·*ko*·ke
banana	*plátano*	*pla*·ta·no
beans	*judías*	khoo·*dee*·as
cabbage	*col*	kol
capsicum	*pimiento*	pee·*myen*·to
carrot	*zanahoria*	sa·na·o·rya
cherry	*cereza*	se·*re*·sa
corn	*maíz*	ma·*ees*
cucumber	*pepino*	pe·*pee*·no
grape	*uvas*	*oo*·vas
lemon	*limón*	lee·*mon*
lettuce	*lechuga*	le·*choo*·ga
mushroom	*champiñón*	cham·pee·*nyon*
nuts	*nueces*	*nwe*·ses
onion	*cebolla*	se·*bo*·ya
orange	*naranja*	na·*ran*·kha
peach	*melocotón*	me·lo·ko·*ton*
peas	*guisantes*	gee·*san*·tes
pineapple	*piña*	*pee*·nya
plum	*ciruela*	seer·*we*·la
potato	*patata*	pa·*ta*·ta
spinach	*espinacas*	es·pee·*na*·kas
strawberry	*fresa*	*fre*·sa
tomato	*tomate*	to·*ma*·te
watermelon	*sandía*	san·*dee*·a

Other

bread	*pan*	pan
cheese	*queso*	*ke*·so
egg	*huevo*	*we*·vo
honey	*miel*	myel
jam	*mermelada*	mer·me·*la*·da
oil	*aceite*	a·*sey*·te
pepper	*pimienta*	pee·*myen*·ta
rice	*arroz*	a·*ros*
salt	*sal*	sal
sugar	*azúcar*	a·*soo*·kar

Drinks

beer	*cerveza*	ser·*ve*·sa
coffee	*café*	ka·*fe*
(orange) juice	*zumo (de naranja)*	*soo*·mo (de na·*ran*·kha)
milk	*leche*	*le*·che
red wine	*vino tinto*	*vee*·no *teen*·to
tea	*té*	te
(mineral) water	*agua (mineral)*	*a*·gwa (mee·ne·*ral*)
white wine	*vino blanco*	*vee*·no *blan*·ko

Signs

Abierto	Open
Cerrado	Closed
Entrada	Entrance
Hombres/Varones	Men
Mujeres/Damas	Women
Prohibido	Prohibited
Salida	Exit
Servicios/Baños	Toilets

EMERGENCIES

Help!	*¡Socorro!*	so·*ko*·ro
Go away!	*¡Vete!*	*ve*·te

Call ...!	*¡Llame a ...!*	*ya*·me a ...
a doctor	*un médico*	oon *me*·dee·ko
the police	*la policía*	la po·lee·*see*·a

I'm lost.
Estoy perdido/a. es·*toy* per·*dee*·do/a (m/f)

I'm ill.
Estoy enfermo/a. es·*toy* en·*fer*·mo/a (m/f)

I'm allergic to (antibiotics).
Soy alérgico/a a (los antibióticos). soy a·*ler*·khee·ko/a a (los an·tee·*byo*·tee·kos) (m/f)

Where are the toilets?
¿Dónde están los baños? *don*·de es·*tan* los *ba*·nyos

SHOPPING & SERVICES

I'd like to buy ...
Quisiera comprar ... kee·*sye*·ra kom·*prar* ...

I'm just looking.
Sólo estoy mirando. *so*·lo es·*toy* mee·*ran*·do

Can I look at it?
¿Puedo verlo? *pwe*·do *ver*·lo

I don't like it.
No me gusta. no me *goos*·ta

How much is it?
¿Cuánto cuesta? *kwan*·to *kwes*·ta

That's too expensive.
Es muy caro. es mooy *ka*·ro

There's a mistake in the bill.
Hay un error en la cuenta. ai oon e·*ror* en la *kwen*·ta

NICA SLANG

Here's a small selection of the huge array of Nicaraguan slang.

¡Chocho!	Wow!
¡Tuani!	Good!/Relaxed!/Cool!
bochinche	an all-in brawl
chele	white person
chunche	a small object
dominguear	to dress up
estar hasta el tronco	to be very drunk
palmado	broke, penniless
pateperro	aimless wanderer

ATM	*cajero automático*	ka·*khe*·ro ow·to·*ma*·tee·ko
internet cafe	*cibercafé*	see·ber·ka·*fe*
post office	*correos*	ko·*re*·os
tourist office	*oficina de turismo*	o·fee·*see*·na de too·*rees*·mo

TIME, DATES & NUMBERS

What time is it?	*¿Qué hora es?*	ke *o*·ra es
It's (10) o'clock.	*Son (las diez).*	son (las dyes)
It's half past (one).	*Es (la una) y media.*	es (la *oo*·na) ee *me*·dya

morning	*mañana*	ma·*nya*·na
afternoon	*tarde*	*tar*·de
evening	*noche*	*no*·che
yesterday	*ayer*	a·*yer*
today	*hoy*	oy
tomorrow	*mañana*	ma·*nya*·na

Monday	*lunes*	*loo*·nes
Tuesday	*martes*	*mar*·tes
Wednesday	*miércoles*	*myer*·ko·les
Thursday	*jueves*	*khwe*·ves
Friday	*viernes*	*vyer*·nes
Saturday	*sábado*	*sa*·ba·do
Sunday	*domingo*	do·*meen*·go

1	*uno*	*oo*·no
2	*dos*	dos
3	*tres*	tres
4	*cuatro*	*kwa*·tro
5	*cinco*	*seen*·ko
6	*seis*	seys
7	*siete*	*sye*·te
8	*ocho*	*o*·cho
9	*nueve*	*nwe*·ve
10	*diez*	dyes
20	*veinte*	*veyn*·te
30	*treinta*	*treyn*·ta
40	*cuarenta*	kwa·*ren*·ta
50	*cincuenta*	seen·*kwen*·ta
60	*sesenta*	se·*sen*·ta
70	*setenta*	se·*ten*·ta
80	*ochenta*	o·*chen*·ta
90	*noventa*	no·*ven*·ta
100	*cien*	syen
1000	*mil*	meel

MISKITO PHRASES

There are more than 150,000 native speakers of Miskito scattered along the Caribbean coast. Here are a few phrases to get you started.

Hello./Goodbye.	*Naksa./Aisabi.*
Yes./No.	*Ow./Apia.*
Please./Thank you.	*Plees./Dingki pali.*
How are you?	*Nakisma?*
Good, fine.	*Pain.*
Bad, lousy.	*Saura.*
friend	*pana*
Does anyone here speak Spanish?	*Nu apo ya Ispel aisee sapa?*
My name is ...	*Yan nini ...*
What's your name?	*An maninam dia?*
Excuse me, could you help me?	*Escyus, man sipsma ilpeimonaya?*
How do I get to ...?	*Napkei sipsna gwaiya ...?*
Is it far/near?	*Nawina lihurasa/ lamarasa?*
Could you tell me where a hotel is?	*Man ailwis hotel ansara barsa?*
Do you have a bathroom?	*Baño brisma?*
Where is the bus station?	*Ansarasa buskaba takaskisa?*
What time does the bus/boat leave?	*Man nu apo dia teim bustaki/duritaki sapa?*
May I cross your property?	*Sipsna man prizcamku nueewaiya?*
Are there landmines?	*Danomite barsakei?*
Where can I change dollars?	*Ansara dalas sismonaya sipsna?*
How much is it?	*Naki preis?*
I'm a vegetarian.	*Yan wal wina kalila pias.*
I feel sick.	*Yan siknes.*

TRANSPORTATION

boat	*barco*	*bar*·ko
bus	*autobús*	ow·to·*boos*
plane	*avión*	a·*vyon*
taxi	*taxi*	*tak*·see
train	*tren*	tren

first	*primero*	pree·*me*·ro
last	*último*	*ool*·tee·mo
next	*próximo*	*prok*·see·mo

A ... ticket, please.	*Un billete de ..., por favor.*	oon bee·*ye*·te de ... por fa·*vor*
1st-class	*primera clase*	pree·*me*·ra *kla*·se
2nd-class	*segunda clase*	se·*goon*·da *kla*·se
one-way	*ida*	ee·da
return	*ida y vuelta*	ee·da ee *vwel*·ta

bus stop	*parada de autobuses*	pa·*ra*·da de ow·to·*boo*·ses
ticket office	*taquilla*	ta·*kee*·ya
timetable	*horario*	o·*ra*·ryo
train station	*estación de trenes*	es·ta·*syon* de *tre*·nes

Does it stop at ...?
¿Para en ...? — *pa*·ra en ...

What stop is this?
¿Cuál es esta parada? — kwal es *es*·ta pa·*ra*·da

What time does it arrive/leave?
¿A qué hora llega/sale? — a ke o·ra *ye*·ga/*sa*·le

Please tell me when we get to ...
¿Puede avisarme cuando lleguemos a ...? — *pwe*·de a·vee·*sar*·me *kwan*·do ye·*ge*·mos a ...

I want to get off here.
Quiero bajarme aquí. — *kye*·ro ba·*khar*·me a·*kee*

I'd like to hire a ...	*Quisiera alquilar ...*	kee·*sye*·ra al·kee·*lar* ...
bicycle	*una bicicleta*	*oo*·na bee·see·*kle*·ta
car	*un coche*	oon *ko*·che
motorcycle	*una moto*	*oo*·na *mo*·to

helmet	*casco*	*kas*·ko
mechanic	*mecánico*	me·*ka*·nee·ko
petrol/gas	*gasolina*	ga·so·*lee*·na
service station	*gasolinera*	ga·so·lee·*ne*·ra

Is this the road to ...?
¿Se va a ... por esta carretera? — se va a ... por es·ta ka·re·*te*·ra

(How long) Can I park here?
¿(Cuánto tiempo) Puedo aparcar aquí? — (*kwan*·to *tyem*·po) *pwe*·do a·par·*kar* a·*kee*

The car has broken down.
El coche se ha averiado. — el *ko*·che se a a·ve·*rya*·do

I have a flat tyre.
Tengo un pinchazo. — *ten*·go oon peen·*cha*·so

I've run out of petrol.
Me he quedado sin gasolina. — me e ke·*da*·do seen ga·so·*lee*·na

GLOSSARY

See p309 for useful words and phrases dealing with food and dining. See the Language chapter (p303) for other useful words and phrases.

alcaldía – mayor's office
arroyo – stream or gully
ave – bird

banco – bank
baño – bathroom
barco – boat
barrio – district, neighborhood
bicicleta – bicycle
bomba – gas station; short funny verse; bomb
bosque – forest

caballo – horse
cabinas – cabins
cacique – chief
calle – street
cama – bed
campesino/a – peasant; person who works in agriculture
campo – field or countryside
carretas – wooden ox carts
carretera – road or highway
cascada – waterfall
catedral – cathedral
caverna – cave
cerro – hill or mountain
chele/a – White/European, from *leche* (milk)
ciudad – city
cocina – kitchen; cooking
colectivo – buses, minivans or cars operating as shared taxis; see also *normal* and *directo*
colibrí – hummingbird
colina – hill
cooperativa – cooperative
cordillera – mountain range
córdoba – Nicaraguan unit of currency
correo – mail service
coyote – moneychanger or people smuggler
cruce – crossing
cueva – cave

dios – god
directo – direct; long-distance bus that has only a few stops

emergencia – emergency
empalme – three-way intersection
estación – station (as in ranger station or bus station); season
estero – estuary

farmacia – pharmacy
fiesta – party or festival
finca – farm or plantation
flor – flower
frontera – border

gringo/a – male/female North American or European visitor (can be affectionate or insulting, depending on the tone used)
guapote – large fish caught for sport, equivalent to rainbow bass

hacienda – a rural estate

iglesia – church
Ineter – Nicaragua Institute for Territorial Studies
Interamericana – Pan-American Hwy
Intur – Nicaraguan Institute of Tourism
isla – island

jardín – garden

laguna – lagoon
lancha – boat (usually small); see also *panga*
lapa – parrot
lavandería – laundry facility, usually offering dry-cleaning services

malecón – pier; sea wall; waterfront promenade
Marena – Nicaragua's Ministry of the Environment & Natural Resources
marimba – xylophone
mercado – market
mesa – table
mestizo – person of mixed descent, usually Spanish and Indian
migración – immigration
mirador – lookout point
mono – monkey
moto – motorcycle
muelle – dock
museo – museum

Nica – Nicaraguan, male or female
normal – long-distance bus with many stops

panga – light boat; *ruteado;* see also *lancha*
pántano – swamp or wetland
parque – park

ADDRESSES

Following are some terms and abbreviations commonly used in Nicaraguan addresses.

abajo	down
arriba	up
costado	beside
entre	between
esq	at the corner of
frente	in front of
int	inside
salida	exit
semaf	traffic lights

parque central – central town square or plaza
parque nacional – national park
pirópos – catcalls
piso – floor (as in 2nd floor)
pista – airstrip
playa – beach
posada – guesthouse
pueblo – village
puerto – port
pulpería – corner grocery store

rancho – thatched-roof hut
refresco – soda or bottled refreshment
refugio nacional de vida silvestre – national wildlife refuge
río – river

salto – waterfall (literally, jump)
sendero – trail; path
sierra – mountain range
soda – very Costa Rican term for a simple cafe; they're all over southern Nicaragua
supermercado – supermarket

tienda – store
típica/o – typical; particularly used to describe food (*comida típica* means 'typical cooking')
tope – dead end or T-intersection
tortuga – turtle
tucán – toucan

Unesco – UN Educational, Scientific and Cultural Organization

viajero – traveler
vivero – plant nursery
volcán – volcano

zona – zone

FOOD GLOSSARY

arroz – rice

baho – dry plantain, yucca and beef stew

camarones – shrimp
chicharrón – fried pork rinds
chile – vinegar with chilli peppers
cuajada – fresh, salty, crumbly cheese

ensalada – salad

frijoles – beans

gallo pinto – rice and beans

hamburguesa – hamburger
huevos del toro – bull testicles
huevos de paslama – turtle eggs
huevos fritos/revueltos – fried/scrambled eggs

maduros – ripe plantains served boiled or fried
mondongo – tripe soup

nacatamales – cornmeal with spices and meat

postre – dessert

raspados – shaved ice flavored with fruit juice
rundown – also *rondon;* thick Caribbean soup with coconut

quesillo – soft cheese with cream wrapped in a *tortilla*
queso – cheese

salchicha – sausage
salsa de ajillo – garlic sauce

tajadas – thin sliced green plantain fries
tortilla – cornmeal pancake
tostones – green plantains cut thick, mashed then fried

Behind the Scenes

SEND US YOUR FEEDBACK

We love to hear from travelers – your comments keep us on our toes and help make our books better. Our well-traveled team reads every word on what you loved or loathed about this book. Although we cannot reply individually to postal submissions, we always guarantee that your feedback goes straight to the appropriate authors, in time for the next edition. Each person who sends us information is thanked in the next edition – the most useful submissions are rewarded with a selection of digital PDF chapters.

Visit **lonelyplanet.com/contact** to submit your updates and suggestions or to ask for help. Our award-winning website also features inspirational travel stories, news and discussions.

Note: We may edit, reproduce and incorporate your comments in Lonely Planet products such as guidebooks, websites and digital products, so let us know if you don't want your comments reproduced or your name acknowledged. For a copy of our privacy policy visit lonelyplanet.com/privacy.

OUR READERS

Many thanks to the travelers who used the last edition and wrote to us with helpful hints, useful advice and interesting anecdotes:

Beate Allmenröder, Nick Atwood, Craig Bachman, Luciano Baracco, Craig Baskett, Roy Bateman, Marisa Bell-Metereau, Ann Blask, Katharina Borg, William Bova, Lindsay Campbell, Dan Caspi, Claudia Christl, Zachary Cohen, Berdina De Boer, Sarah Jane Diehl, Myke Dickens, Esther Eggink, Guntram Ehrlenspiel, Irene En Edwin, Craig Faanes, Alvaro Flores, Richard Folley, Kiehl Fred, June Fujimoto, Phil Gaffey, Peter Gandesbery, Madelon Gielen, Larry Gillispie, Guadalupe González, Richard Gustitis, Andreas Keller Hansen, Lisa Hartley, Edwin Heeregrave, Merritt Helfferich, Ferdinand Hofer, Mikael Holvila, Elizabeth Irwin, Alex Johnston, Colin Jones, Zlata Karpas, Peter Kitchen, Lisa Knappich, Troels Kolln, Wojtek Kosarzecki, Sophie Kosiara, Martin Kráľ, Tim Laslavic, Pierre Lavrijsen, Haninah Levine, Golda Lewin, Fritz Liedtke, Ronald Liefhebber and Nienke Bosschaart, Ash Mahajan, Jacques Malaspina, Carlo Masini, Roberta Mazzoli, Vanessa Mcintyre, Ruth Moesby, Nadine Mooren, James Mordovancey, Mieke Muys, Michael Naumann, Jolien Nicolai, Andrea Ottolina, Jan Popelka, Michael Putnam, Corinna Schneider, Brandee Smith, Michael Smith, Tanya Snyder, Andreanne St Gelais, Cecil Steed, Hanneke Steenis, Mark Tew, Sophie Thostrup-Clemmensen, Jan Tilston, Albertus Valkenburg, Pim Van Campen, Lise Van Den Heuvel, Maja Vinde Folkersen, Julie Vissers, Rivka Wehrens, Johan & Henny Wels, Anthony P White, Cindy Williams, Magdalena Wodyńska, Alan Wyllie

AUTHOR THANKS

Alex Egerton

Thanks to KC, Ras Ariel, Zander, Edwin, Juan Lasso, Arjen, Juana Boyd, Marjiory in San Carlos, Adam Clarke, Shirlene Greene and Rupert Allen, and the multitude of Nicaraguans out on the road whose passion for their country makes research so much easier. Also thanks to Lucas 'Userscript' V and Adam Skolnick for the inspiring prose.

And at home, thanks to Shaun and May for the farm, to mum and Nick for waiting, and Olga for the opportune cups of tea.

Greg Benchwick

Thanks to Cat and crew at Lonely Planet, to my coordinating author, to Pipo in Managua, and my fearless and peerless travel companion, Violeta Benchwick.

ACKNOWLEDGMENTS

Climate map data adapted from Peel MC, Finlayson BL & McMahon TA (2007) 'Updated World Map of the Köppen-Geiger Climate Classification', *Hydrology and Earth System Sciences*, 11, 163344.

Cover photograph: Panga fishing boat, Corn Islands, Nicaragua, Worldwide Photo.

THIS BOOK

This 3rd edition of Lonely Planet's Nicaragua guidebook was researched and written by Alex Egerton (coordinating author) and Greg Benchwick. The previous edition was researched and written by Lucas Vidgen (coordinating author) and Adam Skolnick. The 1st edition was a two-country guide called *Nicaragua & El Salvador* and was written by Paige Penland, Gary Chandler and Liza Prado.

This guidebook was commissioned in Lonely Planet's Oakland office, and produced by the following:

Commissioning Editor Catherine Craddock-Carrillo

Coordinating Editors Anne Mason, Kristin Odijk

Coordinating Cartographers Jeff Cameron, Hunor Csutoros

Coordinating Layout Designer Wendy Wright

Managing Editors Bruce Evans, Angela Tinson

Senior Editor Andi Jones

Managing Cartographers Anita Banh, Alison Lyall

Managing Layout Designer Jane Hart

Assisting Editors Alan Murphy, Charlotte Orr

Cover Research Naomi Parker

Internal Image Research Barbara Di Castro

Language Content Branislava Vladisavljevic

Thanks to Ryan Evans, Larissa Frost, Genesys India, Jouve India, Trent Paton, Raphael Richards, Gerard Walker

Index

Map Pages **000**
Photo Pages **000**

Map Pages **000**
Photo Pages **000**

Map Pages **000**
Photo Pages **000**

Map Legend

Sights
- Beach
- Bird Sanctuary
- Buddhist
- Castle/Palace
- Christian
- Confucian
- Hindu
- Islamic
- Jain
- Jewish
- Monument
- Museum/Gallery/Historic Building
- Ruin
- Sento Hot Baths/Onsen
- Shinto
- Sikh
- Taoist
- Winery/Vineyard
- Zoo/Wildlife Sanctuary
- Other Sight

Activities, Courses & Tours
- Bodysurfing
- Diving/Snorkelling
- Canoeing/Kayaking
- Course/Tour
- Skiing
- Snorkelling
- Surfing
- Swimming/Pool
- Walking
- Windsurfing
- Other Activity

Sleeping
- Sleeping
- Camping

Eating
- Eating

Drinking & Nightlife
- Drinking & Nightlife
- Cafe

Entertainment
- Entertainment

Shopping
- Shopping

Information
- Bank
- Embassy/Consulate
- Hospital/Medical
- Internet
- Police
- Post Office
- Telephone
- Toilet
- Tourist Information
- Other Information

Geographic
- Beach
- Hut/Shelter
- Lighthouse
- Lookout
- Mountain/Volcano
- Oasis
- Park
- Pass
- Picnic Area
- Waterfall

Population
- Capital (National)
- Capital (State/Province)
- City/Large Town
- Town/Village

Transport
- Airport
- Border crossing
- Bus
- Cable car/Funicular
- Cycling
- Ferry
- Metro station
- Monorail
- Parking
- Petrol station
- Subway/Subte station
- Taxi
- Train station/Railway
- Tram
- Underground station
- Other Transport

Note: Not all symbols displayed above appear on the maps in this book

Routes
- Tollway
- Freeway
- Primary
- Secondary
- Tertiary
- Lane
- Unsealed road
- Road under construction
- Plaza/Mall
- Steps
- Tunnel
- Pedestrian overpass
- Walking Tour
- Walking Tour detour
- Path/Walking Trail

Boundaries
- International
- State/Province
- Disputed
- Regional/Suburb
- Marine Park
- Cliff
- Wall

Hydrography
- River, Creek
- Intermittent River
- Canal
- Water
- Dry/Salt/Intermittent Lake
- Reef

Areas
- Airport/Runway
- Beach/Desert
- Cemetery (Christian)
- Cemetery (Other)
- Glacier
- Mudflat
- Park/Forest
- Sight (Building)
- Sportsground
- Swamp/Mangrove

OUR STORY

A beat-up old car, a few dollars in the pocket and a sense of adventure. In 1972 that's all Tony and Maureen Wheeler needed for the trip of a lifetime – across Europe and Asia overland to Australia. It took several months, and at the end – broke but inspired – they sat at their kitchen table writing and stapling together their first travel guide, *Across Asia on the Cheap*. Within a week they'd sold 1500 copies. Lonely Planet was born.

Today, Lonely Planet has offices in Melbourne, London and Oakland, with more than 600 staff and writers. We share Tony's belief that 'a great guidebook should do three things: inform, educate and amuse'.

OUR WRITERS

Alex Egerton

Coordinating Author, Northern Highlands, Caribbean Coast, San Carlos Islas Solentiname & the Río San Juan A journalist by trade, Alex has been based in Nicaragua for almost a decade while working as a travel writer throughout Latin America. After exploring the villages, nature reserves and back roads from Nueva Segovia to Río San Juan, Alex moved to the Caribbean, bought a boat and settled down in Pearl Lagoon where the patchy internet is compensated by the fresh breeze and fantastic food. When not on the road writing, he spends his spare time exploring Nicaragua's nature reserves on foot and by kayak. Alex also wrote the Plan Your Trip and Understand Nicaragua chapters of this book.

Greg Benchwick

Managua, Masaya & Los Pueblos Blancos, Granada, Southwestern Nicaragua, León & Northwestern Nicaragua Greg first traveled through Nicaragua in 1995 with an empty notebook and a backpack full of dreams. Since then he's written dozens of guidebooks to countries throughout Latin America, supported UN missions in Nicaragua and beyond, and discovered lost beaches and new stories one street over.

Read more about Greg at:
lonelyplanet.com/members/gbenchwick

Published by Lonely Planet Publications Pty Ltd
ABN 36 005 607 983
3rd edition – Sept 2013
ISBN 978 1 74179 699 5

10 9 8 7 6 5 4 3 2
Printed in China